AF576557

VOL. 3 ADVERTISING GREETING CARDS

P·I·E BOOKS

VOL. 3 ADVERTISING GREETING CARDS

First Edition, May 1993

P·I·E BOOKS
Villa Phoenix Suite 407, 4-14-6, Komagome,
Toshima-ku, Tokyo 170 Japan
Tel:03-3949-5010 Fax:03-3949-5650

ISBN4-938586-41-X C3070 P16000E

Artwork on cover designed by Steven Guarnaccia

CONTENTS

P・I・E BOOKSではこれまでにDM（ダイレクトメール）デザインの世界を封書タイプの作品を中心に、商業的なものからプライベートなグリーティング・カードまで幅広く『アドバタイジング・グリーティング・カード』として紹介してきました。本書はその第三弾に当たるものです。

封書DMには特有の面白さがあります。ちょっとワクワクした気持ちで封筒を開ける、中のカードを取り出す、手の上で広げてみる、こういった一連の動作が受け手である私たちに一種の緊張感を持った楽しさを与えてくれます。中身が変わった形のカードや招待状だった時の驚きは、思いがけないプレゼントをもらった様な嬉しさではないでしょうか。

封書タイプのDMの良さは、より多くの情報を入れられるという点で、またデザイナーにとっても、他の2次元的なデザインであるポスターやポスト・カードなどとは違って、封筒から取り出すことを考えた3次元的なデザインができる面白みのある題材であると思います。

FOREWORD

今回も日本を含めた海外19ケ国からの応募作品があり、その種類や形態も様々です。磁石付きの移転通知、封筒から取り出すと飛び出して箱形になるカード、素材にアクリル版を使用した年賀状など、作り手の主張や個性を感じさせる作品が多数集まりました。

仕掛けの凝った視覚的に派手なDMが以前より少なくなり、折り方の工夫や色の組み合わせ、また小さな切り込みを入れポップ・アップ・カードにしたものなど、オーソドックスでありながらもちょっとしたアイデアで新鮮な驚きや感動を与えてくれる作品が増えたことが印象的でした。不況と言われる中で広告費が削られているのも事実です。いかにコストをかけずに楽しくて効果的なDMを作るかは今後の課題でもあるでしょう。

本書を見ていただいて、実際に手にした時と同じような驚きや楽しさや、封書DMの世界に新しい発見を感じ取っていただければ嬉しく思います。

ピエ・ブックス編集部

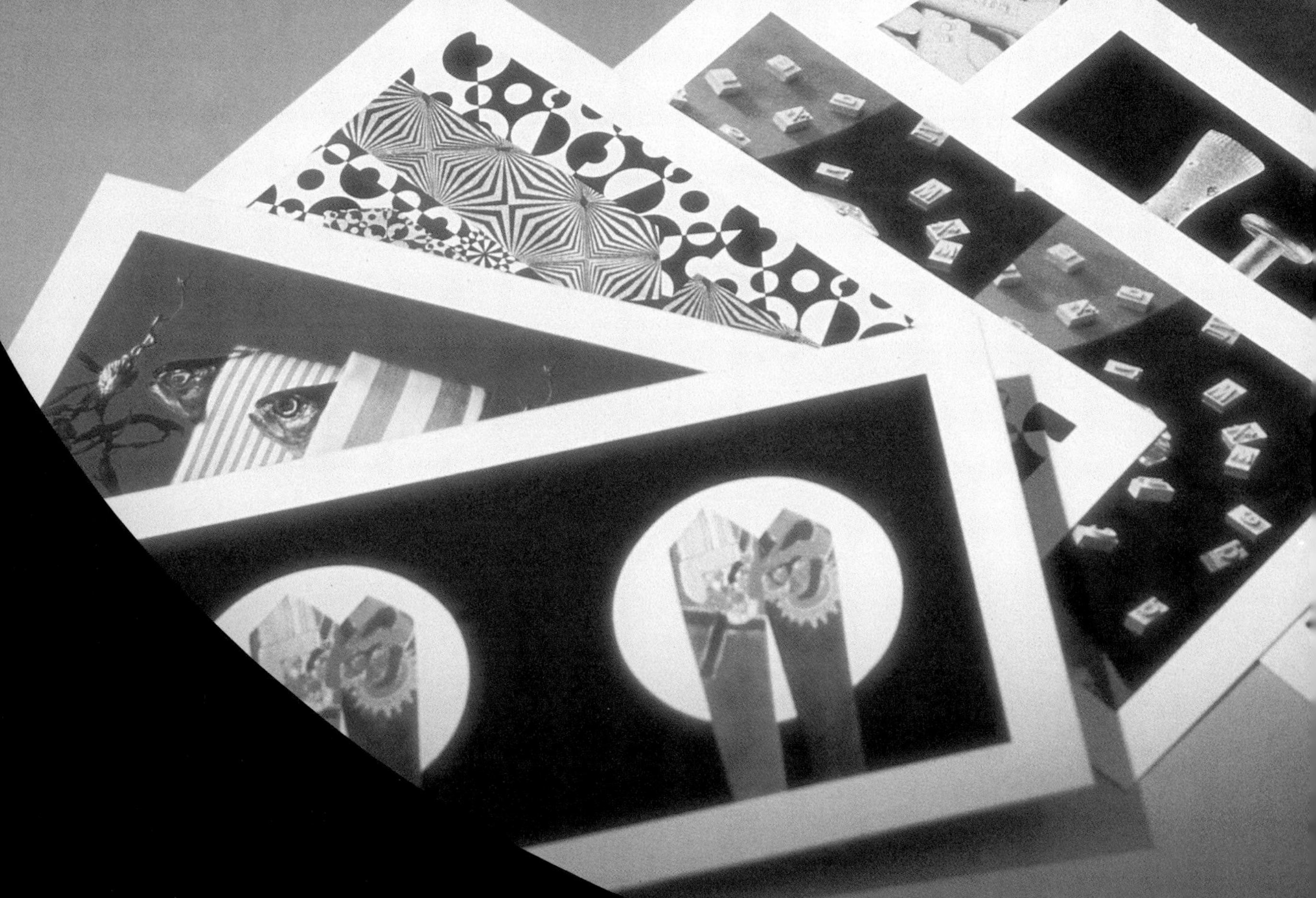
TO OBTAIN THE THIRD DIMENSIONAL EFFECT,
PLACE YOUR STEREO SET OF IMAGES HERE
AND VIEW THROUGH LENSES. YOUR EYES
WILL ADJUST AFTER A FEW SECONDS.
Paul Smith

P·I·E Books has been bringing you outstanding greeting card art of every sort in our "Advertising Greeting Cards" series. We have concentrated on letter-type (enveloped) cards of singular design. Direct mailers from commercial promotion to private greetings, are also included in this theme. This book is the third volume in the series.

Letter-type direct mailers are quite different from postcards in their effect due to the sequence of actions required to access the information within. The process begins with examining and then opening the envelope, the experience of piqued curiosity that goes with revealing something hidden. Then there are the tactile sensations of taking out the card, examining the outside and again opening it with your finger-tips, exposing its hidden massage to the light. This sequence of gestures adds to the fun by involving us in the process of communication. We feel a *frisson* of delight at the prospect of a surprise. Perhaps it comes out into the hand in a surprising shape or a dazzling color. Perhaps it is an invitation to something exciting or a message from a long-lost friend. It is a little like receiving an unexpected present.

One of the advantages of letter-type direct mailers for the sender is that more information can be contained within. This medium is particularly interesting for the designer, because it gives scope to incorporate some unique ideas such as 3-D effects,

FOREWORD

pop-up effects and various surprise effects made possible by the envelope, the folds in the card and so forth.

We had submissions in every imaginable style and form sent to us from 19 countries around the world, including Japan for inclusion in this volume. Each piece speaks eloquently of the creator's individual genius and his idiosyncratic message. Take for example the change-of-address notice with a magnetic compass attached, or the card that spontaneously turns into a box when it is taken out of the envelope, or the New Years card made of acrylic sheet.

We noticed that there are fewer cards this year with that "glitzy look" or the highly contrived visuals and glossy production values that we have seen in previous years. Our impression is that the artwork on today's cards is a little more subdued. Nevertheless, there are plenty of refreshing surprises to be had, and we were impressed with the subtlety of ideas that have replaced the flash that prevailed in the past.

More and more companies are trying to cut back on advertising expenses in this period of economic recession. The challenge this presents for designers and direct mail programs is how to make interesting and effective mailers while incurring less cost.

We feel this book captures the creative energy that has been put into direct mailers over the past year or so. We hope that you will get the sort of pleasure from this book that you would as if you actually held the originals in your hands.

P·I·E BOOKS

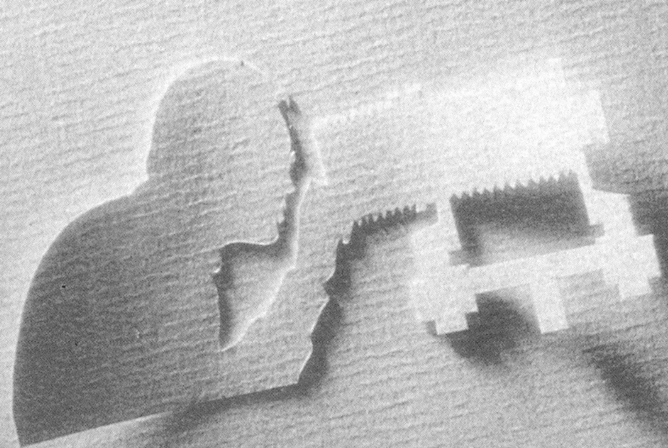
C.K. WONG Photography
ERN CENTRE 1065 KING'S ROAD HONG KONG TEL 5-635277 FAX 5-650290

E d i t o r i a l   N o t e s

CD:Creative Director

AD:Art Director

D:Designer

P:Photographer

I:Illustrator

CW:Copywriter

DF:Design Firm

CL:Client

TC:Type of Company

クレジットのタイトルには、作品の使用目的を
また、国名は出品者の居住国を表記しました。
The credit headings refer to the intended use.
The country indicated for each entry is the
country in which the submittor resides.

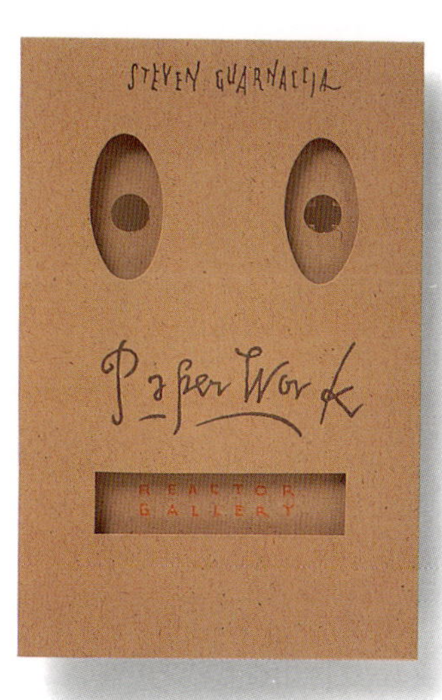
STEVEN GUARNACCIA
PaperWork
REACTOR
GALLERY

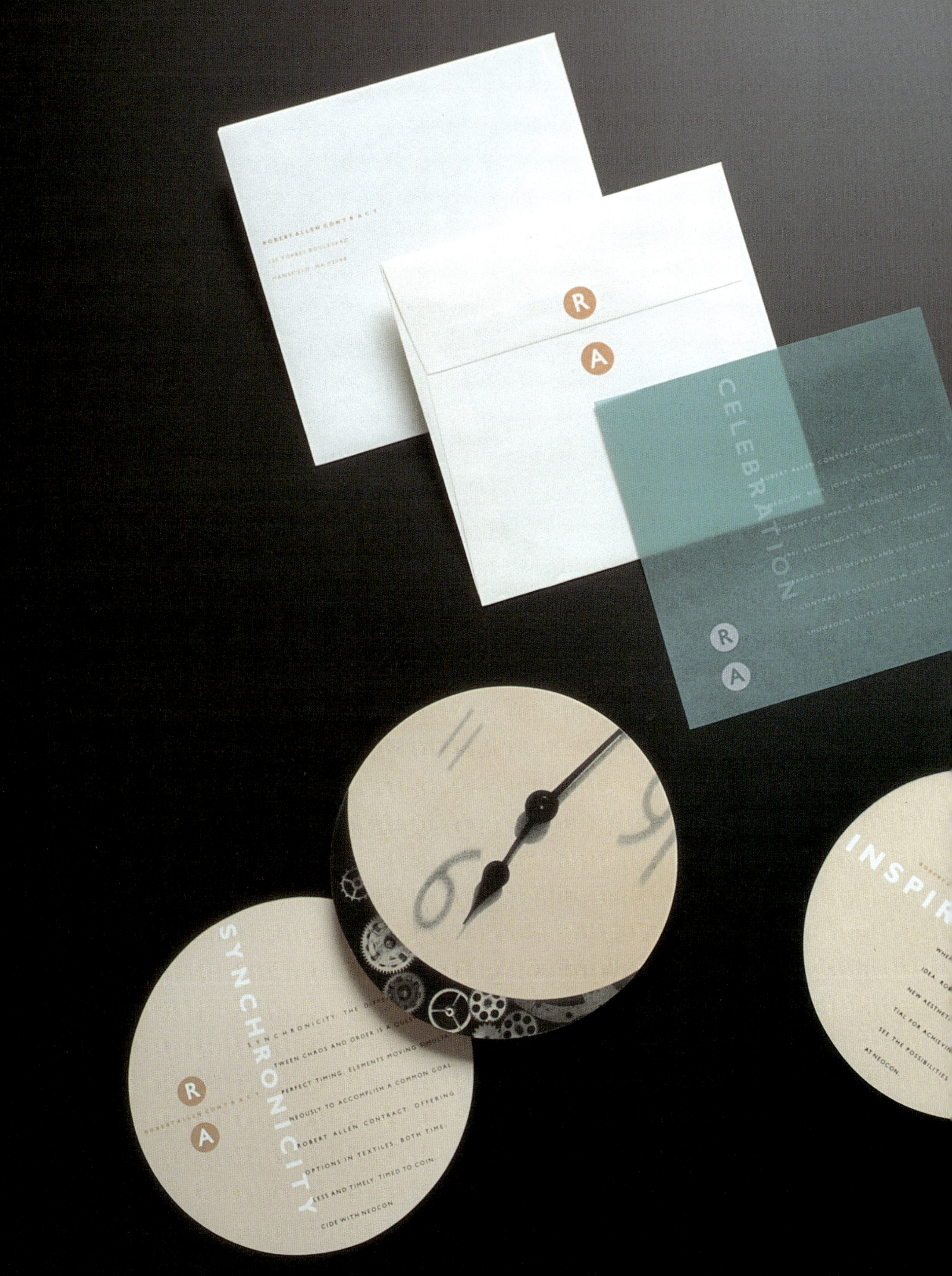

CELEBRATION
R
A
SYNCHRONICITY
ROBERT ALLEN CONTRACT
NEOUSLY TO ACCOMPLISH A COMMON GOAL
ROBERT ALLEN CONTRACT. OFFERING
OPTIONS IN TEXTILES. BOTH TIME-
LESS AND TIMELY. TIMED TO COIN-
CIDE WITH NEOCON.

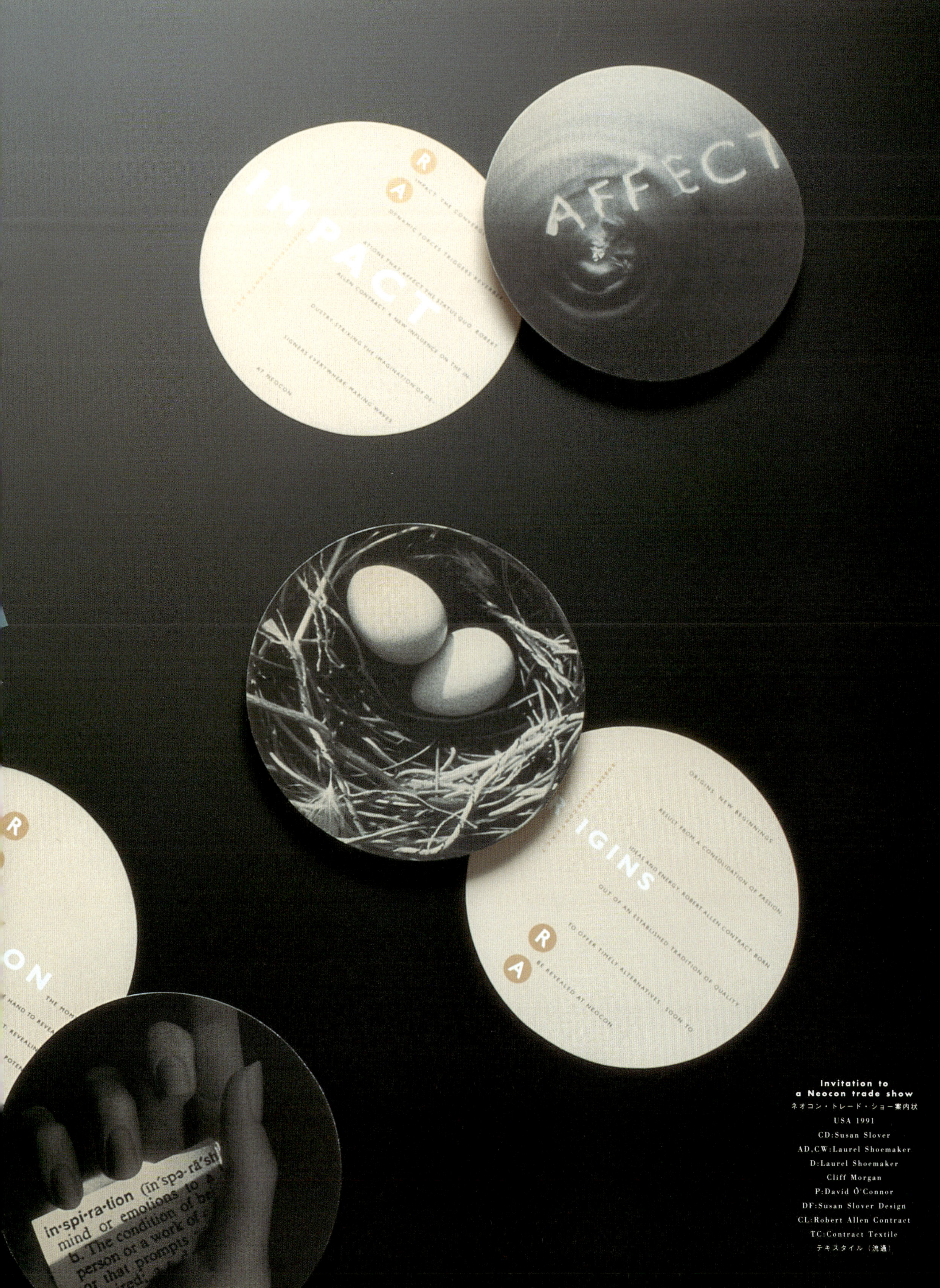

Invitation to a Neocon trade show
ネオコン・トレード・ショー案内状
USA 1991
CD:Susan Slover
AD,CW:Laurel Shoemaker
D:Laurel Shoemaker
Cliff Morgan
P:David O'Connor
DF:Susan Slover Design
CL:Robert Allen Contract
TC:Contract Textile
テキスタイル（流通）

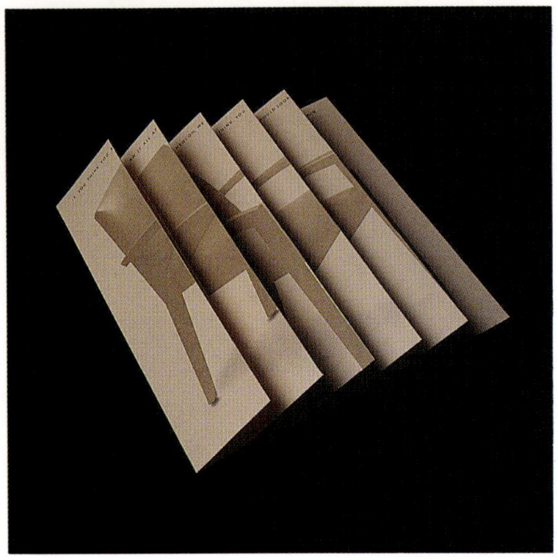

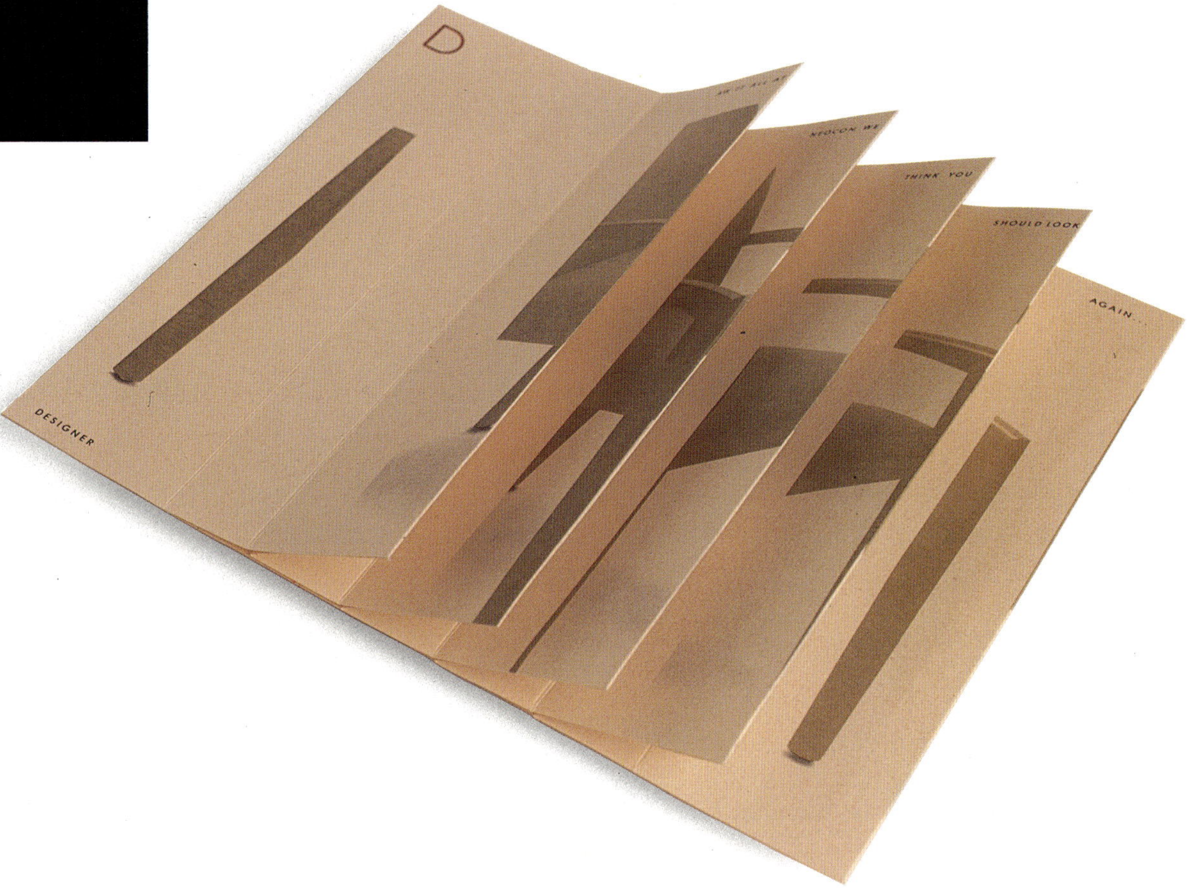

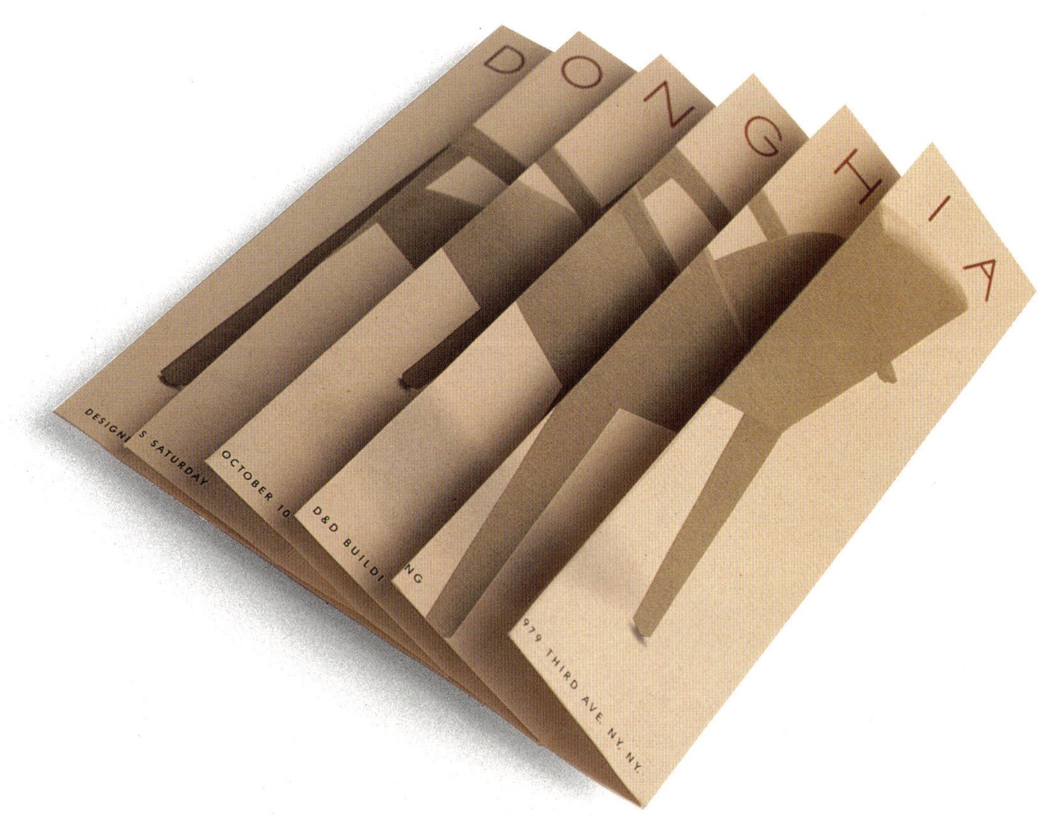

Invitation to a trade show
商品展示会案内状
USA 1989
CD,AD,CW:Susan Slover
D:Thomas Bricker
P:Raeanne Giovanni
DF:Susan Slover Design
CL:Donghia
TC:Designer and Maker of Interior Accessories
インテリア・アクセサリーの
デザイン及び製造
•
The card is folded in such a way that the angle of the chair changes depending on how you turn the folds.
カードがヒダ状になっており、めくり方によって
椅子の向きが変化する。

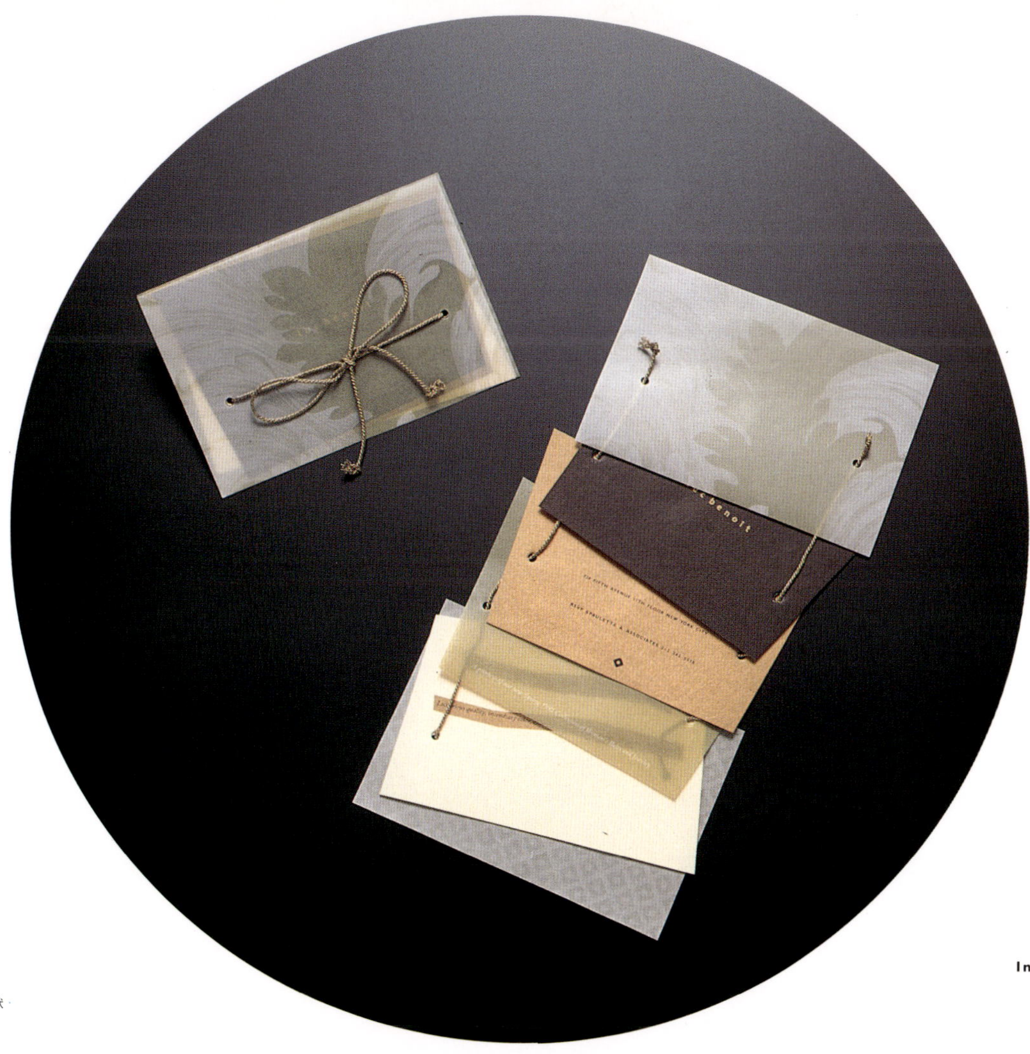

▲
Invitation to a fashion preview
ファッション・プレビュー案内状
USA 1990
CD:Susan Slover
D:Cliff Morgan
CW:Laura Silverman
DF:Susan Slover Design
CL:Luc Bendit
TC:Designer of Lether Accessories
レザー・アクセサリーのデザイン

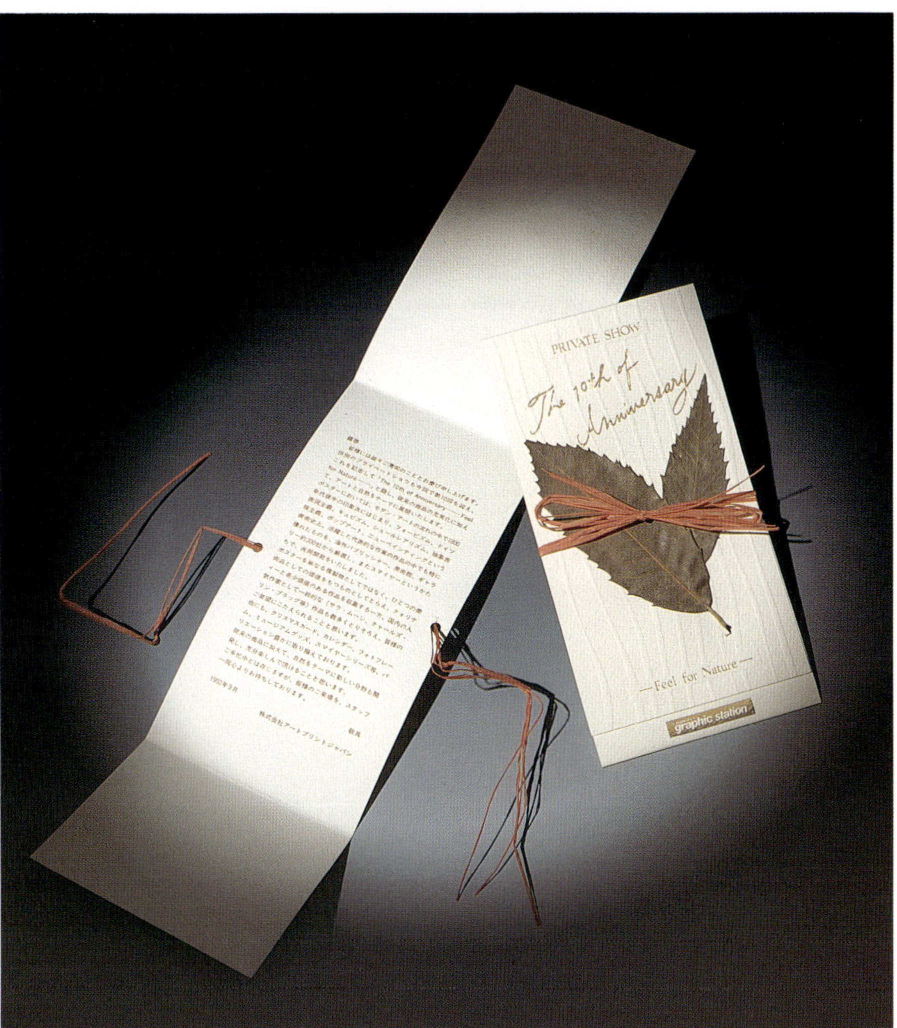

▼
Invitation to an exhibition
展示会案内状
JAPAN 1992
CD,D:Mutsuko Morita
CL:Art Print Japan
TC:Poster,Card Publisher
ポスター、カード制作販売

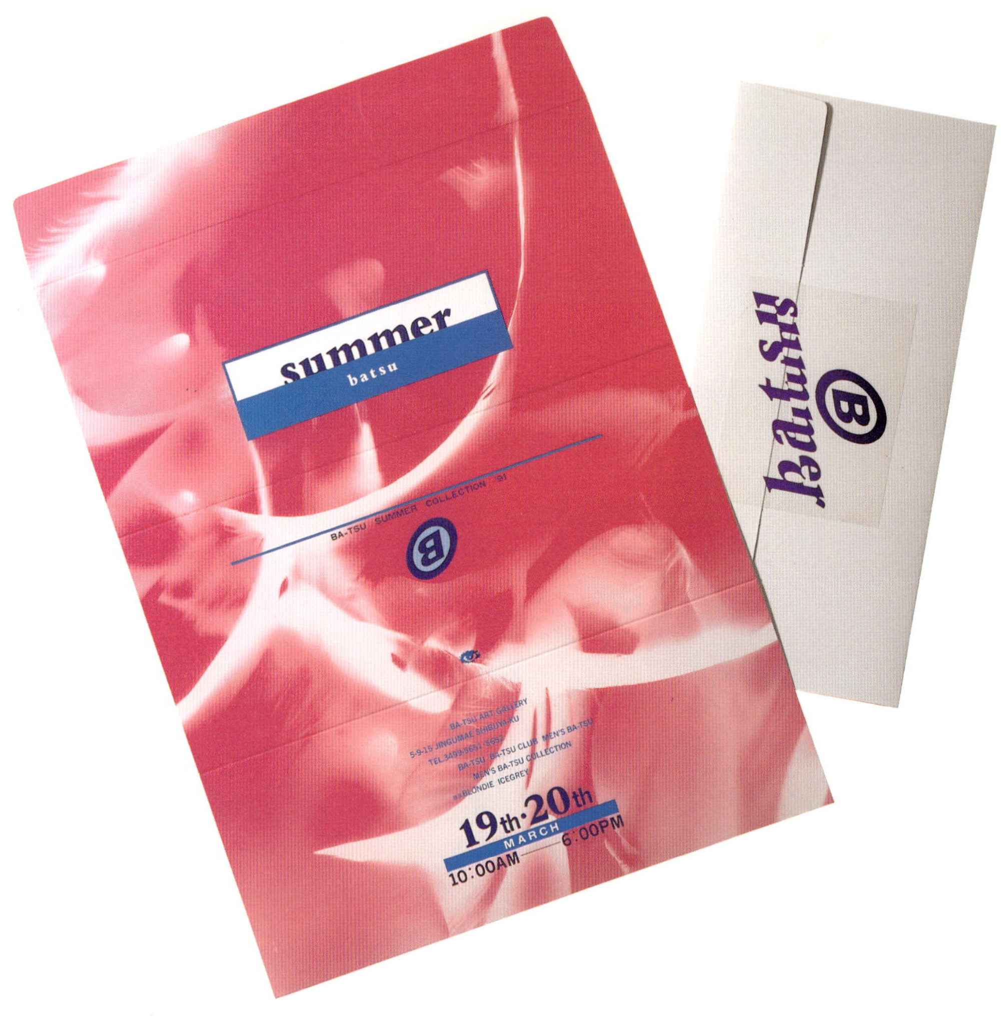

▲
Invitation to a Ba-tsu collection
バツ展示会案内状
JAPAN 1991
AD,D,P:Kiyoko Sakura
CL:BA-TSU
TC:Apparel Maker
アパレル

▼
Invitation to a Ba-tsu collection
バツ展示会案内状
JAPAN 1992
AD,D:Kiyoko Sakura
CL:BA-TSU
TC:Apparel Maker
アパレル

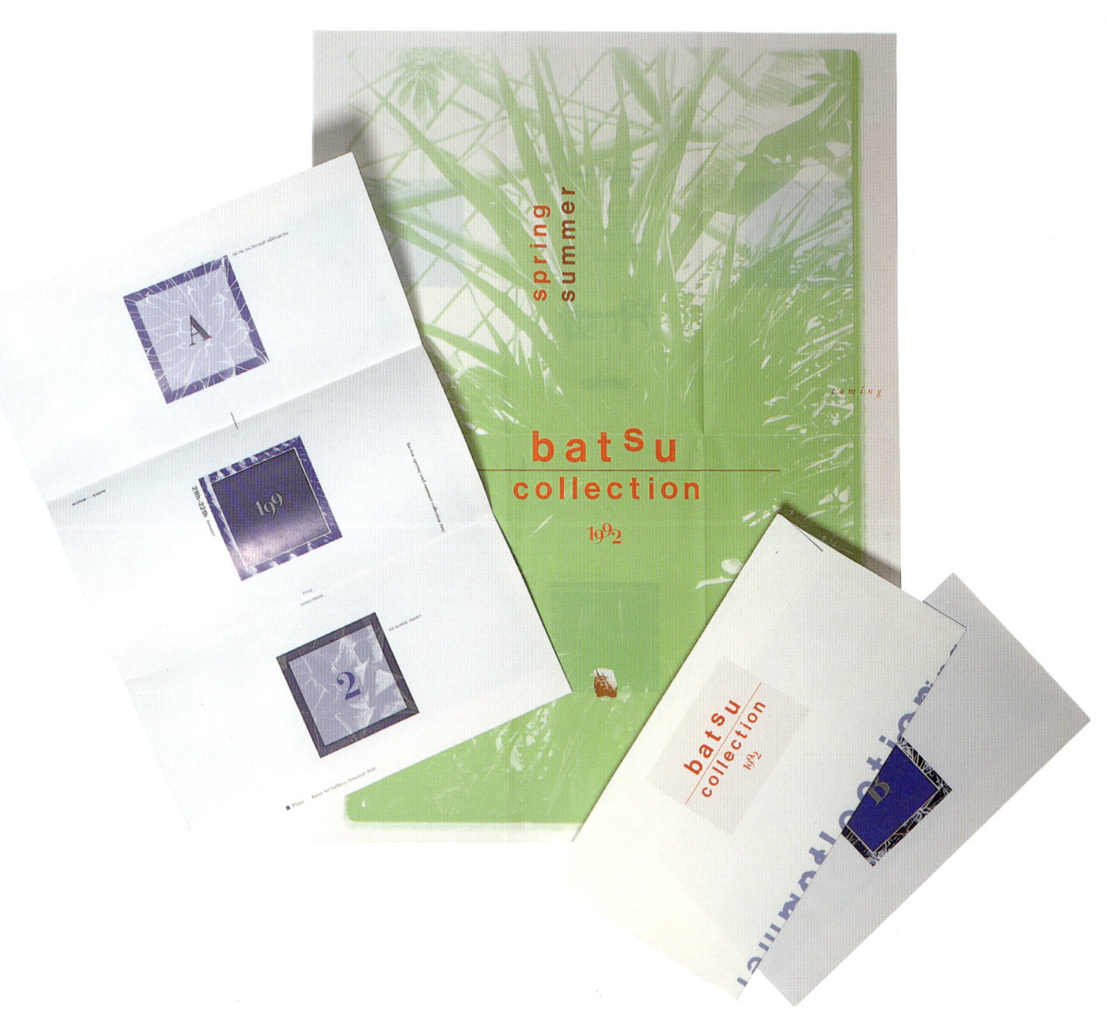

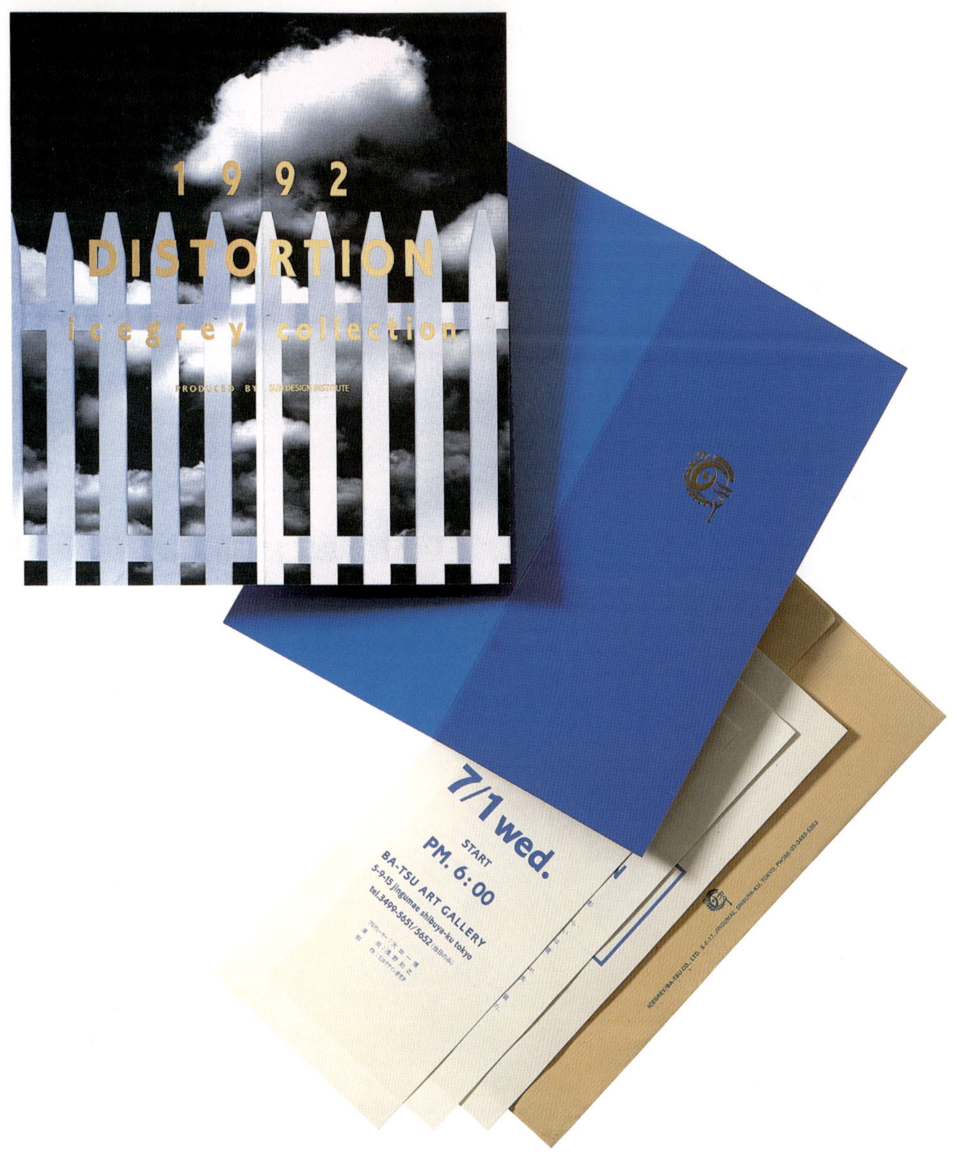

▲
Invitation to an Ice Grey collection
アイス・グレイ展示会案内状
JAPAN 1992
AD:Toshikazu Murata
Kiyoko Sakura
D:Kiyoko Sakura
CL:BA-TSU
TC:Apparel Maker
アパレル

▼
Invitation to a Ba-tsu collection
バツ展示会案内状
JAPAN 1992
AD,D:Kiyoko Sakura
CL:BA-TSU
TC:Apparel Maker
アパレル

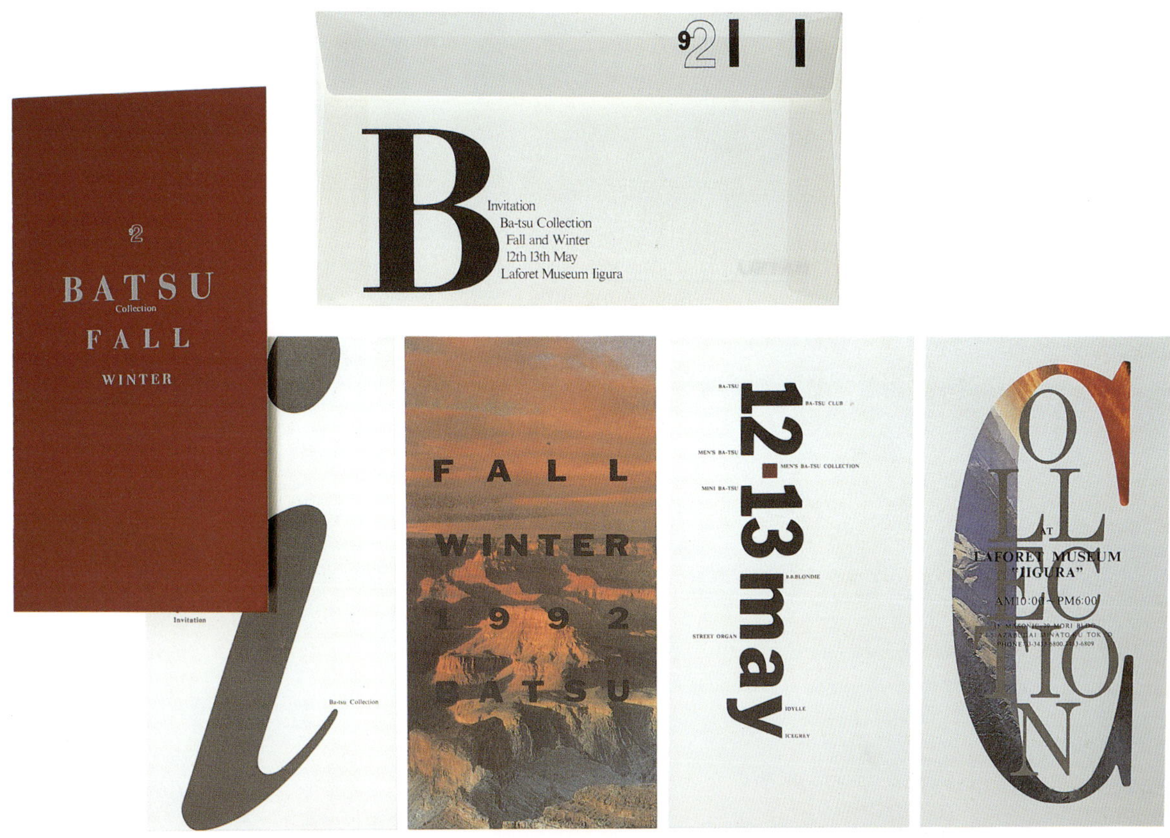

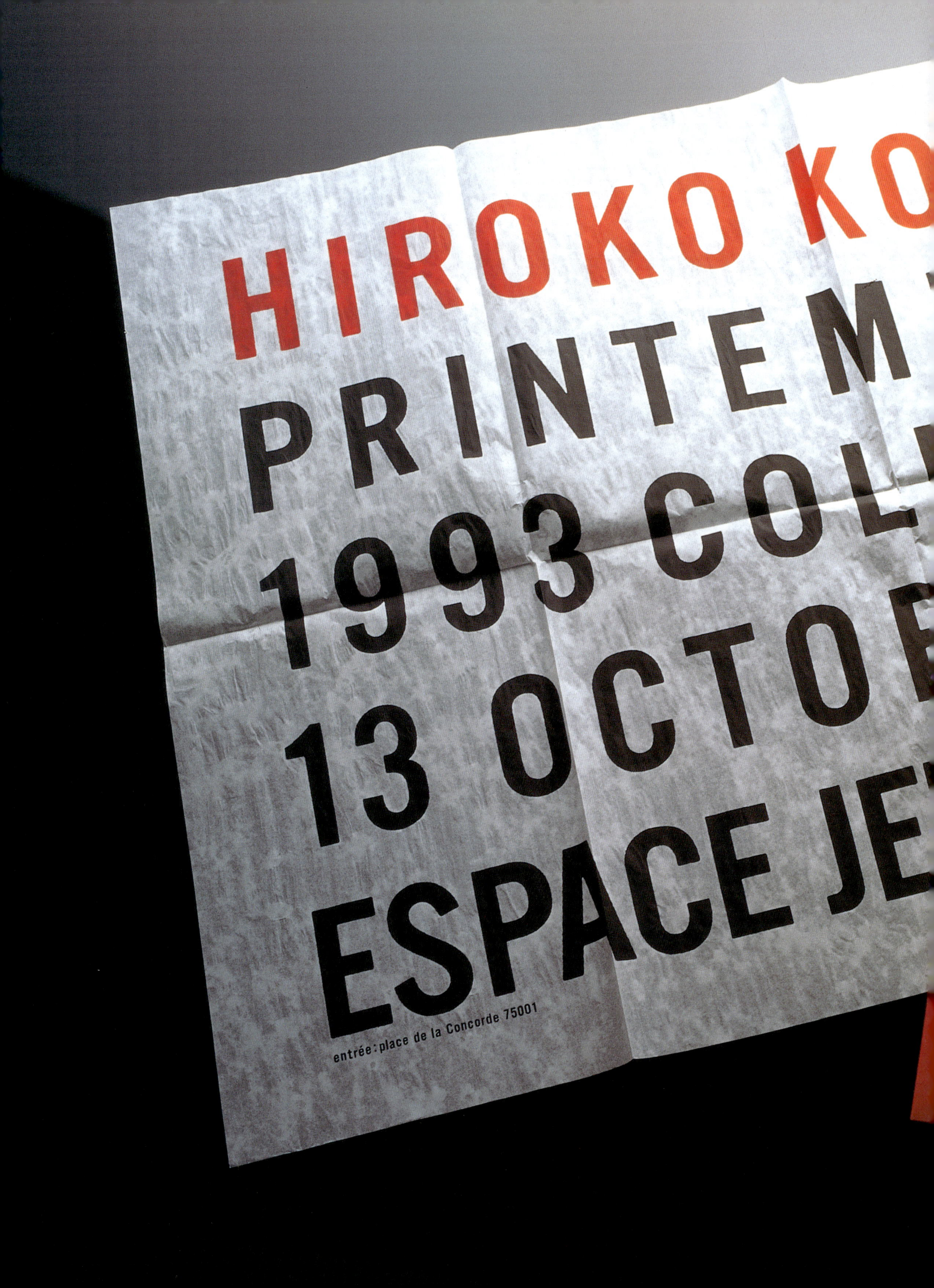

HIROKO KO

PRINTEM

1993 COL

13 OCTO

ESPACE JE

entrée : place de la Concorde 75001

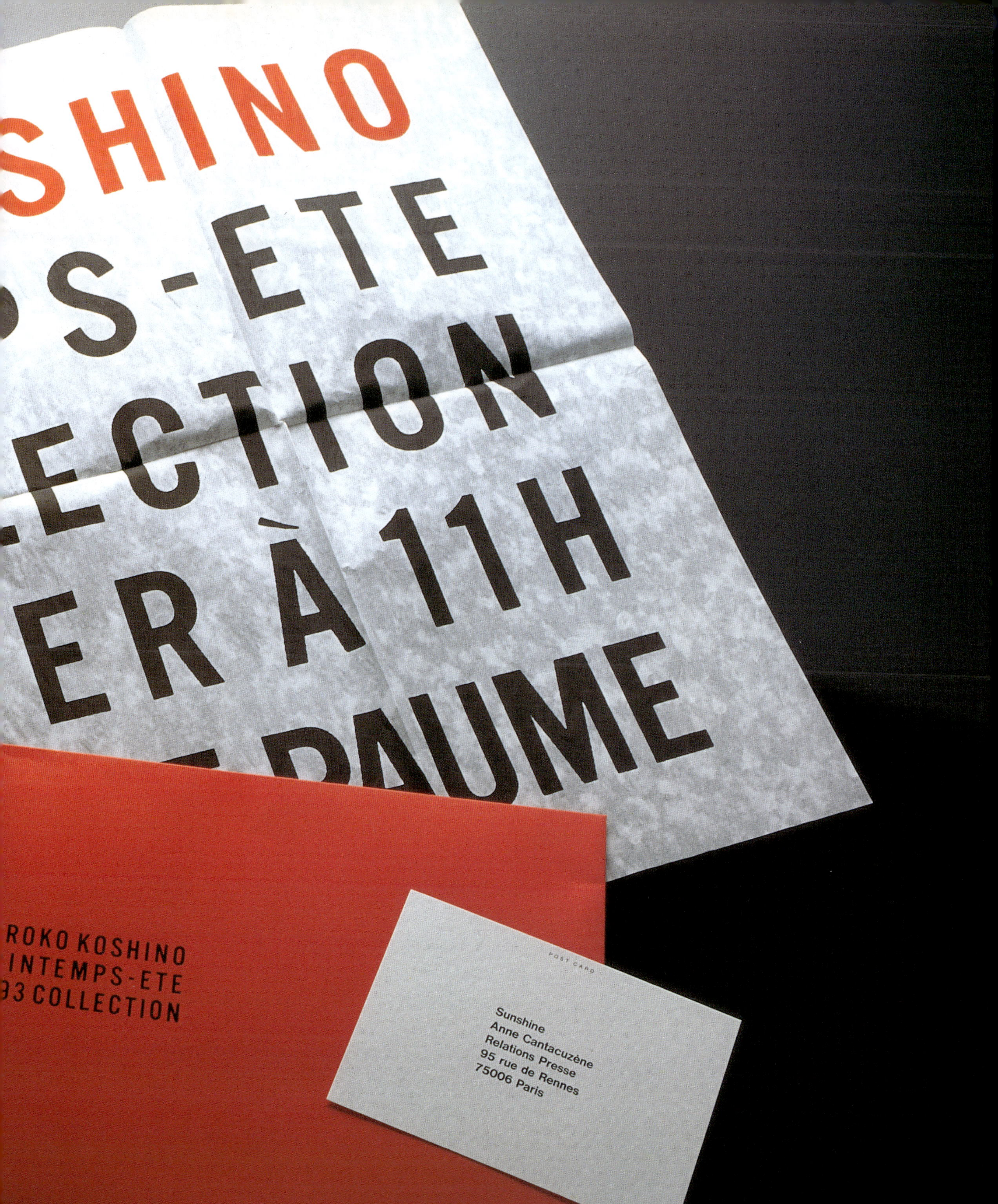

Invitation to a collection

展示会案内状

JAPAN 1993

AD:Koji Mizutani

D:Junko Horiuchi

CL:Hiroko Koshino Design Office

TC:Apparel Maker

アパレル

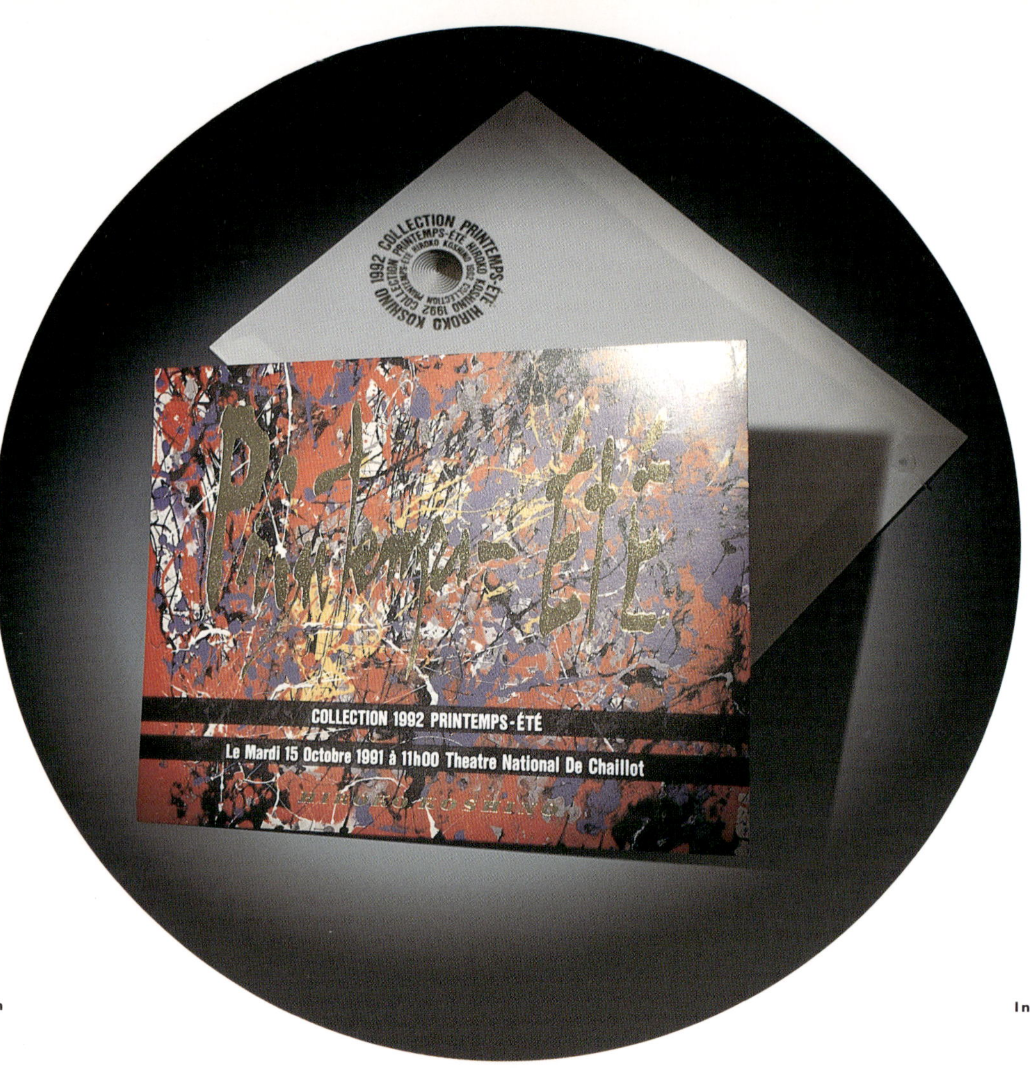

▲
Invitation to a collection
展示会案内状
JAPAN 1992
AD:Koji Mizutani
D:Noriko Shimamoto
CL:Hiroko Koshino Design Office
TC:Apparel Maker
アパレル

▼
Invitation to a collection
展示会案内状
JAPAN 1992
AD:Koji Mizutani
D:Hiroshi Omizo
Junko Horiuchi
CL:Hiroko Koshino Design Office
TC:Apparel Maker
アパレル

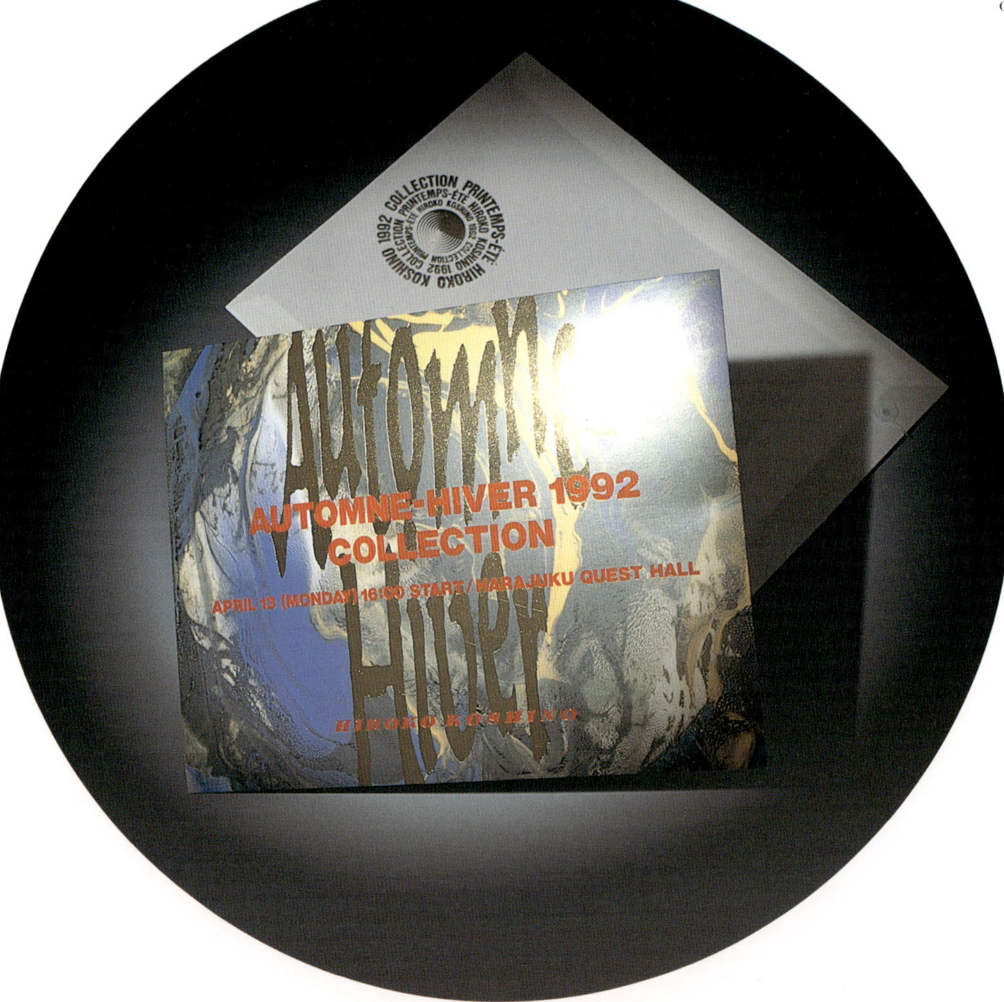

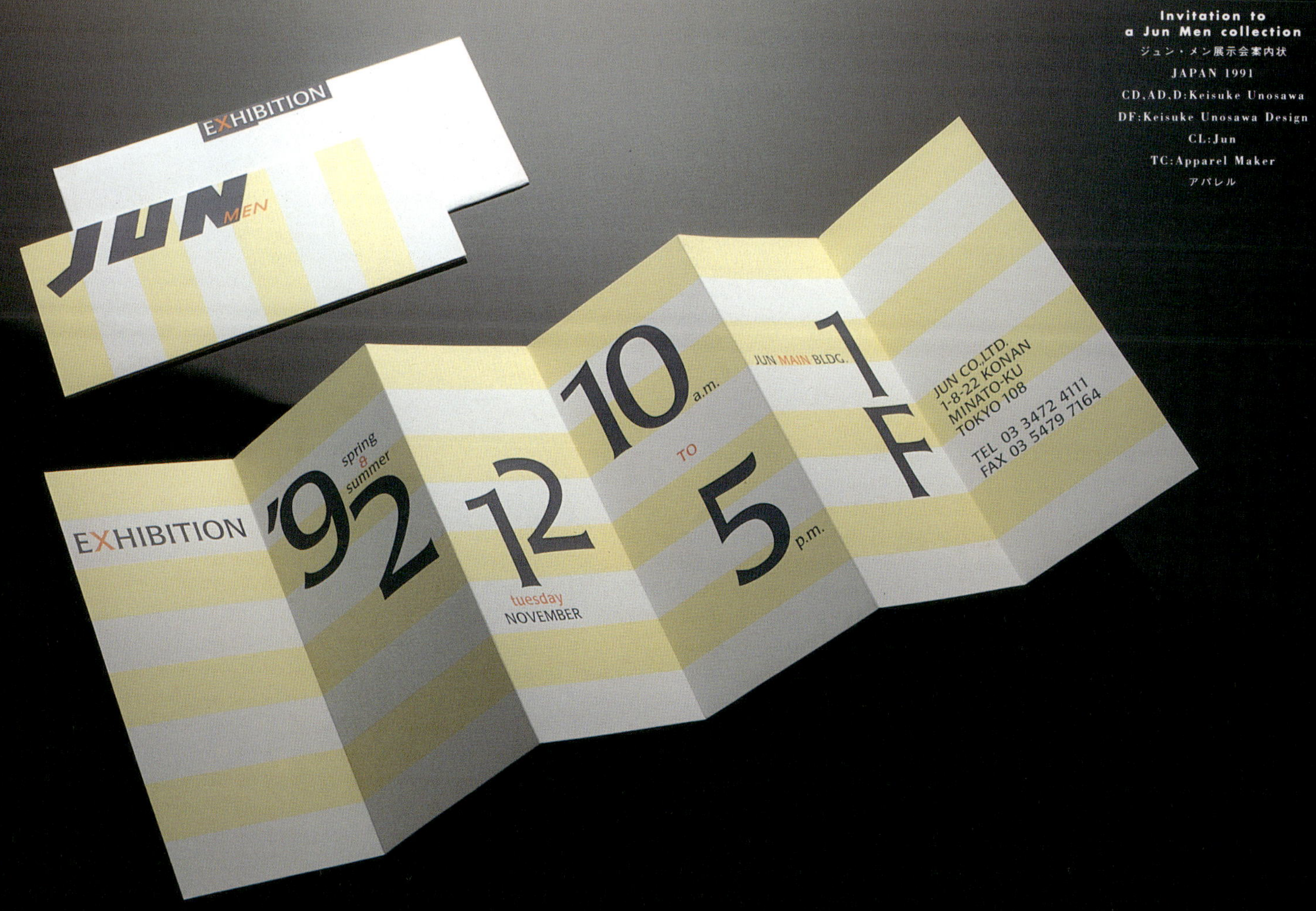

Invitation to a Jun Men collection
ジュン・メン展示会案内状
JAPAN 1991
CD,AD,D:Keisuke Unosawa
DF:Keisuke Unosawa Design
CL:Jun
TC:Apparel Maker
アパレル

Invitation to a Jun Men collection
ジュン・メン展示会案内状
JAPAN 1991
CD,AD,D:Keisuke Unosawa
DF:Keisuke Unosawa Design
CL:Jun
TC:Apparel Maker
アパレル

▲
Invitation to an Oxford Quincy fashion collection
オックスフォード・クインシー展示会案内状
JAPAN 1992
CD:Yozo Fujii
AD,D:Eiji Shimizu
CL:Oxford
TC:Apparel Maker
アパレル

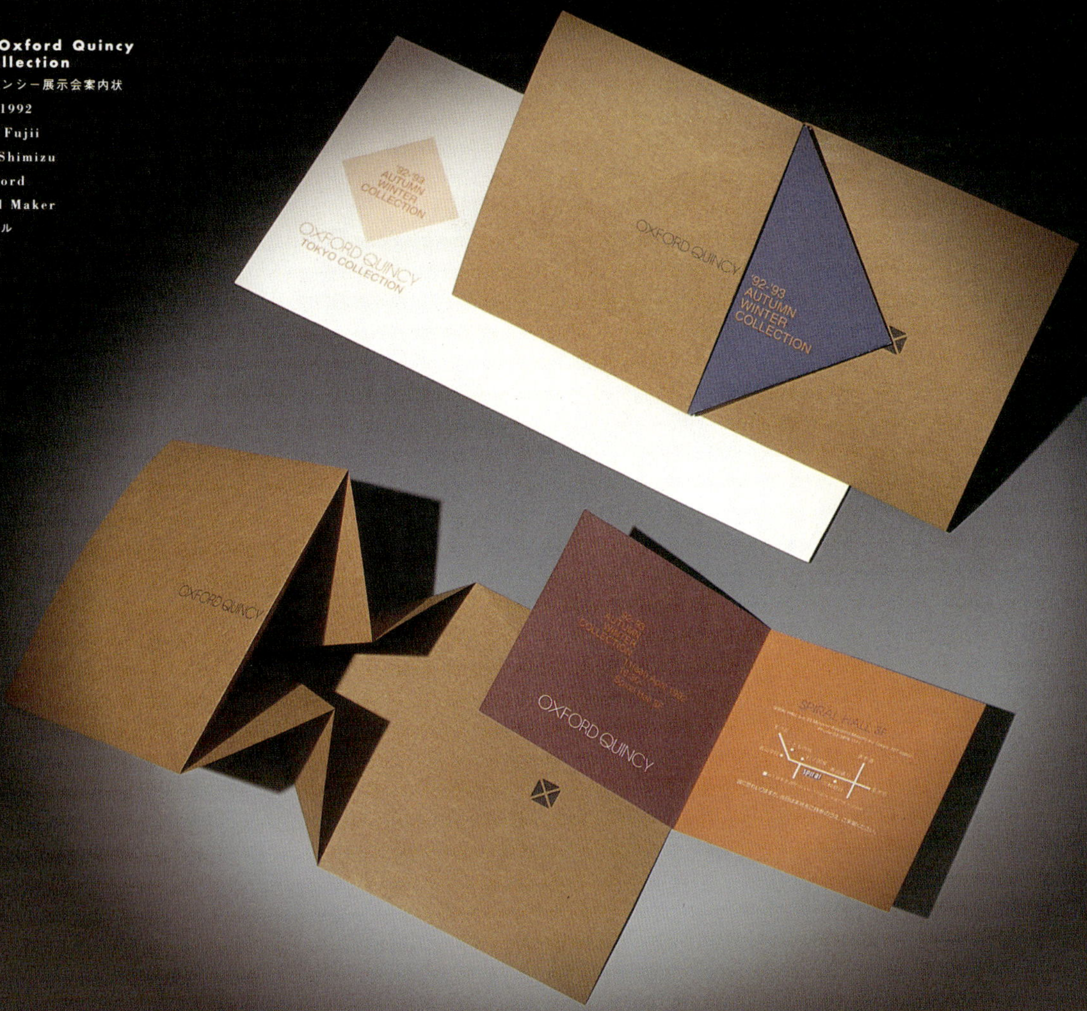

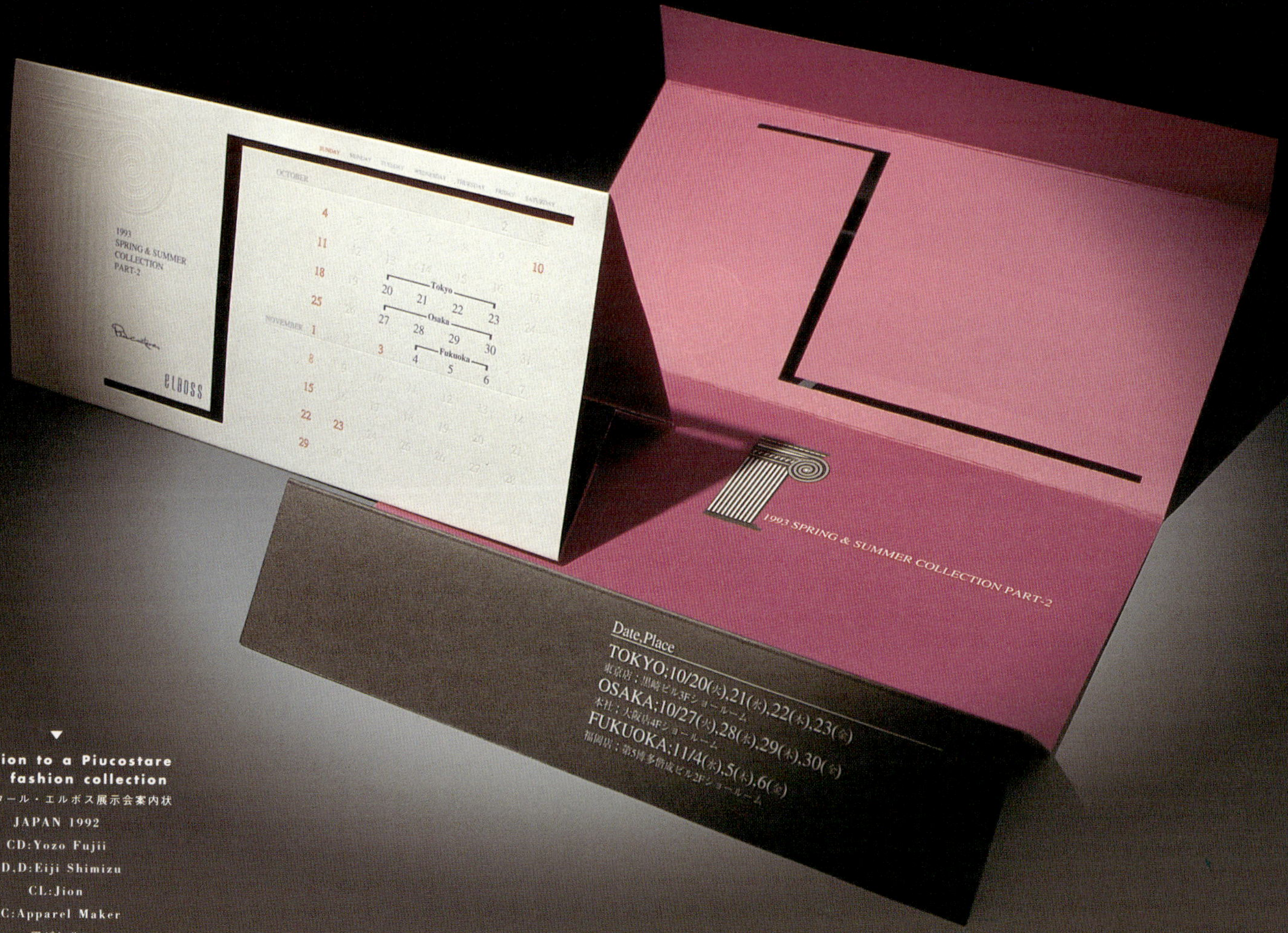

▼
Invitation to a Piucostare Elboss fashion collection
ピュコスタール・エルボス展示会案内状
JAPAN 1992
CD:Yozo Fujii
AD,D:Eiji Shimizu
CL:Jion
TC:Apparel Maker
アパレル

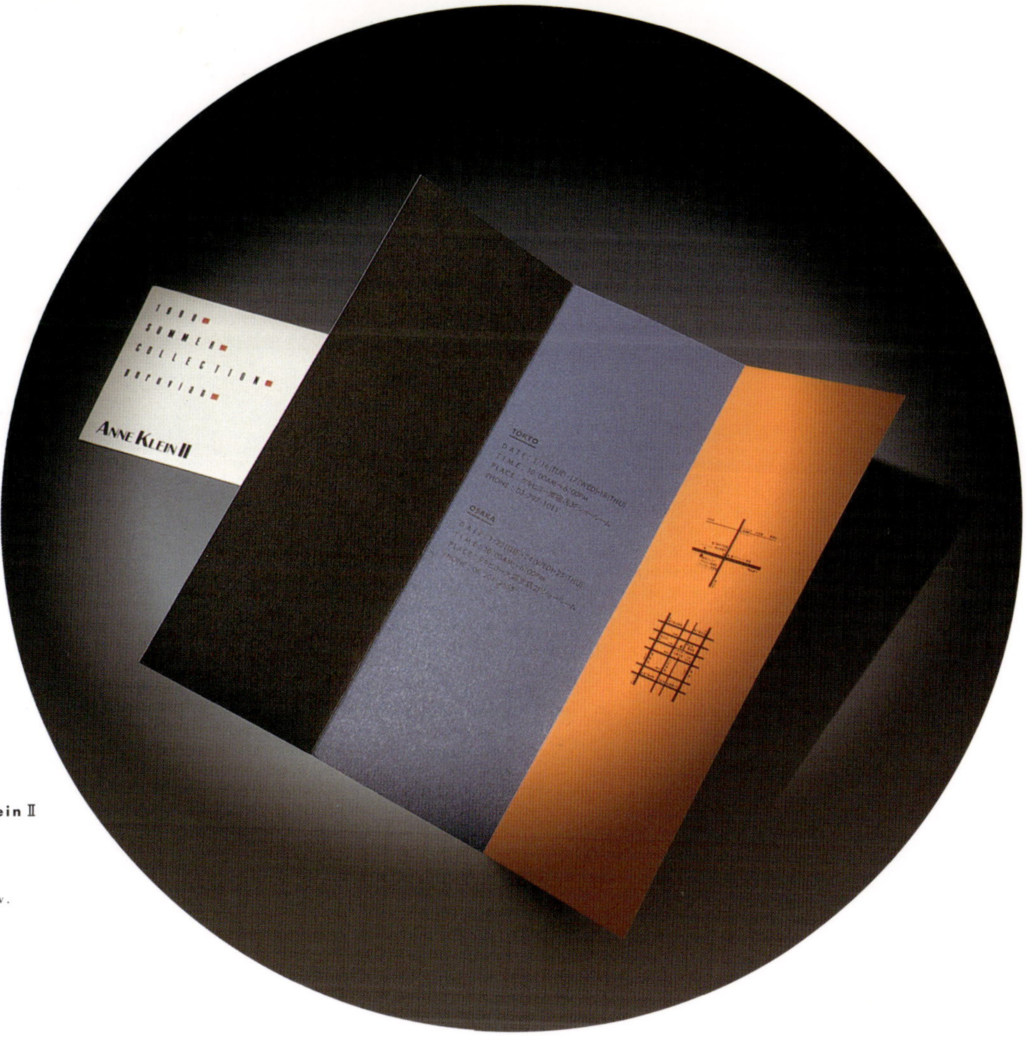

▲
Invitation to an Anne Klein Ⅱ fashion collection
アン・クラインⅡ展示会案内状
JAPAN 1990
CD,D:Hanabusa Plannig Div.
CL:Takihyo
TC:Apparel Maker
アパレル

▼
Invitation to a Kata Eyewear sales exhibition
カタ・アイウェア展示販売会案内状
USA 1991
CD:Richard Seireeni
AD,D:Romane Cameron
CW:Phyllis Hansen
DF:Studio Seireeni
CL:Wilshire Designs
TC:Eyewear Manufacturer
眼鏡製造

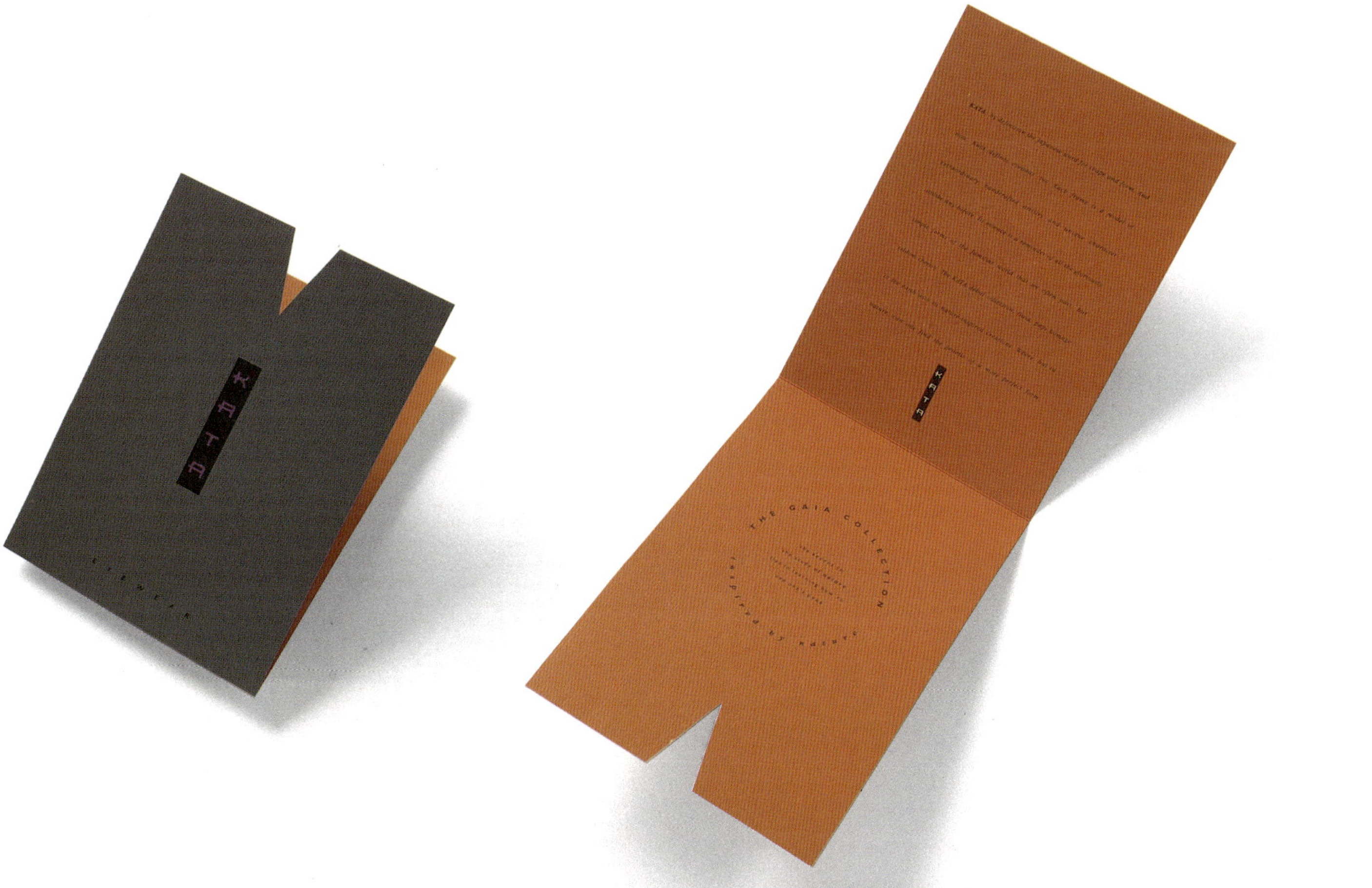

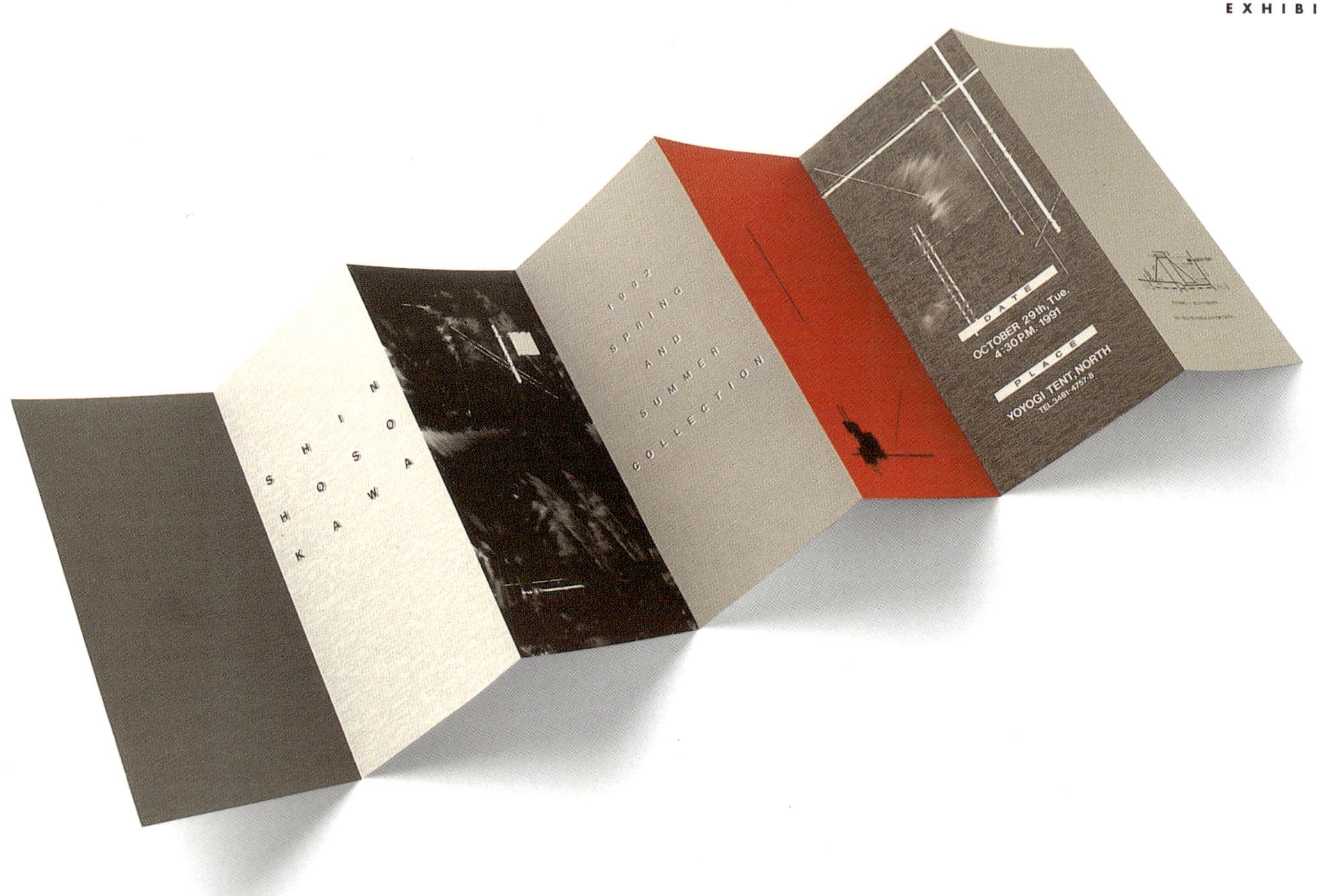

▲
Invitation to a Shin Hosokawa collection
シン・ホソカワ展示会案内状
JAPAN 1991
AD:Hiroshi Takahara
D:Mayumi Oka
CL:Pashu
TC:Apparel Maker
アパレル

▼
Invitation to a Shin Hosokawa collection
シン・ホソカワ展示会案内状
JAPAN 1992
AD:Hiroshi Takahara
D:Mayumi Oka
CL:Pashu
TC:Apparel Maker
アパレル

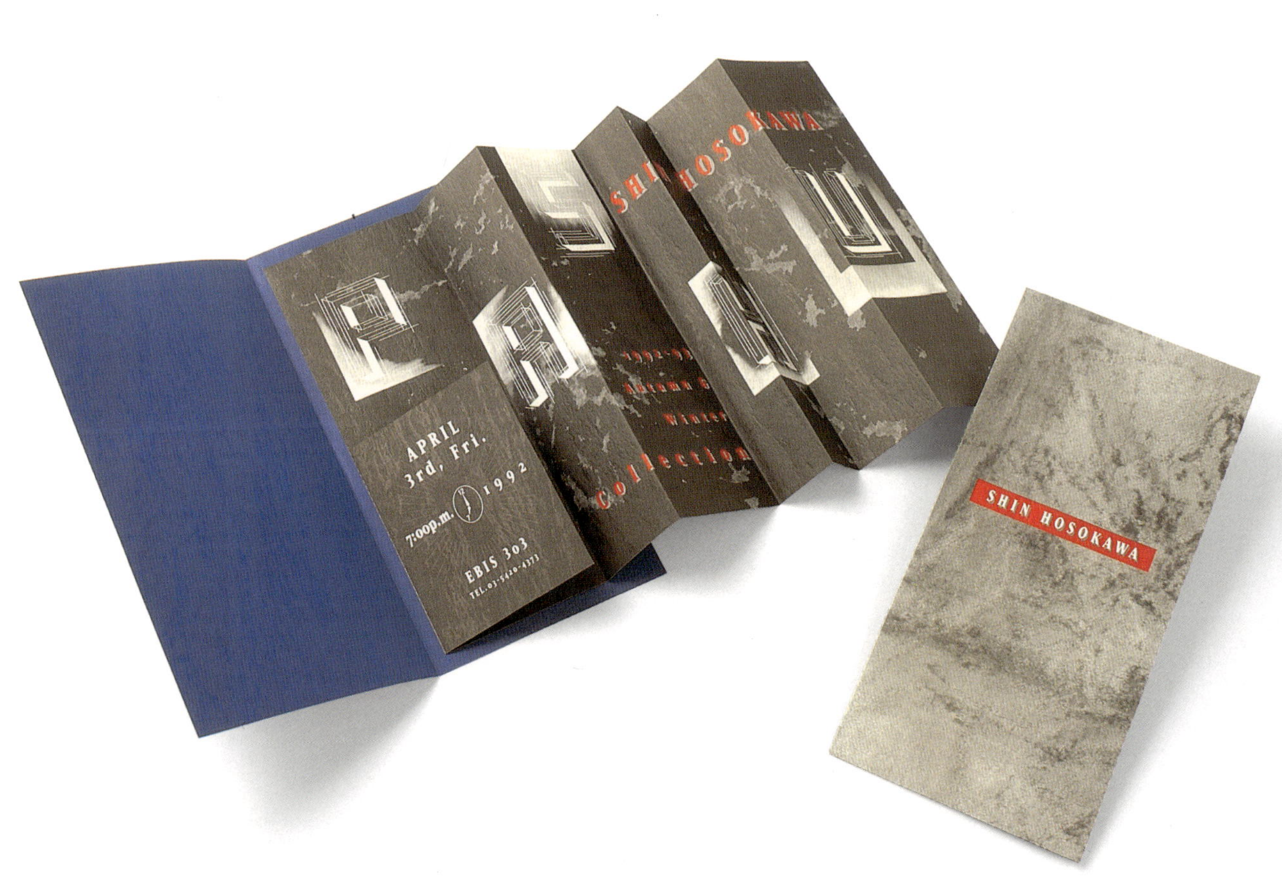

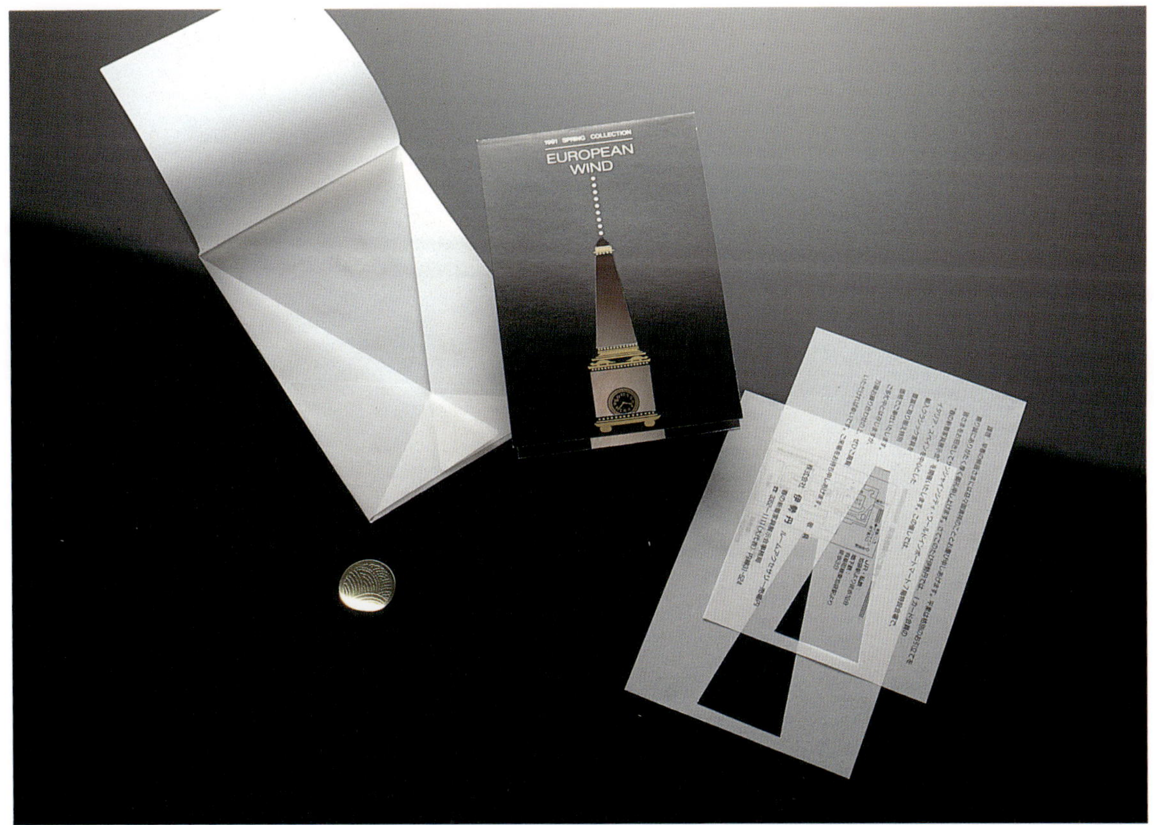

▲
Invitation to an imported furniture sales show
輸入家具展示会案内状
JAPAN 1991
CD,AD,D:Katsuaki Kumakura
CL:Isetan
TC:Department Store
百貨店

▼
Invitation to a sales show
展示会案内状
JAPAN 1990
CD:Setsuko Mataki
AD,D:Akihiko Tsukamoto
CL:Sasaki Keori
TC:Textile Wholesaler
テキスタイル卸売り

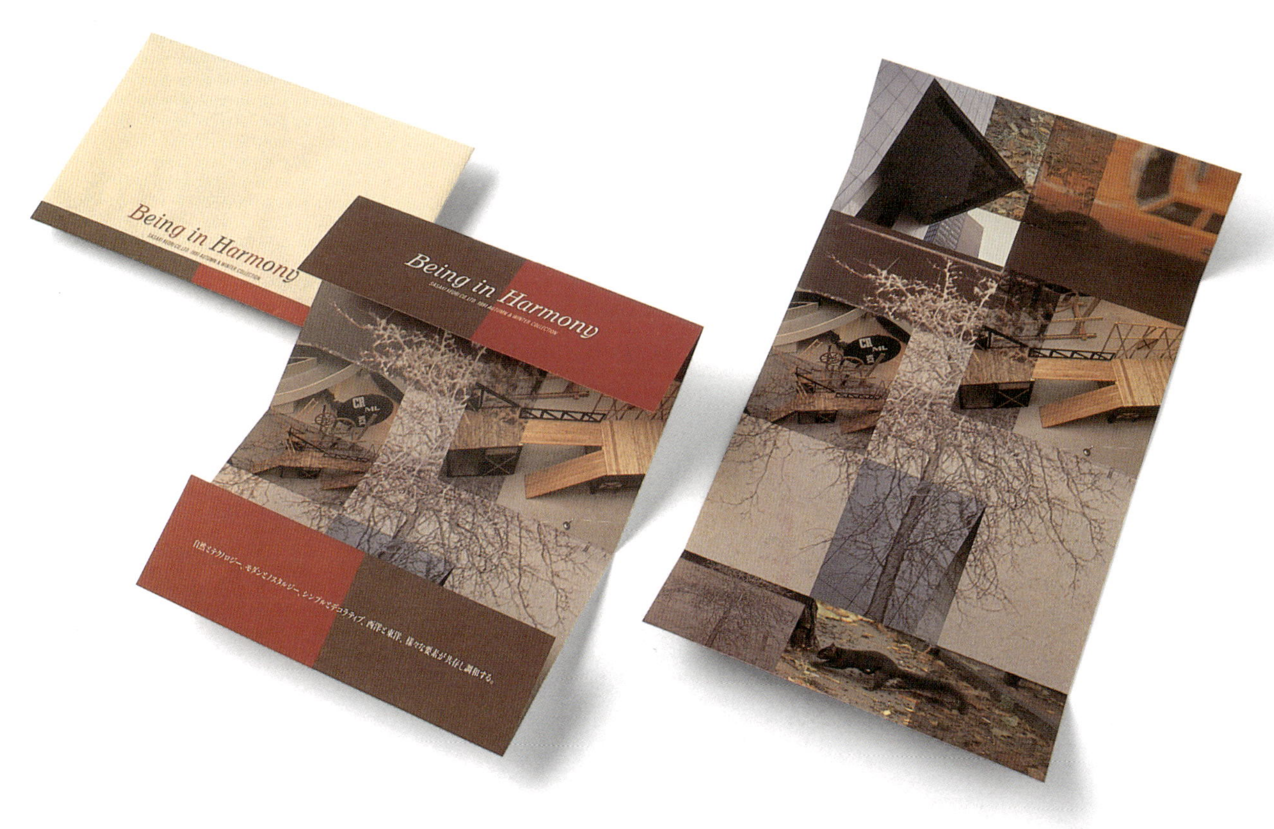

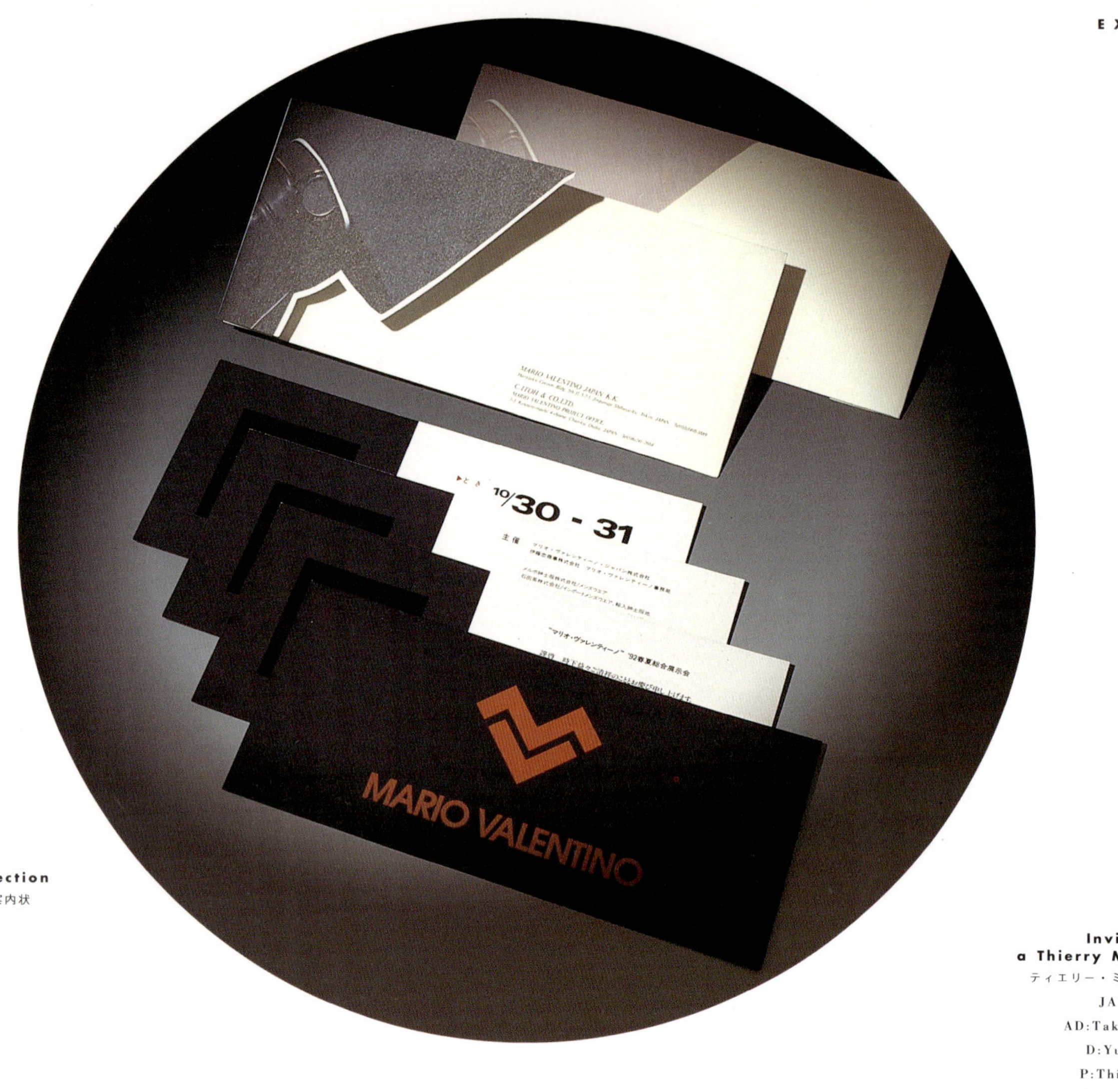

▲
Invitation to a Mario Valentino collection
マリオ・バレンティーノ展示会案内状
JAPAN 1991
CD:Masahiro Okafuji
Ikuko Takahashi
AD,D:taKAKAku
P:TYEN
CW:Nobuaki Otsuki
DF:Otsuki Planing
CL:C.Itoh
TC:Apparel Maker
アパレル

▼
Invitation to a Thierry Mugler collection
ティエリー・ミュグレー展示会案内状
JAPAN 1992
AD:Takashi Matsuura
D:Yumiko Hirai
P:Thierry Mugler
CL:Monte Rosa
TC:Apparel Maker
アパレル

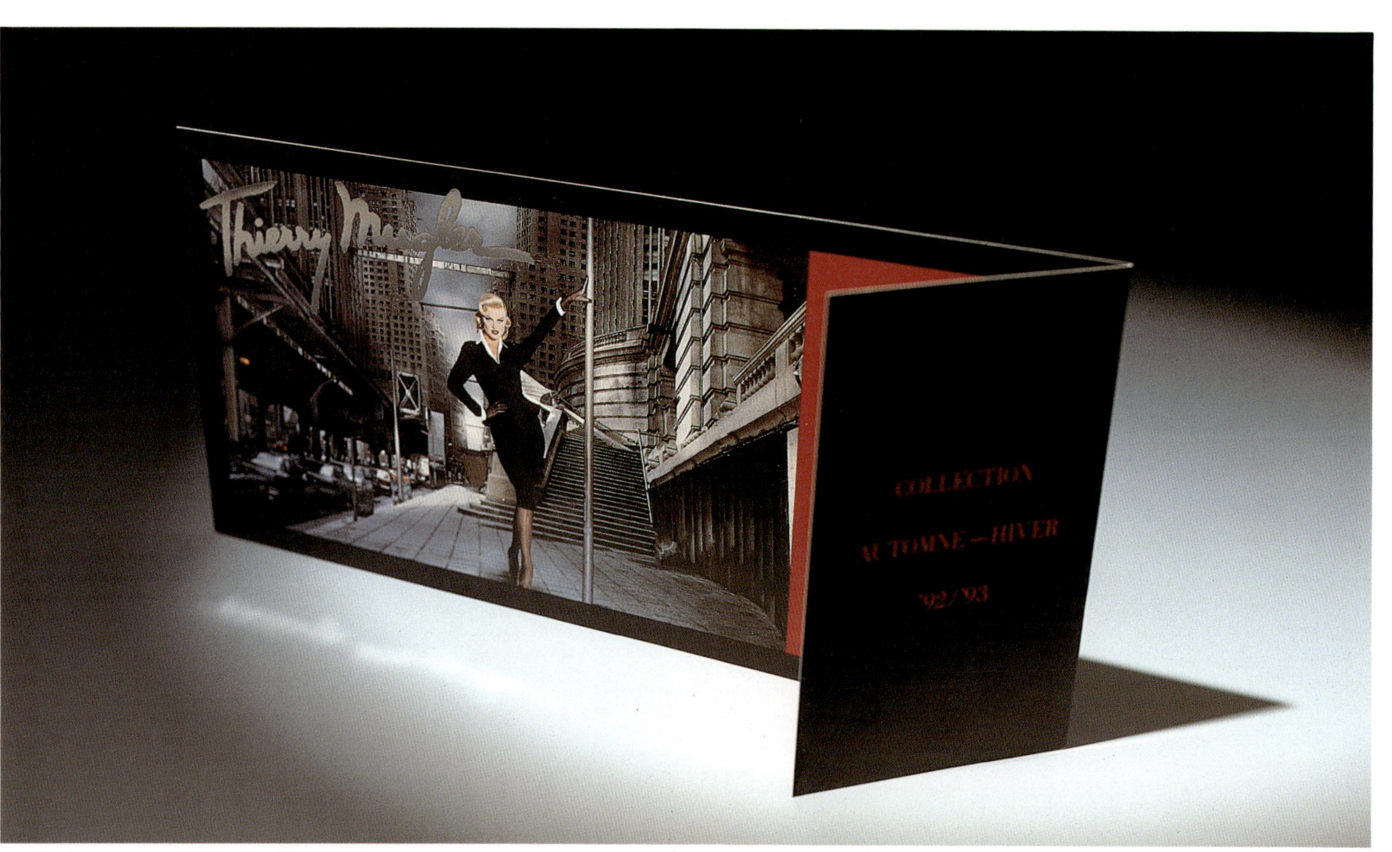

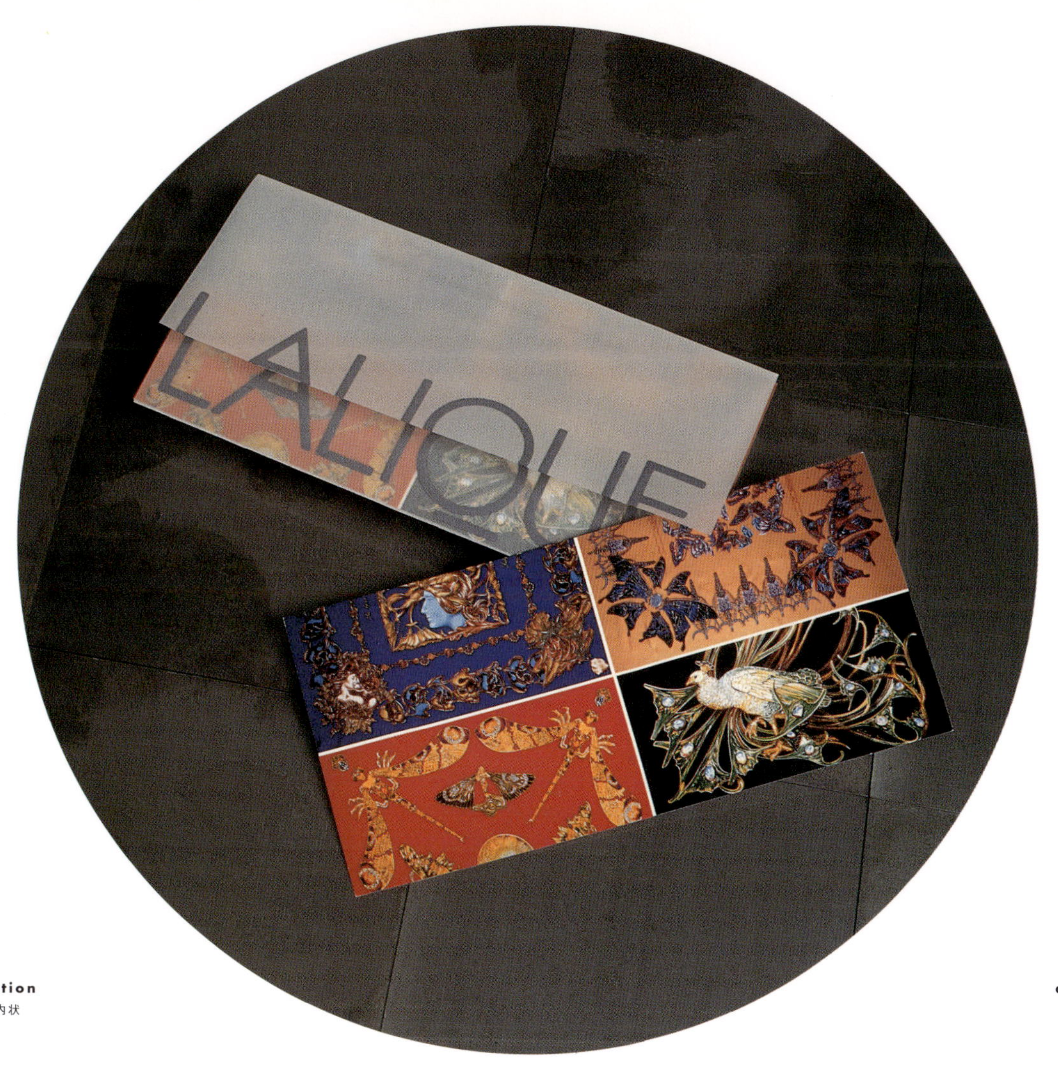

▲
Invitation to
a Lalique Glass exhibition
ラリーク・ガラス製品展示会案内状
ITALY 1992
CD:Claudio Zamperini
CW:Grazia Lotti
CL:Studio Grazia Lotti for Lalique
TC:Art Glass Maker
ガラス製品製造

▼
Invitation to
an accessory collection
アクセサリー展示会案内状
JAPAN 1990
AD,D:Yoshinori Kikuchi
P:Shigemi Suzuki
CL:Orient
TC:Watch,Accessory Maker
時計、アクセサリー製造販売

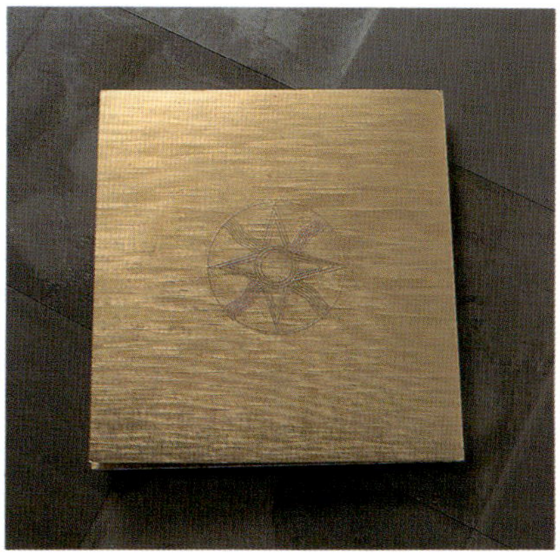

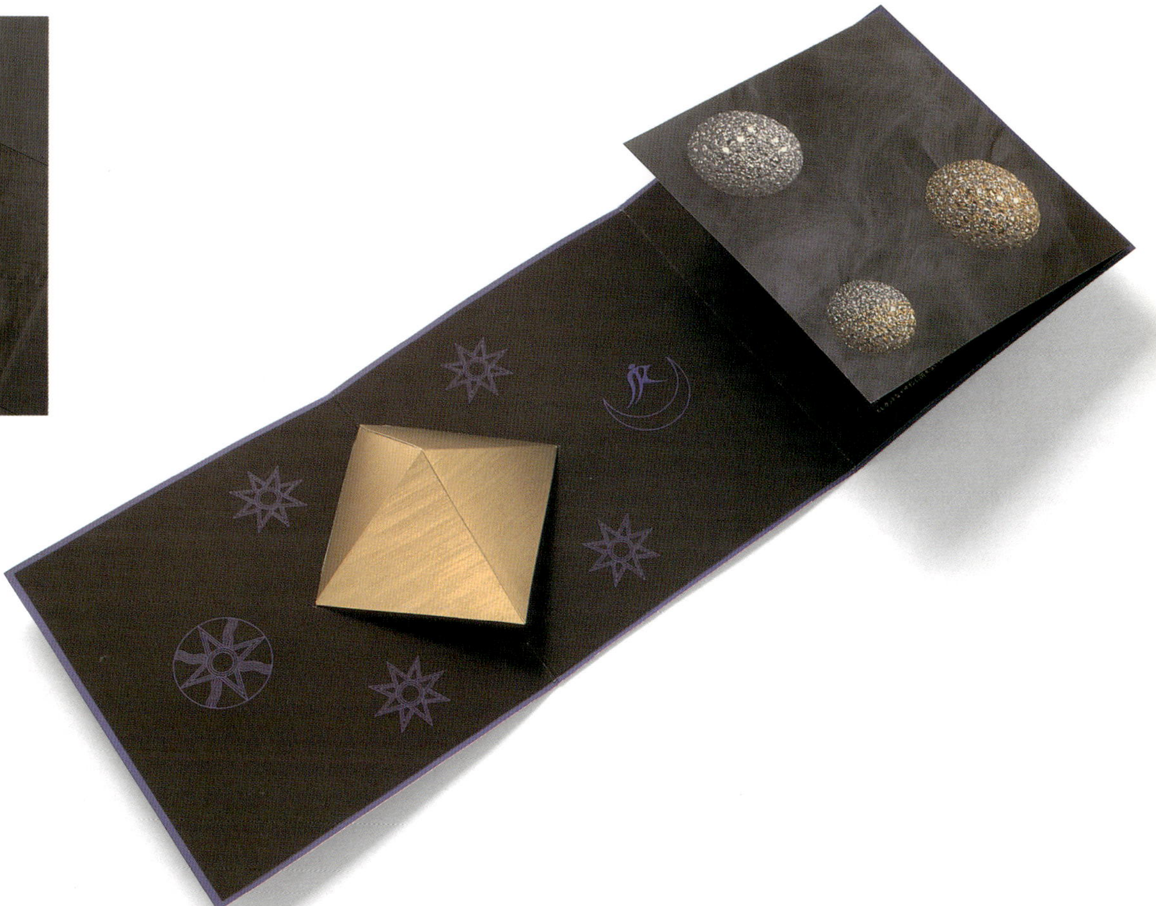

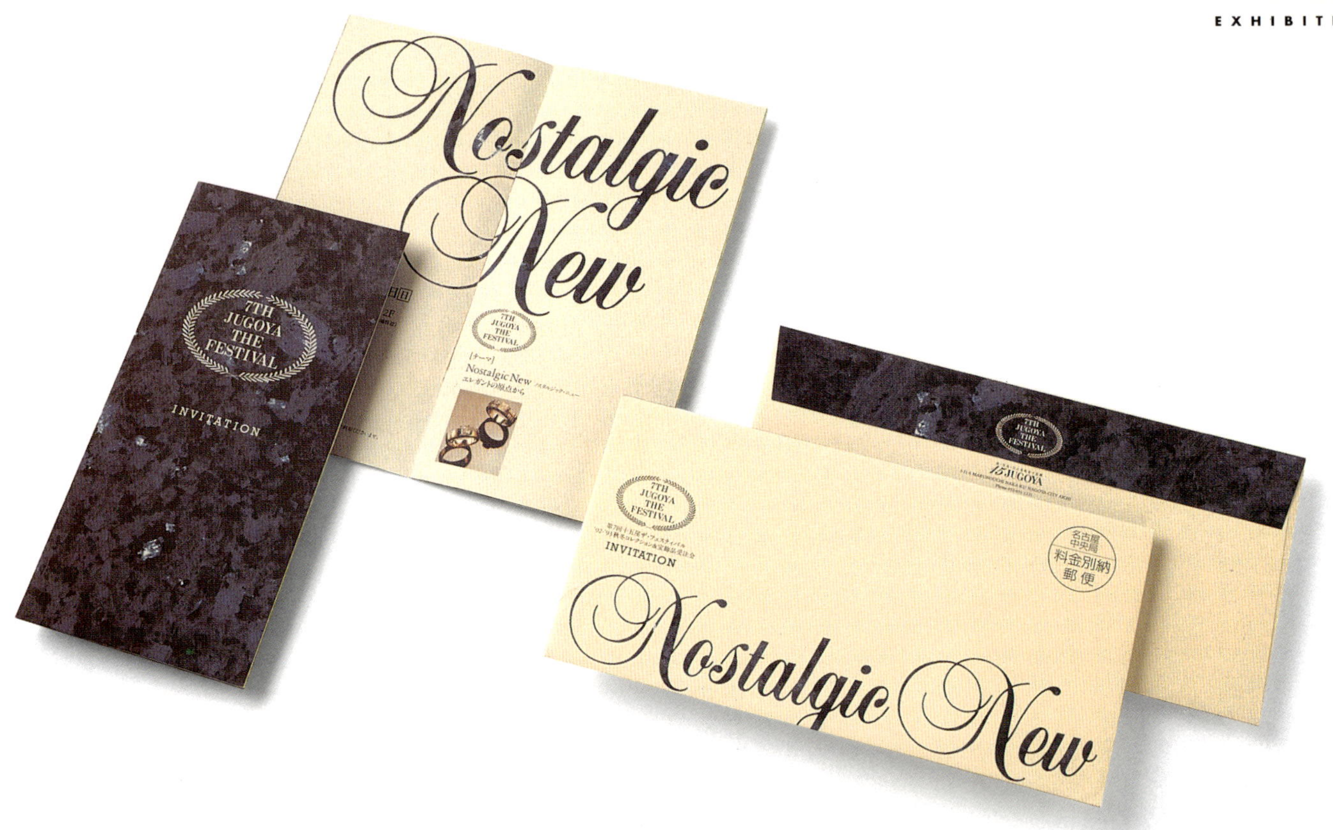

▲
Invitation to an accessory collection
アクセサリー展示会案内状
JAPAN 1992
CD,AD,D:Yasumitsu Iguchi
CL:Jugoya
TC:Apparel Maker
アパレル

▼
Invitation to a collection
展示会案内状
JAPAN 1991
CD:Takazumi Tokuyama
D,I,DF:Kid Design Studio
CL:Lamoi
TC:Hair Accessory Maker
髪飾メーカー

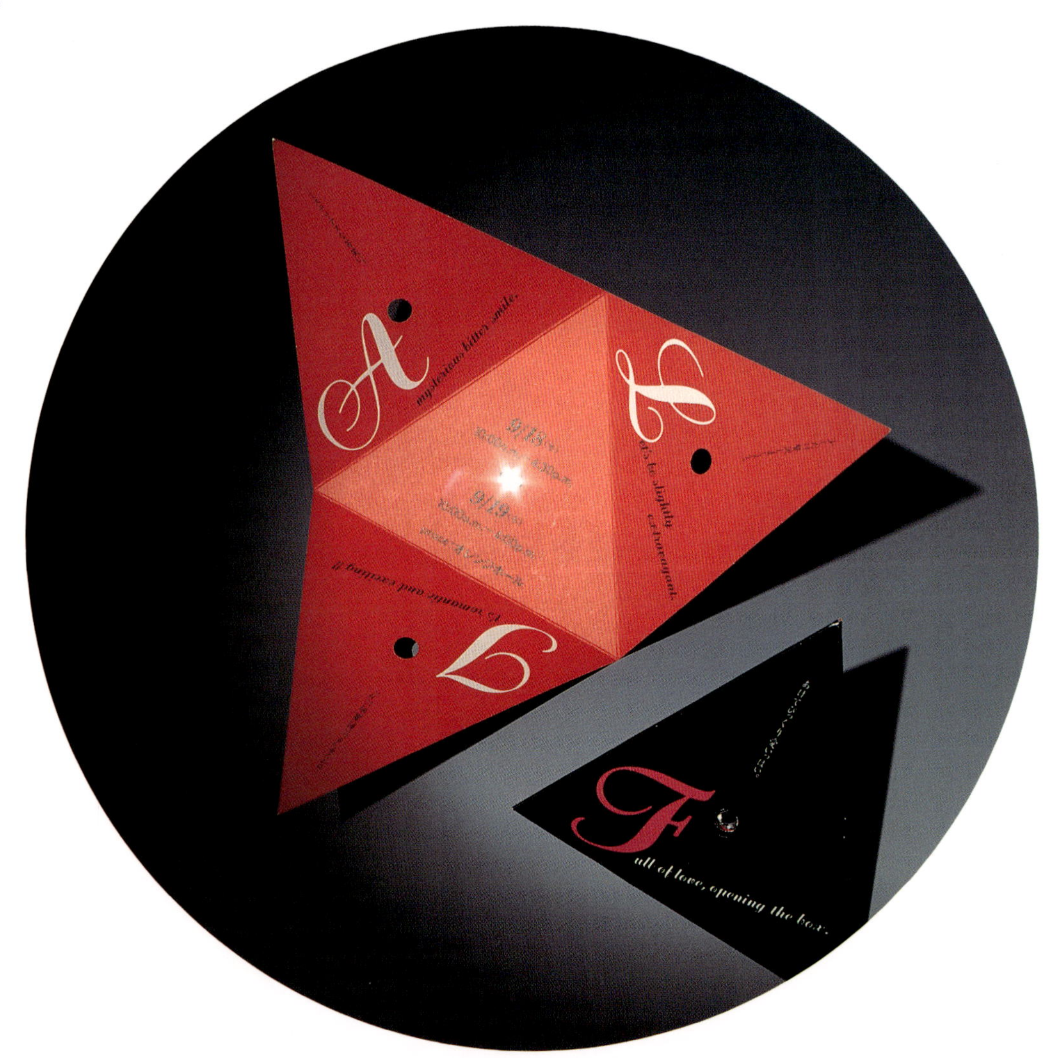

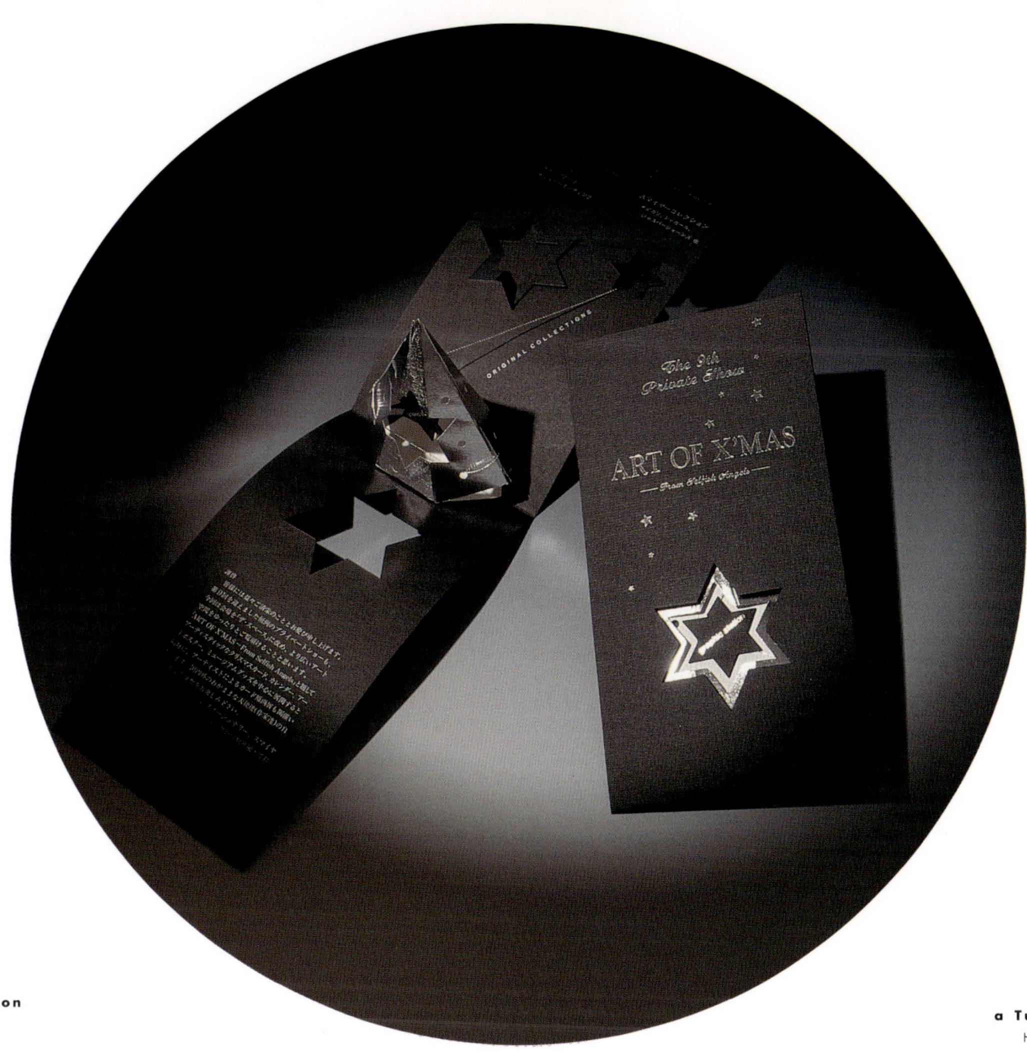

▲
Invitation to an exhibition
展示会案内状
JAPAN 1991
CD,AD,D:Mutsuko Morita
CL:Art Print Japan
TC:Poster,Card Publisher
ポスター、カード制作販売

▼
Invitation to a Tua Rahikainen exhibition
トゥア・ラヒカイネン展示会案内状
JAPAN 1990
CD:Reo Mishima
AD:Akihiko Tsukamoto
D:Harumi Tominaga
CW:Sakiko Yoshihara
CL:Creative Eight
TC:Event Planner
イベント企画

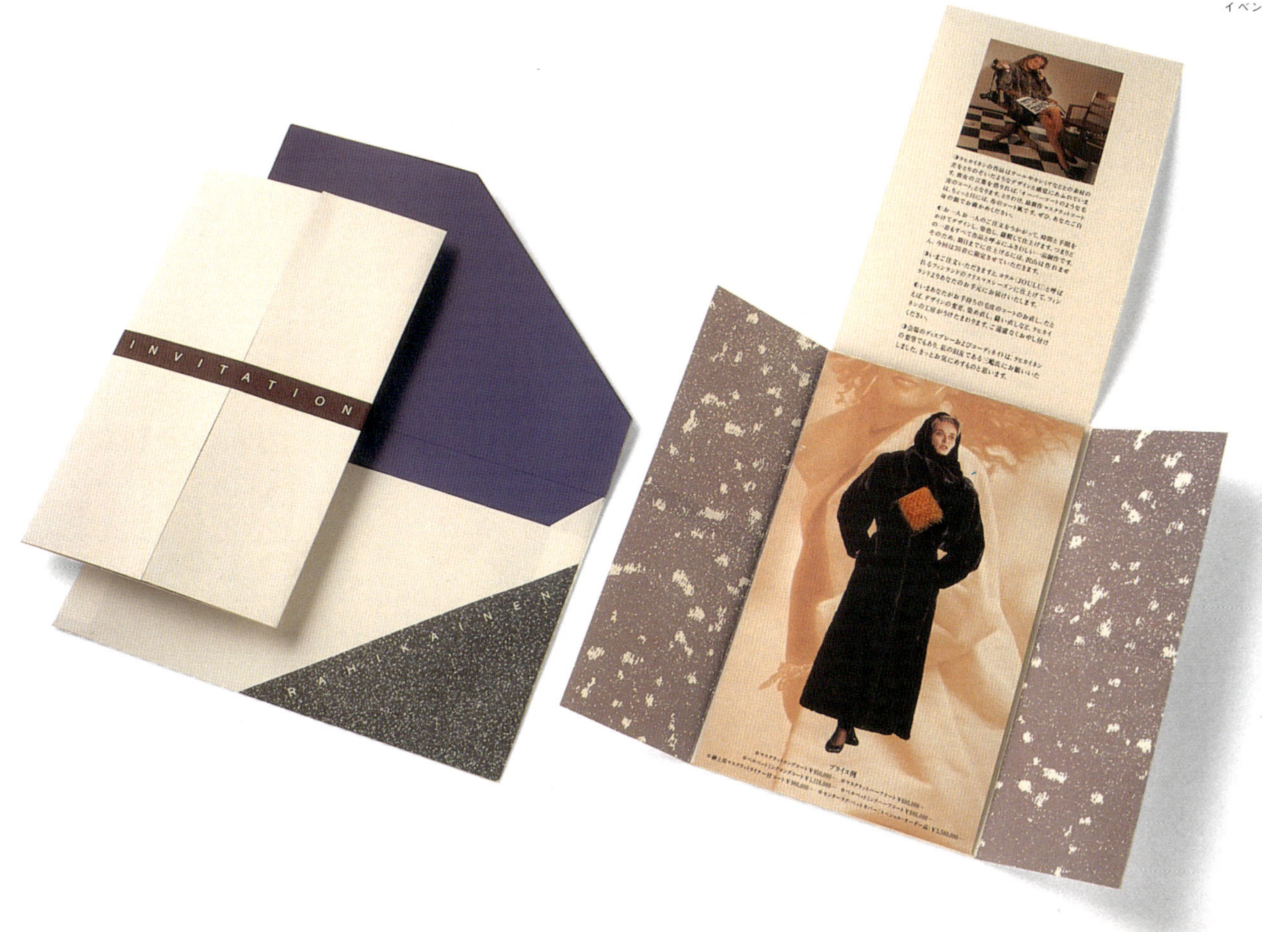

Invitation to a Xenon sales show
キセノン展示会案内状
JAPAN 1991
AD,D,I:Shoujirou Ogushi
CW:Tadasu Inoue
DF:Creative Grace
CL:Naiki
TC:Office Furniture Maker
オフィス用家具製造販売

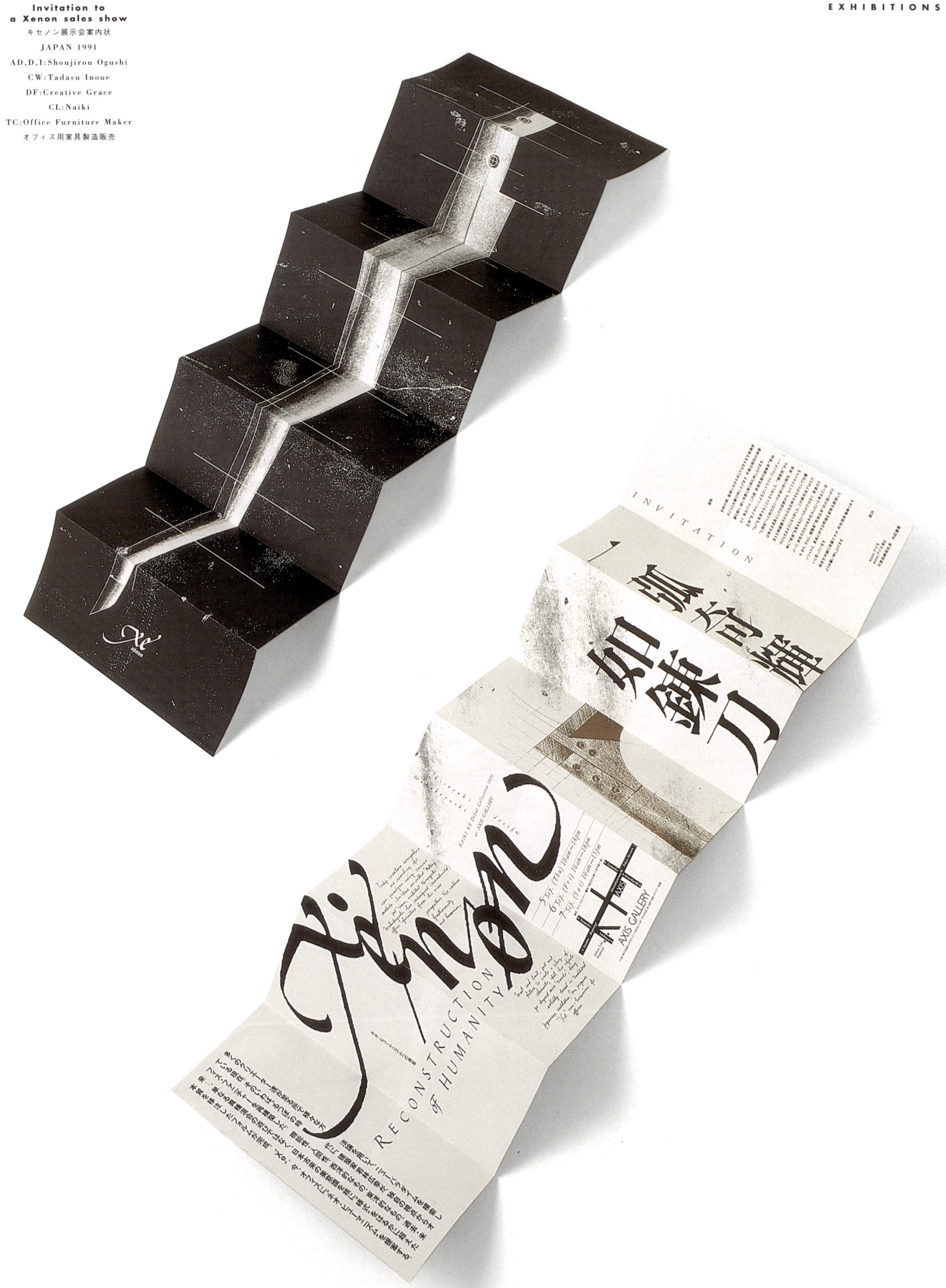

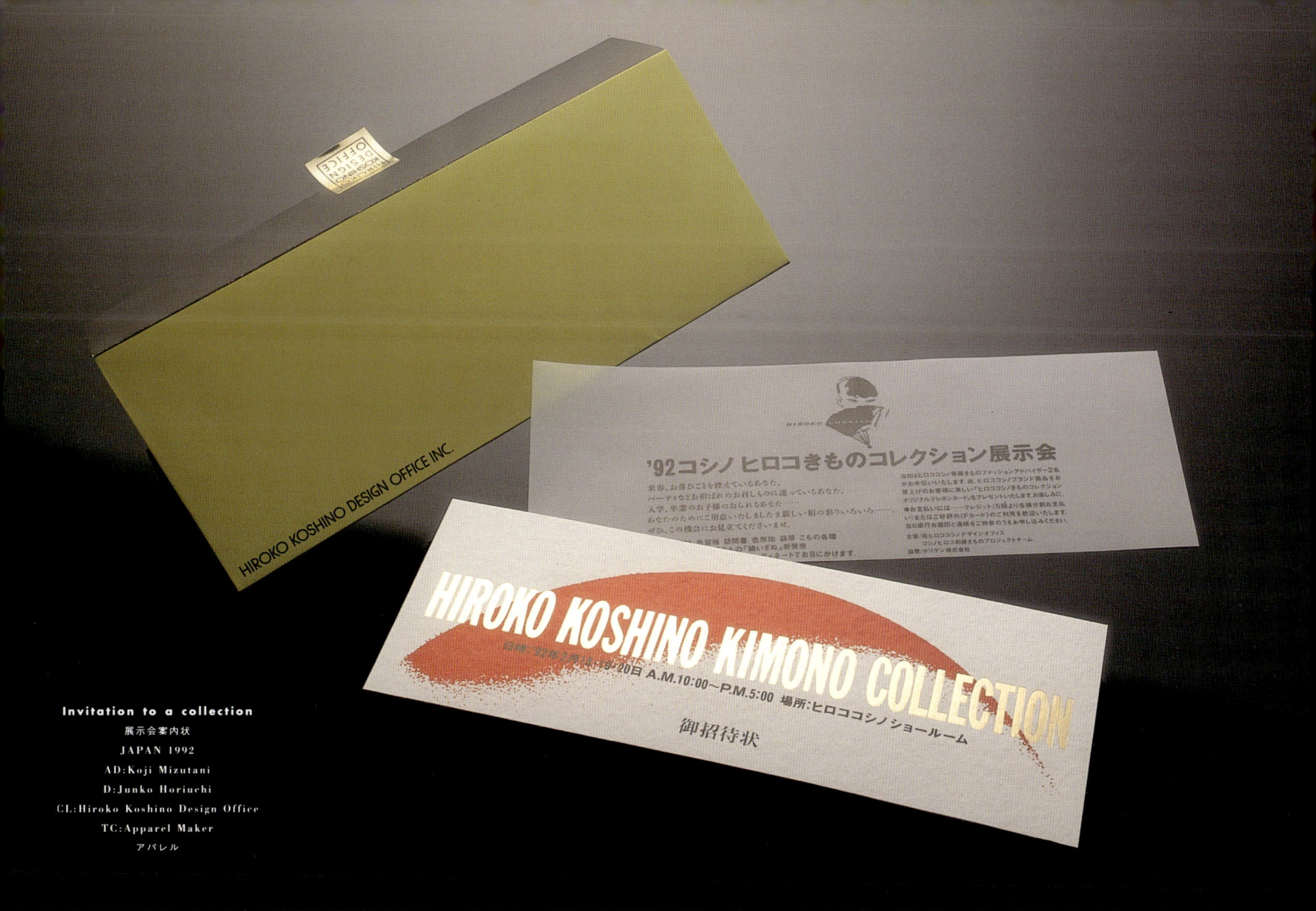

Invitation to a collection
展示会案内状
JAPAN 1992
AD:Koji Mizutani
D:Junko Horiuchi
CL:Hiroko Koshino Design Office
TC:Apparel Maker
アパレル

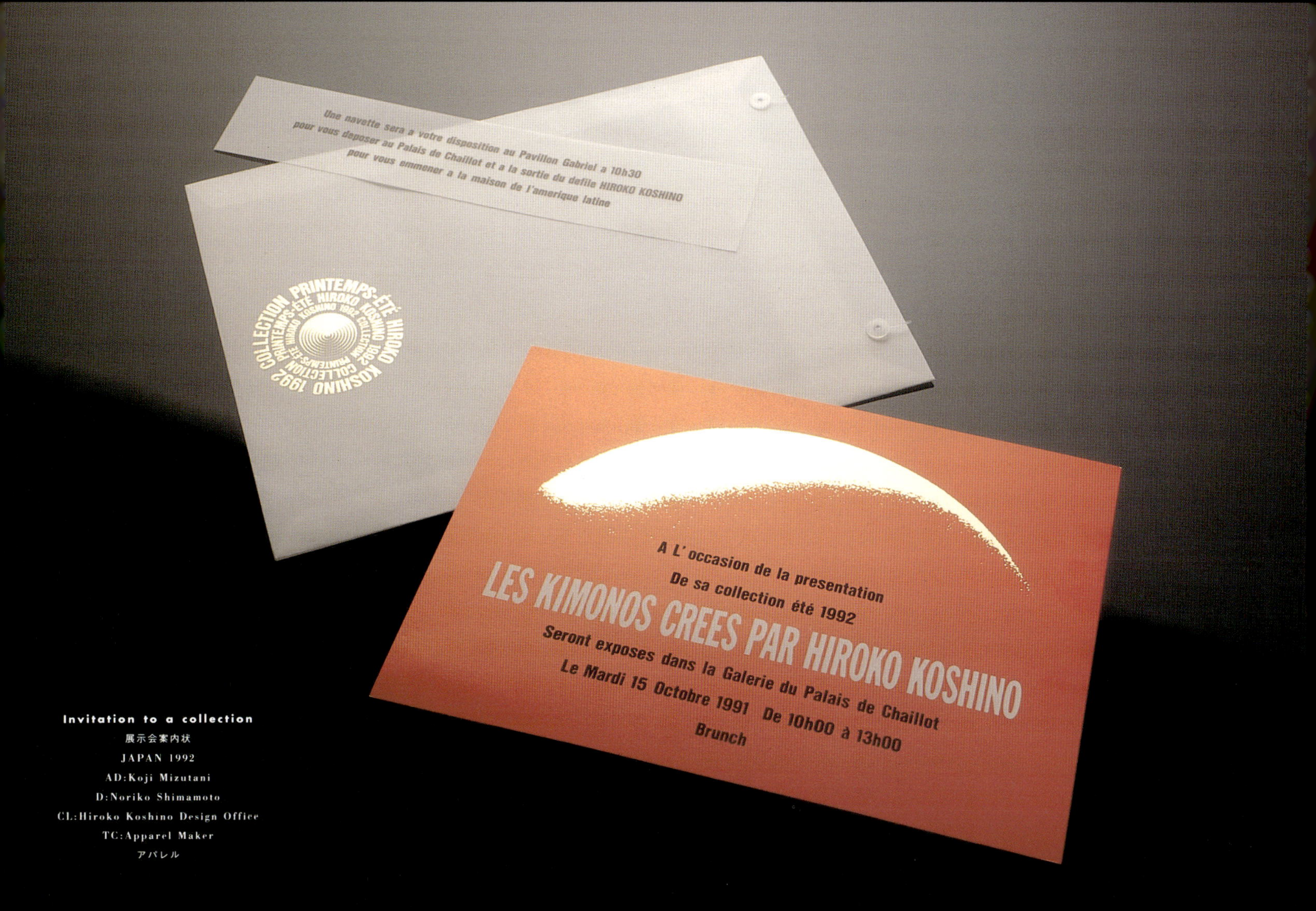

Invitation to a collection
展示会案内状
JAPAN 1992
AD:Koji Mizutani
D:Noriko Shimamoto
CL:Hiroko Koshino Design Office
TC:Apparel Maker
アパレル

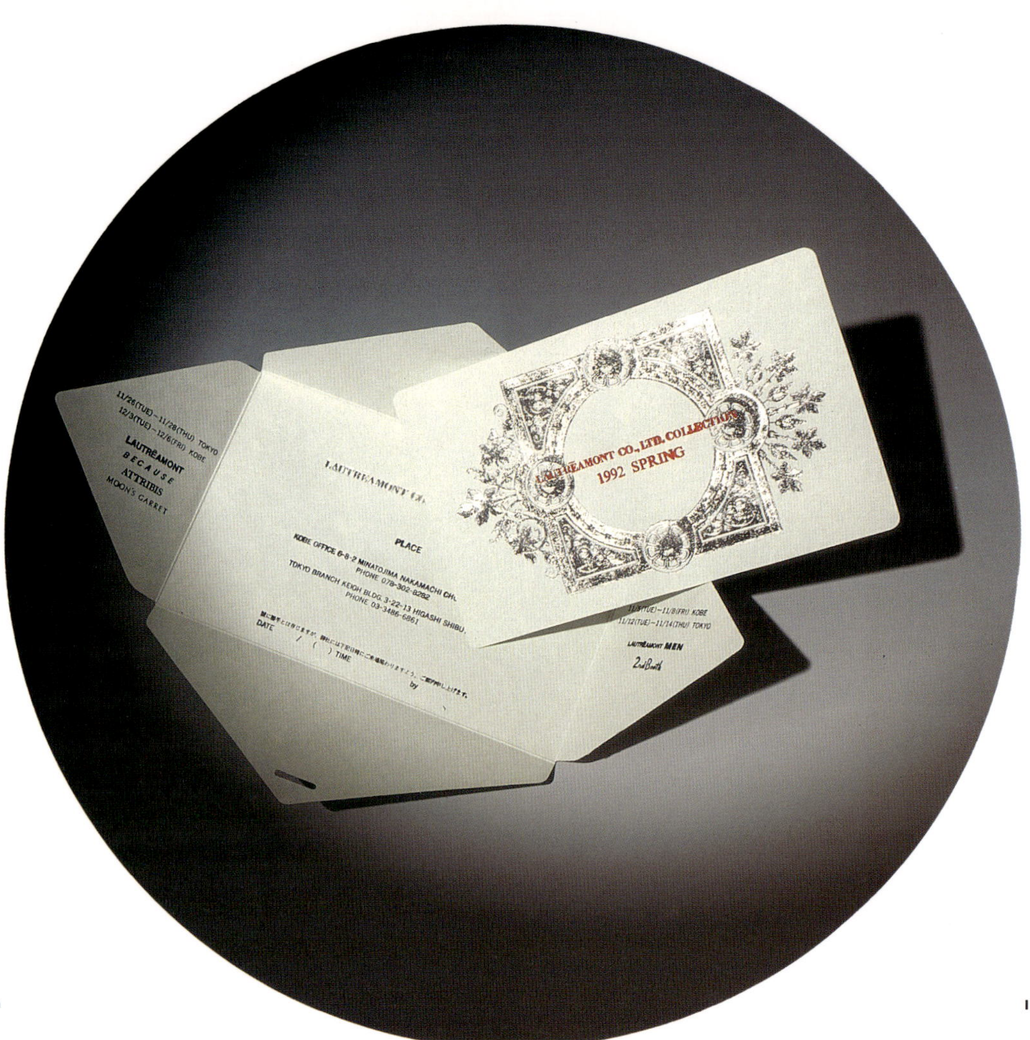

▲
Invitation to a collection
展示会案内状
JAPAN 1991
CD,AD,D:Tatsuya Ishii
Shoko Asada
CL:Lautréamont
TC:Apparel Maker
アパレル

▼
Invitation to a collection
展示会案内状
JAPAN 1991
CD,AD,D:Tatsuya Ishii
Shoko Asada
CL:Lautréamont
TC:Apparel Maker
アパレル

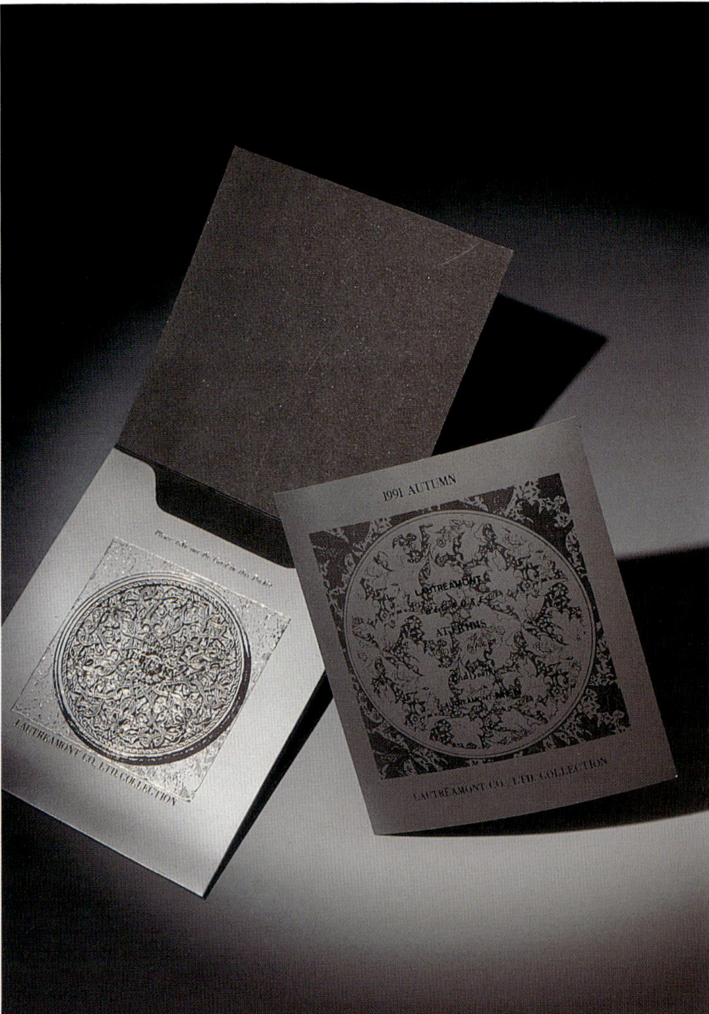

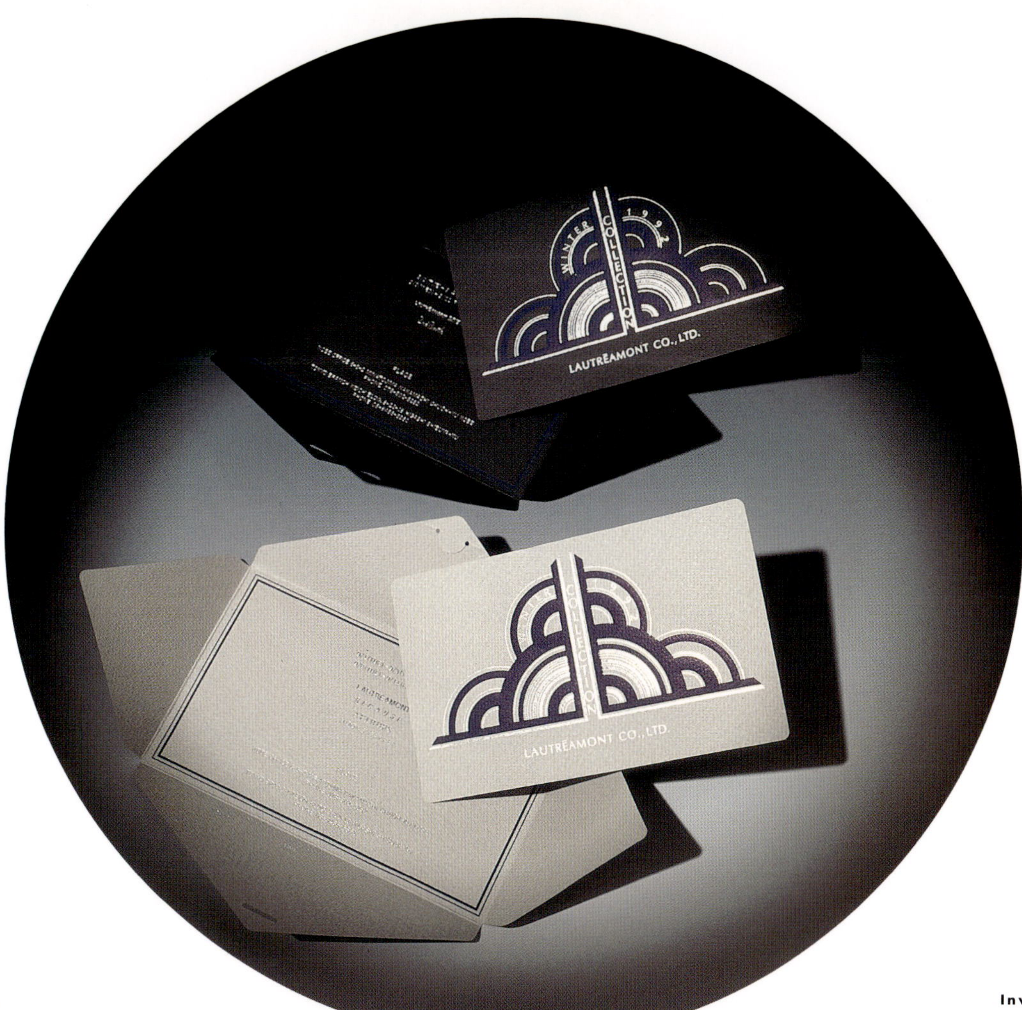

▲
Invitation to a collection
展示会案内状
JAPAN 1992
CD:Tatsuya Ishii
CL:Lautrémont
TC:Apparel Maker
アパレル

▼
Invitation to an exhibition
展示会案内状
JAPAN 1989
DF:Murata Kimpaku
CL:Murata Kimpaku
TC:Distributor of foil material and pressing machines
箔押用機械、素材販売

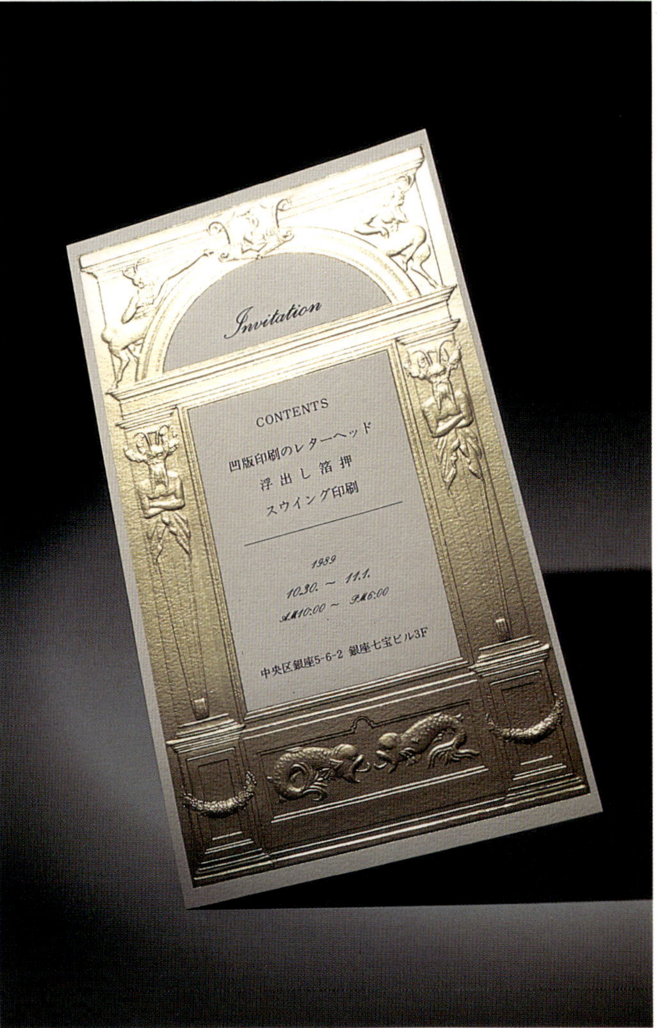

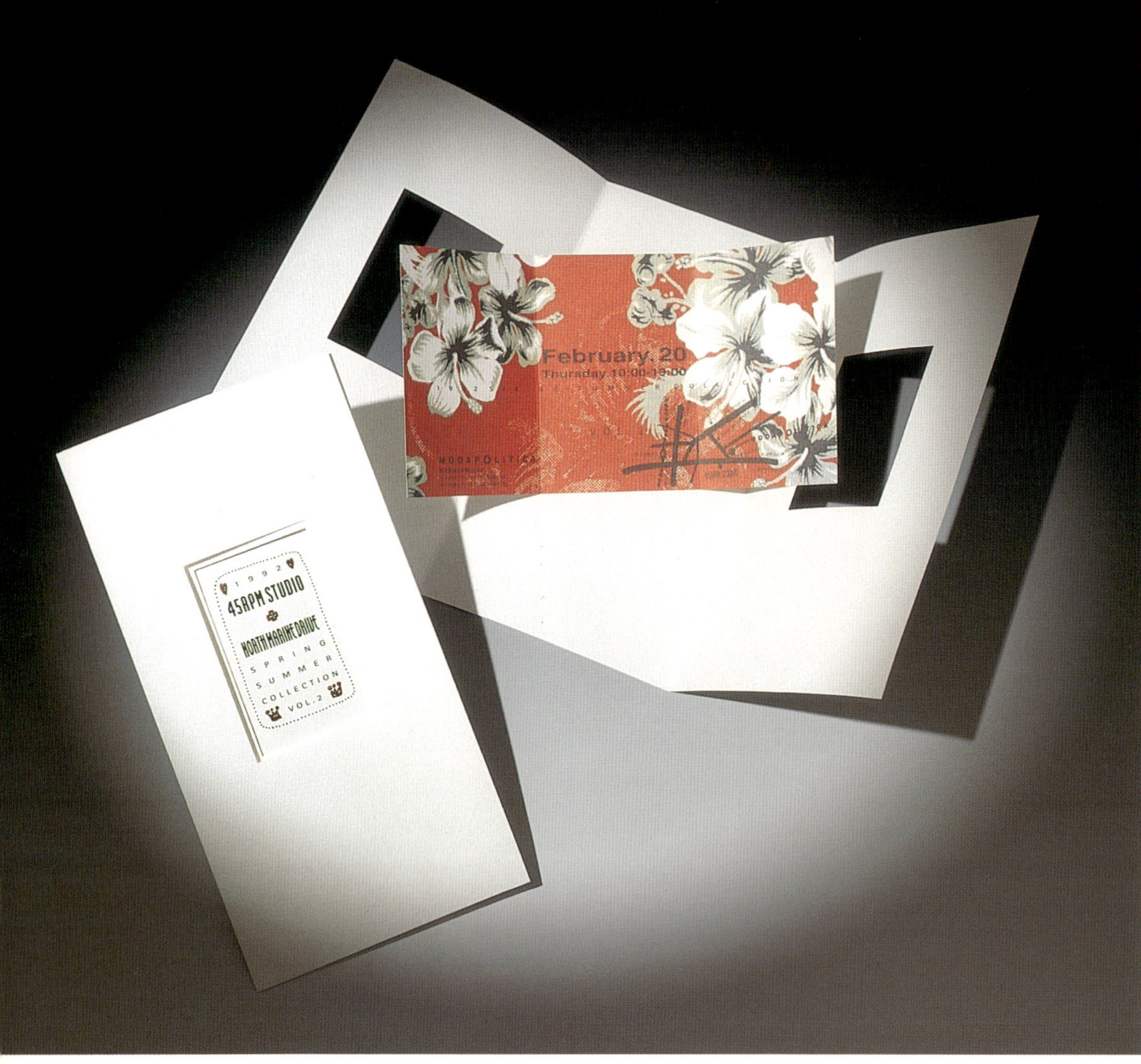

▼
Invitation to a collection
展示会案内状
JAPAN 1991
CD,AD,D,I:Joji Yano
DF:Yano Design Room
CL:45 Rpm-Studio
TC:Apparel Maker
アパレル

▲
Invitation to a collection
展示会案内状
JAPAN 1991
CD,AD,D,I:Joji Yano
DF:Yano Design Room
CL:45 Rpm-Studio
TC:Apparel Maker
アパレル

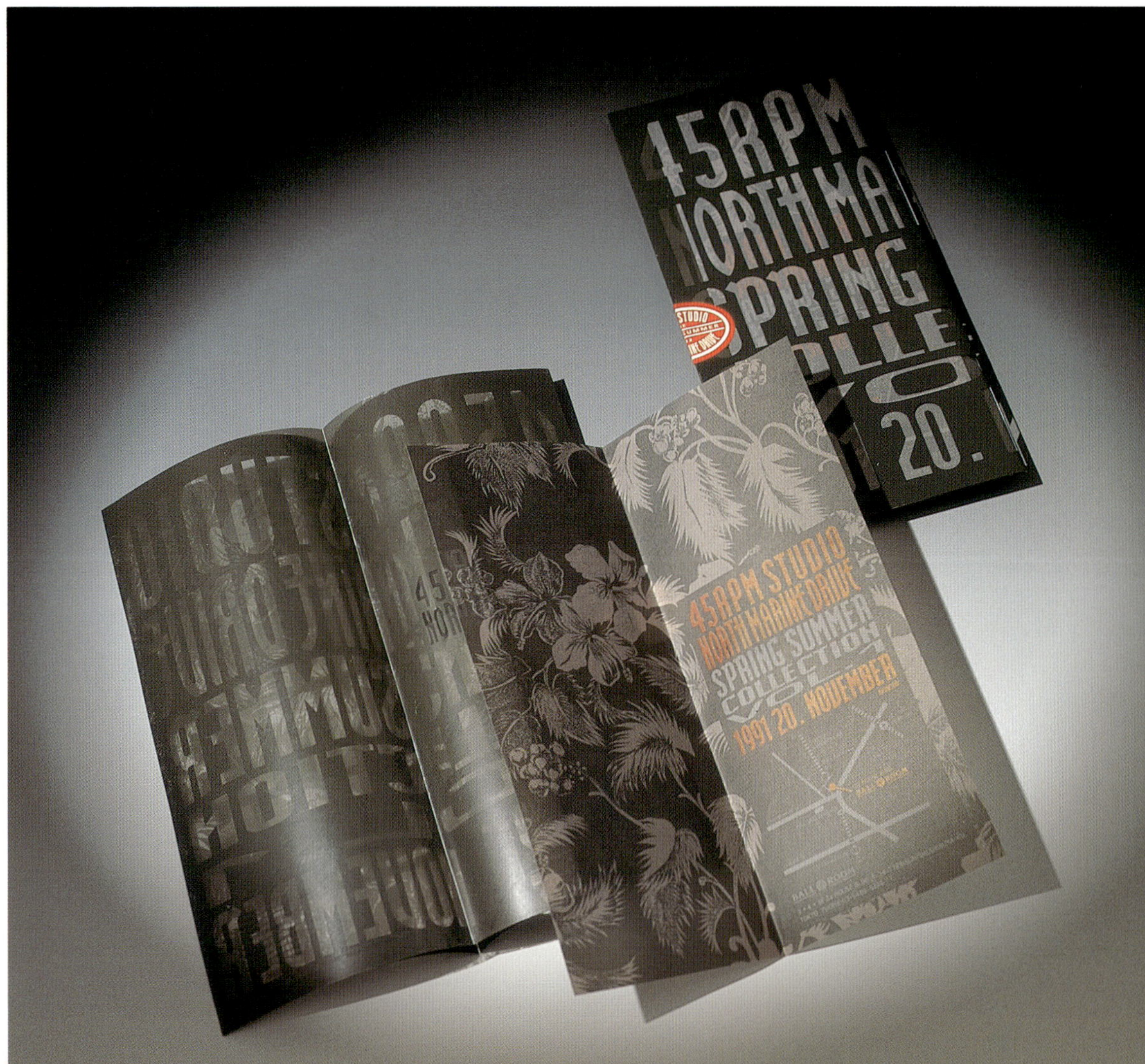

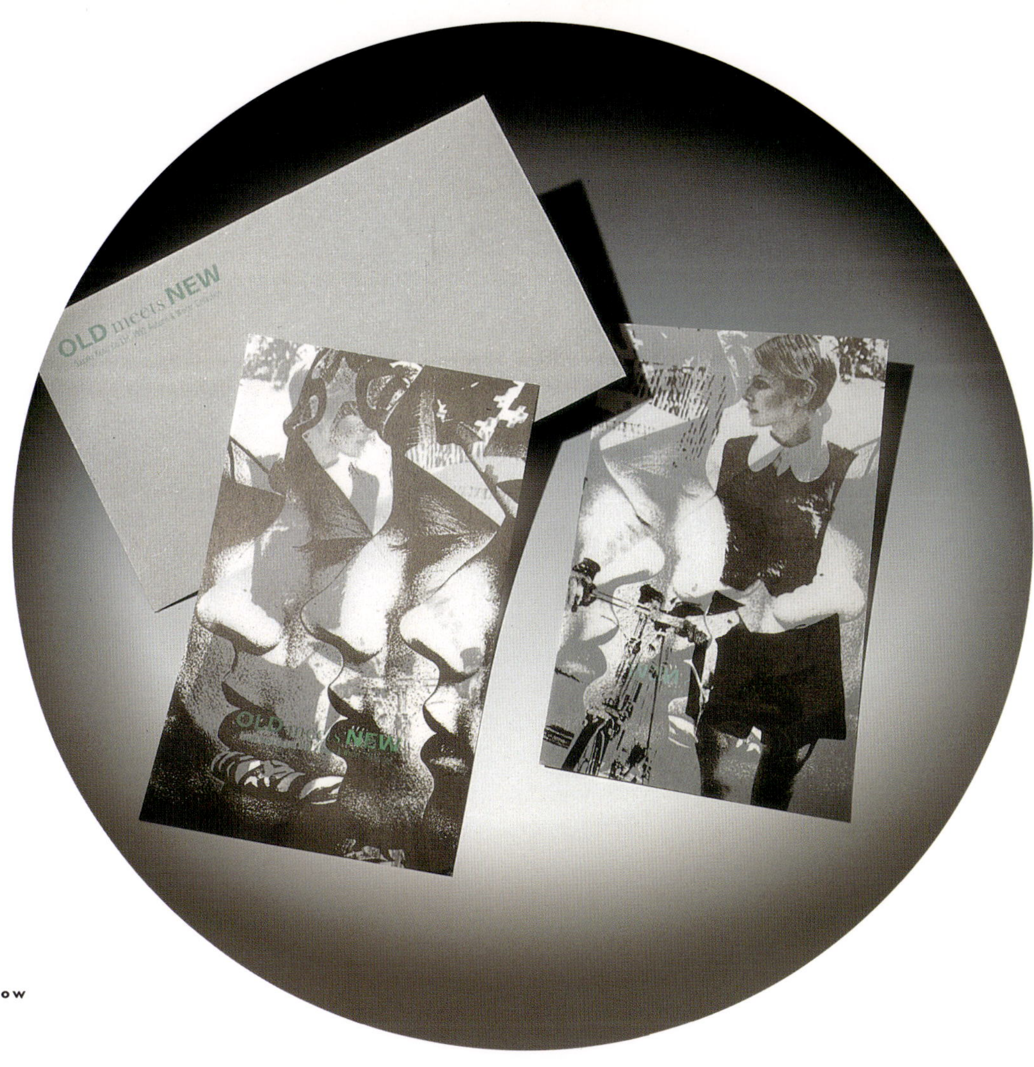

▲
Invitation to a sales show
展示会案内状
JAPAN 1991
CD:Setsuko Mataki
AD,D:Akihiko Tsukamoto
CL:Sasaki Keori
TC:Textile Wholesaler
テキスタイル卸売り

▼
Invitation to an Odds-On collection
オッズ・オン展示会案内状
JAPAN 1988
AD,D:Musée
I:Odds On
CL:Issey Miyake International
TC:Apparel Maker
アパレル

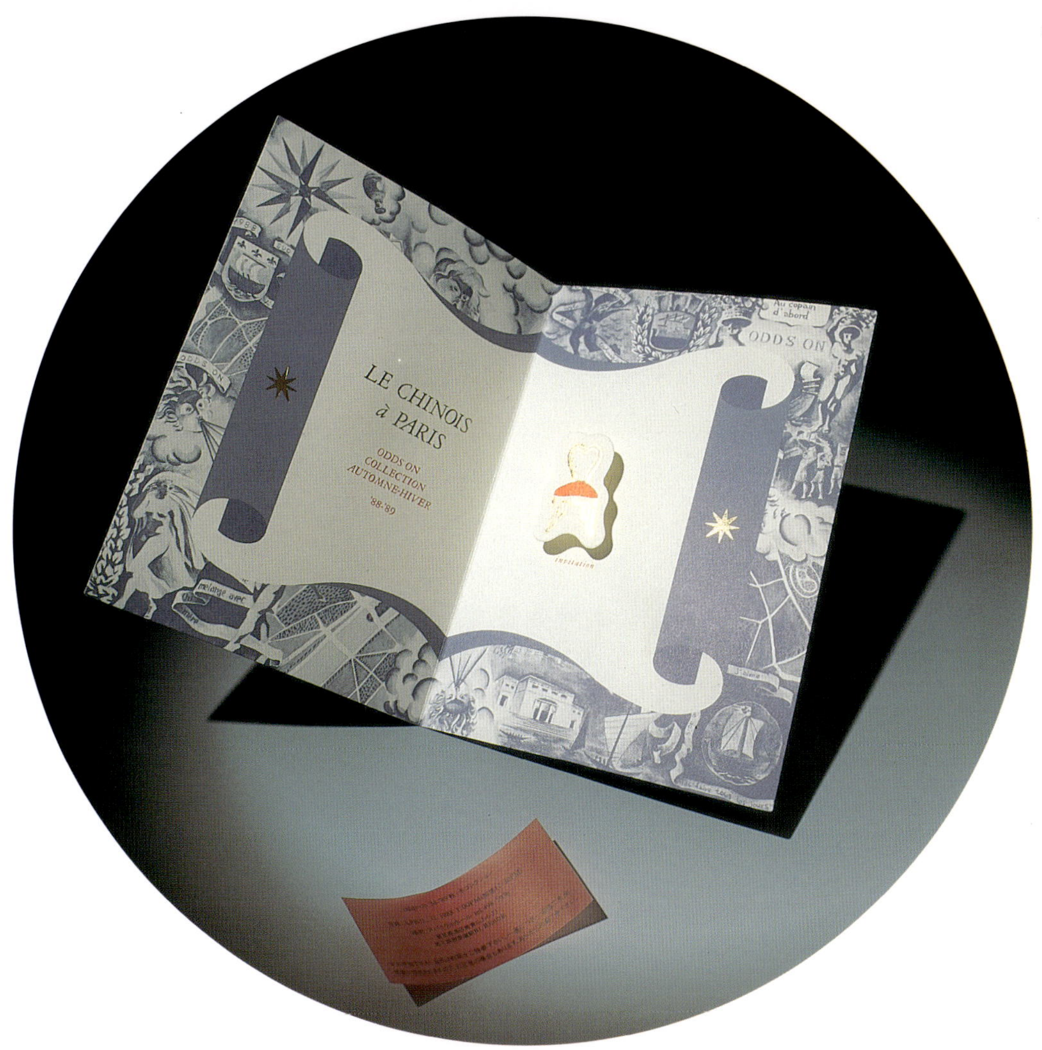

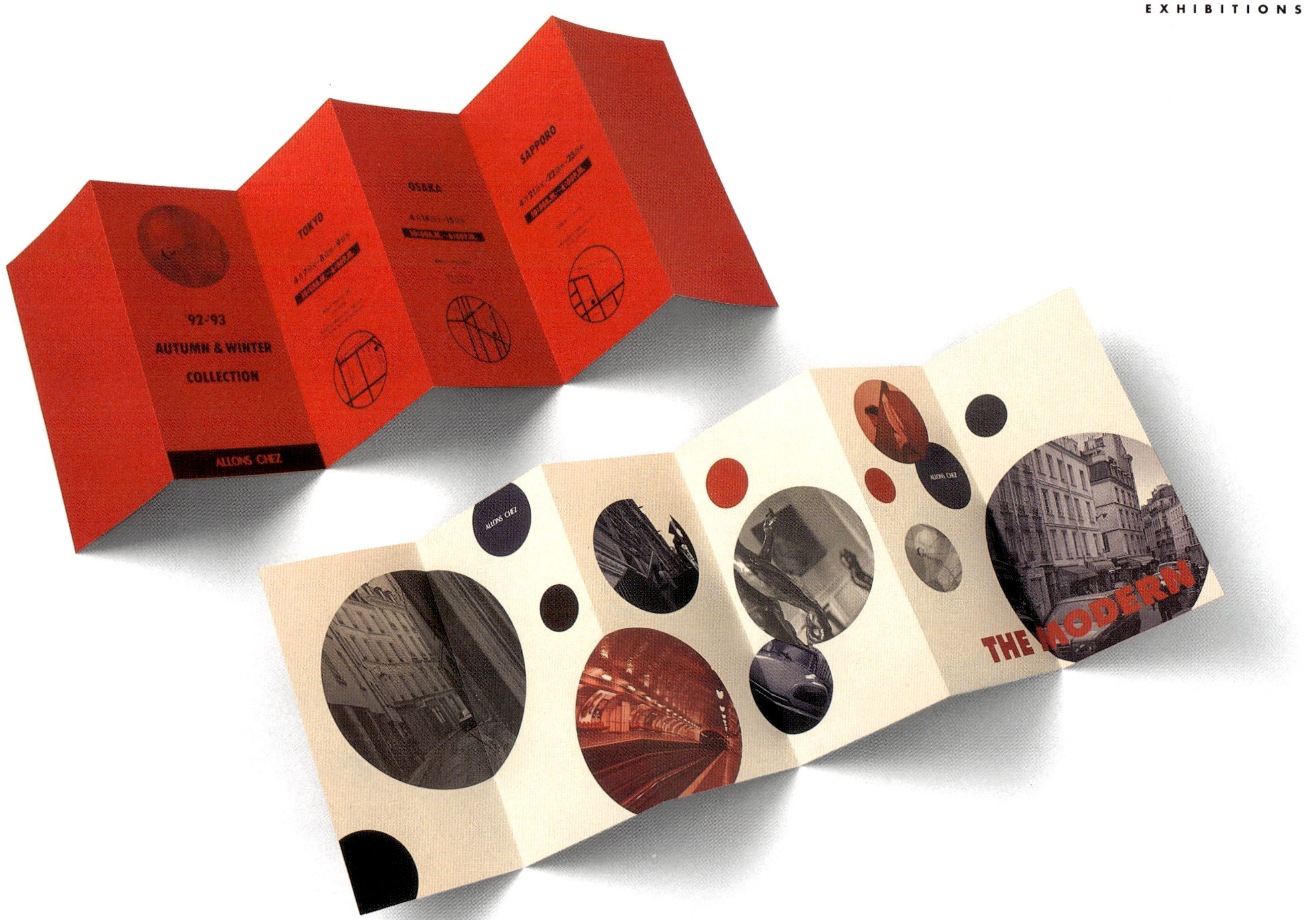

▲

Invitation to
Allons Chez Collection

アロンシュ展示会案内状

JAPAN 1991

AD,D:Akira Utsumi

P:Lai-hai Chiang

CL:Comt

TC:Apparel Maker

アパレル

▼

Invitation to an exhibition

展示会案内状

JAPAN 1993

CD:Takanori Suzuki

AD:Noriaki Kitazato

D:Kazuko Yusa

CL:Daidoh

TC:Apparel Maker

アパレル

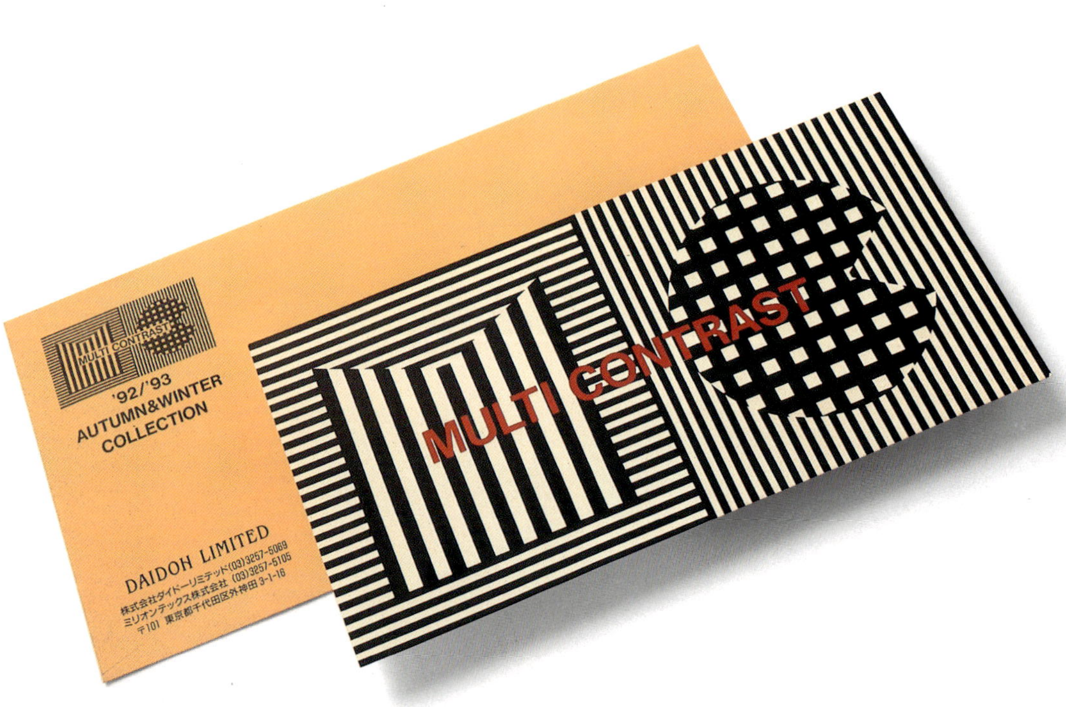

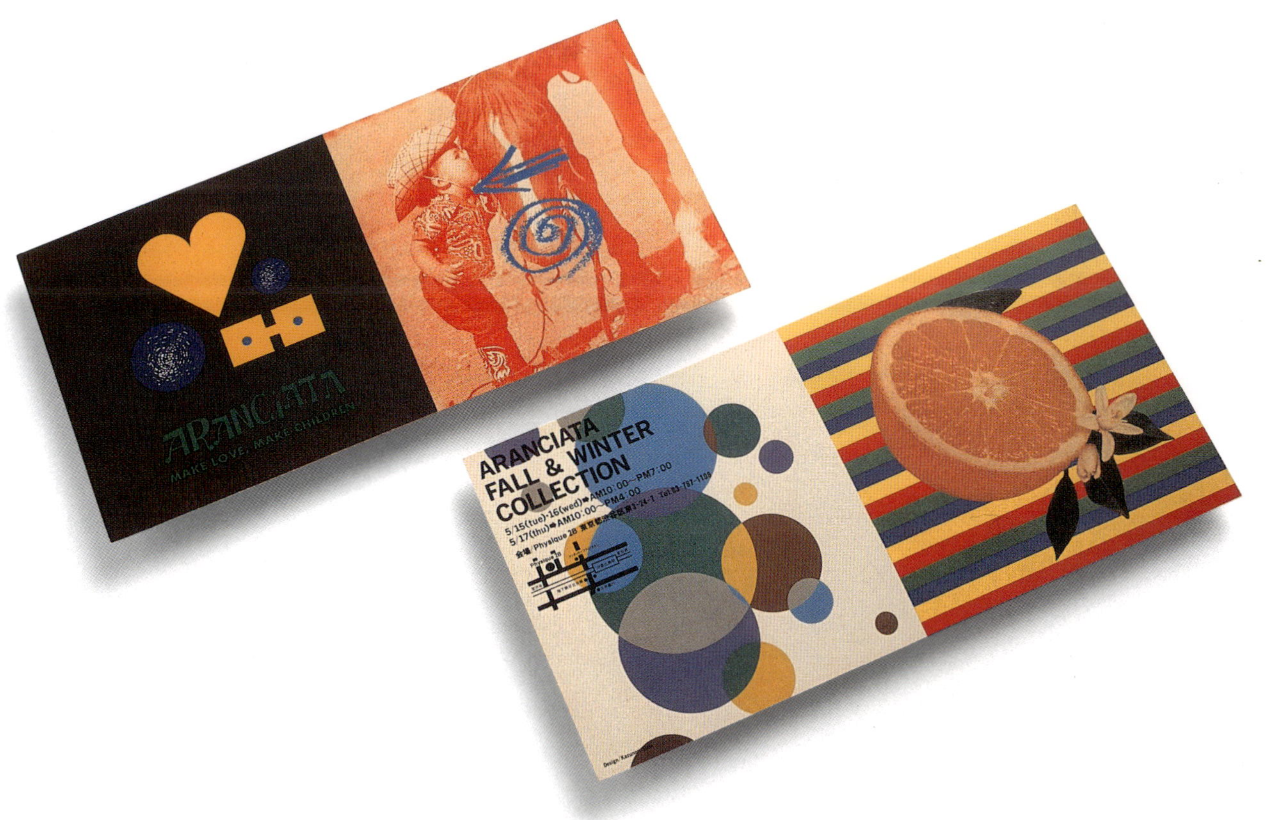

▲
Invitation to a collection
展示会案内状
JAPAN 1990
AD,D:Kazunori Sudo
CL:Aranciata
TC:Apparel Maker
アパレル

▼
Invitation to a collection
展示会案内状
JAPAN 1990
AD,D:Kazunori Sudo
I:Kazuko Furuta
CL:Aranciata
TC:Apparel maker
アパレル

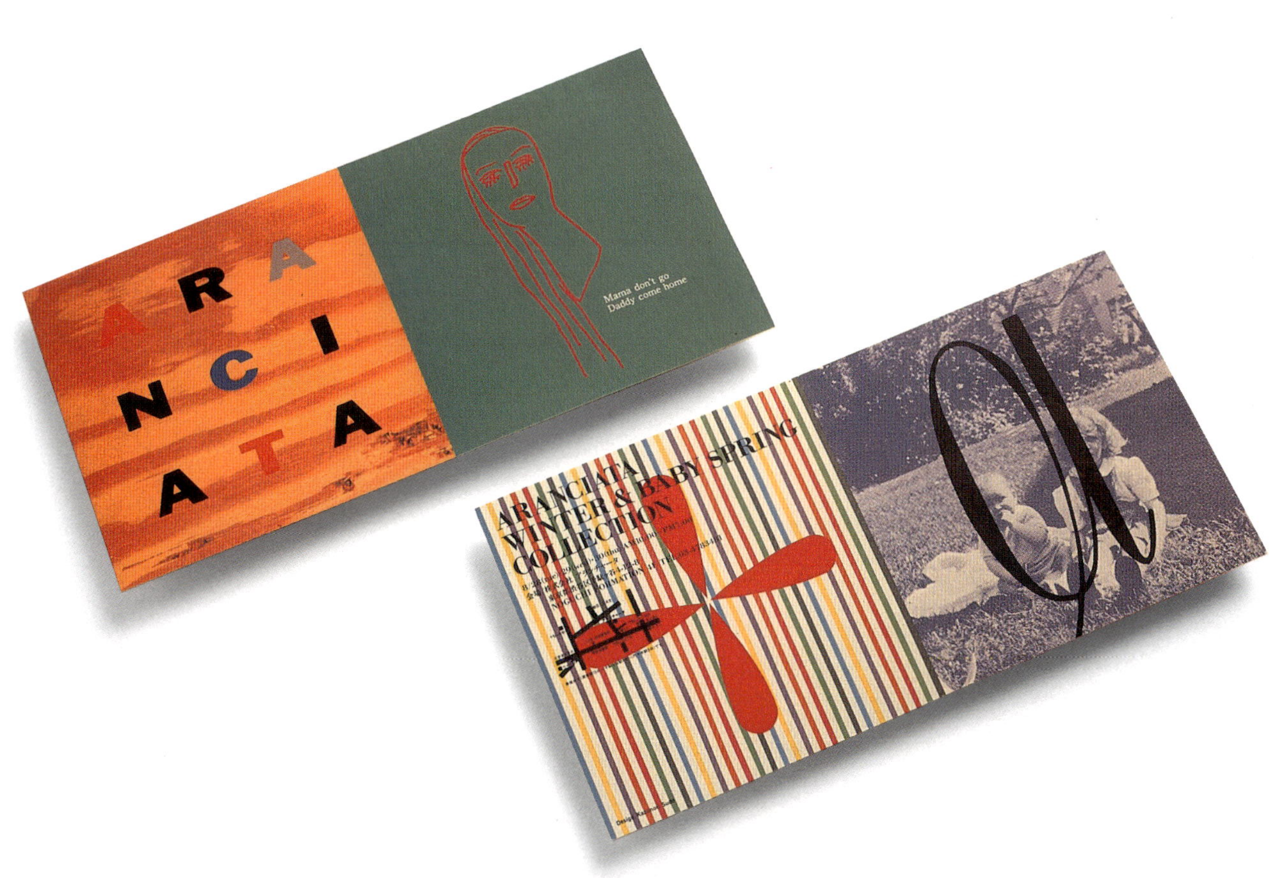

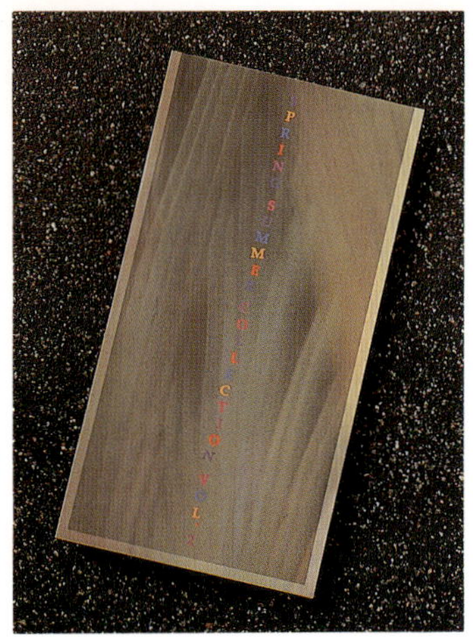

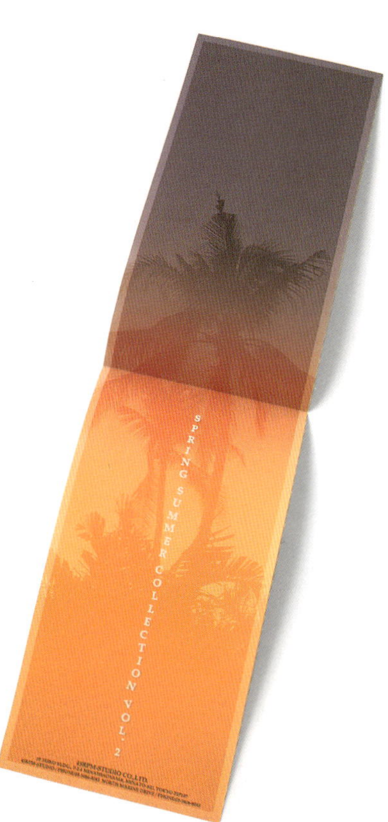

▲
Invitation to a collection
展示会案内状
JAPAN 1991
D:Joji Yano
CL:45 Rpm-Studio
TC:Apparel Maker
アパレル

▼
Invitation to a collection
展示会案内状
JAPAN 1991
D:Joji Yano
CL:45 Rpm-Studio
TC:Apparel Maker
アパレル

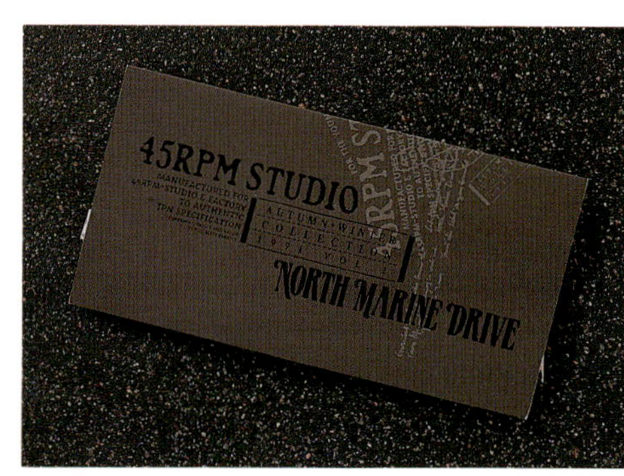

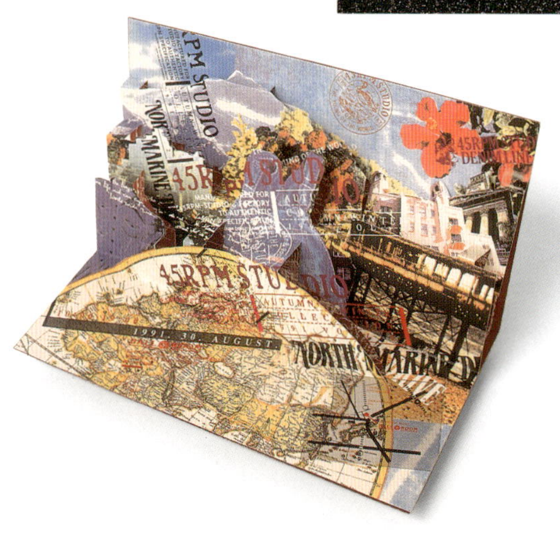

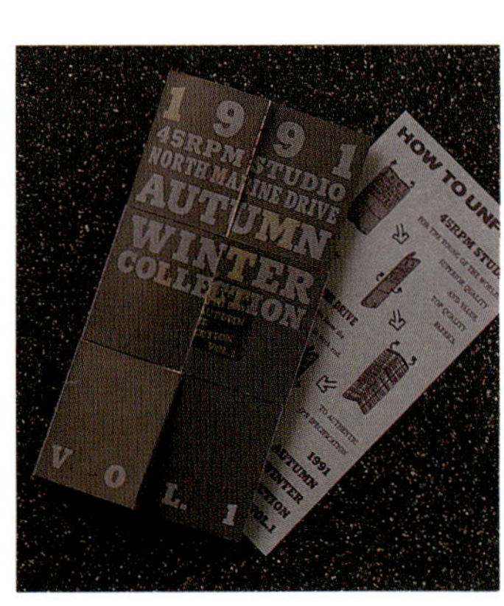

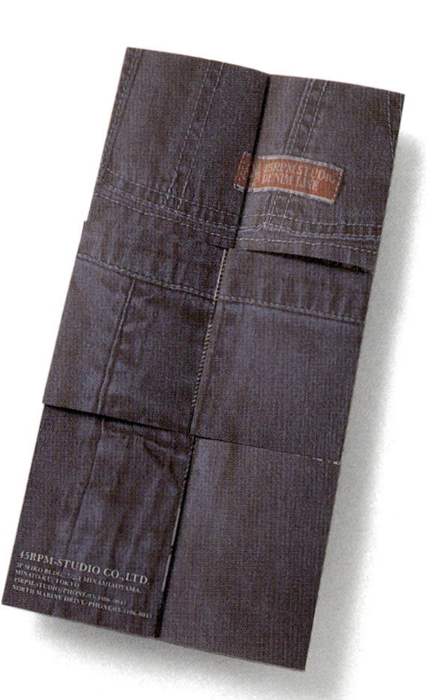

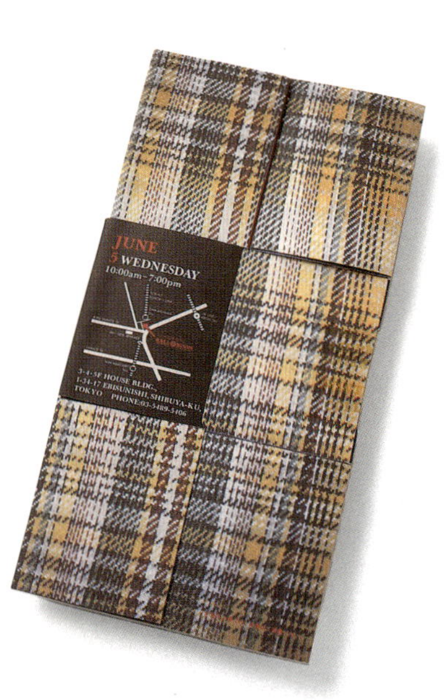

◀
Invitation to a collection
展示会案内状
JAPAN 1991
D:Joji Yano
CL:45 Rpm-Studio
TC:Apparel Maker
アパレル
•
By thumbing through quickly,
the entire picture changes.
めくることによって、
全体の絵柄が変化していく。

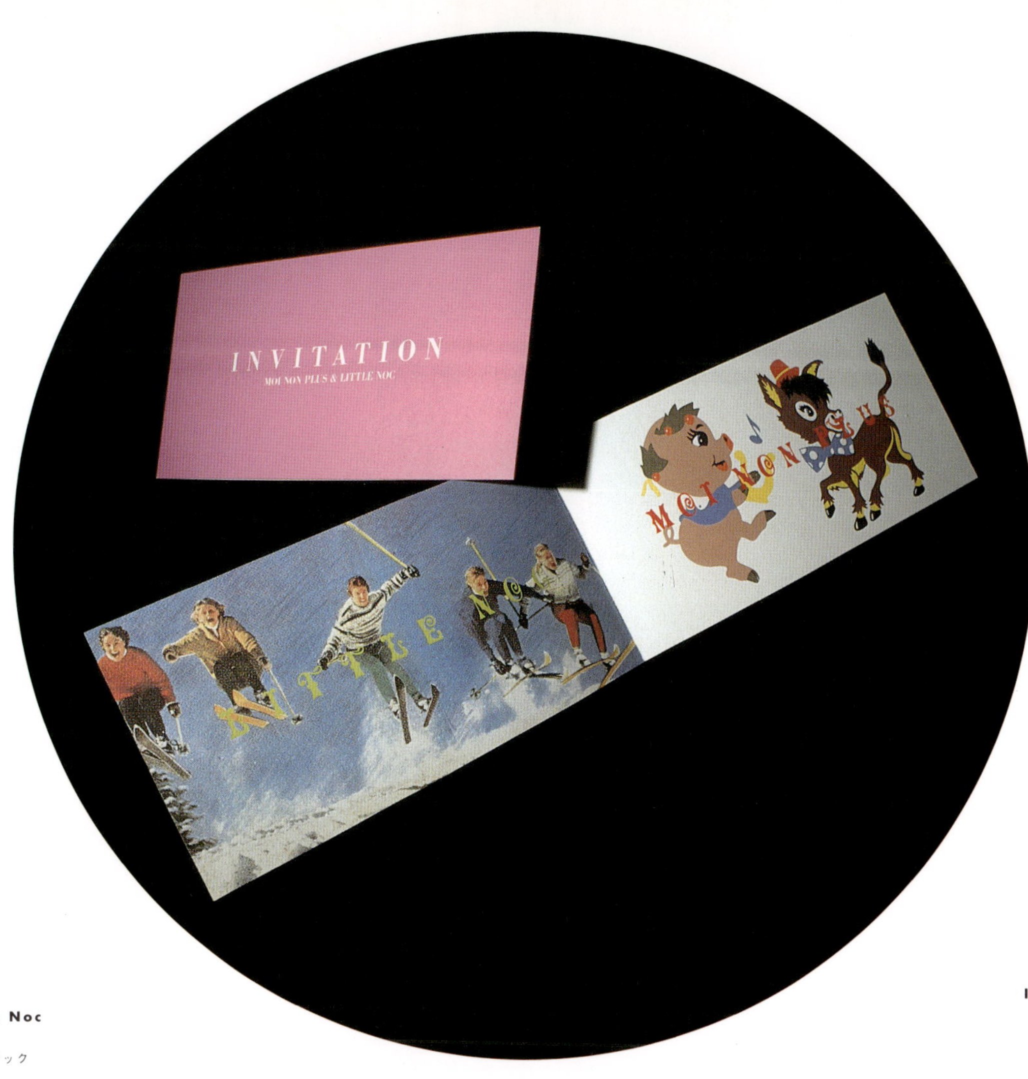

▲
Invitation to a Moi Non Plus & Little Noc collection

モア・ノン・プリュ&リトル・ノック
展示会案内状
JAPAN 1990
AD:Kazunori Sudo
D:Hiroyuki Watanabe
CL:Bun Boy
TC:Apparel Maker
アパレル

▼
Invitation to a sales show

展示会案内状
JAPAN 1991
CD:Setsuko Mataki
AD,D,I:Akihiko Tsukamoto
P:Eiichi Tsukada
CL:Sasaki Keori
TC:Textile Wholesaler
テキスタイル卸売り

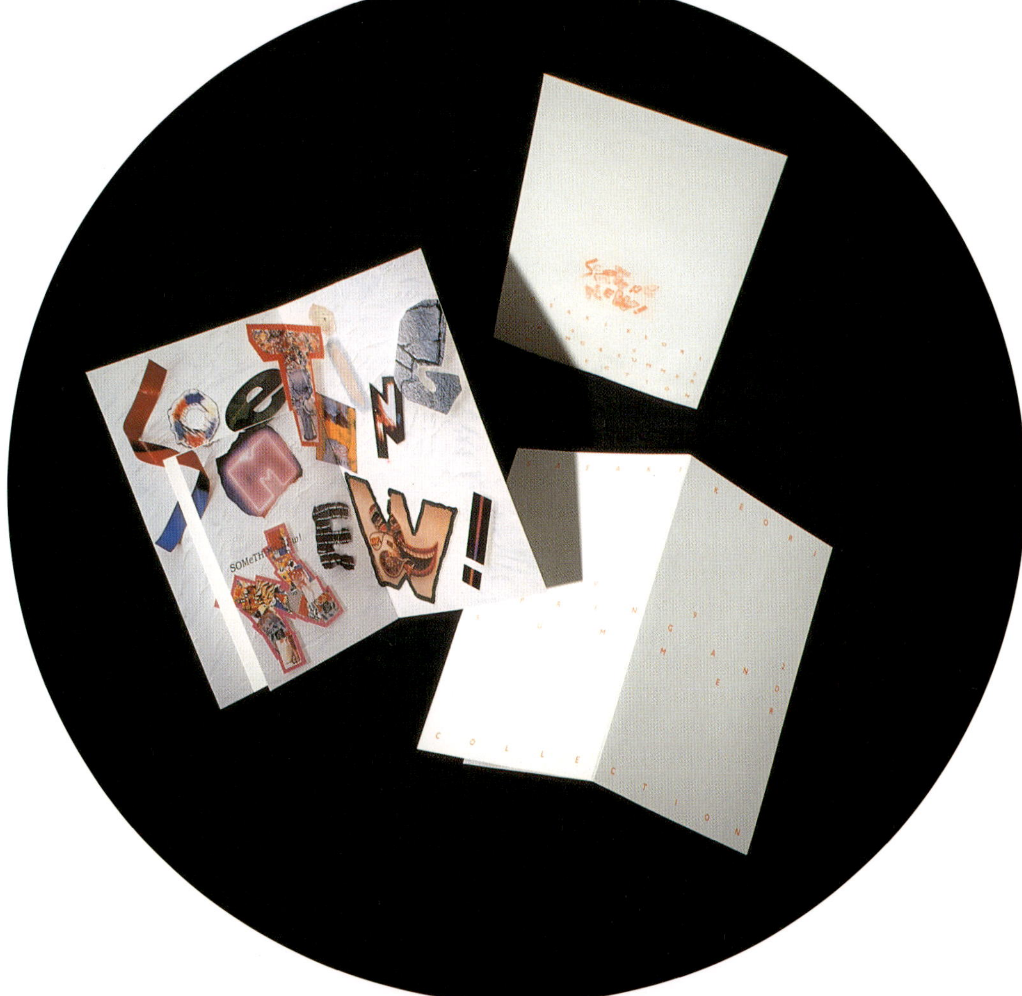

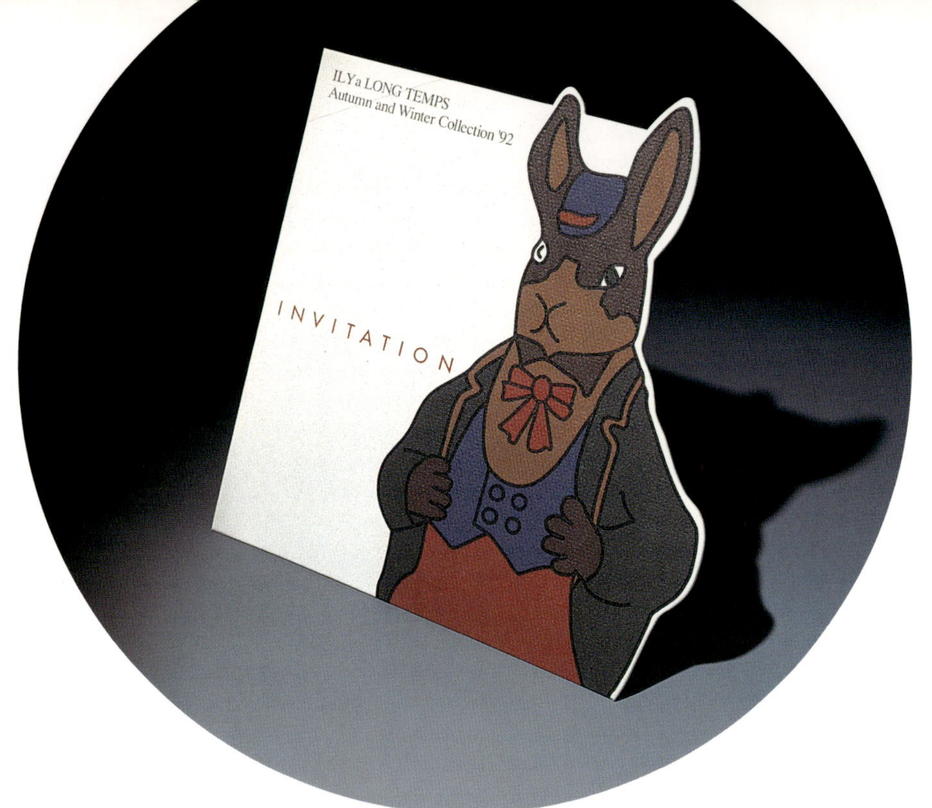
ILYa LONG TEMPS
Autumn and Winter Collection '92
INVITATION

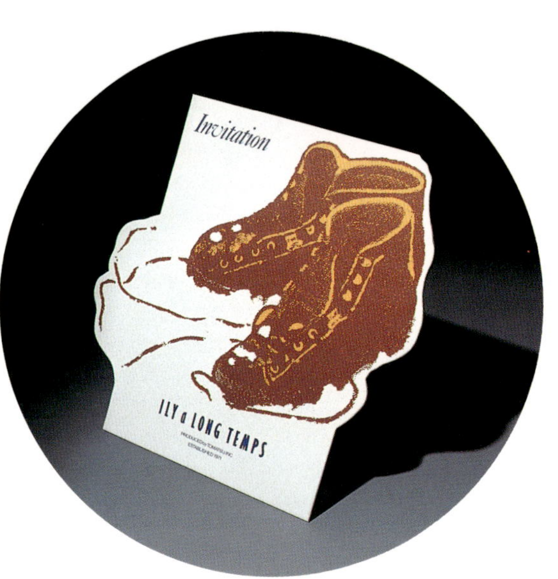
Invitation
ILY a LONG TEMPS

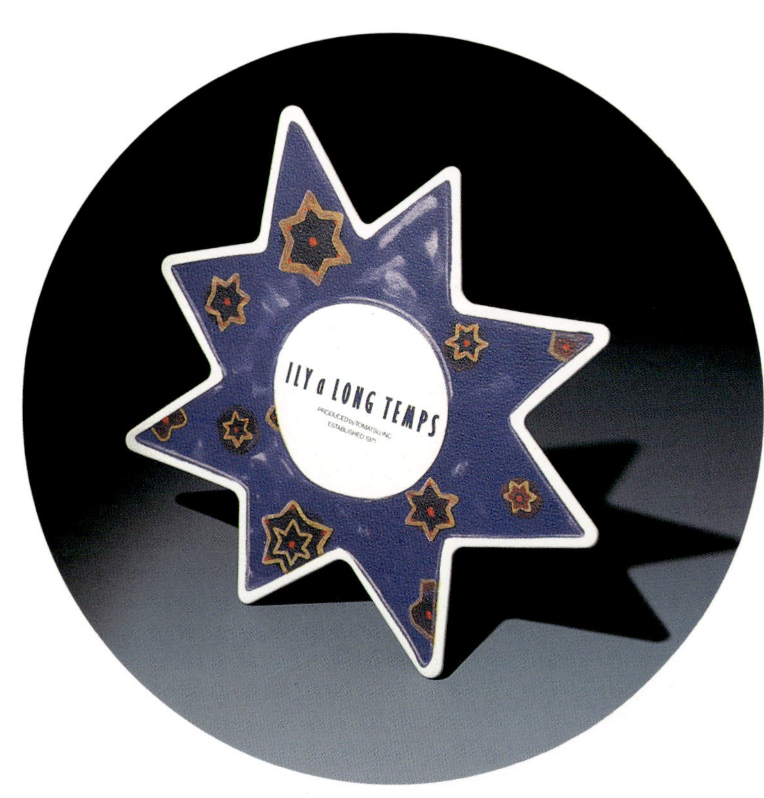
ILY a LONG TEMPS
PRODUCED by TOMATSU INC
ESTABLISHED 1971

Invitation to an Ily a Long Temps collection
イリ・ア・ロンタン展示会案内状
JAPAN 1989~92
CD,AD,D:Takashi Doi
CL:Tomatsu
TC:Apparel Maker
アパレル

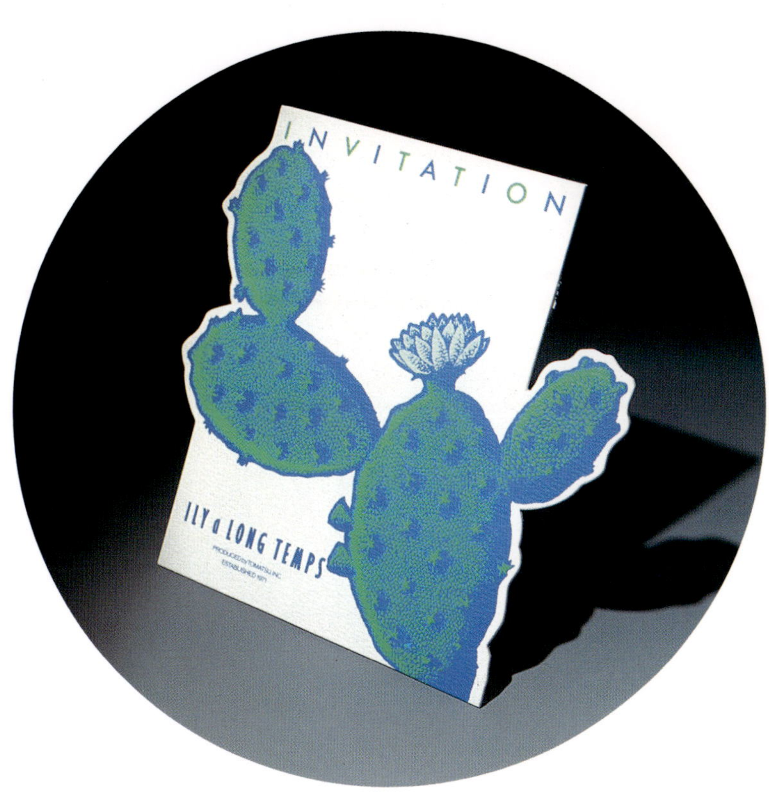

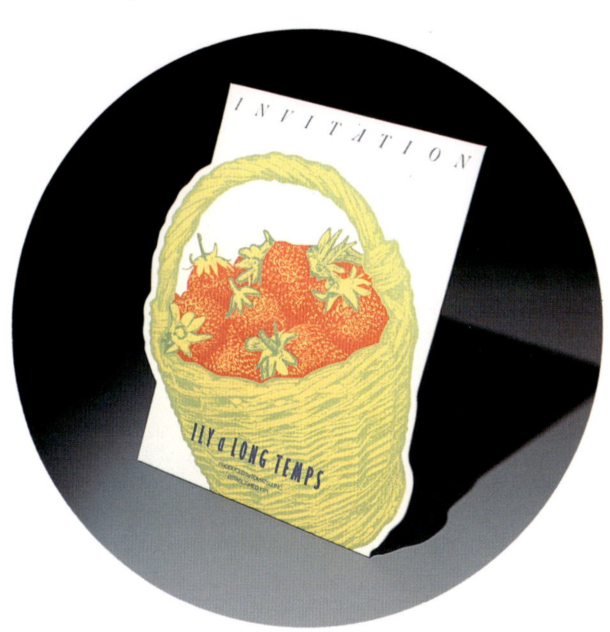

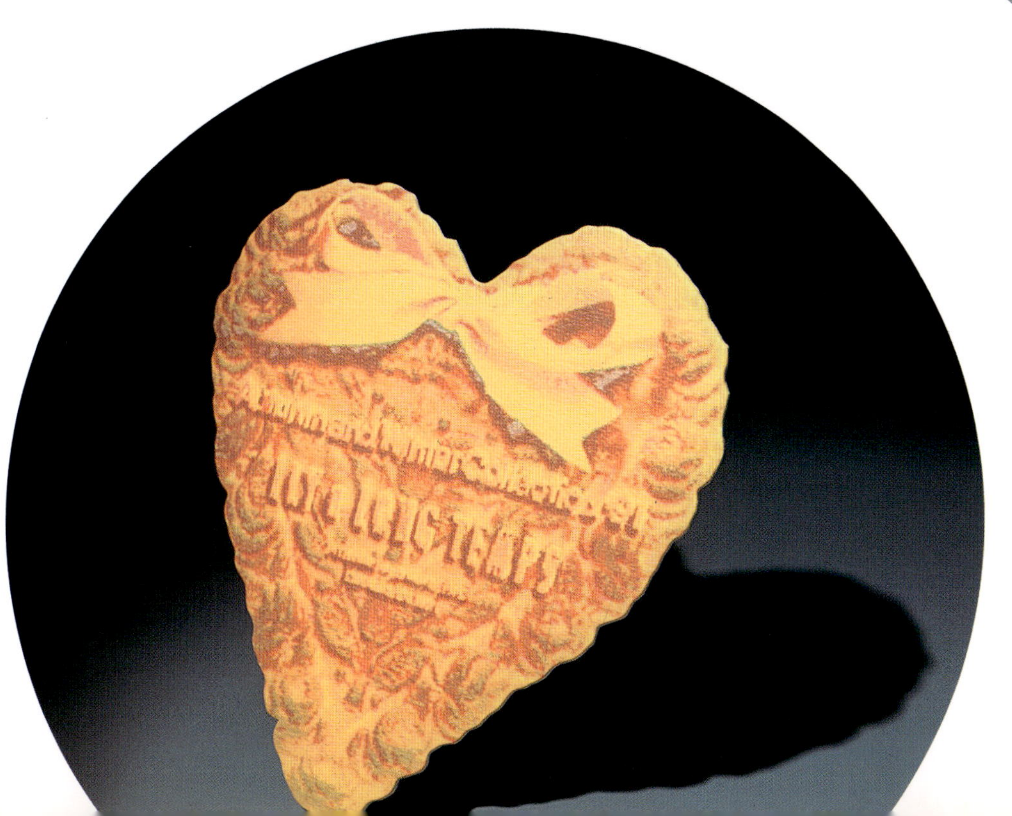

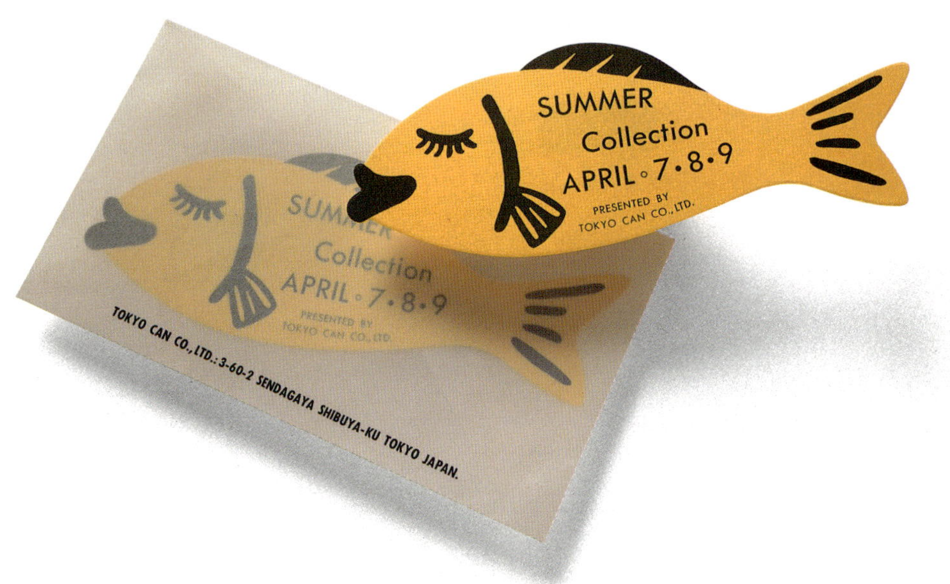

◀
Invitation to a collection
展示会案内状
JAPAN 1992
CD,AD,D:Mikiko Shimizu
CL:Tokyo Can
TC:Apparel Maker
アパレル

▶
Invitation to a collection
展示会案内状
JAPAN 1991
AD,D:Mikiko Shimizu
CL:Tokyo Can
TC:Apparel Maker
アパレル

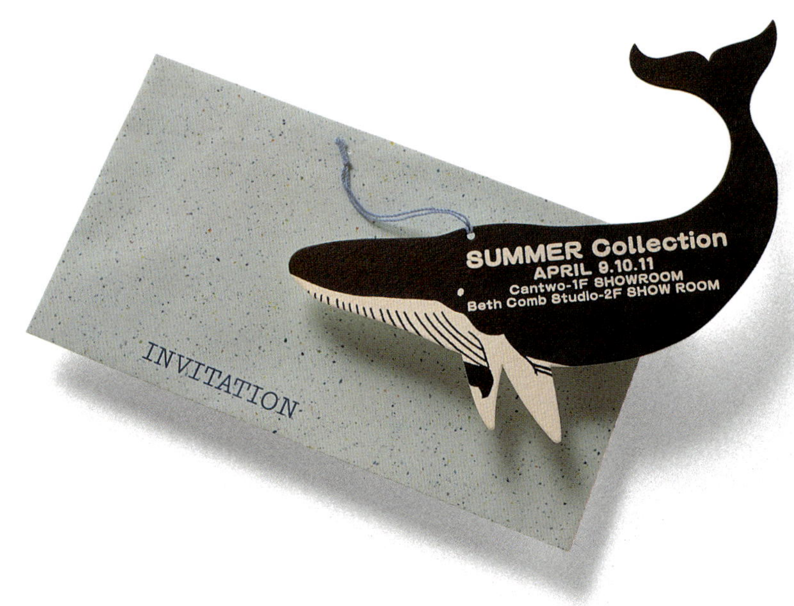

◀
Invitation to an Oxford Traditional collection
オックスフォード・
トラディショナル展示会案内状
JAPAN 1992
CD:Yozo Fujii
AD,D,I:Eiji Shimizu
CL:Oxford
TC:Apparel Maker
アパレル

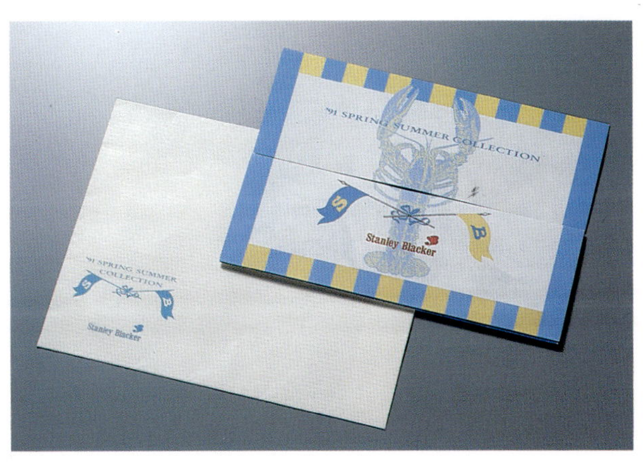

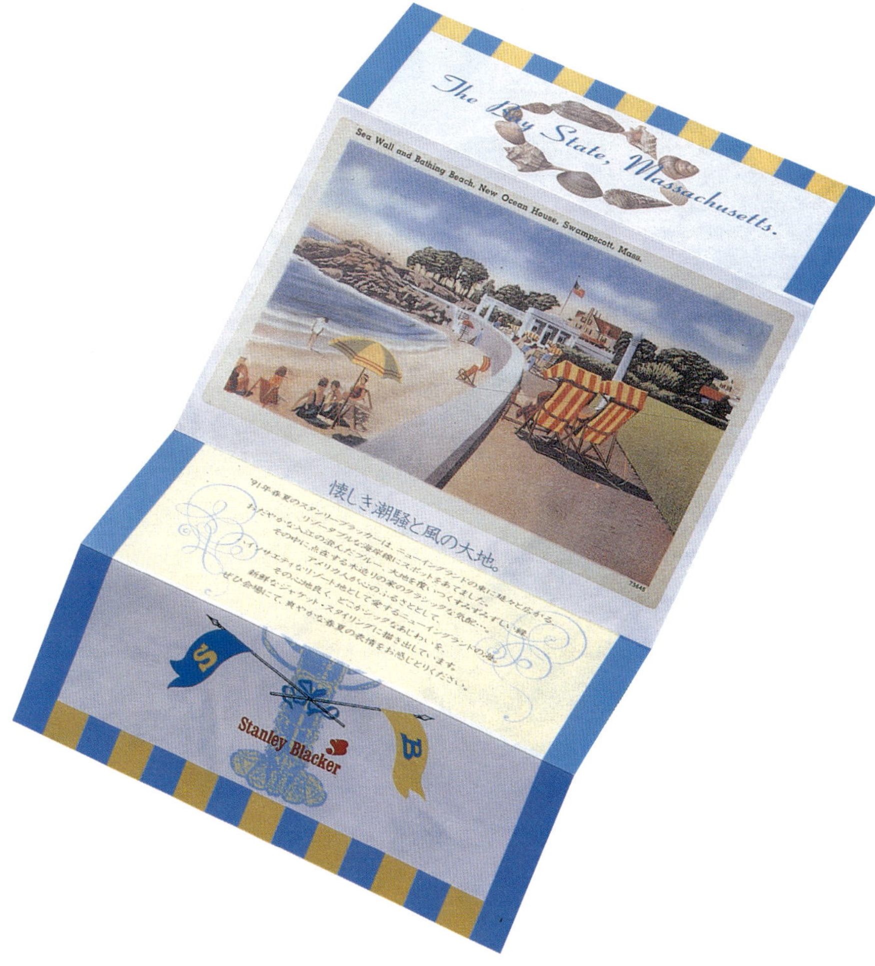

▲
Invitation to
a Stanley Blacker collection
スタンリー・ブラッカー展示会案内状
JAPAN 1990
AD,D:Rie Kikkawa
CW:Koki Kikkawa
CL:Joi'x
TC:Apparel Maker
アパレル

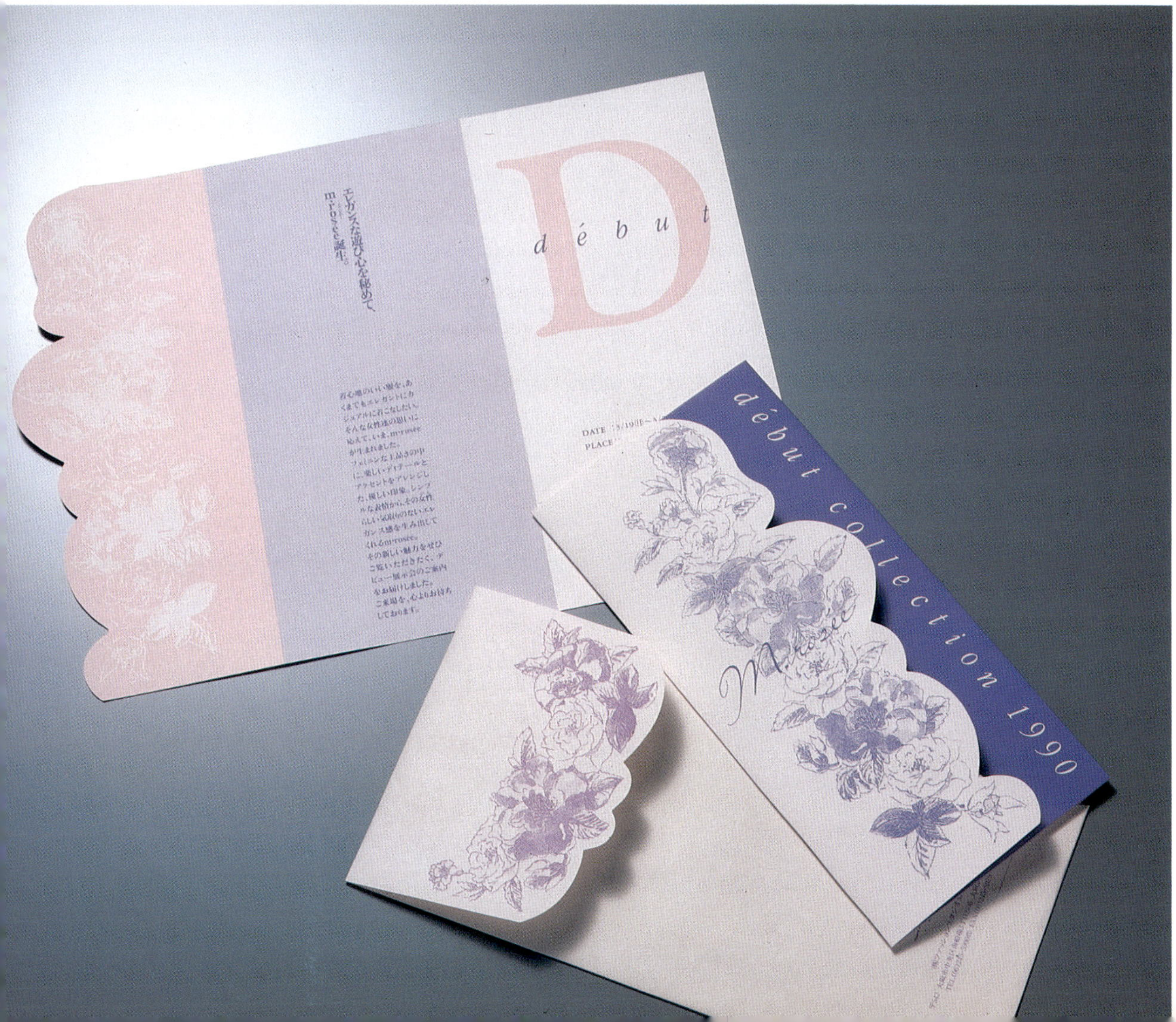

◀
Invitation to
a M,rosse collection
ミアム・エムロゼー展示会案内状
JAPAN 1990
AD:Rie Kikkawa
D:Ako Hirai
CW:Koki Kikkawa
CL:Fashion Studio Miki
TC:Apparel Maker
アパレル

Invitation to a Kansai Kids collection

カンサイ・キッズ展示会案内状

JAPAN 1990

CD:Hisashi Asanuma

AD:Sumio Aoki

D:Toyomi Ohkawa

I:Chizuko Todoroki

CW:Minoru Ohyama

CL:Gunze

TC:Apparel Maker

アパレル

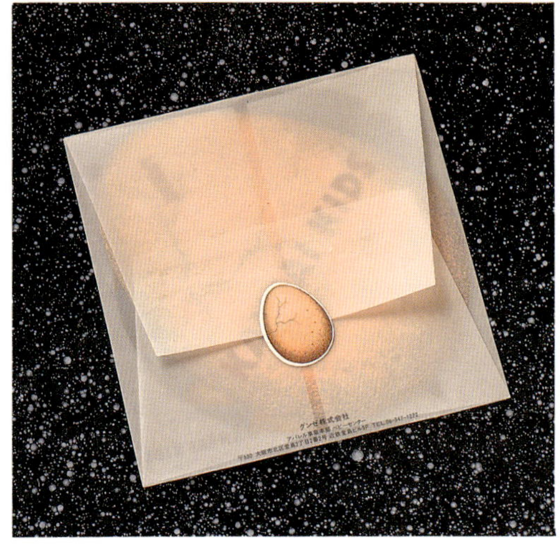

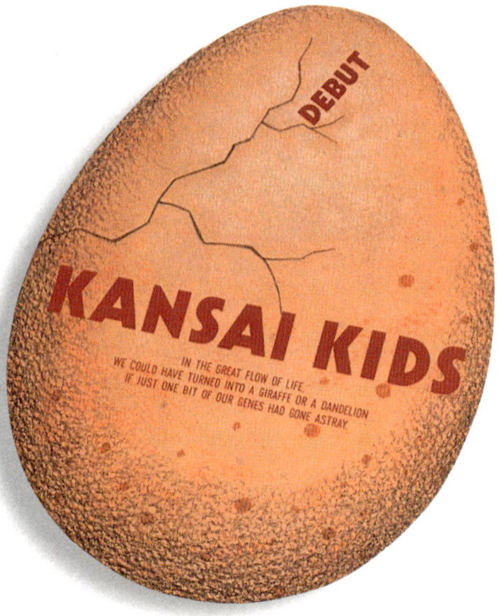

DEBUT

KANSAI KIDS

IN THE GREAT FLOW OF LIFE.
WE COULD HAVE TURNED INTO A GIRAFFE OR A DANDELION
IF JUST ONE BIT OF OUR GENES HAD GONE ASTRAY.

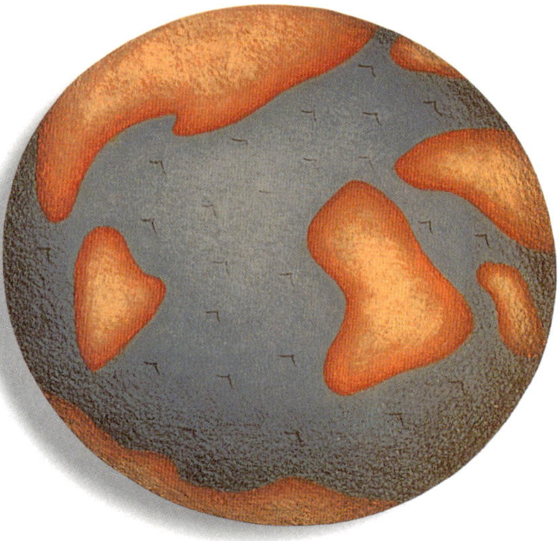

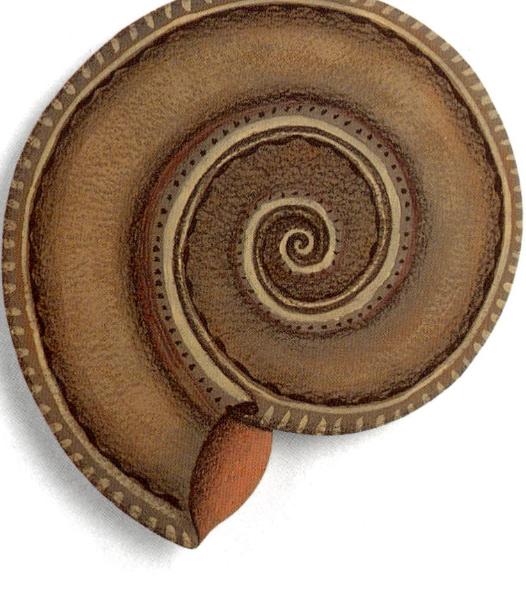

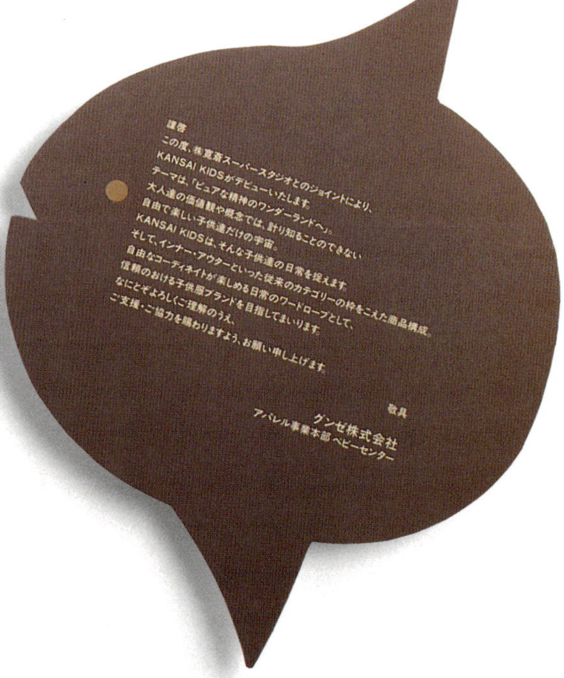

謹啓
この度、株寛斎スーパースタジオとのジョイントにより、
KANSAI KIDSがデビューいたします。
テーマは、「ピュアな精神のワンダーランドへ」。
大人達の価値観や概念では、計り知ることのできない
自由で楽しい子供達だけの宇宙。
KANSAI KIDSは、そんな子供達の日常を捉えます。
そして、インナー・アウターといった従来のカテゴリーの枠をこえた商品構成。
自由なコーディネイトが楽しめる日常のワードローブとして、
信頼のおける子供服ブランドを目指してまいります。
なにとぞよろしくご理解のうえ、
ご支援・ご協力を賜わりますよう、お願い申し上げます。

敬具
グンゼ株式会社
アパレル事業本部 ベビーセンター

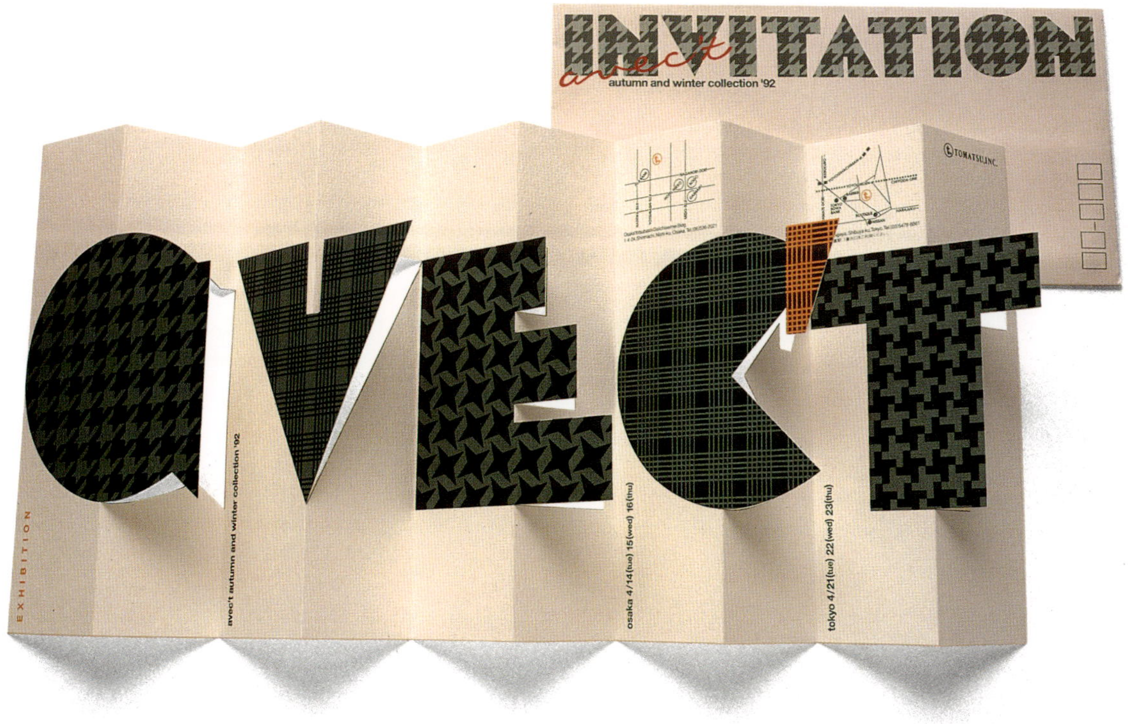

▲
Invitation to an Avec't collection
アヴェクテ展示会案内状
JAPAN 1992
AD,D:Takashi Doi
CL:Tomatsu
TC:Apparel Maker
アパレル

▼
Invitation to a Tomatsu Boutique collection
トマツ・ブティック展示会案内状
JAPAN 1991
AD,D:Takashi Doi
CL:Tomatsu
TC:Apparel Maker
アパレル

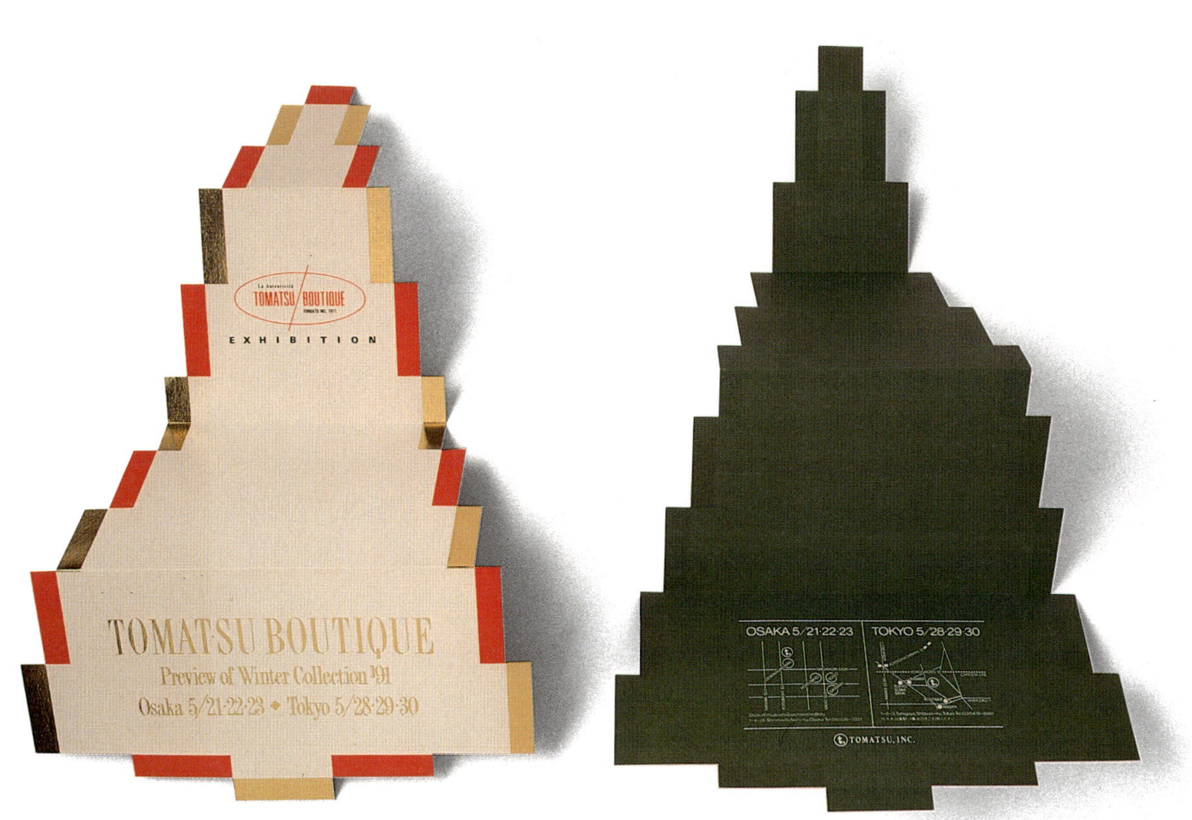

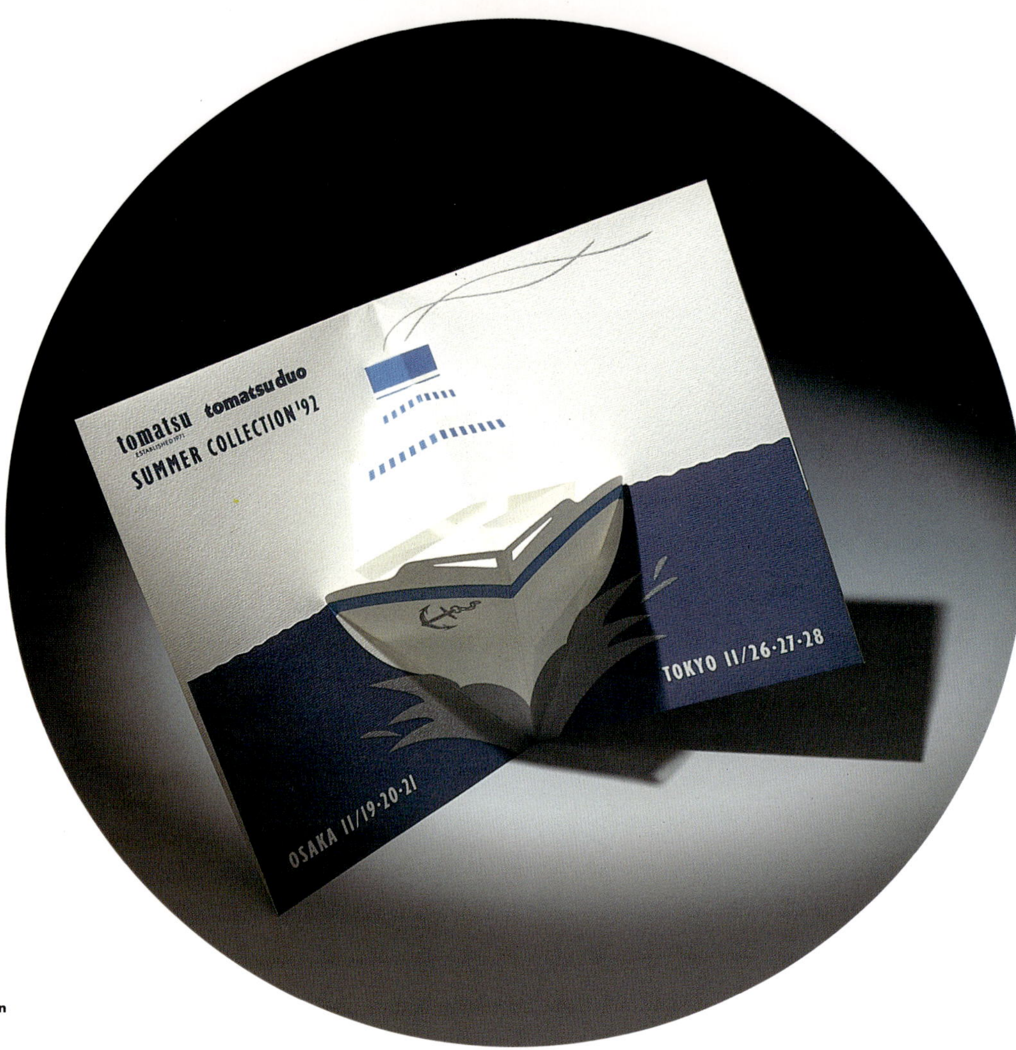

Invitation to a collection
展示会案内状
JAPAN 1990~92
AD,D:Kazuki Konishi
CL:Tomatsu
TC:Apparel Maker
アパレル

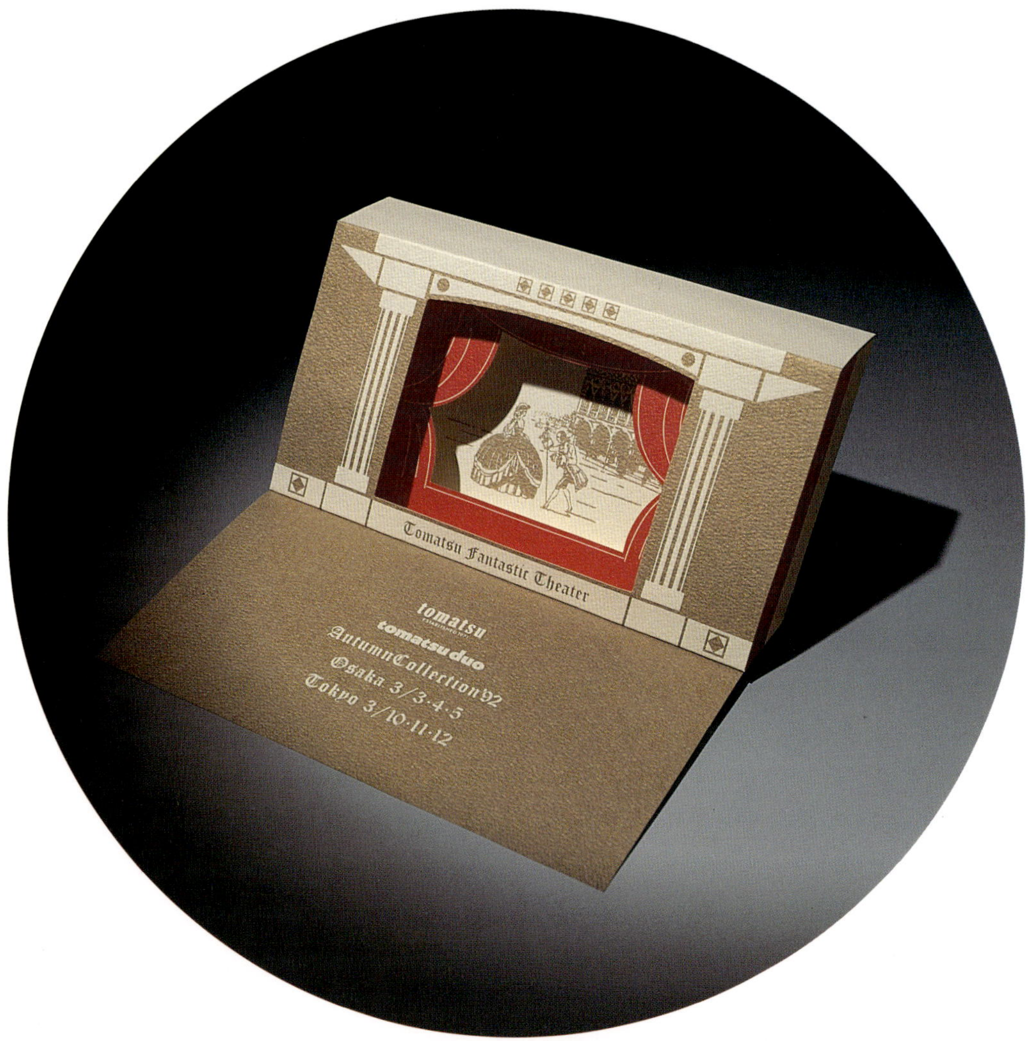

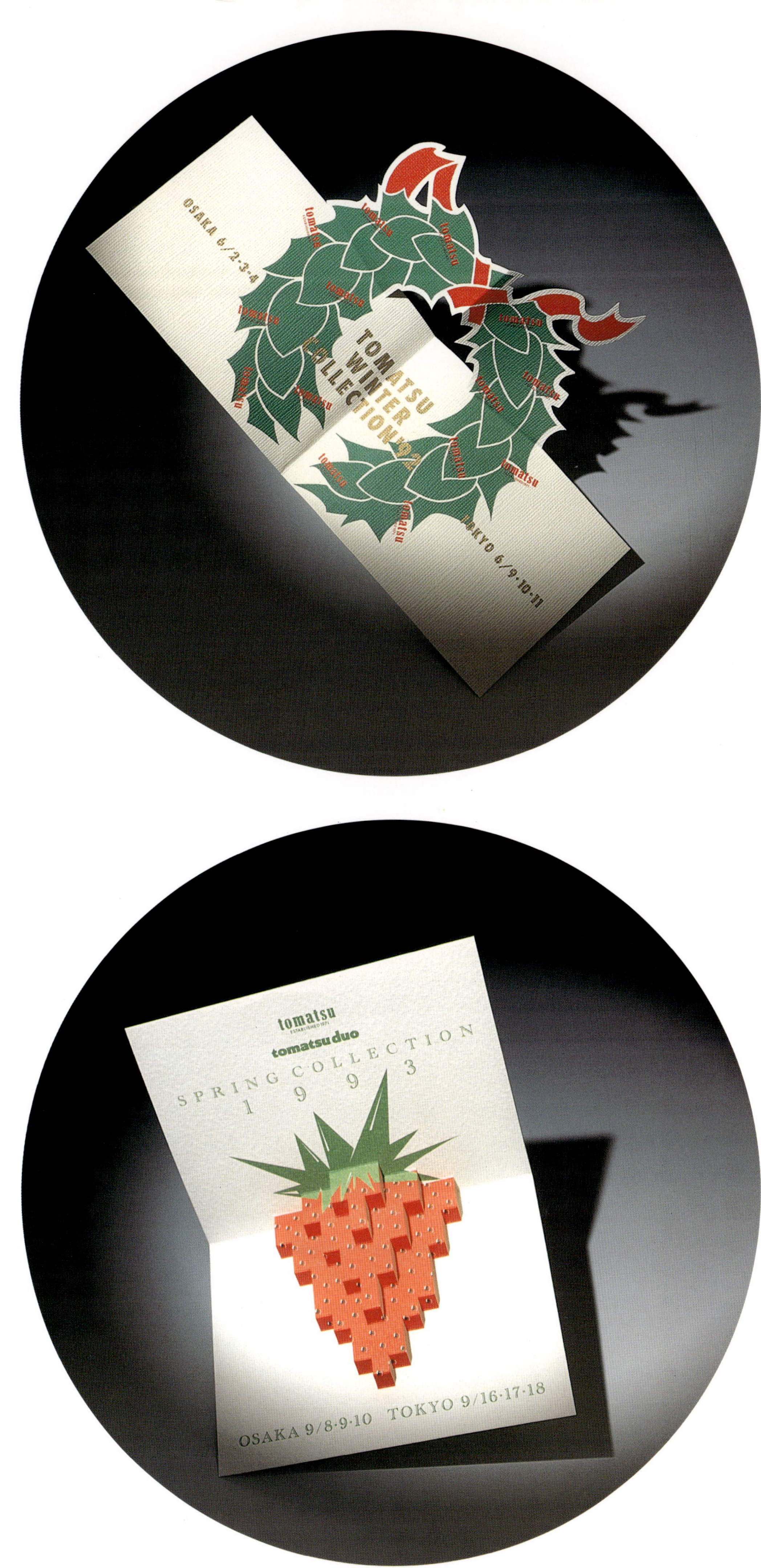
OSAKA 6/2·3·4
TOMATSU
WINTER
COLLECTION
TOKYO 6/9·10·11
tomatsu
tomatsu duo
SPRING COLLECTION
1 9 9 3
OSAKA 9/8·9·10 TOKYO 9/16·17·18

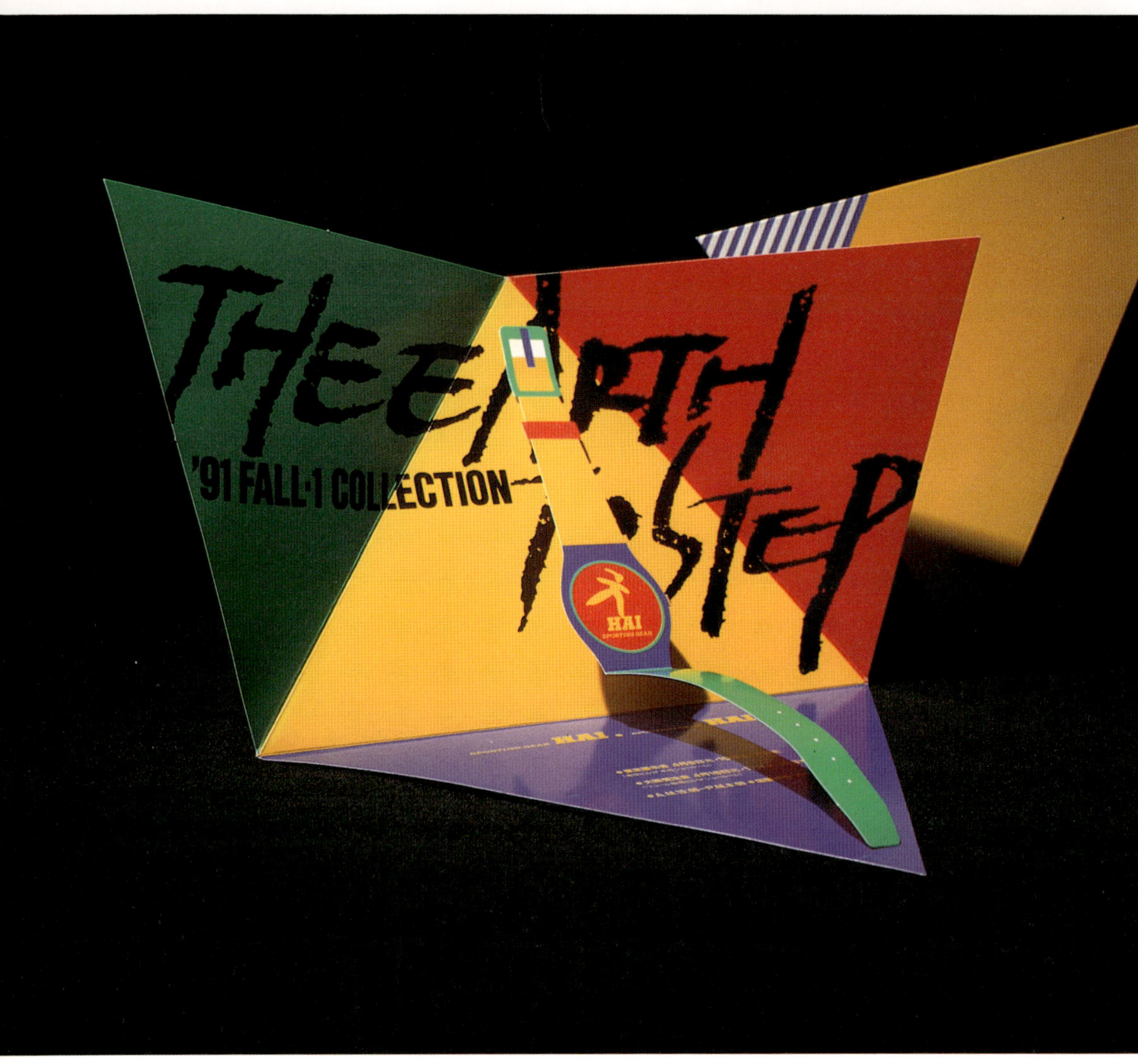

Invitation to a Sporting Gear Hai collection
スポーティング・ギア・ハイ展示会案内状
JAPAN 1991
AD:Prop/Kunihiko Ukita
CL:Point Up
TC:Apparel Wholesaler
アパレル

Invitation to the opening of an Expo stand
万博スタンド・オープニング招待状
AUSTRALIA 1988
CD:Garry Emery
AD,D,DF:Emery Vincent Design
CL:Australia Post
TC:Australia Postal Authority
オーストラリア郵政省

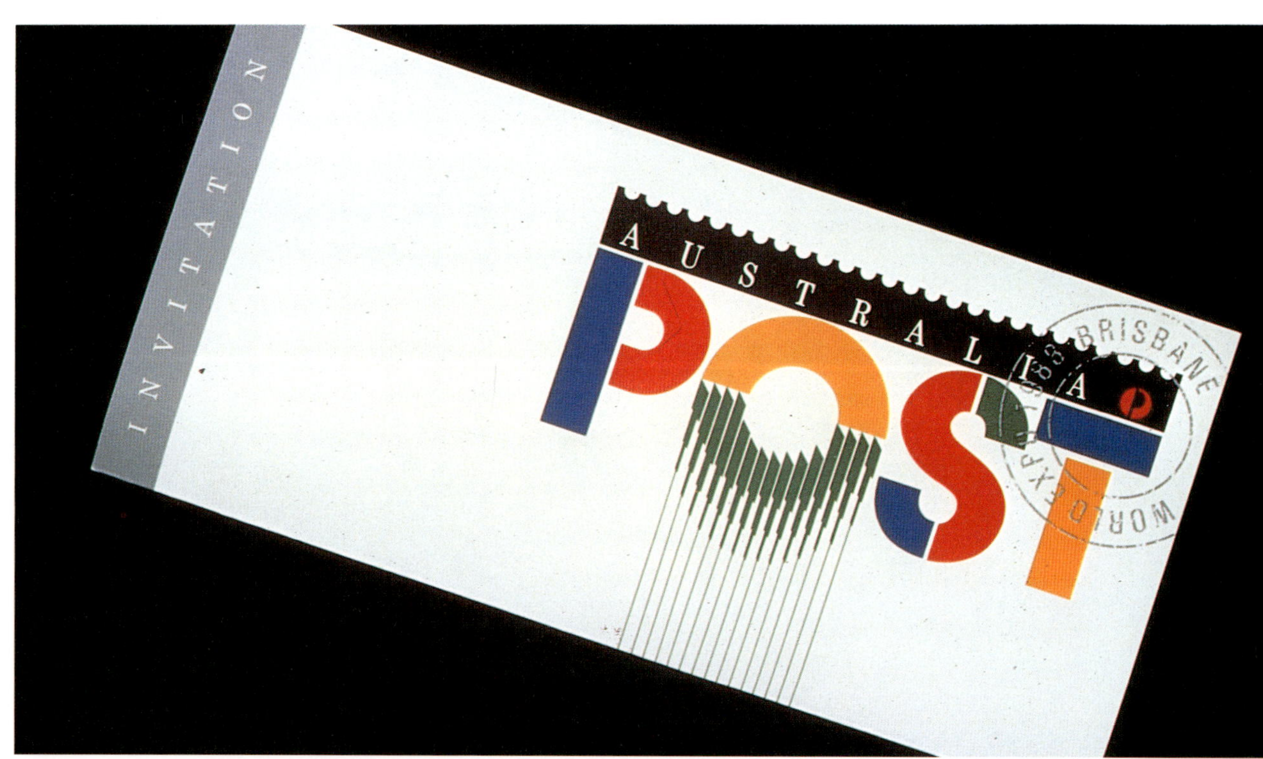

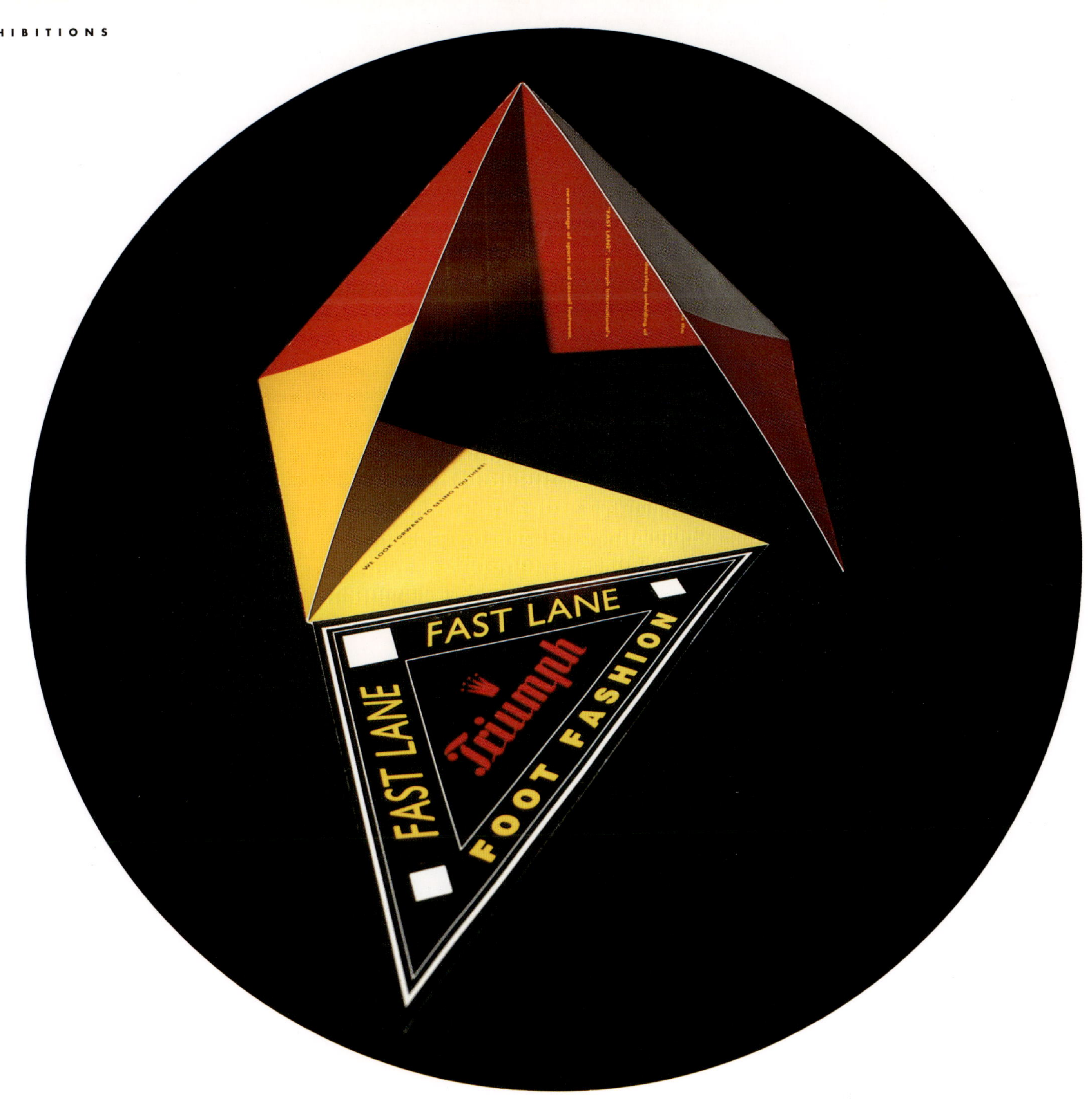

Invitation to a Fast Lane fashion show

ファースト・レーン・
ファッション・ショー案内状

HONG KONG 1990

D:Catherine Lam Siu Hung

DF:Triump Int'l (H.K)

CL:Triump Int'l (H.K)

TC:Apparel Maker

アパレル

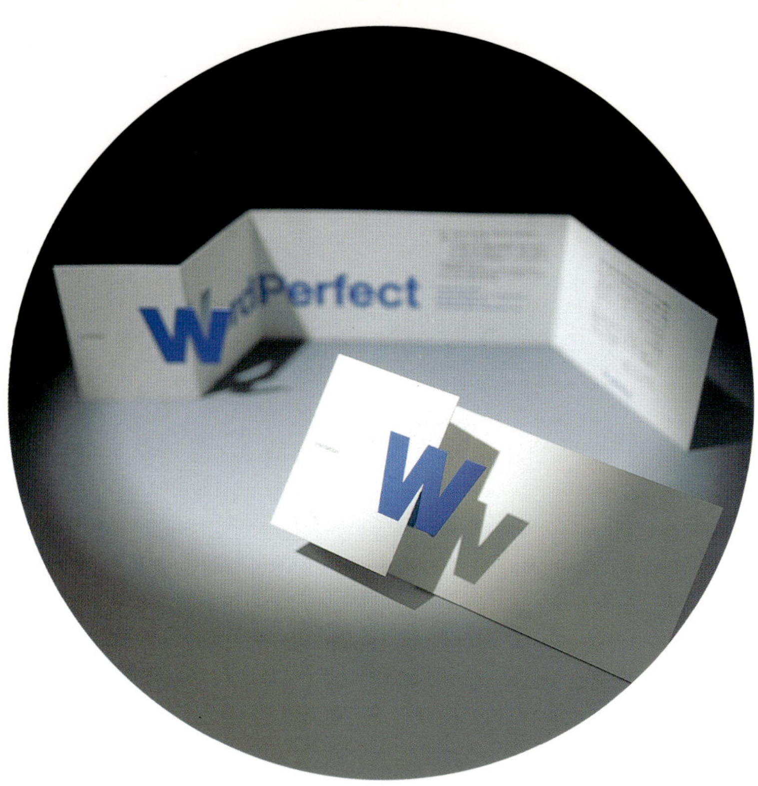

◀
Invitation to a new product presentation
新製品発表説明会案内状
JAPAN 1992
D:Akihiko Tsukamoto
CL:Word Perfect Japan
TC:Computer Software Developer
コンピューター・ソフトウェア開発

▶
Invitation to an art exhibition
美術展案内状
AUSTRIA 1988
CD,AD,D,I,CW:Sigi Ramoser
CL:Kunst Raum Dornbirn
TC:Cultural Organization
文化団体

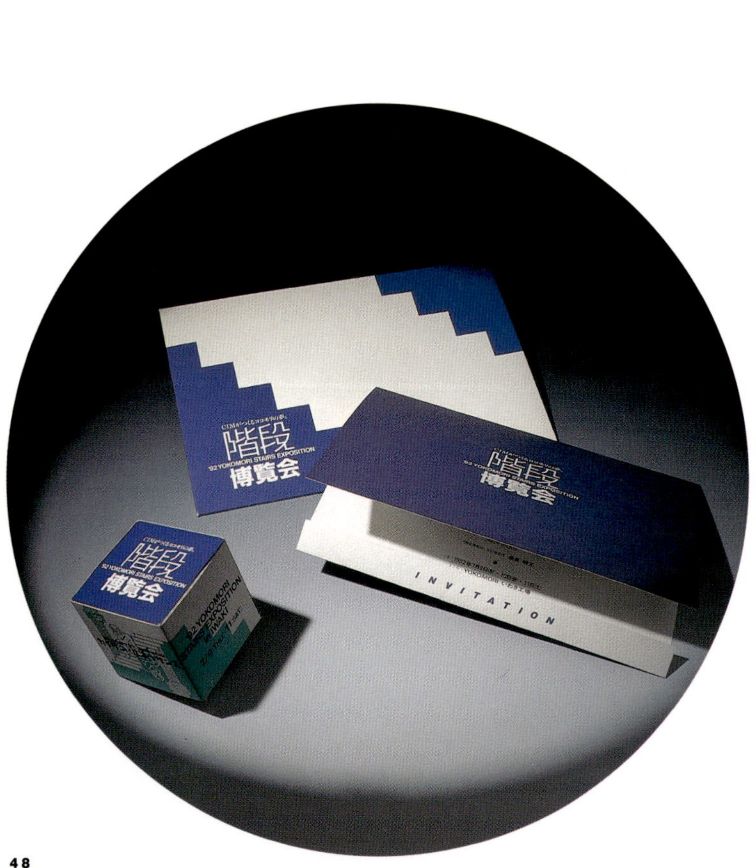

◀
Invitation to a stairway exhibition
階段博覧会案内状
JAPAN 1992
CD,AD:Motohiro Saito
D:Masahiro Kurusu
I:Daisuke Kimura
CW:Hiroaki Yamada
DF:Crossover
CL:Yokomori
TC:Stair Maker
階段製造
•
When taken out of the envelope, the contents spring into a box shape.
封筒から出すと、ゴムの力で箱型になる。

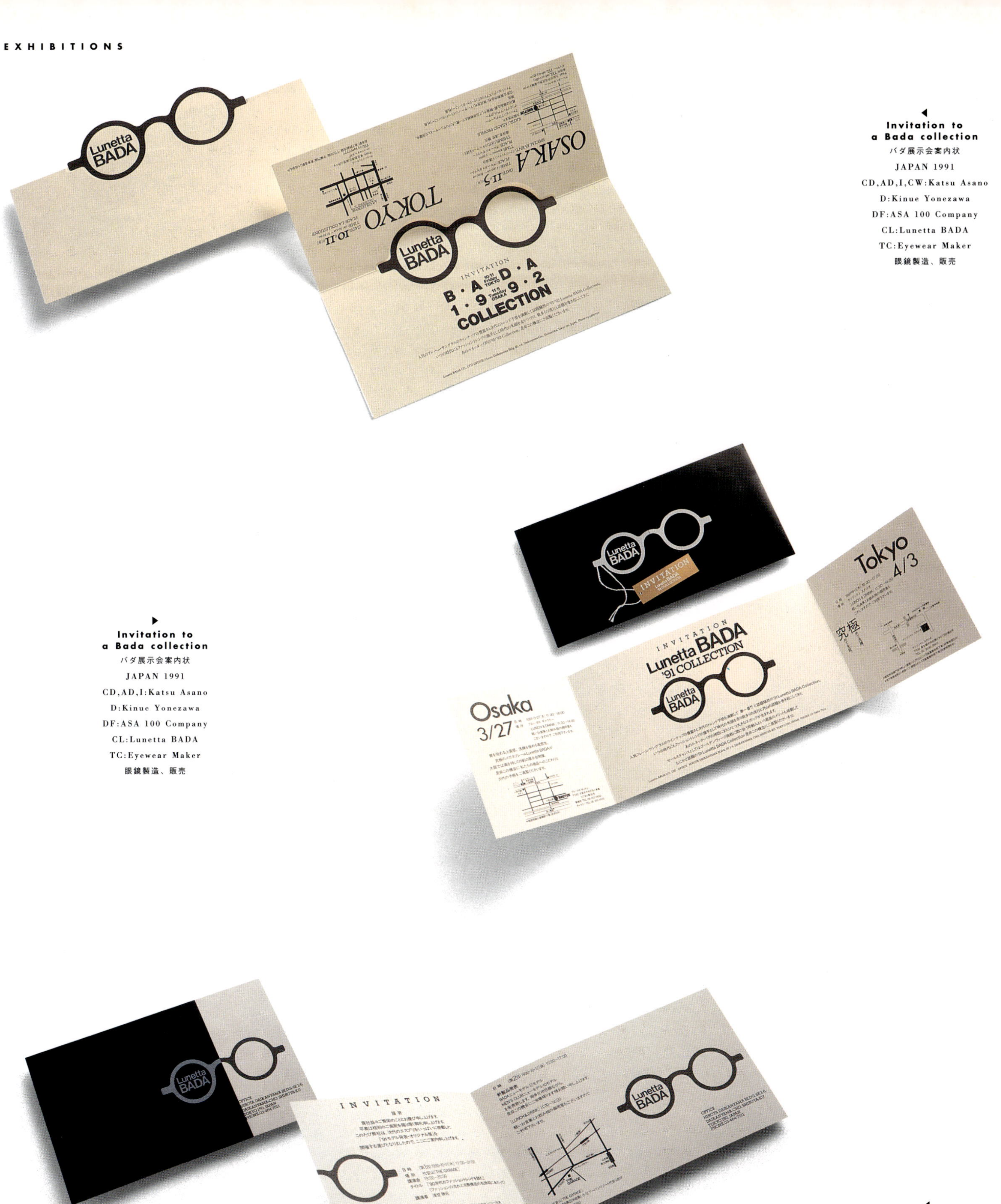

◀
Invitation to a Bada collection
バダ展示会案内状
JAPAN 1991
CD,AD,I,CW:Katsu Asano
D:Kinue Yonezawa
DF:ASA 100 Company
CL:Lunetta BADA
TC:Eyewear Maker
眼鏡製造、販売

▶
Invitation to a Bada collection
バダ展示会案内状
JAPAN 1991
CD,AD,I:Katsu Asano
D:Kinue Yonezawa
DF:ASA 100 Company
CL:Lunetta BADA
TC:Eyewear Maker
眼鏡製造、販売

◀
Invitation to a Bada collection
バダ展示会案内状
JAPAN 1990
CD,AD,I,CW:Katsu Asano
D:Kinue Yonezawa
DF:ASA 100 Company
CL:Lunetta BADA
TC:Eyewear Maker
眼鏡製造、販売

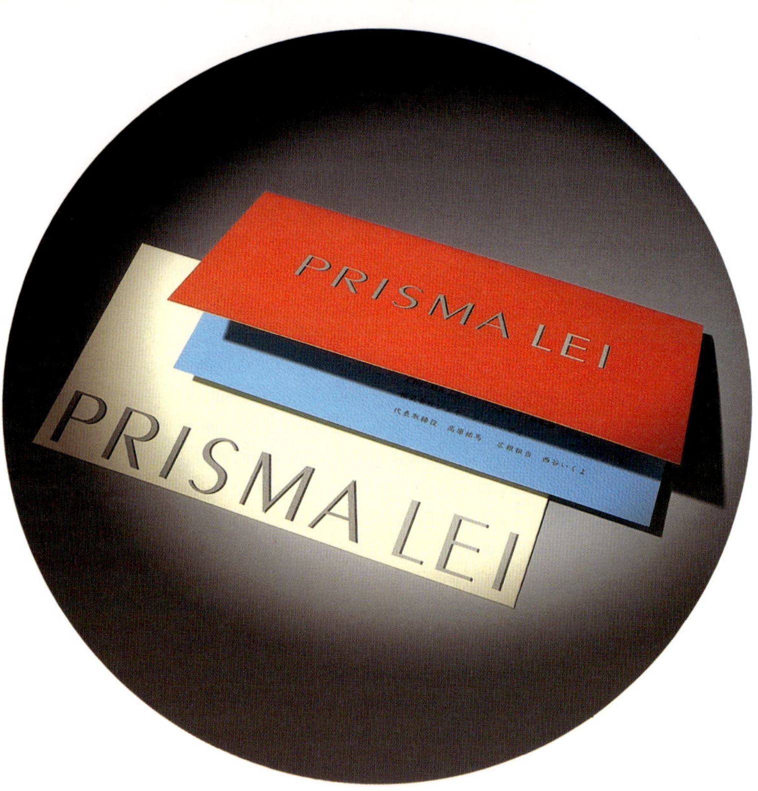

◀
Invitation to a Prisma Lei collection
プリズマ・レイ展示会案内状
JAPAN 1992
AD:Koji Mizutani
D:Hiroshi Omizo/Junko Horiuchi
CL:J.D.I.
TC:Apparel Maker
アパレル

▶
Invitation to a mirror and candle-holder exhibition
鏡・燭台展示会案内状
SWITZERLAND 1991
CD,AD,D,I,CW:Michael Baviera
DF:BBV Michael Baviera
CL:Wohnflex
TC:Furniture and Accessories Retailer
家具・アクセサリー販売

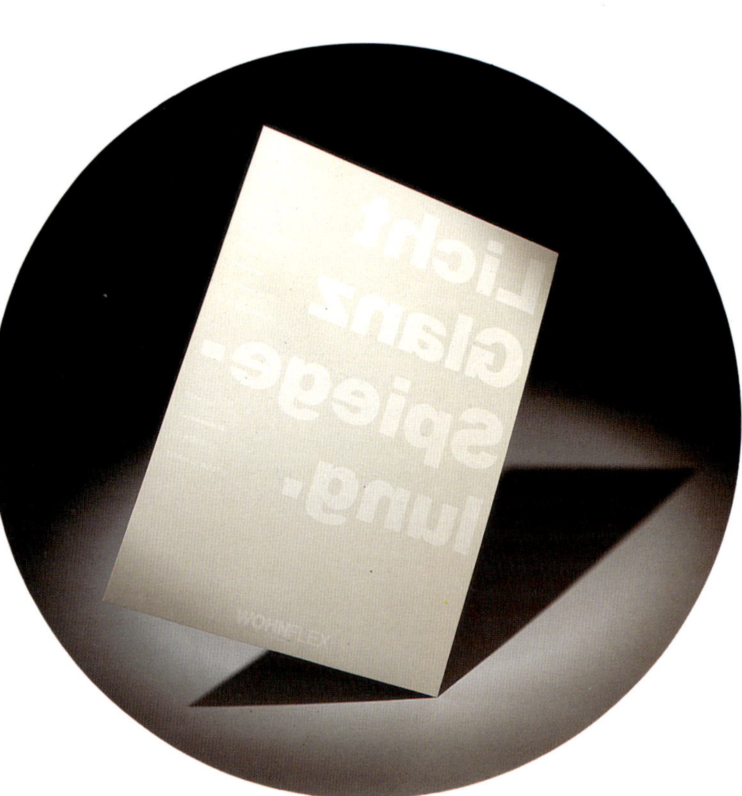

◀
Invitation to an exhibition
展示会案内状
JAPAN 1992
CD:Takanori Suzuki
AD:Noriaki Kitazato
D:Kazuko Yusa
CL:Daidoh
TC:Apparel Maker
アパレル

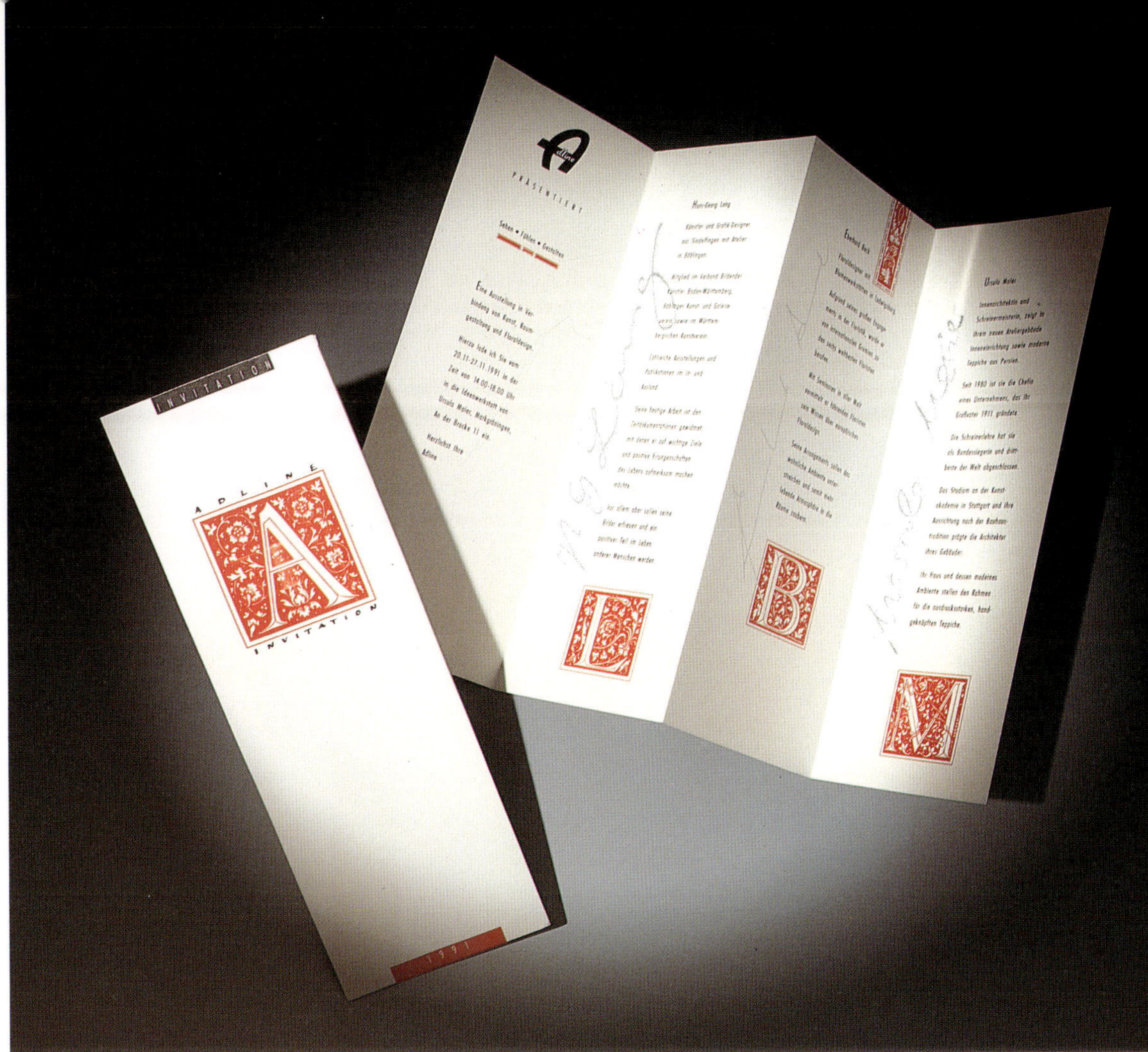

Invitation to an art and design exhibition

美術、デザイン展案内状

GERMANY 1991

D,I:Hans Georg lang

DF:Lane Art + Graphic Design

CL:Adline Exclusive Lady Fashion

TC:Fashion Boutique

ファッション・ブティック

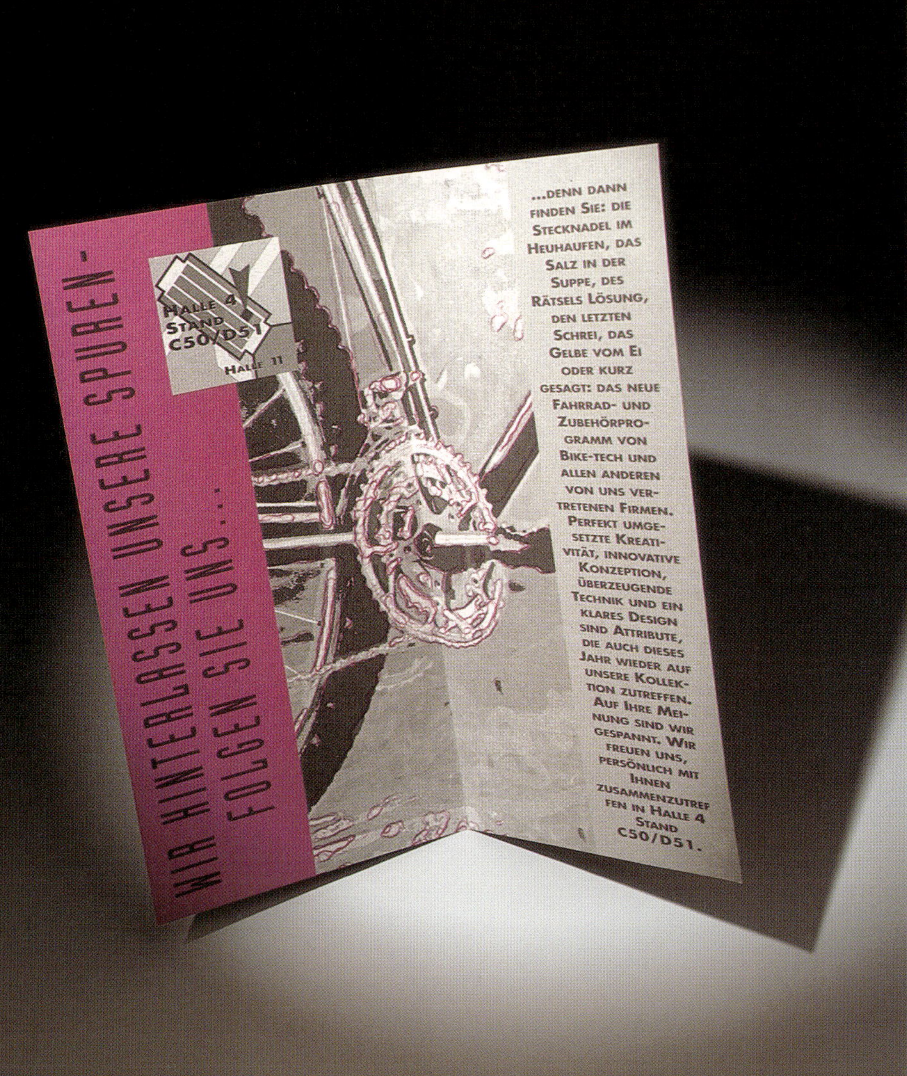

Invitation to the International Bike and Motor Exhibition

国際バイク＆モーター展案内状

GERMANY 1992

CD,AD:Werner Liebchen

CW:Ilona Liebchen

CL:Storck Bike-tech Trading

TC:Bicycle Distributor

自転車販売

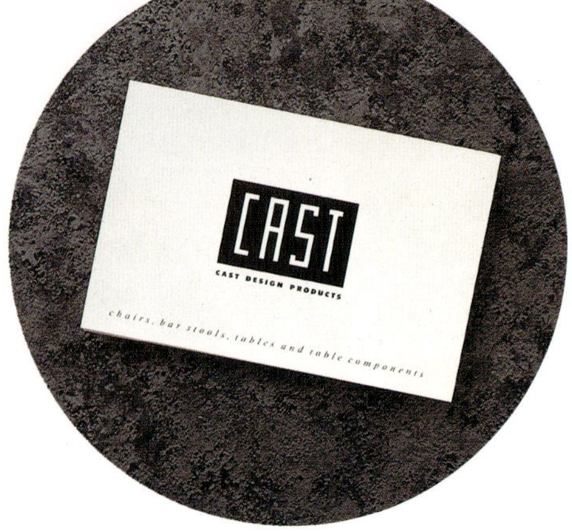

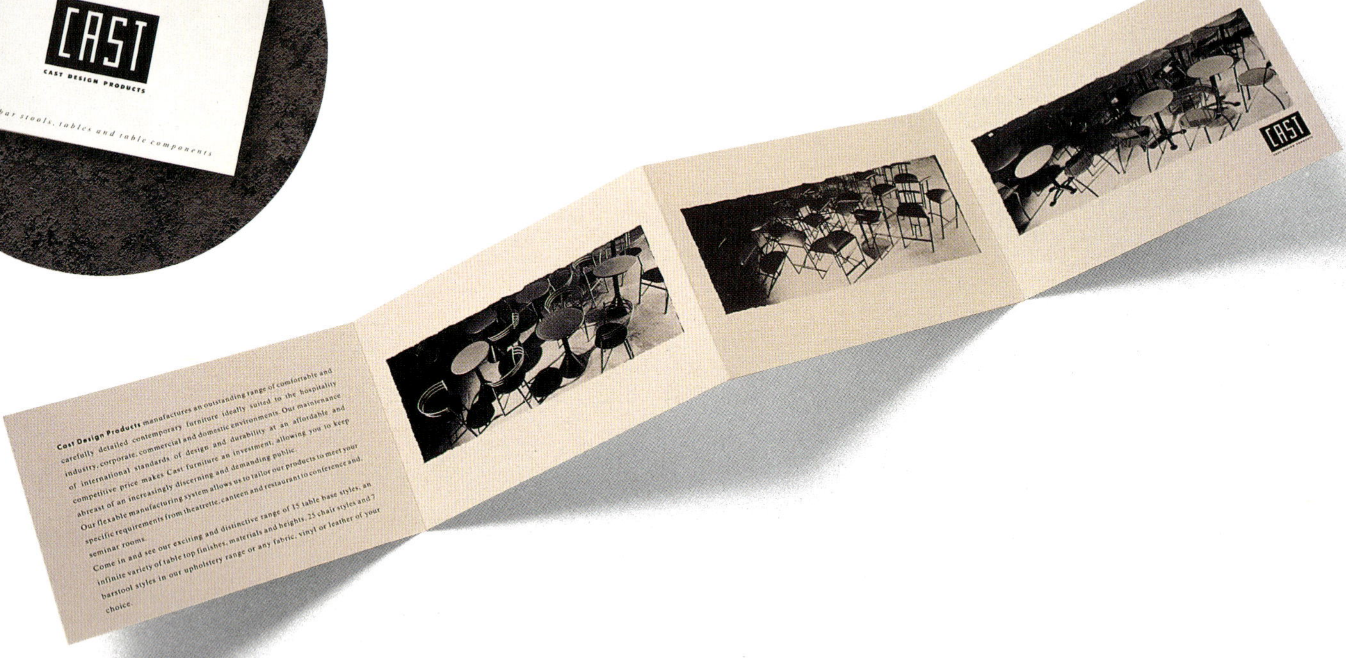

▲

Invitation to a furniture exhibition

家具展示会案内状

AUSTRALIA 1990

CD,AD,D: Michael Trudgeon

P: Elli

DF: Crowd Productions

CL: Cast Design Products

TC: Furniture Maker

家具製造

▼

Invitation to a sales show

展示会案内状

JAPAN 1989

AD: Takashi Fukuda

D: Musée

P: Masaaki Miyazawa

CL: Idée

TC: Furniture Maker

家具製造、販売

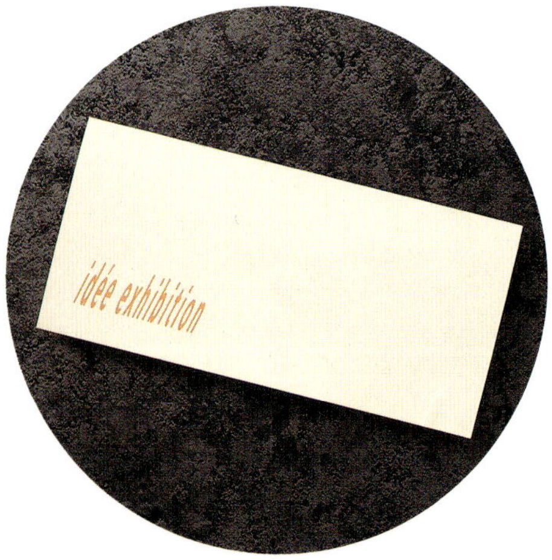

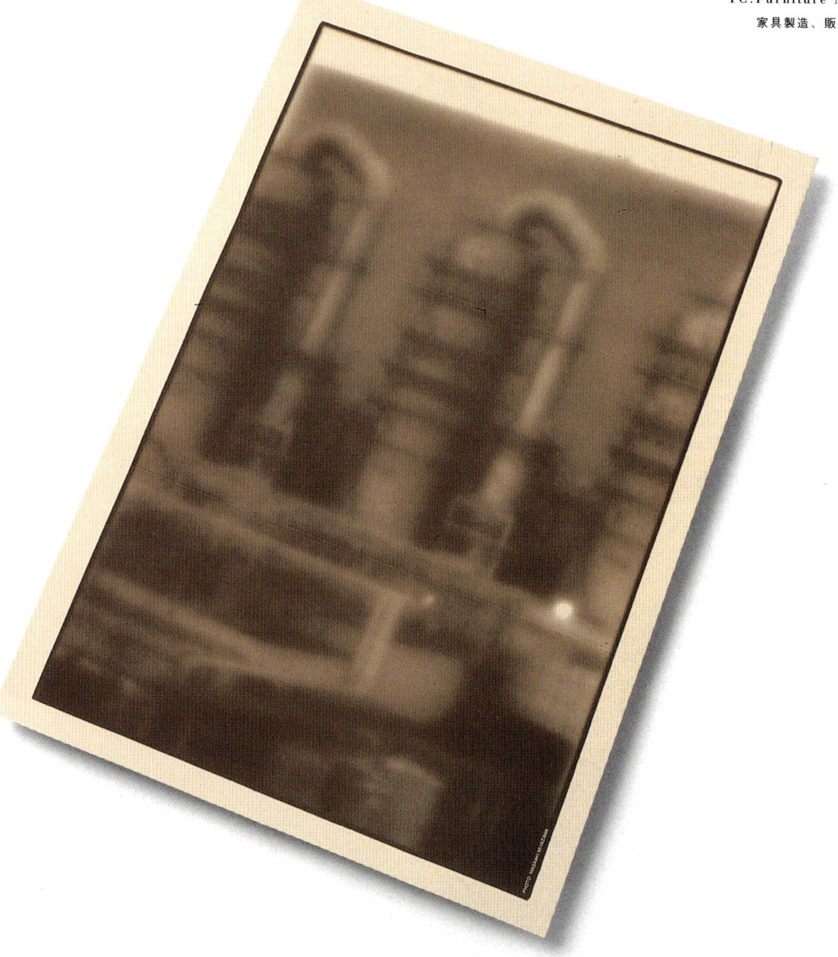

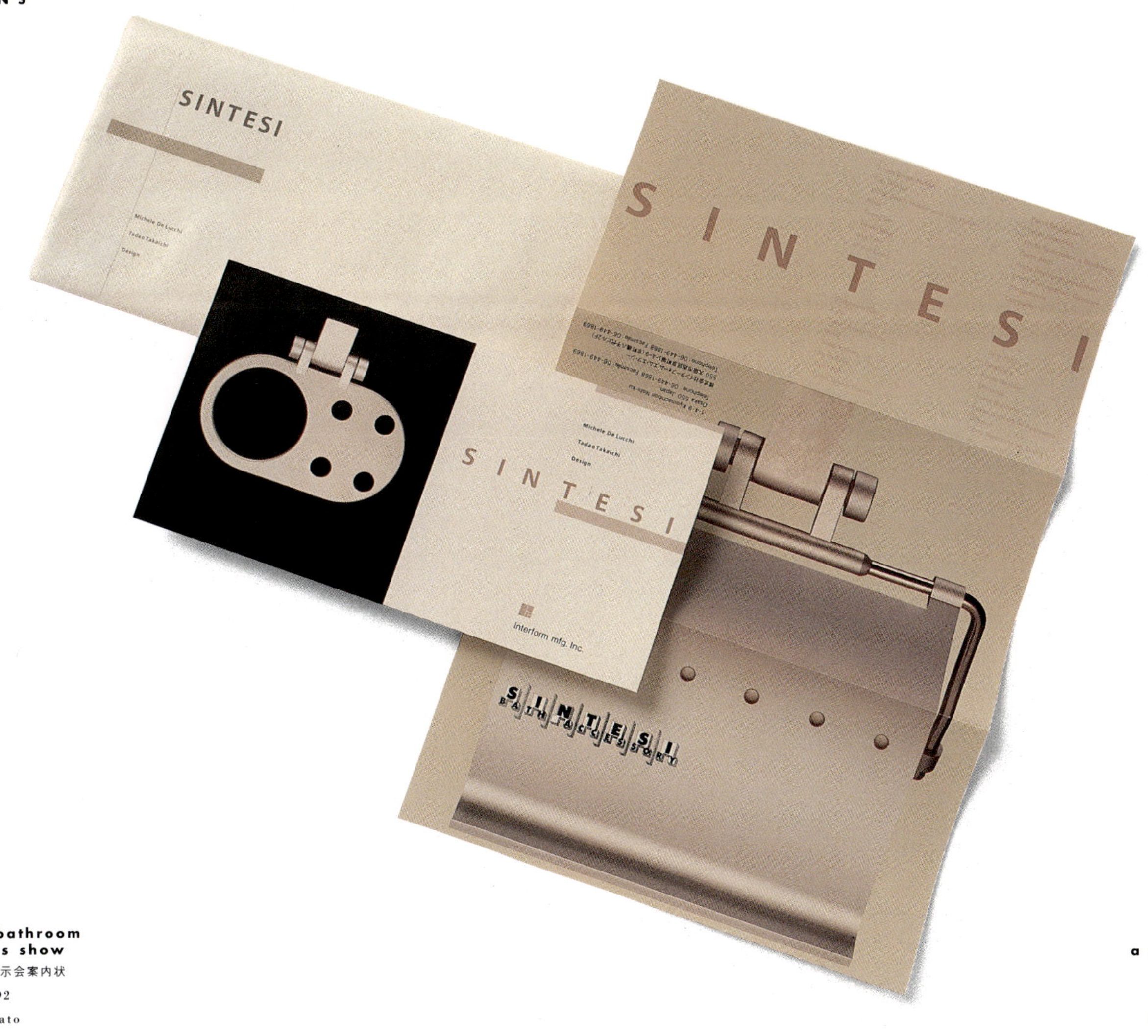

▲
Invitation to a bathroom accessory sales show
バス・アクセサリー展示会案内状
JAPAN 1992
AD,D:Jun Sato
P:Joe Sugino
DF:Jun Sato Design
CL:Interform mfg.
TC:Metal Fixture Maker
建築金物企画、制作

▼
Invitation to a Forme sales show
フォルム展示会案内状
JAPAN 1989
AD:Takashi Fukuda
D:Musée
P:Masaaki Miyazawa
CL:Idée
TC:Furniture Maker
家具製造、販売

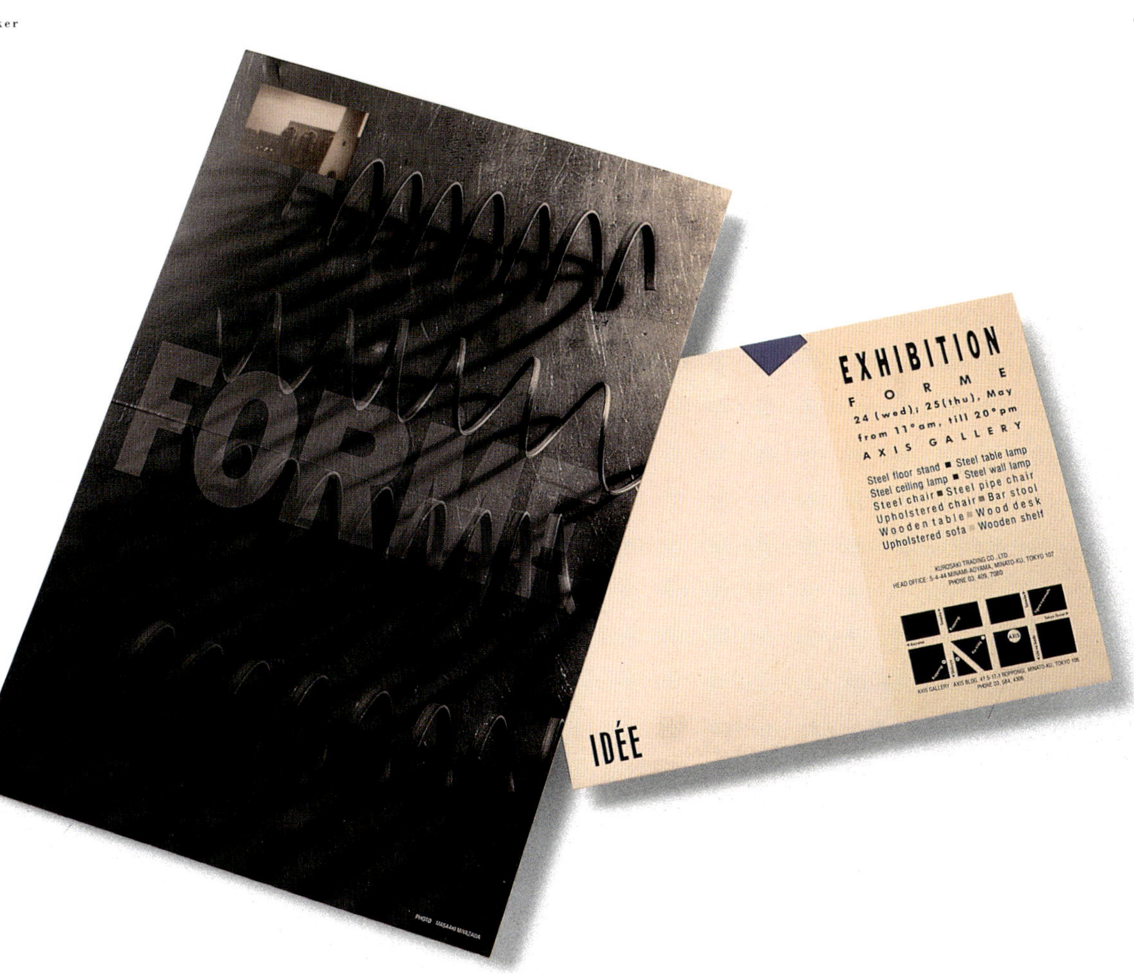

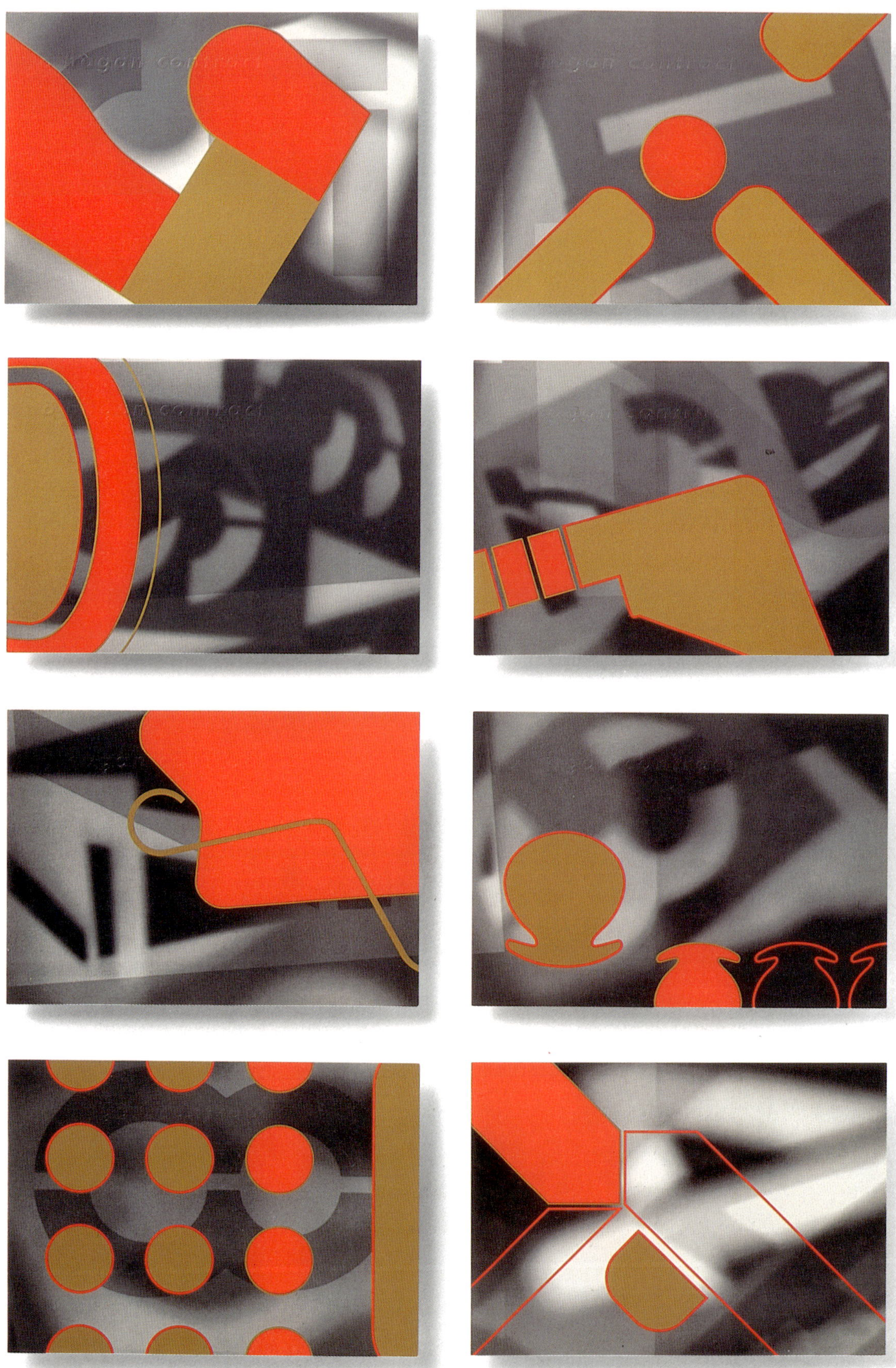

Invitation to a furniture exhibition

家具展示会案内状

ENGLAND 1992

AD:Alan Aboud

D:Alan Aboud

Sandro Sodano

P:Sandro Sodano

DF:Aboud Sodano

CL:O'Hagan Contract

TC:Furniture Retailer

家具販売

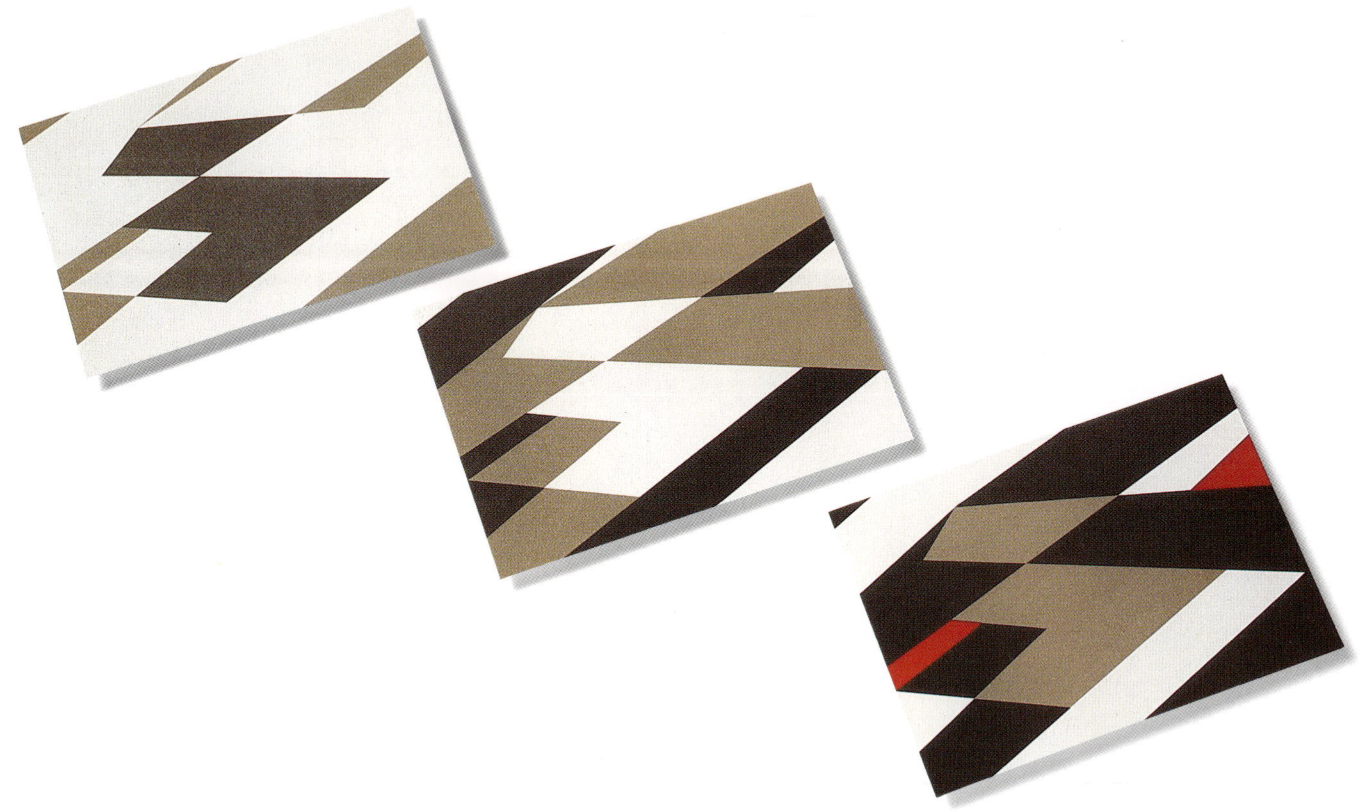

▲
Invitation to an Art Deco furniture and art exhibition

アール・デコ家具、美術展案内状

AUSTRIA 1991

AD,D:Kurt Dornig

CW:Hermann Brändle

DF:Dornig Grafik Design

CL:Sabine Moskat Art Deco und Jugendstil

TC:Antique Dealer

アンティーク・ディラー

▼
Invitation to a HOM fashion show

HOMファッション・ショー案内状

HONG KONG 1990

D:Catherine Lam Siu Hung

DF:Triump Int'l (H.K)

CL:Triump Int'l (H.K)

TC:Apparel Maker

アパレル

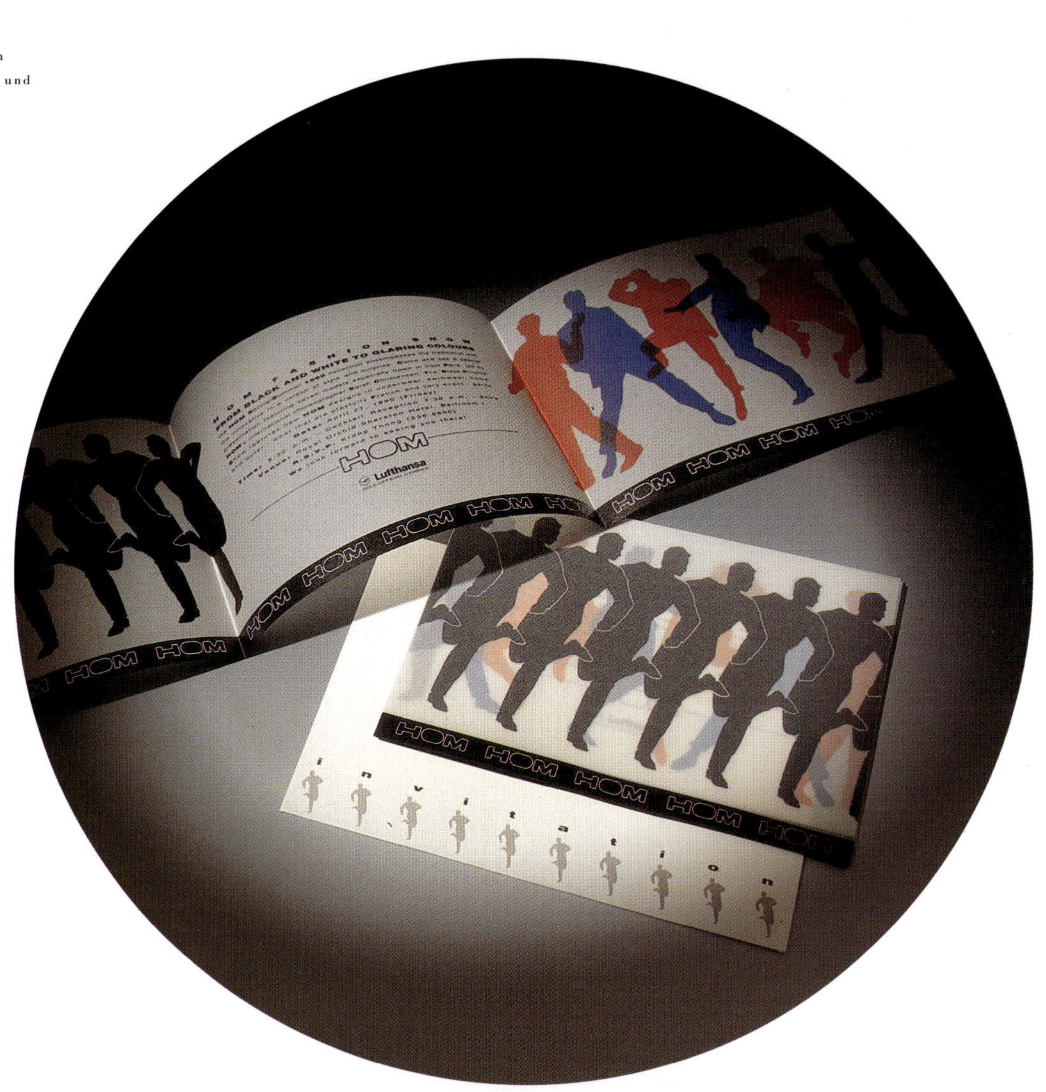

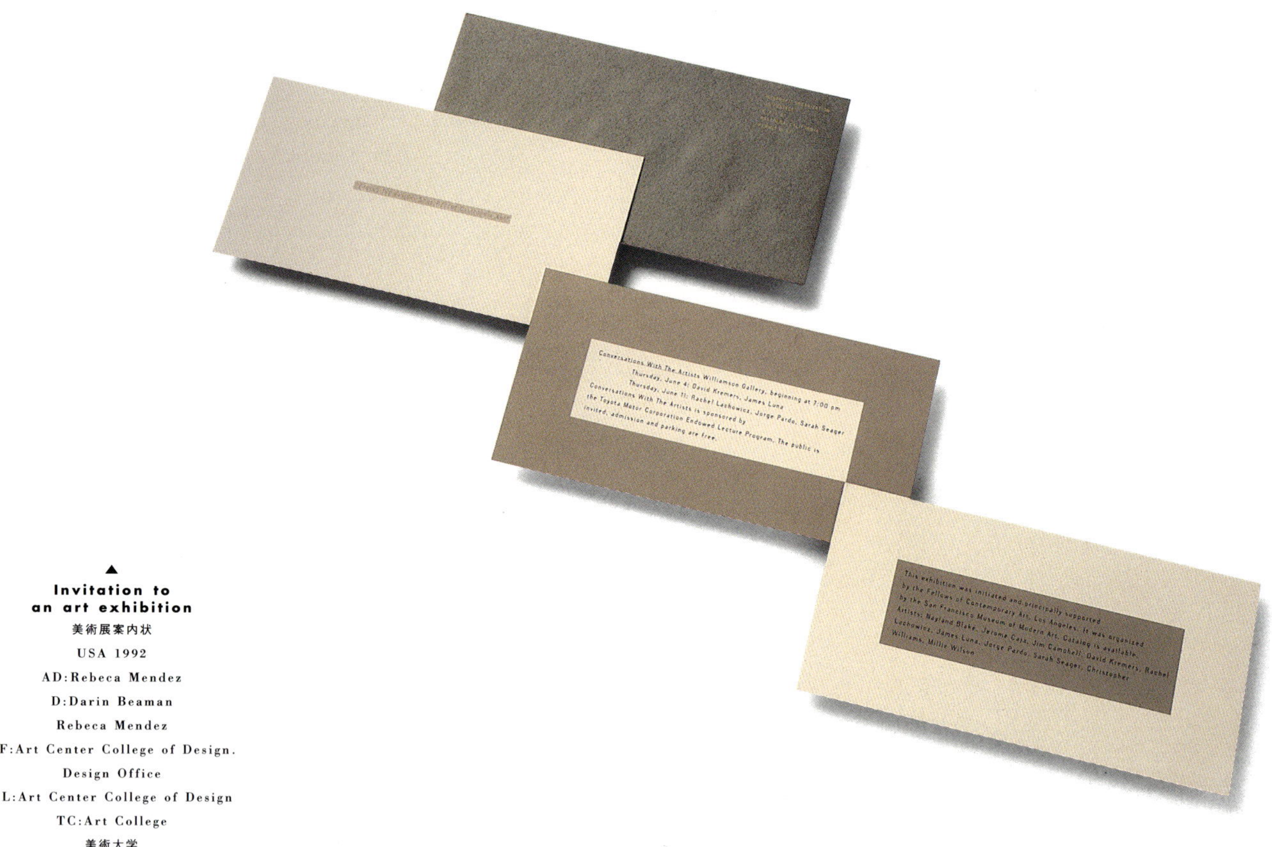

▲
Invitation to an art exhibition
美術展案内状
USA 1992
AD:Rebeca Mendez
D:Darin Beaman
Rebeca Mendez
DF:Art Center College of Design.
Design Office
CL:Art Center College of Design
TC:Art College
美術大学

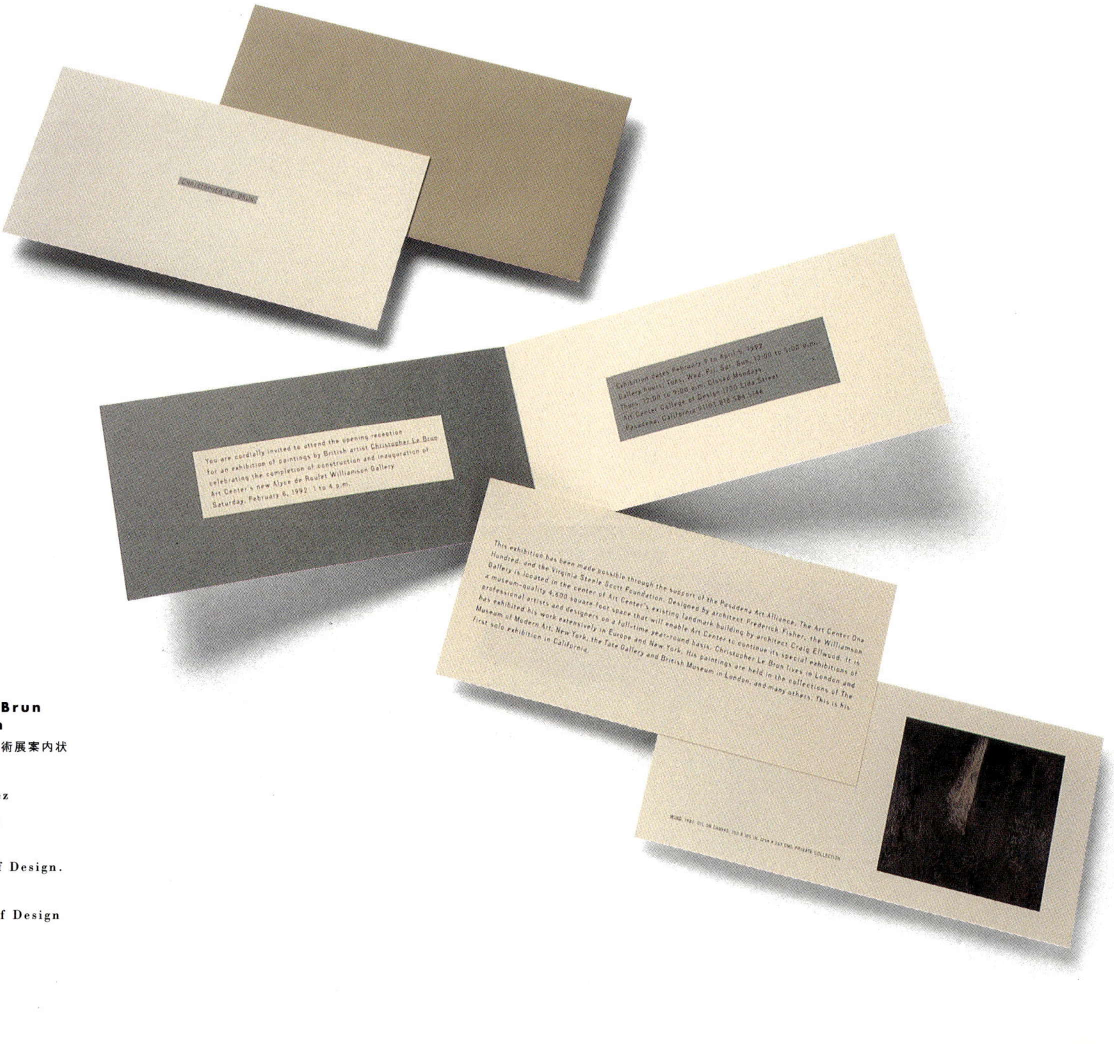

▲
Invitation to a Christopher Le Brun art exhibition
クリストファー・ル・ブラン美術展案内状
USA 1992
AD:Rebeca Mendez
D:Darin Beaman
Rebeca Mendez
DF:Art Center College of Design.
Design Office
CL:Art Center College of Design
TC:Art College
美術大学

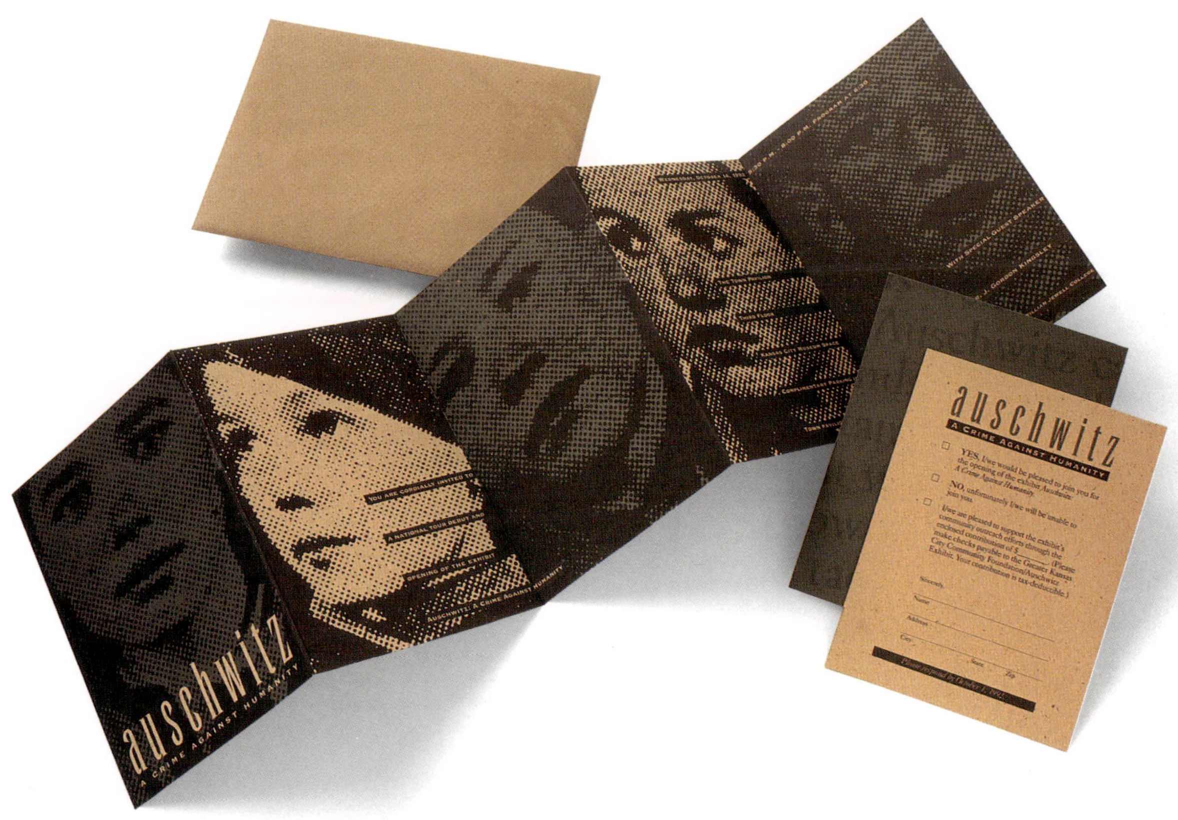

▲
Invitation to an Auschwitz exhibit
アウシュヴィッツ展案内状
USA 1992
AD,D:David Shultz
CW:Parris Communications
DF:Muller
CL:A Kansas City Campaign to Remember
TC:Community Foundation
地域団体

▼
Invitation to an art exhibition
美術展案内状
USA 1986
CD,AD:Rick Eiber
D:Rick Eiber
Red Staff
P:Ben Kerns
CL:Bellevue Art Museum
TC:Museum of Art
美術館

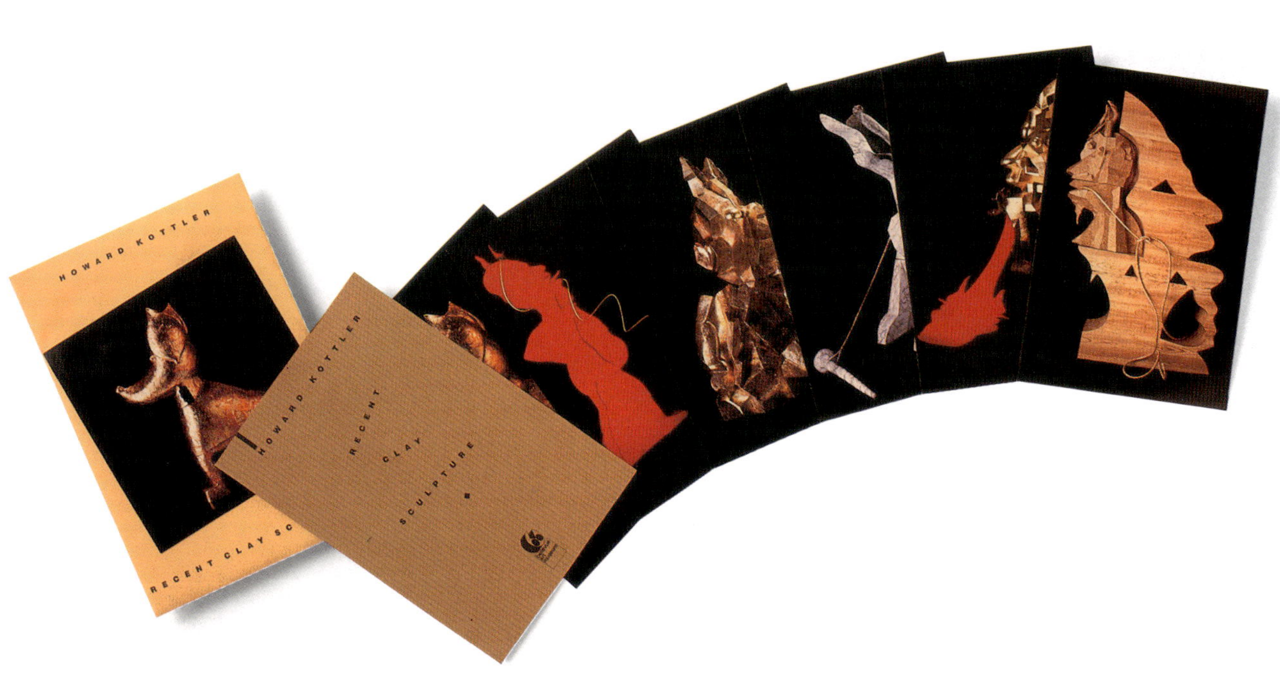

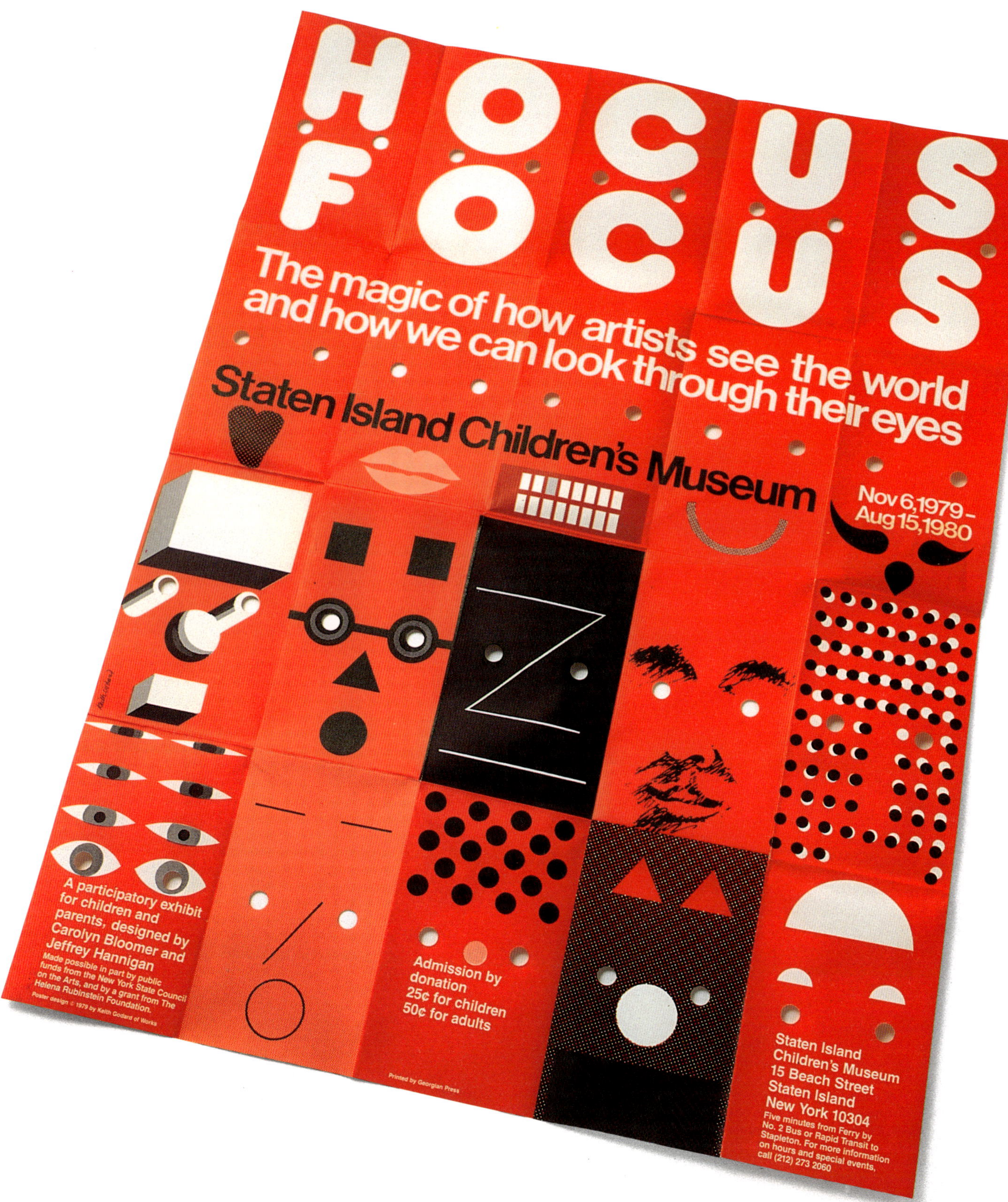

Announcement of an art exhibition
展覧会案内状
USA 1979
AD,D,I:Keith Godard
CW:Children's Museum Staff
DF:Studioworks
CL:Staten Island Children's Museum
TC:Children's Museum
子供博物館

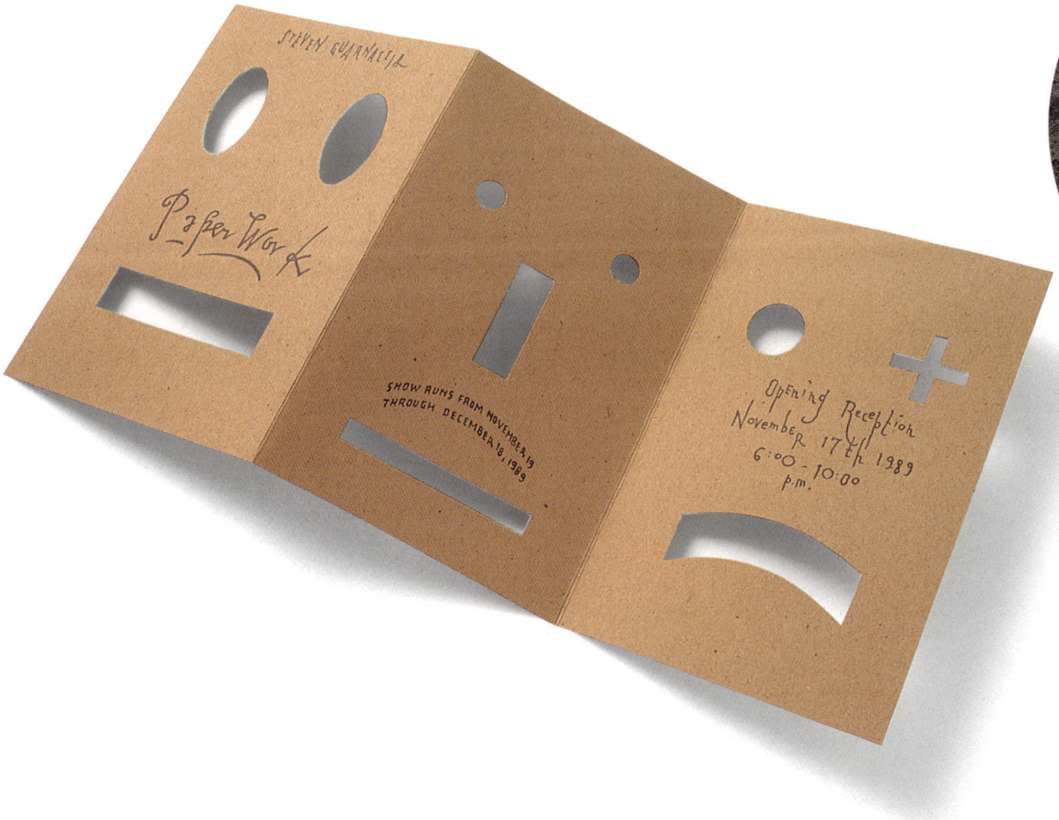

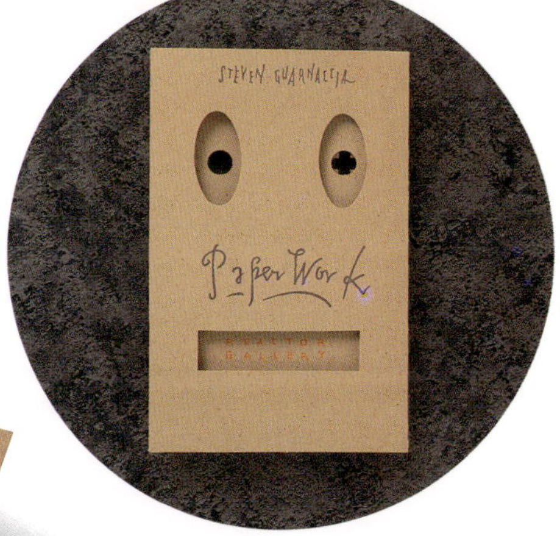

▲
Invitation to an art exhibition
美術展案内状
USA 1989
CD,AD:Bill Grigsby
I:Steven Guarnaccia
CL:The Reactor Gallery,Toronto
TC:Art Gallery
アート・ギャラリー

▼
Invitation to an art exhibition
美術展案内状
USA 1991
CD,AD:Bill Grigsby
D,I:Steven Guarnaccia
CL:The Reactor Gallery, Toronto
TC:Art Gallery
アート・ギャラリー

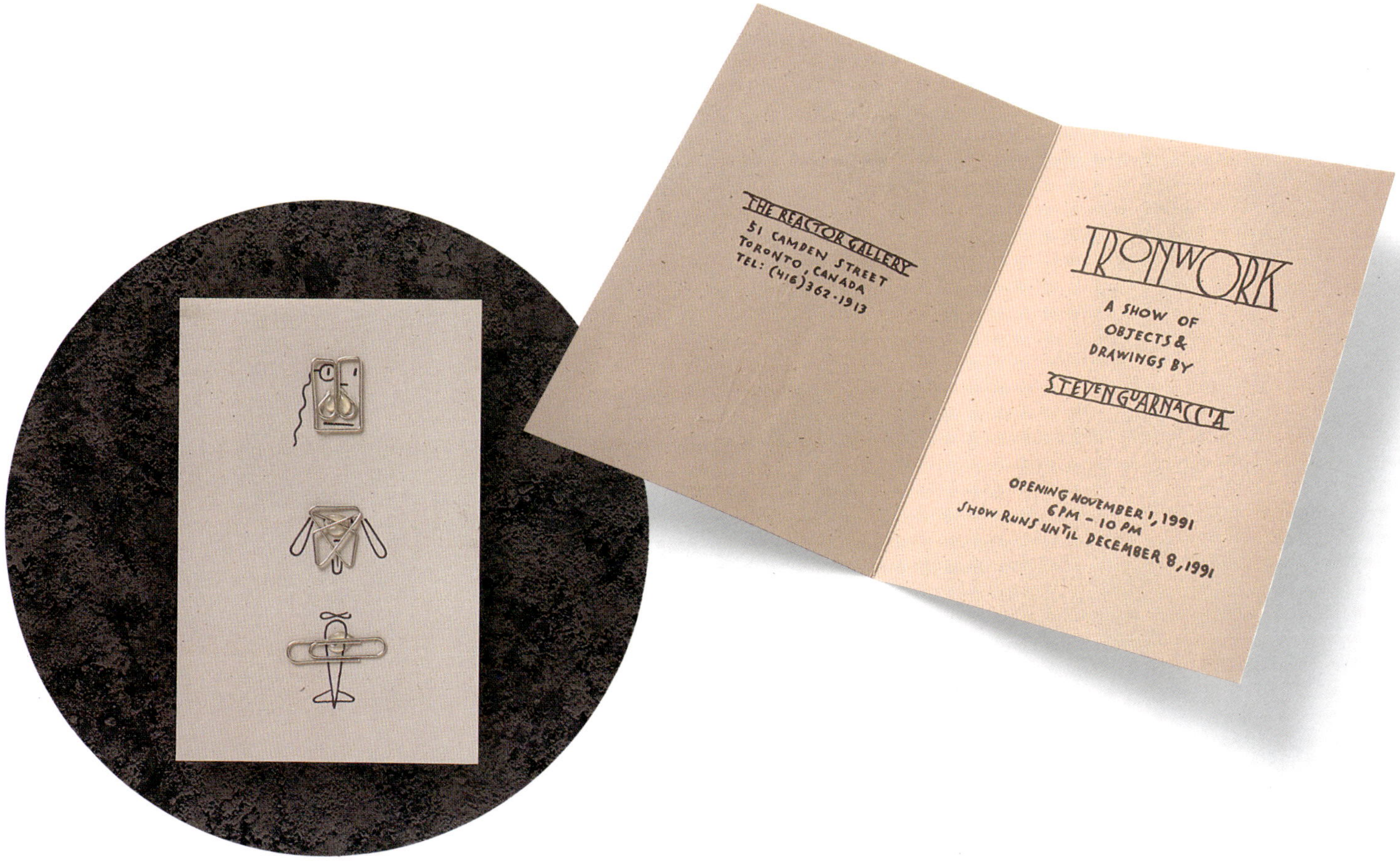

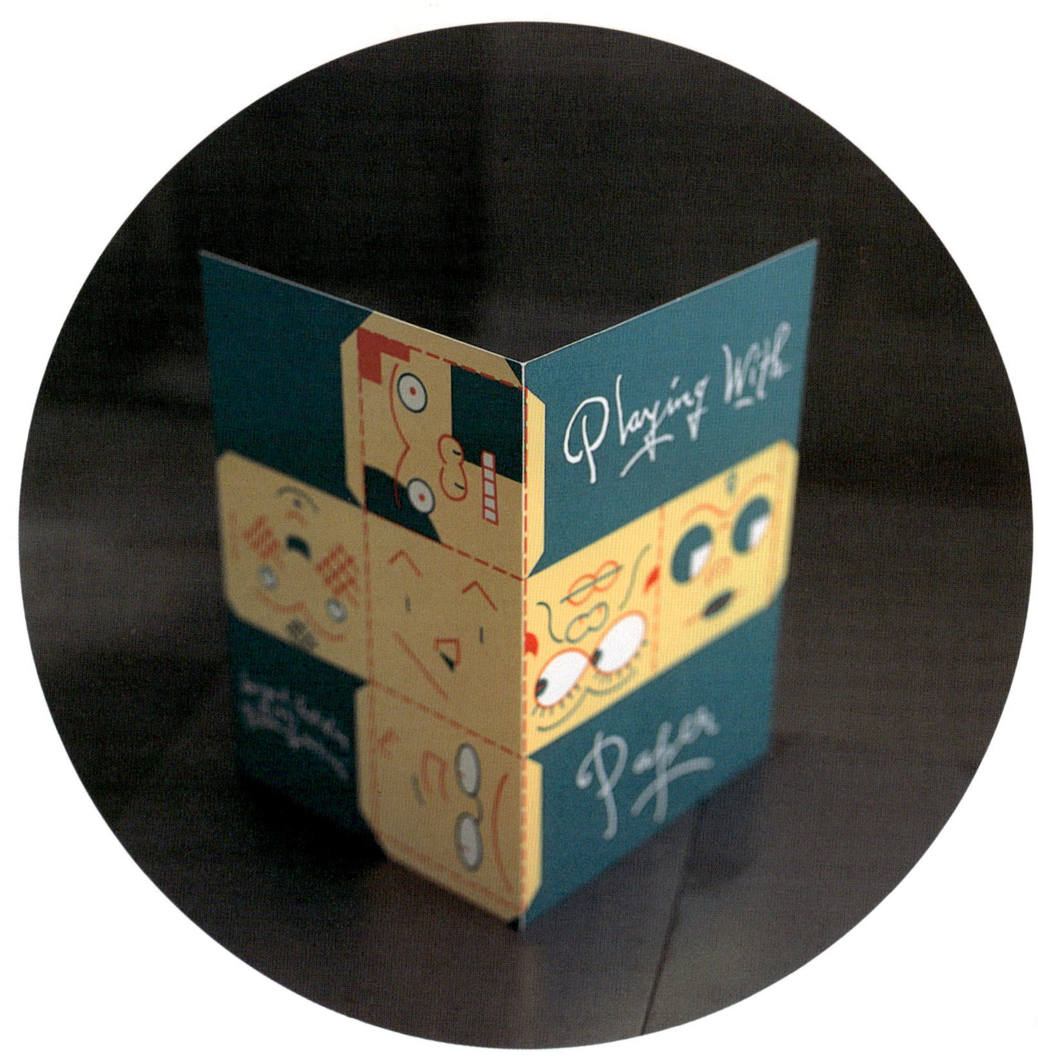

▲
Invitation to an art exhibition
美術展案内状
USA 1991
AD:Debbie Ketchum
D,I,CW:Steven Guarnaccia
CL:Hallmark
TC:Card Publisher
カード制作

▼
Invitation to a publishing trade show
出版トレード・ショー案内状
USA 1990
CD:Susan Slover
D:Laurel Shoemaker
CW:Licia Hahn
DF:Susan Slover Design
CL:European Travel and Life
TC:Magazine
雑誌

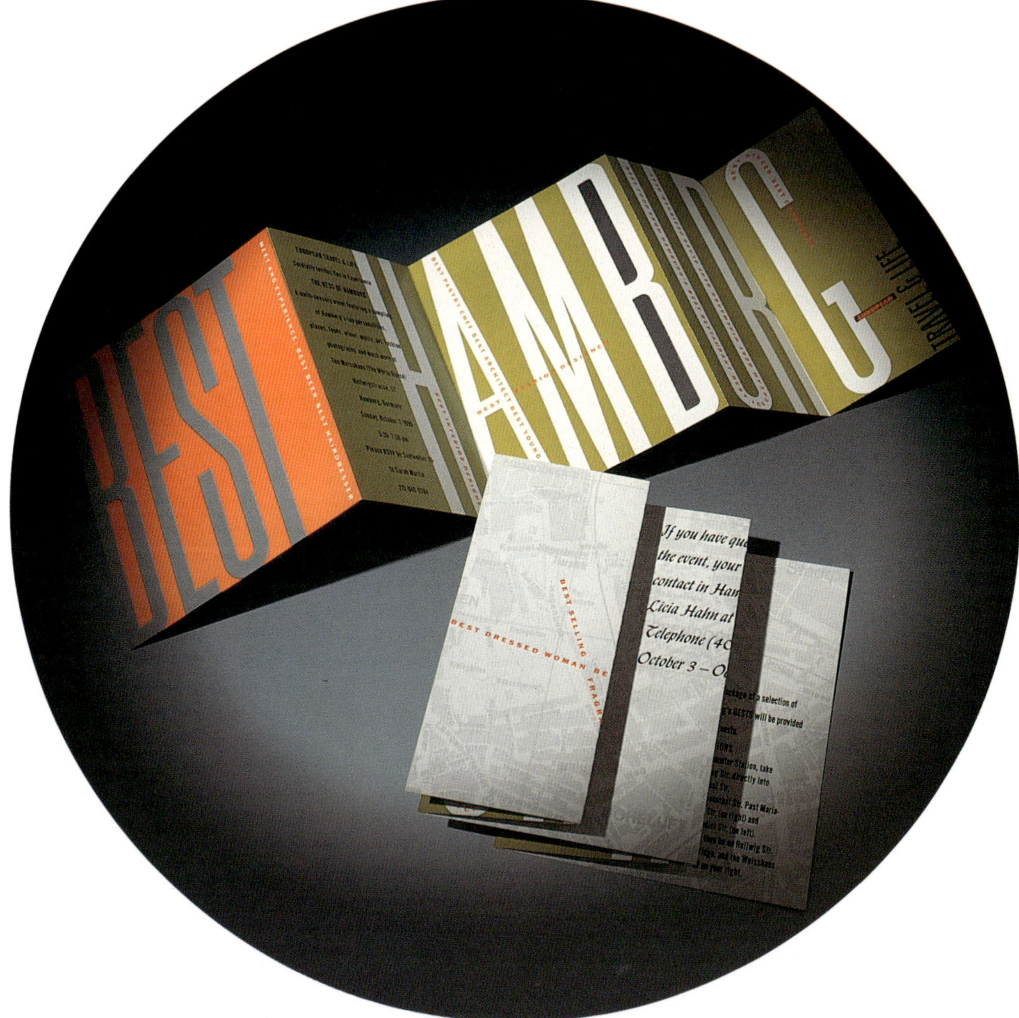

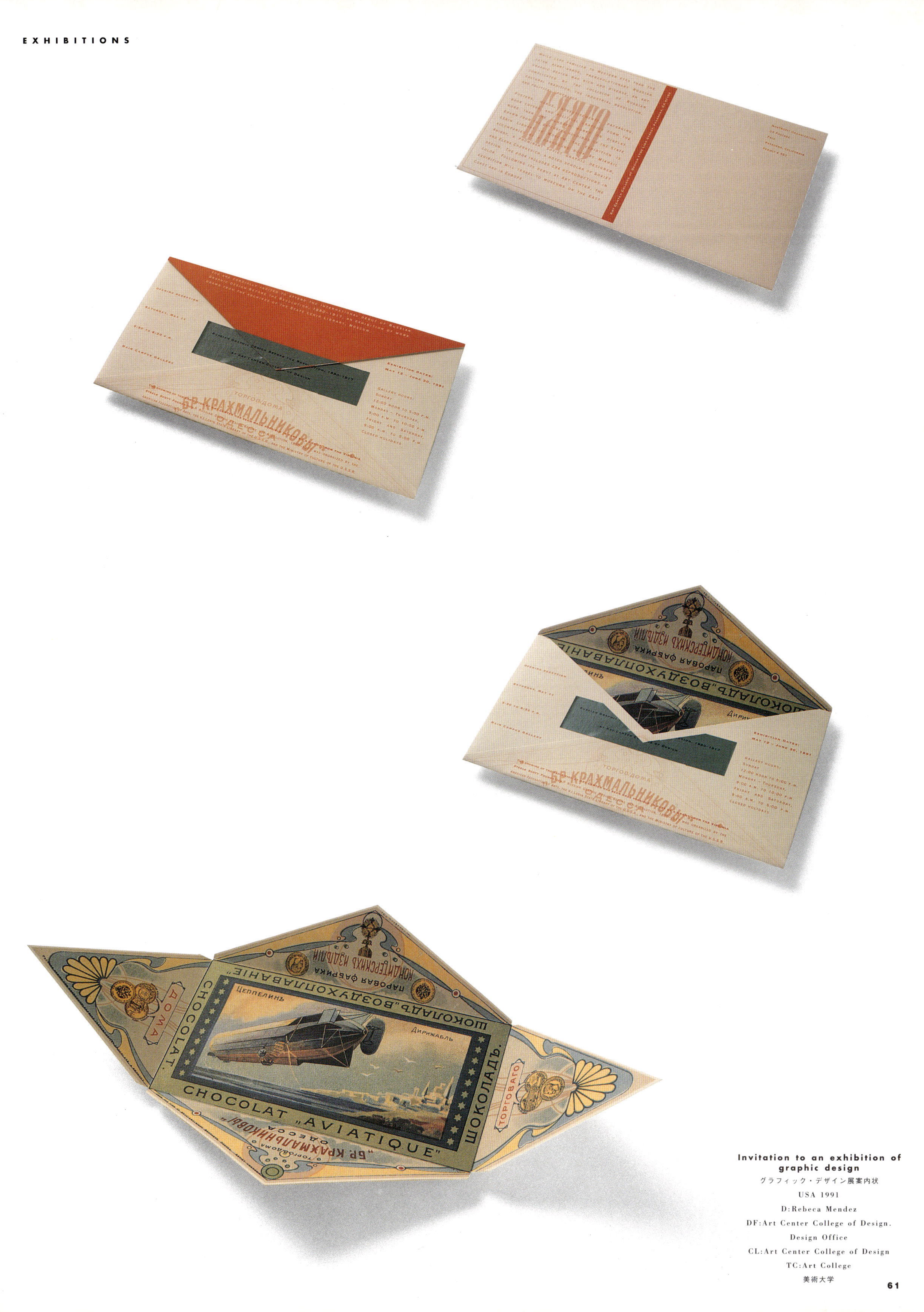

Invitation to an exhibition of graphic design
グラフィック・デザイン展案内状
USA 1991
D:Rebeca Mendez
DF:Art Center College of Design. Design Office
CL:Art Center College of Design
TC:Art College
美術大学

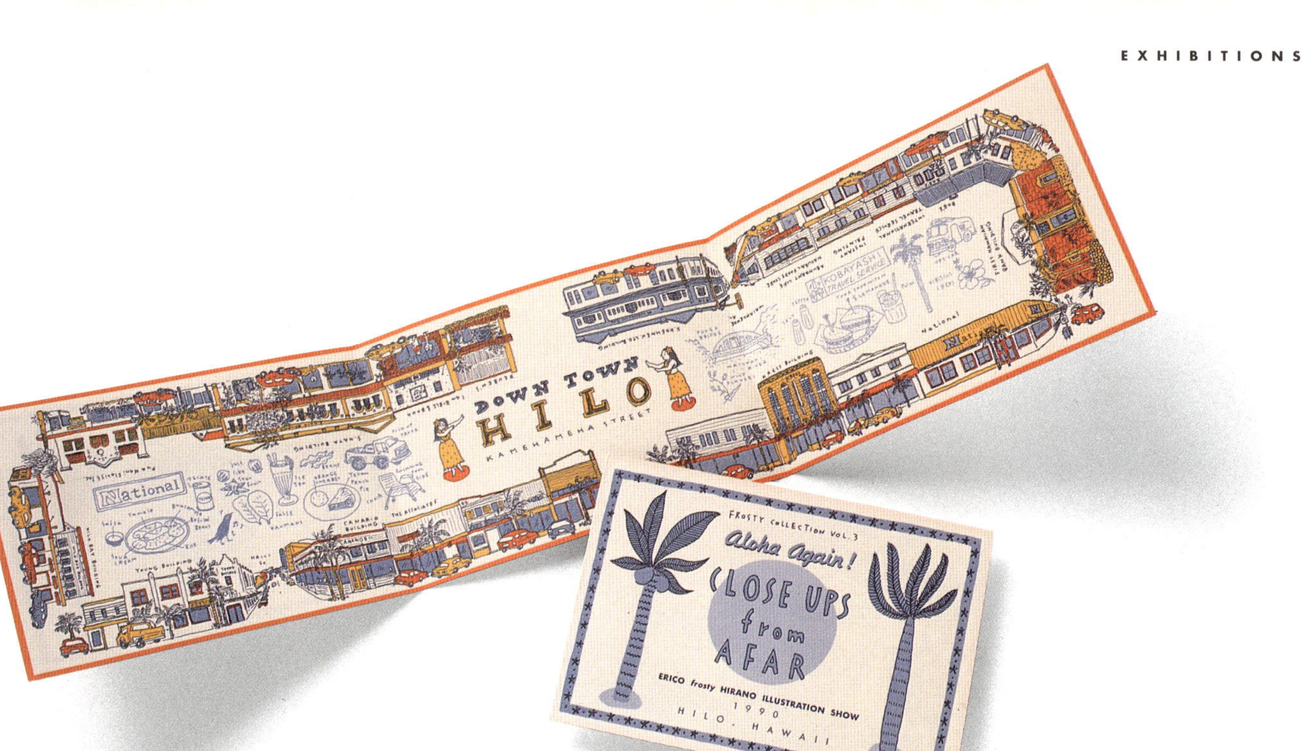

▲
Invitation to a solo exhibition
個展案内状
JAPAN 1990
D,I:Eriko Hirano
CL:Eriko Hirano
TC:Illustrator
イラストレーター

▼
Invitation to a solo exhibition
個展案内状
JAPAN 1988
D,I:Eriko Hirano
CL:Eriko Hirano
TC:Illustrator
イラストレーター

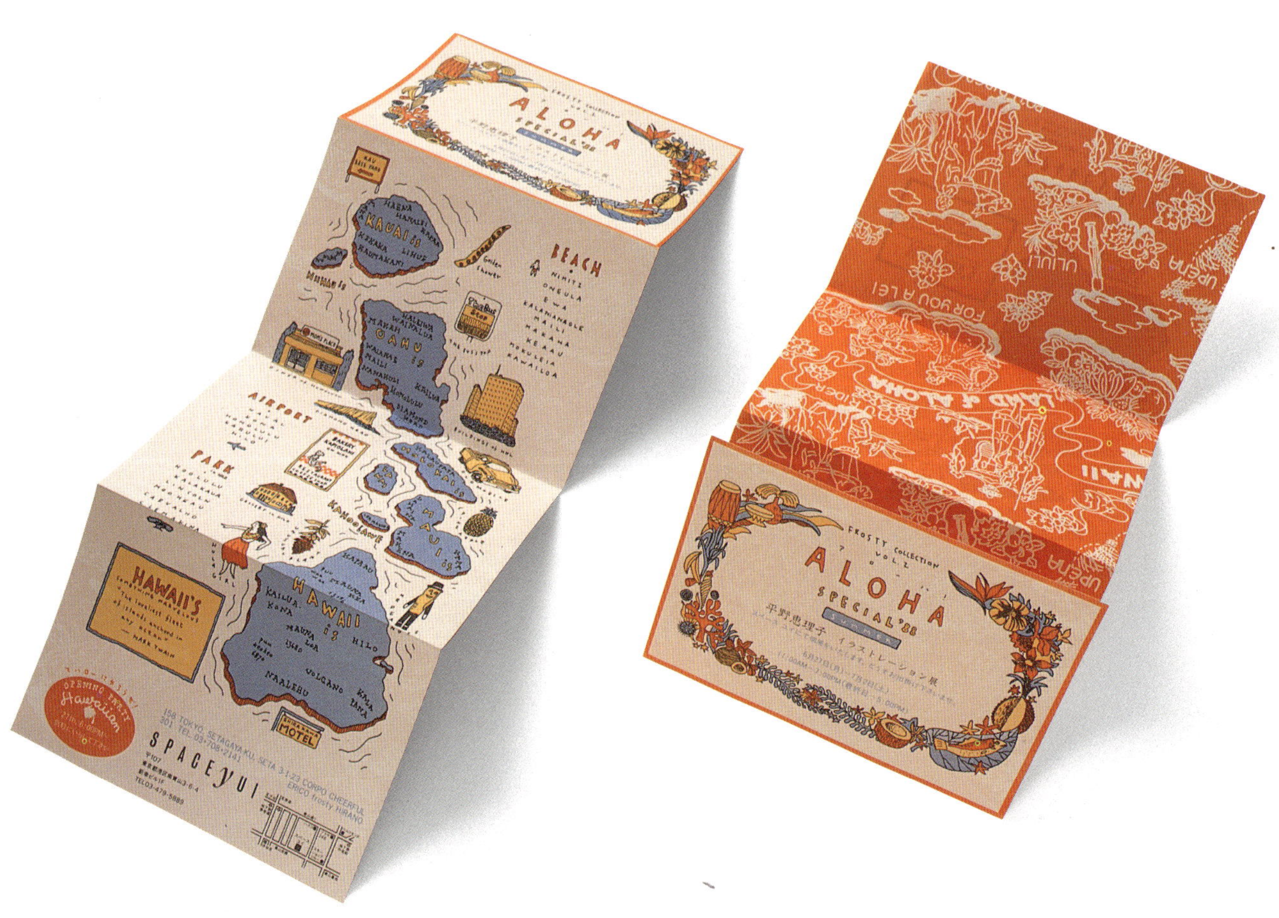

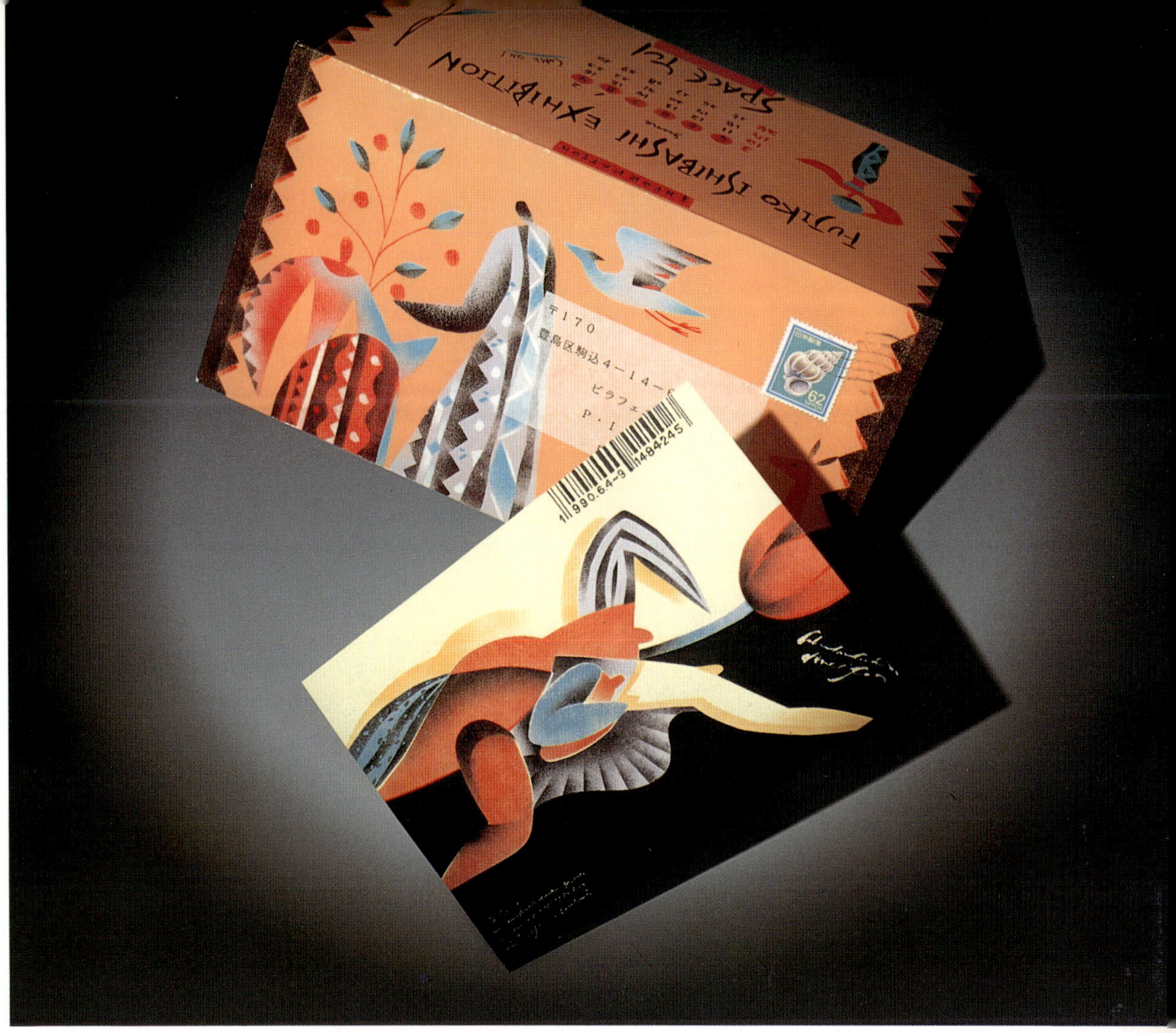

▶

Invitation to a solo exhibition

個展案内状

JAPAN 1990

I:Fujiko Ishibashi

CL:Fujiko Ishibashi

TC:Illustrator

イラストレーター

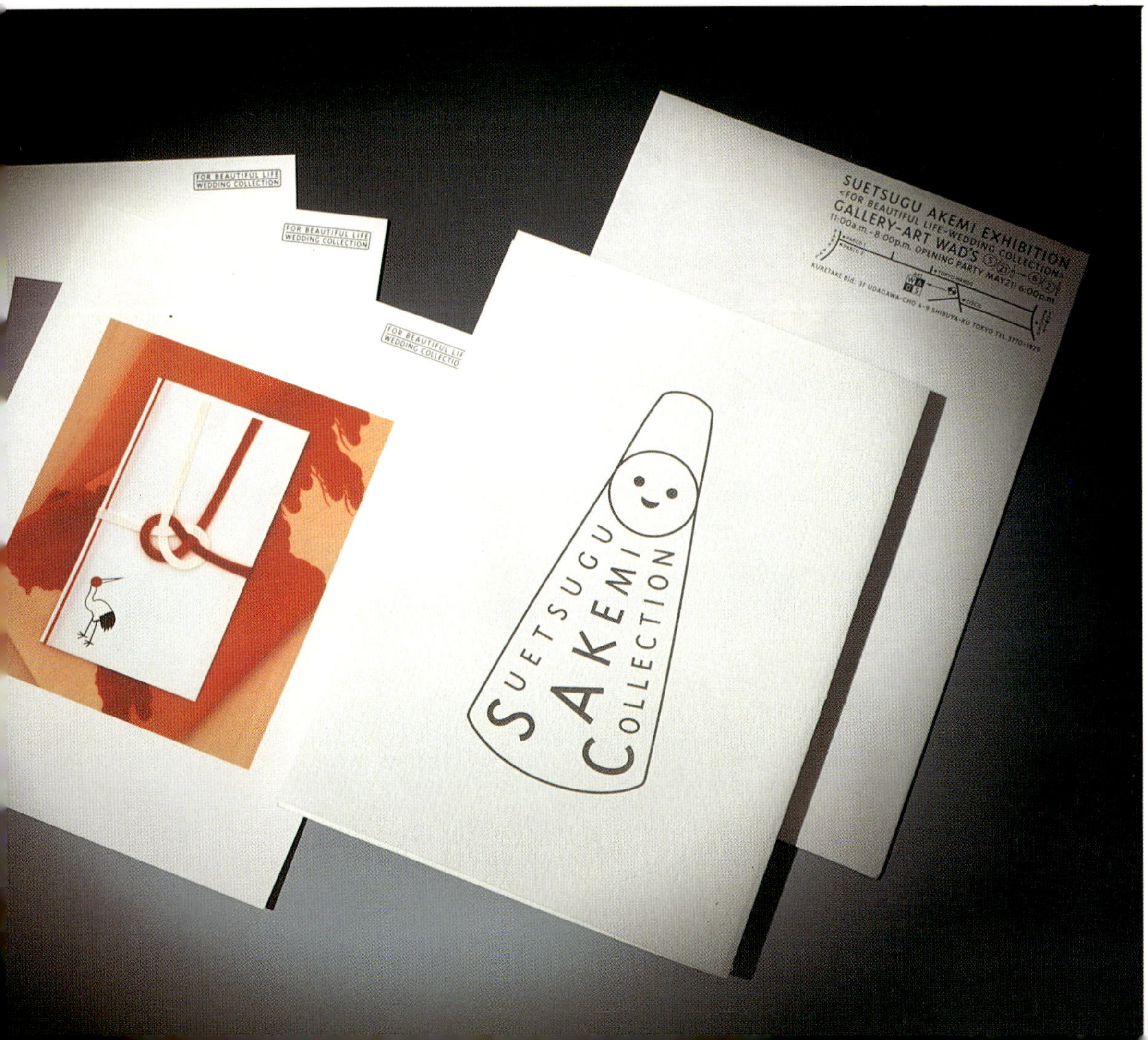

◀

Invitation to a solo exhibition

個展案内状

JAPAN 1992

D:Katsunori Aoki

P:Hideki Morikawa

I:Akemi Suetsugu

CL:Akemi Suetsugu

TC:Illustrator

イラストレーター

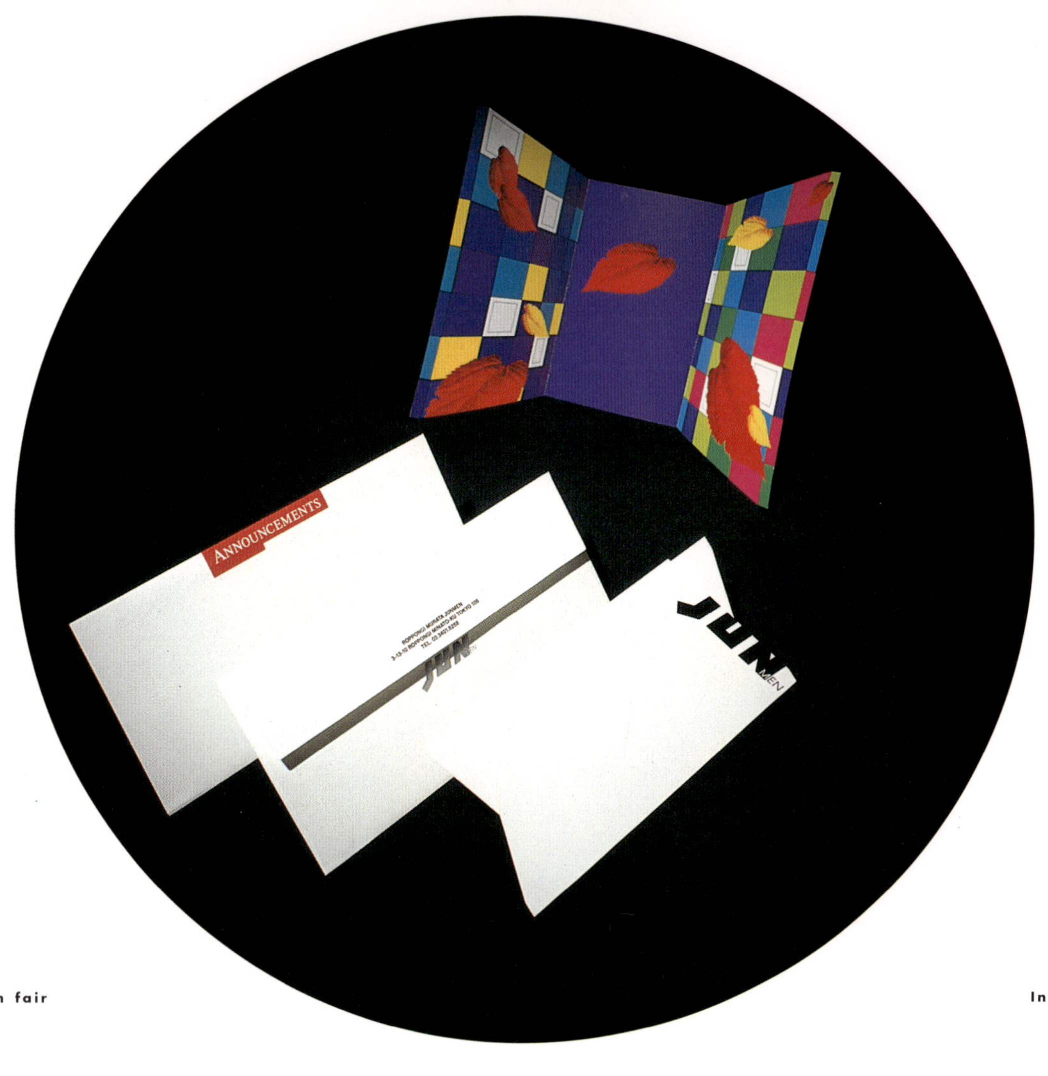

▲
Invitation to an autumn fair
オータム・フェア案内状
JAPAN 1991
AD,D:Keisuke Unosawa
DF:Keisuke Unosawa Design
CL:Jun
TC:Apparel Maker
アパレル

▼
Invitation to a resort fair
リゾート・フェア案内状
JAPAN 1991
AD,D:Keisuke Unosawa
DF:Keisuke Unosawa Design
CL:Jun
TC:Apparel Maker
アパレル

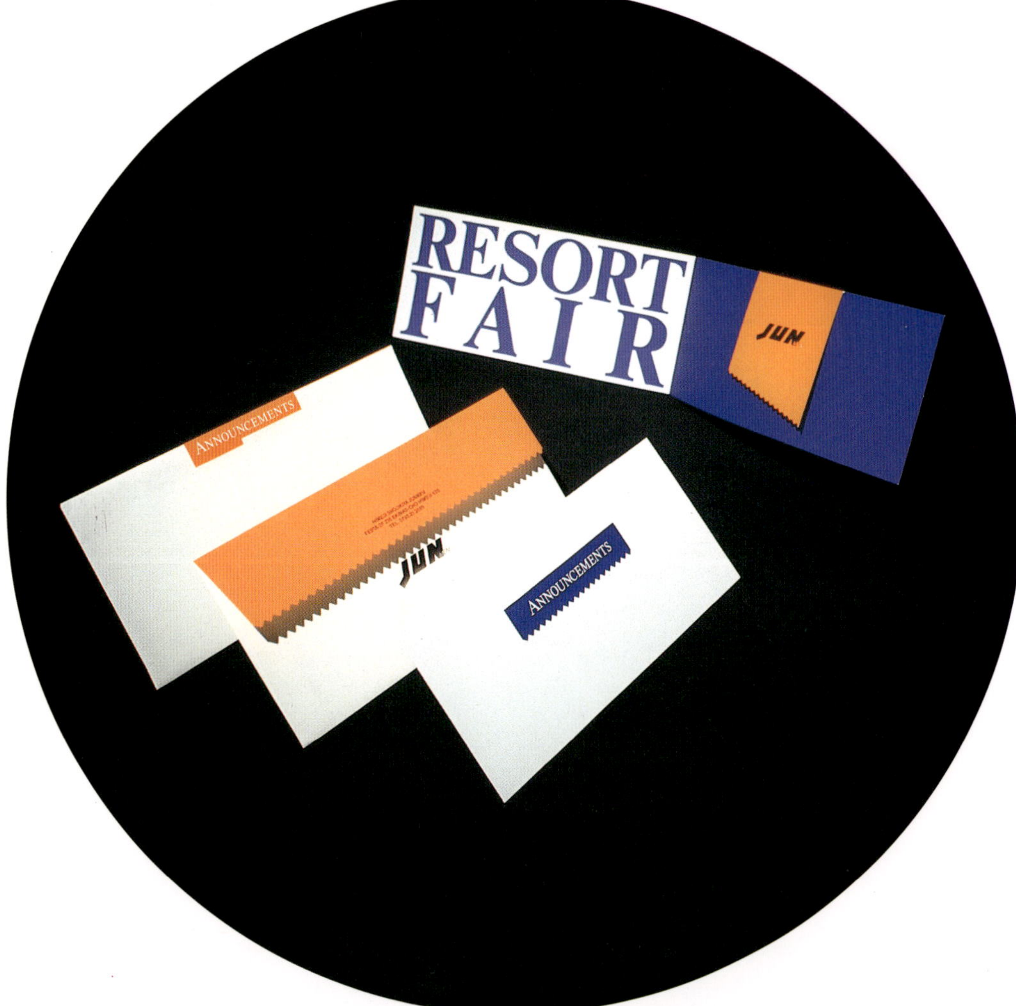

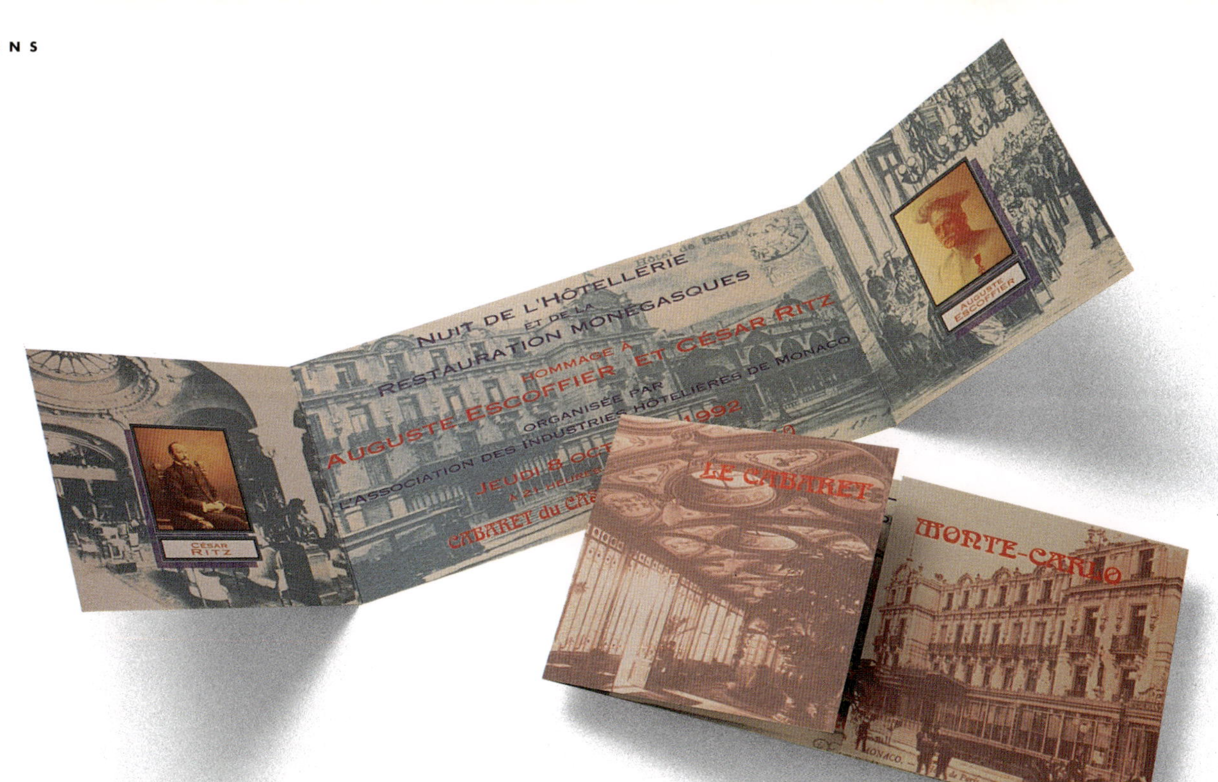

▲

Invitation to a hotel cabaret

ホテル・キャバレー招待状

ITALY 1992

CD,AD,D,I:Amedeo M.Turello

CW:Juliette Bouhanna

CL:Souété Des Bains De Mer

TC:Hotel, Casino

ホテル、カジノ

▼

Invitation to a spring fair

スプリング・フェア案内状

JAPAN 1991

AD,D:Keisuke Unosawa

DF:Keisuke Unosawa Design

CL:Jun

TC:Apparel Maker

アパレル

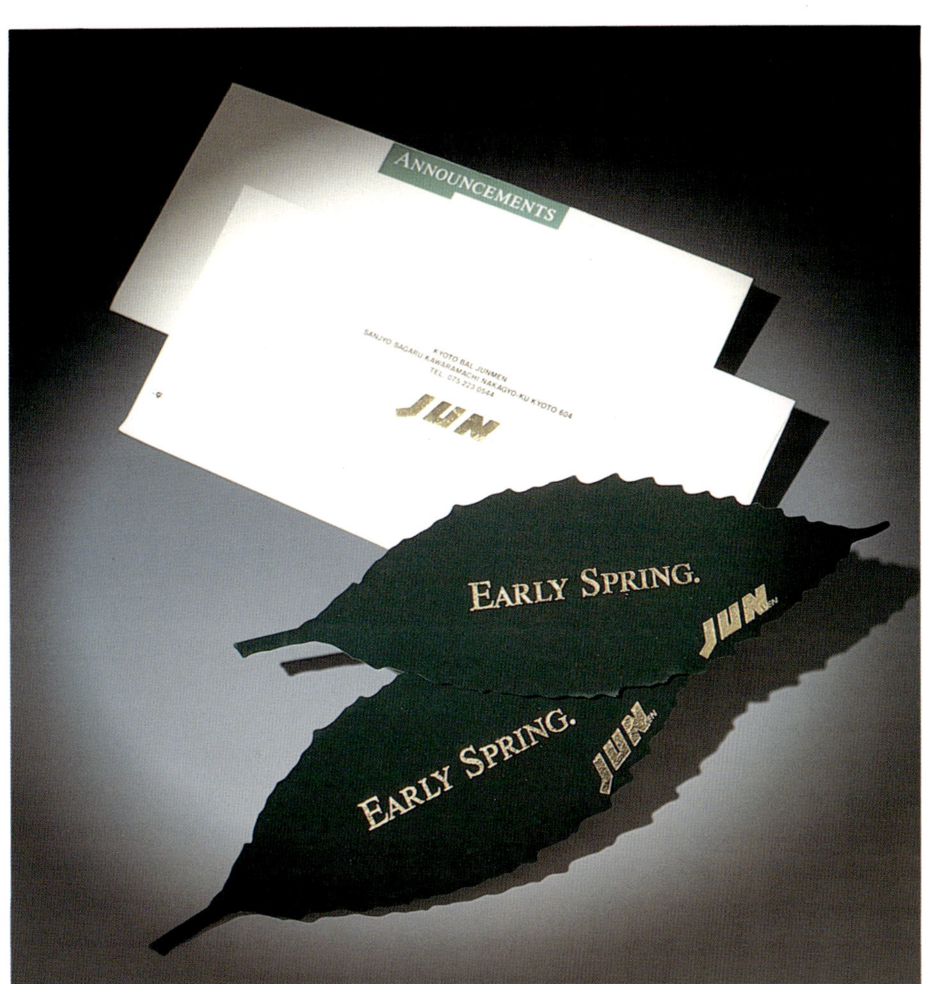

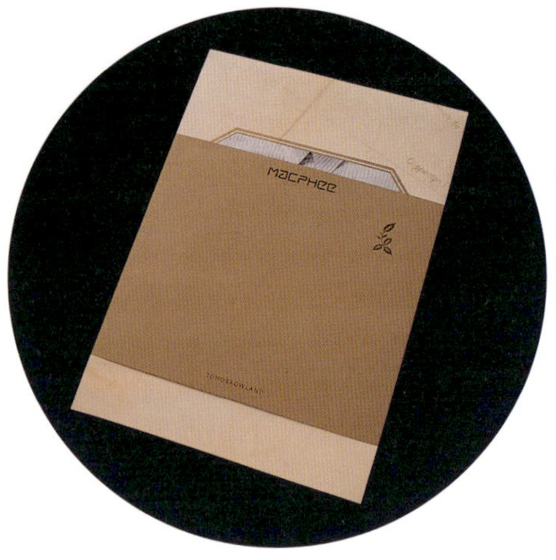

Promotional card

プロモーショナル・カード

JAPAN 1989

AD:Masaaki Hiromura

D:Seigo Kaneko

P:Masayuki Hayashi

DF:Hiromura Design Office

CL:Tomorrowland

TC:Apparel Maker

アパレル

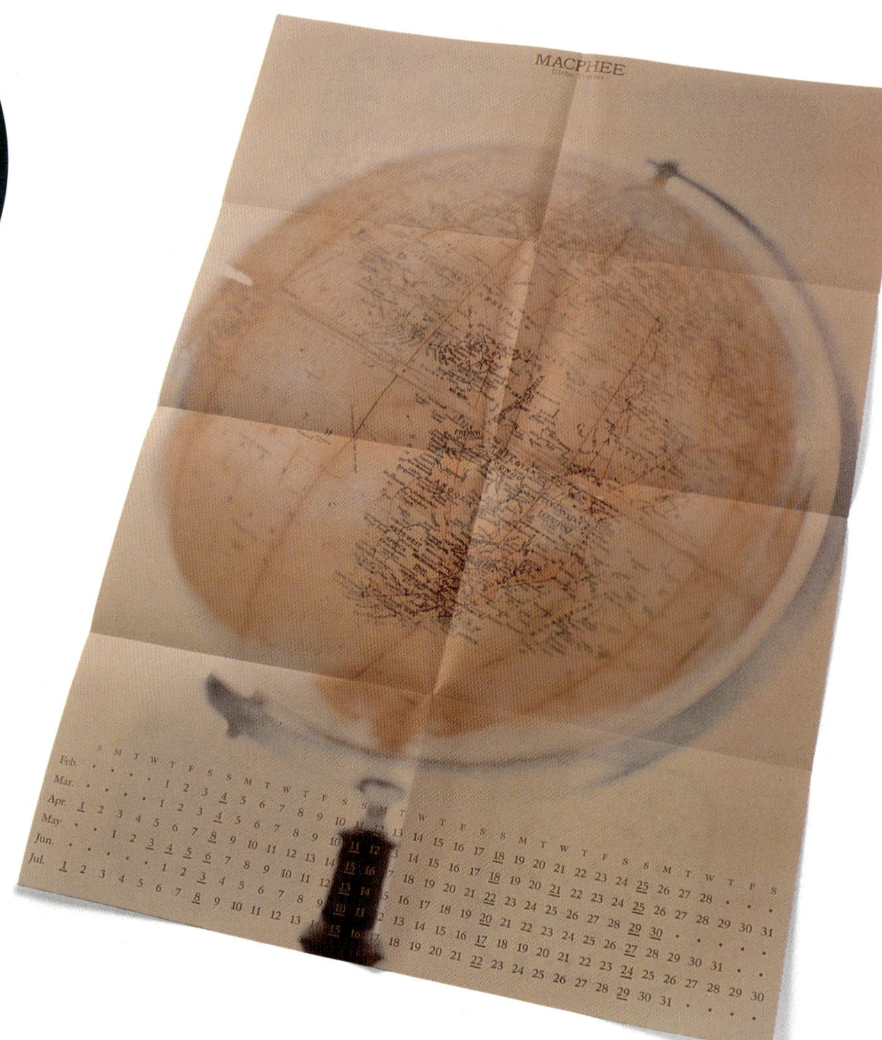

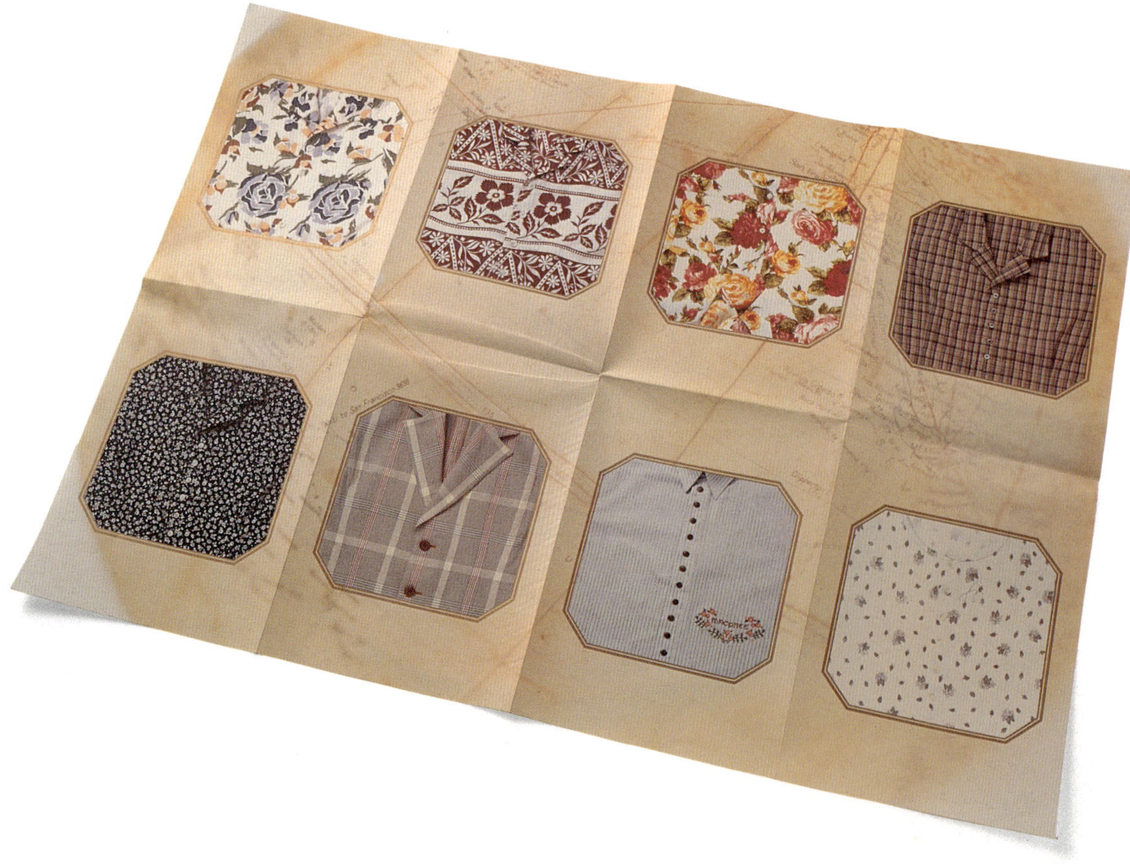

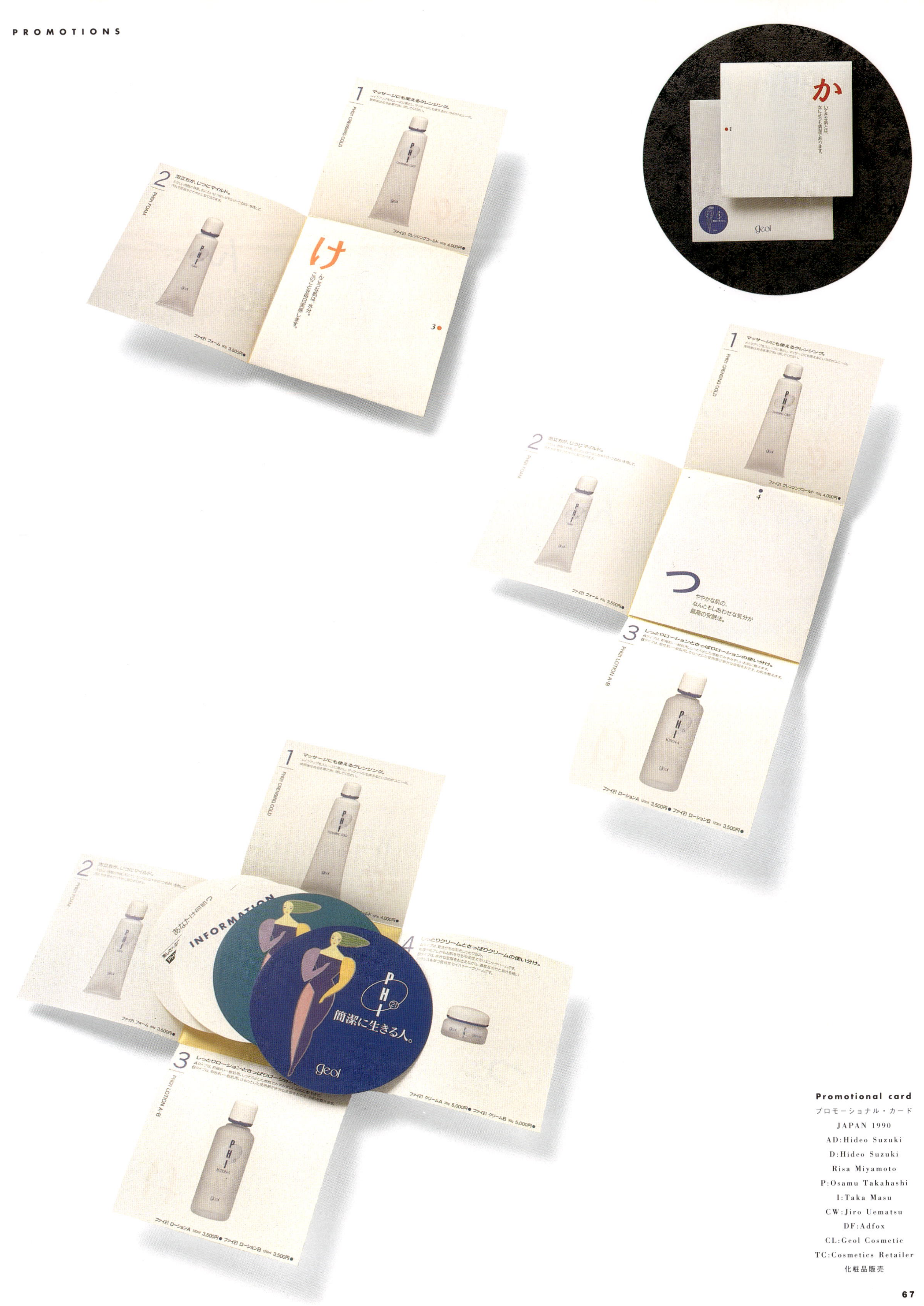

Promotional card
プロモーショナル・カード
JAPAN 1990
AD:Hideo Suzuki
D:Hideo Suzuki
Risa Miyamoto
P:Osamu Takahashi
I:Taka Masu
CW:Jiro Uematsu
DF:Adfox
CL:Geol Cosmetic
TC:Cosmetics Retailer
化粧品販売

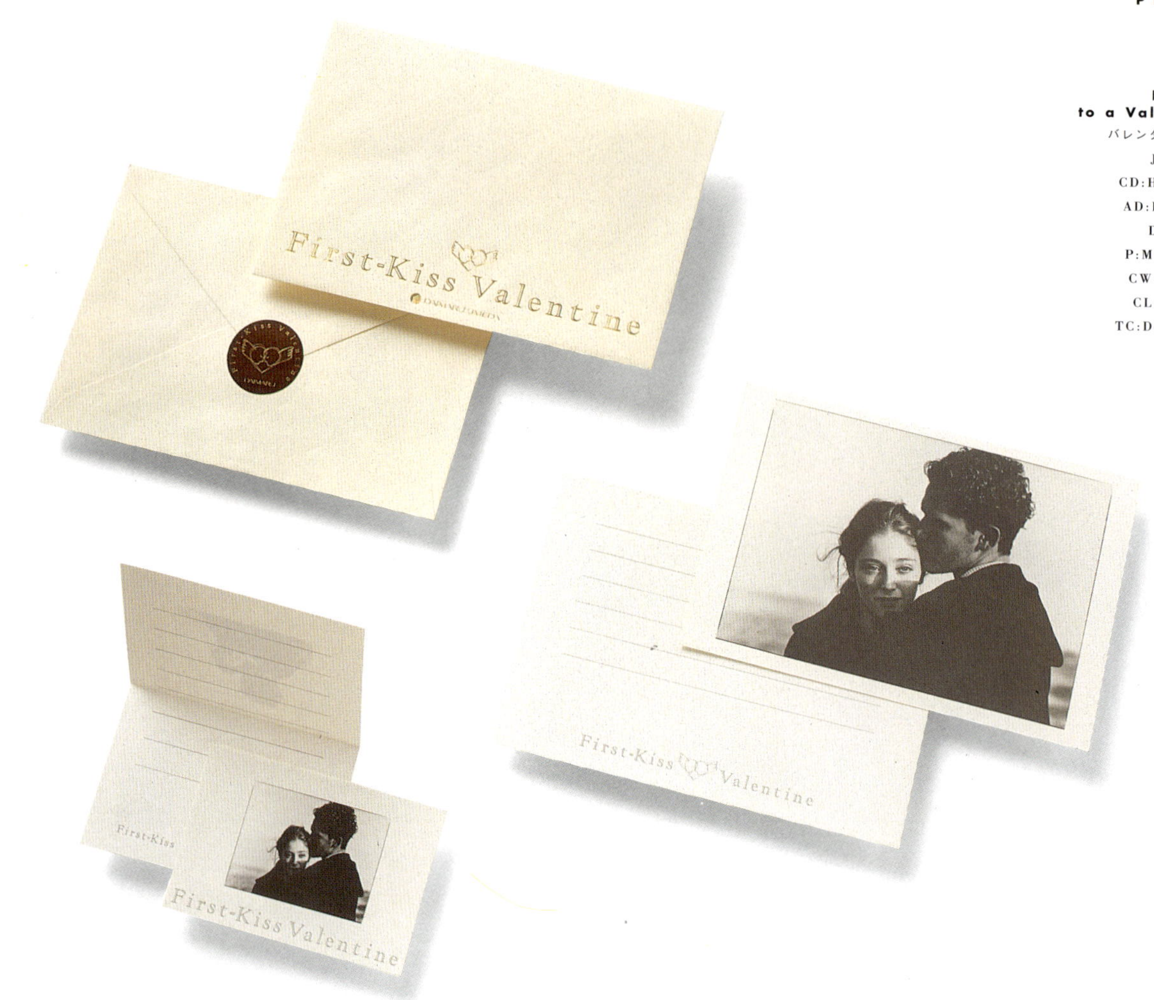

Invitation to a Valentine's Day fair
バレンタイン・フェア案内状
JAPAN 1991
CD:Hiroki Nakagami
AD:Hajime Shimizu
D:Ikuo Ueda
P:Minsei Tominaga
CW:Nobuyuki Ogi
CL:The Daimaru
TC:Department Store
百貨店

Help wanted card
求人案内
JAPAN 1992
CD:Akira Chiyoda
AD:Hiroyuki Suzuki
D:Hiroatsu Matsushita
Kazuya Okamura
CL:Daini Denden
TC:Telecommunications
電信電話

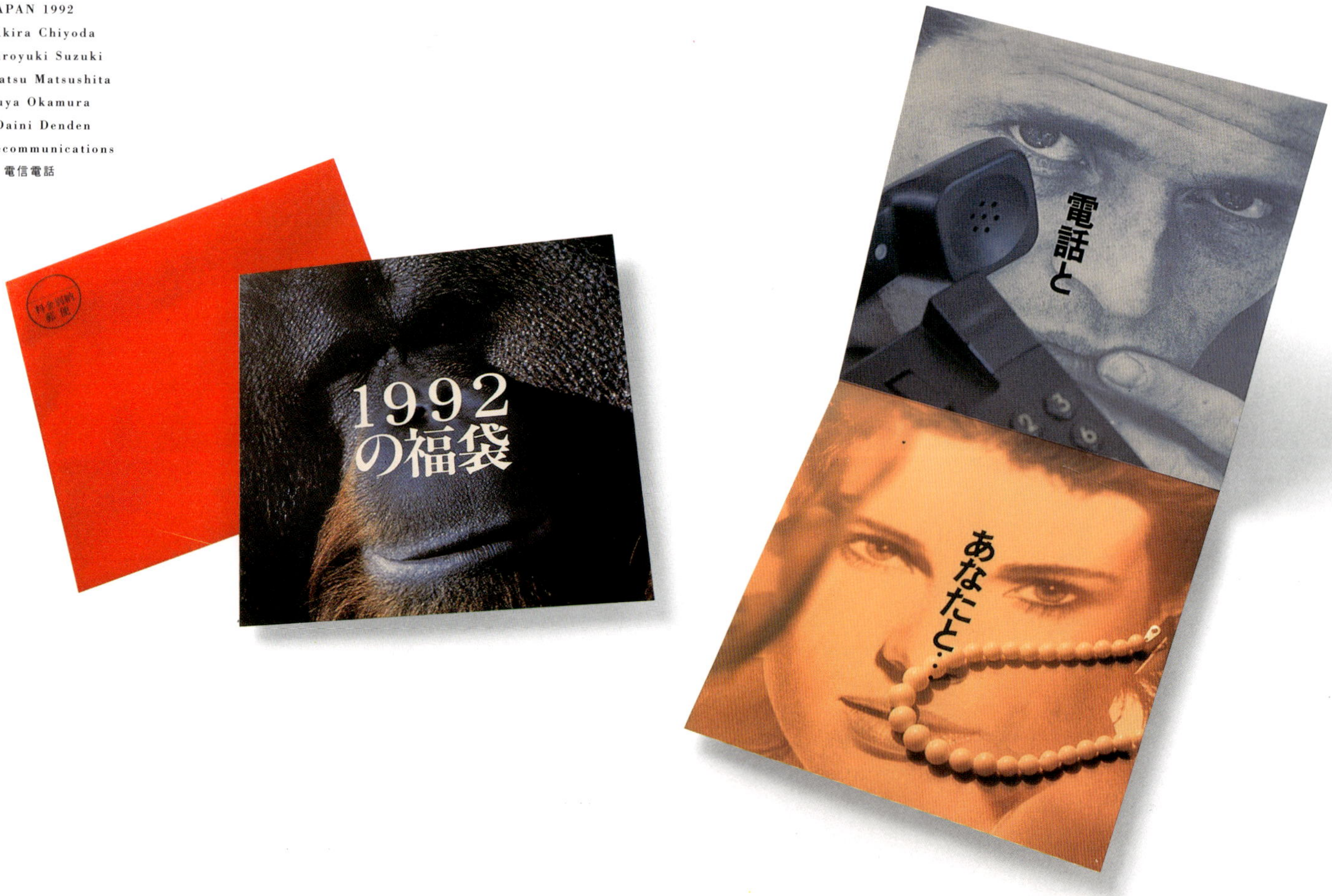

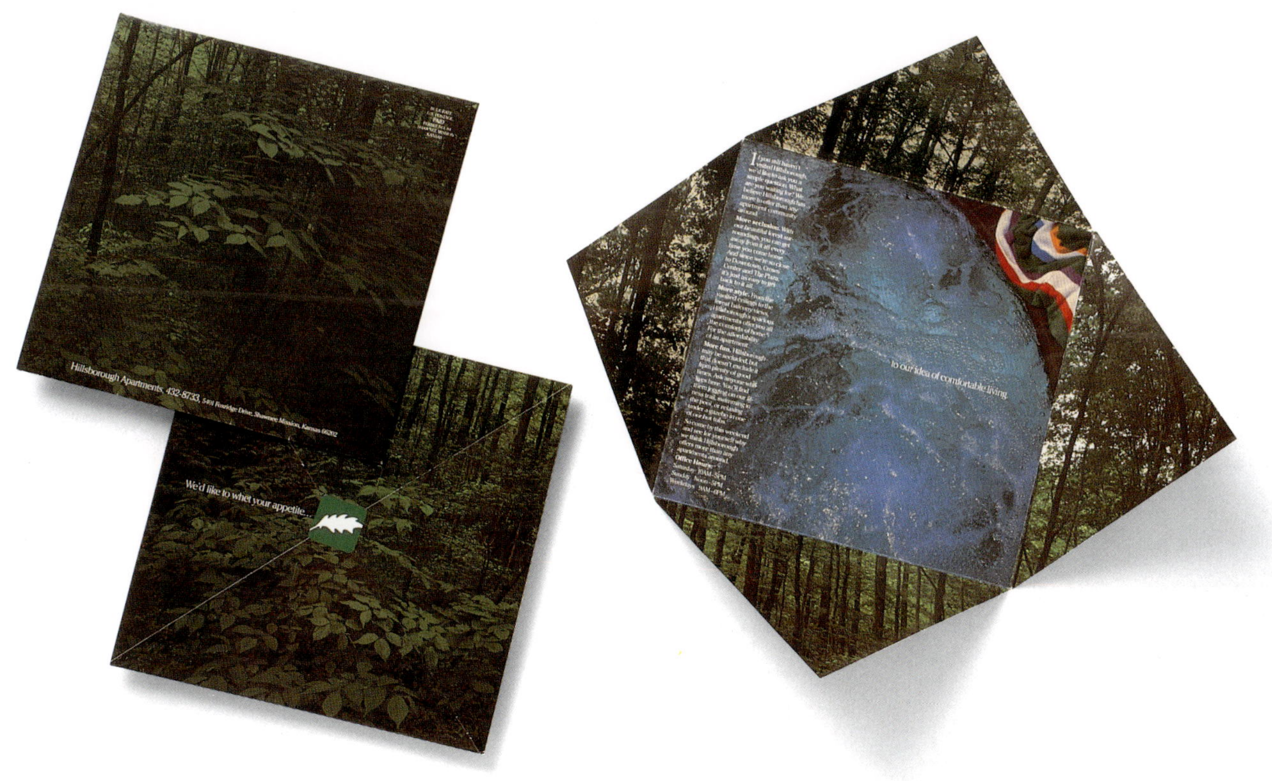

▼
Invitation to a concert
コンサート招待状
JAPAN 1990
CD:Michiyo Saito
Yuzo Toda
AD,D:Michiyo Saito
CL:Epic/Sony Records
TC:Recording Company
音楽ソフト制作

▲
Promotional card
プロモーショナル・カード
USA 1988
AD,D:John Muller
Jane Weers
CW:David Marks
DF:Muller
CL:Hills Borough Apartments
TC:Apartment Management
アパート管理

▼
Promotional card
プロモーショナル・カード
USA 1991
AD,D,I:Dan Collins
CL:Collins Illustration
TC:Independent Artist
アーティスト

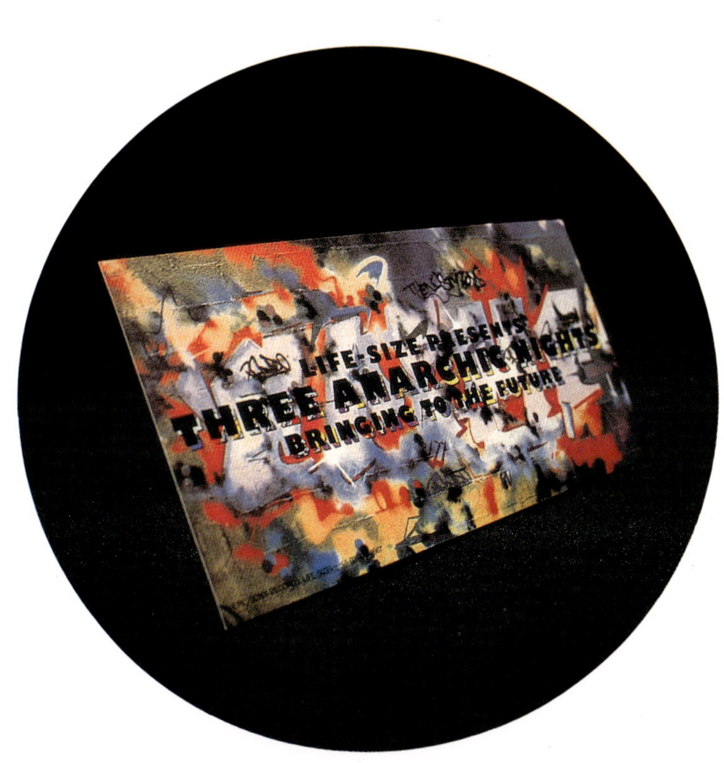

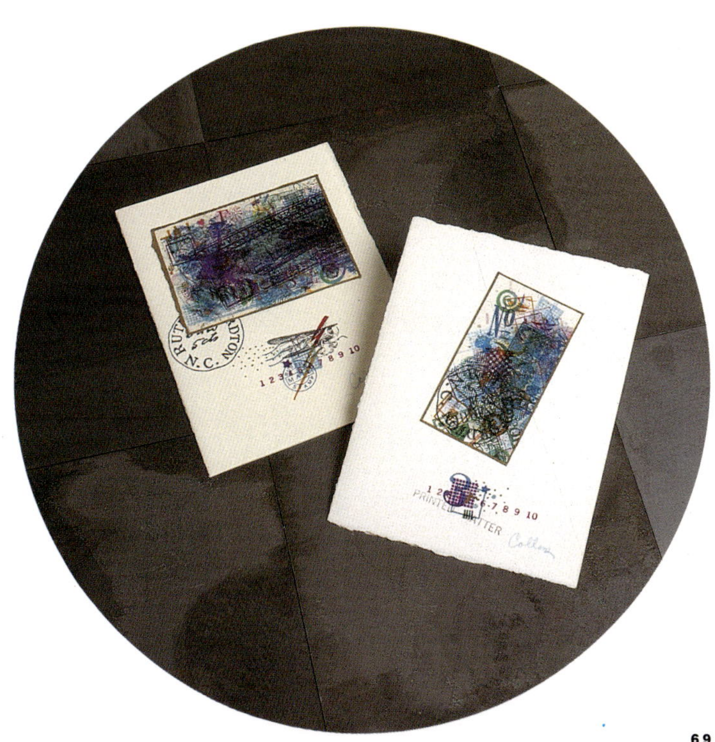

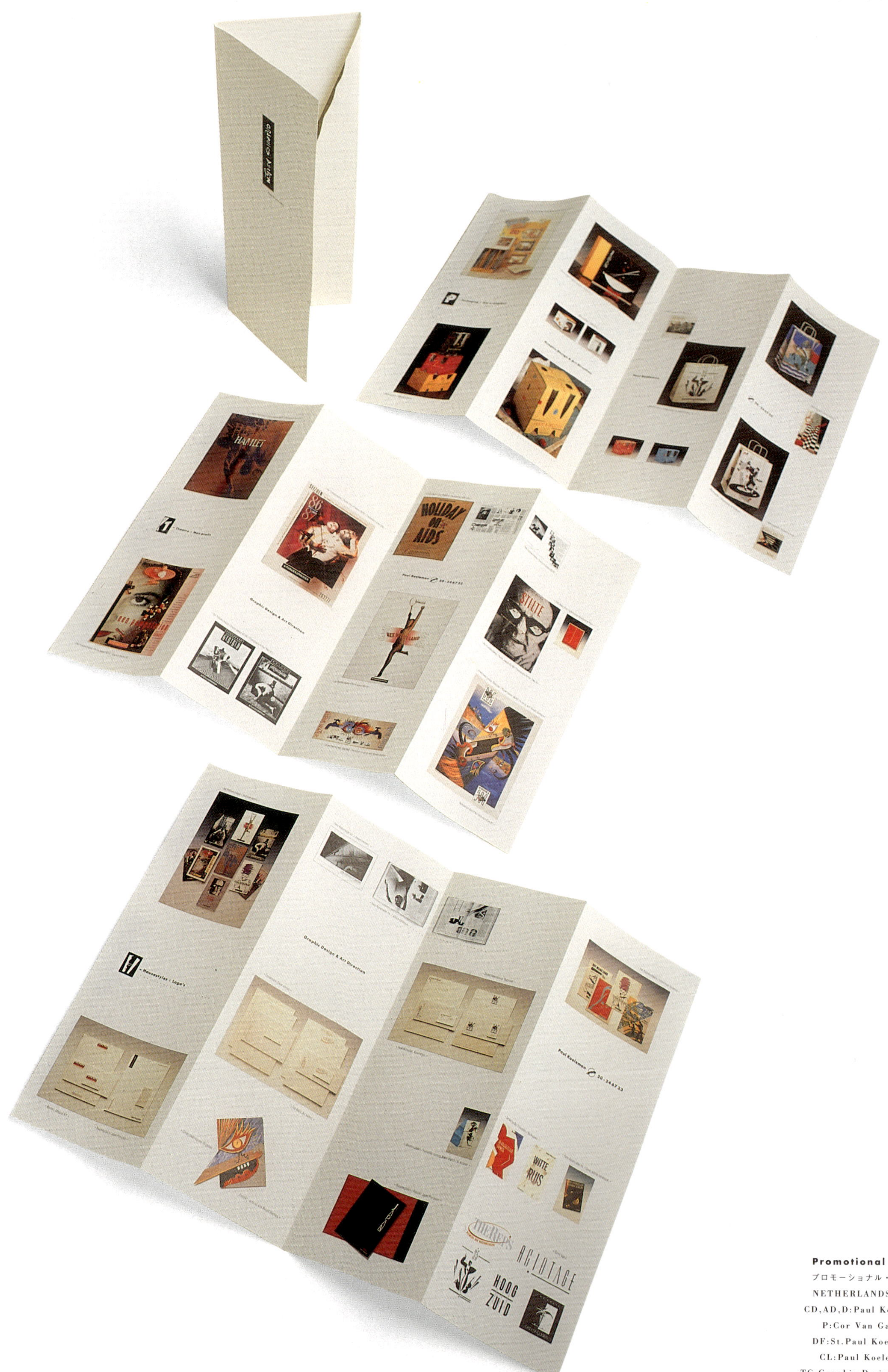

Promotional card
プロモーショナル・カード
NETHERLANDS 1989
CD,AD,D:Paul Koeleman
P:Cor Van Gastel
DF:St.Paul Koeleman
CL:Paul Koeleman
TC:Graphic Design Studio
グラフィック・デザイン

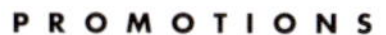

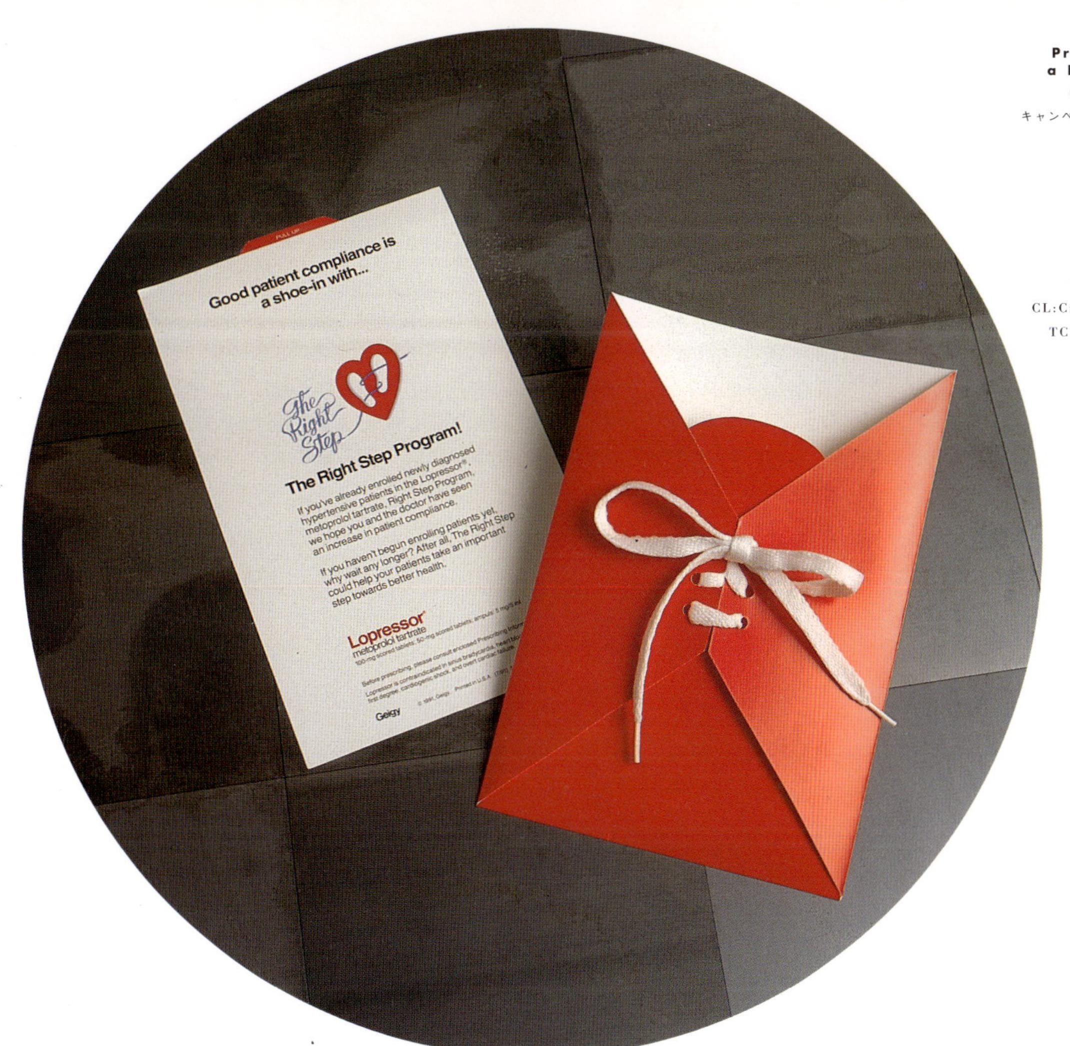

◀

Promotional card for a Lopressor campaign

ロープレッサー（薬品）・
キャンペーン用プロモーショナル・カード
USA 1991
CD:Myrtle Johnson
Silvio Coccia
AD,D:Loren Mork
I:Tom Carnase
CW:Kevin Purcell
DF:C+G Advertising
CL:Ciba-Geigy Pharmaceuticals
TC:Pharmaceuticals Maker
製薬

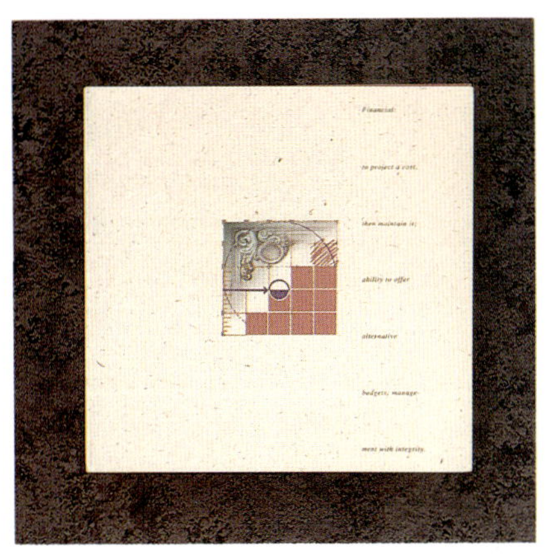

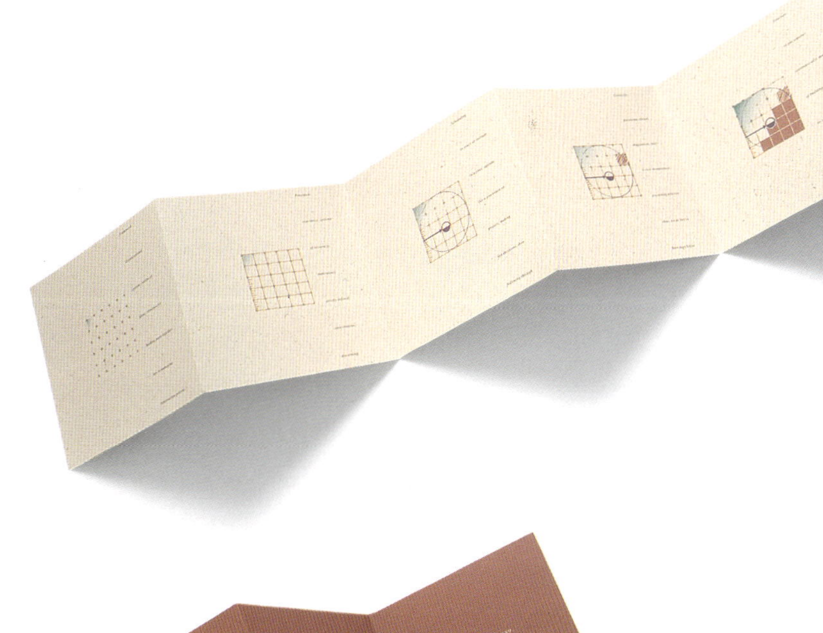

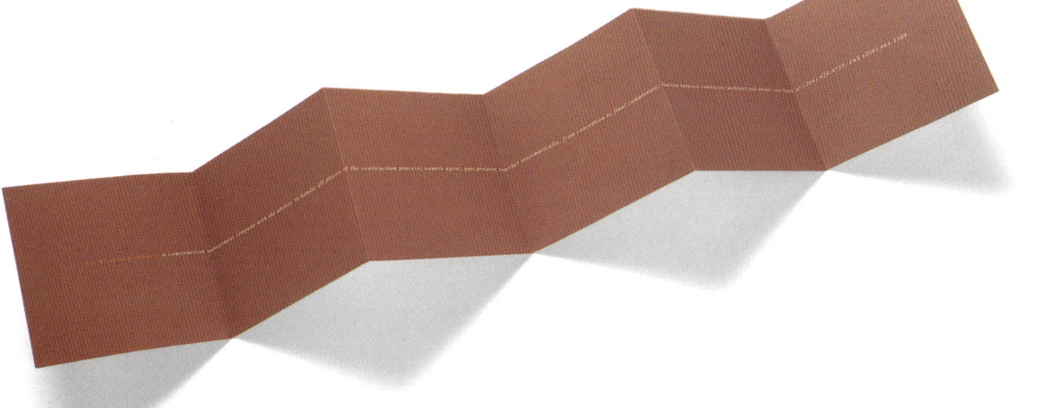

▲

Promotional card

プロモーショナル・カード
USA 1989
AD:Jack Anderson
D:Jack Anderson
David Bates
I:Yutaka Sasaki
Hornall Anderson Design Works
CW:Dory Toft
DF:Hornall Anderson Design Works
CL:The Klinkam
TC:Builder
建設

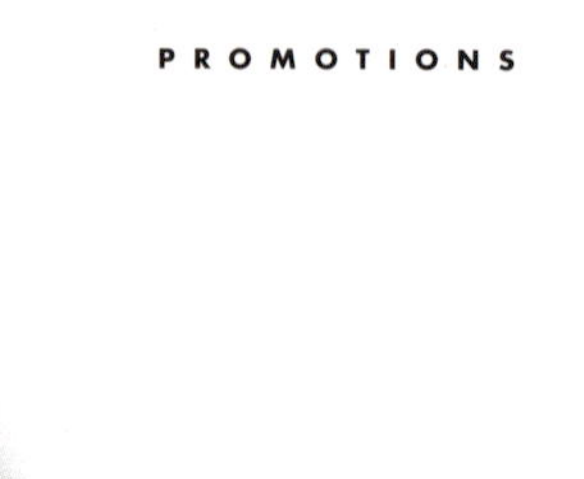

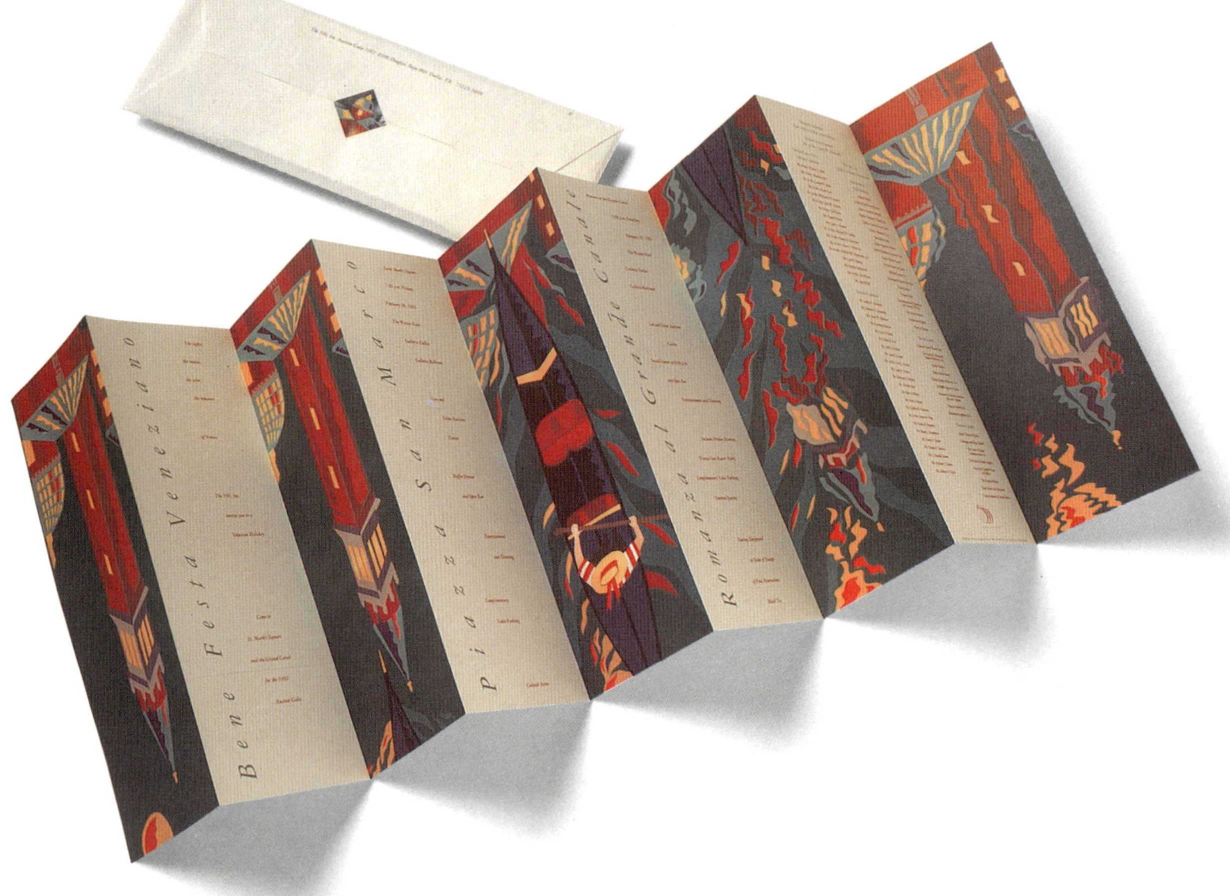

▲
Invitation to a gala
ガラ招待状
USA 1991
AD,D,I:Joe Rattan
DF:Joseph Rattan Design
CL:500
TC:Non-profit Corporation for Sponsoring the Arts
アート推進団体

▼
Promotional card
プロモーショナル・カード
CANADA 1992
CD,I:Dan Wheaton
AD:Ric Riordon
D:Shirley Riordon
CW:Shirley Riordon
Susan Masterson
DF:The Riordon Design Group
CL:Masterson & Associates
TC:Communications Consultant
コミュニケーション・コンサルタント

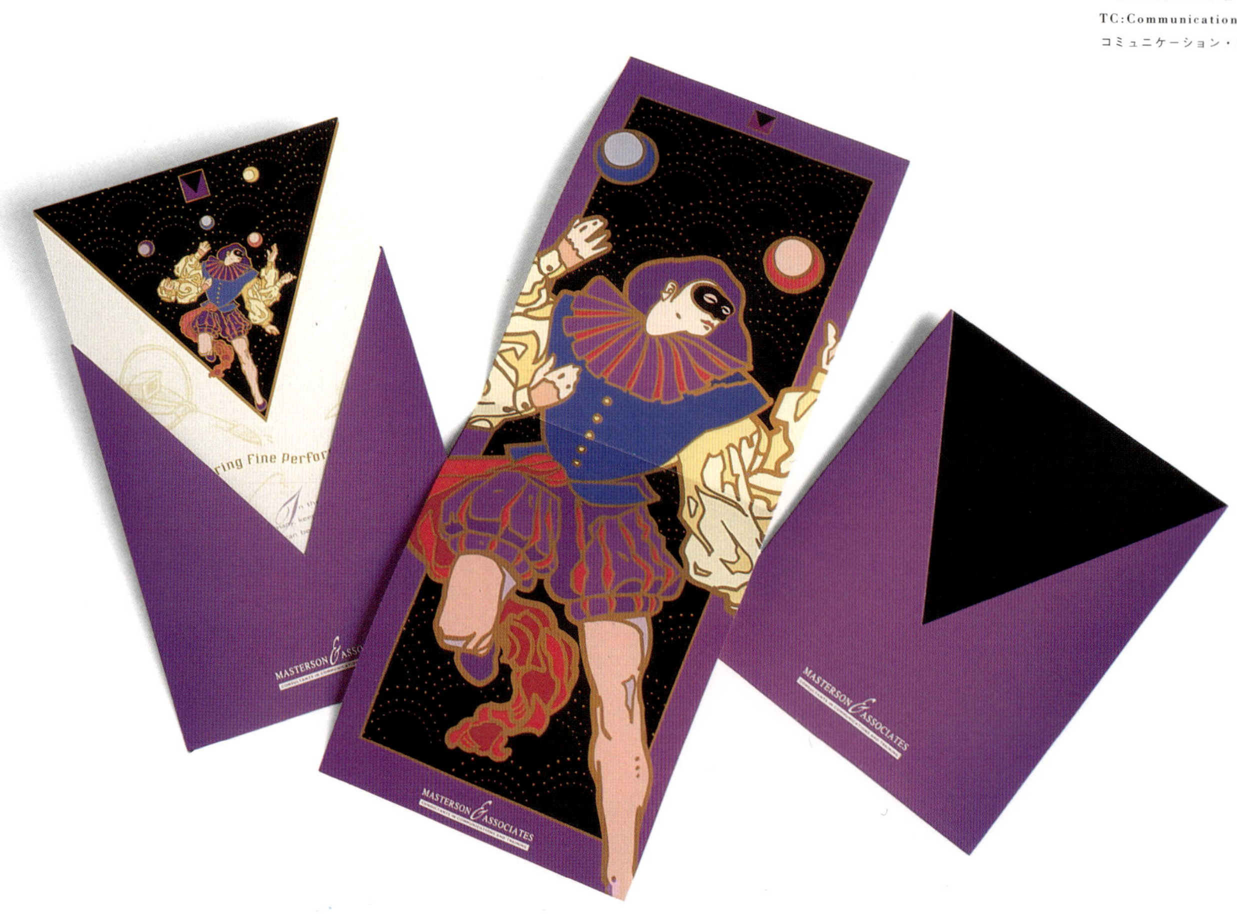

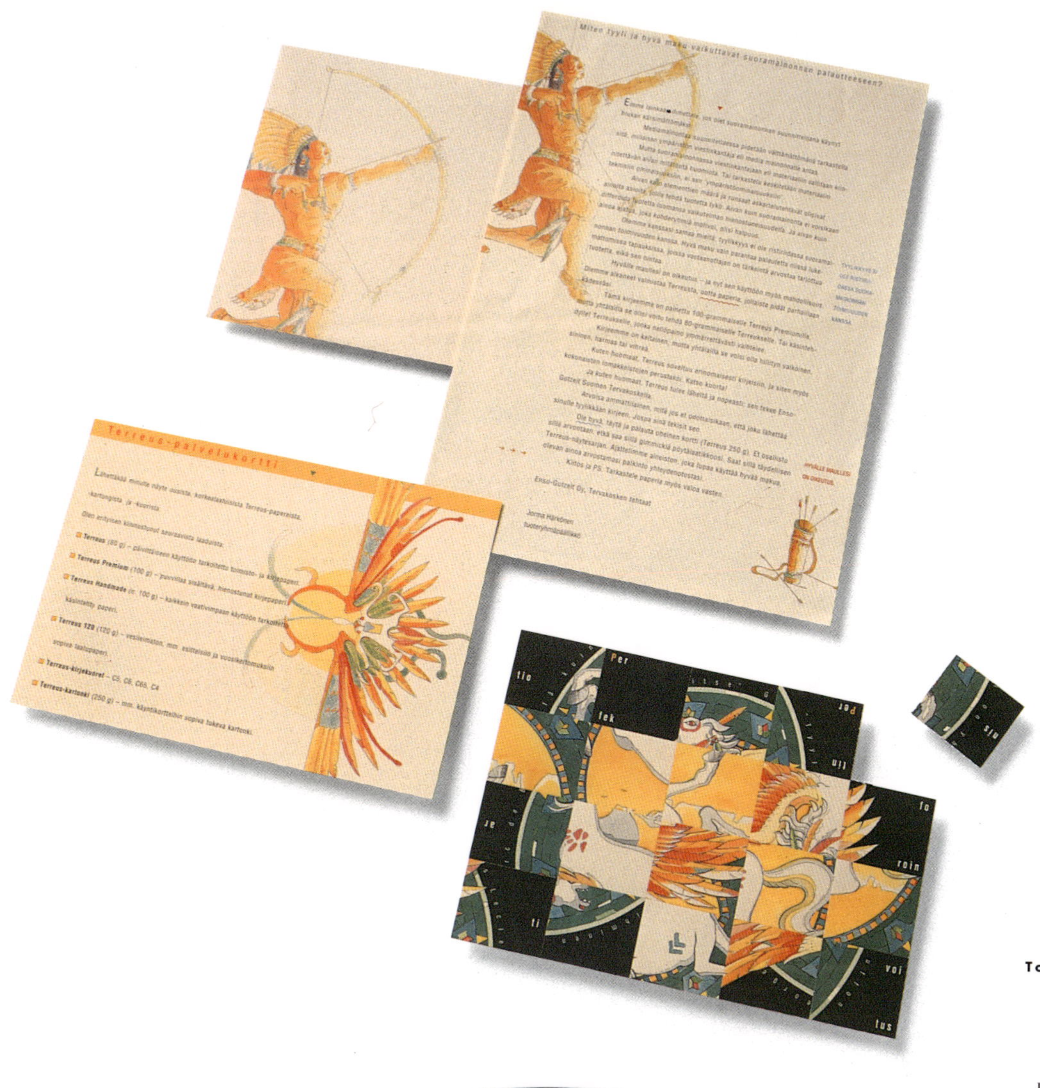

▲
Promotional card
プロモーショナル・カード
FINLAND 1991
AD,I:Viktor Kaltala
D:Viktor Kaltala
Eero Raunio
CW:Timo Kivi
DF:Konsepti Oy
CL:Enso-Gutzeit Oy
Fine Paper Division
TC:Paper Mill
製紙

▼
To solicit entries for a book
投稿募集
AUSTRALIA 1992
AD:Janet Giampietro
I:Jeff Fisher
DF:Black Book Marketing Group
CL:Black Book Marketing Group
TC:Publisher
出版

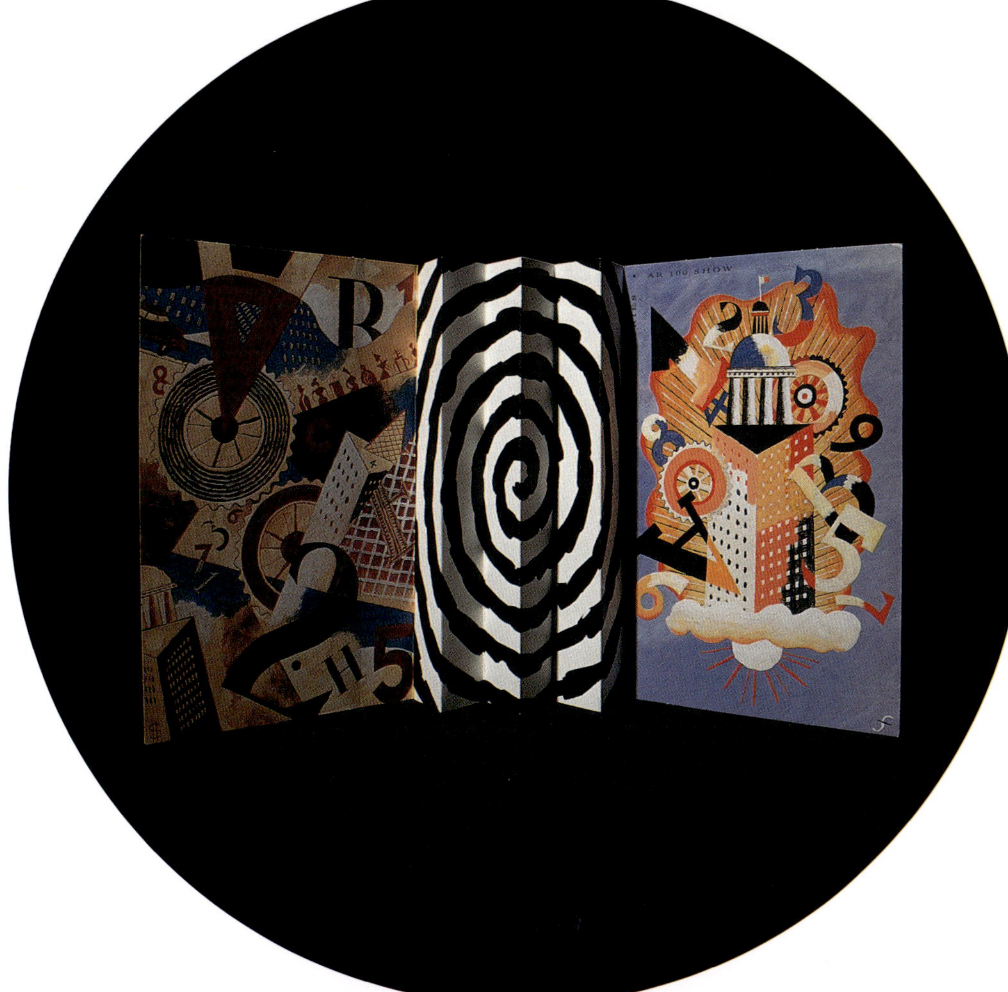

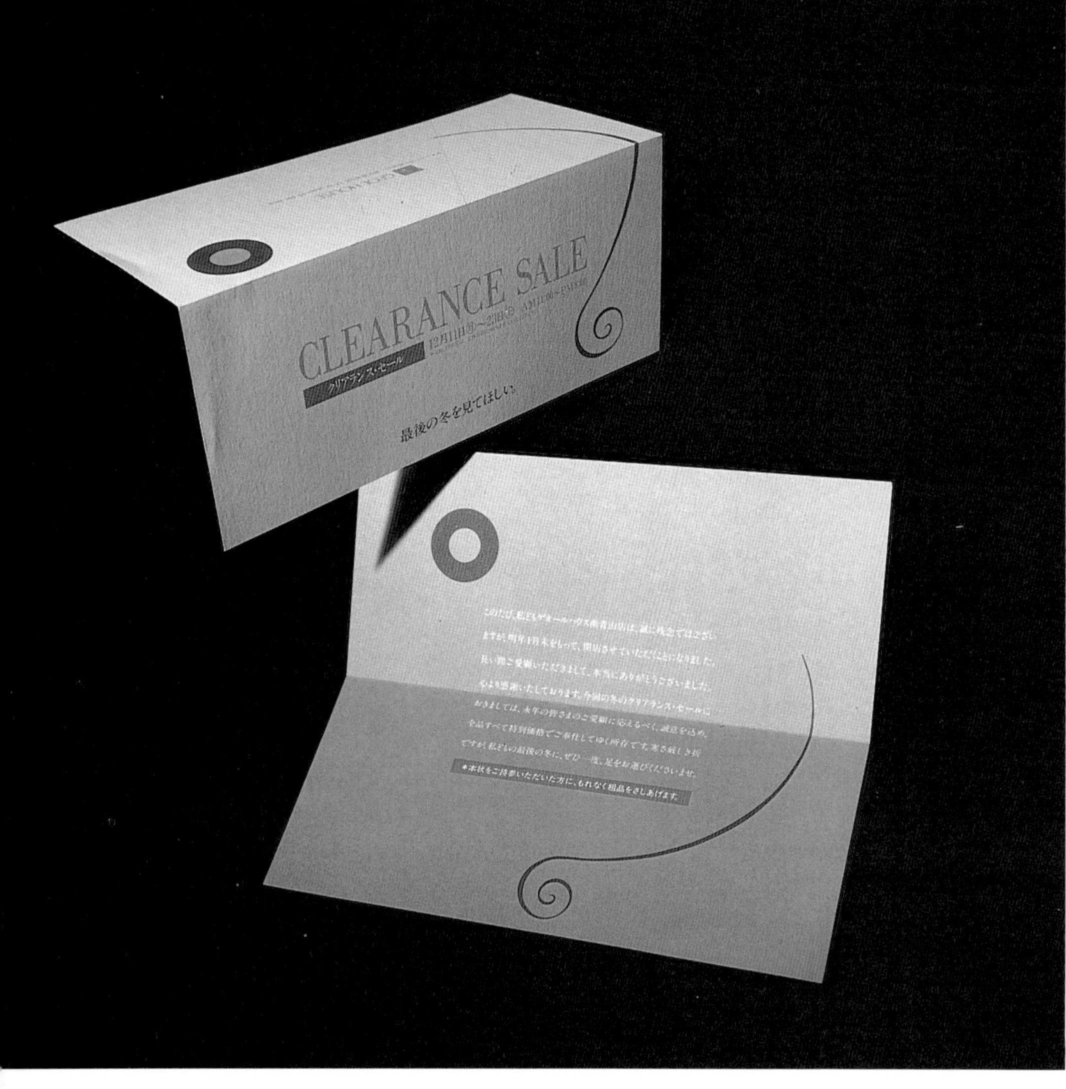

Invitation to a clearance sale
クリアランス・セール案内状
JAPAN 1990
AD,D:Hideo Suzuki
CW:Yuji Nii
DF:Adfox
CL:Geol House
TC:Apparel Retailer
アパレル

Help wanted card
求人案内
JAPAN 1992
CD:Noriyuki Tanaka
AD,D:Hiroaki Konya
CW:Hiroko Kodaka
DF:Kokokunojyo
CL:Bunkahoso Brains
TC:Employment Information Service
就職情報サービス

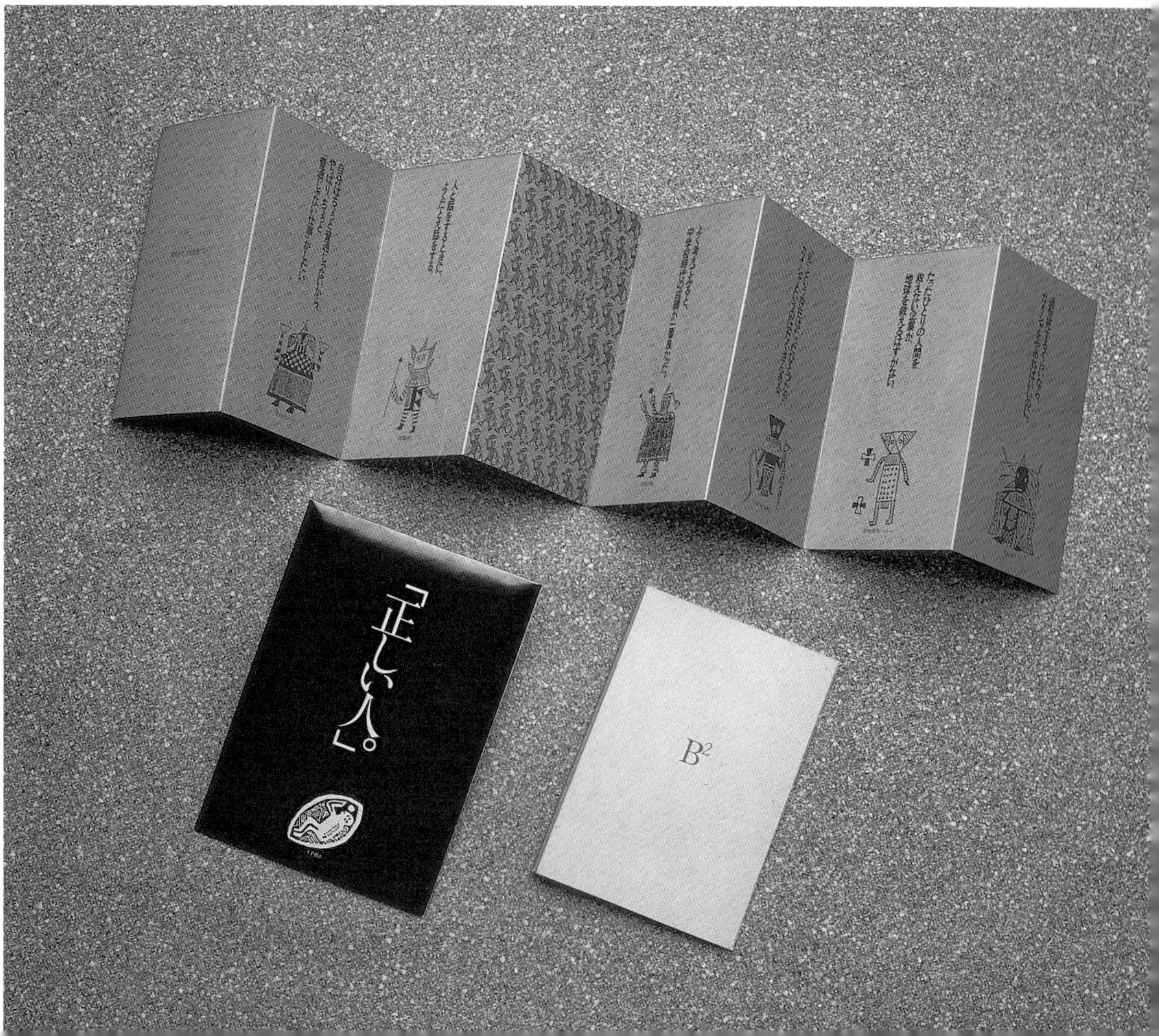

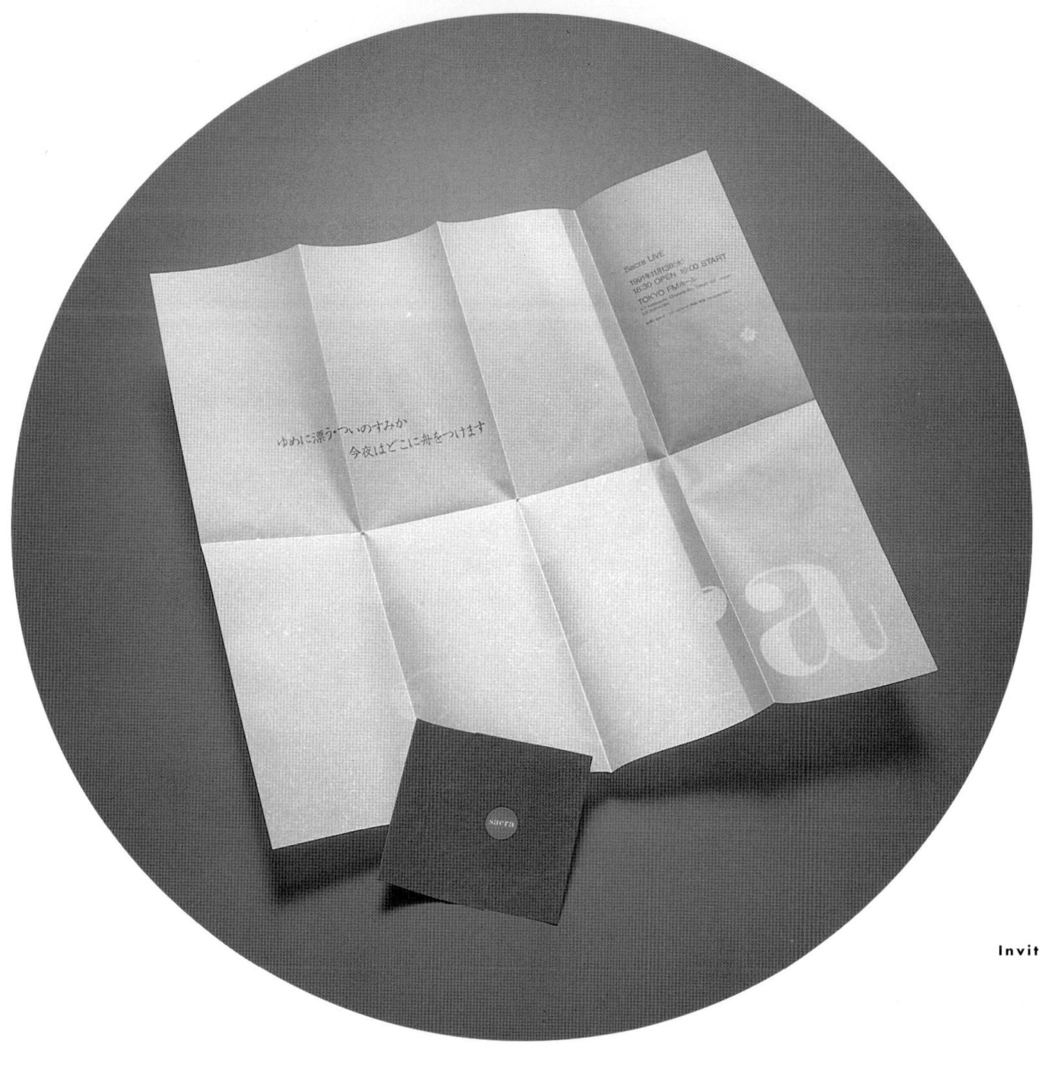

▲
Concert announcement
コンサート案内状
JAPAN 1991
AD,D:Hiroshi Takahara
D:Eiko Nara
CL:Sony Records
TC:Record Producer
レコード制作

▼
Invitation to a charity event
チャリティ・イベント招待状
USA 1992
CD,D:Gail Rigelhaupt
I:Janette Evsebio
CW:Susie Aarons
Lerner Aarons
DF:Rigelhaupt Design
CL:The Center for
Children & Families
TC:Social Service Organization
社会奉仕団体

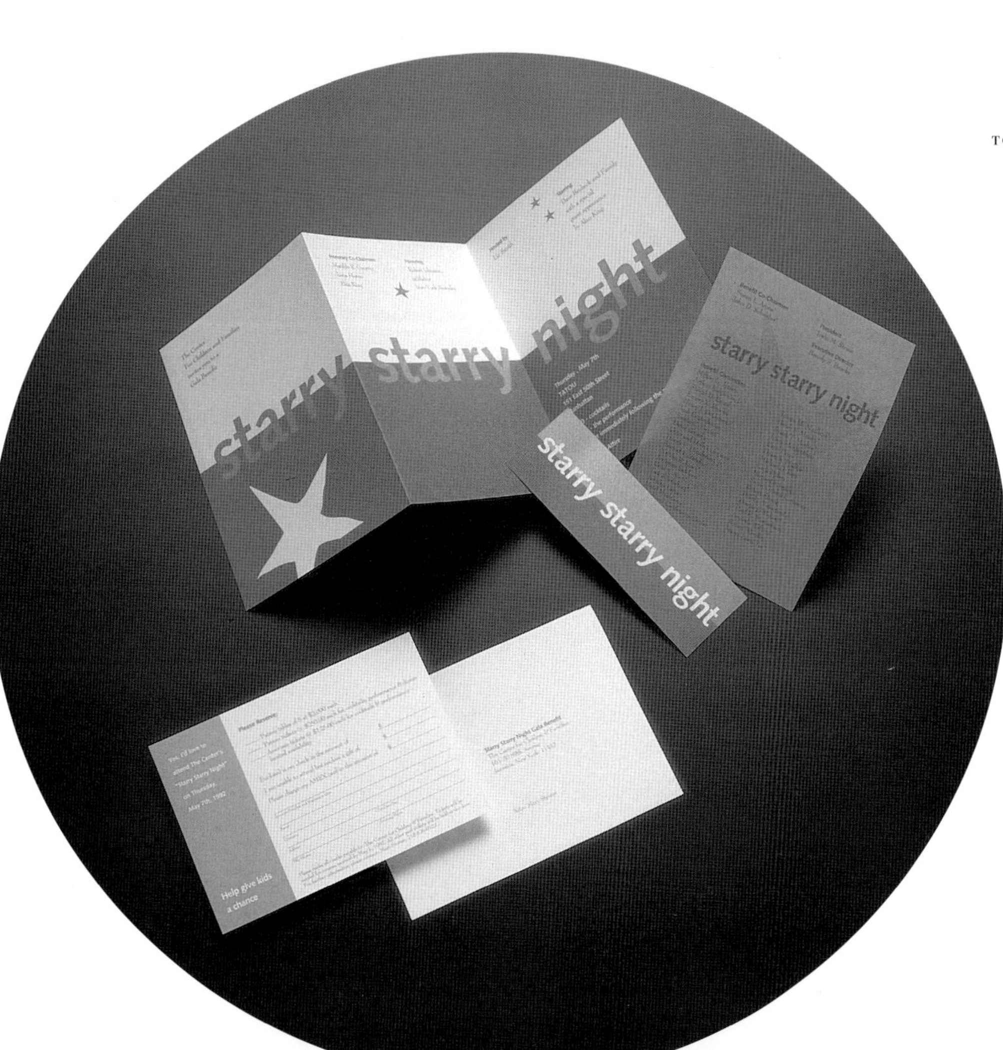

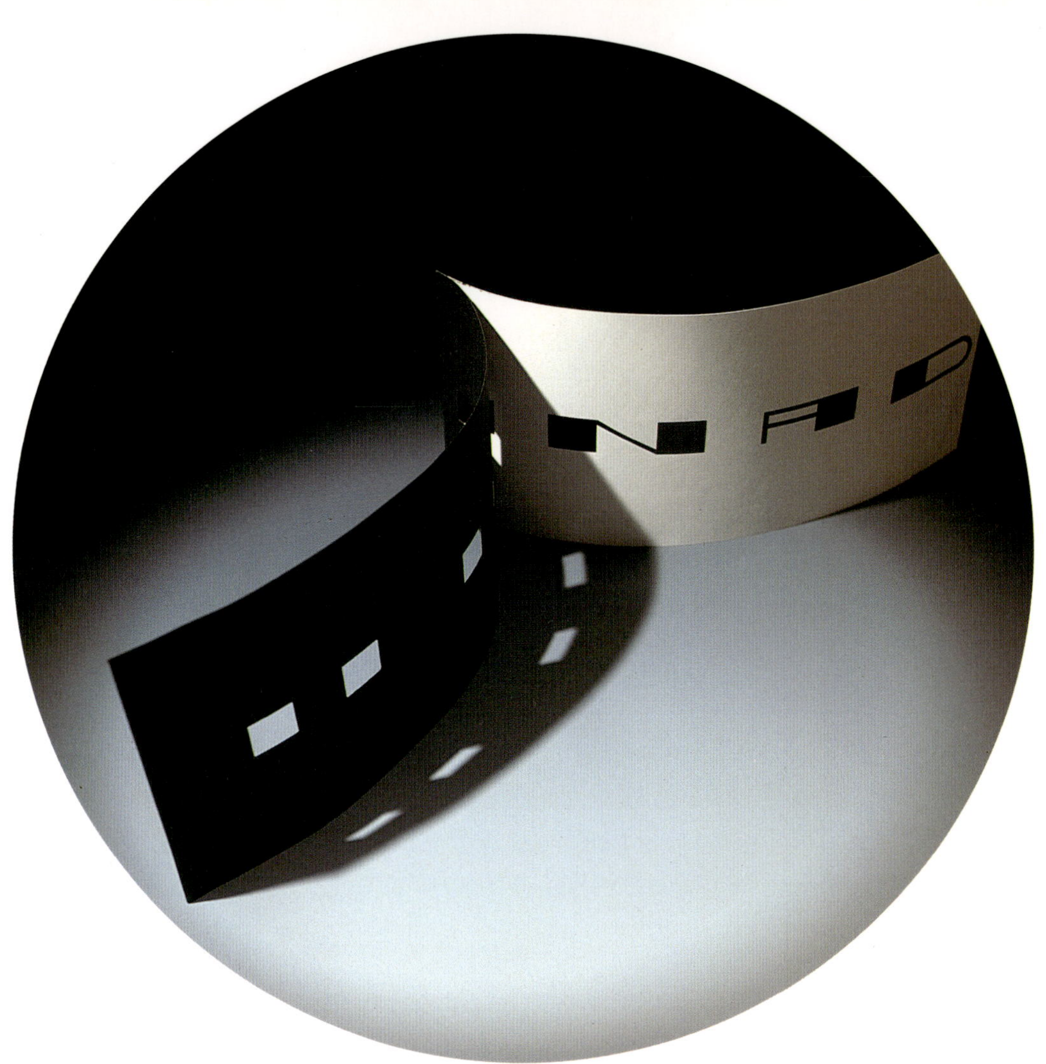

▲
Promotional card
会社案内状
JAPAN 1989
AD,D:Toshihiro Tabuchi
CL:Inad
TC:Architects
建築事務所

▼
Promotional card
プロモーショナル・カード
ENGLAND 1991
CD,AD,D,I:Glenn Tutssel
DF:Michael Peters
CL:Tutssel Warne
TC:Joinery
大工

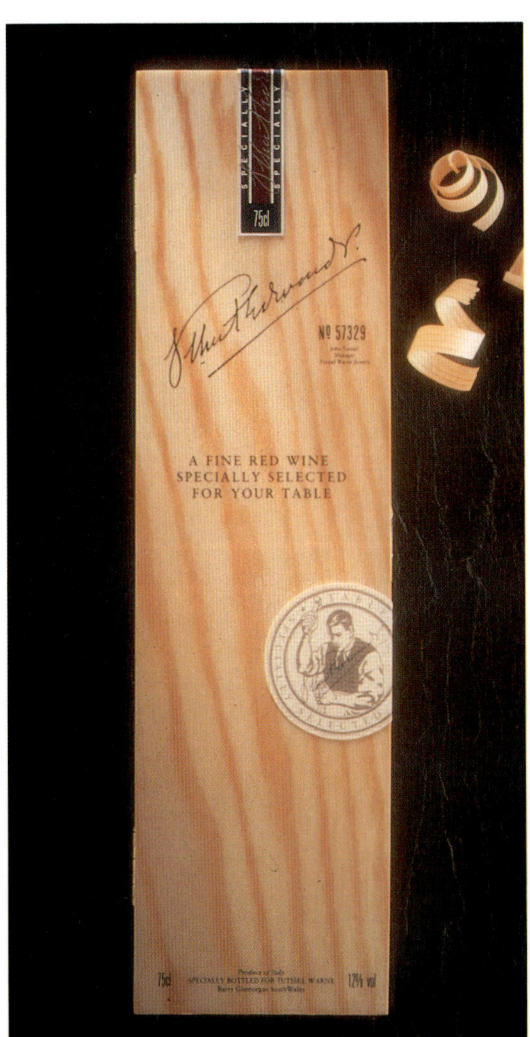

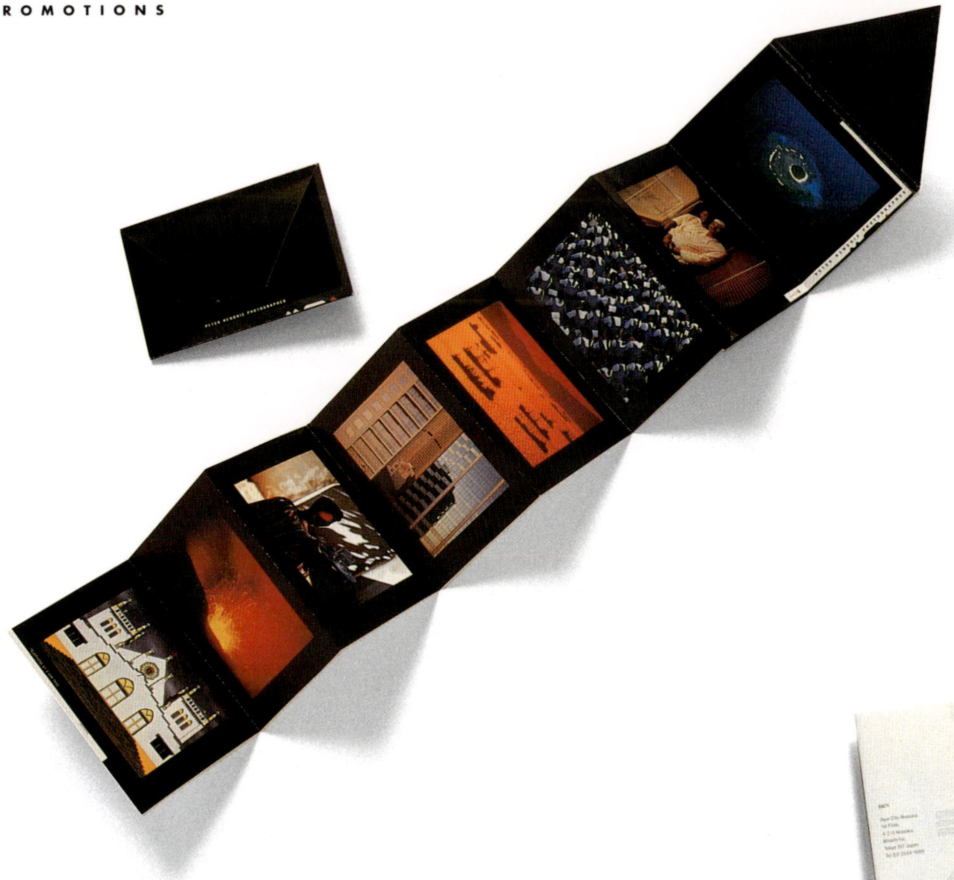

Promotional card
プロモーショナル・カード
AUSTRALIA 1991
CD:Garry Emery
AD,D,DF:Emery Vincent Design
CL:Peter Hendrie
TC:Photographer
フォトグラファー

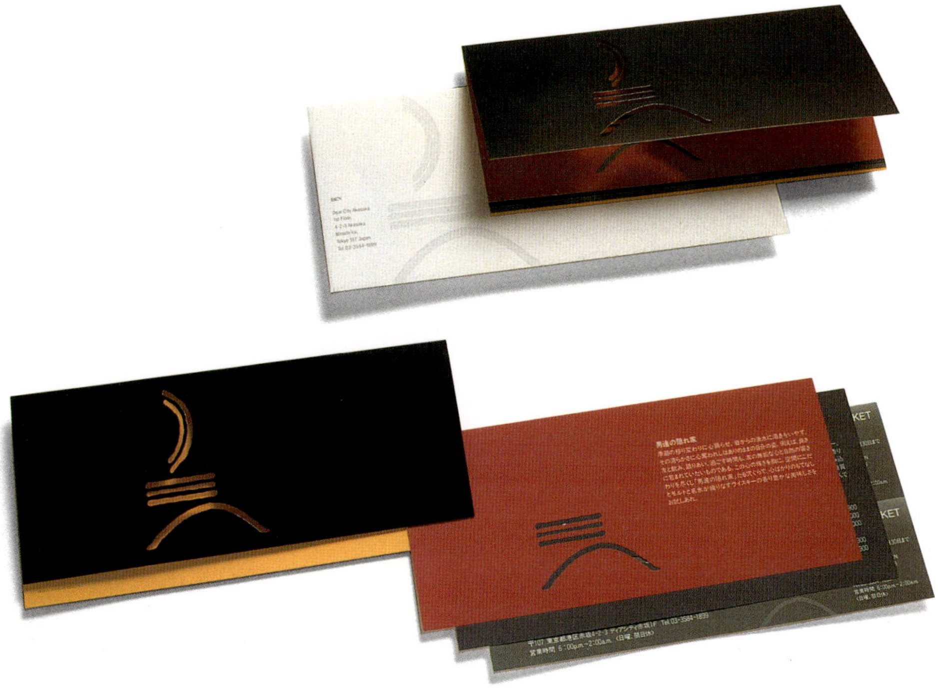

Invitation to a bar
バー招待状
JAPAN 1992
AD:Douglas Doolittle
CL:Myu Planning & Operators
TC:Store and Event Planning;Agent for Suntory
サントリーの店舗、イベント企画、代行

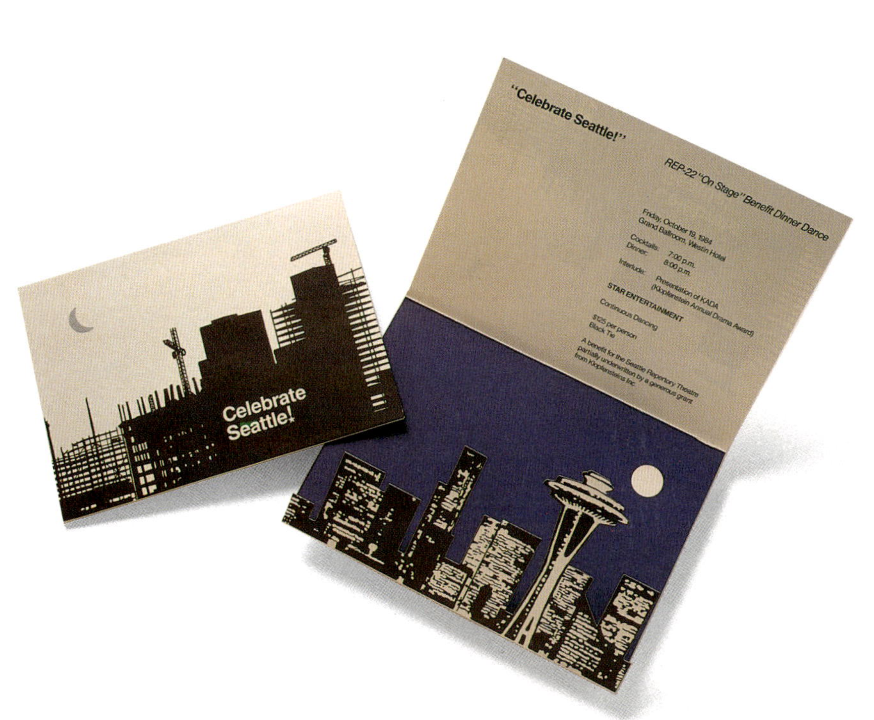

Invitation to a benefit dinner
募金夕食会招待状
USA 1984
CD,AD:Rick Eiber
DF:Rick Eiber Design
CL:Seattle Repertory Theatre
TC:Repertory Theater
劇場

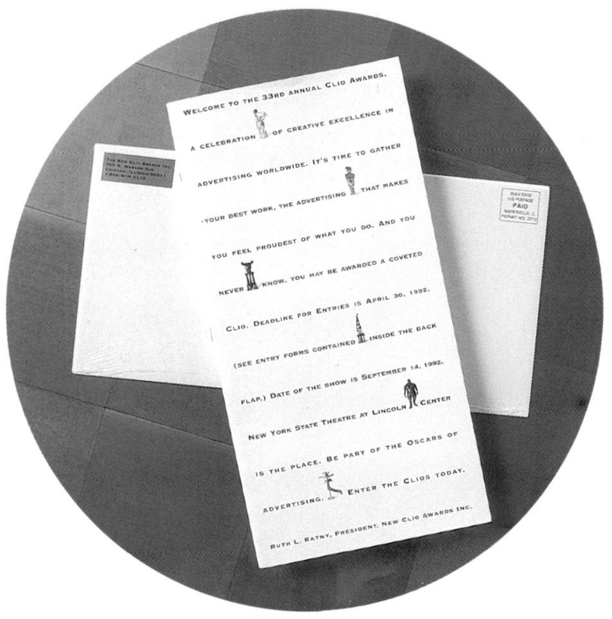

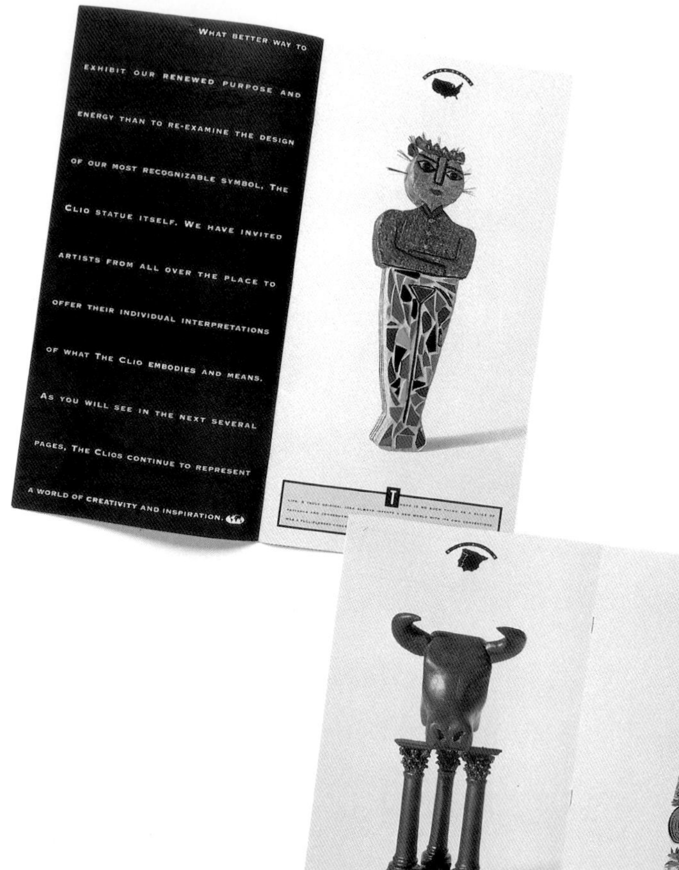

▲

Promotional card
プロモーショナル・カード
USA 1992
AD,D:John Muller
James Dettner
Peter Corcoran
P:Michael Regnier
CW:David Marks
DF:Muller
CL:The New Clio Awards
TC:Advertising Awards
広告大賞

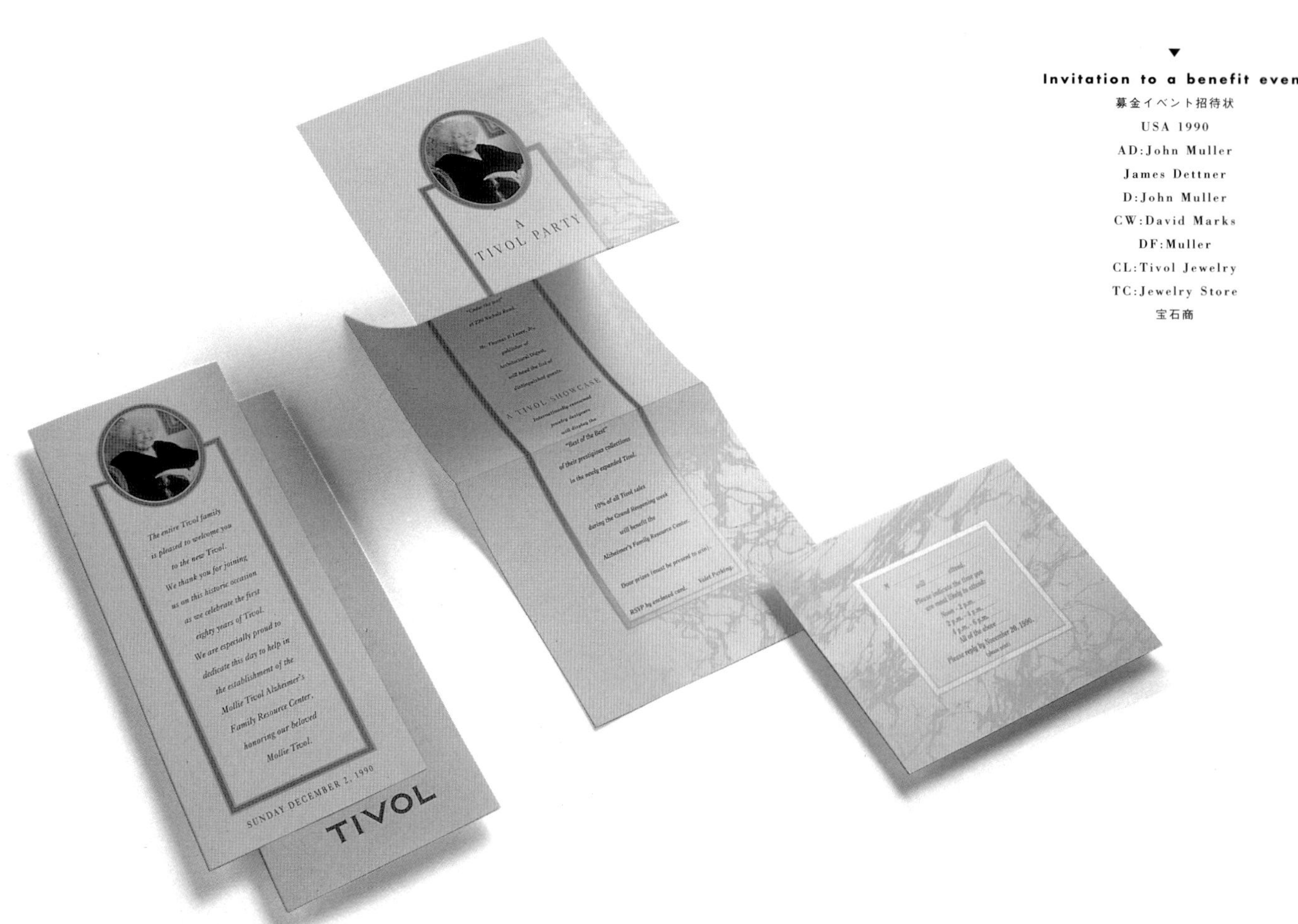

▼

Invitation to a benefit event
募金イベント招待状
USA 1990
AD:John Muller
James Dettner
D:John Muller
CW:David Marks
DF:Muller
CL:Tivol Jewelry
TC:Jewelry Store
宝石商

Invitation to a fund raiser

基金調達イベント招待状

USA 1992

AD:Peter Corcoran

John Muller

D,P:Peter Corcoran

CW:Judy Spaar

Paula Halsey

DF:Muller

CL:Nelson Atkins Museum of Art

TC:Museum of Art

美術館

•

Invitation cards and application forms for various events.

各イベント案内のカードと申込書。

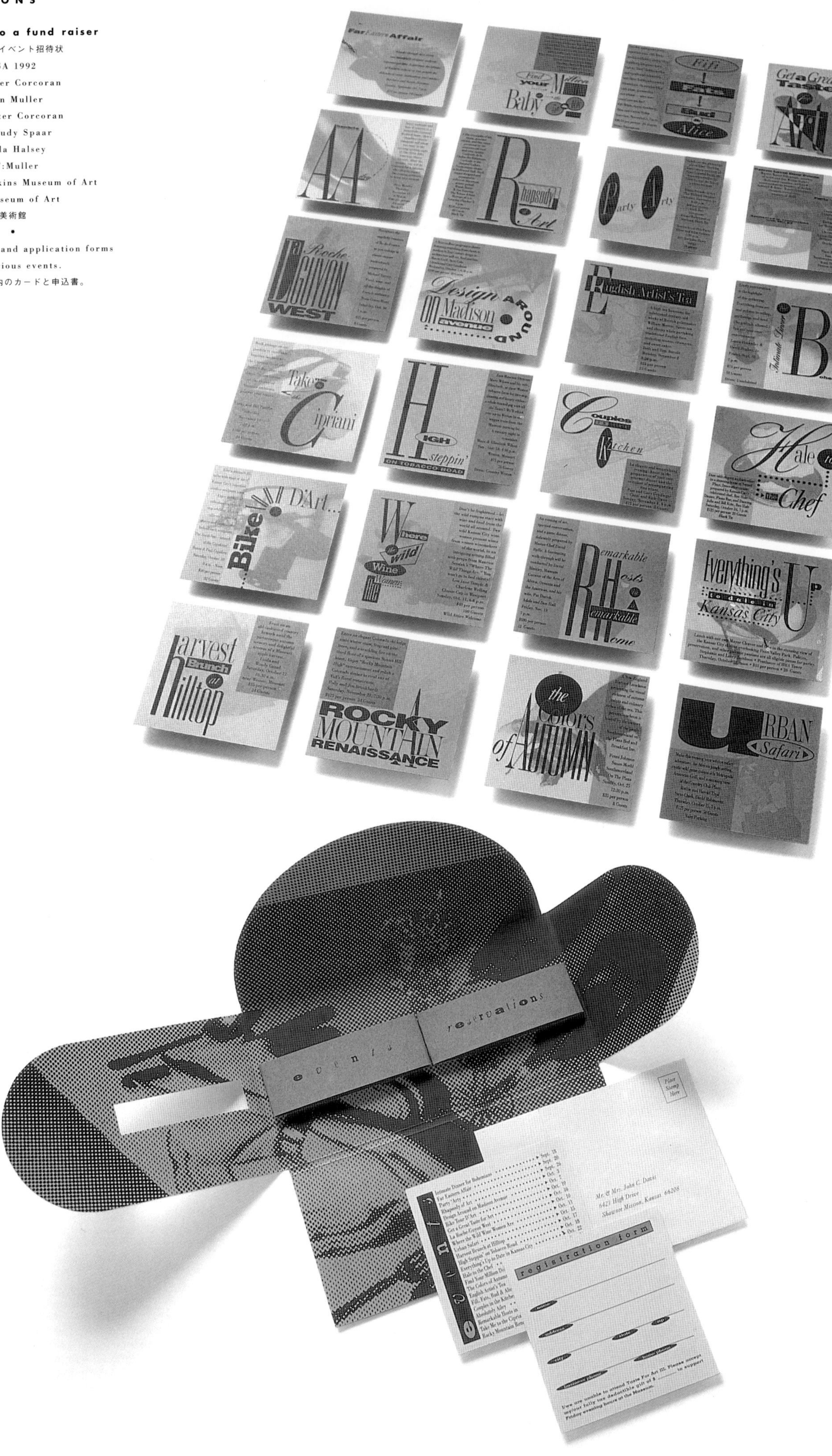

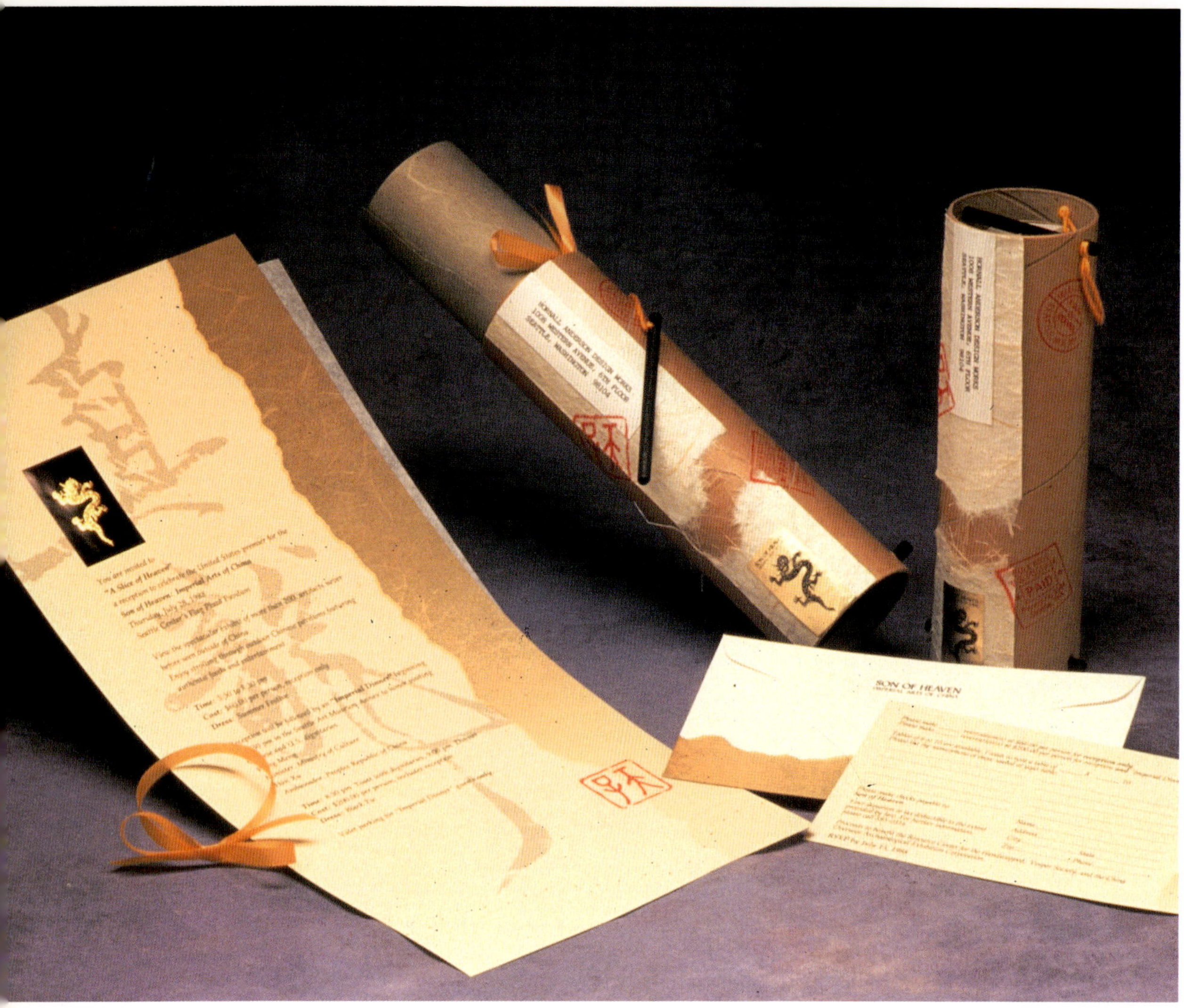

◀
Invitation to a cultural dinner
カルチャー・ディナー招待状
USA 1988
AD:Jack Anderson
D:Jack Anderson
Julie Tanagi-Lock
I:Kenneth Pai
CW:Alex Glant
DF:Hornall Anderson Design Works
CL:Son of Heaven Committee
TC:Fund Raiser
基金調達

▶
Invitation to a cinema event
映画イベント案内状
JAPAN 1990
CD:Yoshikuni Taki
AD,D:Yukashi Wakamatsu
CW:Akihito Sugiyama
CL:Tokyu Bunkamura
TC:Multicultural Facility
複合文化施設

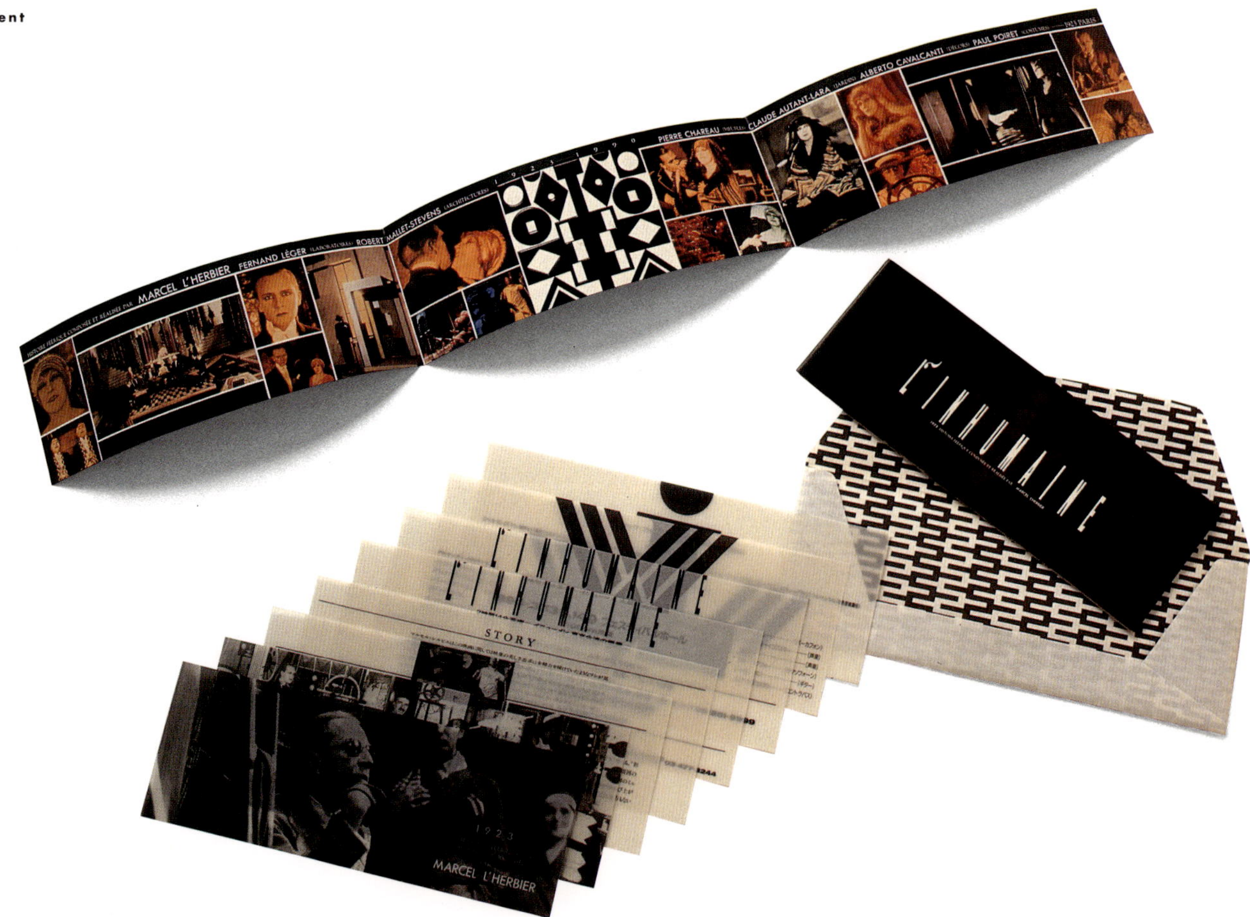

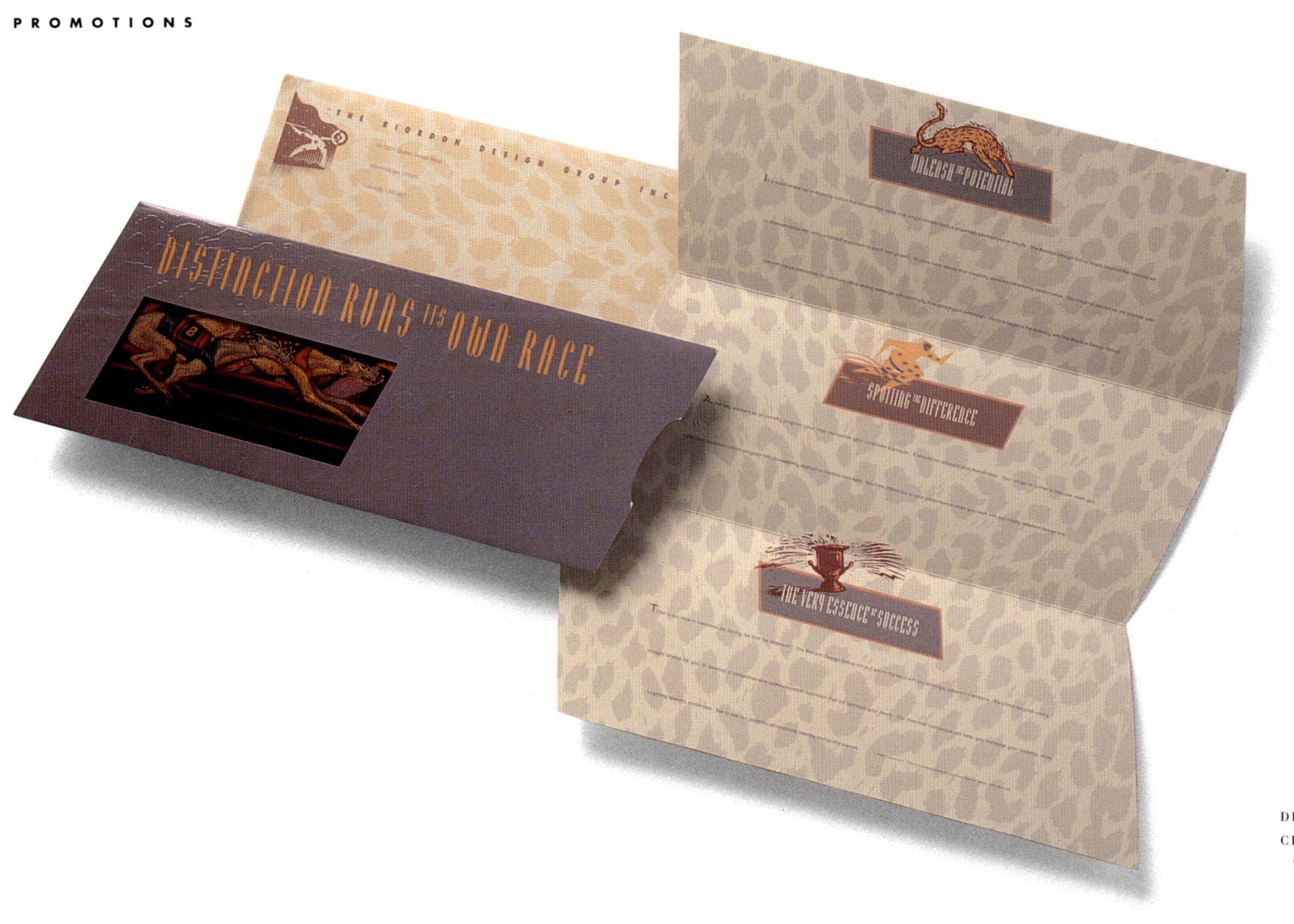

◀

Promotional card

プロモーショナル・カード

CANADA 1992

CD,D:Dan Wheaton

AD:Ric Riordon

I:Harvey Chan

CW:Shirley Riordon

Susan Masterson

DF:The Riordon Design Group

CL:The Riordon Design Group

TC:Graphic Design Studio,

Print Media

グラフィック・デザイン、印刷

▶

Promotional card

プロモーショナル・カード

ENGLAND 1991

AD,D:Alan Aboud

P:Sandro Sodano

CL:Paul Smith, London

TC:Apparel Maker

アパレル

•

Seen through the included glasses, the picture on the card looks 3dimensional.

付属の眼鏡をとおして見ると、カードの写真が立体的に見える。

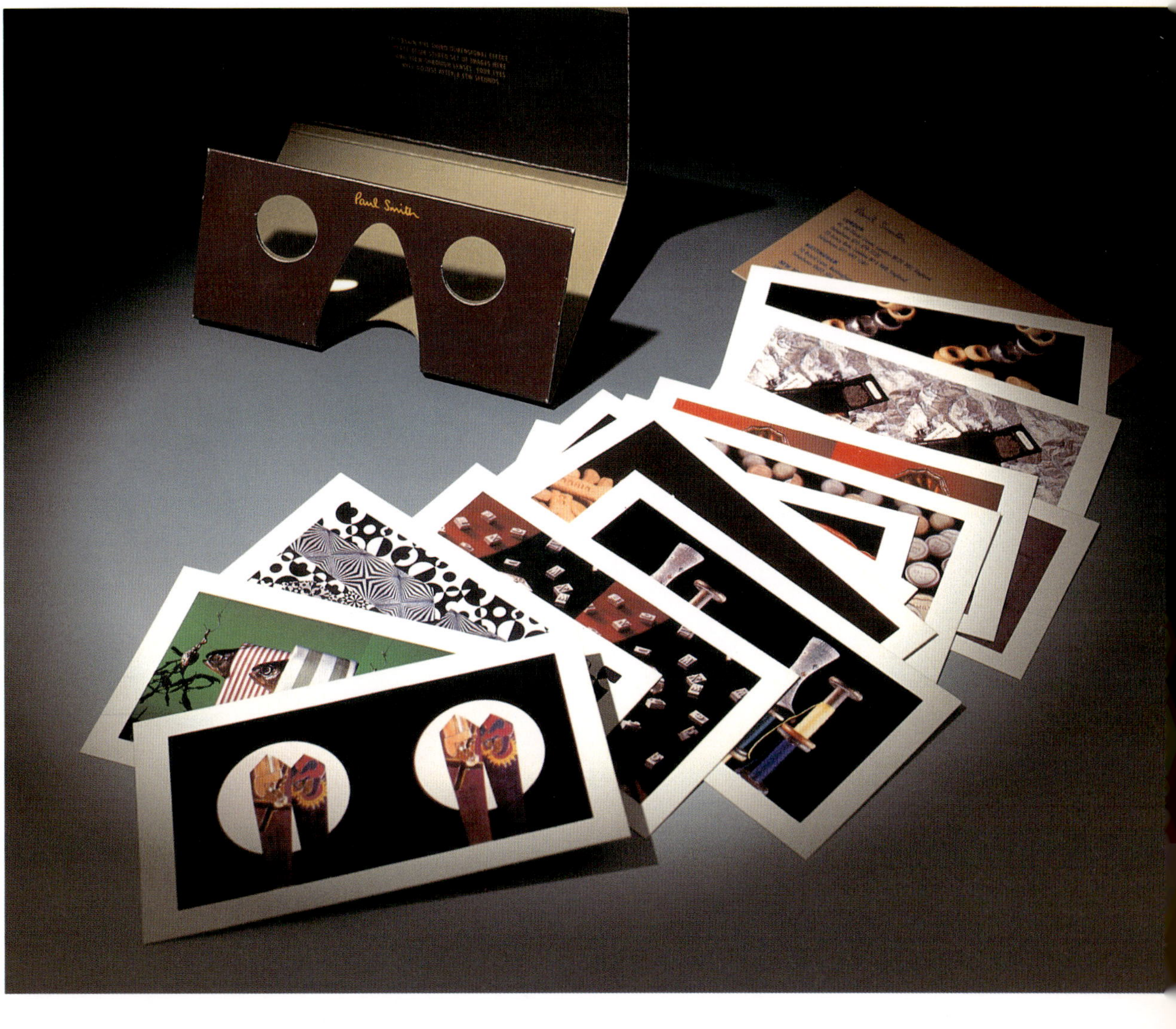

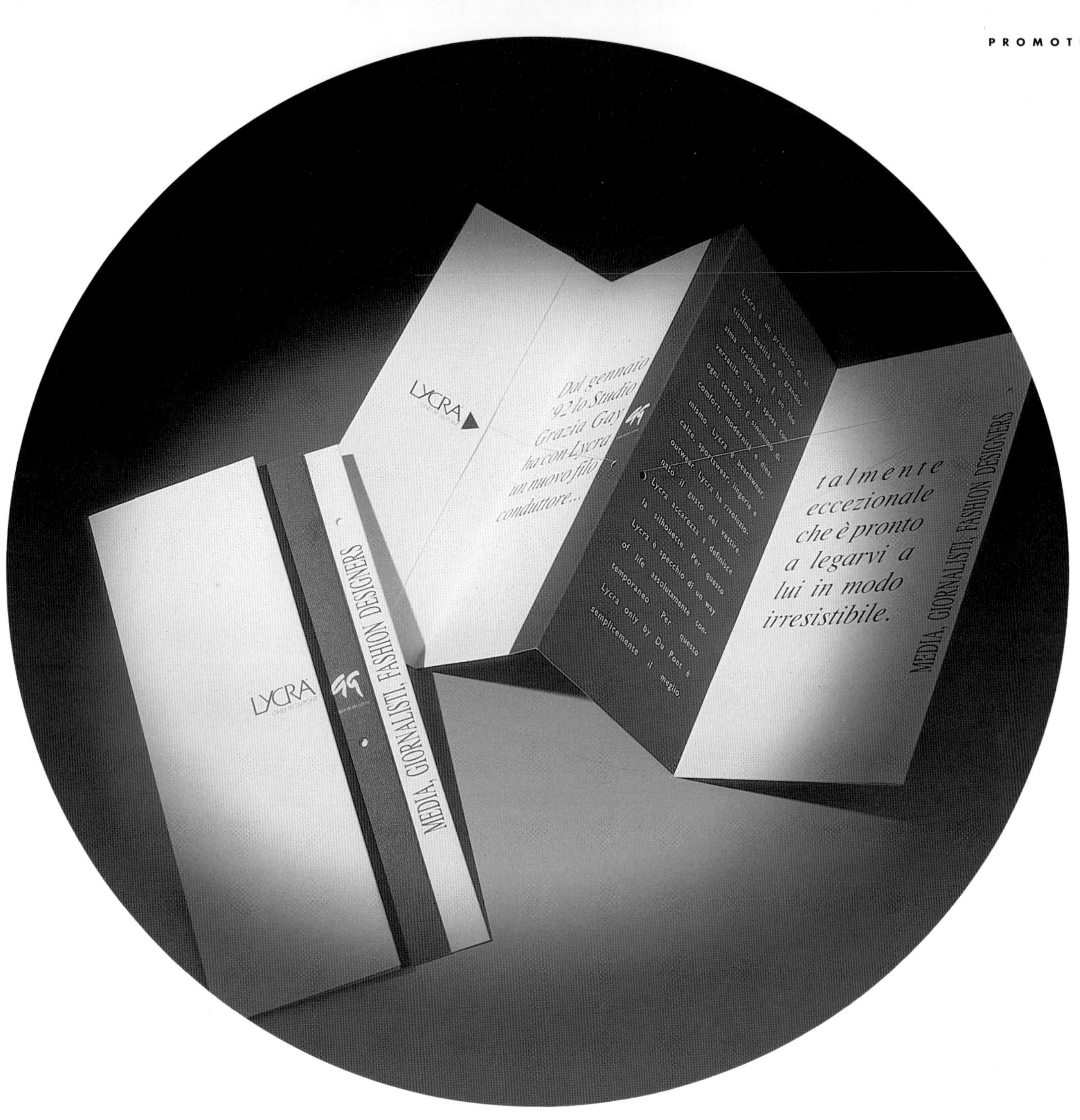

Press release for a fiber promotion

ファイバー製品プロモーション用
プレス・リリース

ITALY 1992

CD:Antonella Sala

CW:Grazia D'Annunzio

DF:Art Work Alas

CL:Studio Grazia Gay for Lycra

TC:Textile Maker
テキスタイル

▼

Promotional card

プロモーショナル・カード

USA 1992

AD:Charles Spencer Anderson

D:Todd Hauswirth

DF:Charles S.Anderson Design

CL:Charles S.Anderson Design

TC:Graphic Design Studio

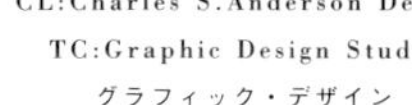

グラフィック・デザイン

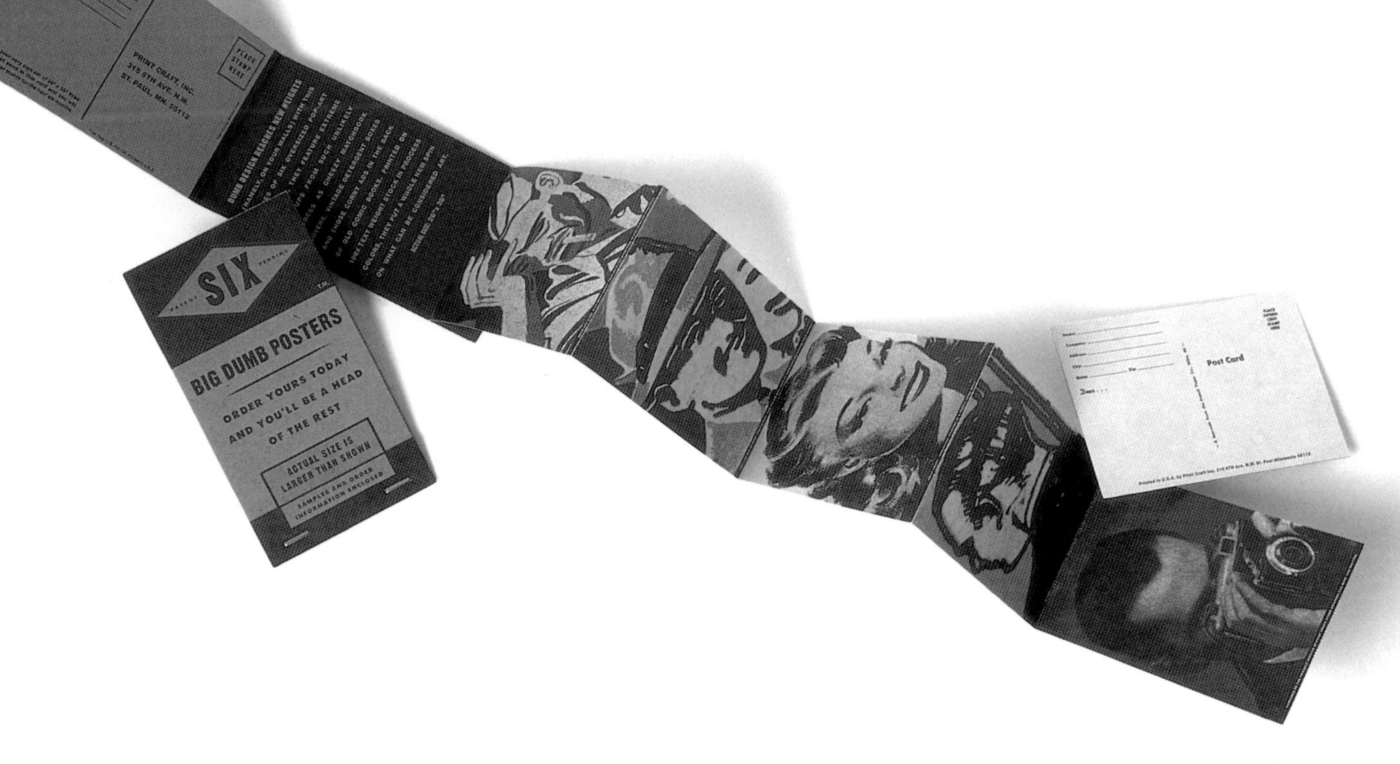

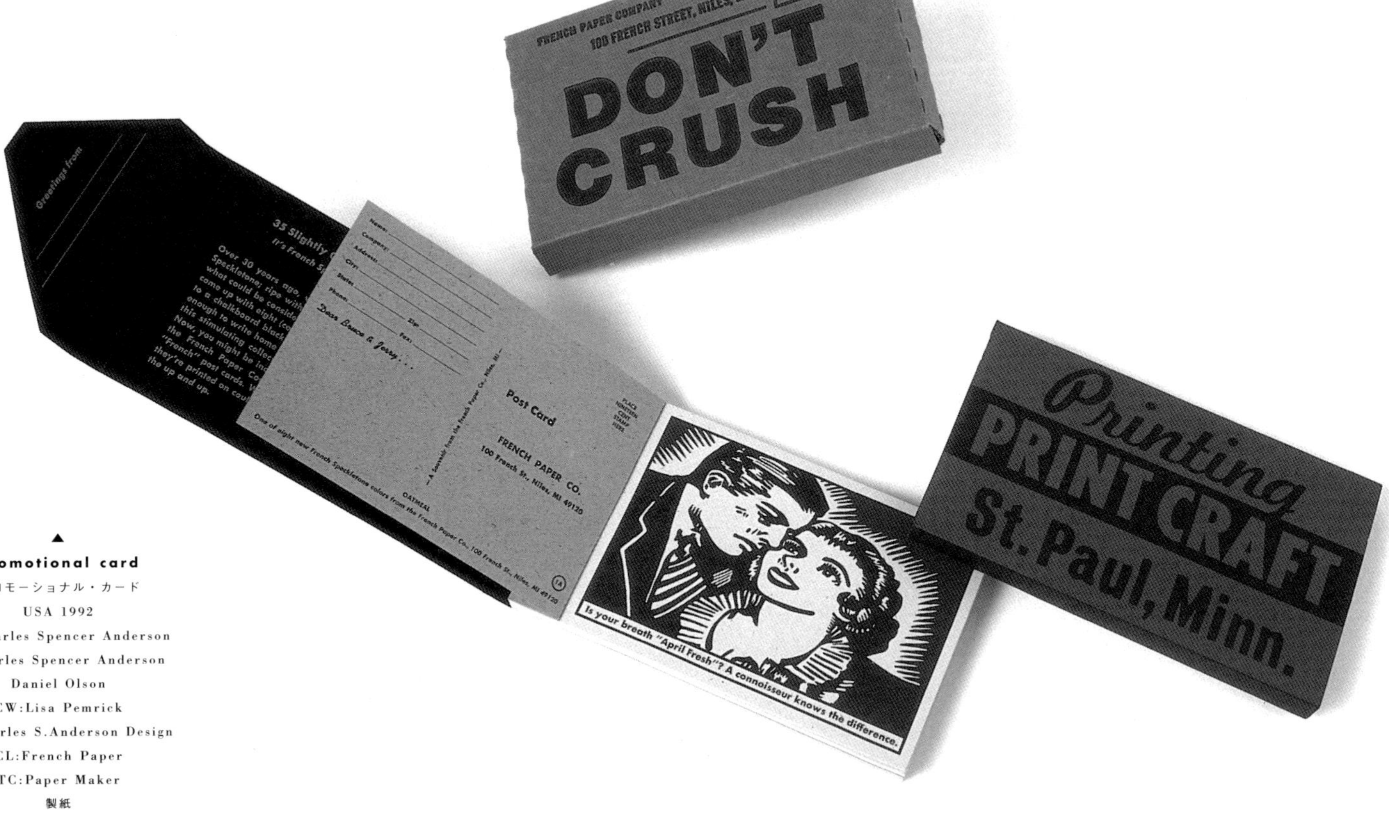

▲

Promotional card

プロモーショナル・カード

USA 1992

AD:Charles Spencer Anderson

D:Charles Spencer Anderson

Daniel Olson

CW:Lisa Pemrick

DF:Charles S.Anderson Design

CL:French Paper

TC:Paper Maker

製紙

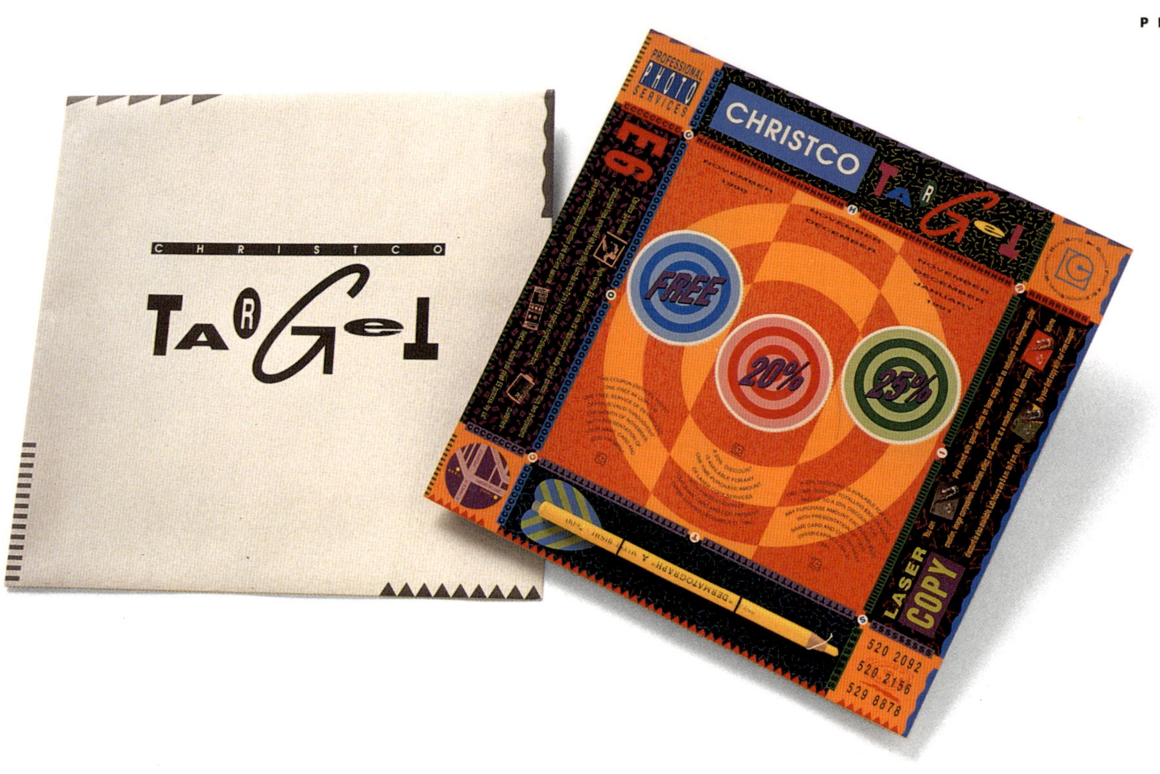

▲

Promotional card
プロモーショナル・カード
HONG KONG 1991
CD:Kan Tai-keung
AD:Lau Siu-hong,Freeman
D:Lau Siu-hong,Freeman
Au Tak-shing,Benny
DF:Kan Tai-keung
Design & Associates
CL:Christco (Hong Kong)
TC:Photographic Service
写真

▼

Promotional card
プロモーショナル・カード
JAPAN 1991
D,I,CW:Toriko Kino
CL:Toriko Kino
TC:Illustrator
イラストレーター

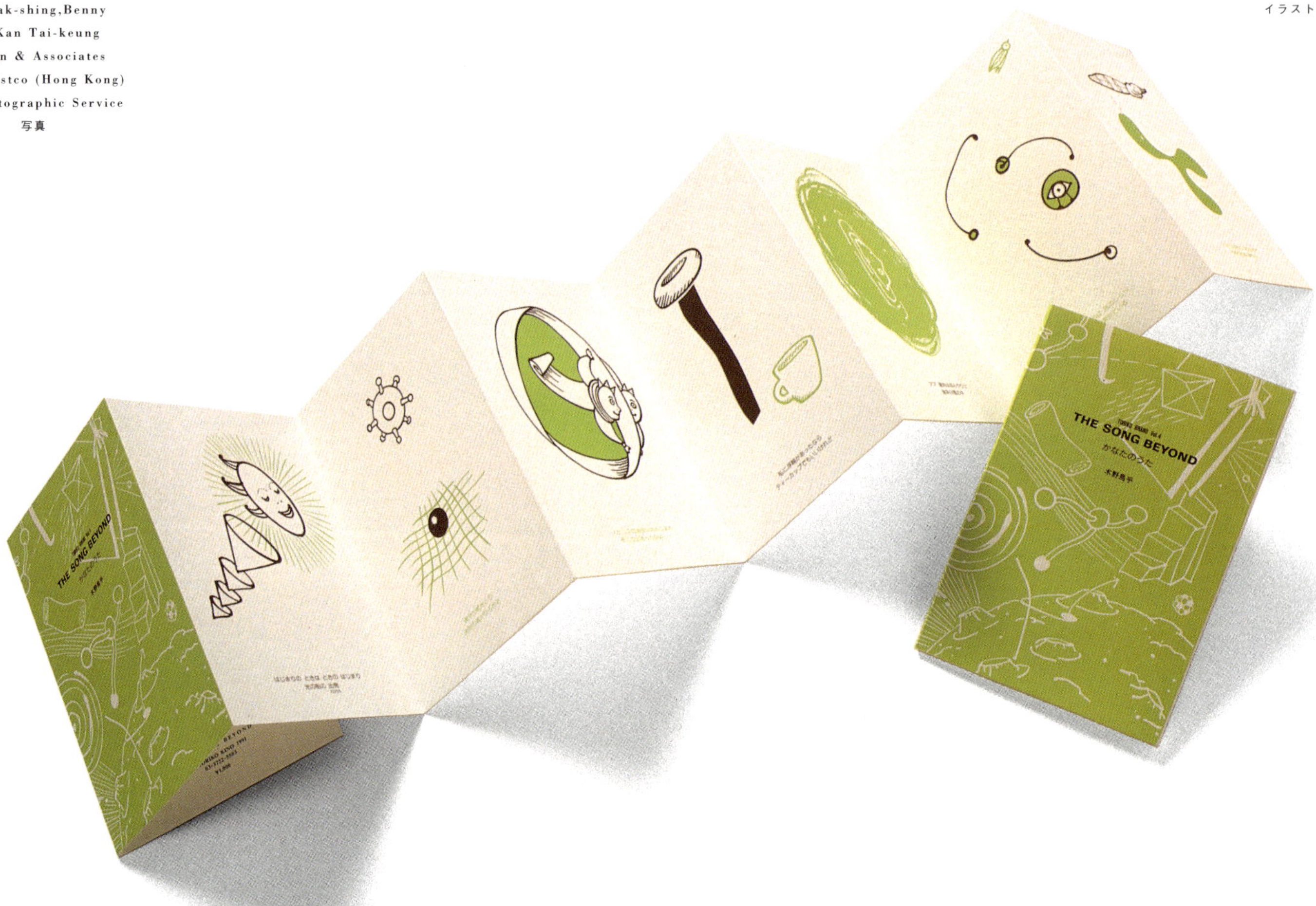

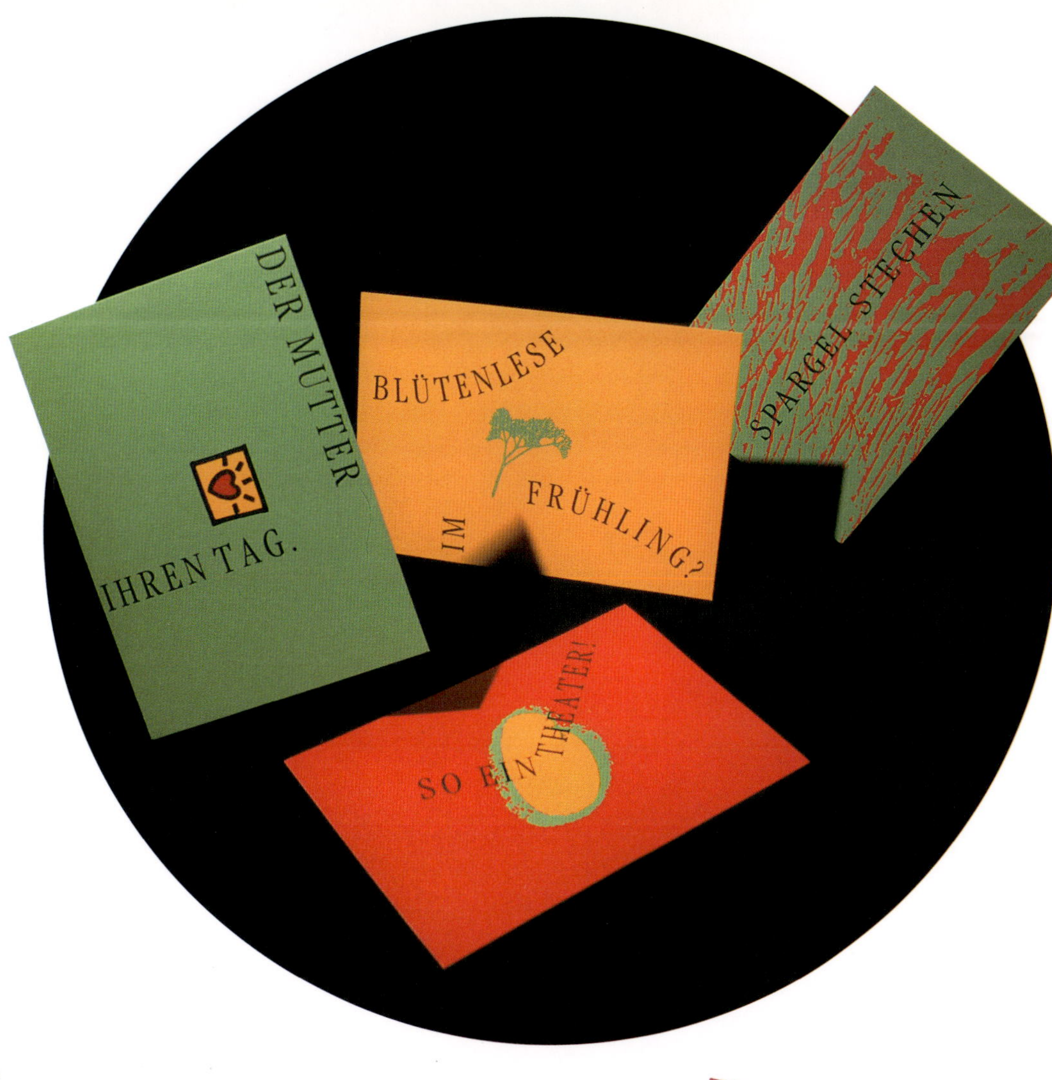

▲
Promotional card
プロモーショナル・カード
AUSTRIA 1991
AD,D,I:Kurt Dornig
CW:Hermann Brändle
DF:Dornig Grafik Design
CL:Le Miserable Quellenstr
TC:Restaurant
レストラン

▼
Promotional card
プロモーショナル・カード
ENGLAND 1992
CD:Jo Mirowski
AD:Peter Hayward
DF:Mainartery
CL:Mainartery
TC:Design Studio
デザイン

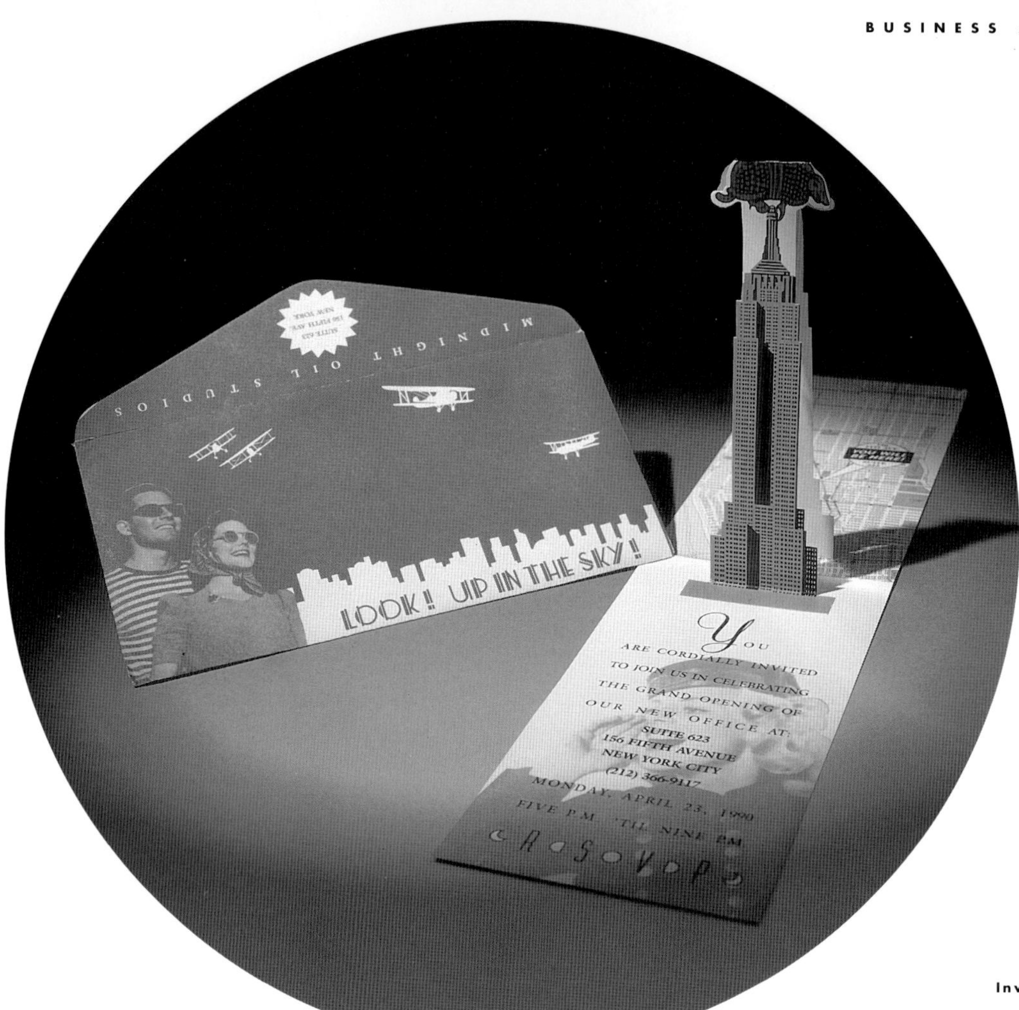

▲
Invitation to an office opening
オフィス・オープニング招待状
USA 1990
CD,I:James M.Skiles
AD,CW:Kathryn A.Klein
D:Tim Megrath
DF:Midnigth Oil Studios
CL:Midnigth Oil Studios
TC:Design Studio
デザイン

▼
Invitation to an open house
オープン・ハウス案内状
USA 1986
CD,AD,D:Eric Rickabaugh
P:Tom Watson
DF:Rickabaugh Graphics
CL:Vantage Companies
TC:Real Estate Developer
不動産開発

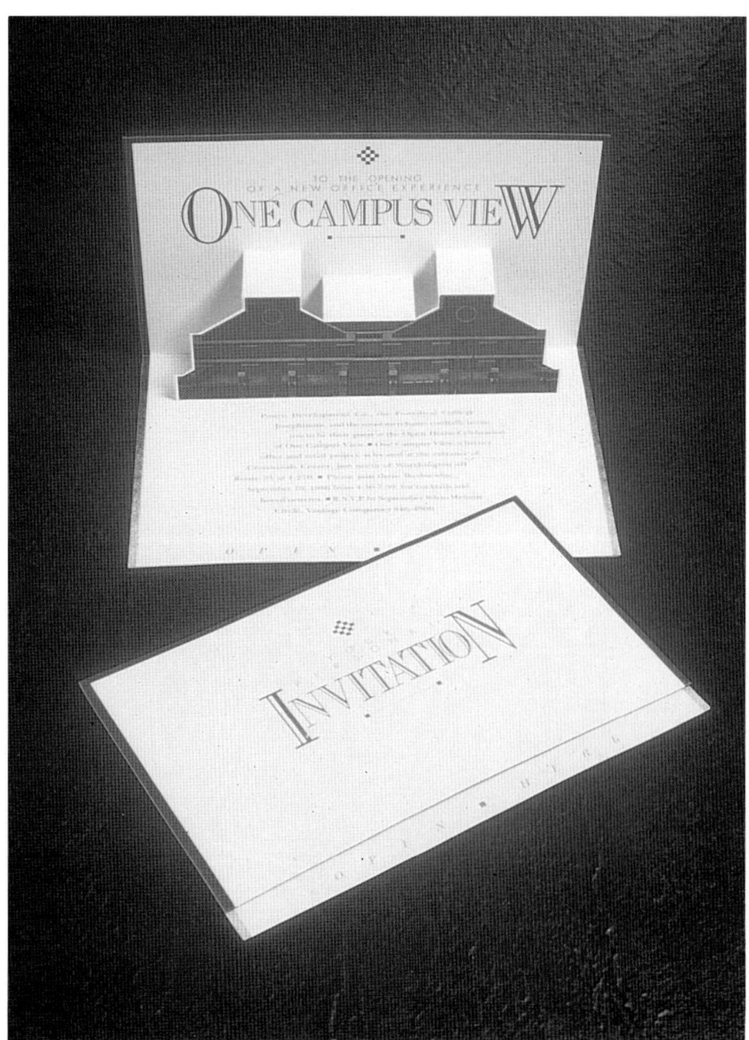

Invitation to the opening of a new gallery

ギャラリー・オープニング招待状

USA 1992

AD:Rebeca Mendez

D:Darin Beaman

P:Steven A. Heller

DF:Art Center College of Design. Design Office

CL:Art Center College of Design

TC:Art College

美術大学

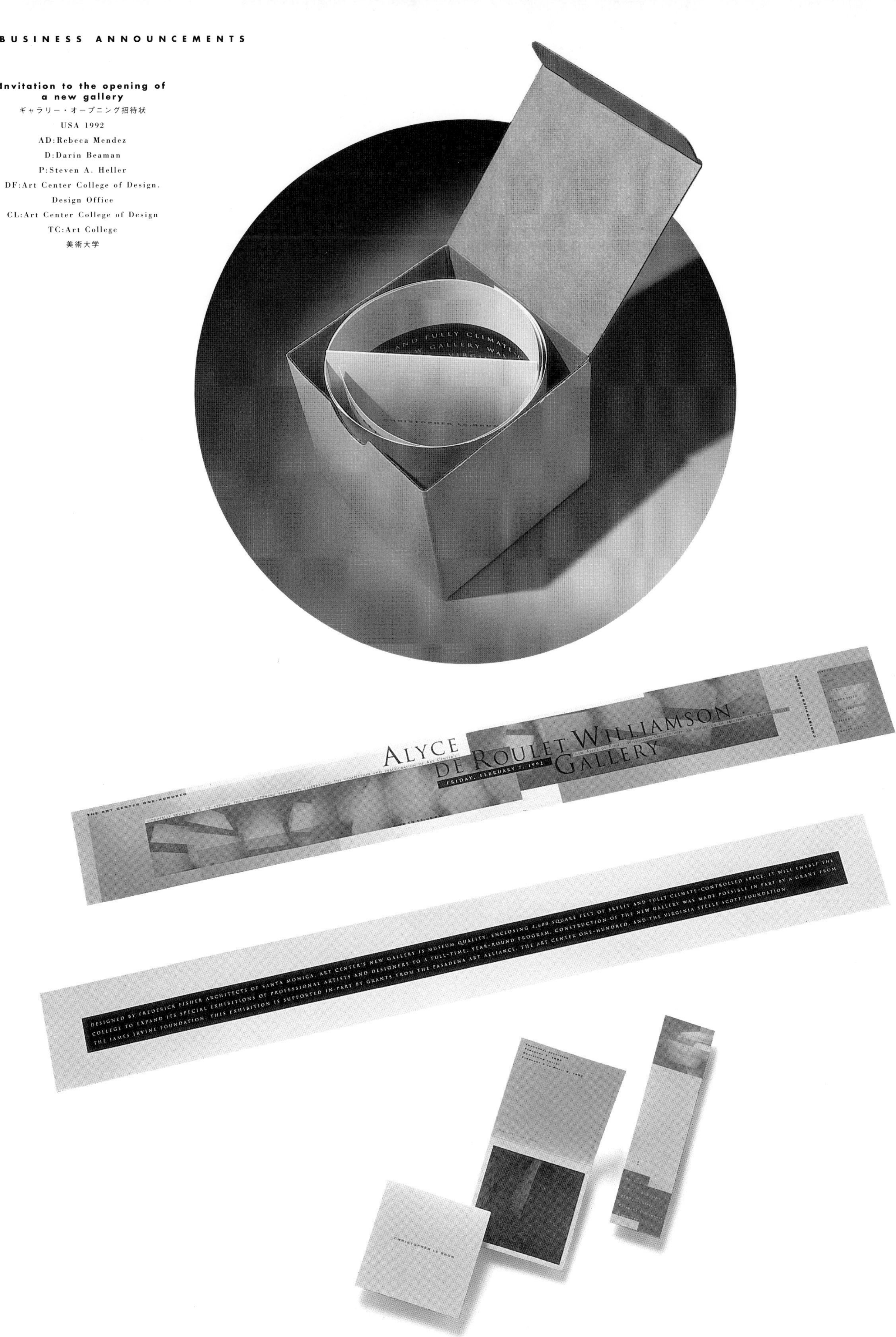

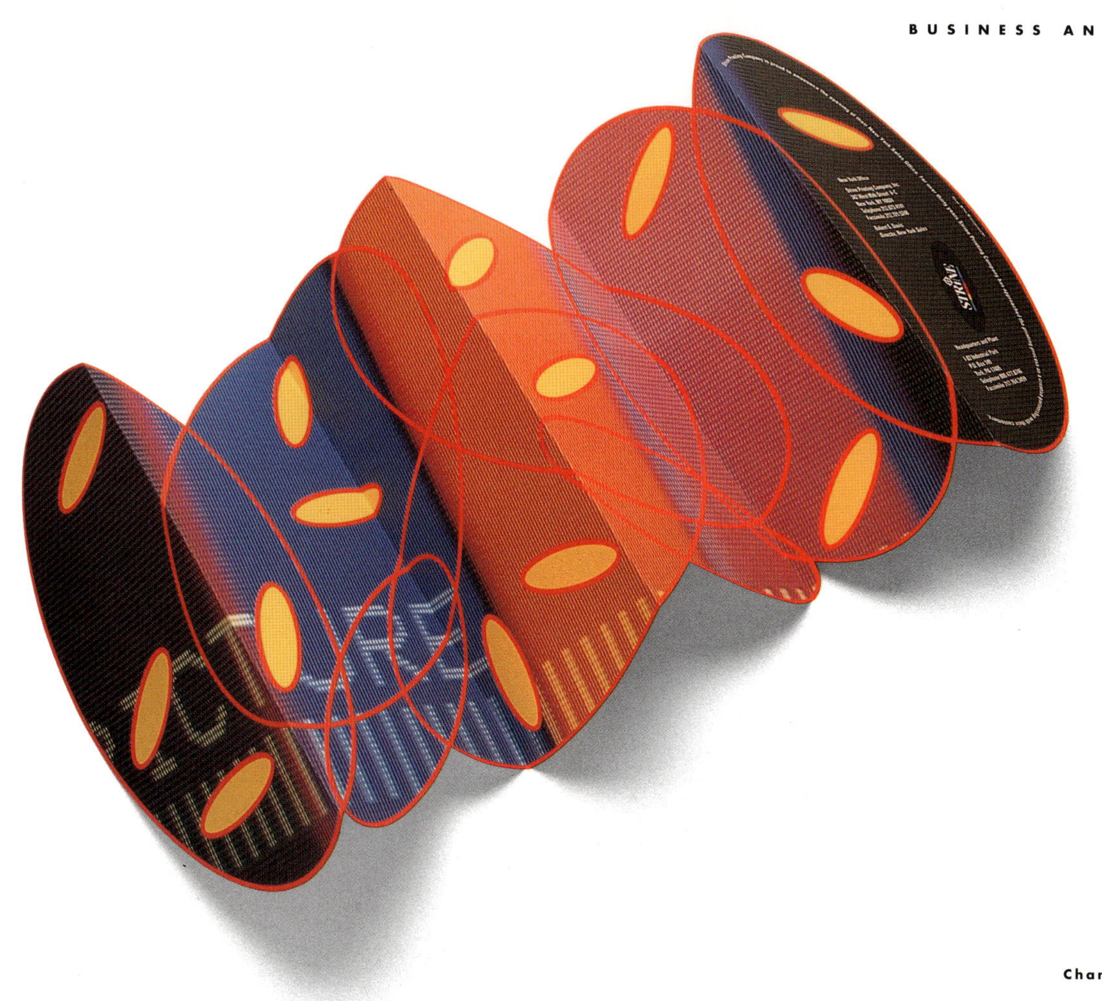

▲
Office opening announcement
オフィス・オープニング通知
USA 1991
AD:Takaaki Matsumoto
Michael McGinn
D:Takaaki Matsumoto
DF:M Plus M
CL:Strine Printing
TC:Printer
印刷

▼
Change-of-address notice
移転通知
HONG KONG 1992
AD,D:Andrea Koura
Percy Chung
CW:Mary O'Malley
Percy Chung
Andrea Koura
DF:Emphasis (Hong Kong)
CL:Emphasis (Hong Kong)
TC:Publisher
出版

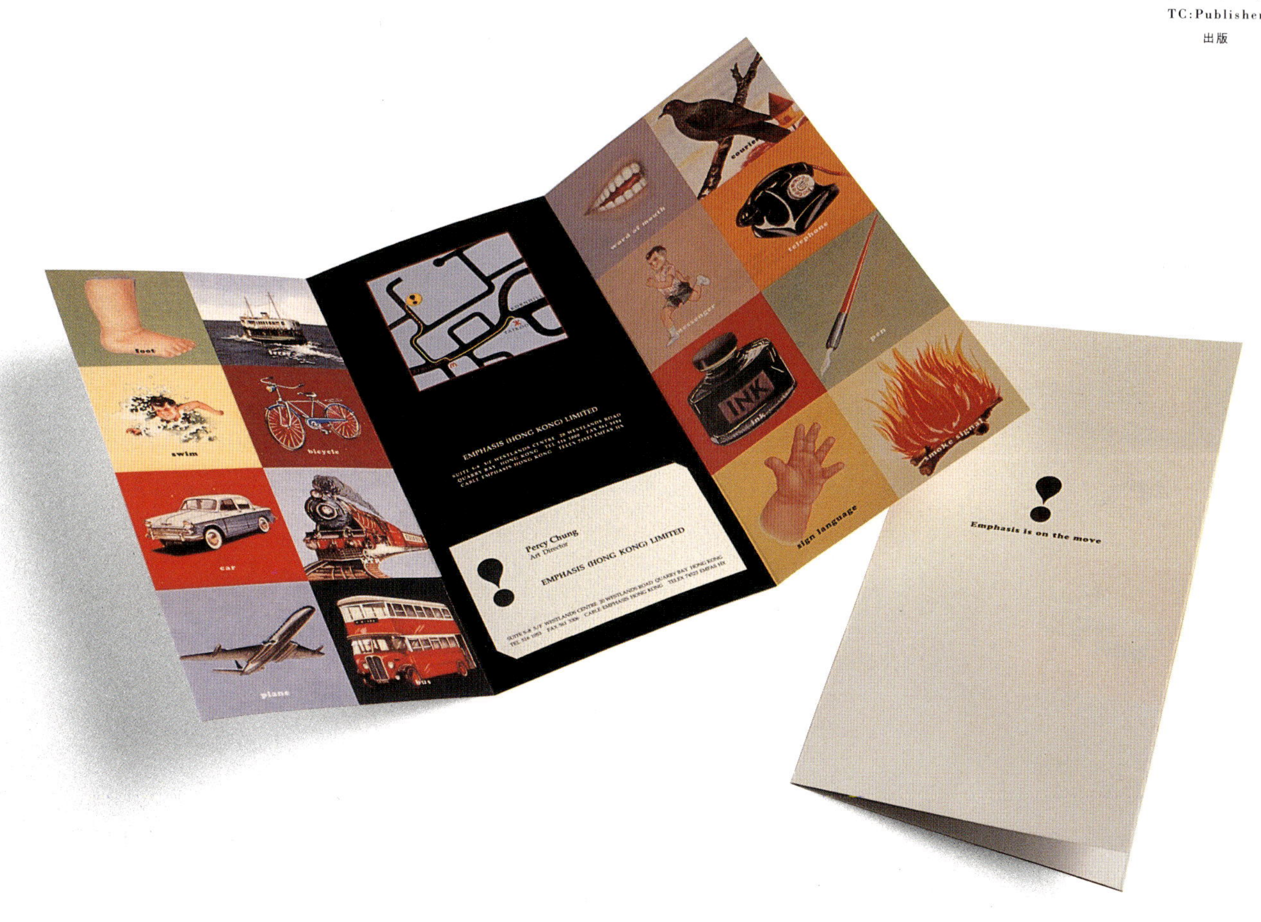

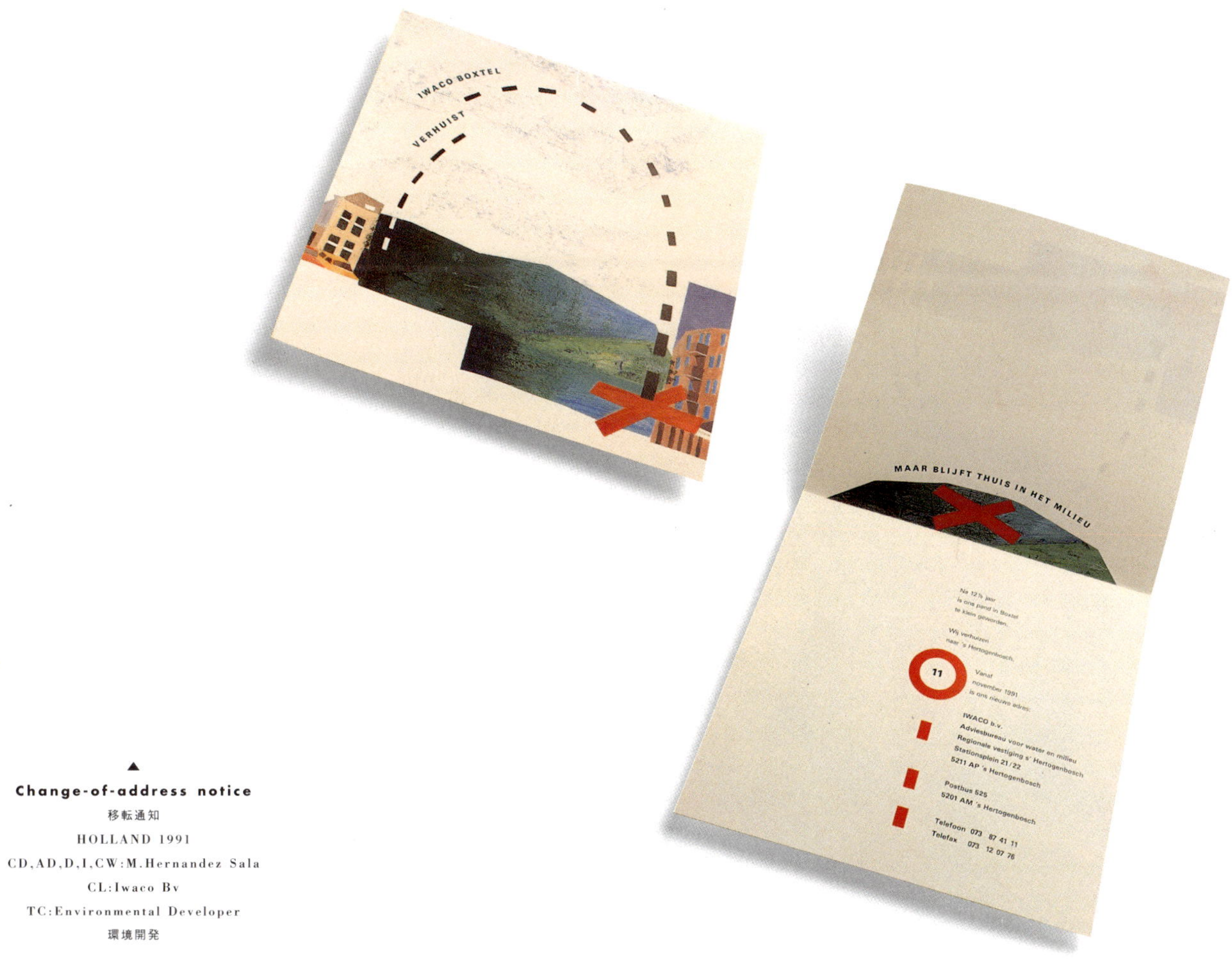

▲
Change-of-address notice
移転通知
HOLLAND 1991
CD,AD,D,I,CW:M.Hernandez Sala
CL:Iwaco Bv
TC:Environmental Developer
環境開発

▼
Invitation to an inauguration party
開業記念パーティー招待状
HOLLAND 1992
CD,AD,D,I,CW:M.Hernandez Sala
CL:Iwaco Bv
TC:Environmental Developer
環境開発

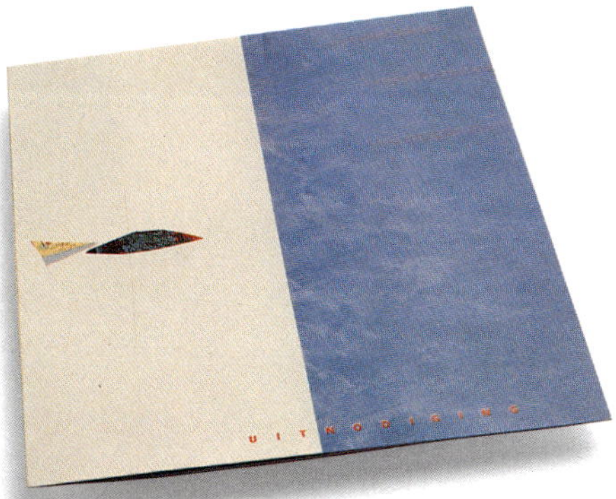

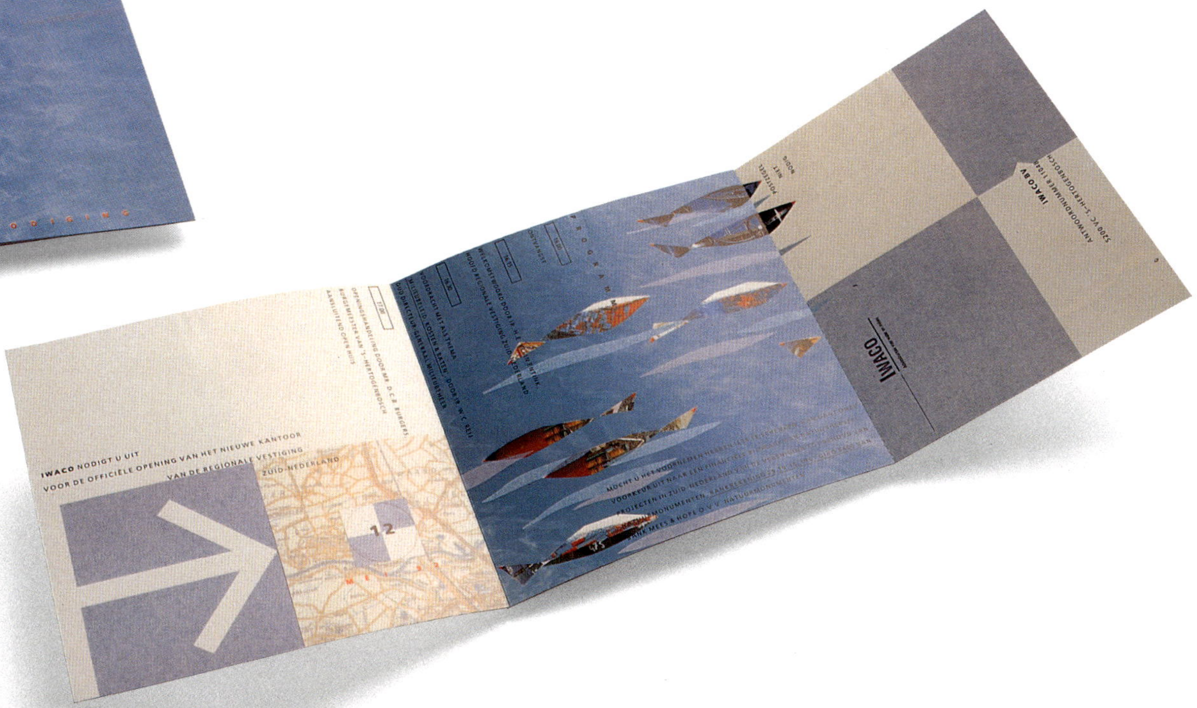

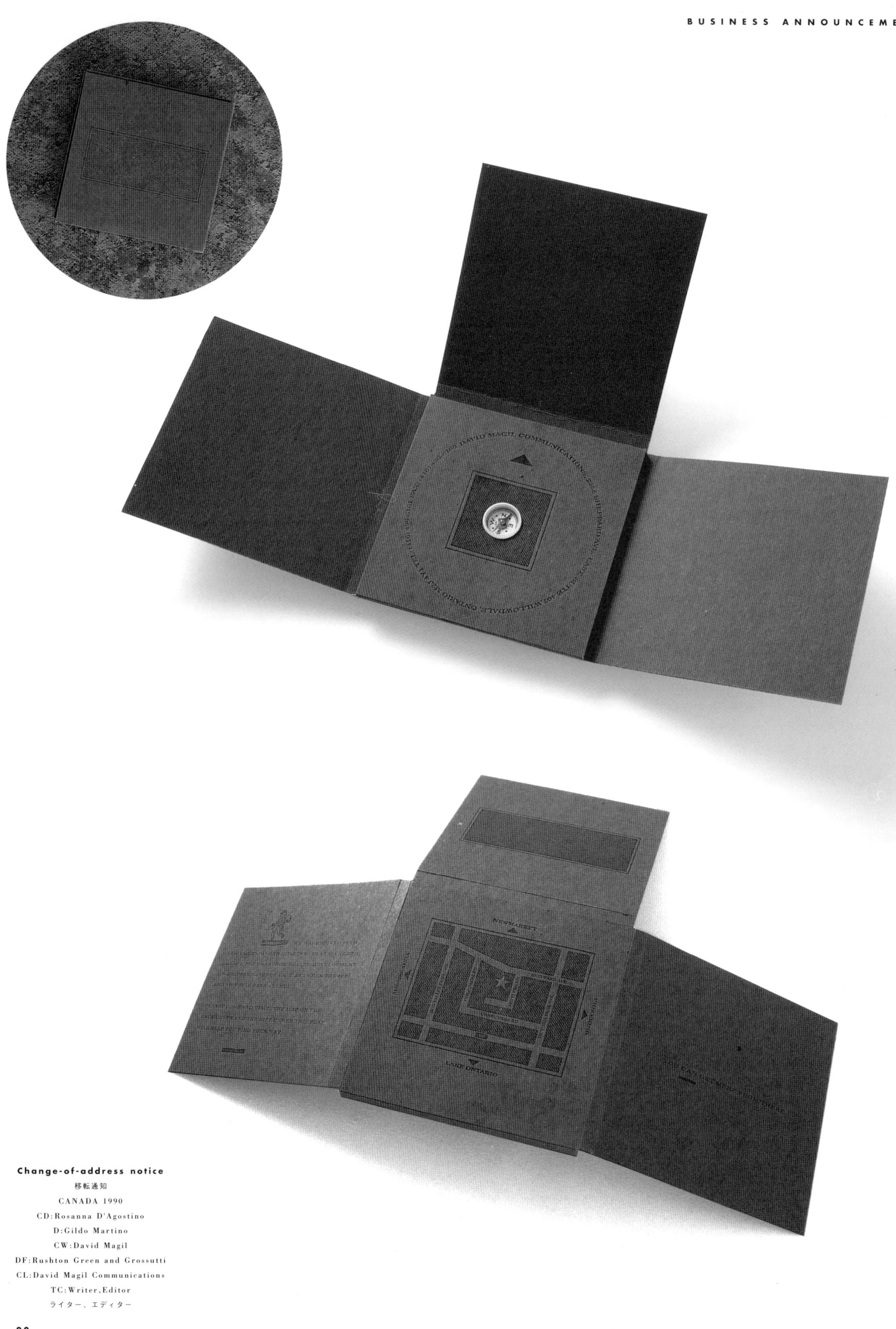

Change-of-address notice
移転通知
CANADA 1990
CD:Rosanna D'Agostino
D:Gildo Martino
CW:David Magil
DF:Rushton Green and Grossutti
CL:David Magil Communications
TC:Writer,Editor
ライター、エディター

Change-of-address notice
移転通知
CANADA 1989
CD:Marcello Grossutti
AD,D:David Craib
I:Michael Custode
DF:Rushton Green and Grossutti
CL:Michael Mitchell
TC:Photographer
フォトグラファー

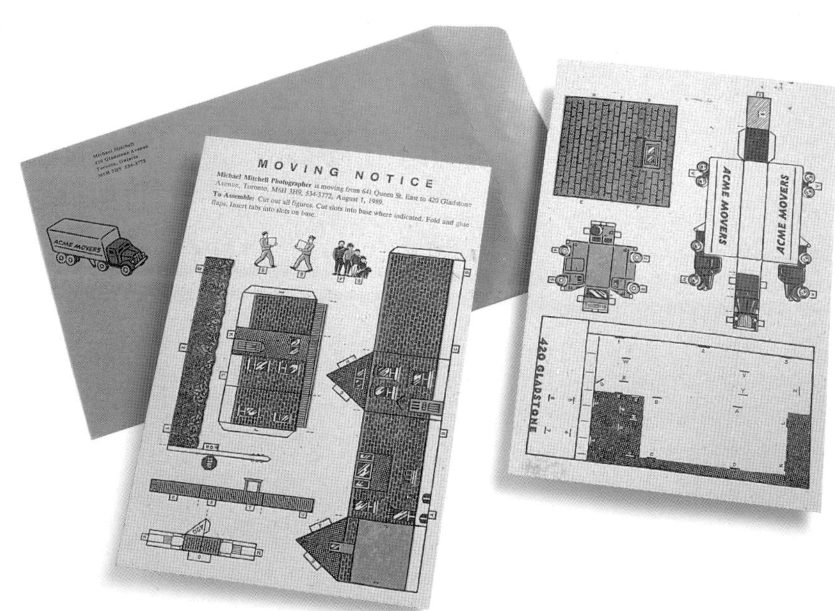

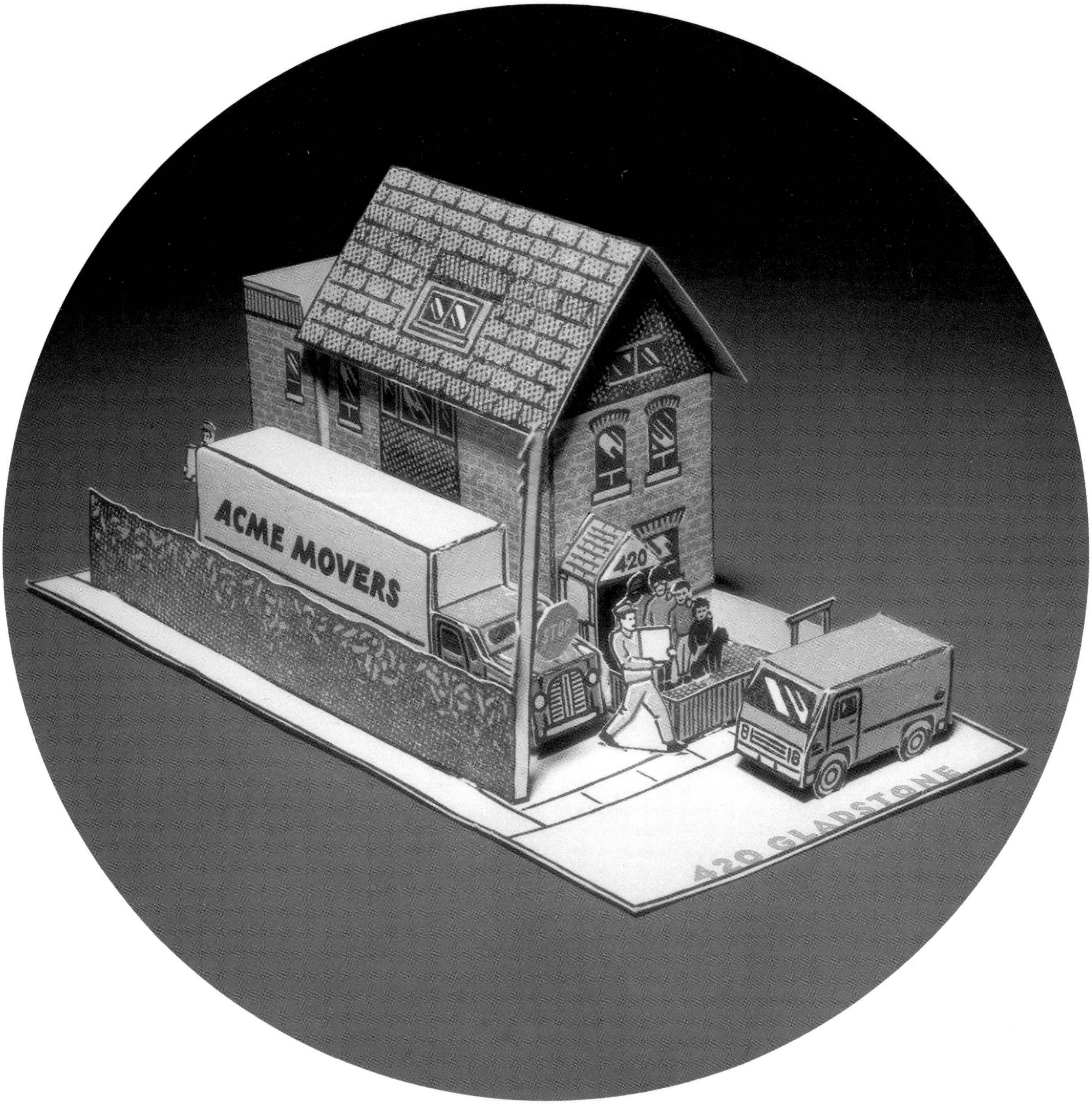

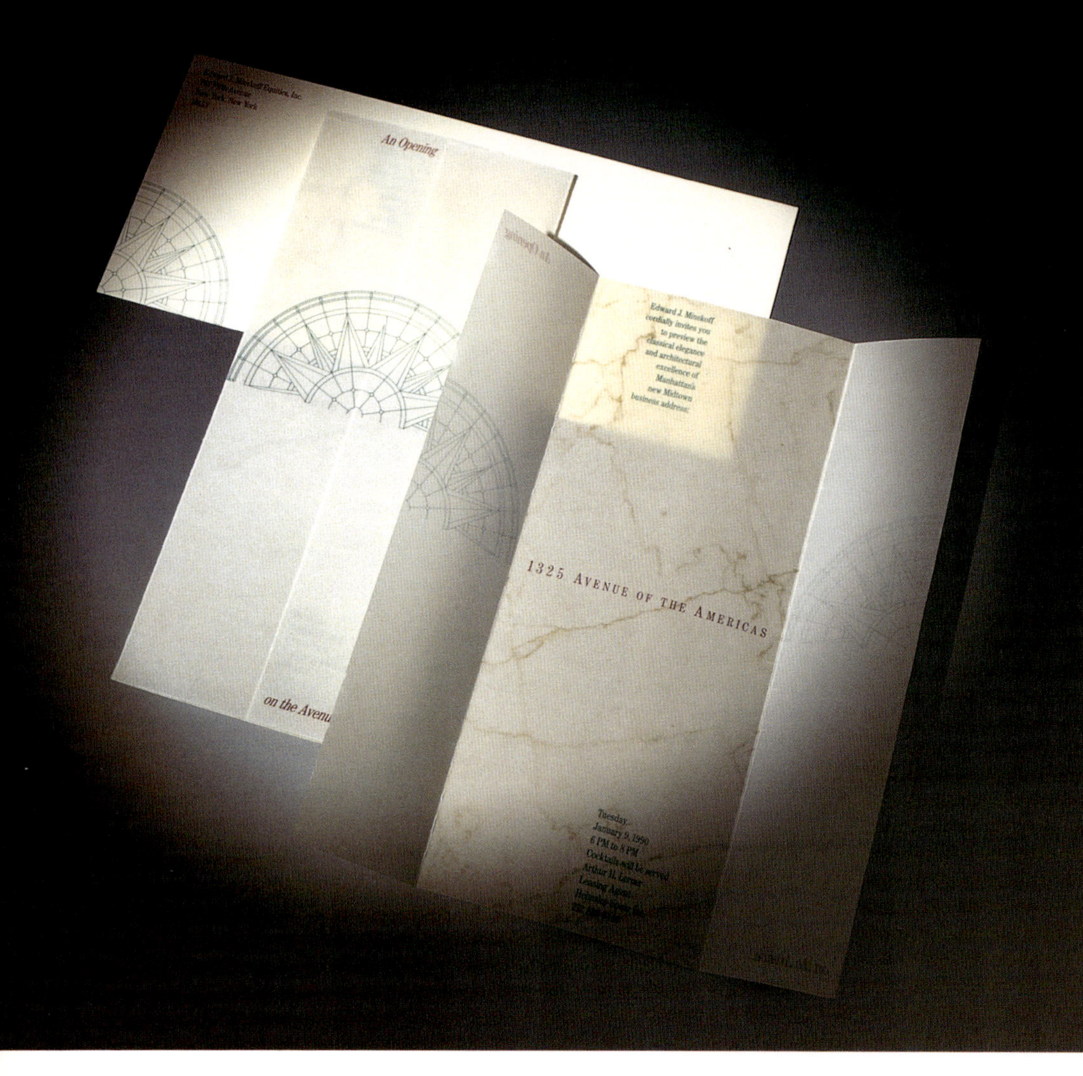

◀
Invitation to an office building opening
オフィス・ビル・オープニング招待状
USA 1989
CD,AD:Richard Poulin
D:Richard Poulin
Rosemary Simpkins
CW,DF:De Harak &
Poulin Associates
CL:Edward J. Minskoff Equities
TC:Real Estate Developer
不動産開発

▶
Office opening announcement
オフィス・オープニング通知
USA 1987
AD:Takaaki Matsumoto
Michael McGinn
D:Michael McGinn
DF:M Plus M
CL:M Plus M
TC:Design Studio
デザイン

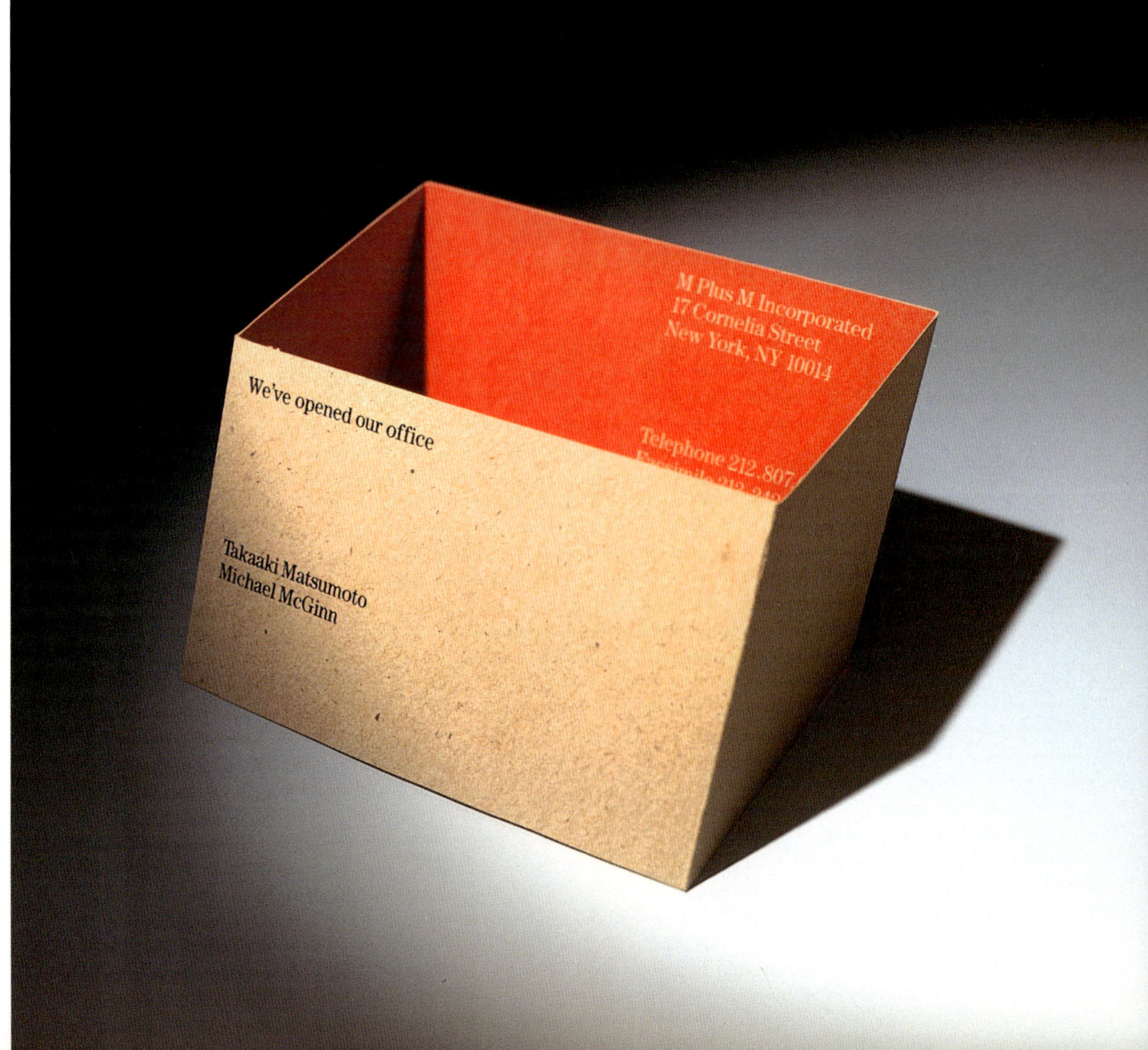

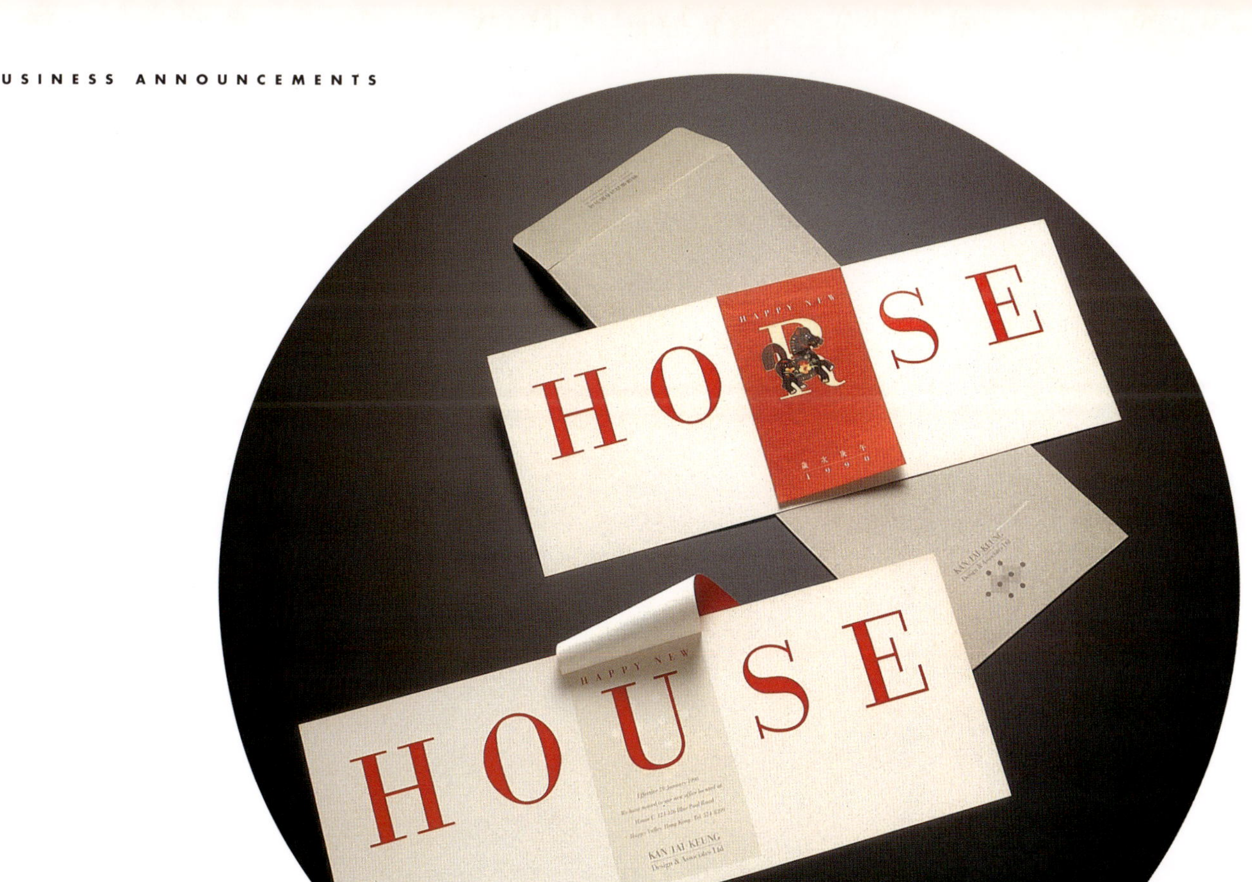

LA TROBE UNIVERSITY OPEN DAY

'Flying Start' Sunday 26 July 11am to 4pm

Abbotsford St Heliers Street
Bundoora Plenty Road
Carlton 625 Swanston Street
Enquiries 03) 479 2738

La Trobe University

▲

Change-of-address notice and New year's card

移転通知＆ニューイヤーズ・カード

HONG KONG 1990

CD:Kan Tai-keung

AD,D:Kan Tai-keung
Lau Siu-hong,Freeman
Yu Chi-kong,Eddy

DF:Kan Tai-keung
Design & Associates

CL:Kan Tai-keung
Design & Associates

TC:Graphic Design Studio
グラフィック・デザイン

●

A New Year's card for the year of the horse. When you turn over the illustration of the horse, a change of office address notice "Happy New House" appears.

馬年のニューイヤーズ・カード。
馬のイラストをめくると
"Happy New House"という事務所移転通知になる。

◀

Invitation to a university open day

大学一般公開日案内状

AUSTRALIA 1992

CD:Garry Emery

AD,D,DF:Emery Vincent Design

CL:La Trobe University

TC:University
大学

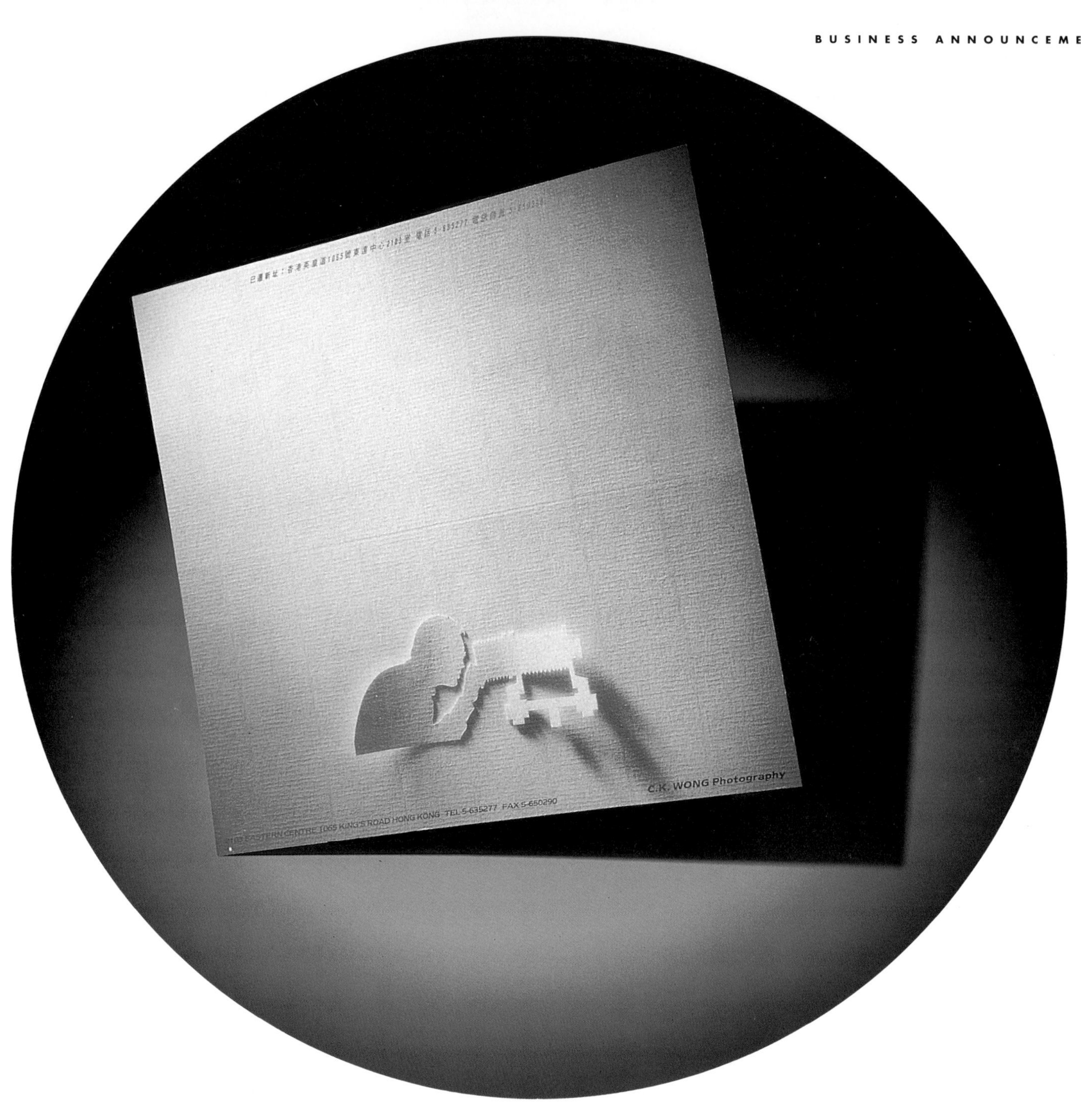

Change-of-address notice
移転通知
HONG KONG 1991
CD:Kan Tai-keung
AD,D:Eddy Yu Chi Kong
DF:Kan Tai-keung Design & Associates
CL:C.K.Wong Photography
TC:Photographer
フォトグラファー

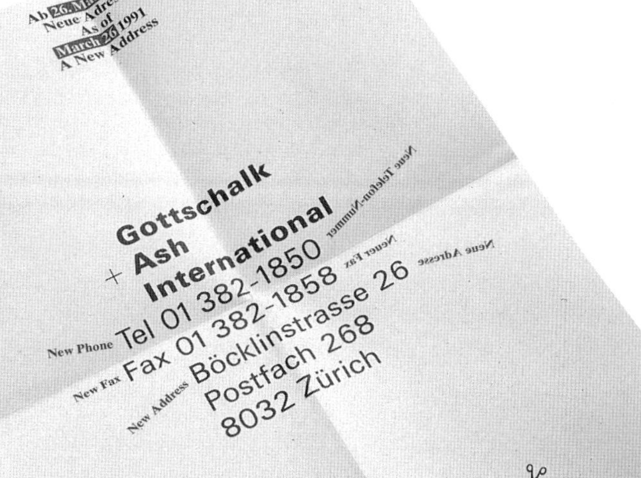

▲

Change-of-address notice

移転通知

SWITZERLAND 1991

CD,AD,D,CW:Fritz Gottschalk

DF:Gottschalk+Ash International

CL:Gottschalk+Ash International

TC:Design Consultant

デザイン・コンサルタント

▼

Change-of-address notice

移転通知

AUSTRALIA 1992

CD:Garry Emery

AD,D,DF:Emery Vincent Design

CL:Carmen Furniture

TC:Furniture Maker

家具製造

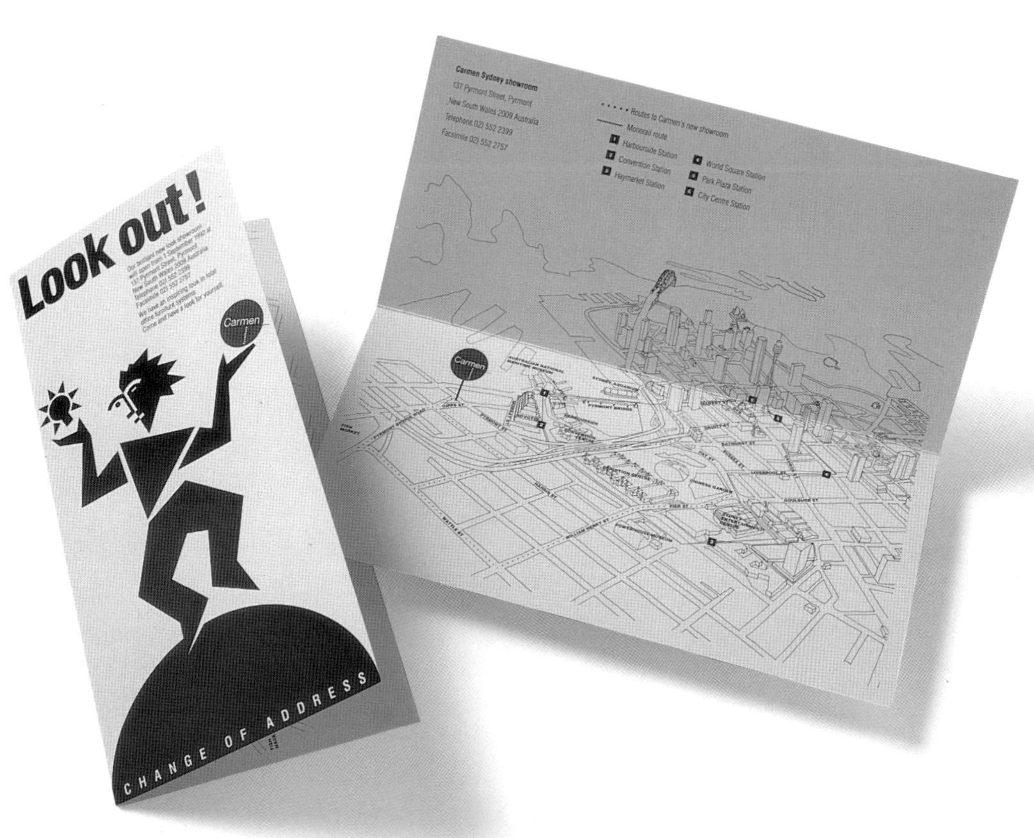

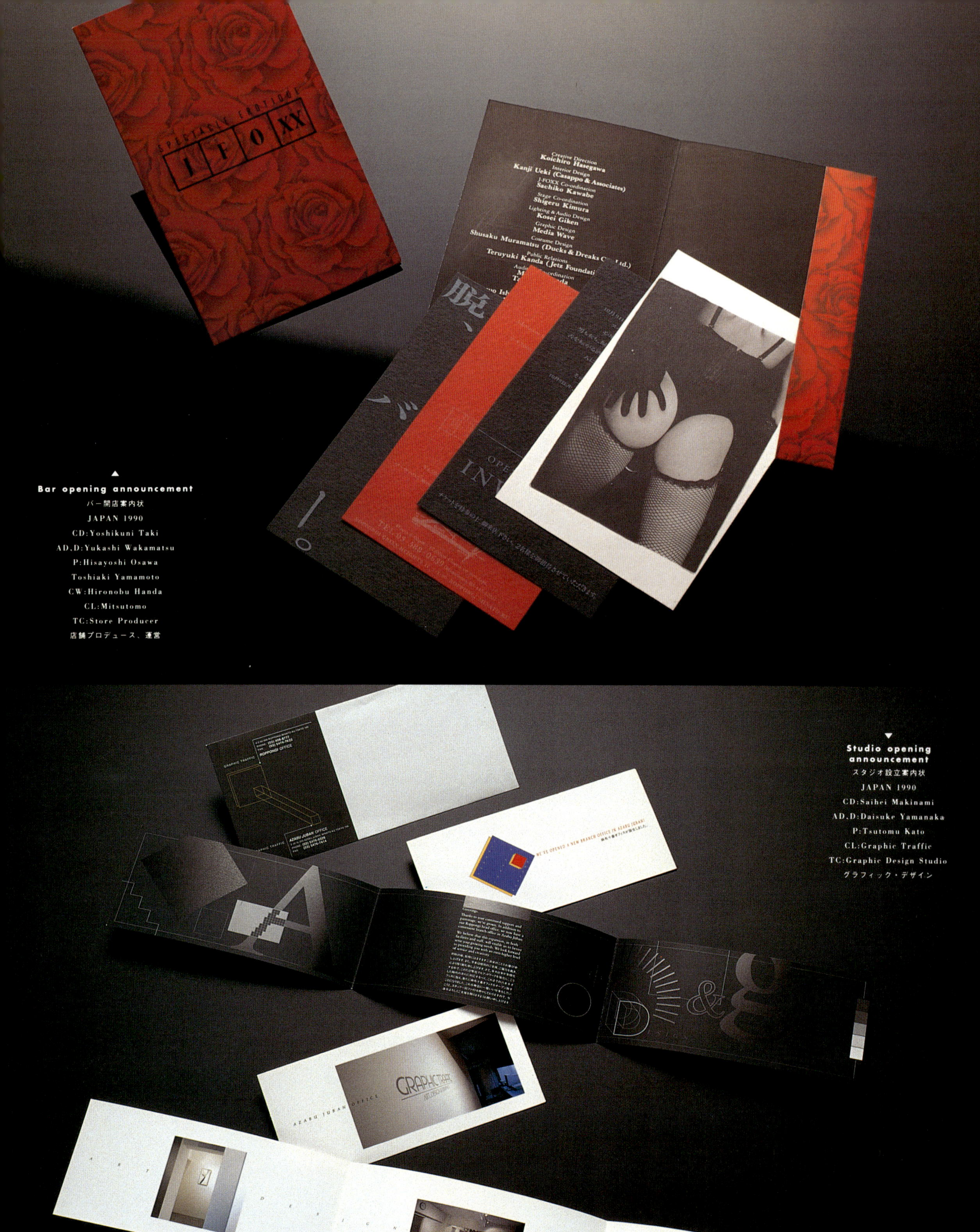

▲
Bar opening announcement
バー開店案内状
JAPAN 1990
CD:Yoshikuni Taki
AD.D:Yukashi Wakamatsu
P:Hisayoshi Osawa
Toshiaki Yamamoto
CW:Hironobu Handa
CL:Mitsutomo
TC:Store Producer
店舗プロデュース、運営

▼
Studio opening announcement
スタジオ設立案内状
JAPAN 1990
CD:Saihei Makinami
AD.D:Daisuke Yamanaka
P:Tsutomu Kato
CL:Graphic Traffic
TC:Graphic Design Studio
グラフィック・デザイン

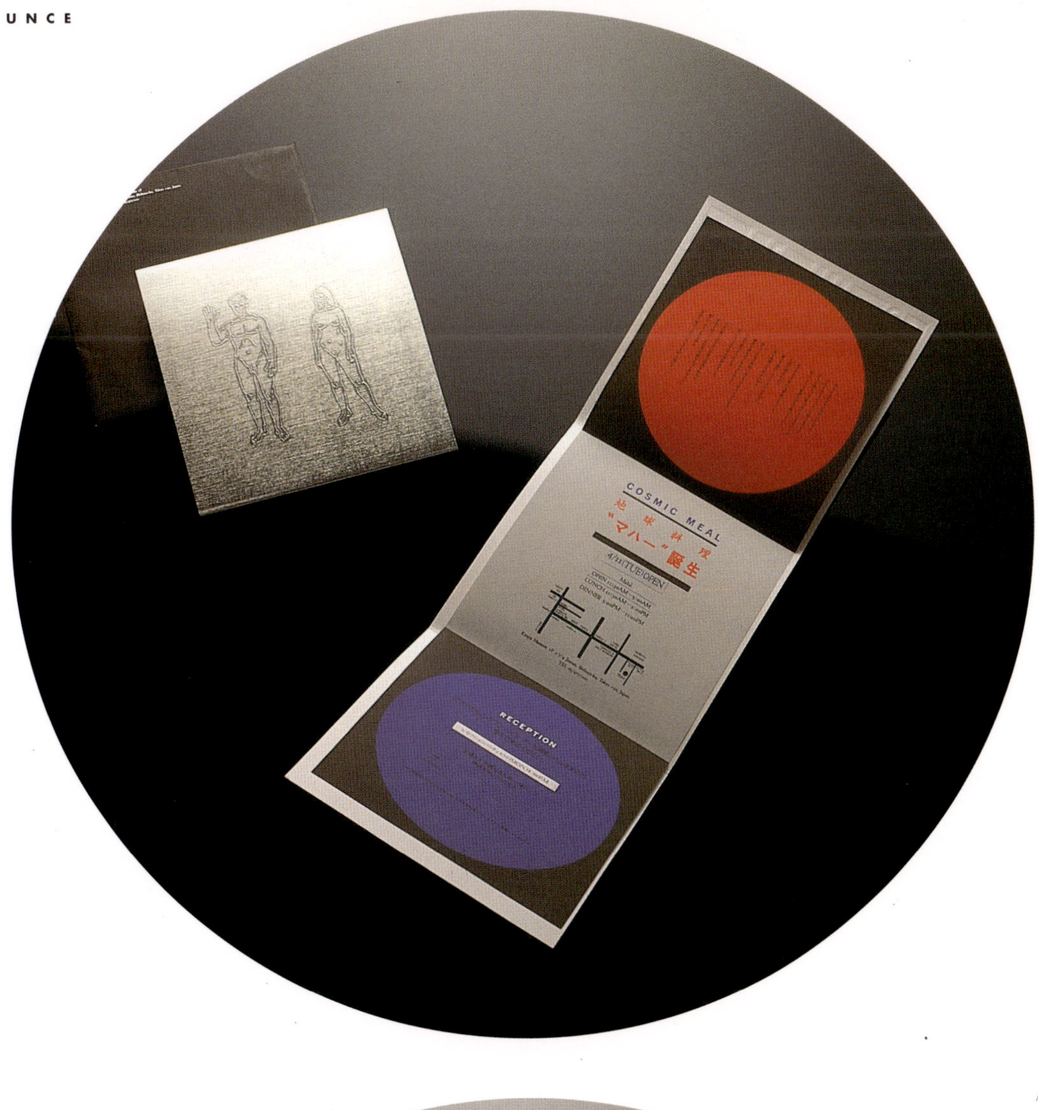

▲
Restaurant opening announcement
レストラン開店案内状
JAPAN 1989
CD:Takakazu Tanaka
AD,D:Yoshinori Kikuchi
CL:Artlex
TC:Resort Tourism Developer
リゾート観光開発

▼
Invitation to an office opening
オフィス・オープニング招待状
AUSTRALIA 1991
CD:Garry Emery
AD,D,DF:Emery Vincent Design
CL:The Hassell Group
TC:Architectural Consultants
建築コンサルタント

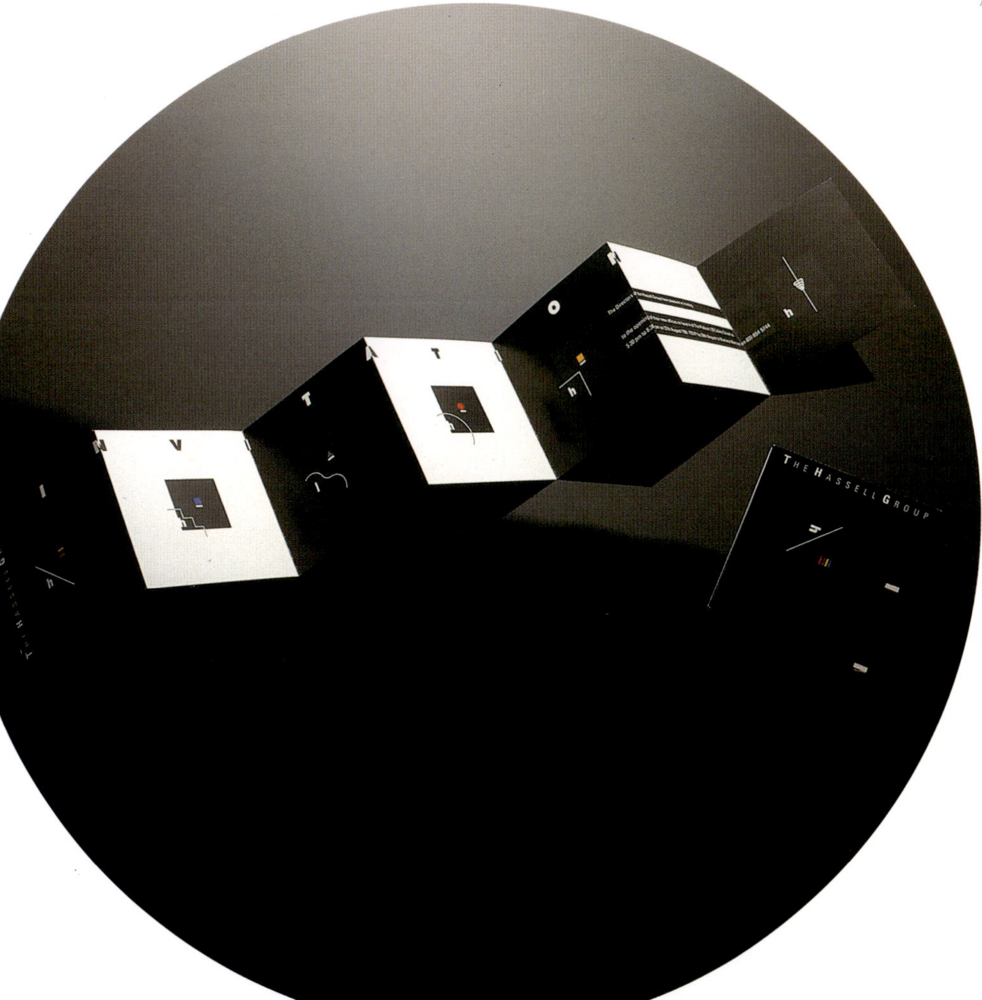

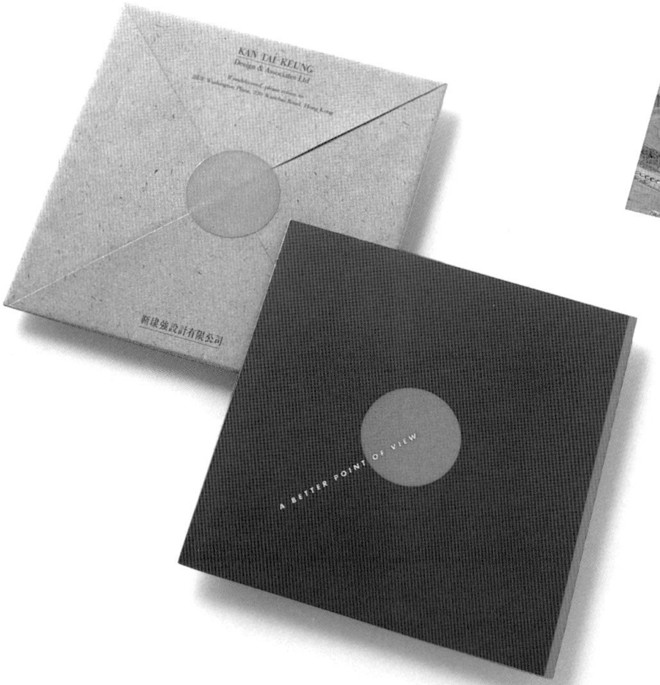

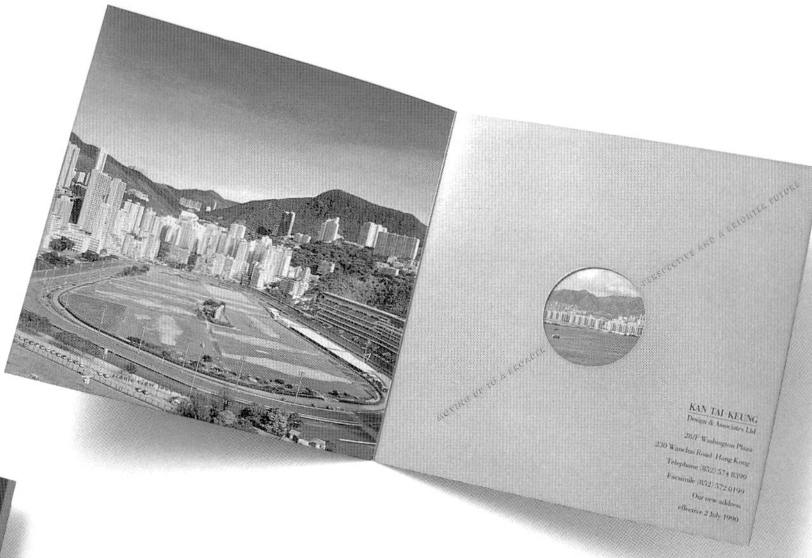

▲
Change-of-address notice
移転通知
HONG KONG 1990
CD:Kan Tai-keung
AD:Kan Tai-keung
Lau Siu-hong,Freeman
Yu Chi-kong,Eddy
D:Wong On-ming,Barry
DF:Kan Tai-keung
Design & Associates
CL:Kan Tai-keung
Design & Associates
TC:Graphic Design Studio
グラフィック・デザイン
•
Features a photo of
the neighborhood of
the new address.
移転先付近の写真が印刷されている。

▼
Change-of-address notice
移転通知
USA 1991
CD,AD:Kathy Forsythe
D,P:Jane Cuthbertson
DF:Forsythe Design
CL:Forsythe Design
TC:Design Studio
デザイン

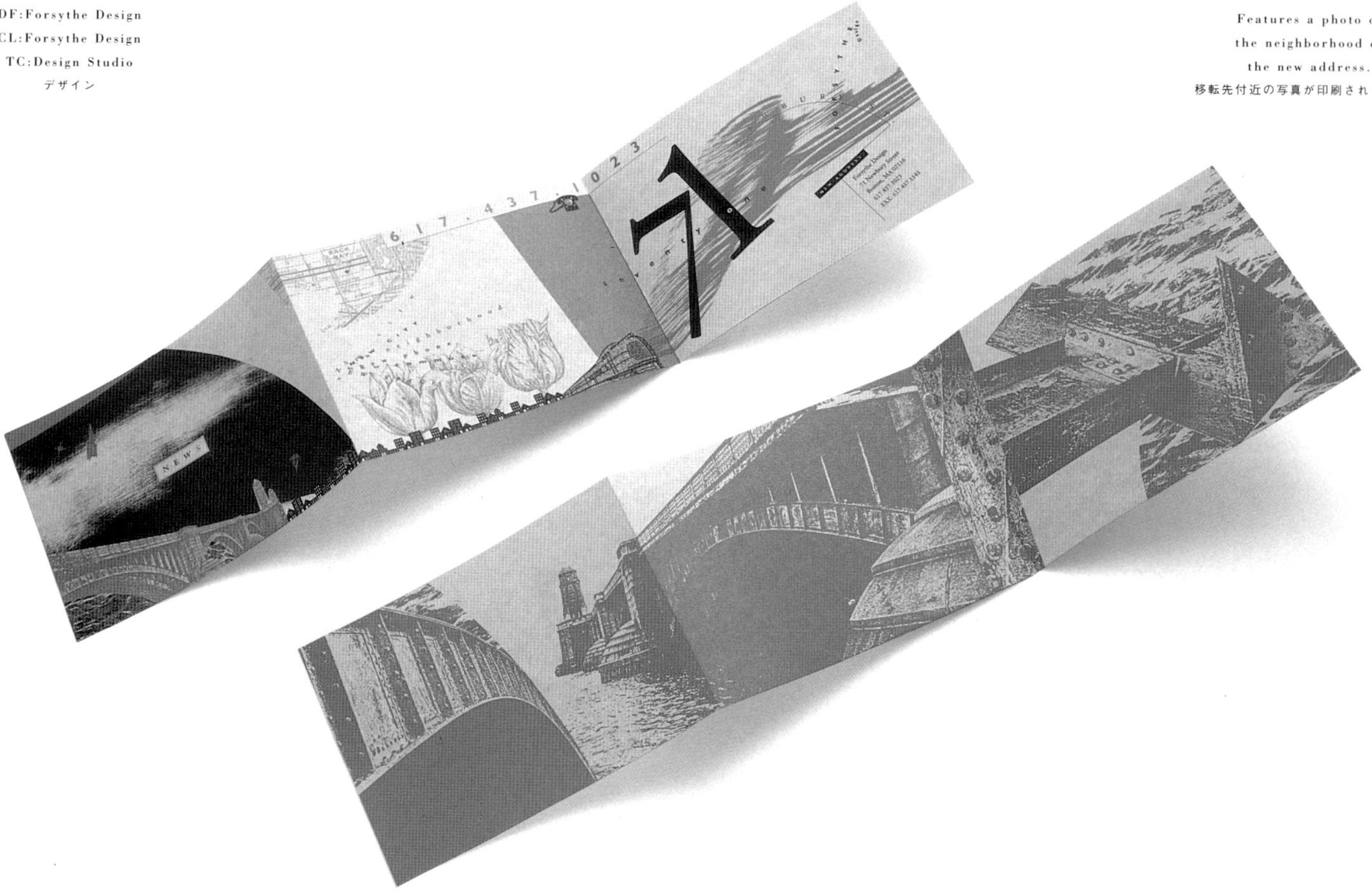

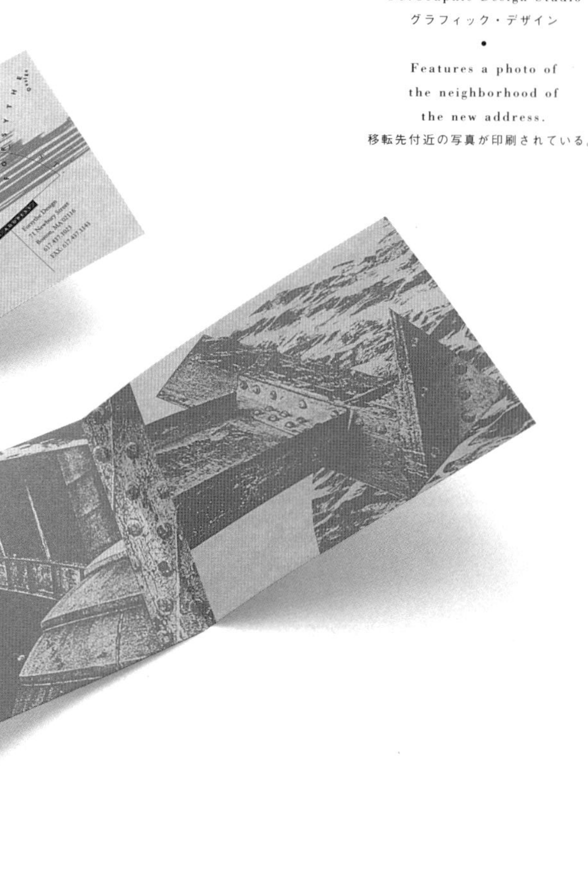

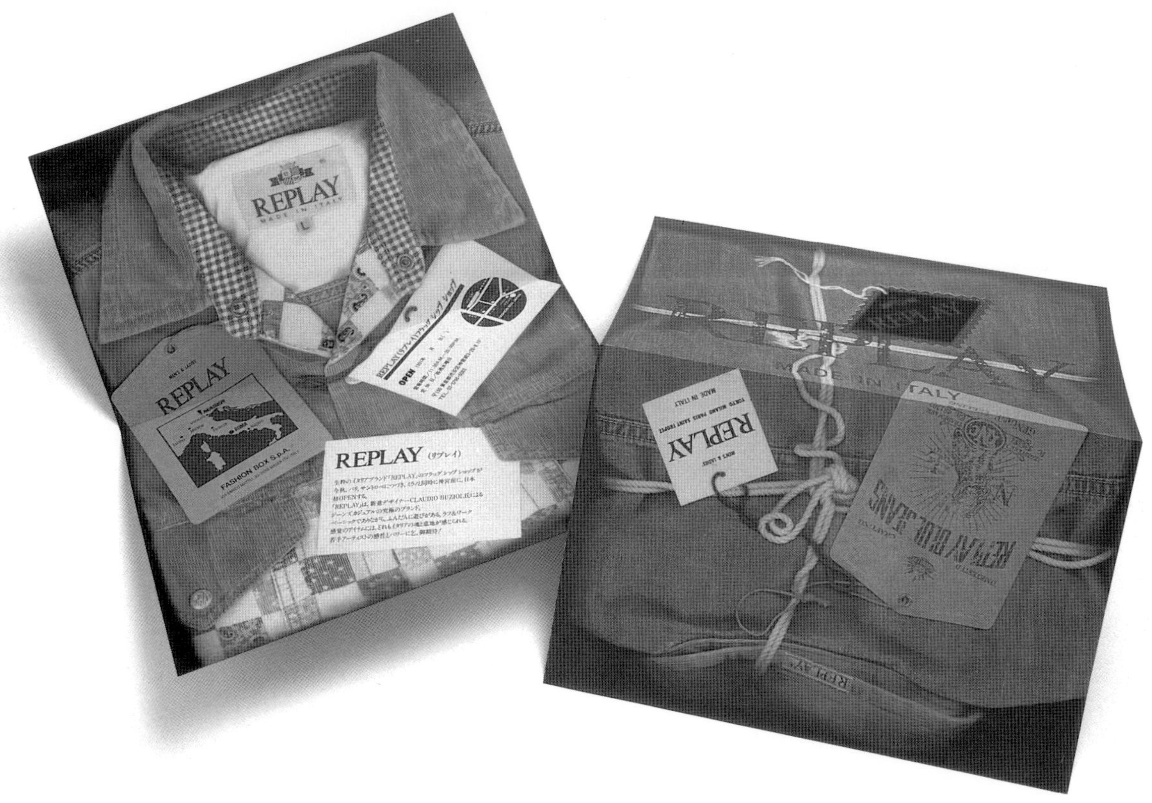

▲
Boutique opening announcement
ブティック開店案内状
JAPAN 1991
AD,D:Akira Utsumi
P,I:Lai-hai Chiang
CL:Fashion Box Japan
TC:Apparel Maker
アパレル

▼
New company announcement
会社設立案内状
JAPAN 1990
CD,AD:Miyuki Yoshida
D:Miyuki Yoshida
Koji Takamatsu
CL:Shitsunai Sobi
TC:Interior Construction
内装施工業

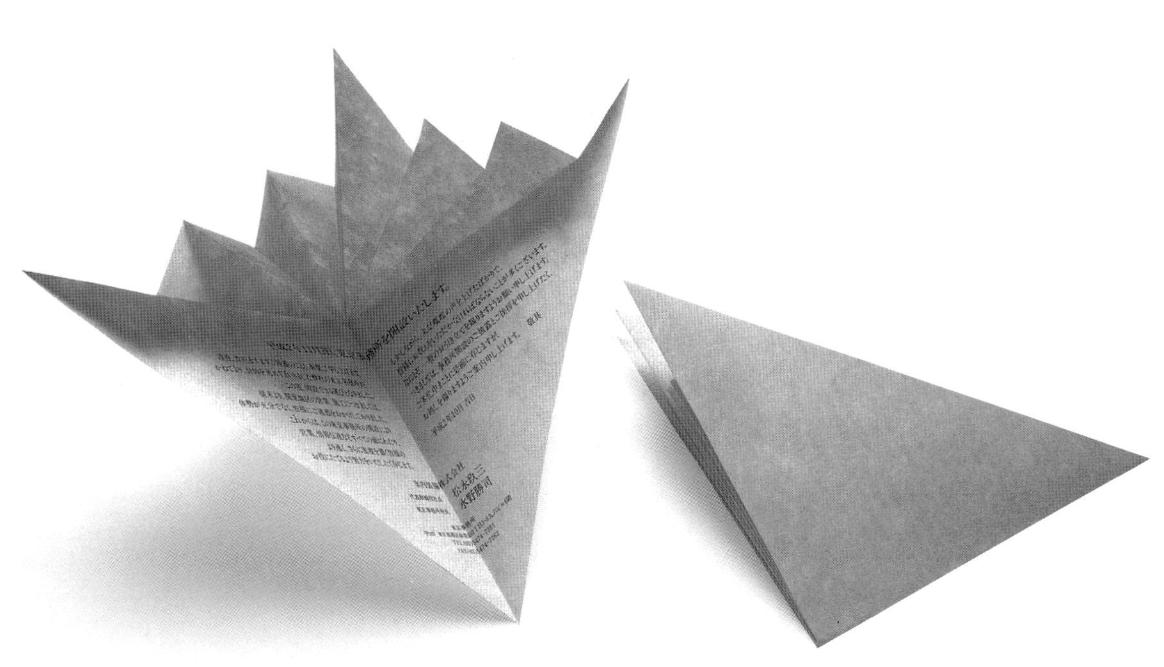

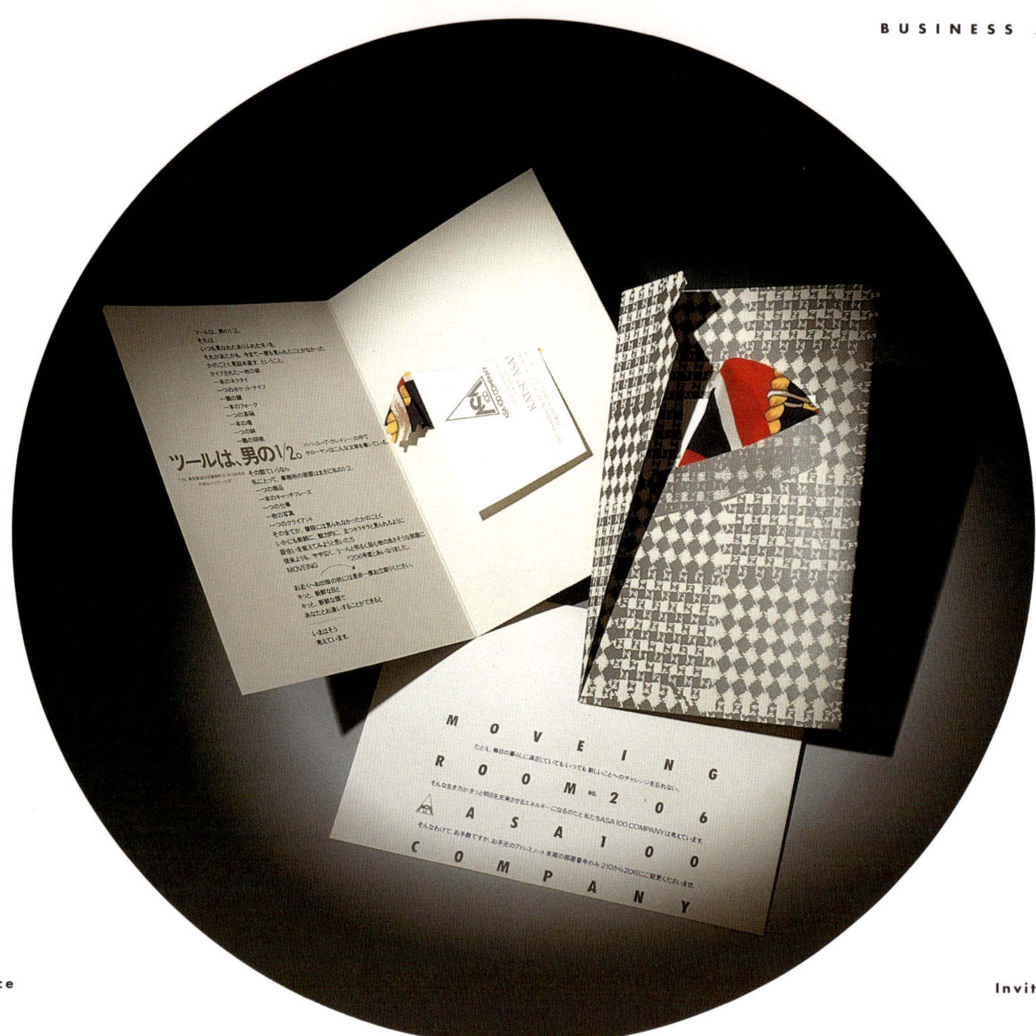

▲
Change-of-address notice
移転通知
JAPAN 1992
CD,AD,P,CW:Katsu Asano
D:Kinue Yonezawa
DF:ASA 100 Company
CL:ASA 100 Company
TC:Design Studio
デザイン

▼
Invitation to a disco opening
ディスコ・オープニング招待状
HOLLAND 1992
CD:T.Langenbach
D,I,DF:Limage Dangereuse
P:Bas Wilders
CL:Lightvessel
TC:Discothéque
ディスコ

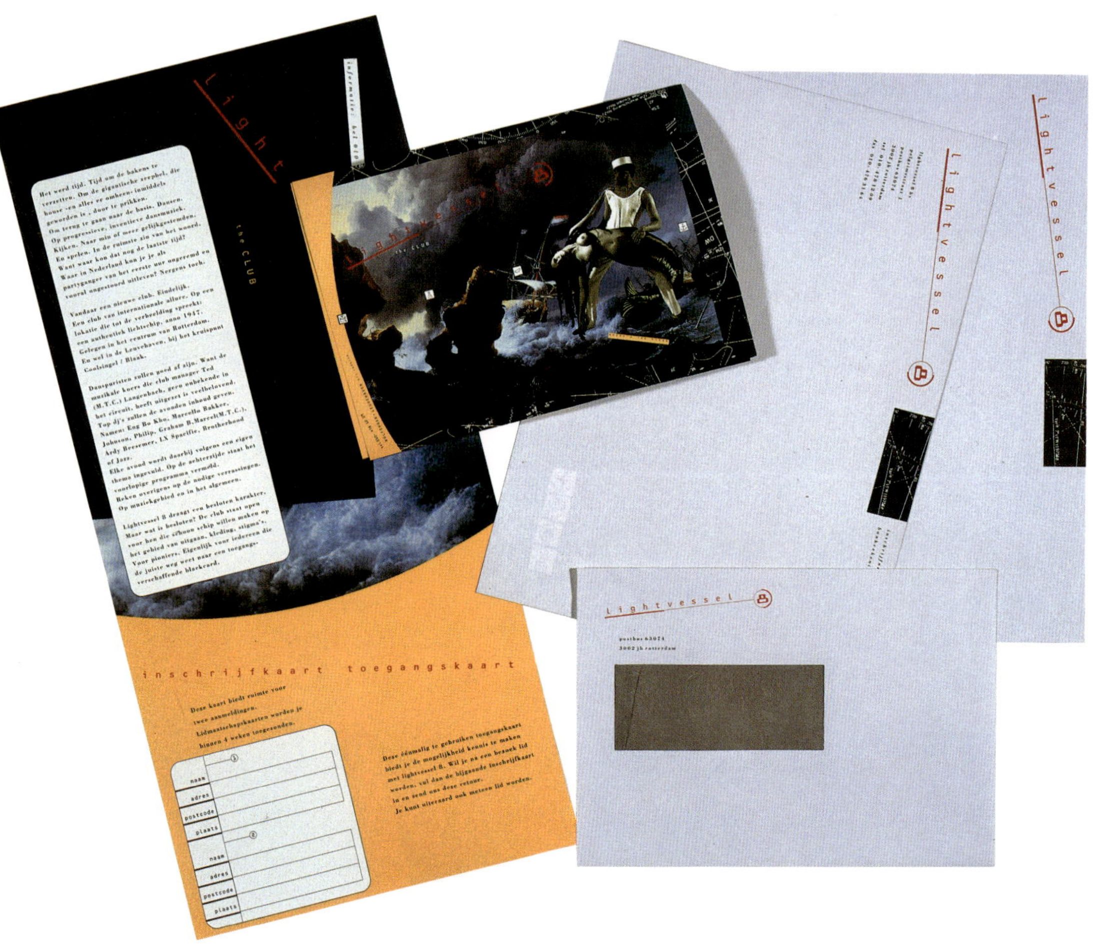

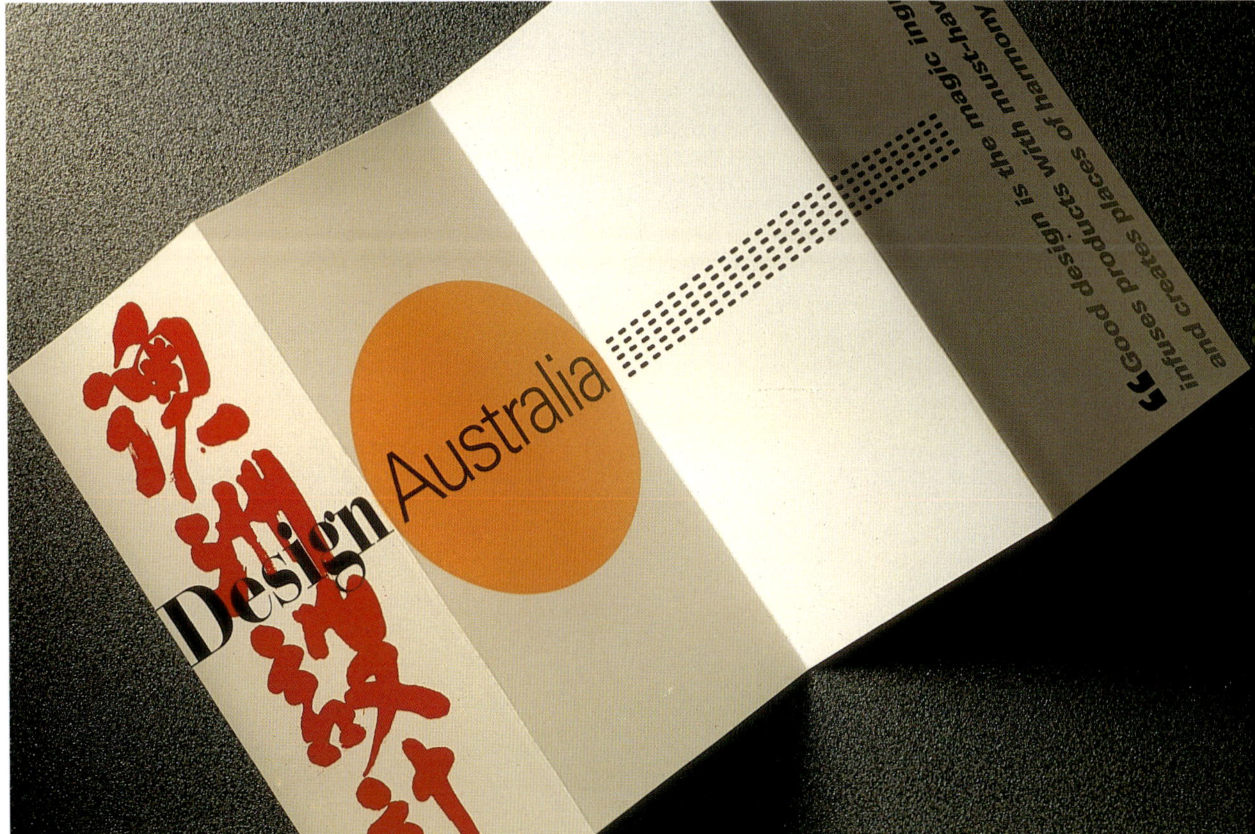

▶

Invitation to a new consortium opening
企業グループ発足式招待状
AUSTRALIA 1991
CD:Garry Emery
AD,D,DF:Emery Vincent Design
CL:Australian Design Services
TC:Design Consortium
デザイン・コンソルティウム（共同体）

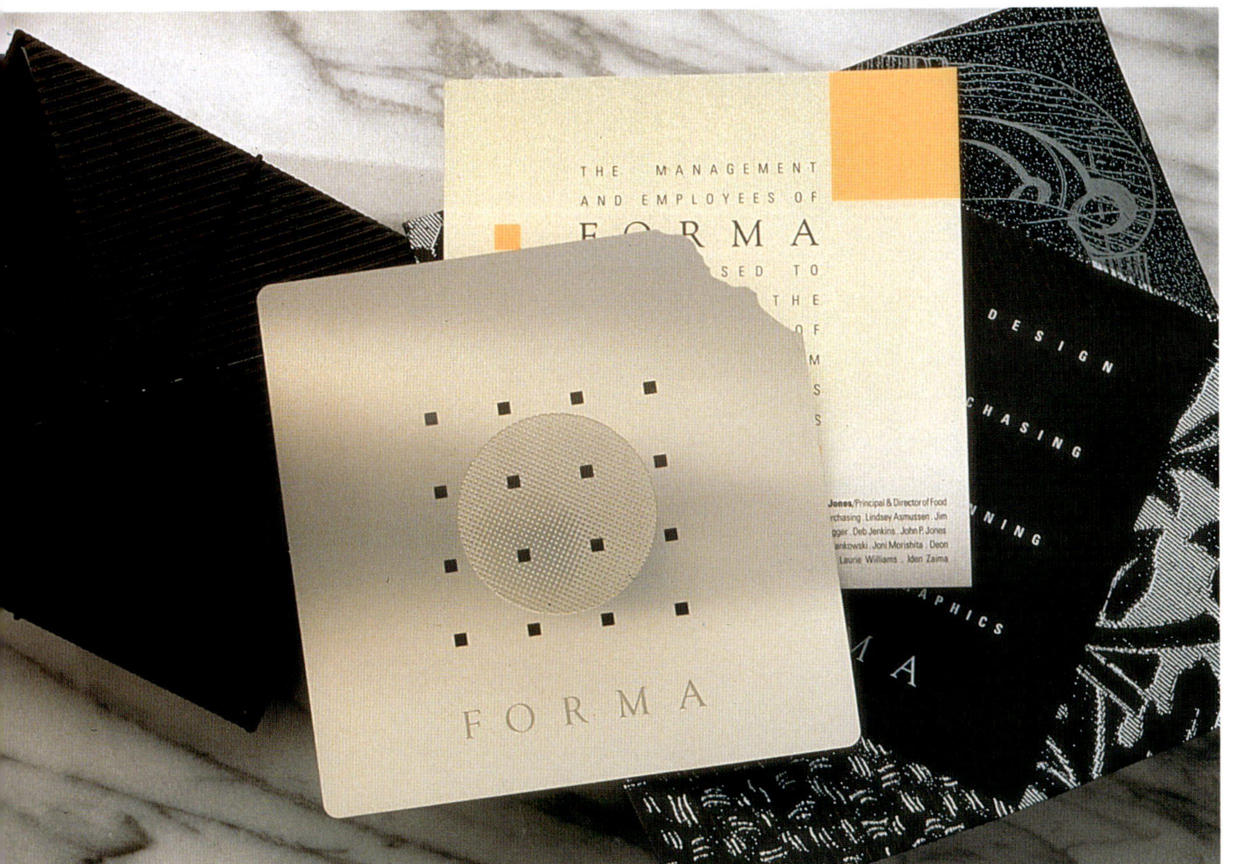

◀

Acquisition announcement
事業吸収通知
USA 1992
AD:John Hornall
D:John Hornall
David Bates
CW:Forma
DF:Hornall Anderson Design Works
CL:Forma
TC:Interior Material Supplier
内装材販売

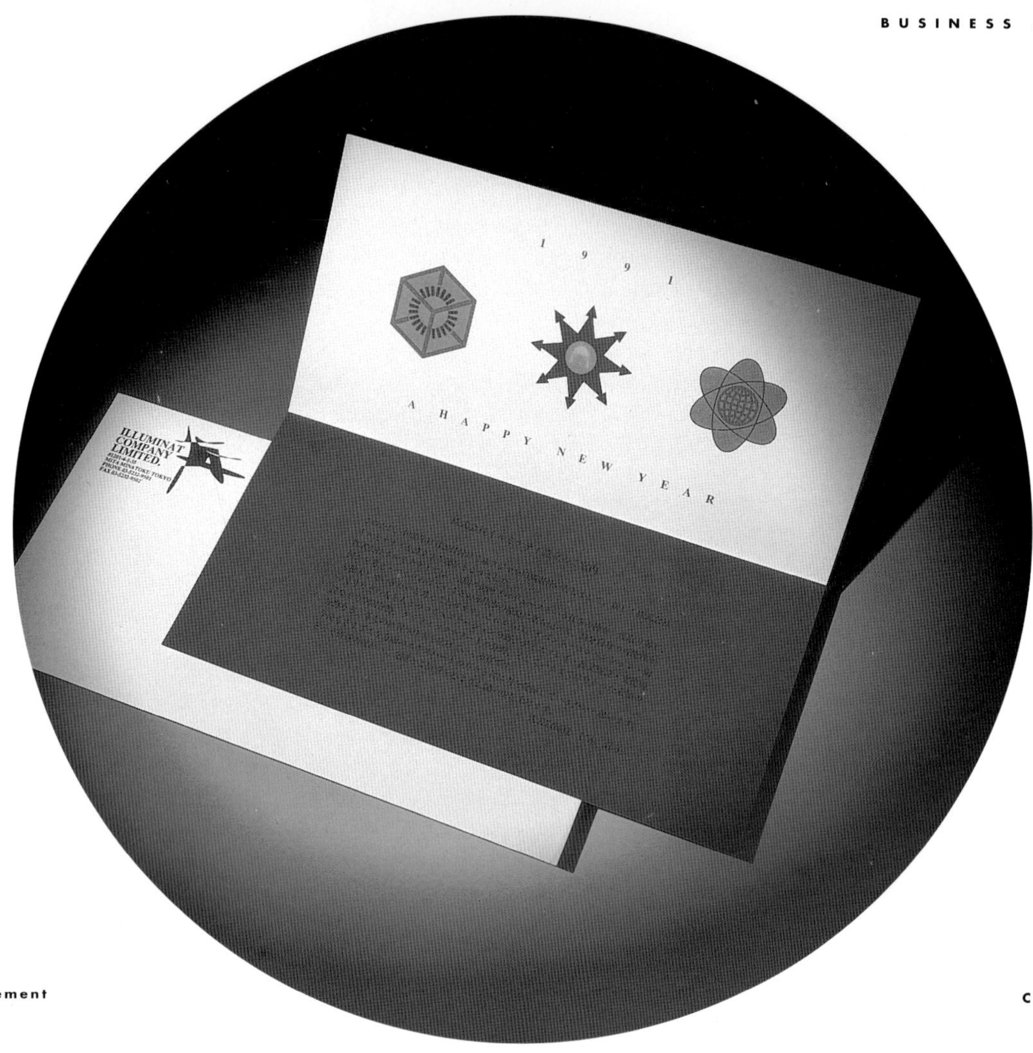

▲
New company announcement
会社設立案内状
JAPAN 1990
AD:Osamu Sato
D:Akio Kodaira
CL:Illuminat
TC:Commercial Display Design
空間プロデュース

▼
Change-of-address notice
移転通知
JAPAN 1992
AD,D,I:Hiroyuki Kurokawa
CL:Paragon
TC:TV Commercial Film Producer
TV-CF制作

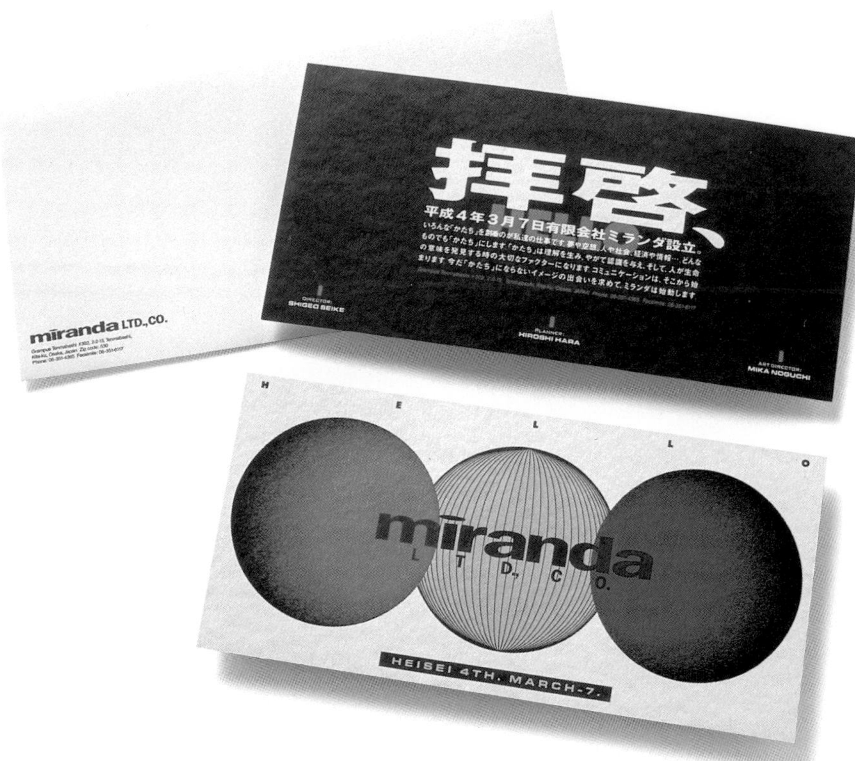

▲
New company announcement
会社設立案内状
JAPAN 1992
CD,CW:Hiroshi Hara
AD,D:Mika Noguchi
DF:miranda
CL:miranda
TC:Graphic Design Studio
グラフィック・デザイン

▼
New company announcement
会社設立案内状
JAPAN 1991
AD,D,P,I:Mieko Misawa
CW:Jun Takabatake
CL:Jungle Mom
TC:Graphic Design Studio
グラフィック・デザイン

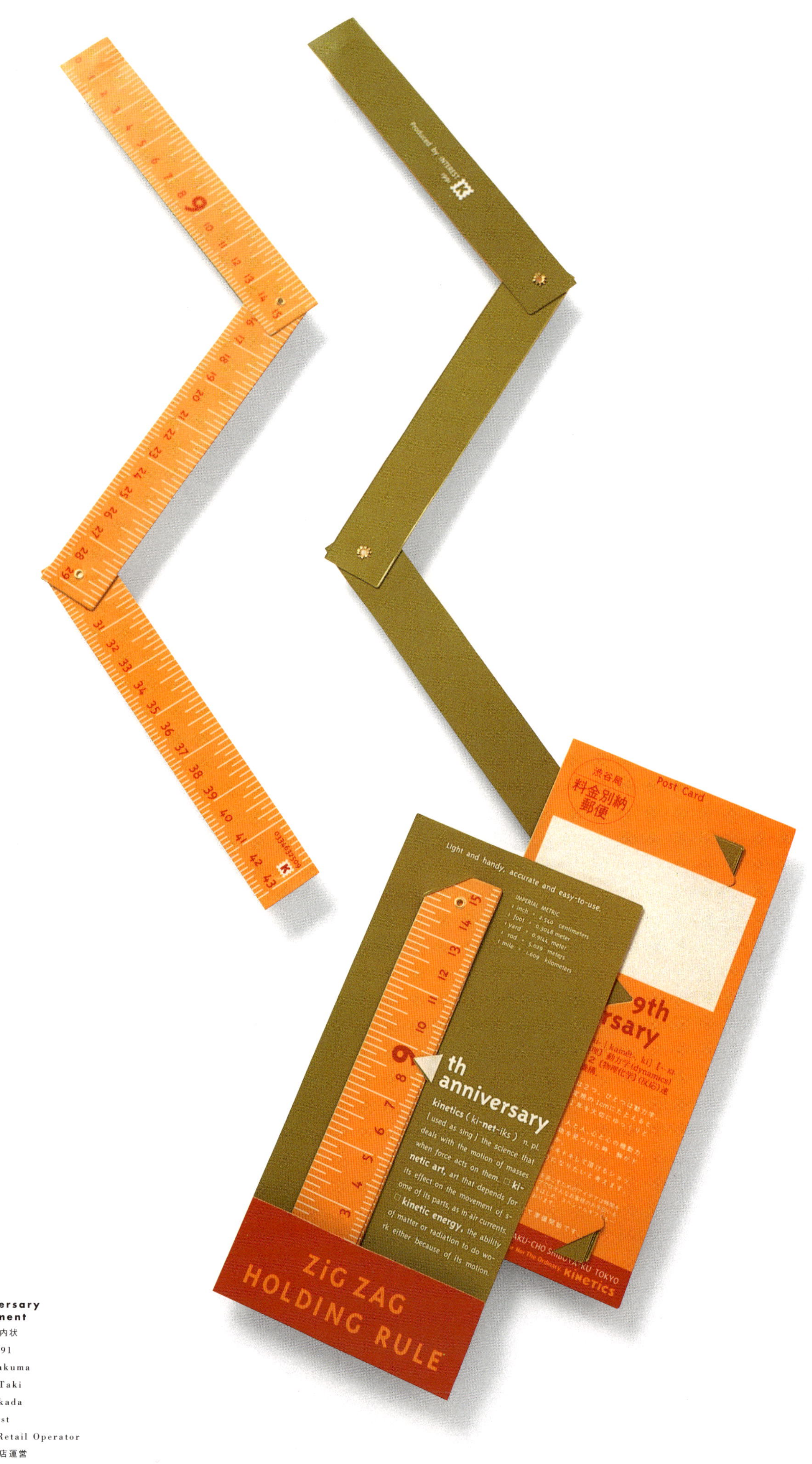

Ninth anniversary announcement
設立9周年案内状
JAPAN 1991
CD:Yukiko Sakuma
AD:Yukari Taki
D:Sumie Takada
CL:Interest
TC:Product Planning,Retail Operator
商品企画、小売店運営

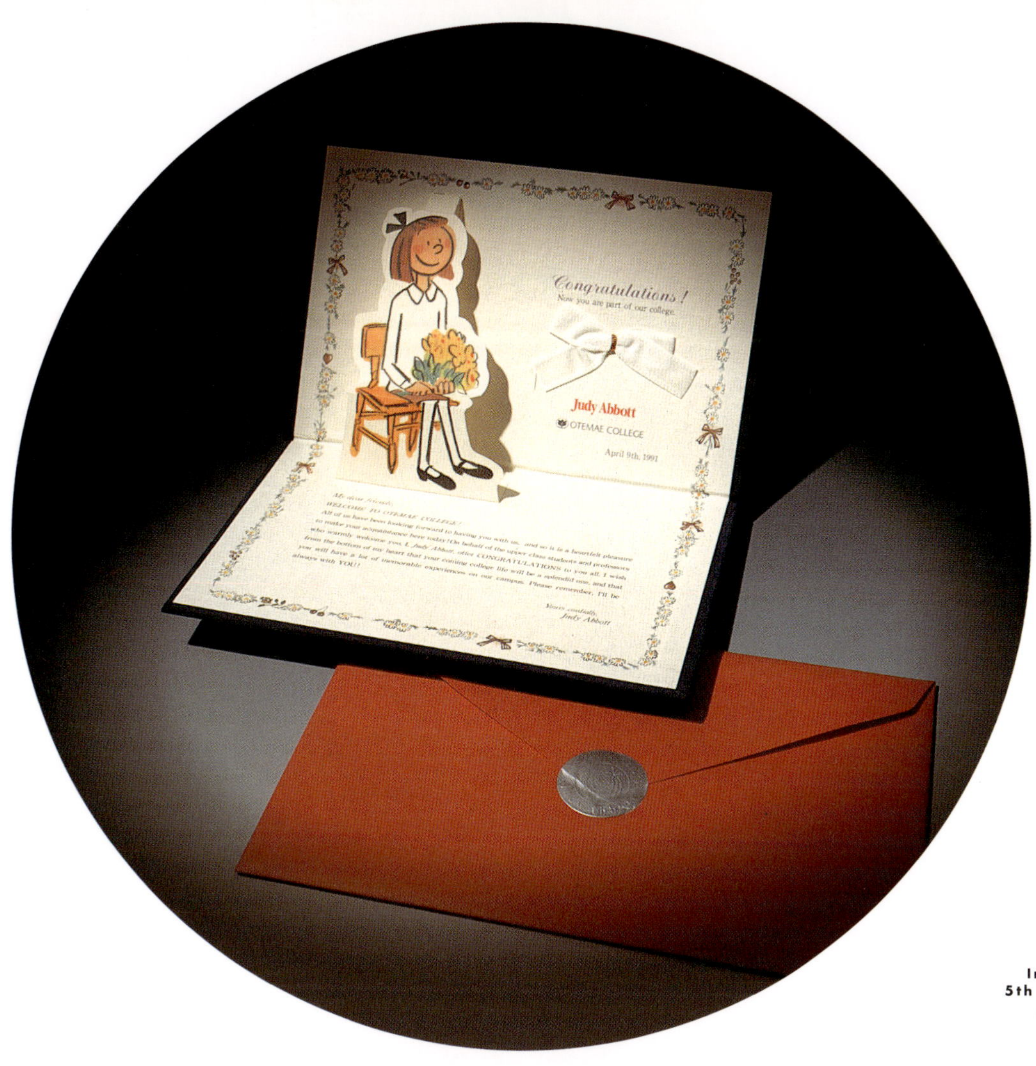

▲
Welcome-to-school card
入学記念カード
JAPAN 1991
CD:Akihide Ogahara
AD:Kohji Yamamoto
D:Hideo Shimohara
I:Asako Nakase
CW:Eiko Okada
CL:Otemae College
TC:School
学校

▼
Invitation to a Dockers 5th anniversary celebration
ドッカーズ5周年記念式典招待状
USA 1992
CD,AD,D:Bruce Yelaska
DF:Bruce Yelaska Design
CL:Levi Strauss
TC:Apparel Maker
アパレル

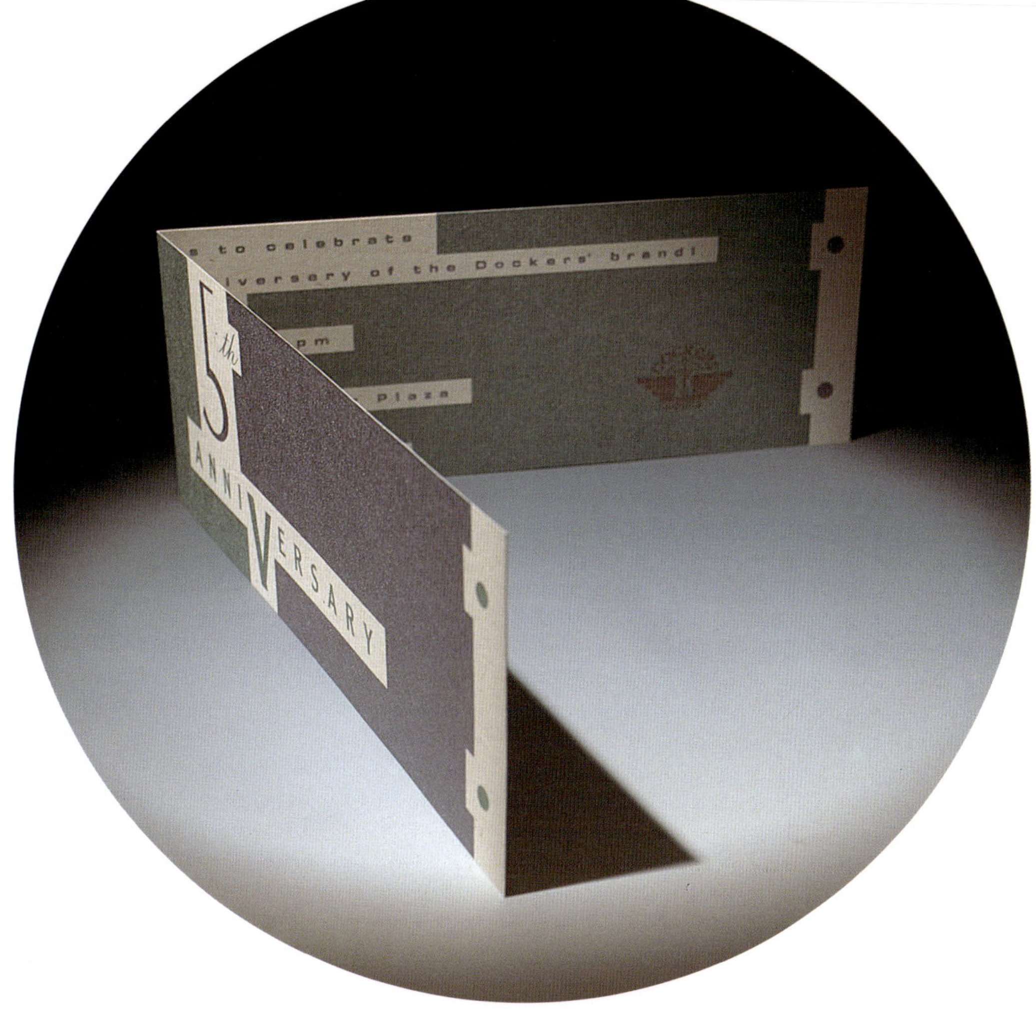

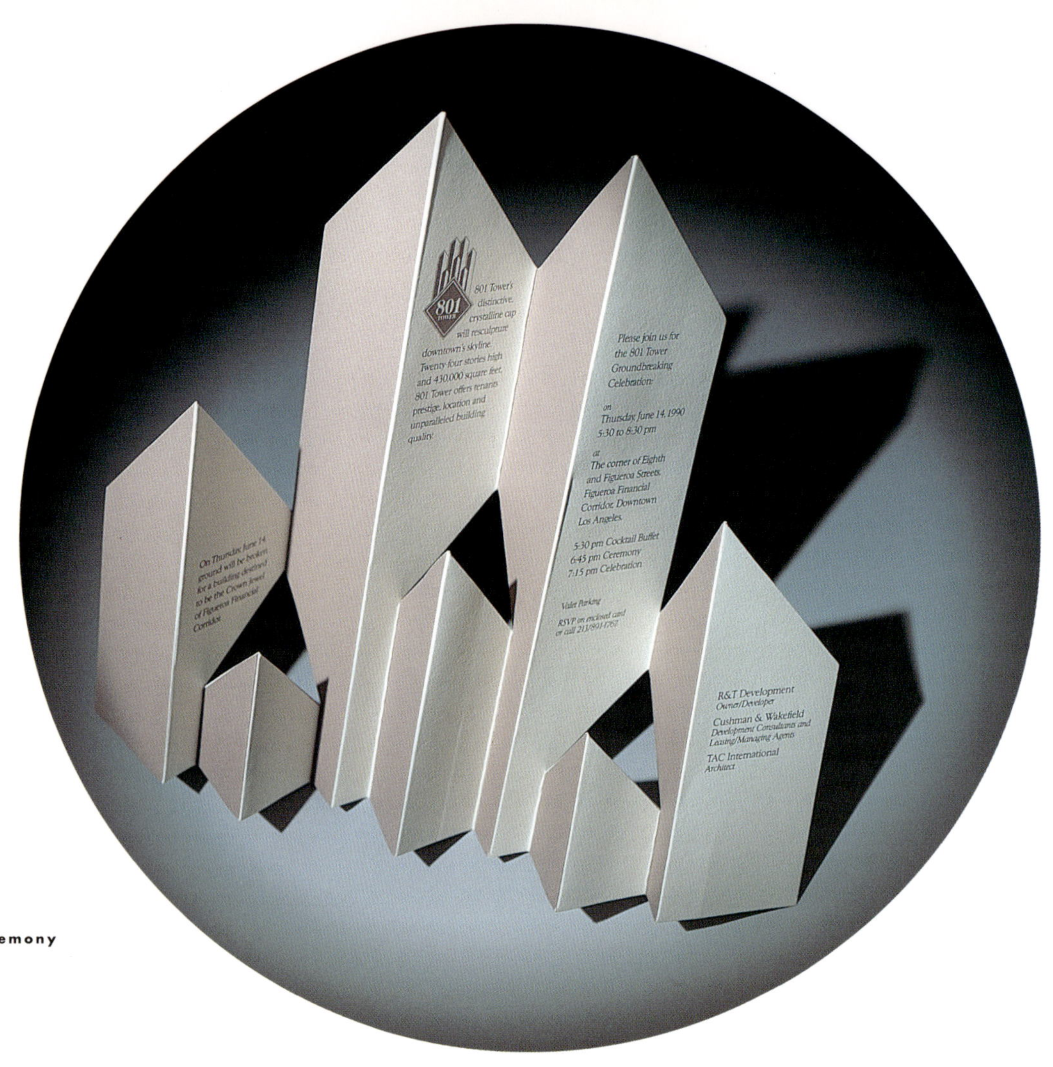

▲
Invitation to a ground-breaking ceremony
起工式招待状
USA 1990
AD:Noel Davies
D:Meredith Kamm
Cathy Tetef-Davies
DF:Davies Associates
CL:R+T Development
TC:Real Estate Developer
不動産開発

Player of the Year Nominations for 1990/91
14
Premier Division — Motherwell, Celtic, Rangers, Rangers
Young Player — Celtic, Aberdeen, Rangers, Rangers
First Division — Raith Rovers, Dundee, Partick Thistle, Falkirk
Second Division — Stirling Albion, Stirling Albion, Berwick Rangers, Berwick Rangers
IRN-BRU
GMB
Scottish Professional Footballers' Association
14th Annual Presentation Dinner
The IRN-BRU Players of the Year Awards 1990/91
THE HOSPITALITY INN, GLASGOW
SUNDAY 19TH MAY 1991

▼
Invitation to the Professional Football Association Players of the Year awards event
プロ・フットボール
年間最優秀選手賞授与式招待状
ENGLAND 1991
AD,I:Paul Khera
D:Paul Khera
Maria Beddoes
CL:Shilland
TC:Marketing Service
マーケティング

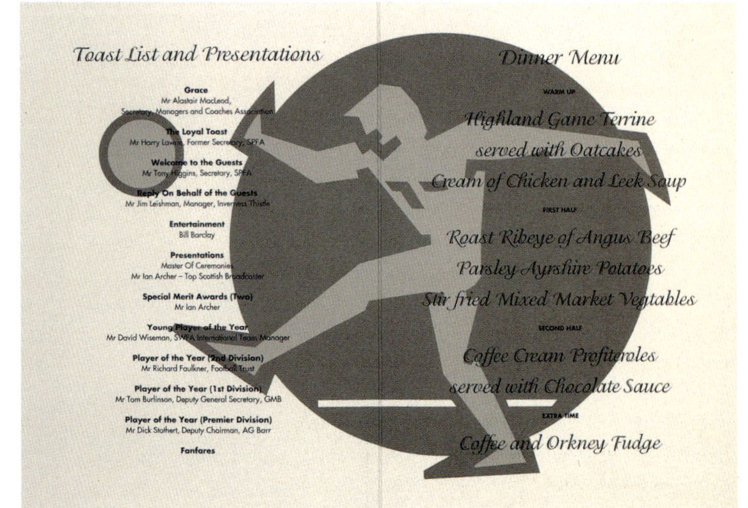
Toast List and Presentations

Grace
Mr Alastair MacLeod, Secretary, Managers and Coaches Association
The Loyal Toast
Mr Harry Lawrie, Former Secretary, SPFA
Welcome to the Guests
Mr Tony Higgins, Secretary, SPFA
Reply On Behalf of the Guests
Mr Jim Leishman, Manager, Inverness Thistle
Entertainment
Bill Barclay
Presentations
Master Of Ceremonies
Mr Ian Archer – Top Scottish Broadcaster
Special Merit Awards (Two)
Mr Ian Archer
Young Player of the Year
Mr David Wiseman, SWFA International Team Manager
Player of the Year (2nd Division)
Mr Richard Faulkner, Football Trust
Player of the Year (1st Division)
Mr Tom Burlinson, Deputy General Secretary, GMB
Player of the Year (Premier Division)
Mr Dick Stothert, Deputy Chairman, AG Barr
Fanfares

Dinner Menu

WARM UP
Highland Game Terrine served with Oatcakes
Cream of Chicken and Leek Soup
FIRST HALF
Roast Ribeye of Angus Beef
Parsley Ayrshire Potatoes
Stir fried Mixed Market Vegtables
SECOND HALF
Coffee Cream Profiteroles served with Chocolate Sauce
EXTRA TIME
Coffee and Orkney Fudge

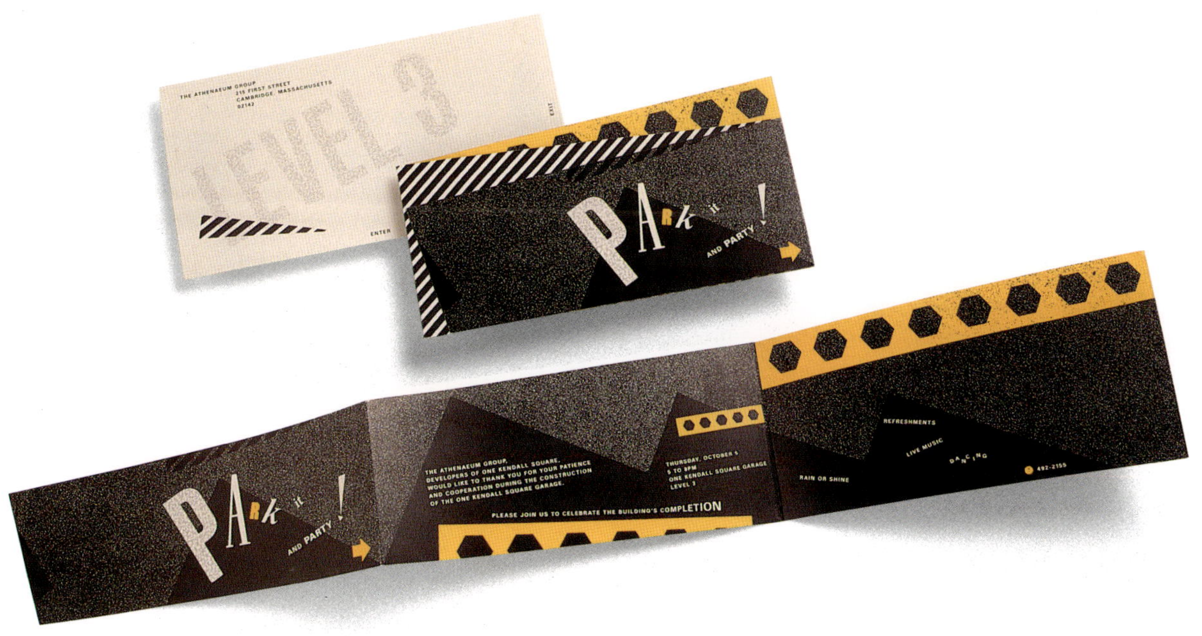

▲
Invitation to a building completion party
ビル完成記念パーティー招待状
USA 1989
CD:Kathy Forsythe
D:Julie Steinhilber
DF:Forsythe Design
CL:The Athenaem Group
TC:Real Estate Agency
不動産

▼
Invitation to a ground-breaking ceremony
起工式招待状
USA 1990
AD:Rebeca Mendez
D:Sze Tsung Leong
DF:Art Center College of Design. Design Office
CL:Art Center College of Design
TC:Art College
美術大学

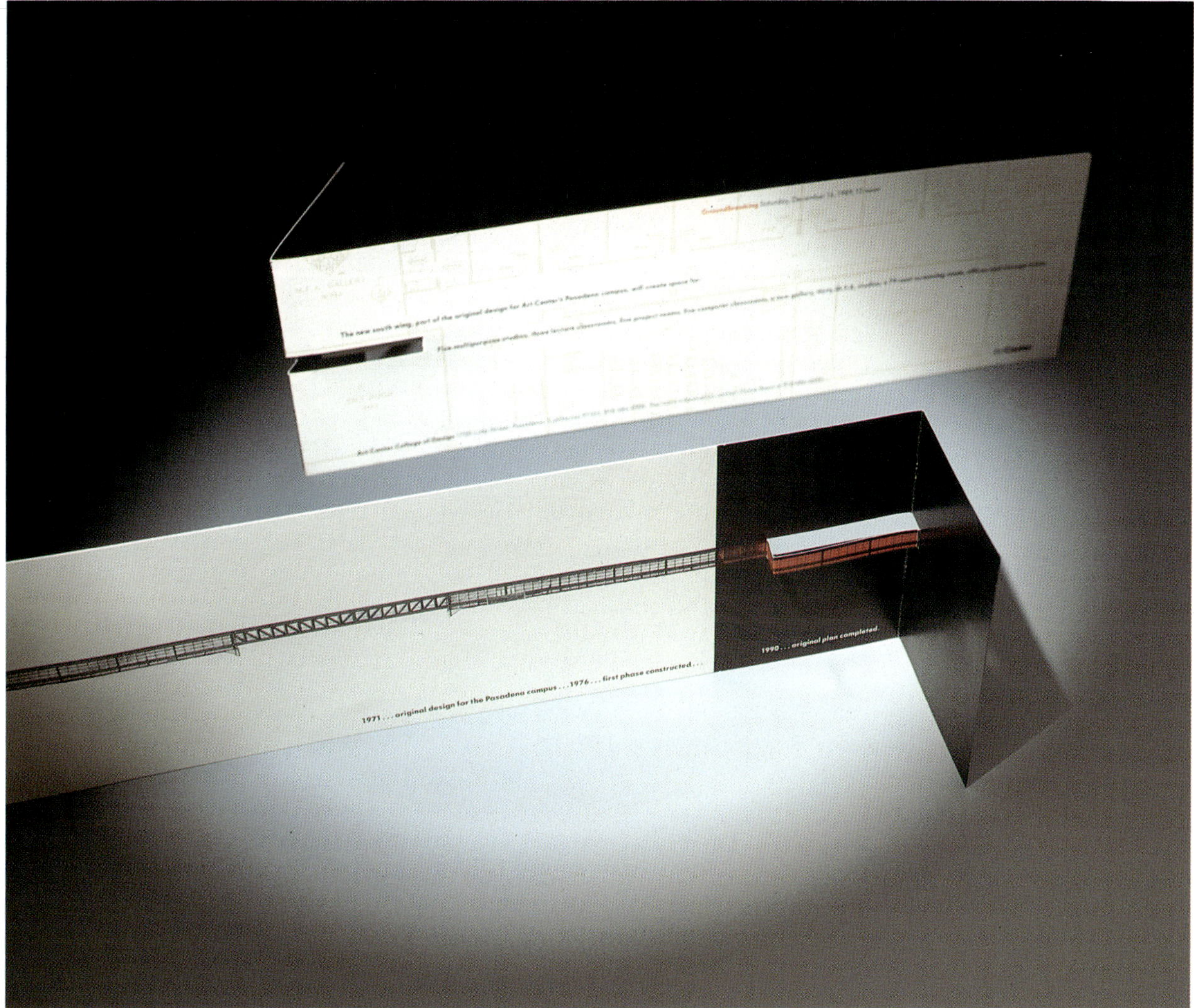

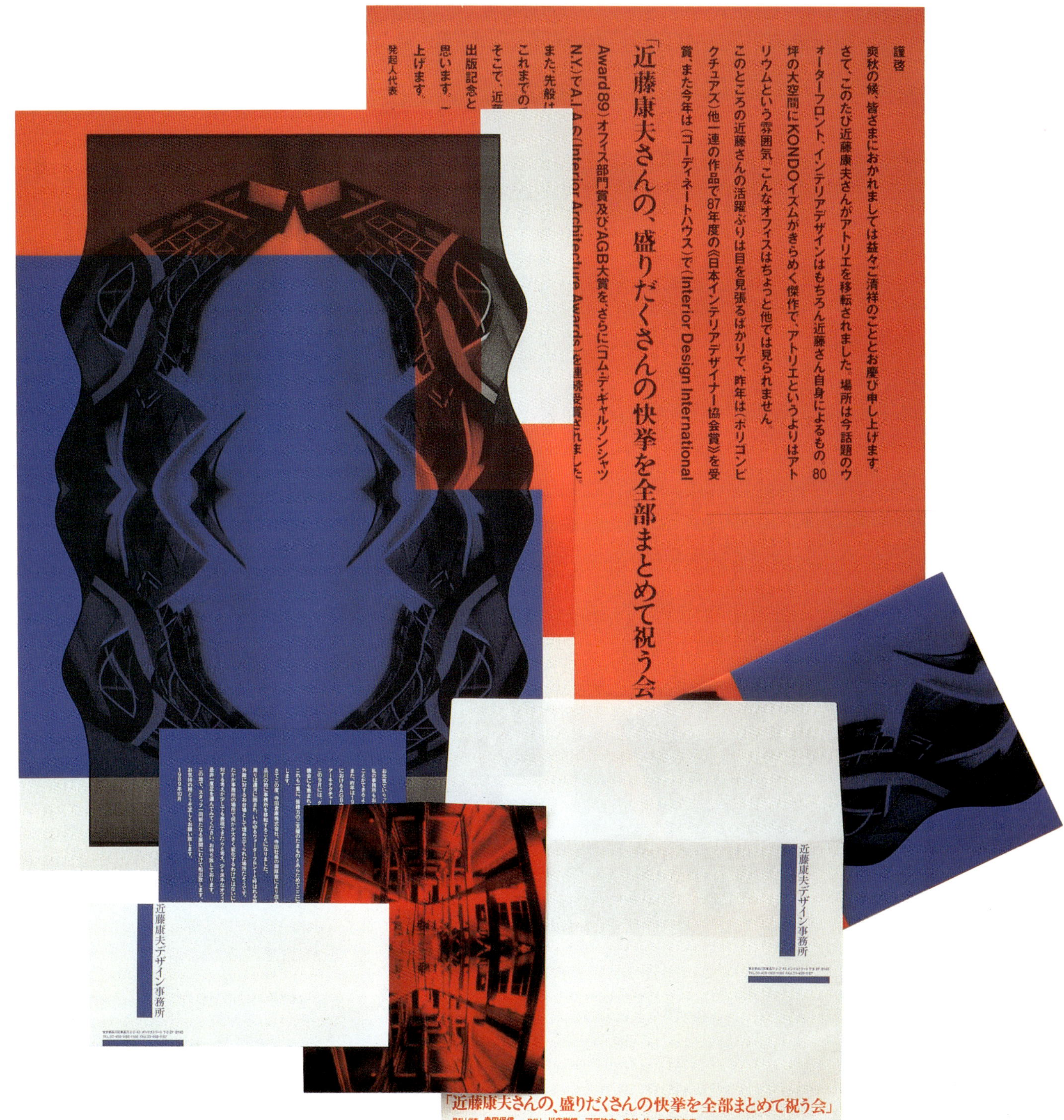

Invitation to
an award celebration
授賞祝賀会招待状
JAPAN 1989
AD,D:Motoko Naruse
CL:Kondo Yasuo Design Office
TC:Interior Design
インテリア・デザイン

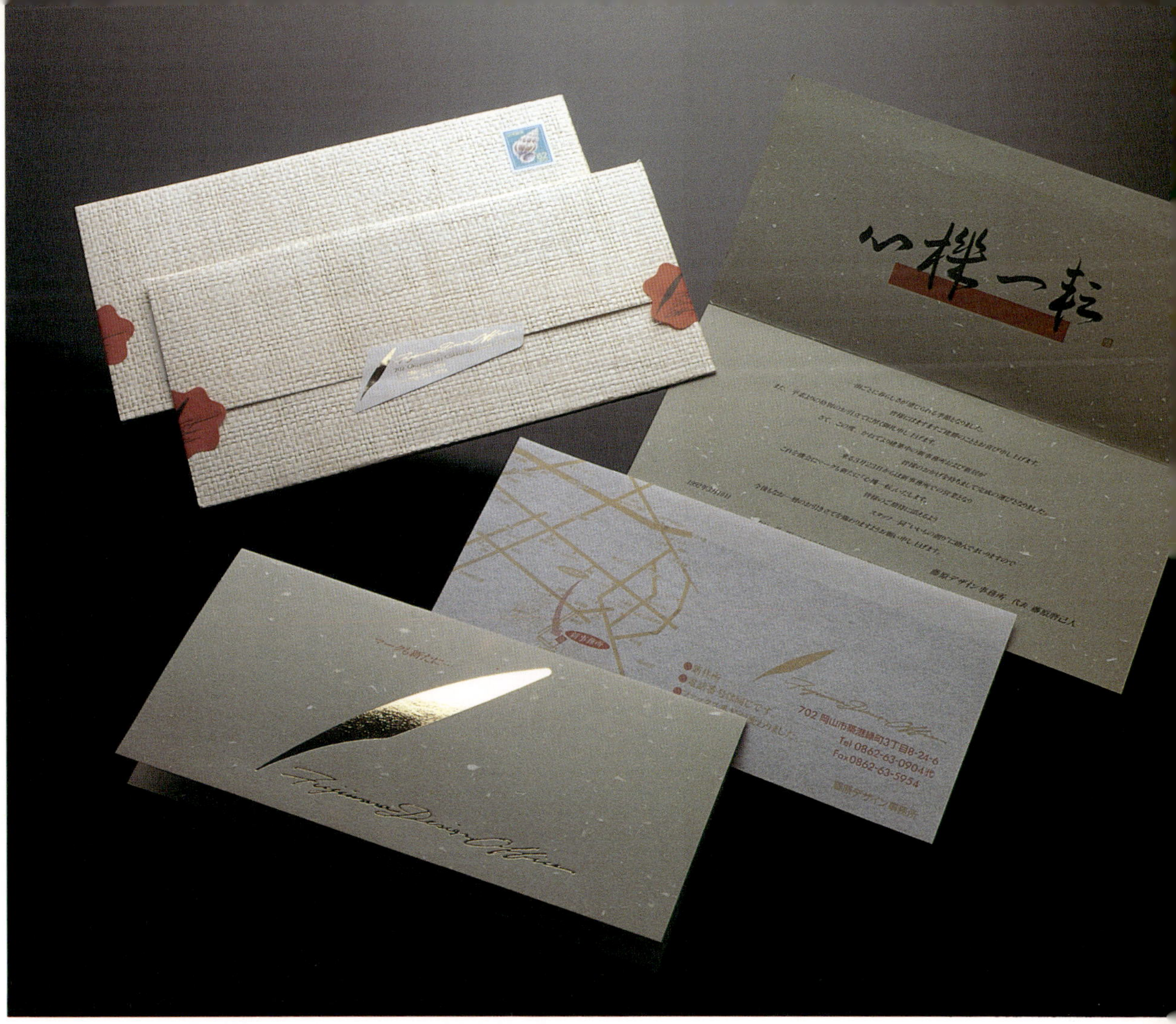

▶

Change-of-address notice

移転通知

JAPAN 1992

CD,AD,D:Makoto Fujiwara

CW:Yoshiko Shimomura

CL:Fujiwara Design Office

TC:Graphic Design Studio

グラフィック・デザイン

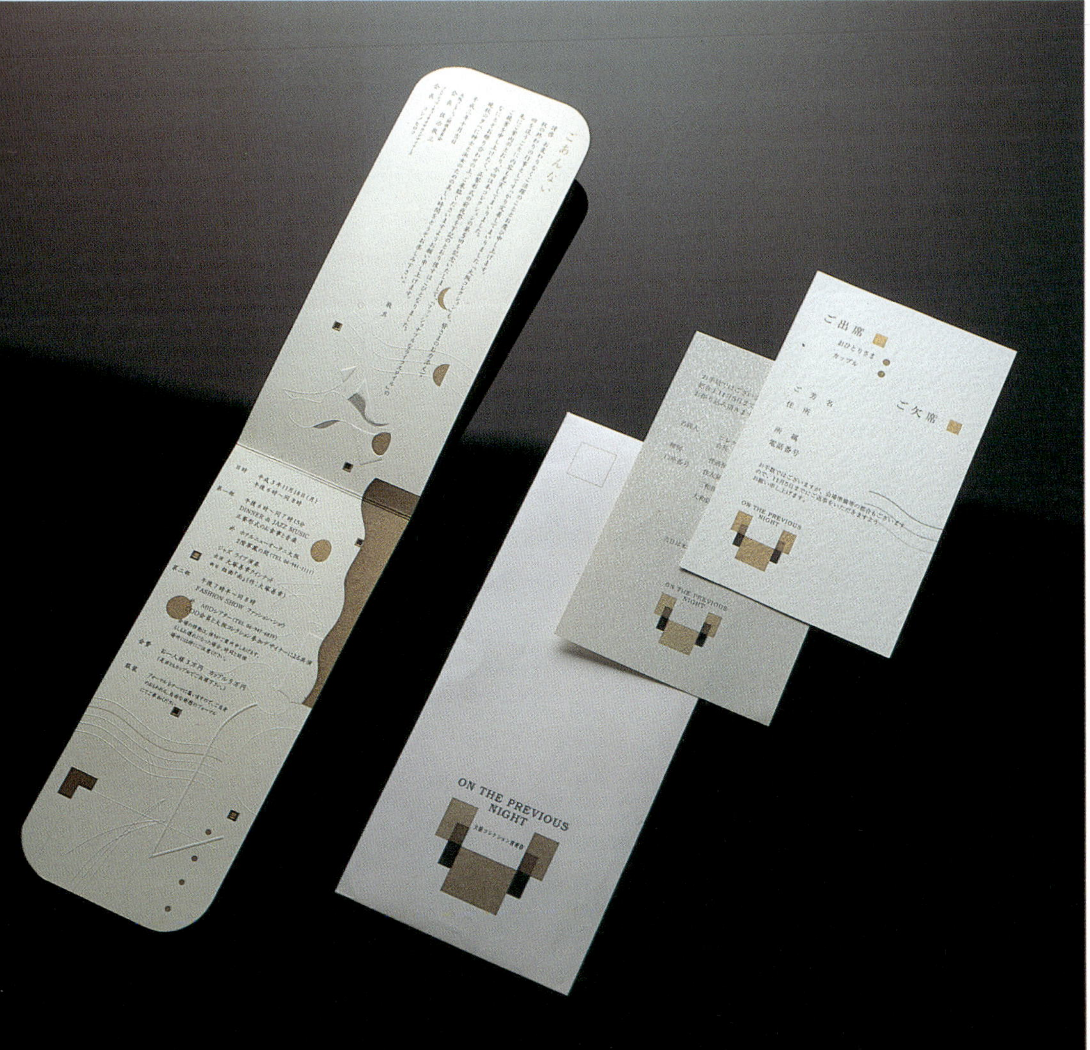

◀

Invitation to the Osaka Collection eve party

大阪コレクション前夜祭招待状

JAPAN 1991

CD:Masaaki Orime

AD:Masayuki Shimizu

D:Masayuki Shimizu

Nio Kimura

DF:Heter-O-Doxy Protprast

CL:Osaka Collection

Organizing Committee

TC:Event Planning Committee

イベント開催委員会

▶
Invitation to a Marty Awards event
マーティ賞授与式招待状
USA 1990
CD,AD:Richard Seireeni
D:Romane Cameron
P:Geoff Kern
DF:Studio Seireeni
CL:California Mart
TC:Apparel Retailer
アパレル

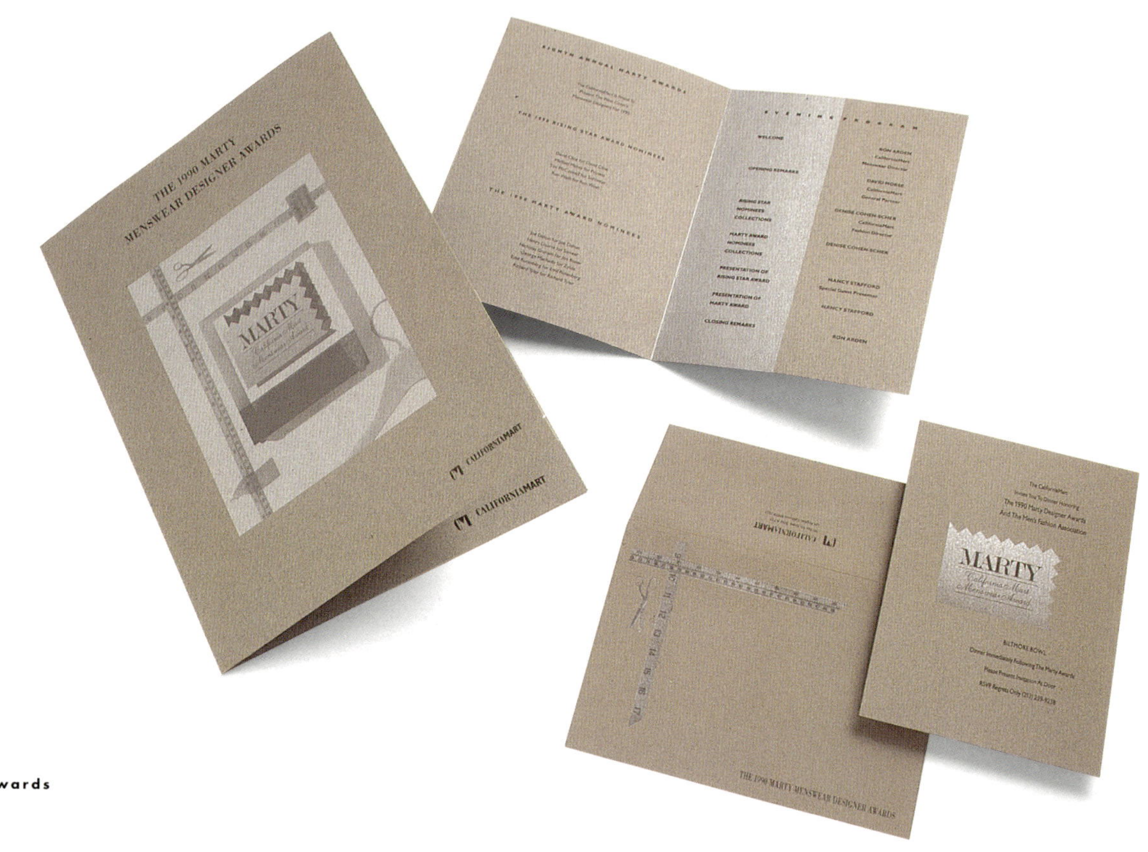

▼
Invitation to the Eddy awards ceremony
エディー賞授与式招待状
USA 1991
CD,AD:Mitchell Mauk
D:Lucia Matioli
P:Carol Droebek
DF:Mauk Design
CL:MacUser Magazine
TC:Magazine Publisher
雑誌出版

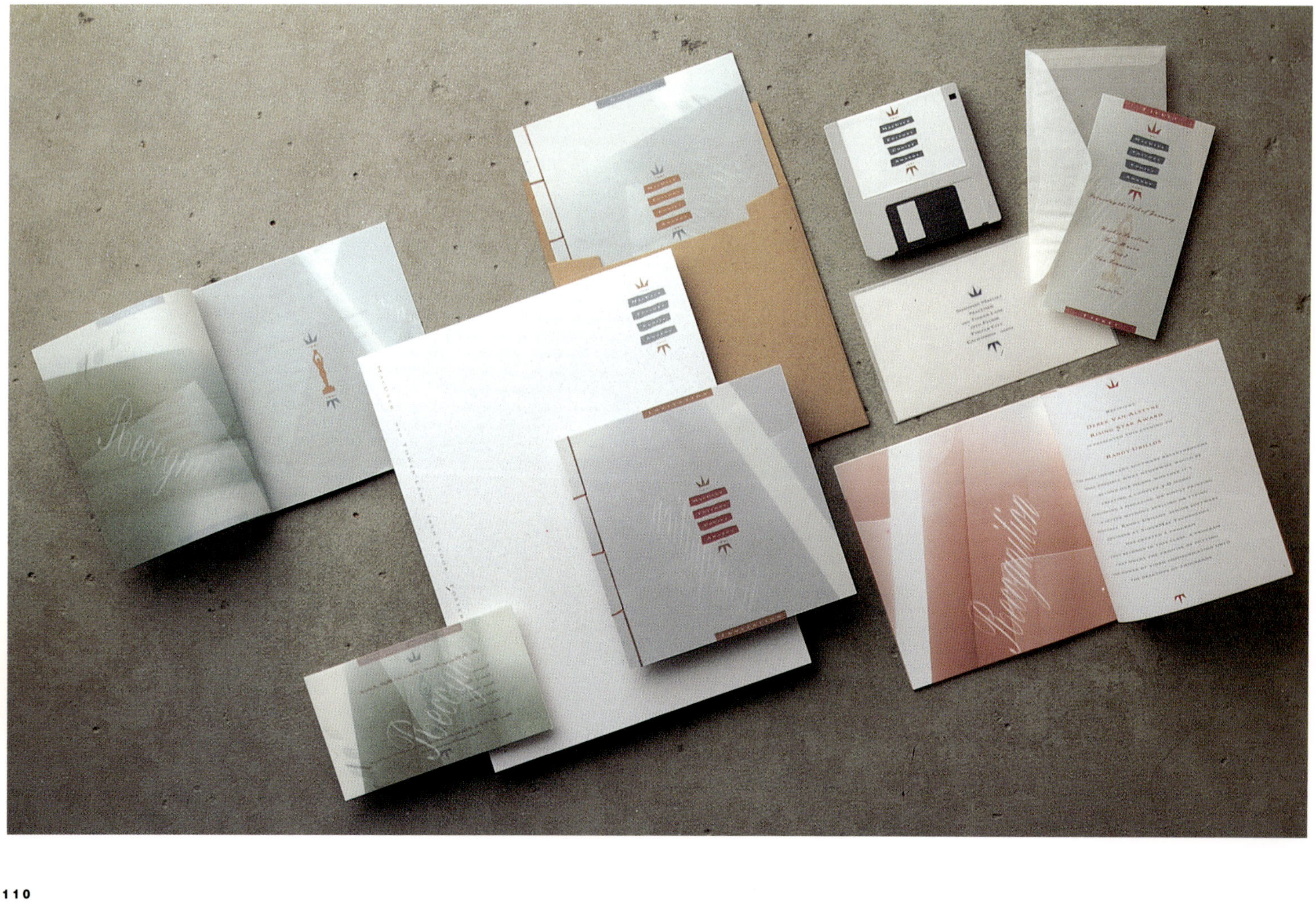

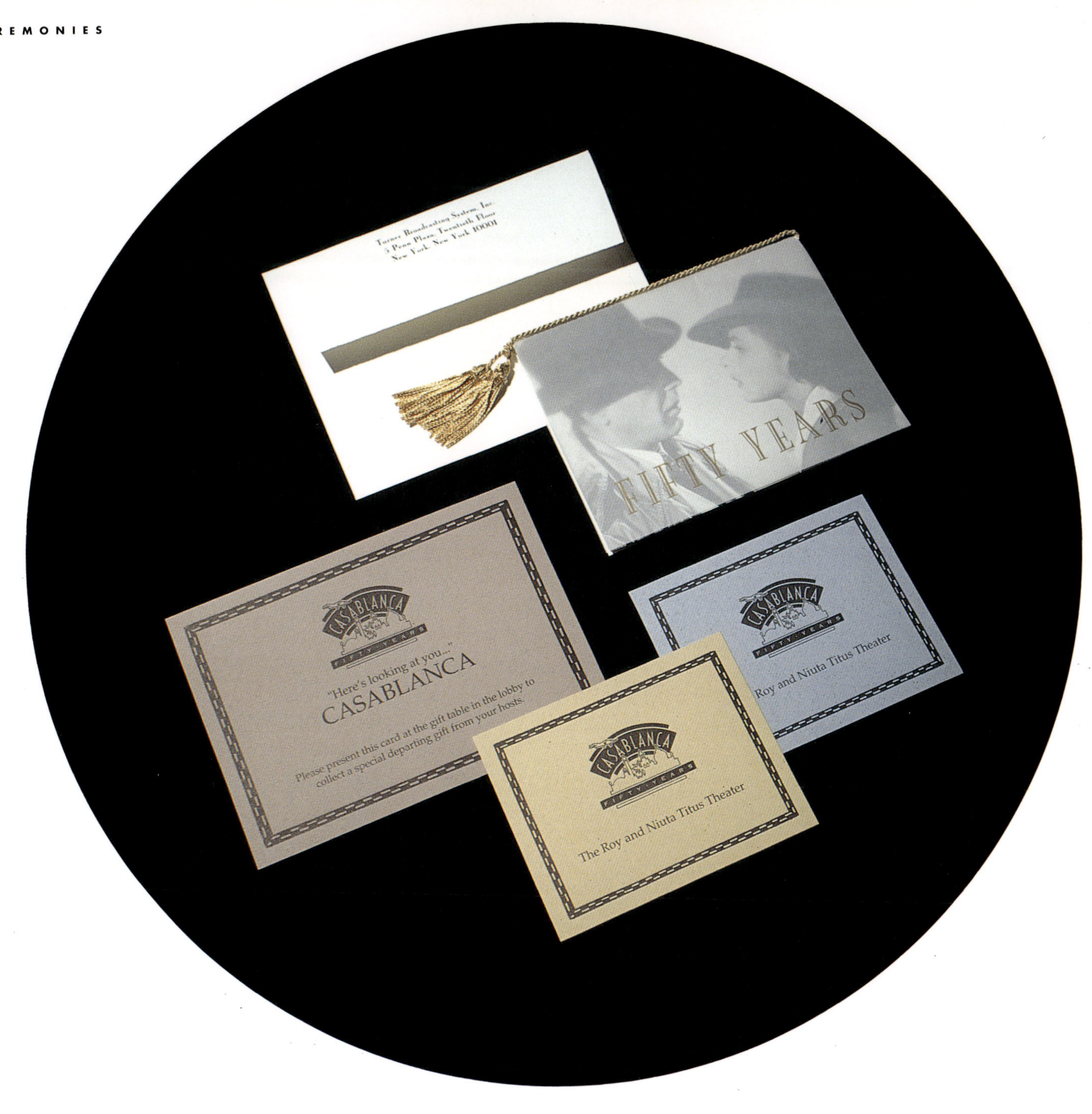

Invitation to a 50th anniversary screening of Casablanca

カサブランカ50周年記念上映会招待状

USA 1992

CD:Joe Swaney

D,I:Tracy Sabin

DF:Sabin Design

CL:Turner Broadcasting System

TC:Film and Video Media

映画、ビデオ・メディア

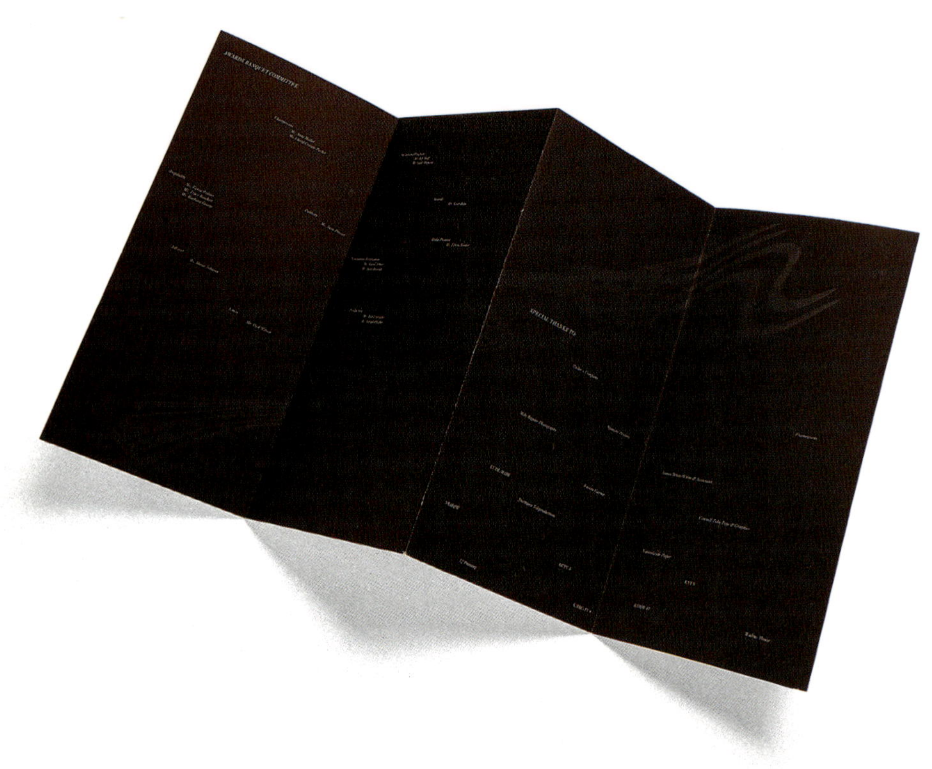

Invitation to an awards event
アワード・イベント招待状
USA 1990
CD:John Muller
D:Jane Weeks
P:Mike Regnier
CW:David Marks
DF:Muller
CL:Kansas City Media Professionals
TC:Organization of Media Buyers
広告主団体

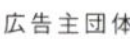

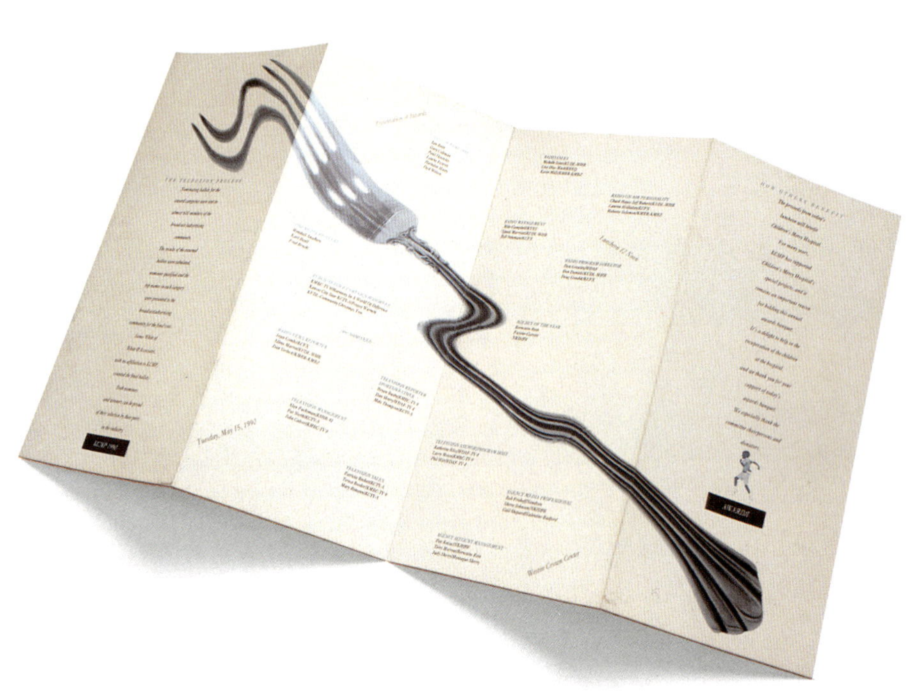

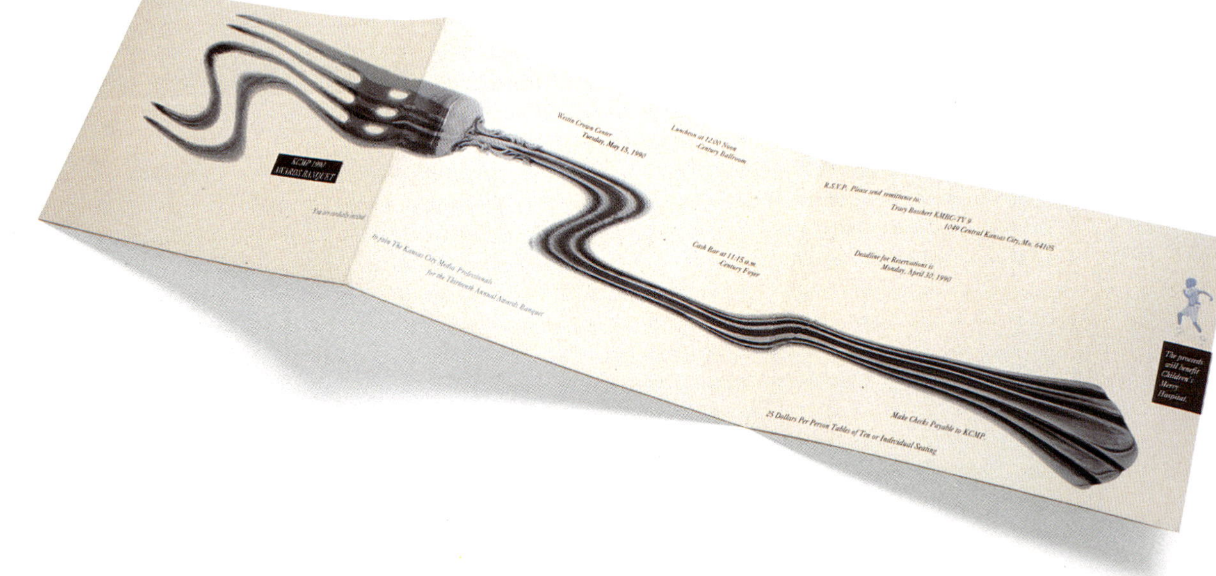

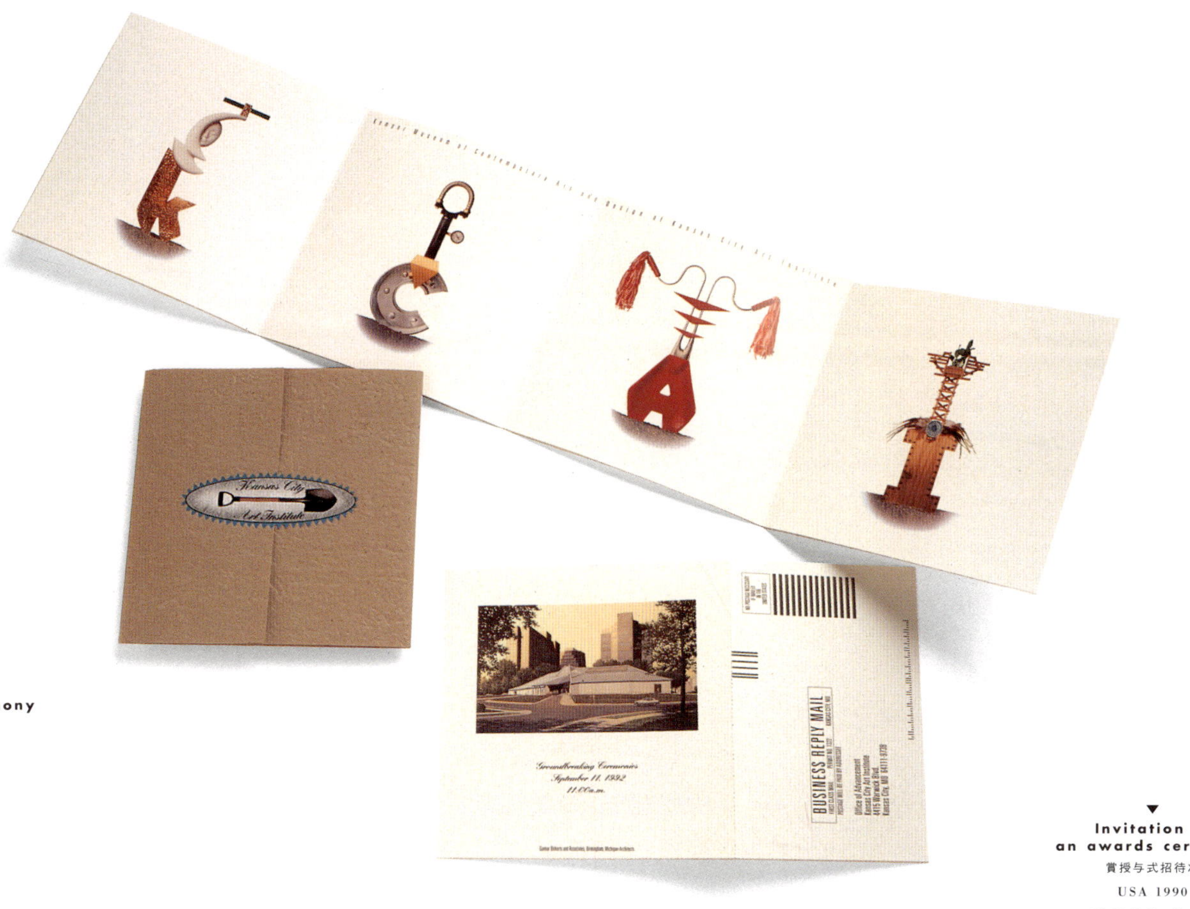

▲
Invitation to
a ground-breaking ceremony
起工式招待状
USA 1992
AD,D:Sal Costello
P:Steve Curtis
I:Sal Costello
David Schultz
Craig Bissell
Peter Corcor
Jennifer Brosnahan
CW:Judy Spaar
DF:Muller
CL:Kansas City Art Institute
TC:Art School
美術学校

▼
Invitation to
an awards ceremony
賞授与式招待状
USA 1990
AD,D:John Sayles
CW:Mary Langen-Goldstien
DF:Sayles Graphic Design
CL:Sayles Graphic Design
TC:Graphic Design Studio
グラフィック・デザイン

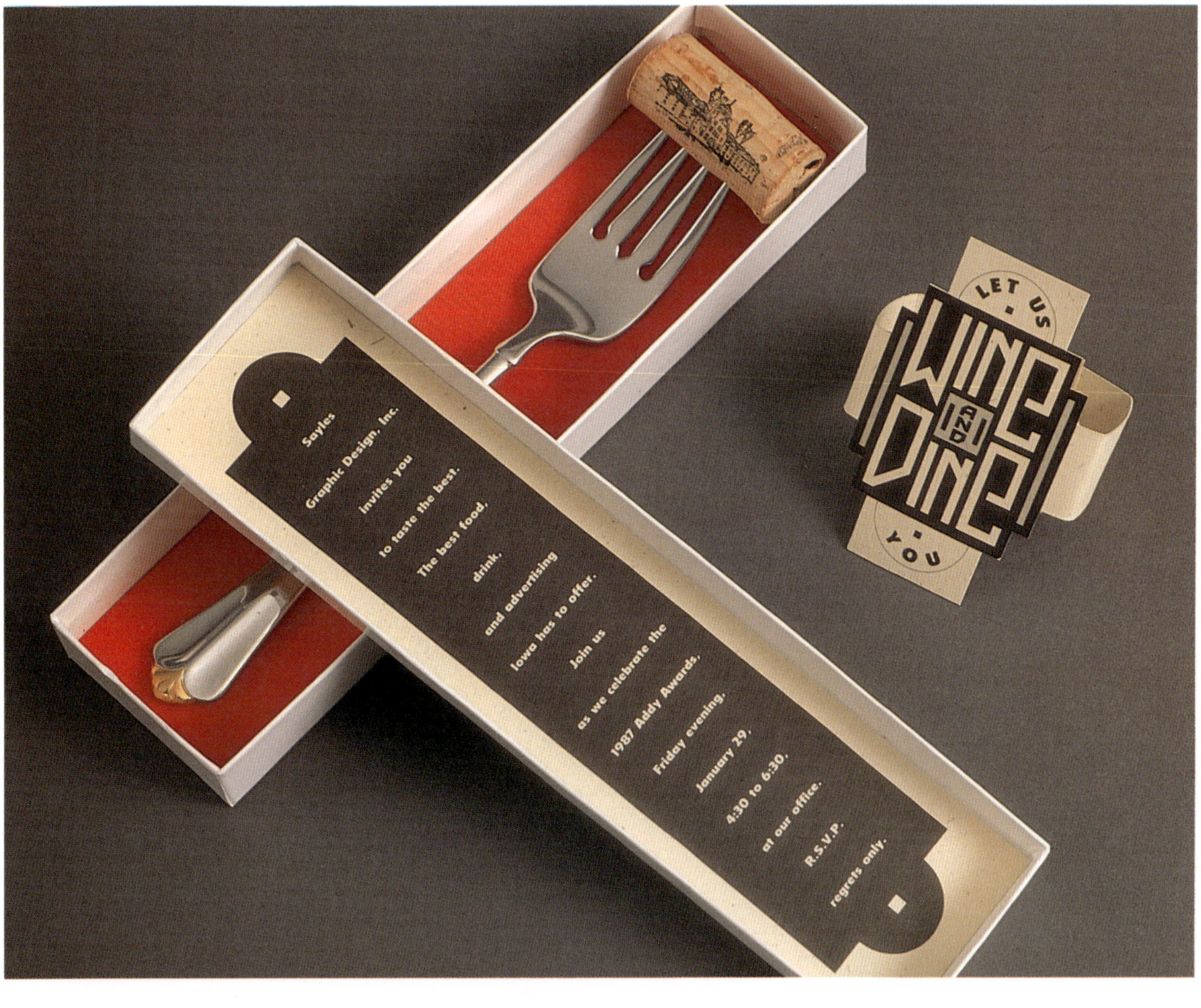

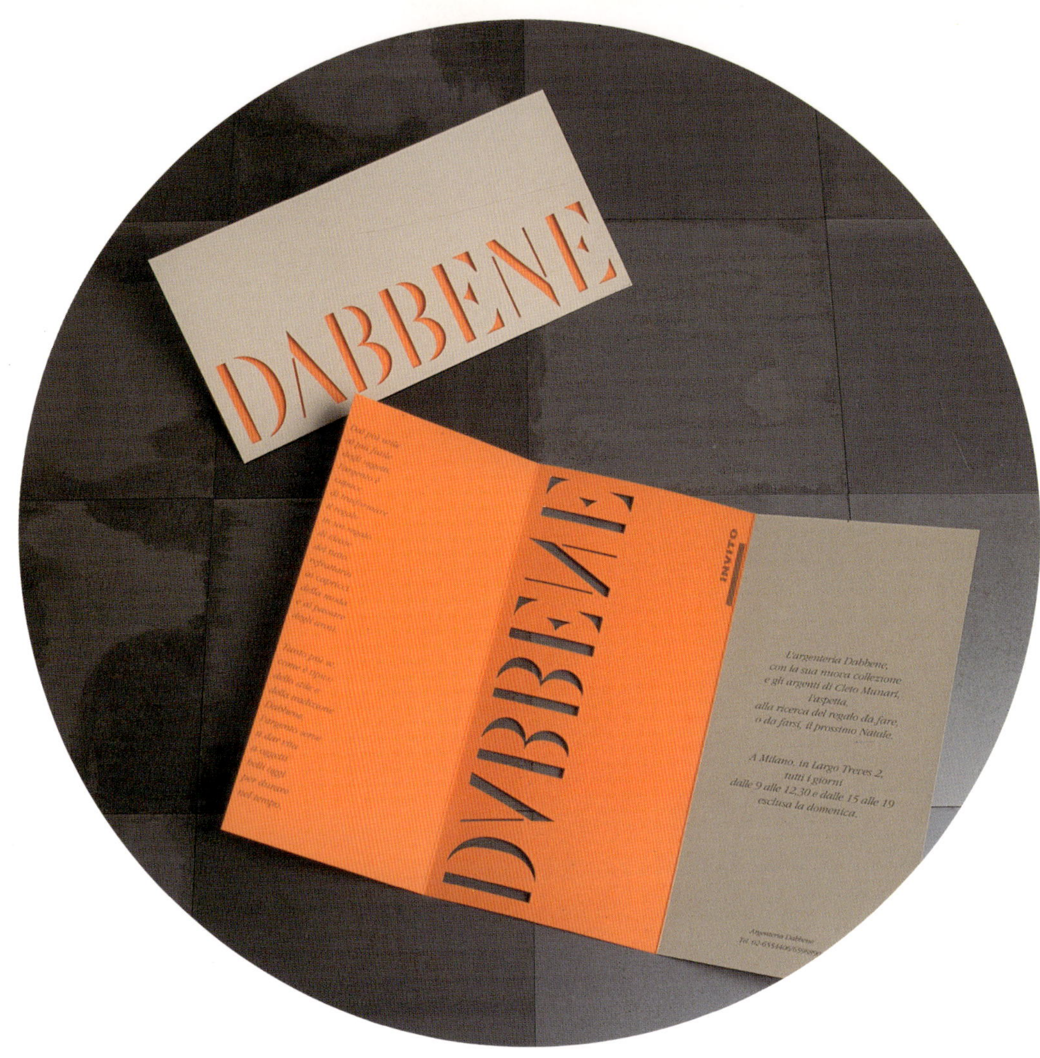

▲

Invitation to a party

パーティー招待状

ITALY 1991

CD,AD:Antonella Sala

CW:Grazia Lotti

DF:Art Work Alas

CL:Dabbene

TC:Silversmith

銀加工

▼

Invitation to a Christmas party

クリスマス・パーティー招待状

USA 1991

D,CW:Peter Crockett

DF:Group Z

CL:Group Z

TC:Design Studio

デザイン

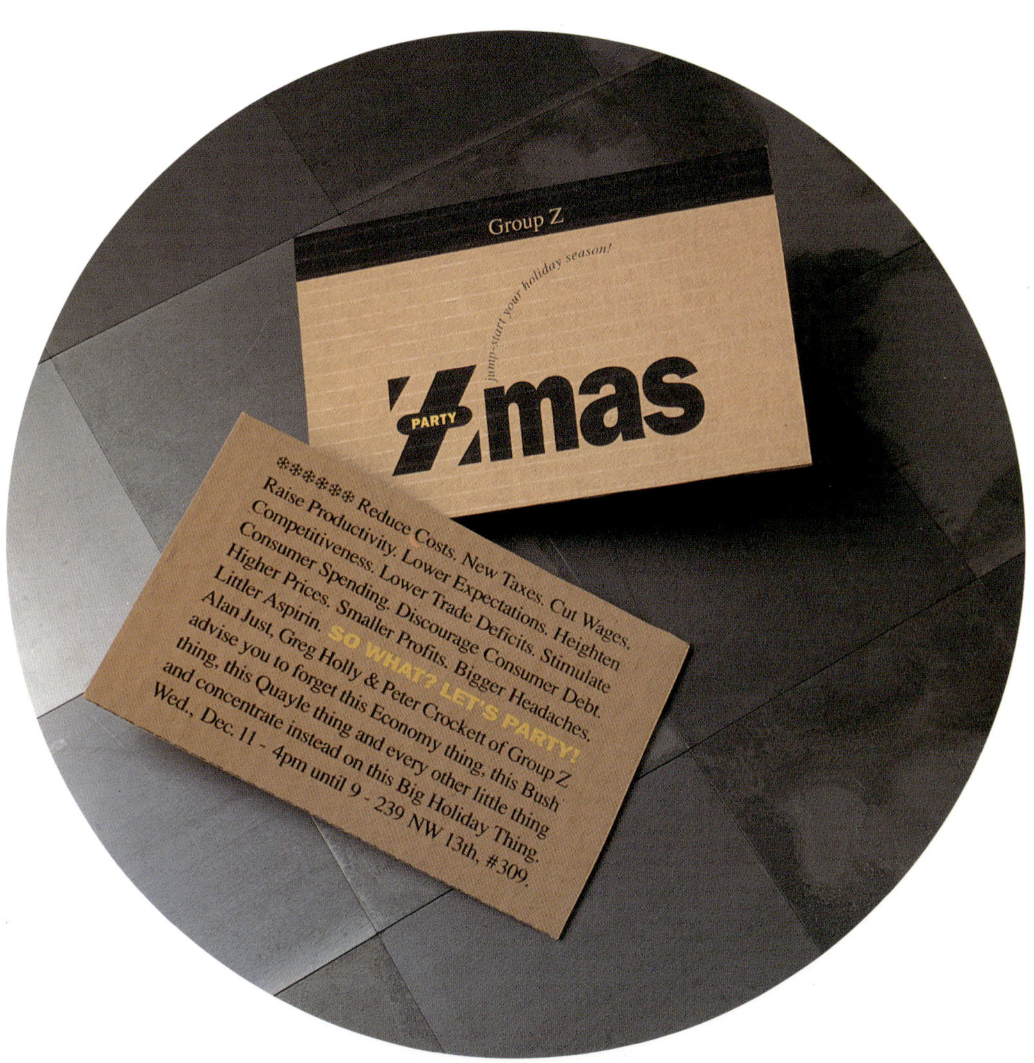

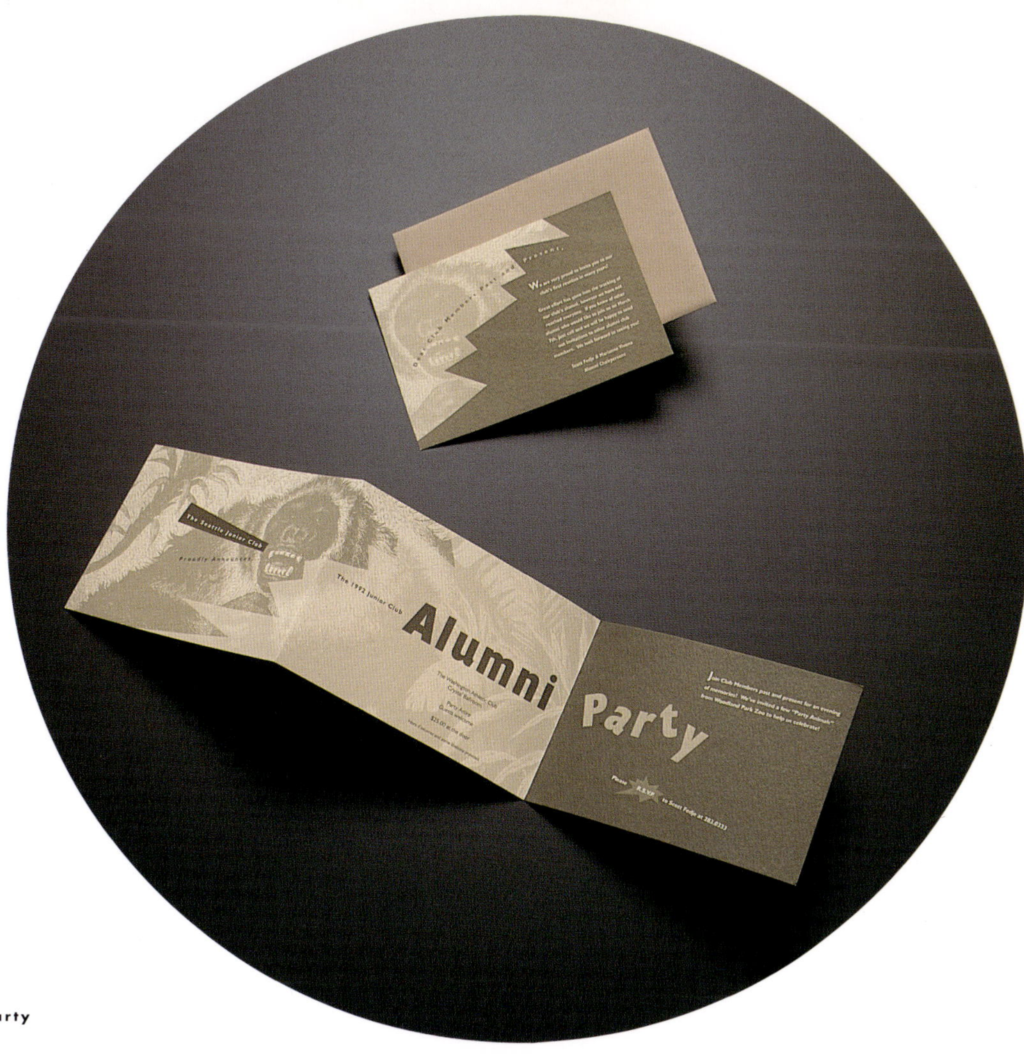

▲
Invitation to a theme party
テーマ・パーティー招待状
USA 1992
CD,AD,D:Stefanie Choi
CL:The Junior Club of Seattle
TC:Social Club
社交クラブ

▼
Invitation to a Grammy party
グラミー賞記念パーティー招待状
USA 1992
AD,D:Craig Yamashita
P:Tom Keller
DF:Georgopoulos Design
CL:MCA Records
TC:Record Producer
レコード制作

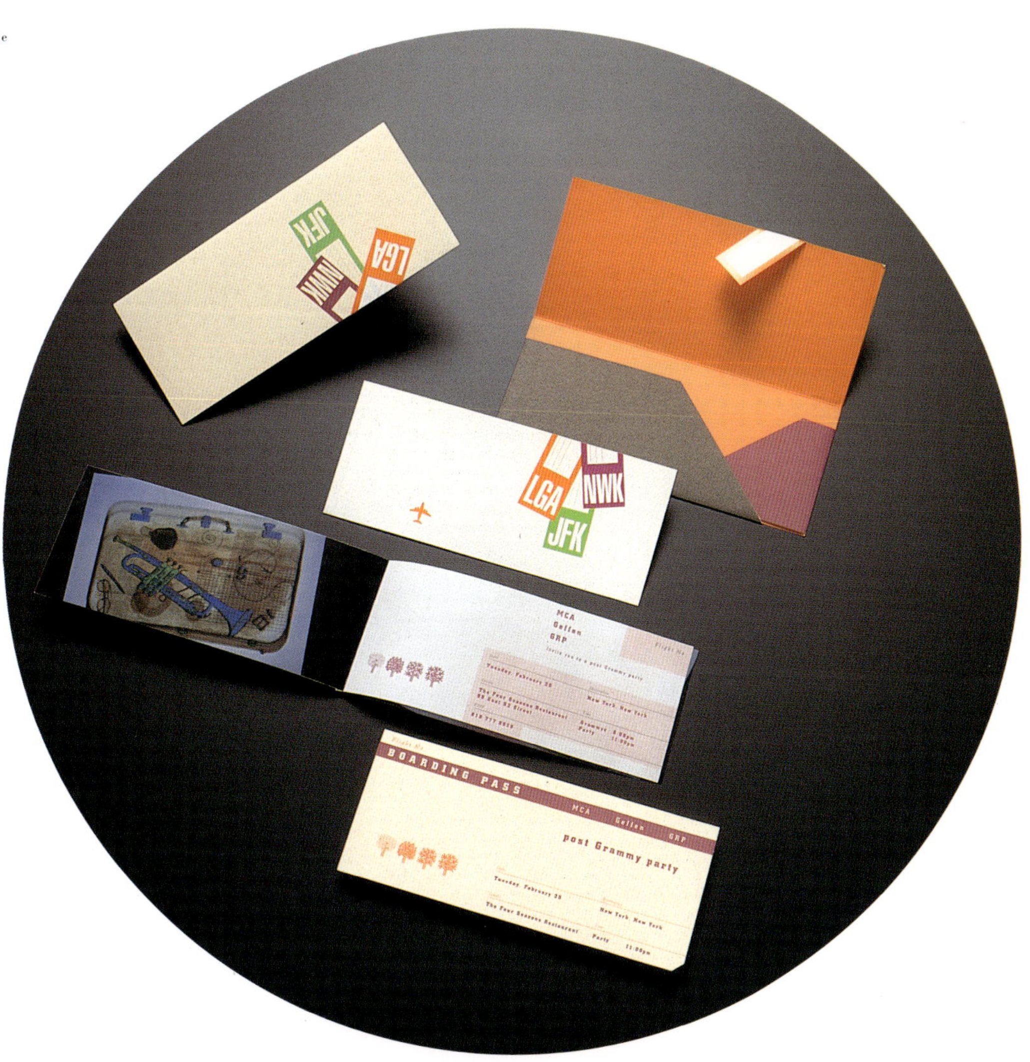

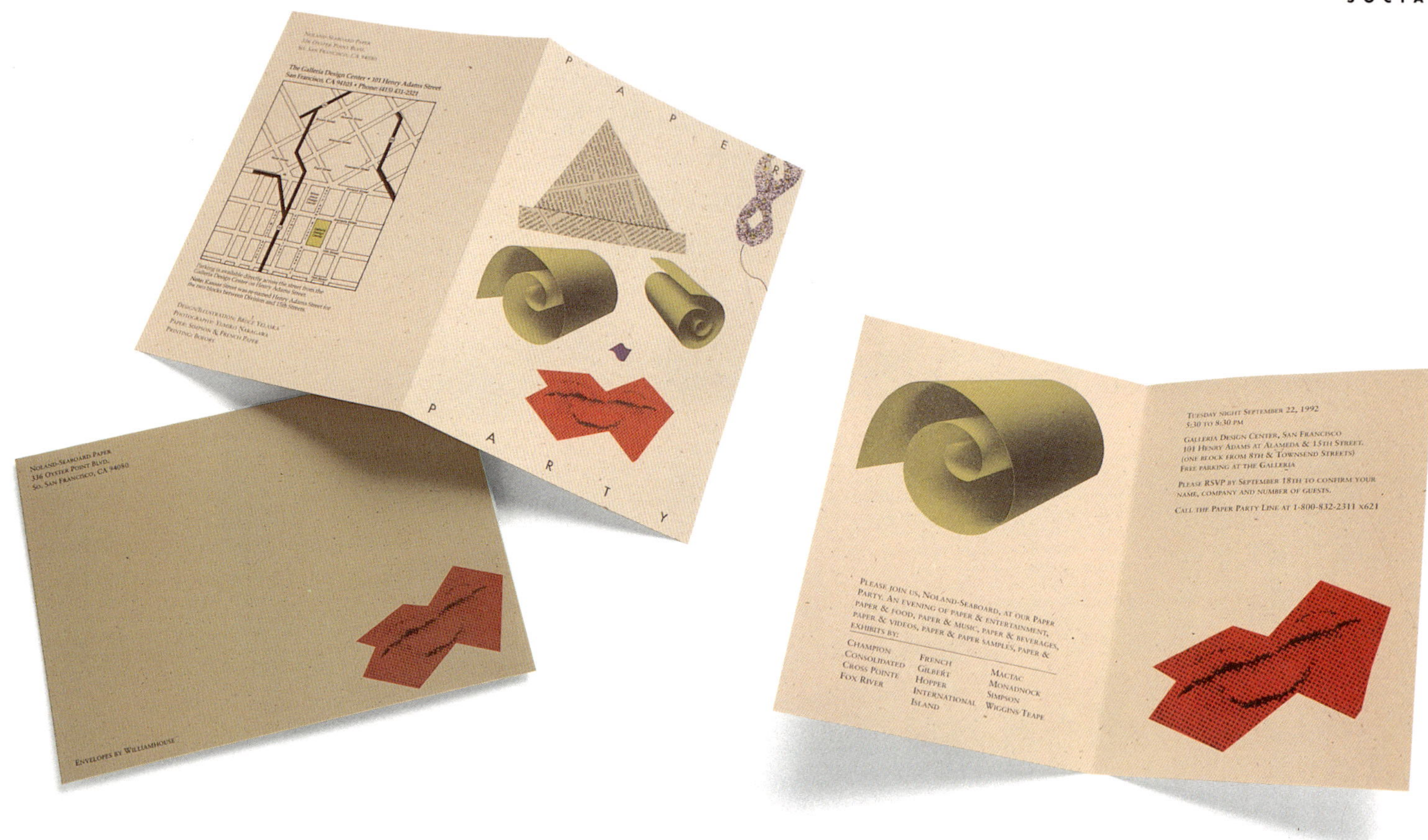

▲

Invitation to a promotional party

プロモーショナル・パーティー招待状

USA 1992

CD,AD,D,I:Bruce Yelaska

P:Yumiko Nakagawa

DF:Bruce Yelaska Design

CL:Noland Seaboard

TC:Paper Maker

製紙

▼

Invitation to a Christmas party

クリスマス・パーティー招待状

AUSTRALIA 1990

AD,D,I:Annette Harcus

CW:Direct Connection

DF:Annette Harcus Design

CL:Direct Connection

TC:Marketing Consultants

マーケティング・コンサルタント

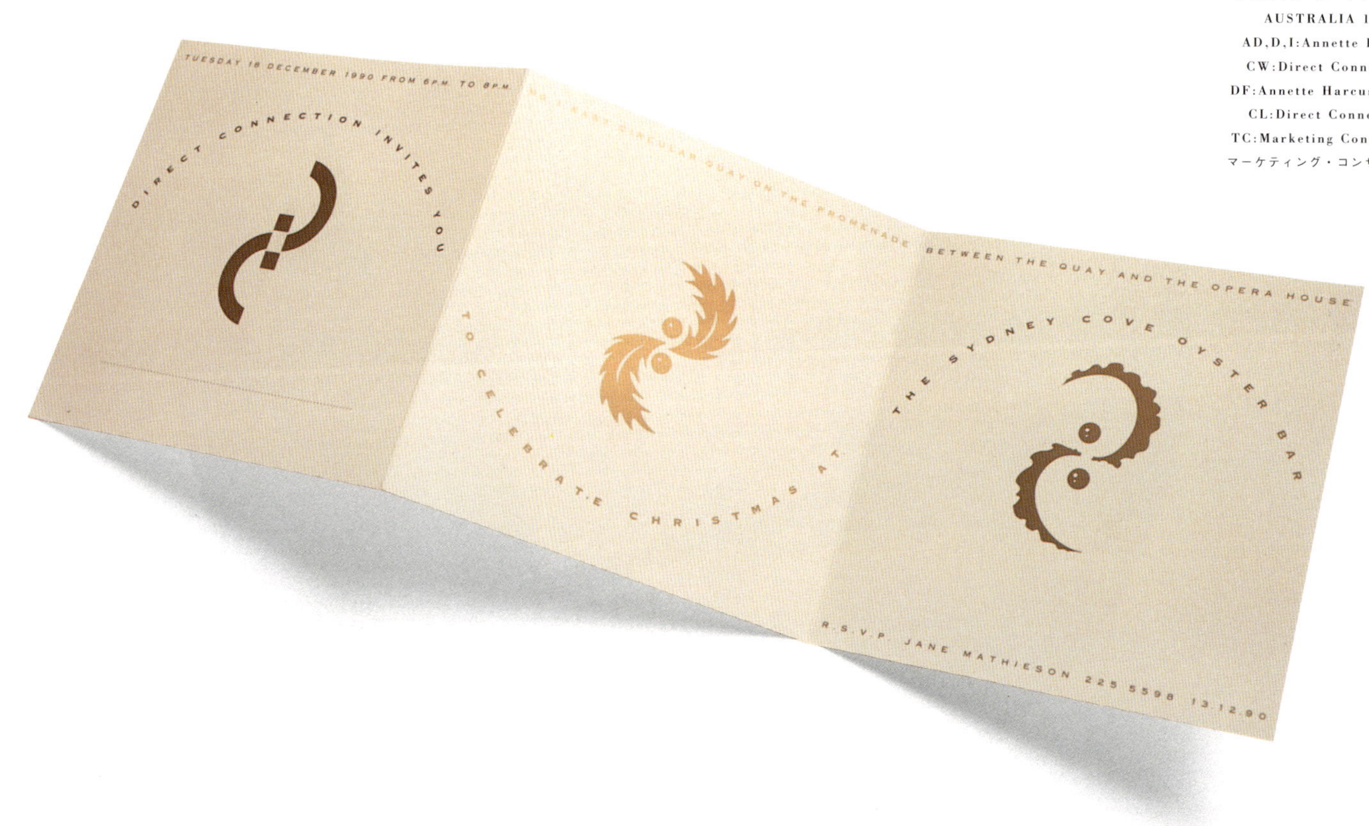

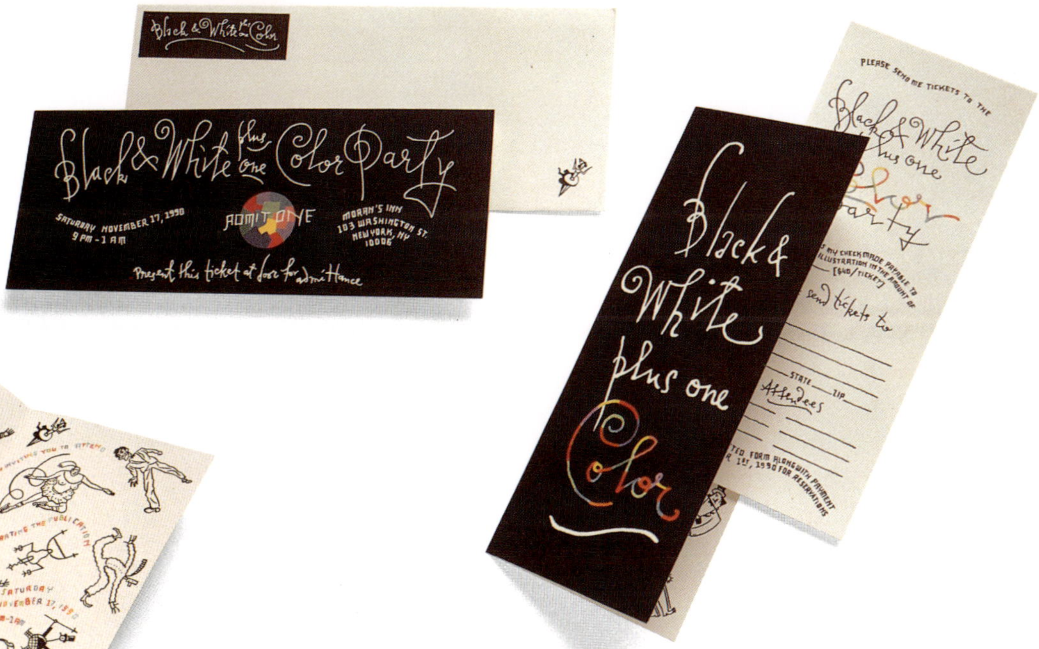

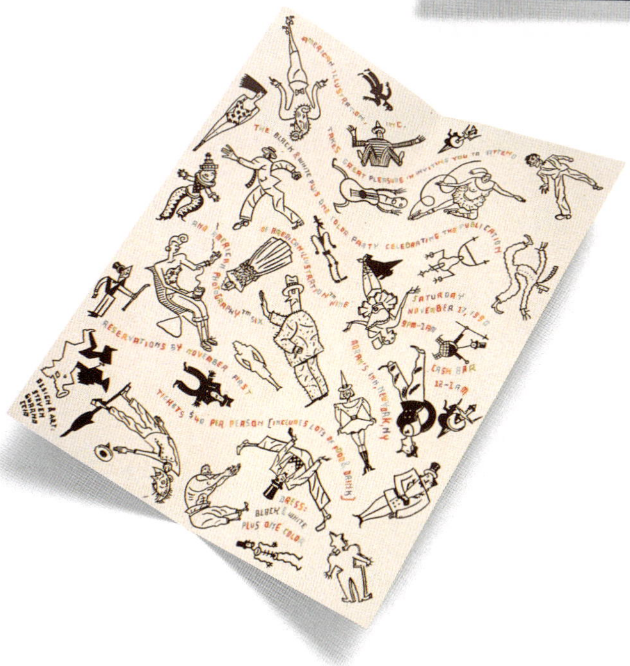

▲
Invitation to a party
パーティー招待状
USA 1990
AD,D,I:Steven Guarnaccia
CL:American Illustration
TC:Illustrators' Organization
イラストレーター協会

▼
Invitation to an Asian American Arts society gathering
アジア系アメリカン・アート協会行事招待状
USA 1992
AD:Alex Jay
D:George Cheng
CL:Inner Circle and Asian New Yorker
TC:Publisher
出版

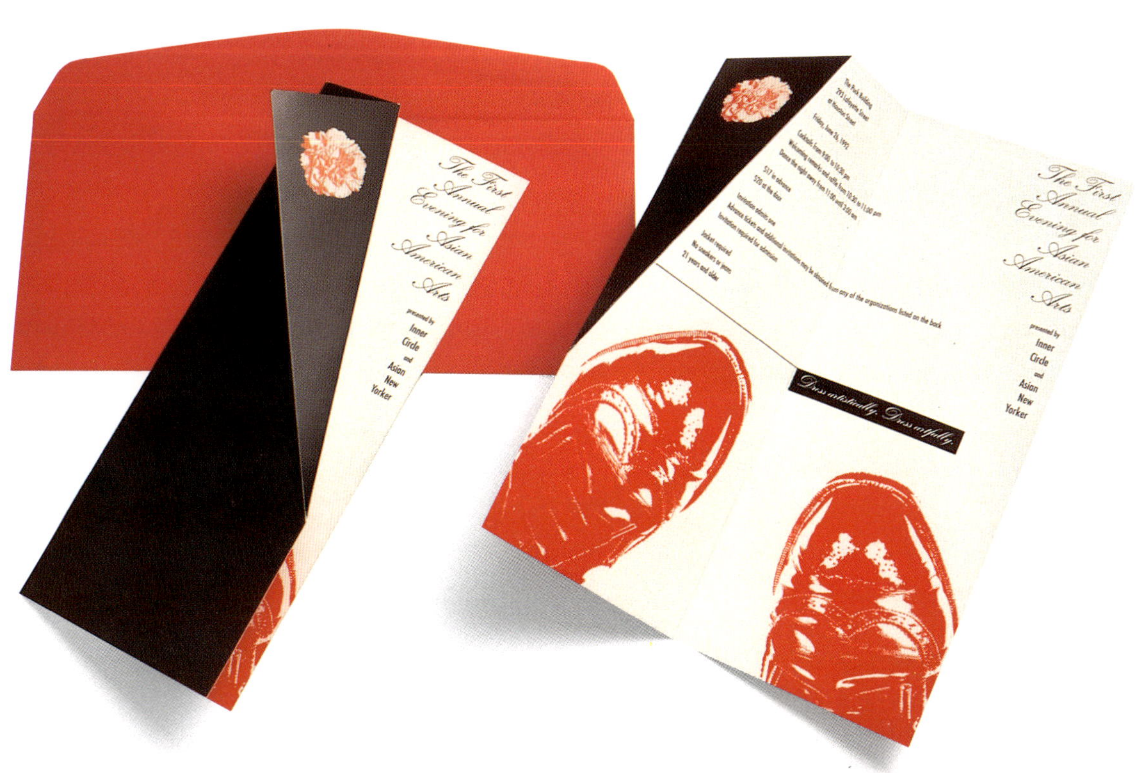

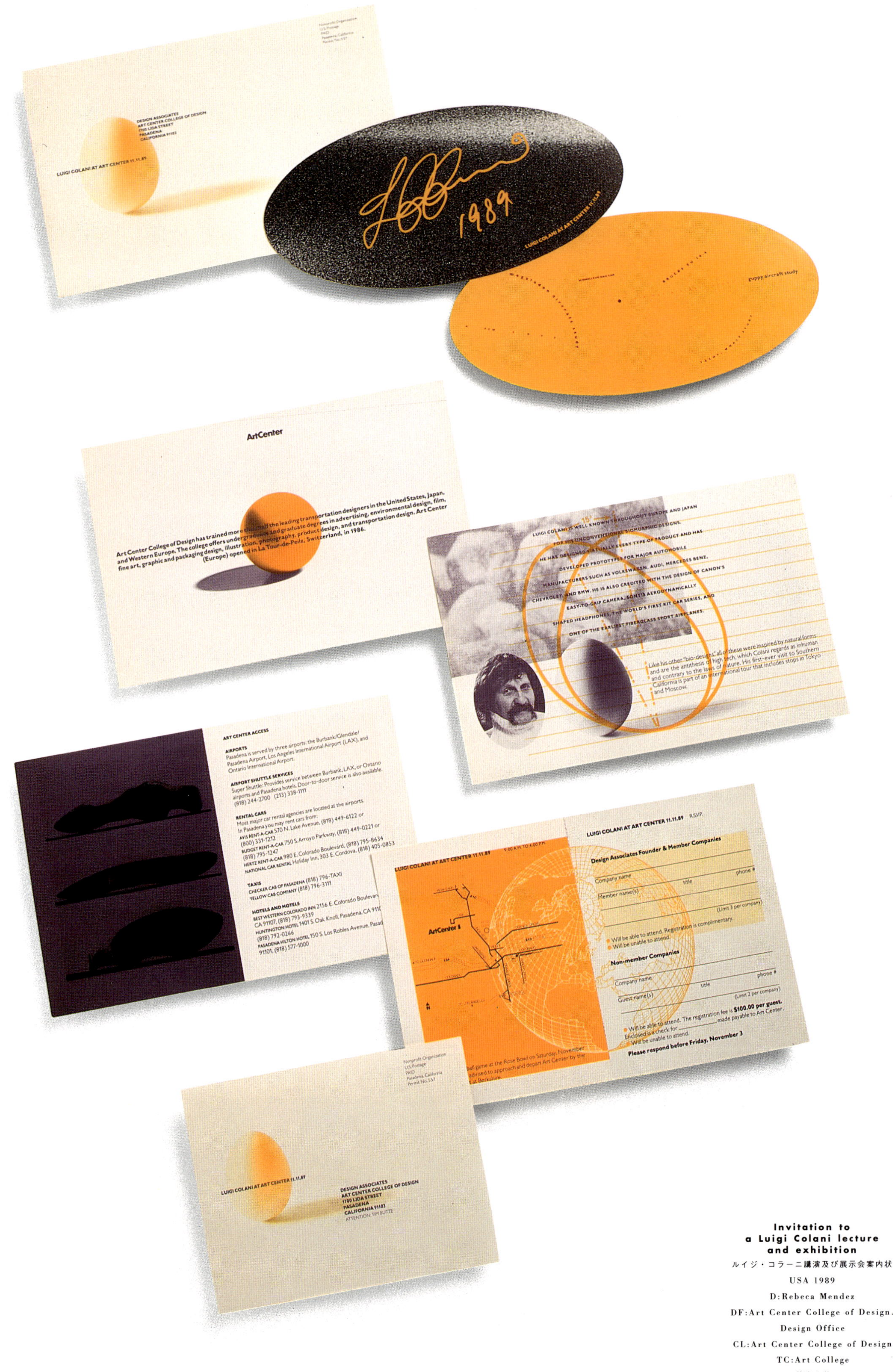

Invitation to a Luigi Colani lecture and exhibition

ルイジ・コラーニ講演及び展示会案内状

USA 1989

D:Rebeca Mendez

DF:Art Center College of Design. Design Office

CL:Art Center College of Design

TC:Art College

美術大学

Invitation to an alumni annual meeting
同窓会招待状
USA 1991
AD:Rebeca Mendez
D:Rebeca Mendez
Darren Namaye
CW:Anna Ganahl
DF:Art Center College of Design.
Design Office
CL:Art Center College of Design
TC:Art College
美術大学

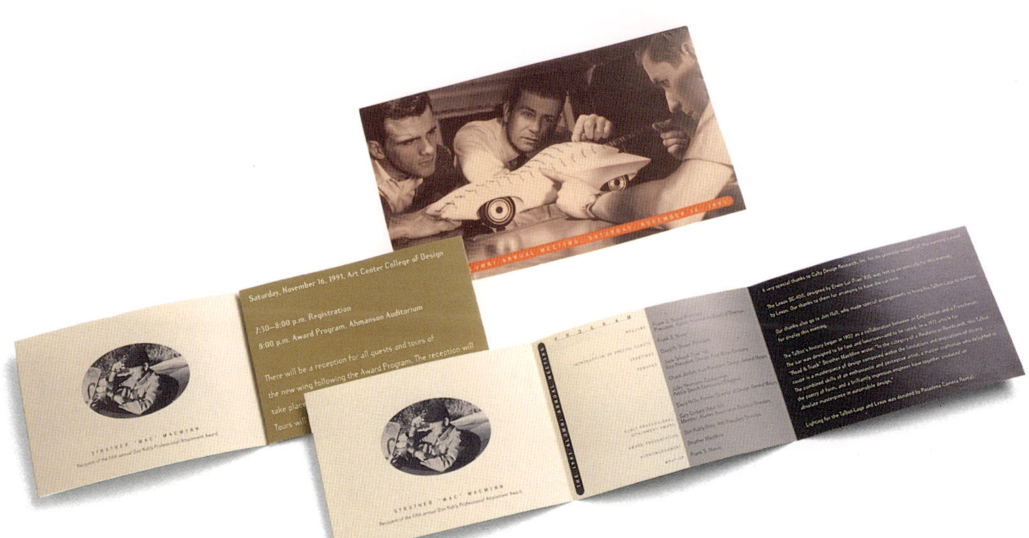

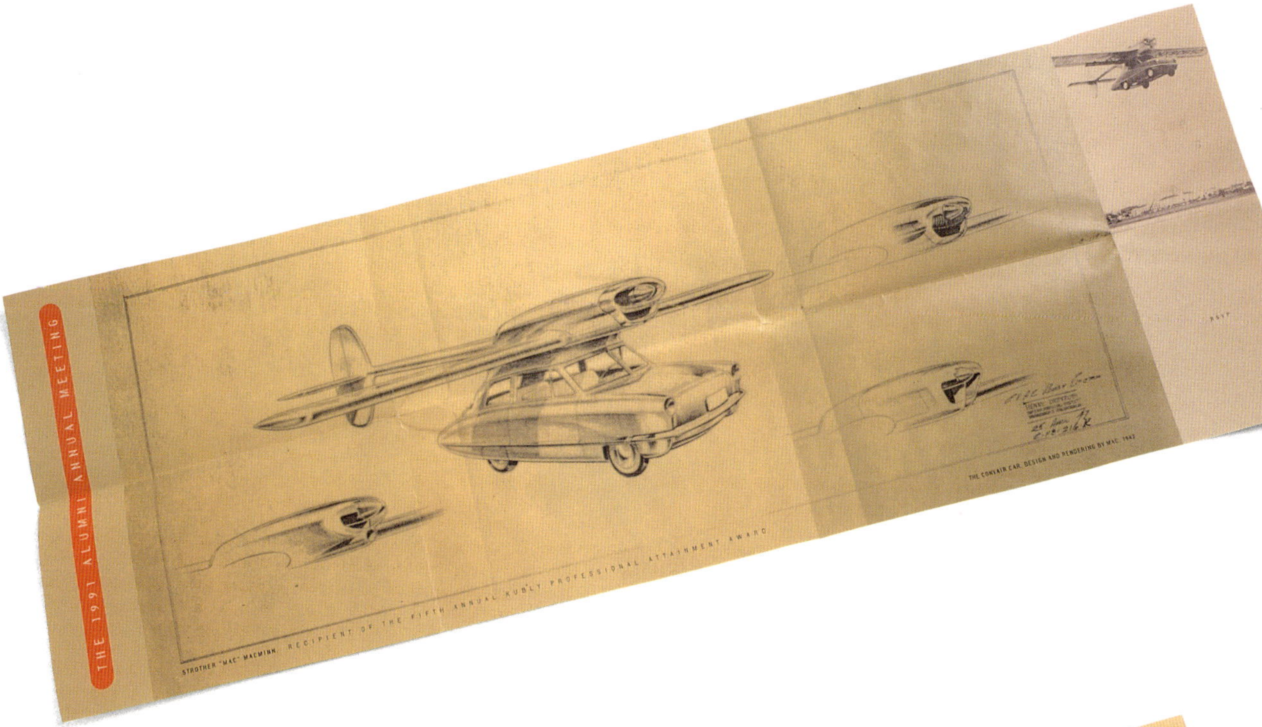

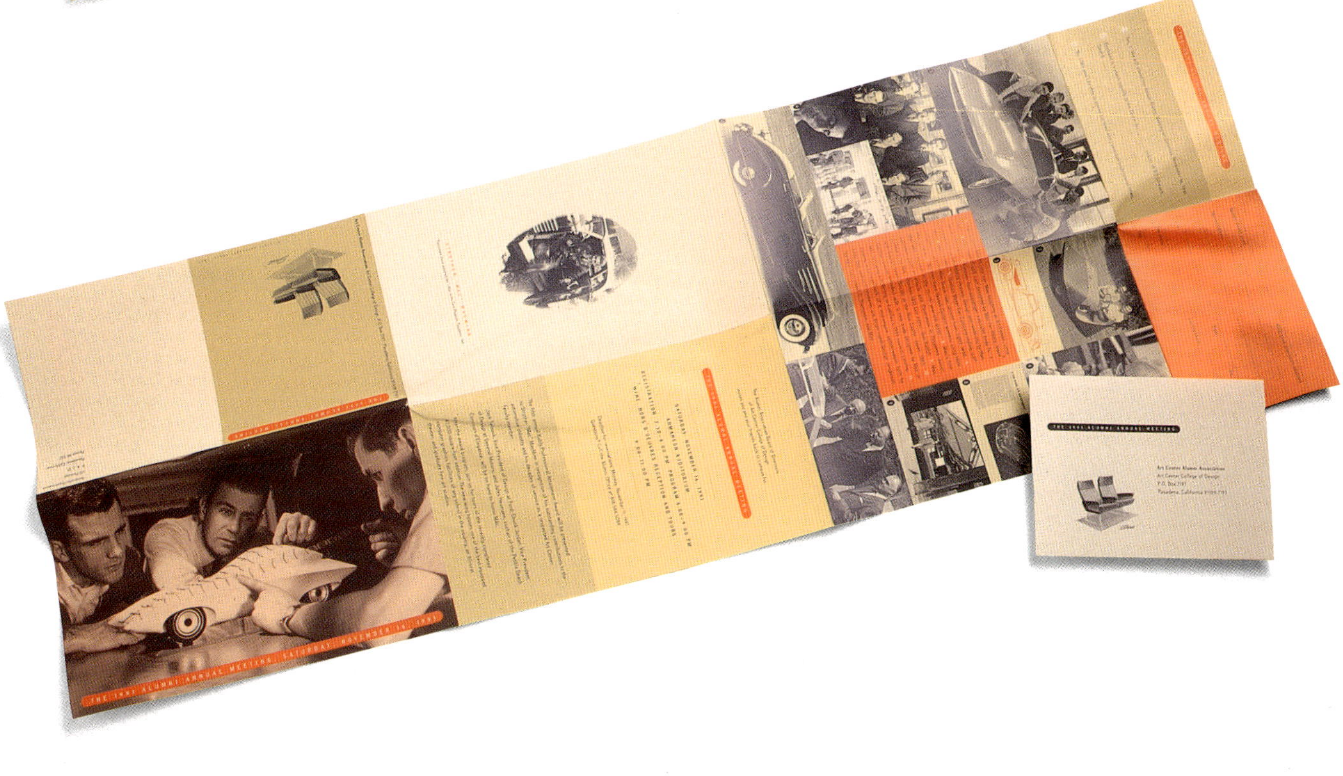

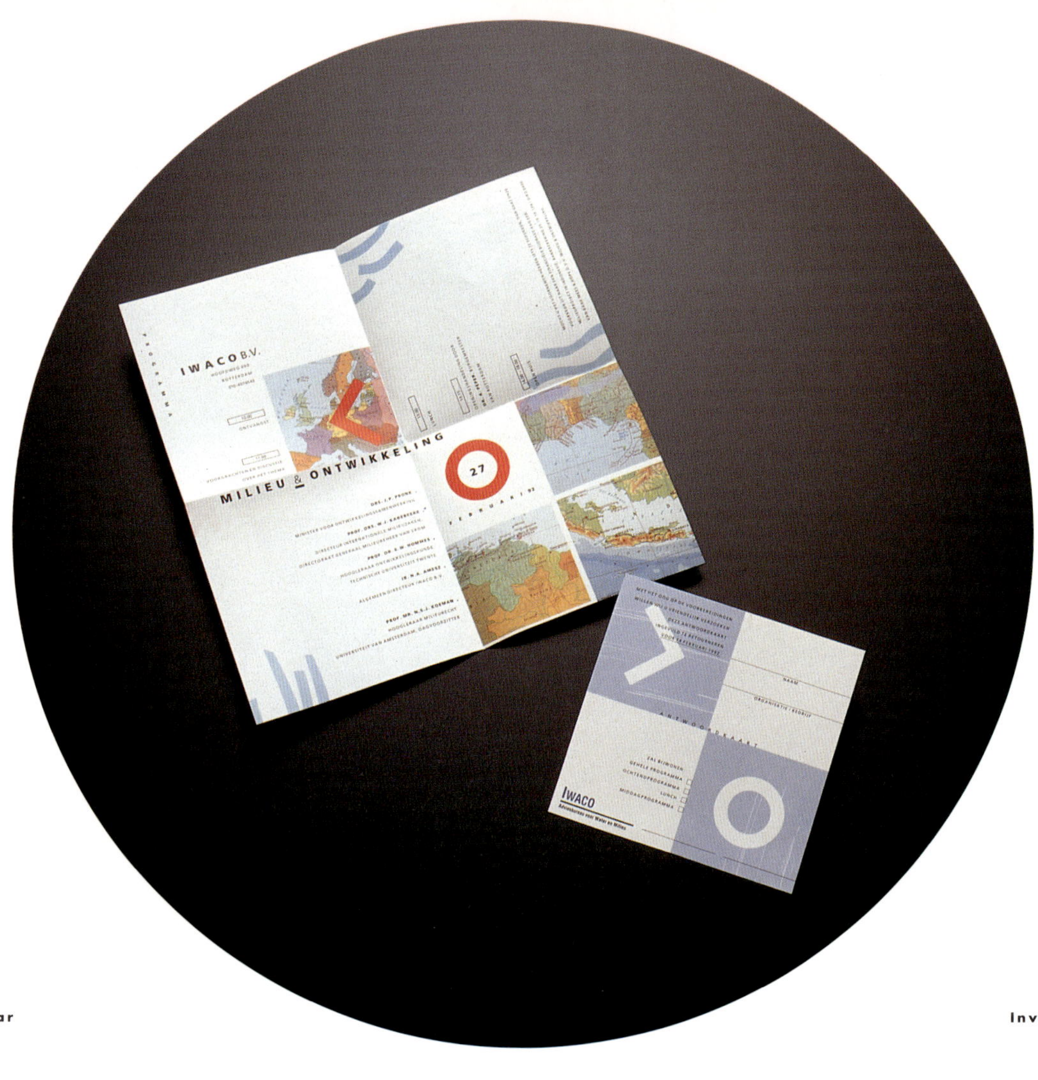

▲
Invitation to a seminar
セミナー案内状
HOLLAND 1992
CD,AD,D,I,CW:M.Hernandez Sala
CL:Iwaco Bv
TC:Environmental Developer
環境開発

▼
Invitation to meet lecturers
講師との懇談会招待状
AUSTRALIA 1991
CD:Garry Emery
AD,D,DF:Emery Vincent Design
CL:Center for Design at Royal Melbourne Institute of Technology
TC:Design School
デザイン学校

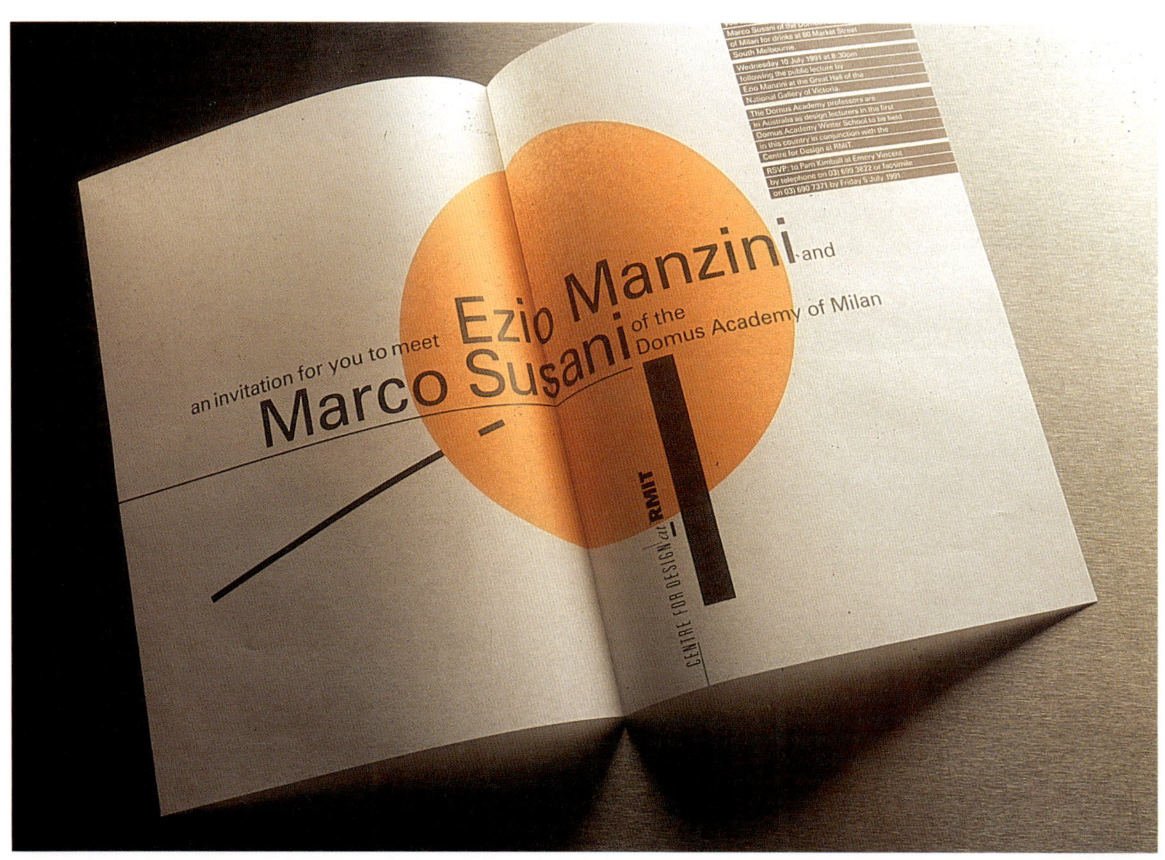

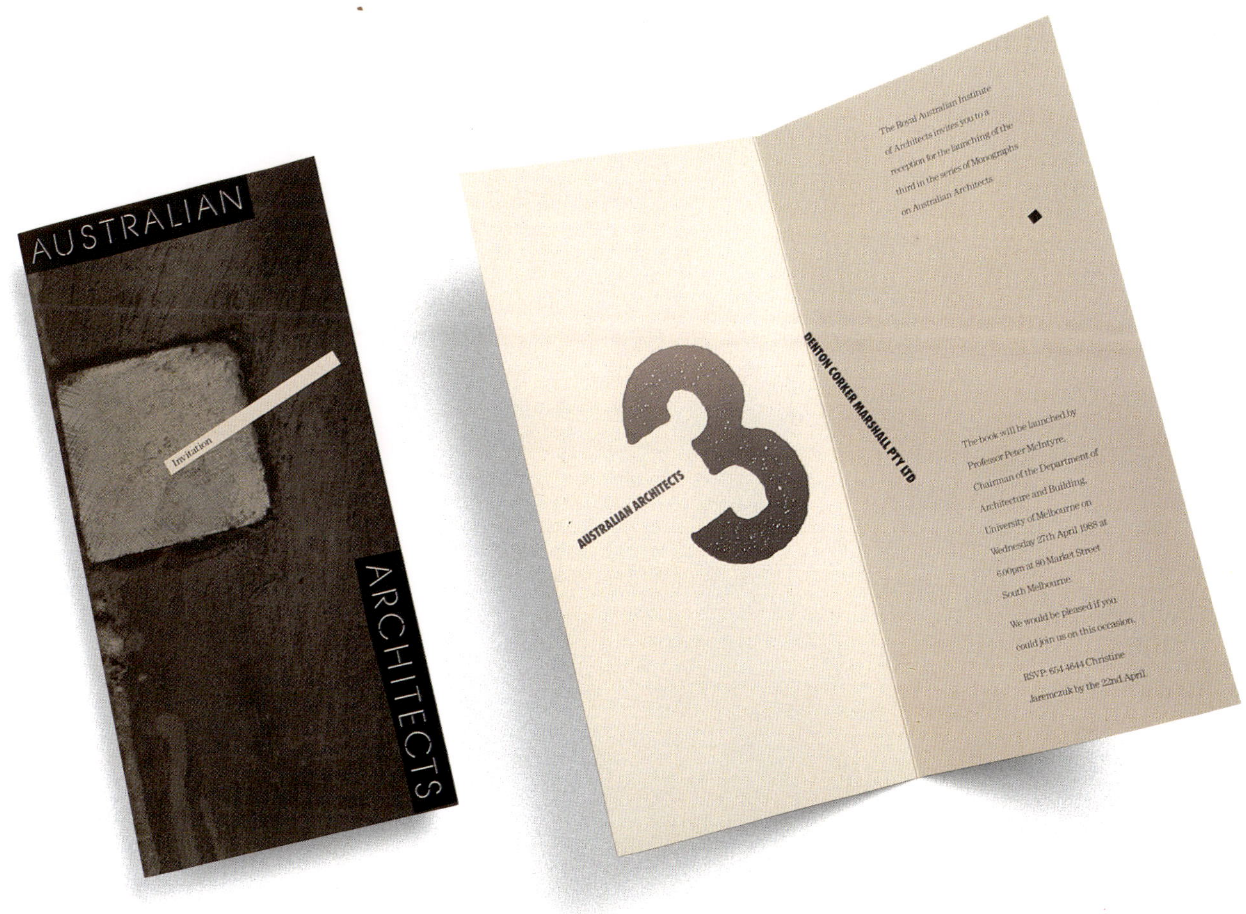

▲
Invitation to a book-launching reception
出版記念レセプション招待状
AUSTRALIA 1988
CD:Garry Emery
AD,D,DF:Emery Vincent Design
CL:Royal Australian Institute of Architects
TC:Architectural Institute
建築協会

▼
Invitation to a promotional party
プロモーショナル・パーティー招待状
AUSTRALIA 1991
CD:Garry Emery
AD,D,DF:Emery Vincent Design
CL:Denton Corker Marshall
TC:Architects
建築

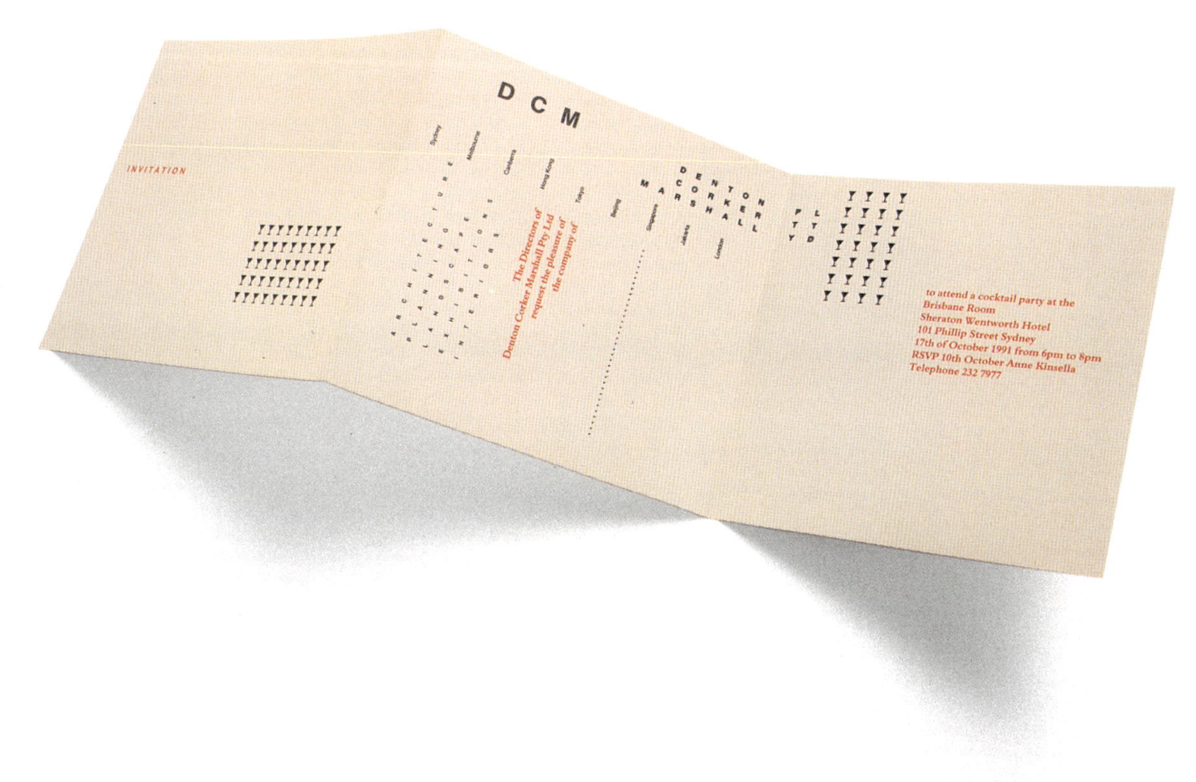

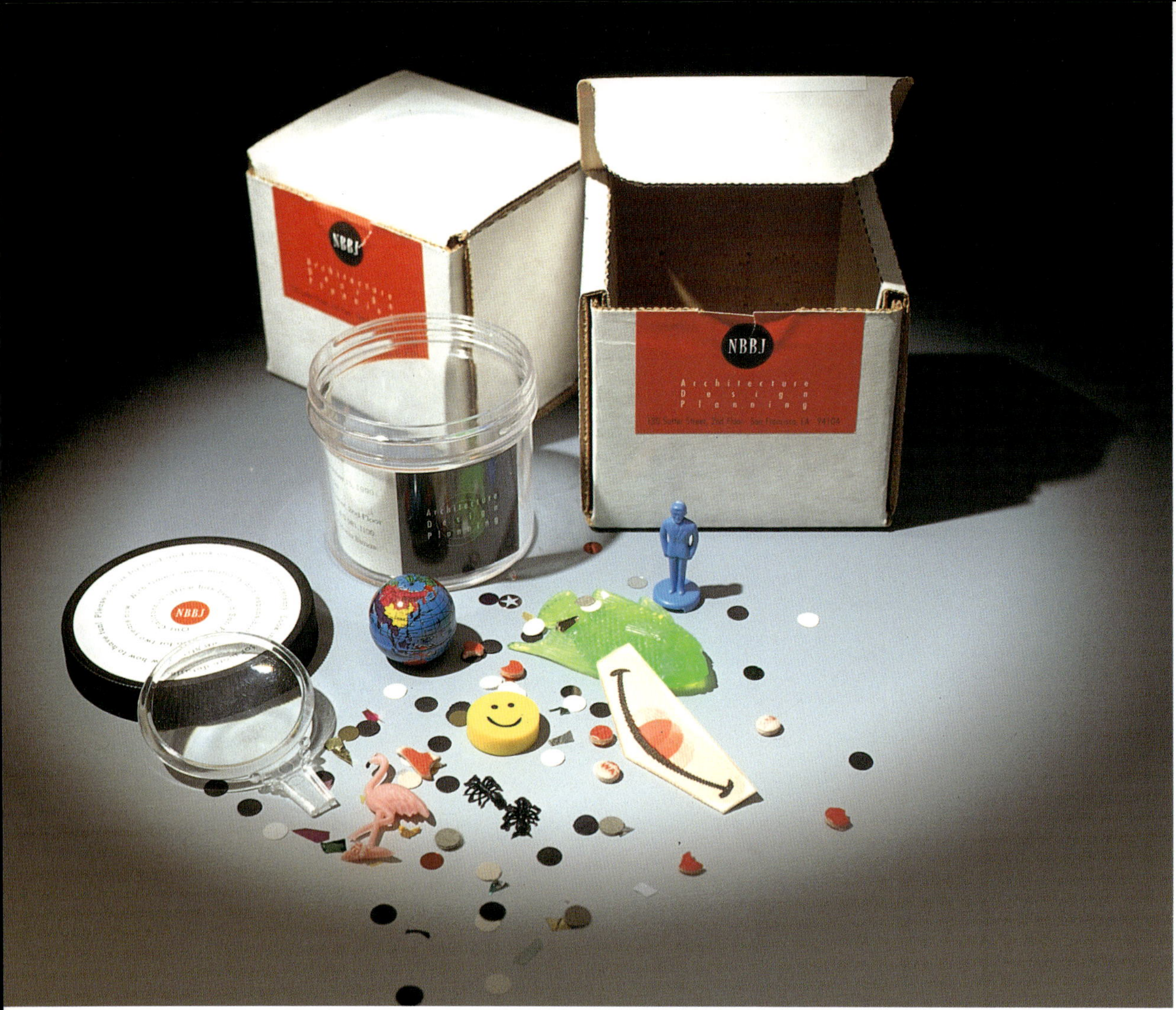

◀

Invitation to an open house party

オープン・ハウス・パーティー招待状

USA 1990

CD:Kerry Burg

AD,D,I,CW:Doug Keyes

DF:NBBJ - Graphic Design

CL:NBBJ - San Francisco

TC:Architects

建築

▶

Invitation to a party

パーティー招待状

USA 1990

D,CW:Patricia Belyea

DF:Belyea Design

CL:Thomas & Kennedy

TC:Typesetter

写植

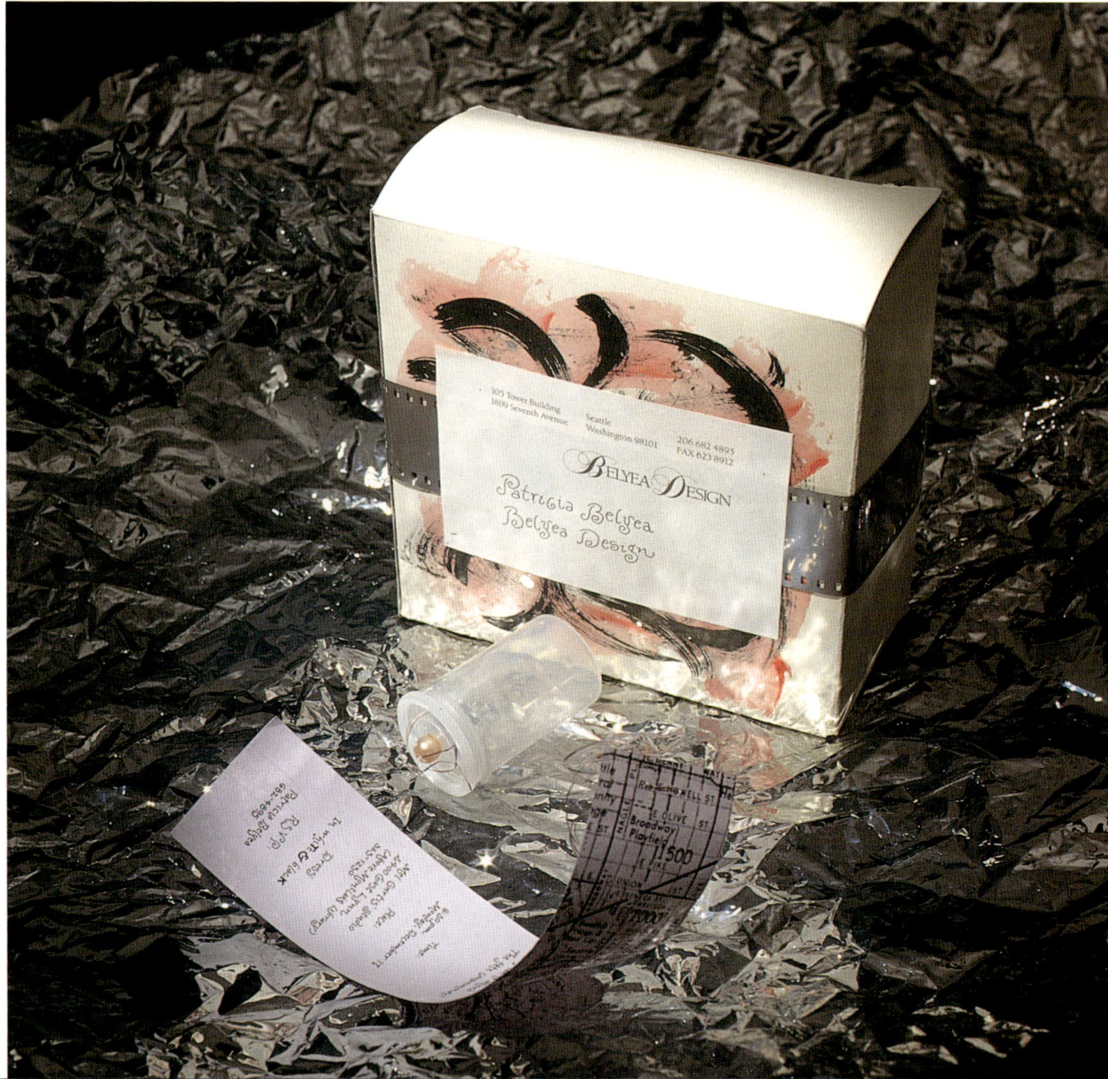

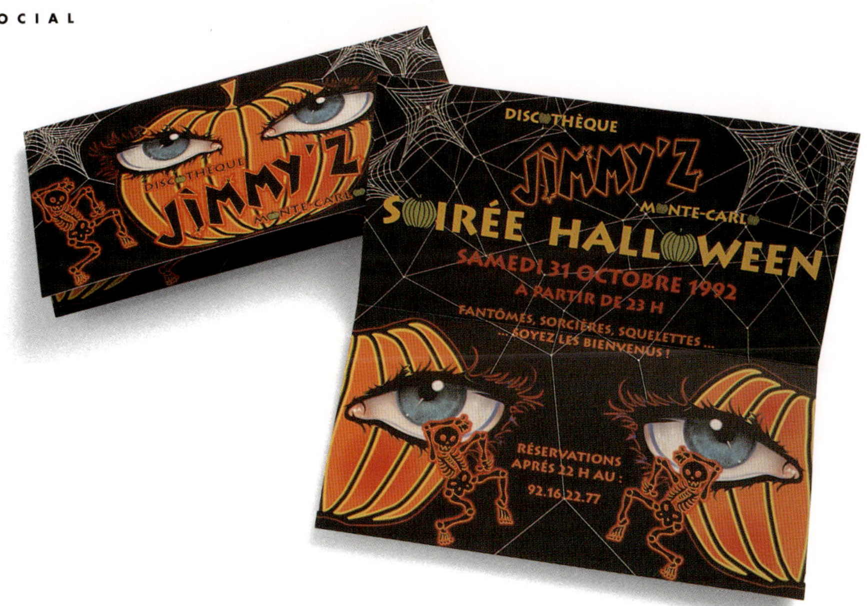

Invitation to a disco Halloween party

ディスコ・ハロウィーン・パーティー招待状

ITALY 1992

CD,AD,D,P,I:Amedeo M.Turello

CW:Ferdinand Martelli

CL:Souété Des Bains De Mer

TC:Hotel, Casino

ホテル、カジノ

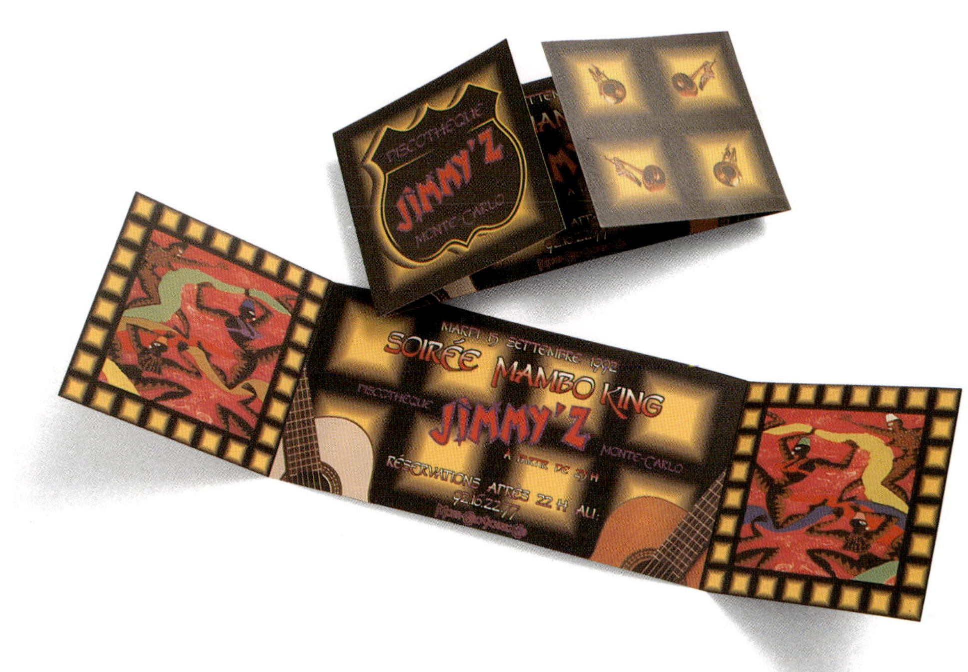

Invitation to a disco party

ディスコ・パーティー招待状

ITALY 1992

CD,AD,D,P:Amedeo M.Turello

CW:Maruel Bataillard

CL:Souété Des Bains De Mer

TC:Hotel, Casino

ホテル、カジノ

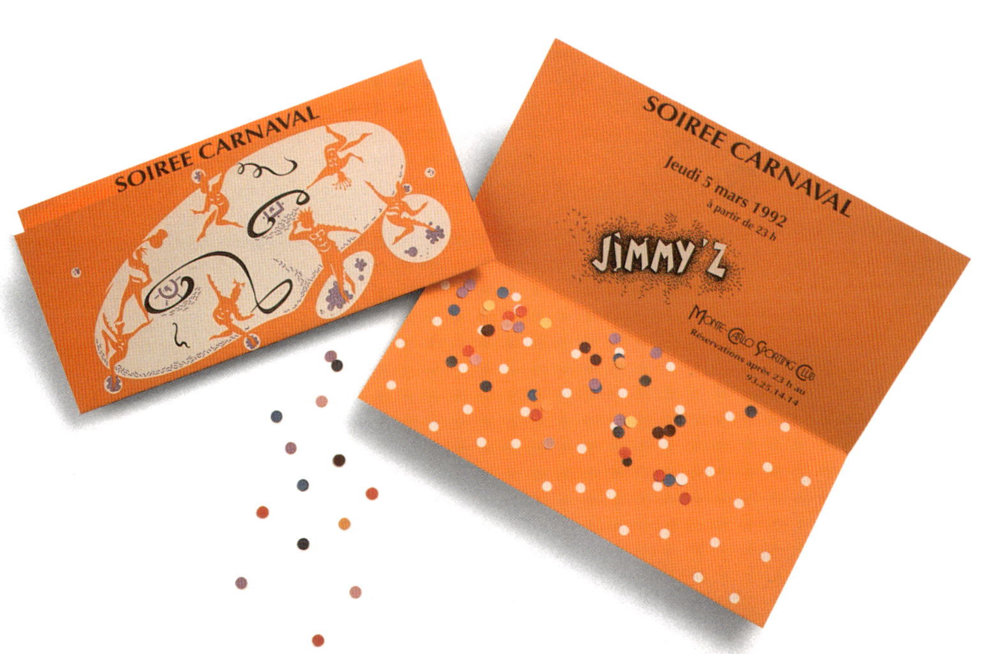

Invitation to a disco carnival

ディスコ・カーニバル招待状

ITALY 1992

CD,AD,D,I:Amedeo M.Turello

CW:Juliette Bouhanna

CL:Souété Des Bains De Mer

TC:Hotel, Casino

ホテル、カジノ

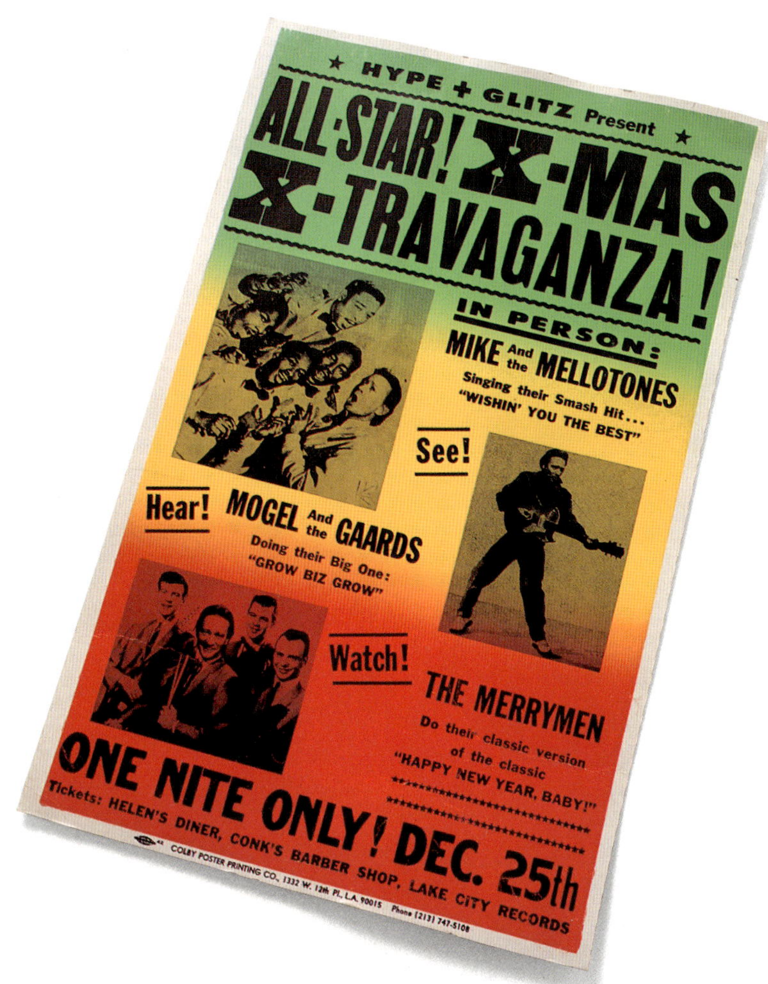

▲
Christmas card
クリスマス・カード
USA 1987
CD,AD,D:Art Chantry
P:Tom Collicott
CW:Mike Mogelgaard
DF:Art Chantry Design
CL:Mogelgaard Associates
TC:Advertising Agency
広告

▼
Christmas card
クリスマス・カード
USA 1988
CD,AD,D:Art Chantry
P:Tom Collicott
CW:Charies Dizkens
DF:Art Chantry Design
CL:Mogelgaard Associates
TC:Advertising Agency
広告

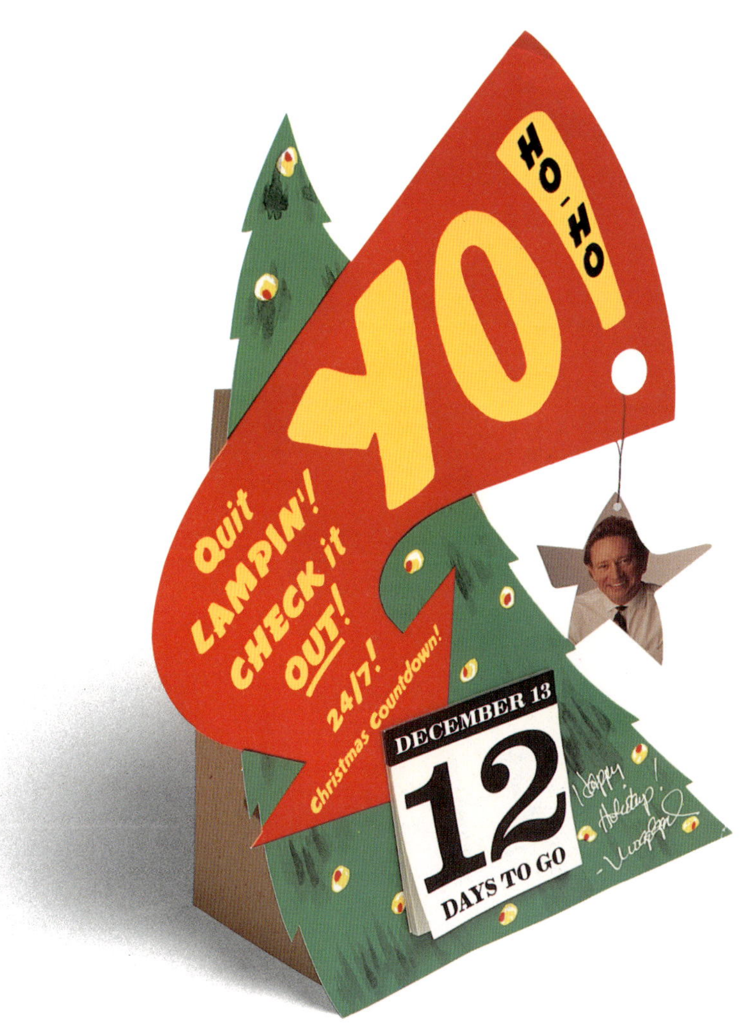

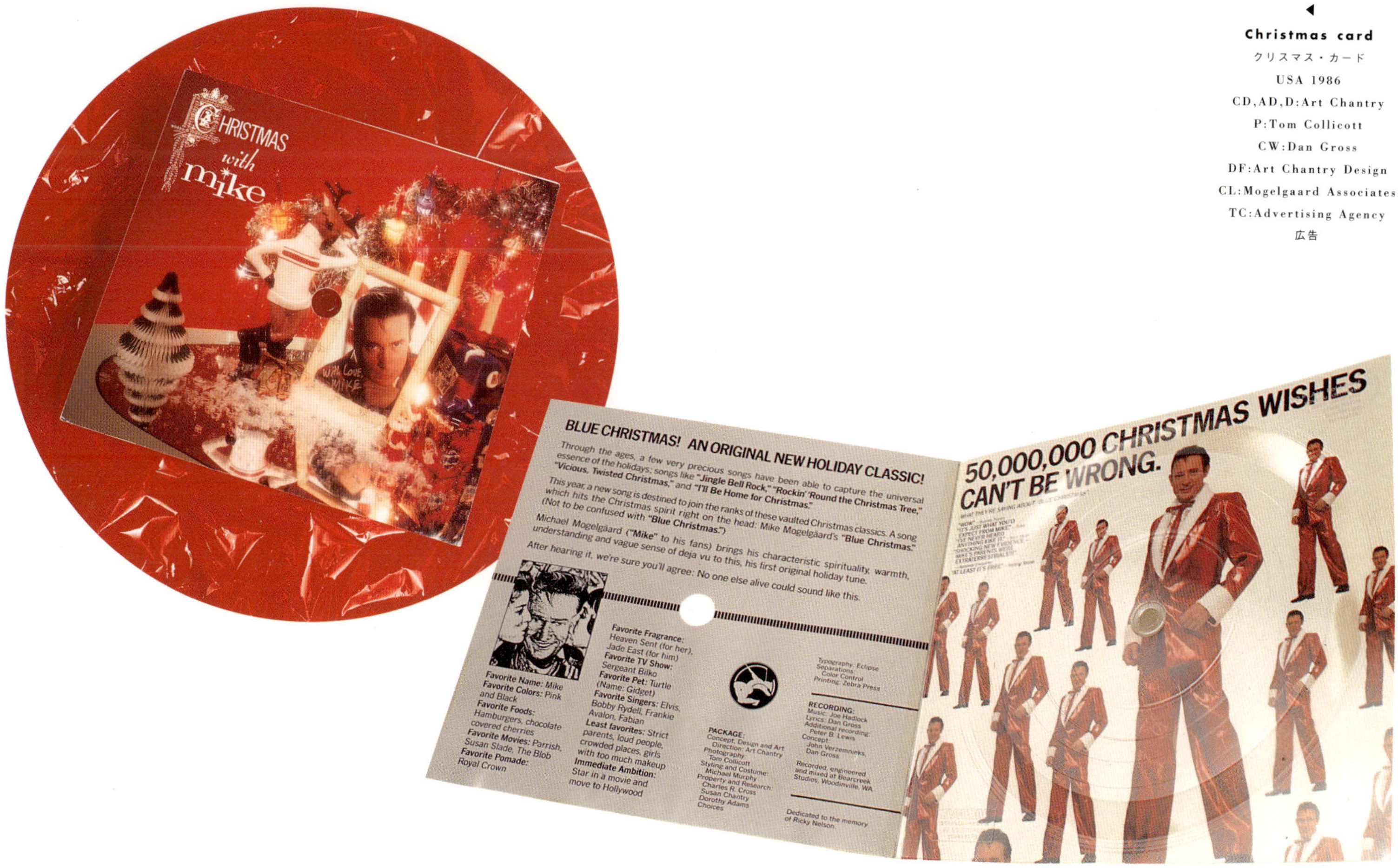

◀
Christmas card
クリスマス・カード
USA 1986
CD,AD,D:Art Chantry
P:Tom Collicott
CW:Dan Gross
DF:Art Chantry Design
CL:Mogelgaard Associates
TC:Advertising Agency
広告

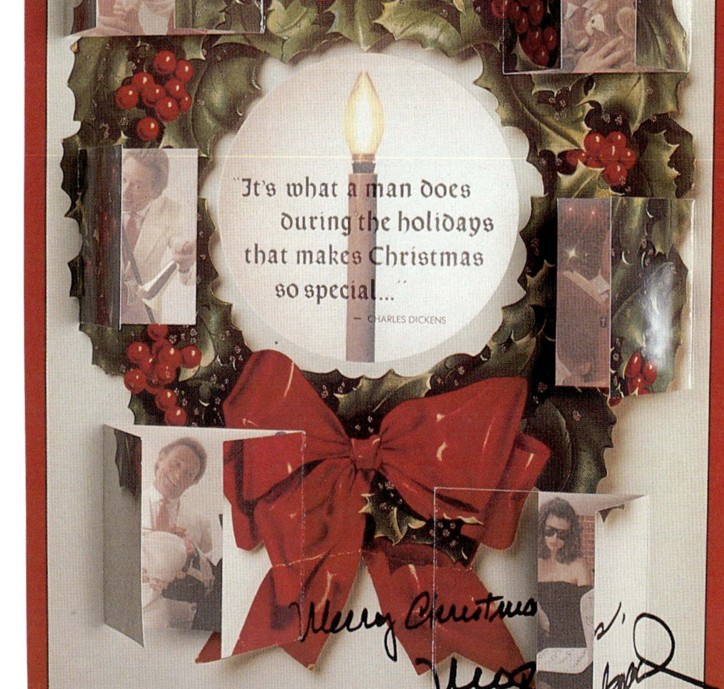

▶
Christmas card
クリスマス・カード
USA 1989
CD,AD,D:Art Chantry
P:Tom Collicott
I:Megan Adcock
DF:Art Chantry Design
CL:Mogelgaard Associates
TC:Advertising Agency
広告

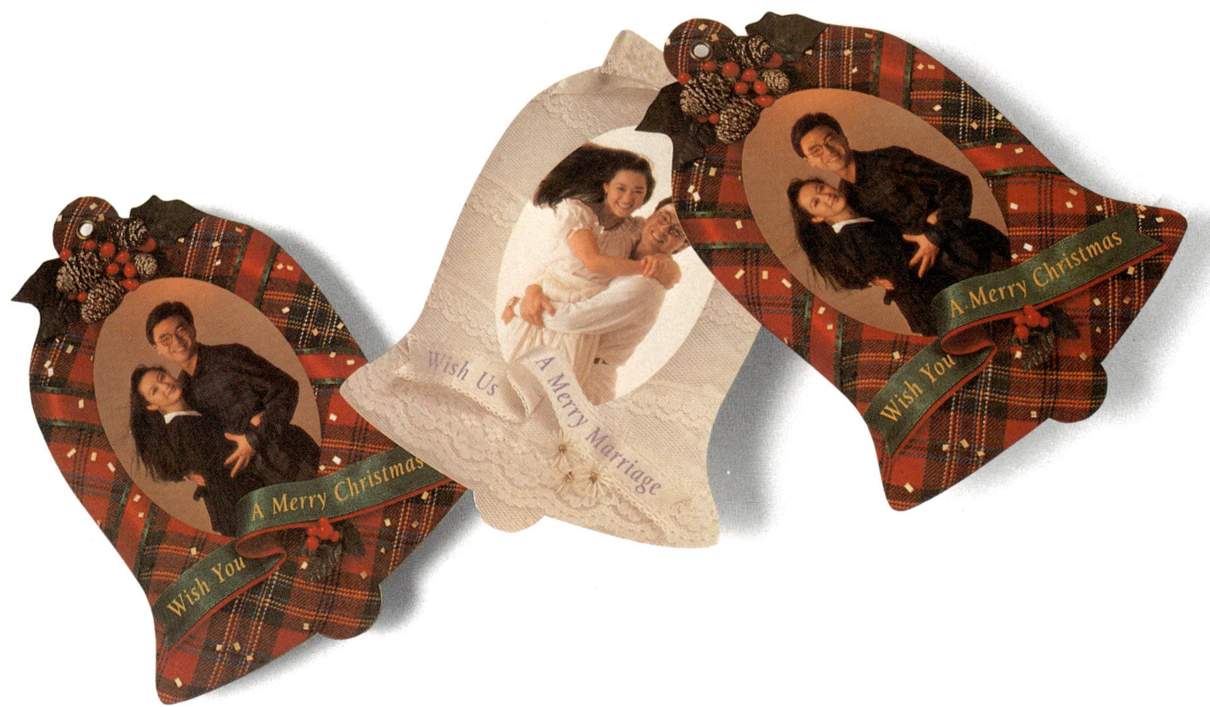

▲
Christmas card
クリスマス・カード
HONG KONG 1987
CD:Kan Tai-keung
AD:Kan Tai-keung
Freeman Lau Siu-hong
D:Chau So-hing,Delphine
DF:Kan Tai-keung
Design & Associates
CL:Teresa & Kenny Bee

▼
Christmas card
クリスマス・カード
USA 1989
CD:Kris Kagelmann Holtz
AD,D:Tracy Gibbons
I:Malcolm Farley
CW:Sandy Siegrist
DF:Janis Boehm Design
CL:Manpower
TC:Personnel Agency
人材派遣

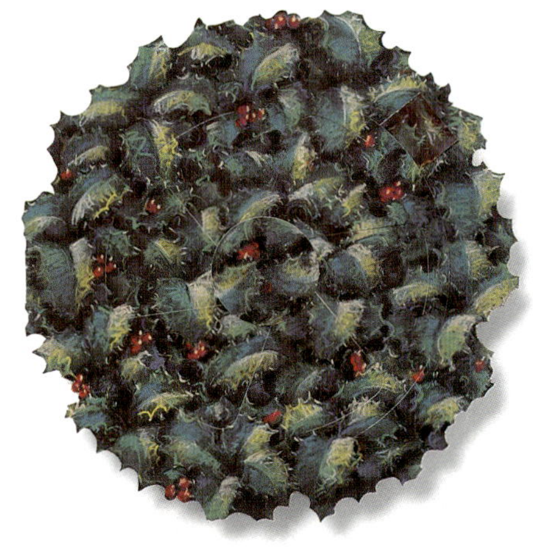
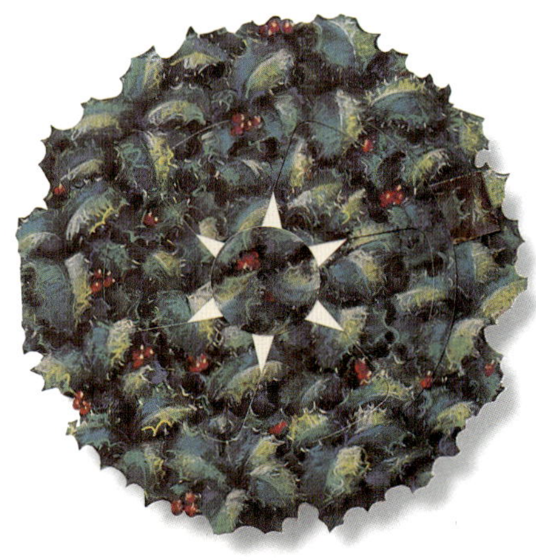
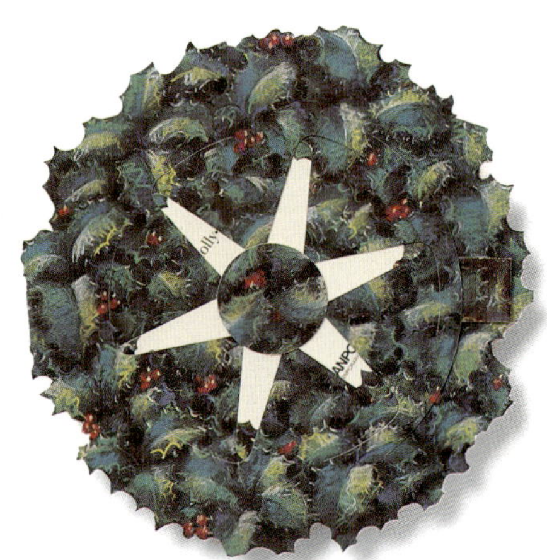
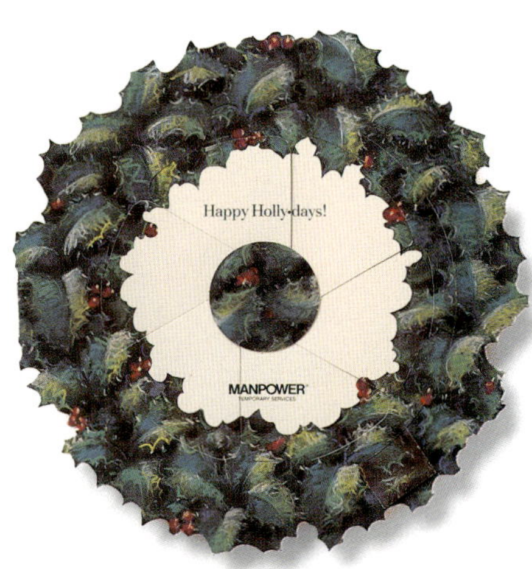

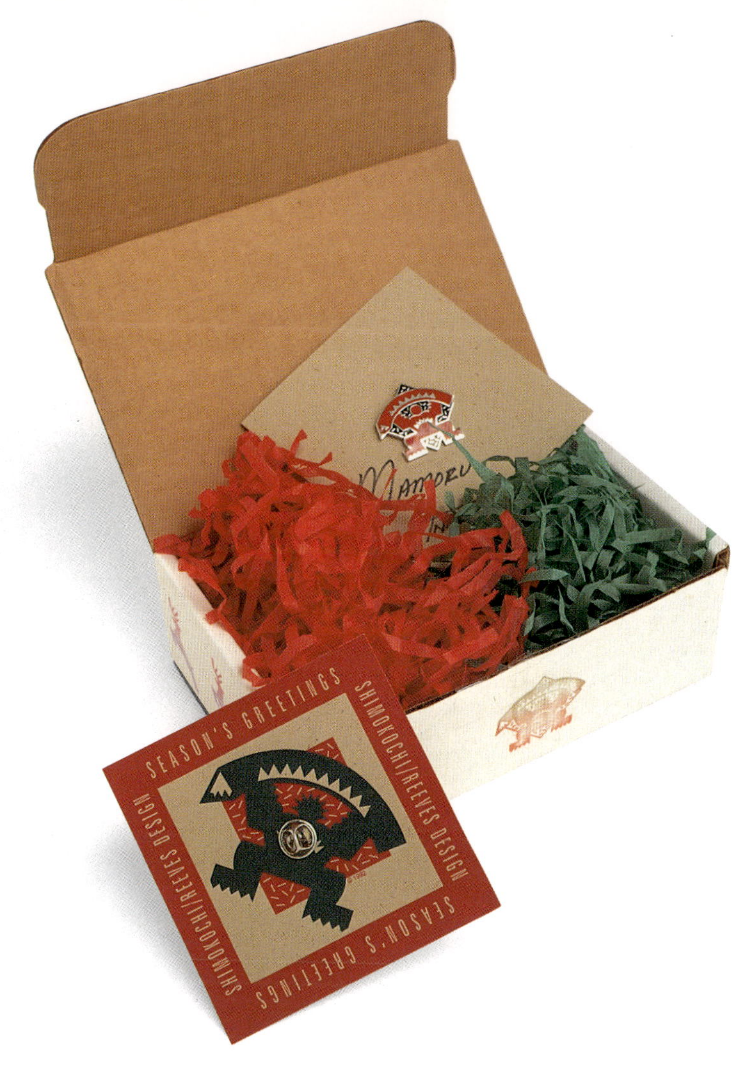

▲
Christmas card
クリスマス・カード
USA 1992
CD,D,I:Mamoru Shimokochi
AD:Anne Reeves
DF:Shimokochi/Reeves
CL:Shimokochi/Reeves
TC:Design Studio
デザイン

▼
Christmas card
クリスマス・カード
CANADA 1990
CD,AD,D,I:Andy Ip
Catherine Lam
DF:Andy Ip Design
CL:Rising Sun Typesetting
TC:Computer Typesetters
コンピューター写植

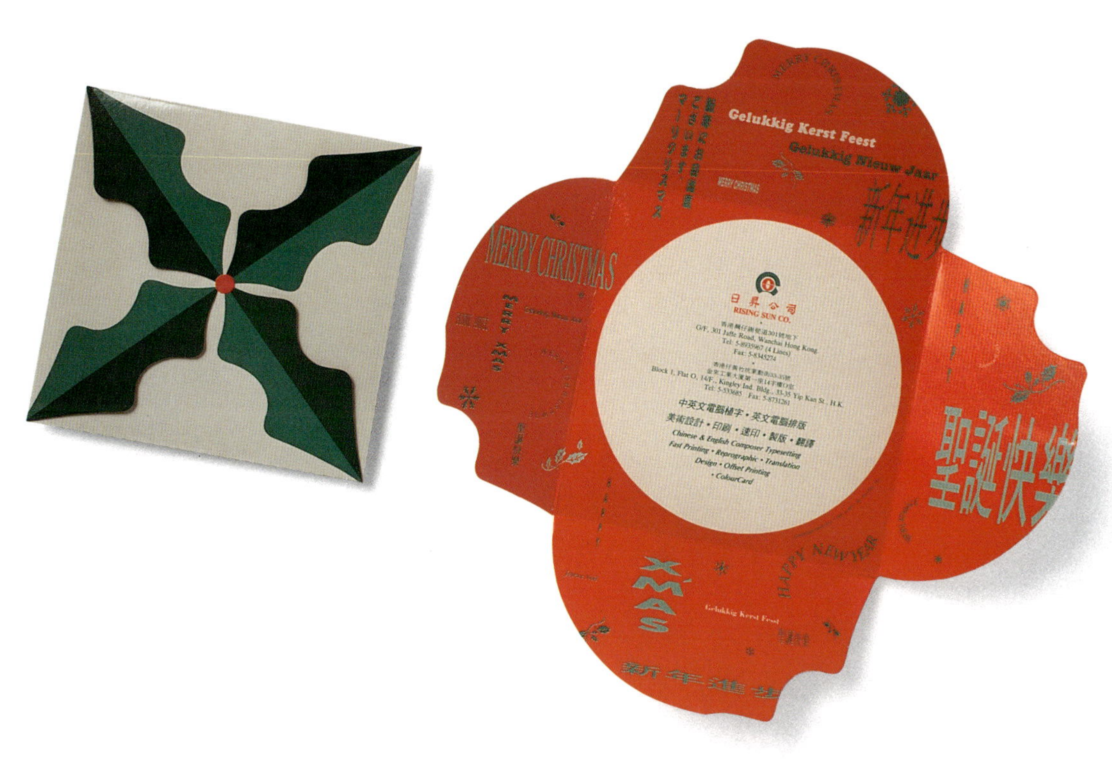

Christmas card
クリスマス・カード
CANADA 1990
CD:Marcello Grossutti
AD,D:John Hardaker
DF:Rushton Green and Grossutti
CL:Rushton Green and Grossutti
TC:Design Studio
デザイン

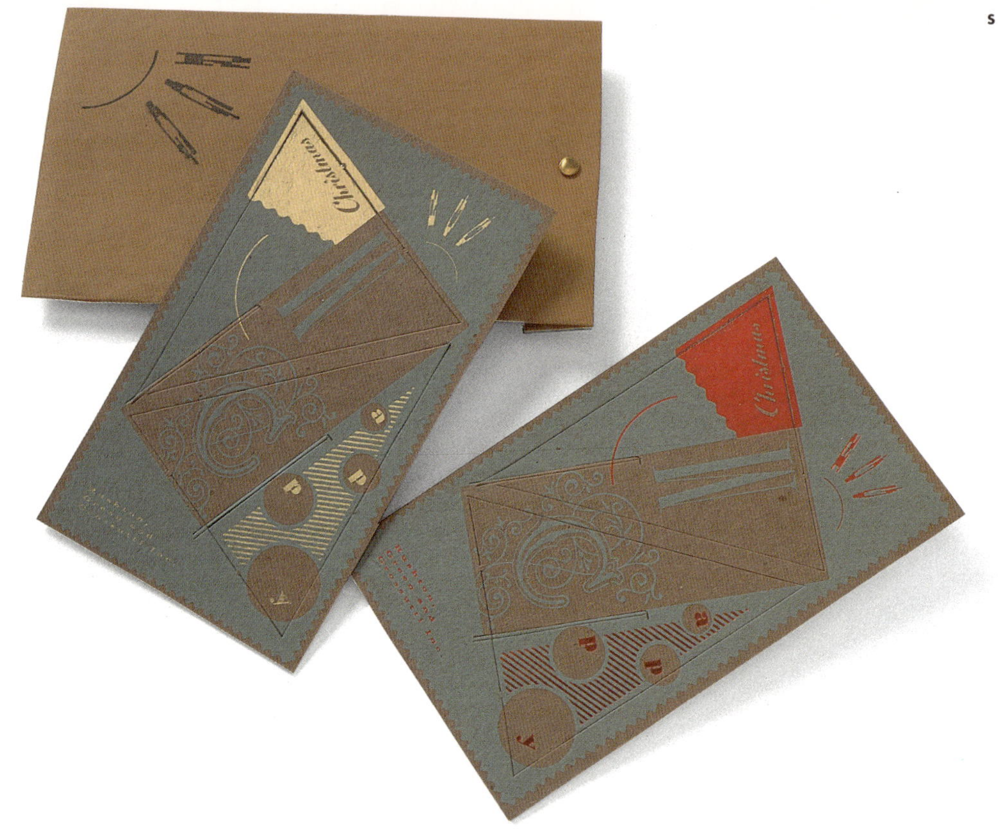

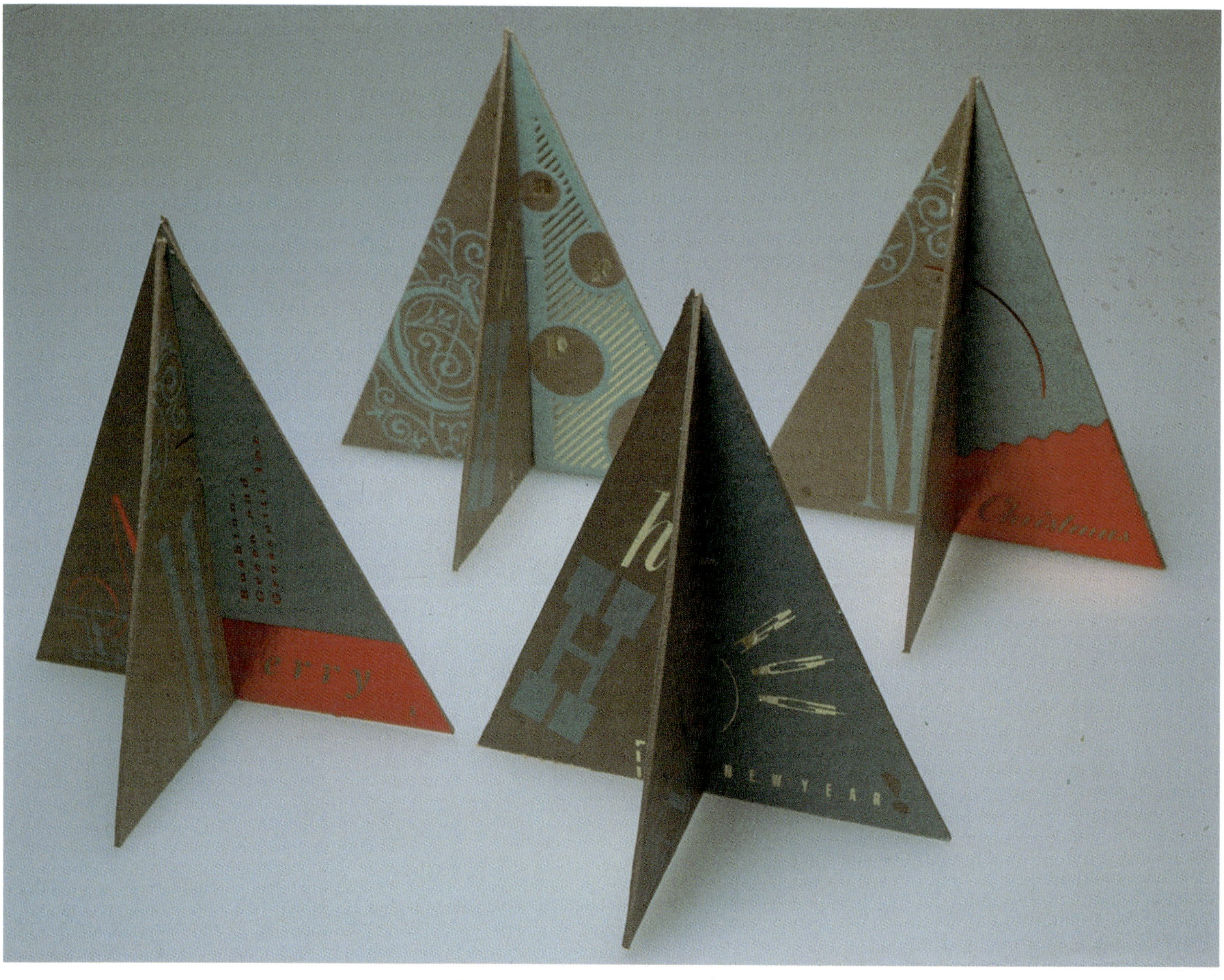

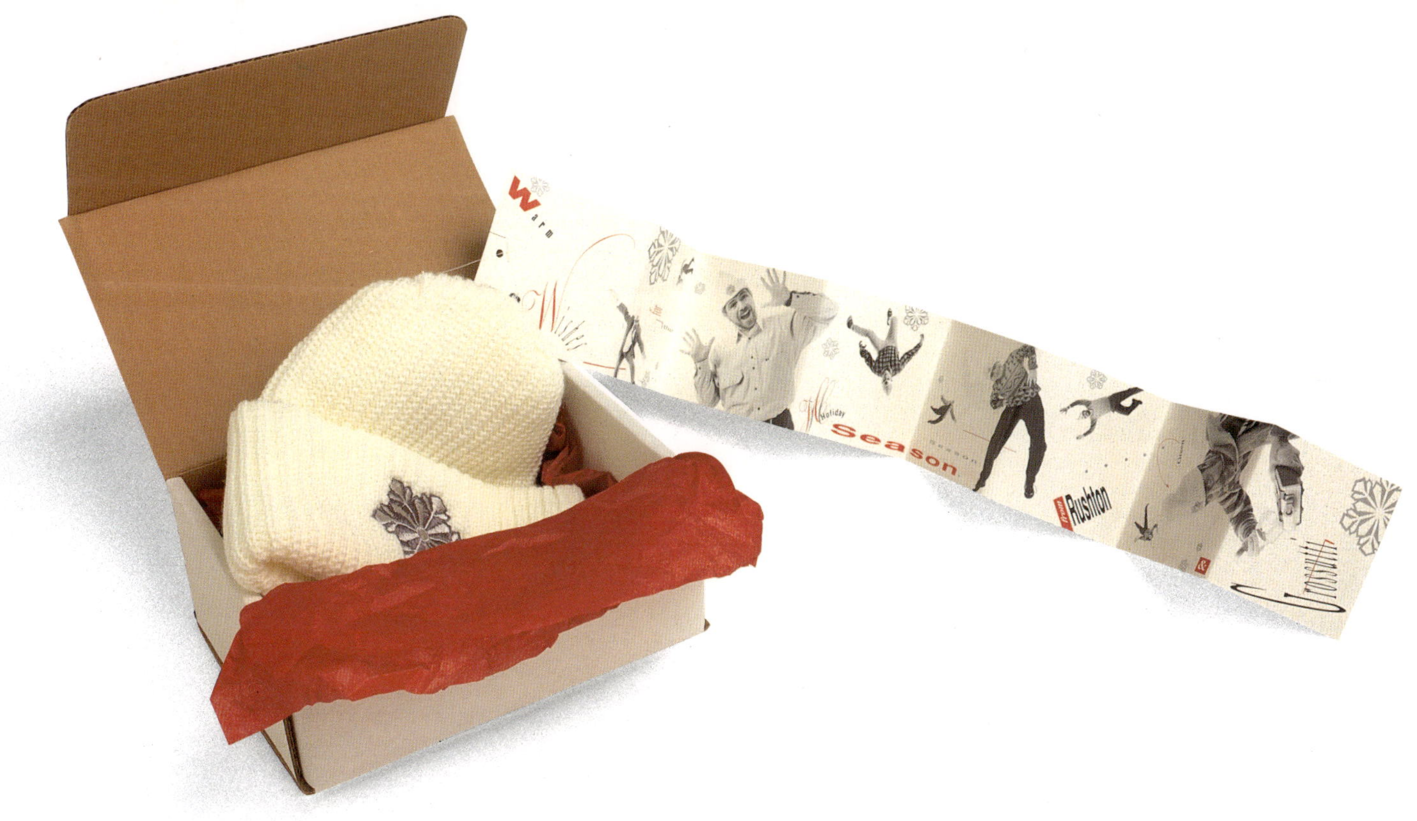

▲
Christmas card
クリスマス・カード
CANADA 1989
CD:Marcello Grossutti
AD,D:John Hardaker
P:Sidney Tabak
DF:Rushton Green and Grossutti
CL:Rushton Green and Grossutti
TC:Design Studio
デザイン

▼
Christmas card
クリスマス・カード
USA 1989
AD,D:Charles Spencer Anderson
Daniel Olson
CW:Lisa Pemrick
DF:Charles S.Anderson Design
CL:Charles S.Anderson Design
TC:Graphic Design Studio
グラフィック・デザイン

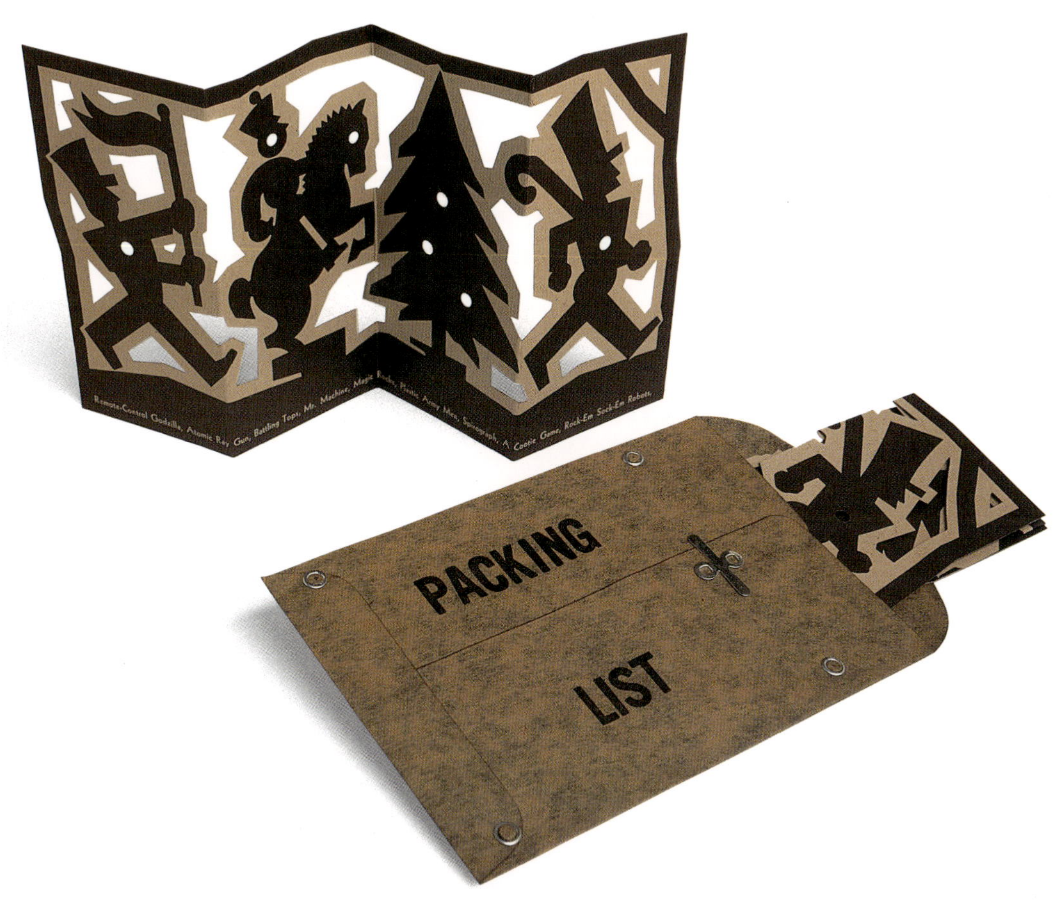

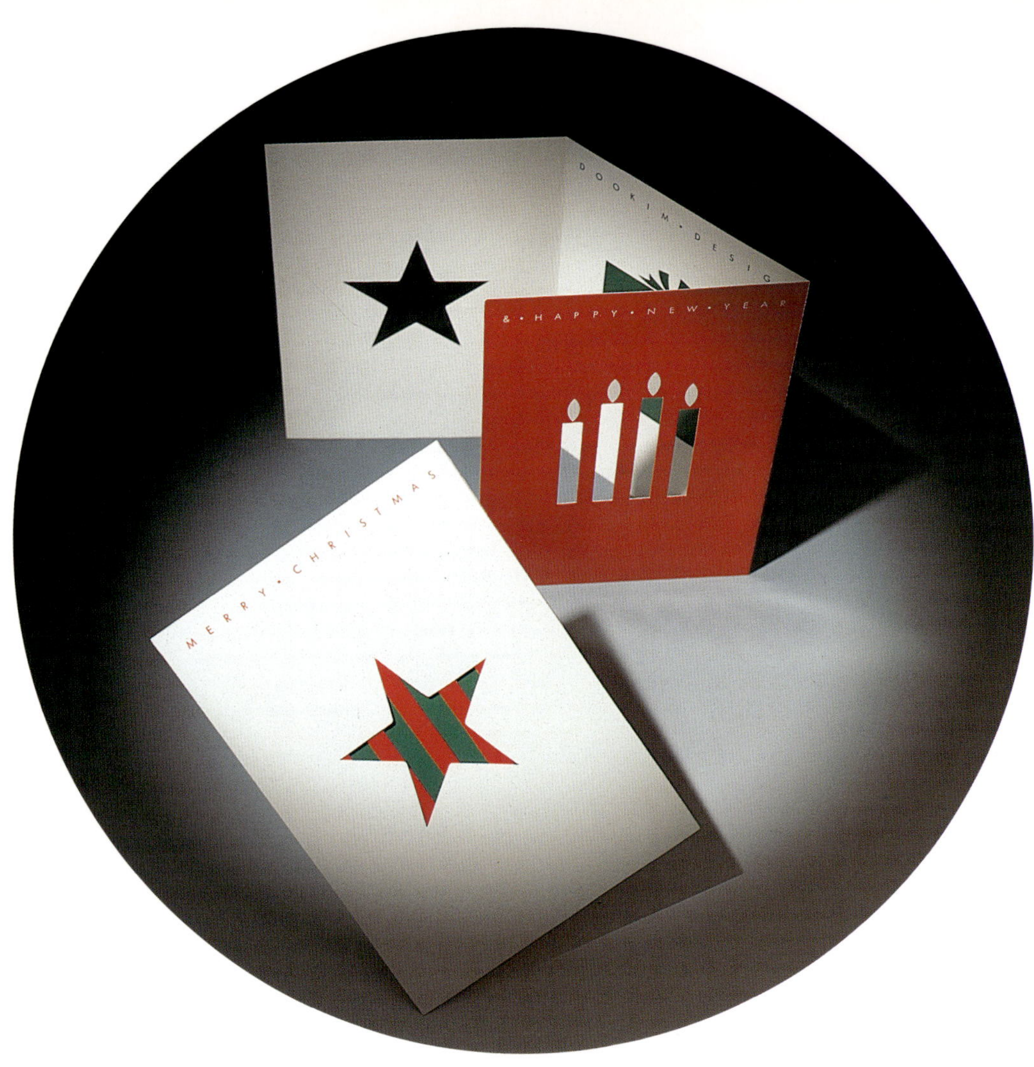

▲
Christmas card
クリスマス・カード
KOREA 1990
CD:Doo Hwang Kim
AD:Dongil Lee
D:Ji-won Shin
Seung Hee Lee
DF:Dookim Design
CL:Dookim Design
TC:Graphic Design Studio
グラフィック・デザイン

▼
Christmas card
クリスマス・カード
AUSTRALIA 1989
AD:Annette Harcus
D,I,CW:Stephanie Martin
DF:Annette Harcus Design
CL:Film Australia
TC:Film Maker
映画制作

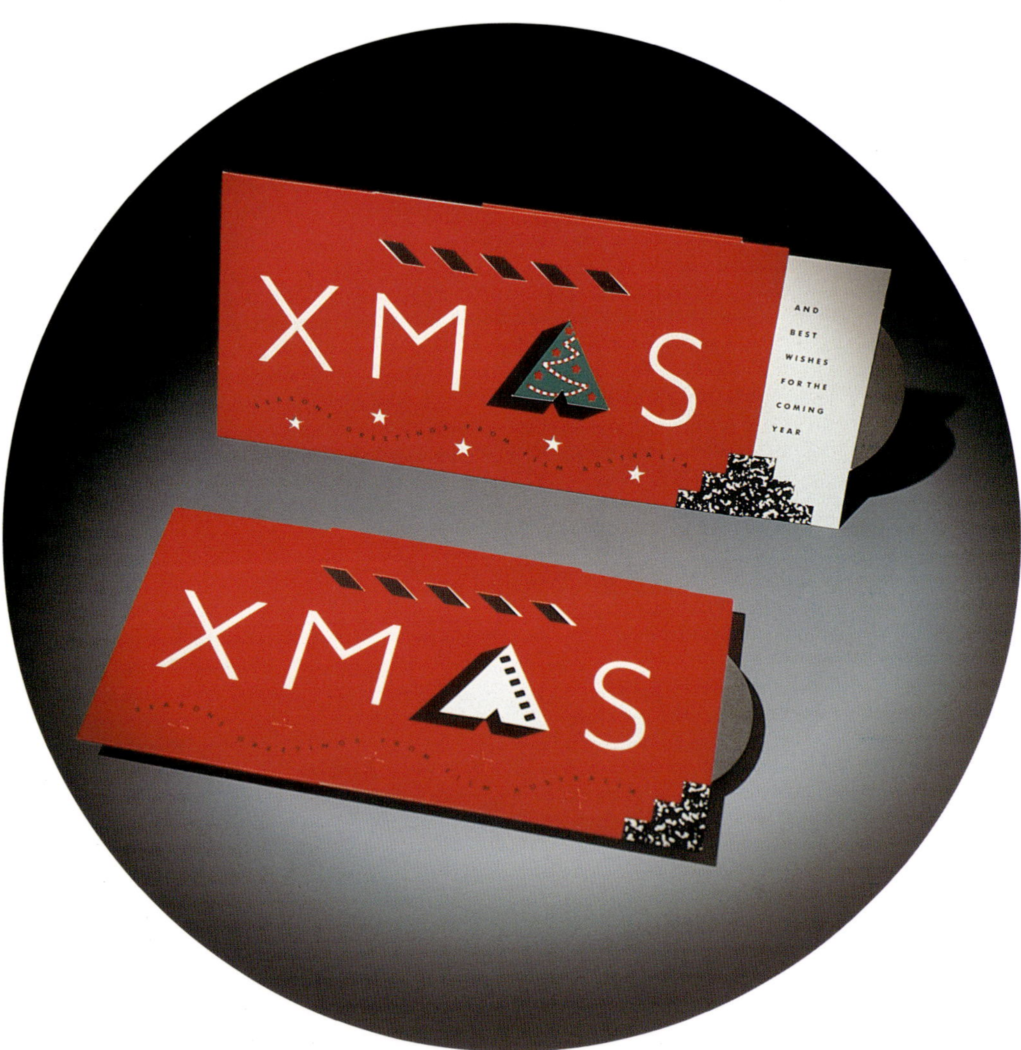

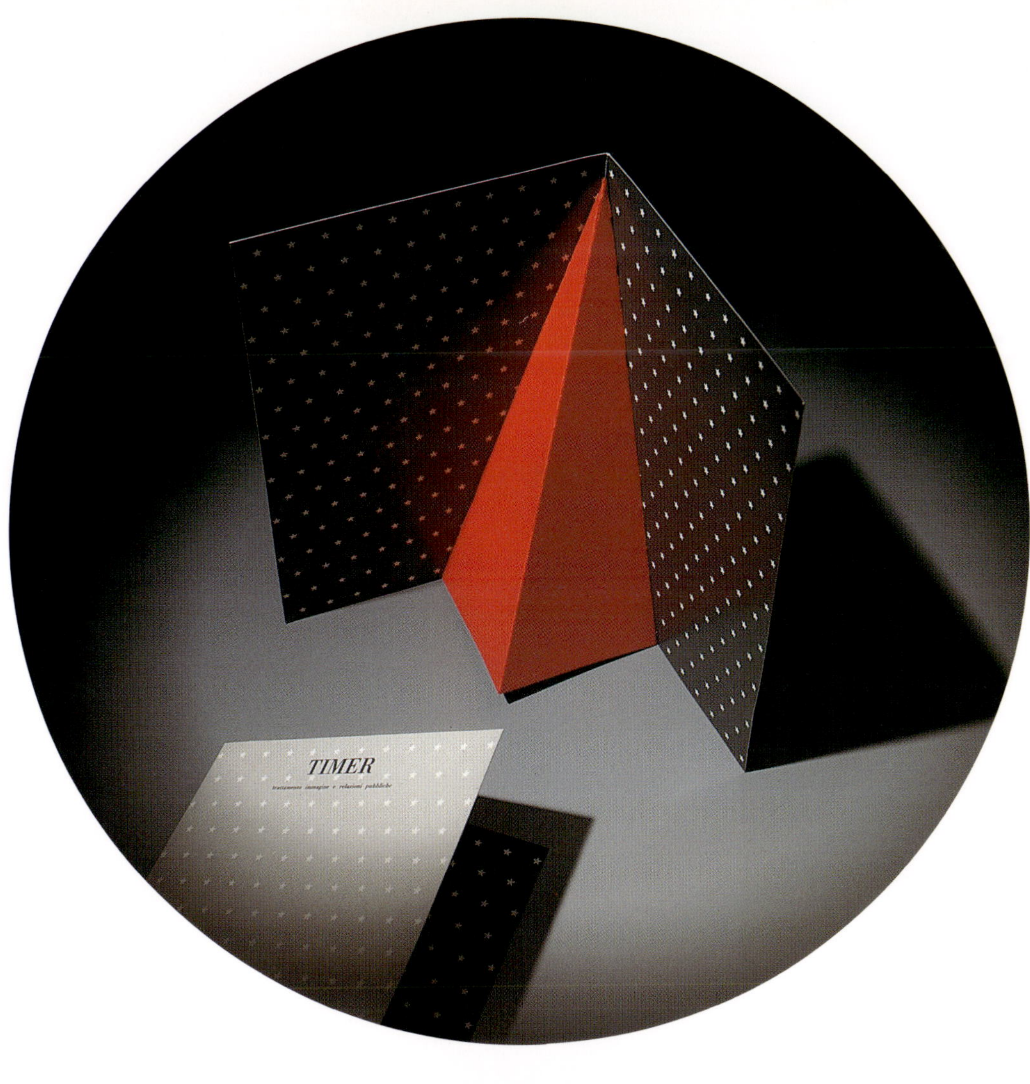

▲
Christmas card
クリスマス・カード
ITALY 1991
AD,D,DF:Susanna Vallebona
CL:Timer
TC:Public Relations Agency
広報

▼
Christmas card
クリスマス・カード
KOREA 1990
CD:Doo Hwang Kim
AD:Dongil Lee
D:Ji-won Shin
Seung Hee Lee
DF:Dookim Design
CL:Dookim Design
TC:Graphic Design Studio
グラフィック・デザイン

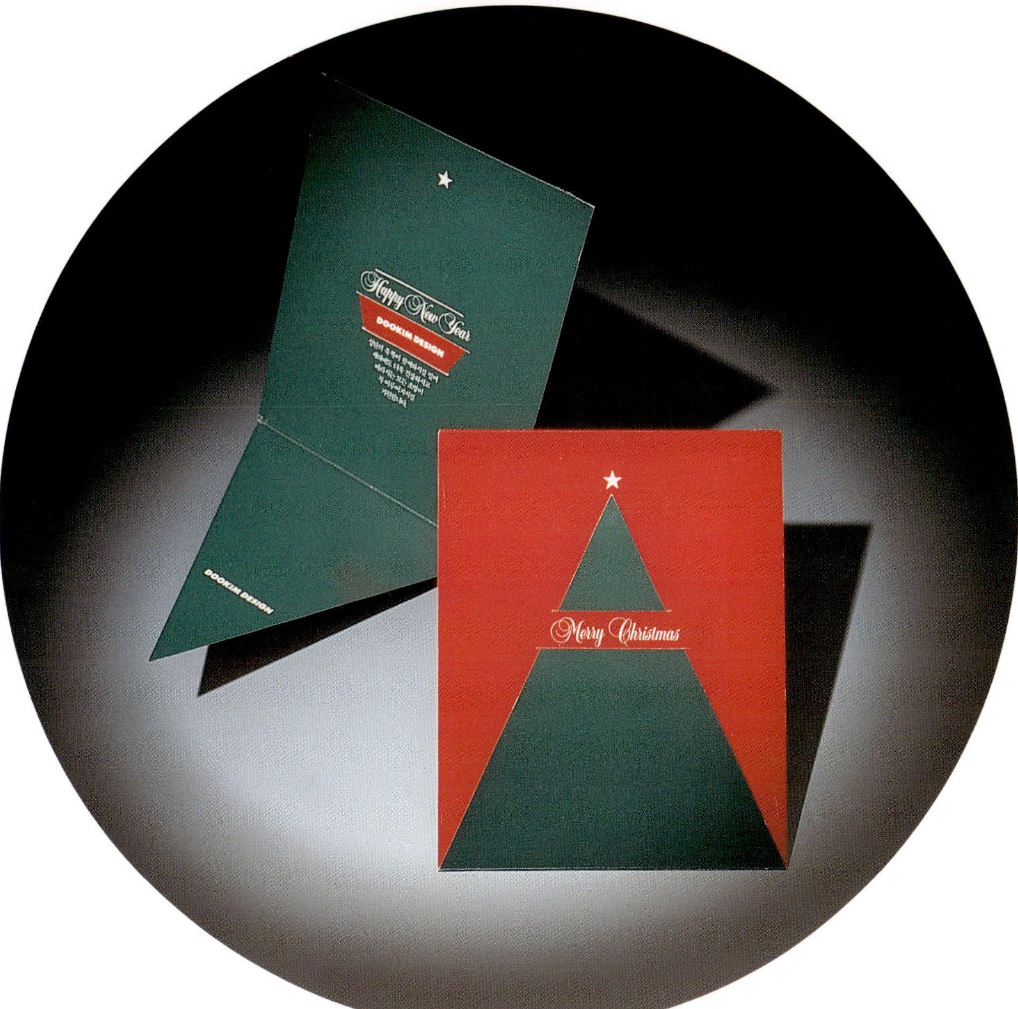

▲

Christmas card

クリスマス・カード

JAPAN 1991

CD:Saihei Makinami

AD.D:Daisuke Yamanaka

CL:Graphic Traffic

TC:Graphic Design Studio

グラフィック・デザイン

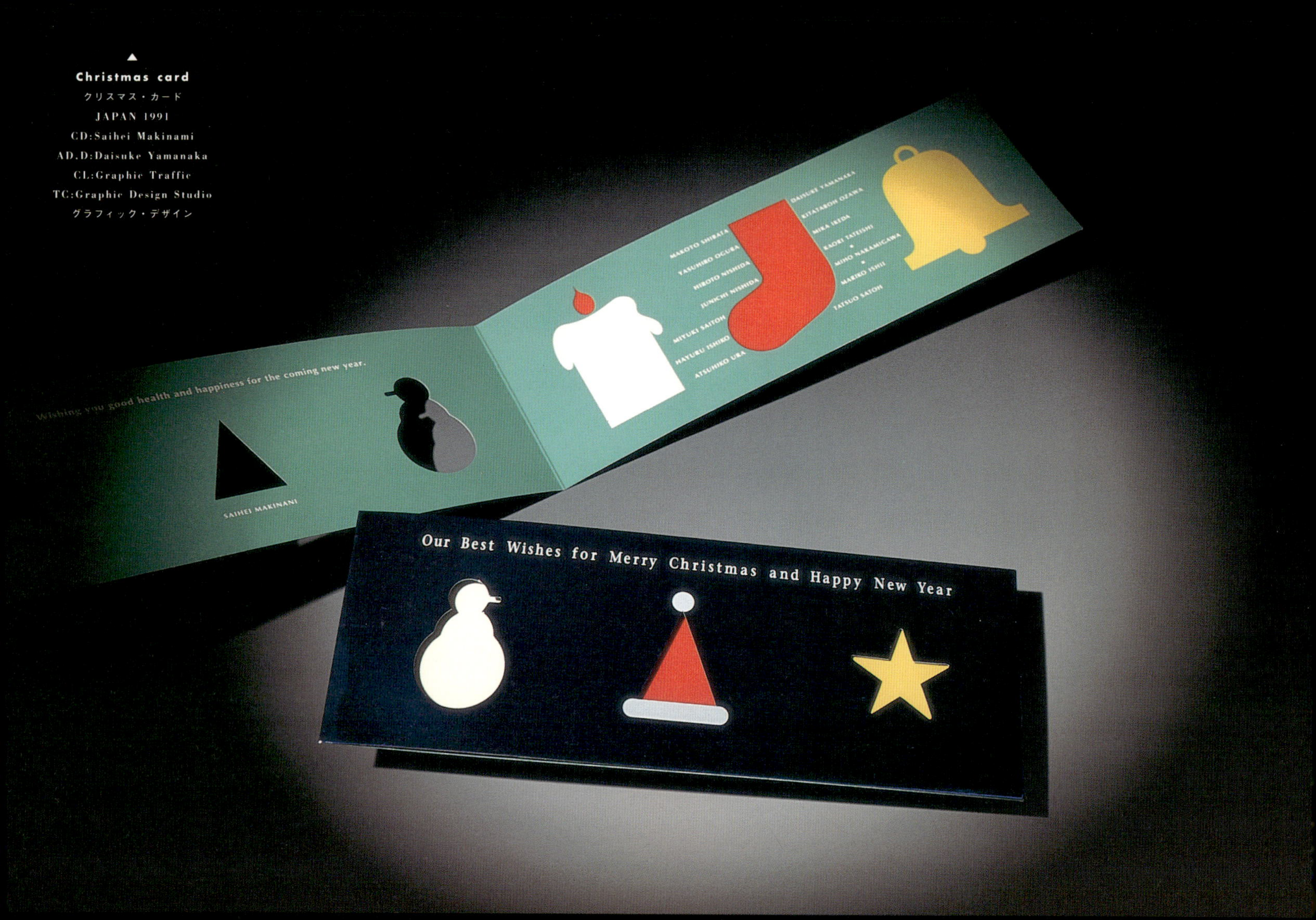

▼

Christmas card

クリスマス・カード

HONG KONG 1989

D:Catherine Lam Siu Hung

DF:Triump Int'l (H.K)

CL:Triump Int'l (H.K)

TC:Apparel Maker

アパレル

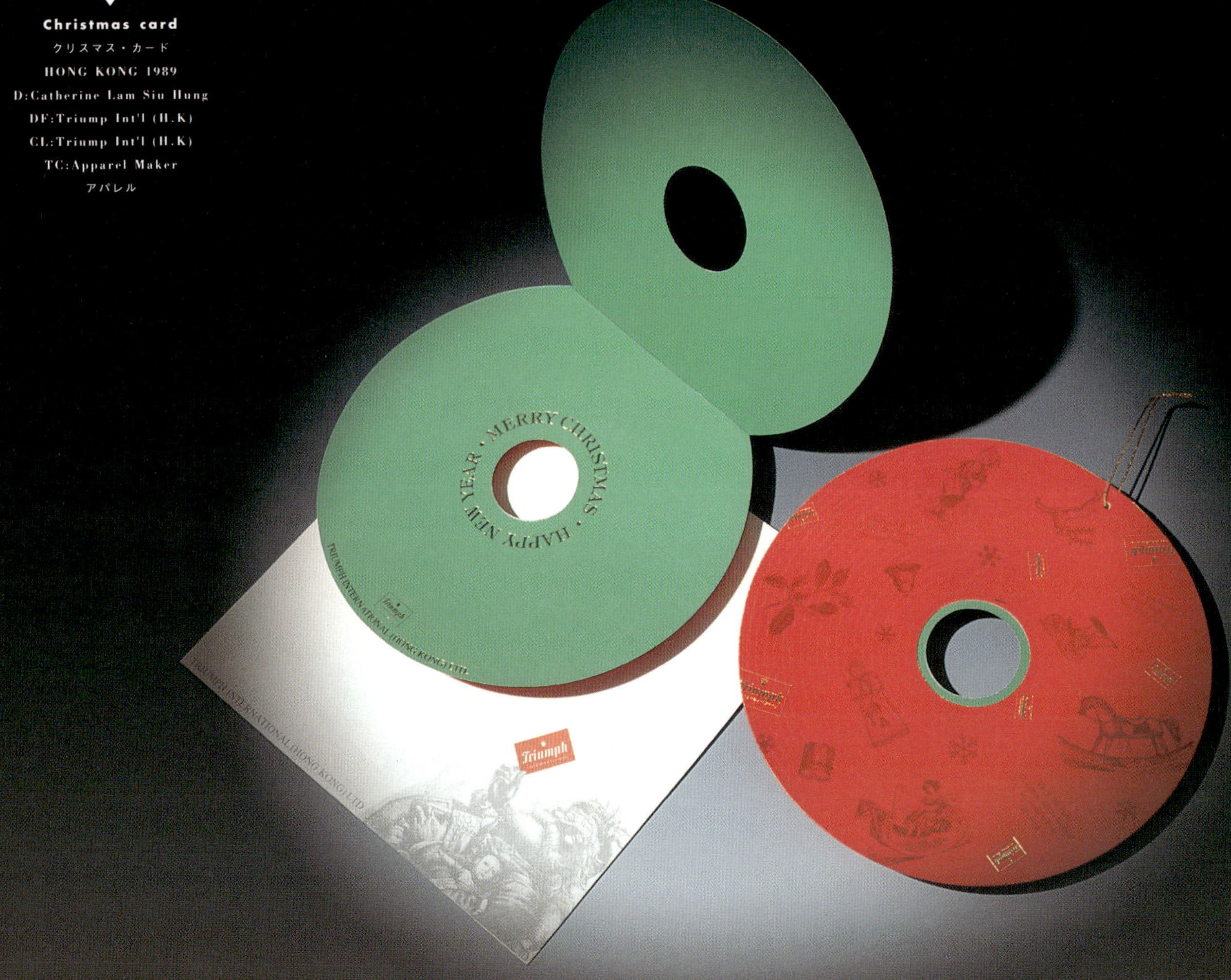

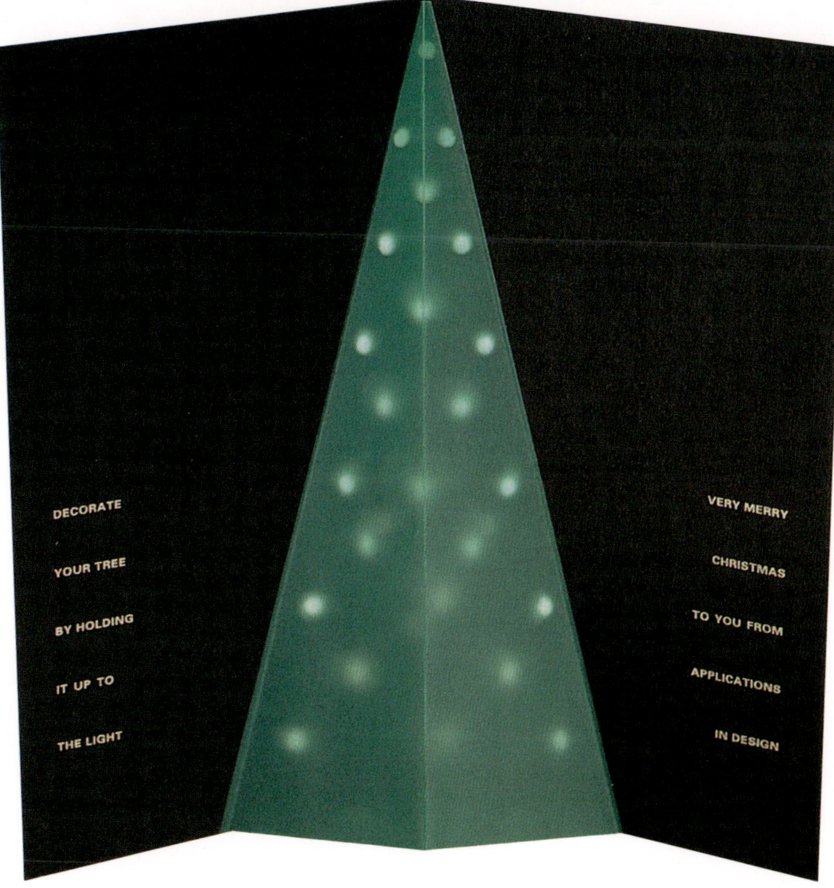

▲
Christmas card
クリスマス・カード
CANADA 1992
AD,D:Michéle Miodonski
CW:Christina Corner
DF:Applications in Design
CL:Applications in Design
TC:Graphic Design Studio
グラフィック・デザイン

▼
Christmas and New year's card
クリスマス&ニューイヤーズ・カード
CANADA 1991
AD,D:Michéle Miodonski
DF:Applications in Design
CL:Applications in Design
TC:Design Studio
デザイン

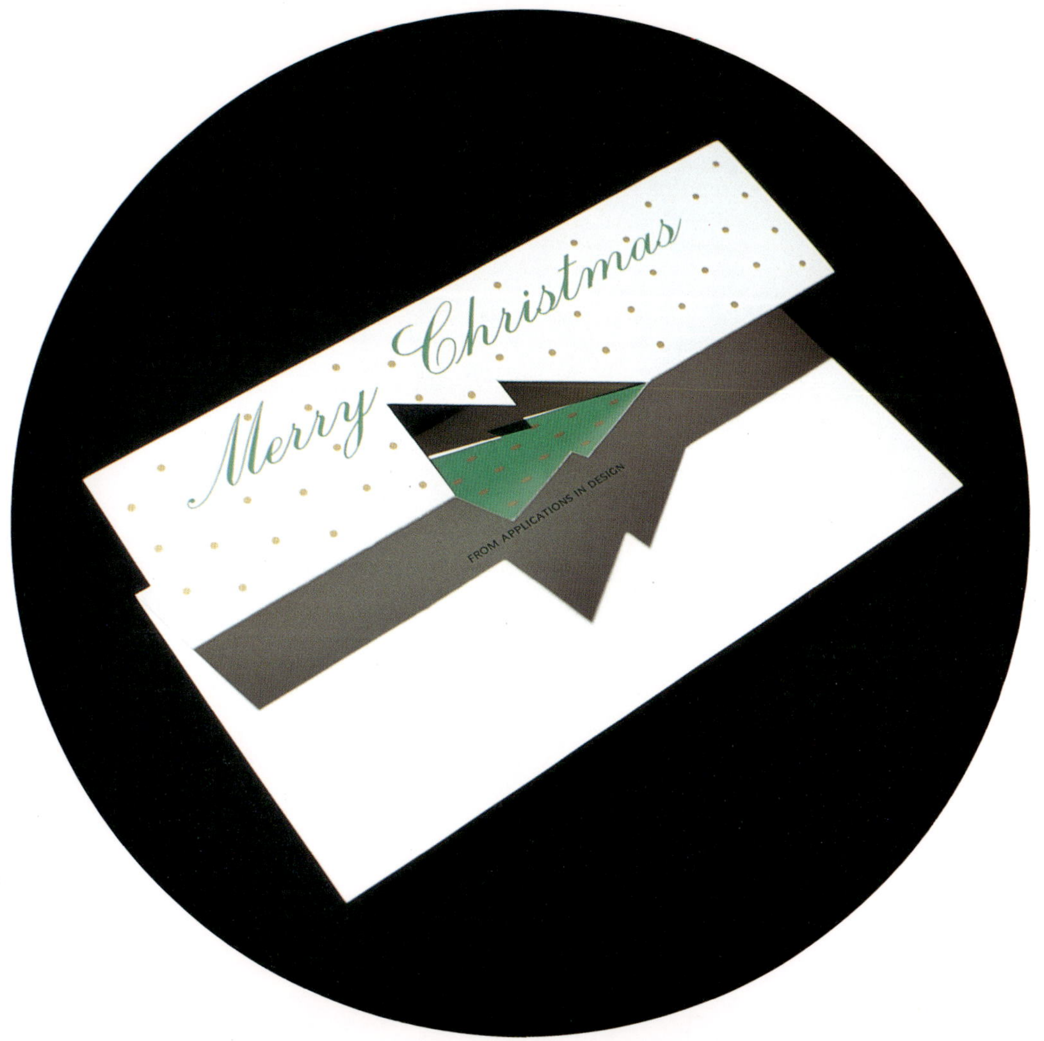

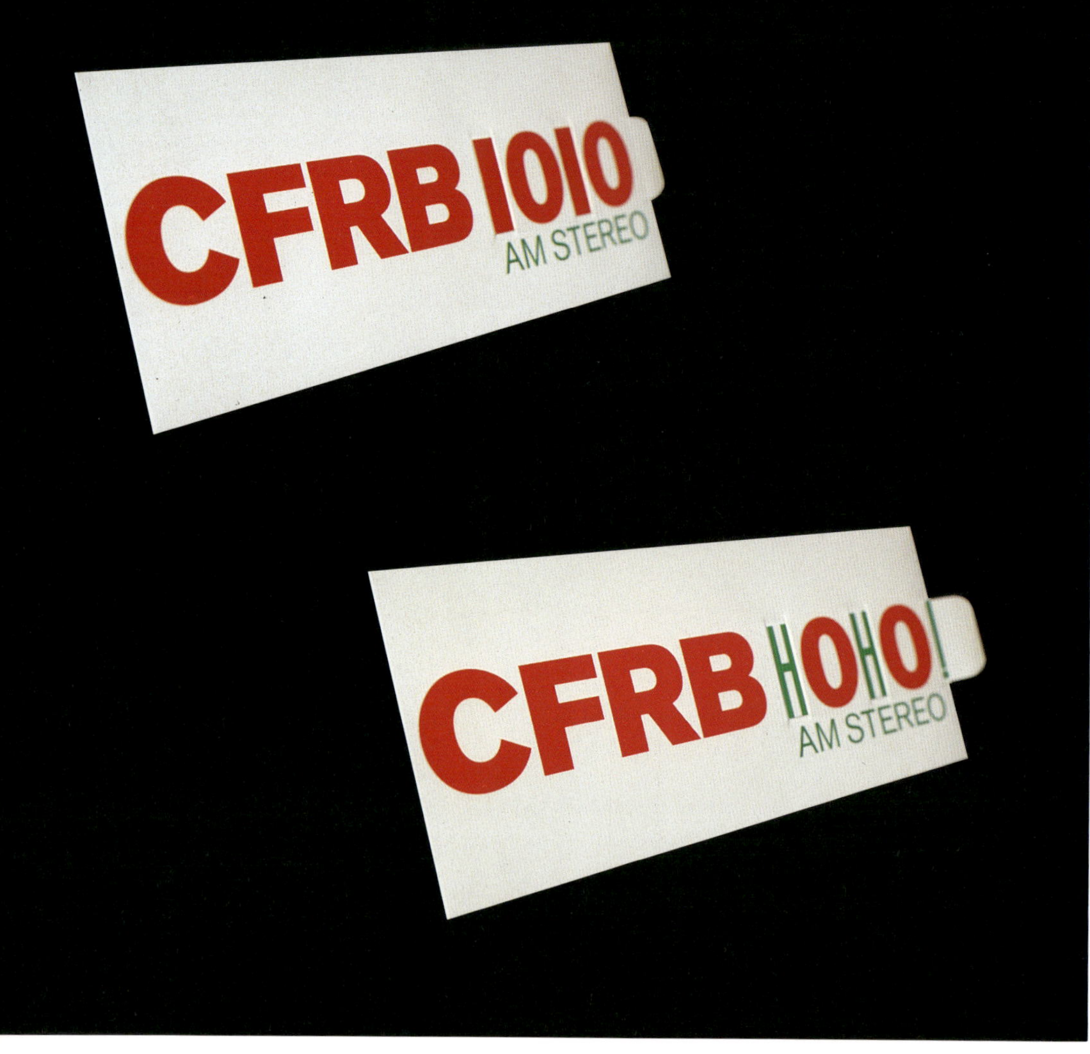

◀
Christmas card
クリスマス・カード
CANADA 1989
AD,D:Michéle Miodonski
DF:Applications in Design
CL:CFRB 1010
Standard Broadcast
TC:Radio Broadcaster
ラジオ局

▶
Christmas card
クリスマス・カード
CANADA 1990
AD,D:Michéle Miodonski
DF:Applications in Design
CL:CFRB 1010
Standard Broadcast
TC:Radio Broadcaster
ラジオ局

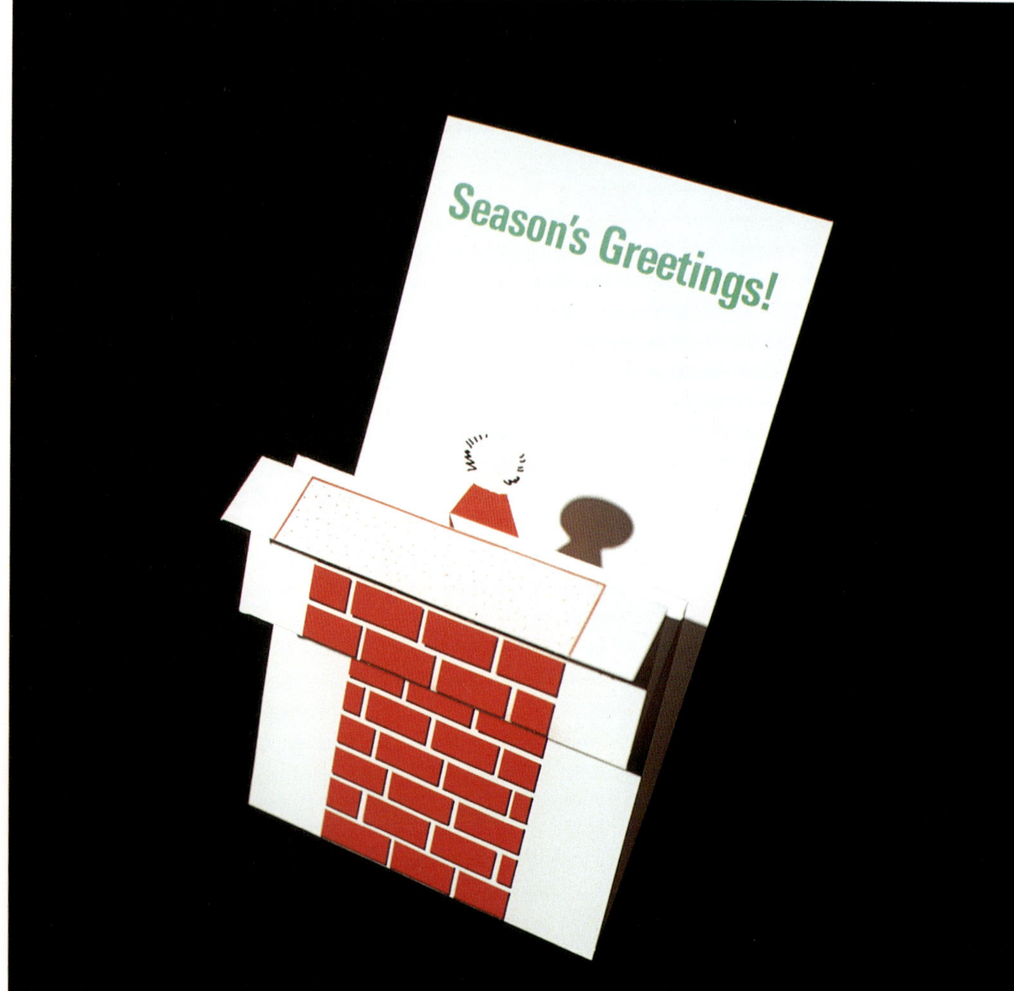

▶
New year's card
ニューイヤーズ・カード
ITALY 1991~92
AD,D,DF:Susanna Vallebona
P:Fabrizio Sartorelli
CL:Esseblu
TC:Graphic Design Studio
グラフィック・デザイン

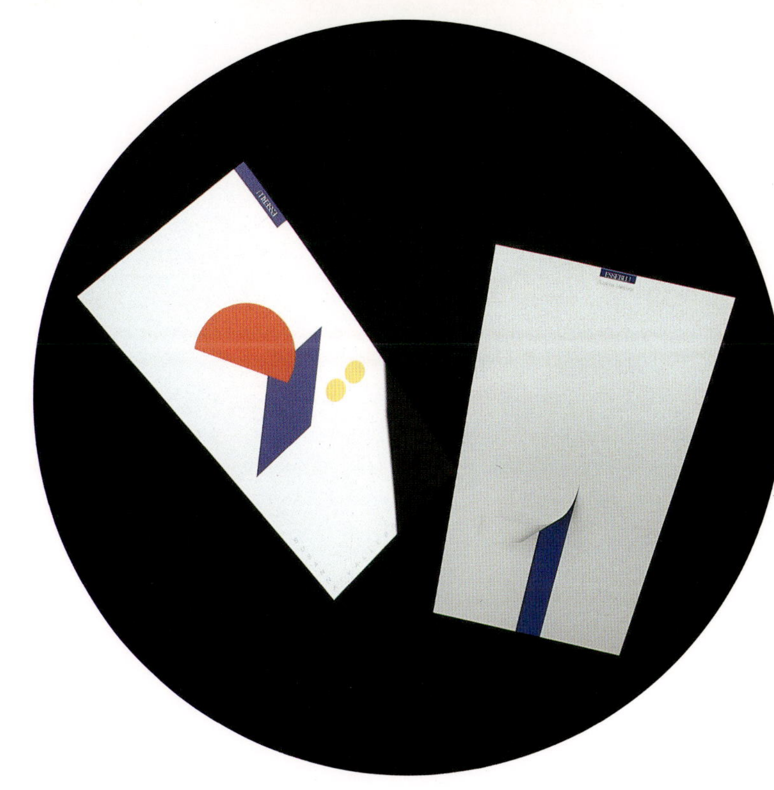

◀
Christmas card
クリスマス・カード
AUSTRIA 1991
AD:Sigi Ramoser
CL:Blit & Blank
TC:Cleaner
清掃

▶
Christmas card
クリスマス・カード
BRASIL 1991
CD:Hugo Kovadloff
Milton Cipis
Claudio Novaes
D,I:Milton Cipis
CW:Maria Pia Parente
DF:D Designers Associados
CL:Copas-Companhia Paulista de
Fertilizantes
TC:Chemicals Maker
化学薬品

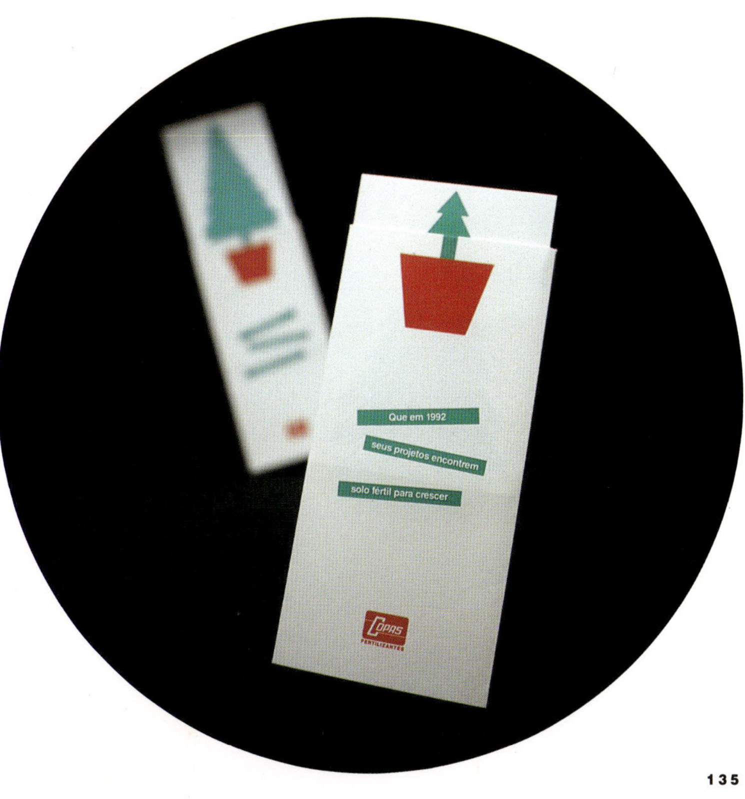

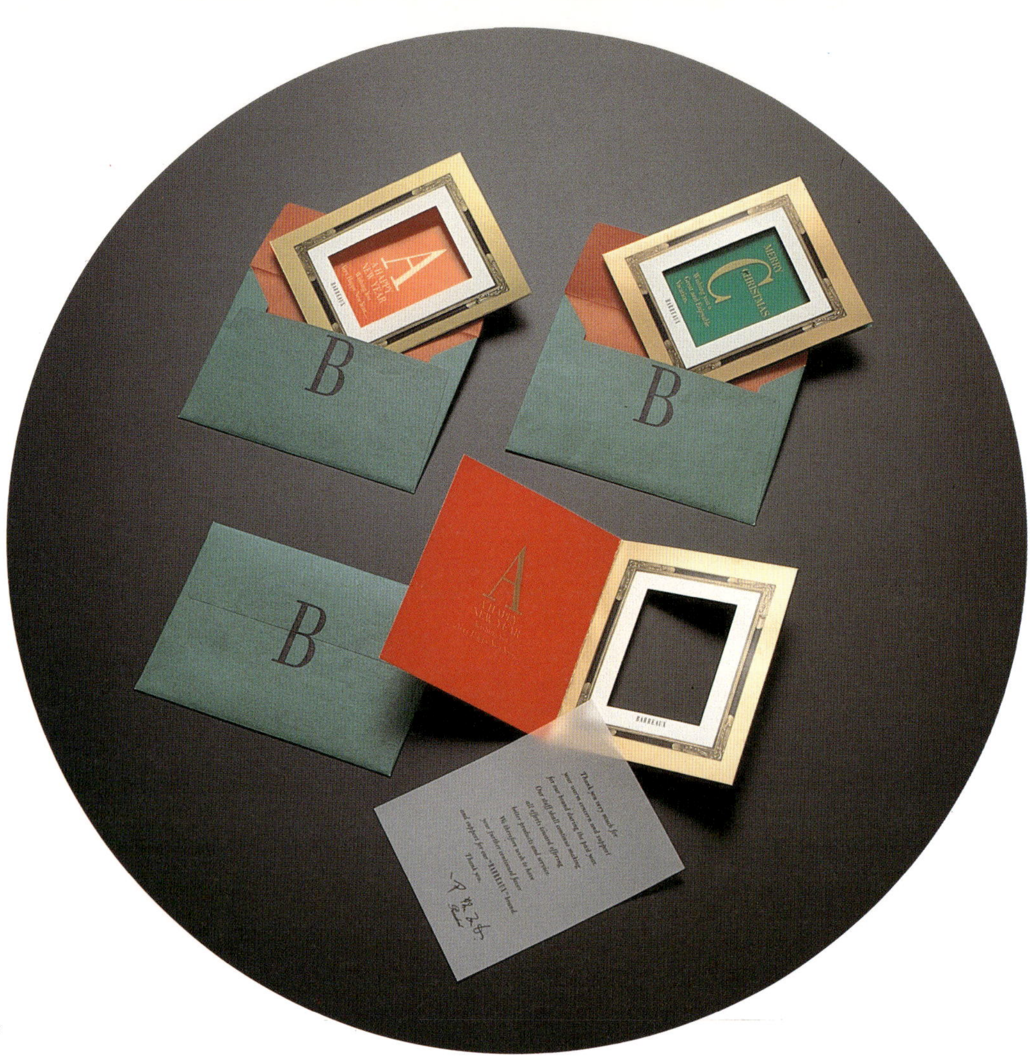

▲
Christmas and New year's card
クリスマス&ニューイヤーズ・カード
JAPAN 1991
CD,AD:Katsu Asano
D:Kinue Yonezawa
DF:ASA 100 Company
CL:Barreaux Division Scoop
TC:Apparel Maker
アパレル

▼
Christmas card
クリスマス・カード
AUSTRIA 1990
D:Sigi Ramoser
CL:Wenin Ohg
TC:Printer
印刷

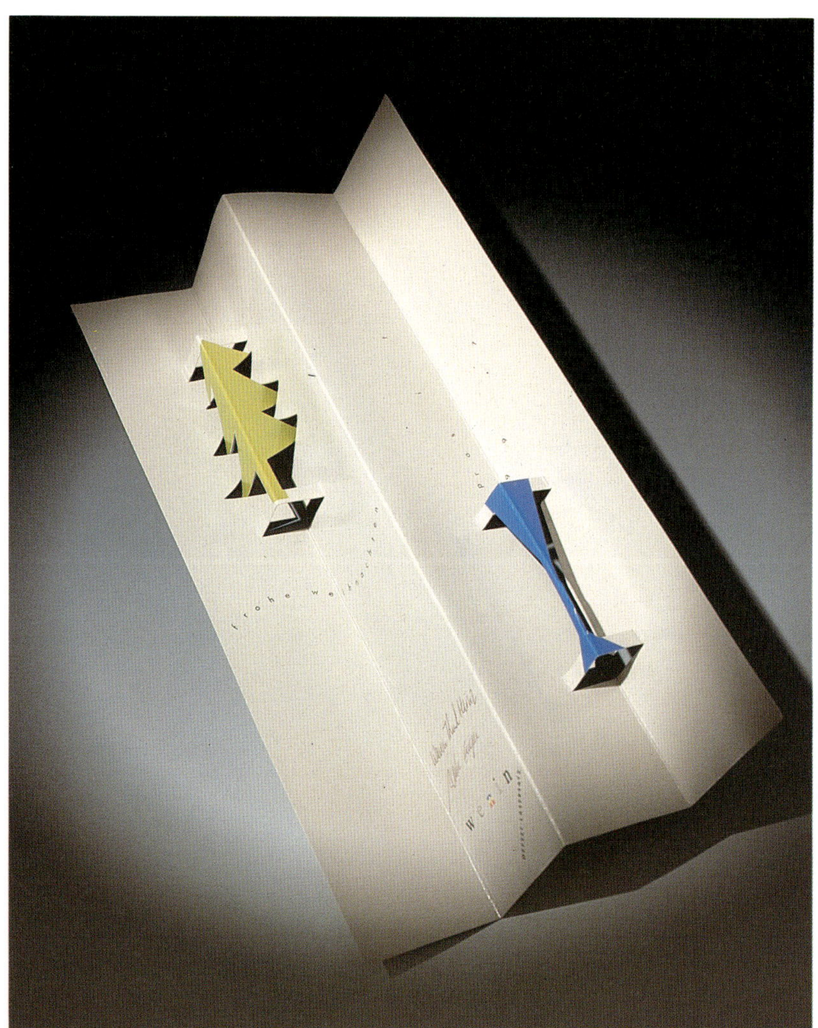

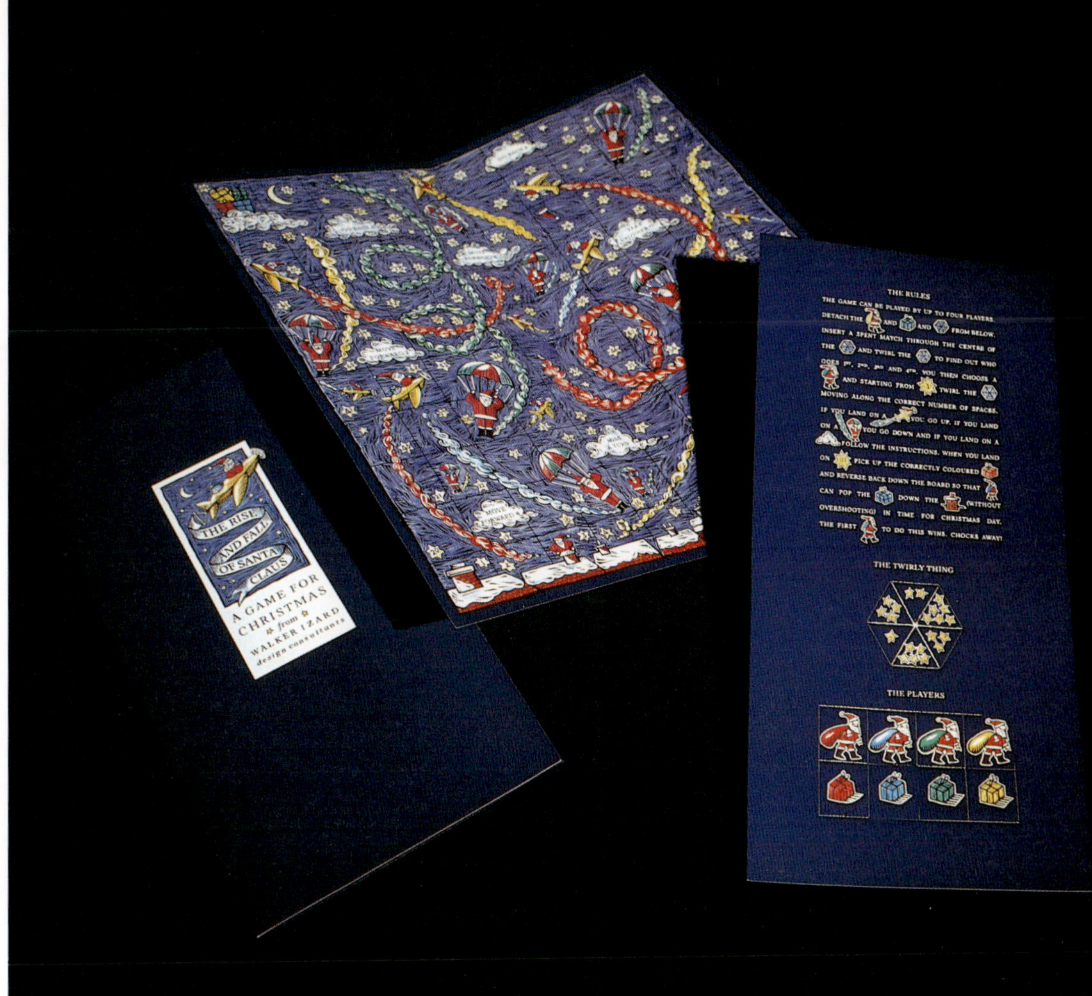

▶

Christmas card

クリスマス・カード

ENGLAND 1988

CD,D,CW:Tim Walker

AD:Paul Izard

I:Jayne Morris

DF:Walker Izard

CL:Guitty Talberg Illustration Agency

TC:Illustration Agency

イラストレーション・エージェンシー

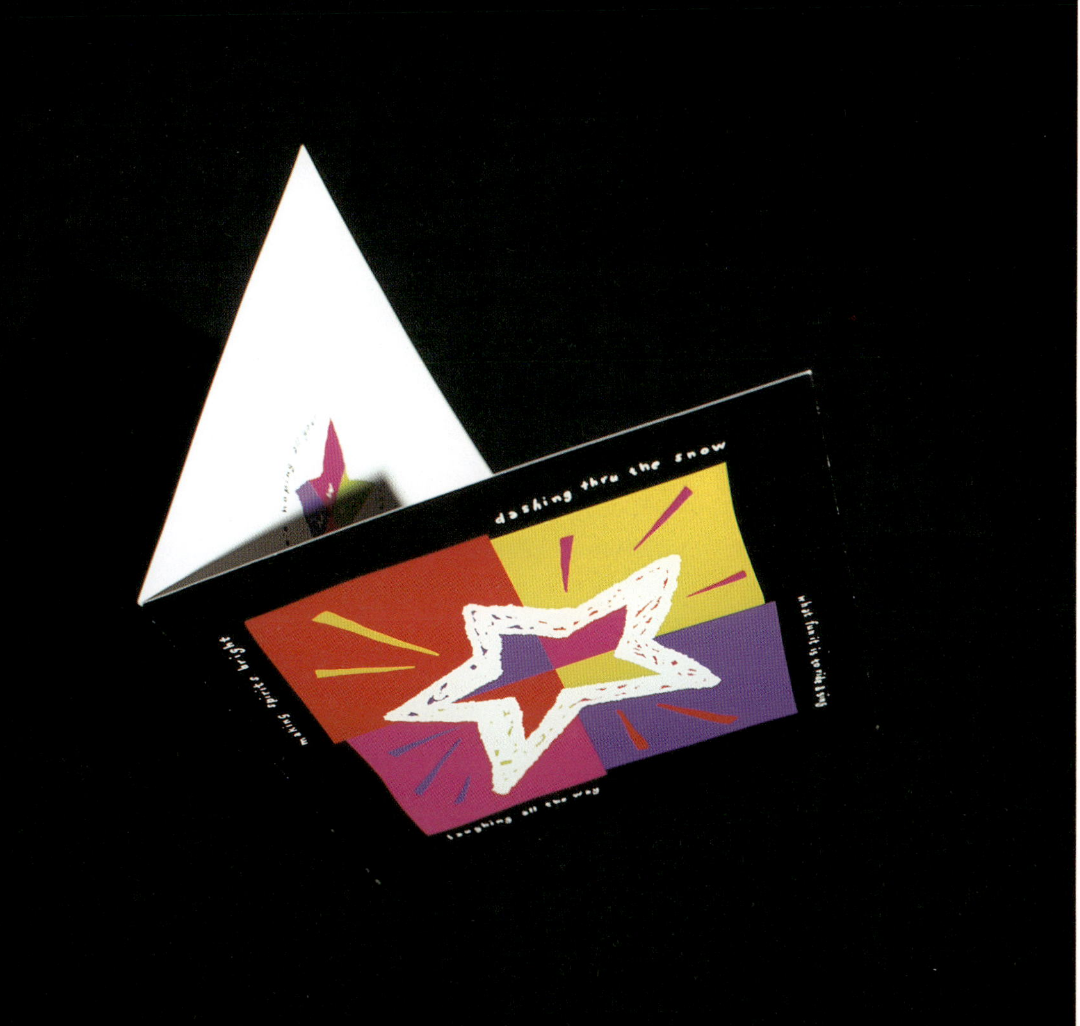

◀

Christmas card

クリスマス・カード

USA 1991

CD,D:Kate McSherry

DF:Murrie, White, Drummond, Lienhart, & Assoc.

CL:Murrie, White, Drummond, Lienhart, & Assoc.

TC:Package Design Studio

パッケージ・デザイン

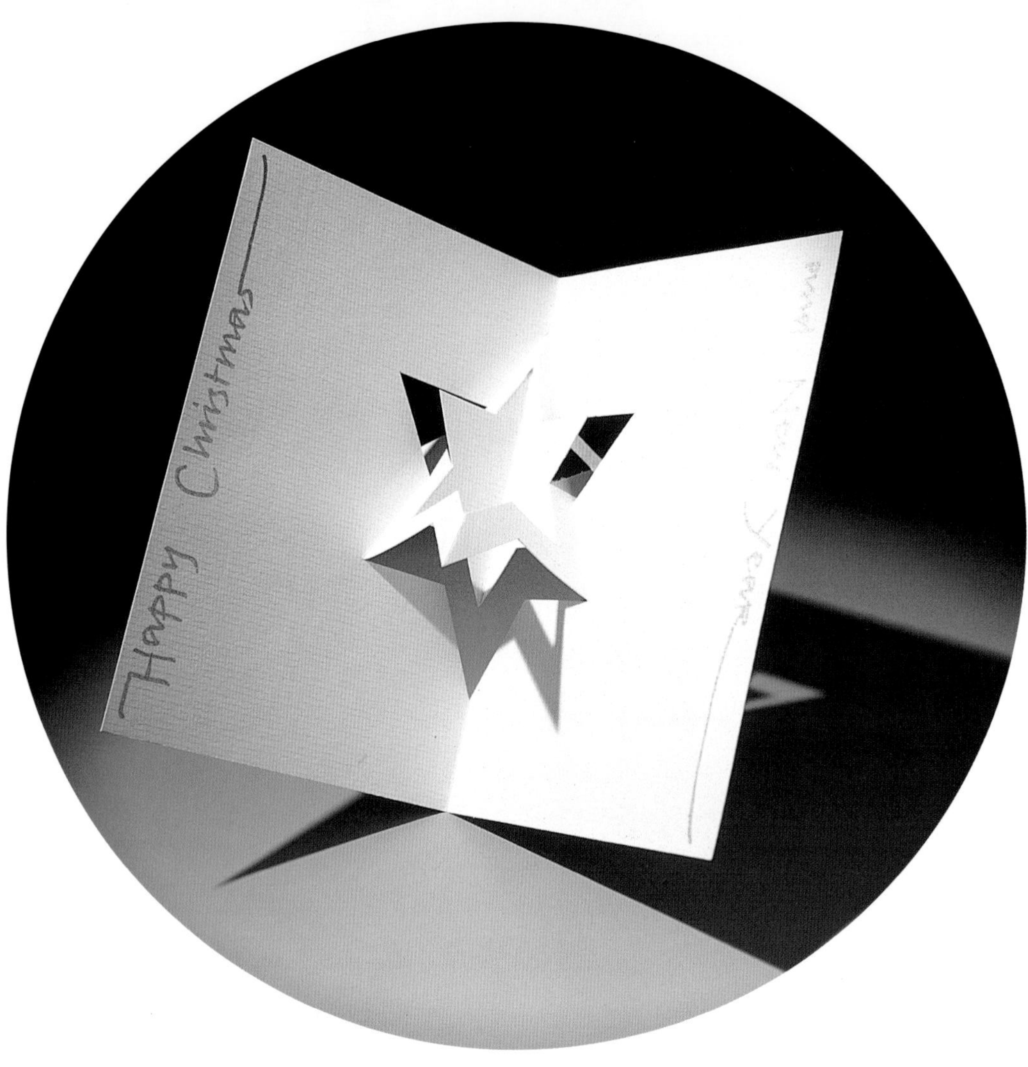

▲
Christmas card
クリスマス・カード
ENGLAND 1991
D:Bramante Architects
CL:Bramante Architects
TC:Architects
建築

▼
Christmas card
クリスマス・カード
ENGLAND 1991
CD,D:Lyn Hourahine
DF:Paper Power
CL:L.H.D.A.
Paper Power
TC:Graphic Consultant
グラフィック・コンサルタント

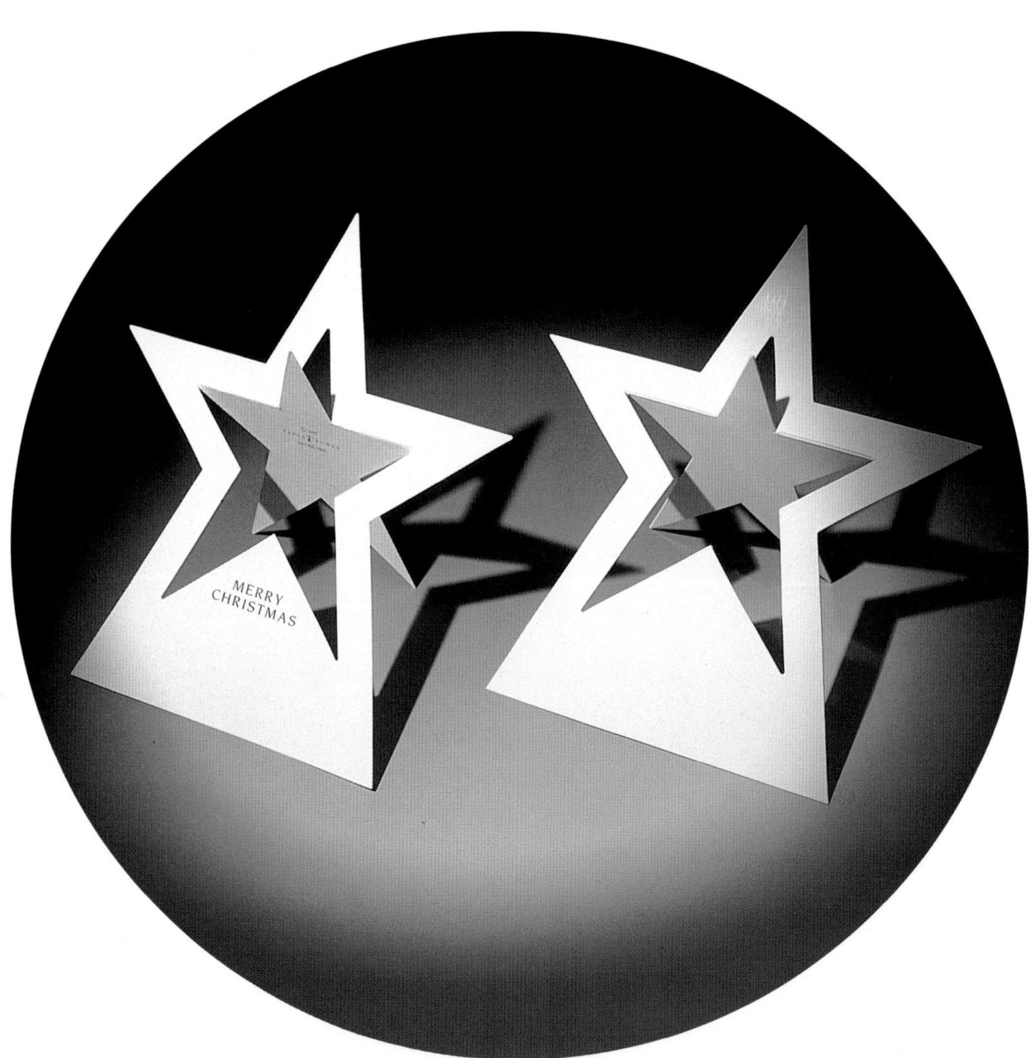

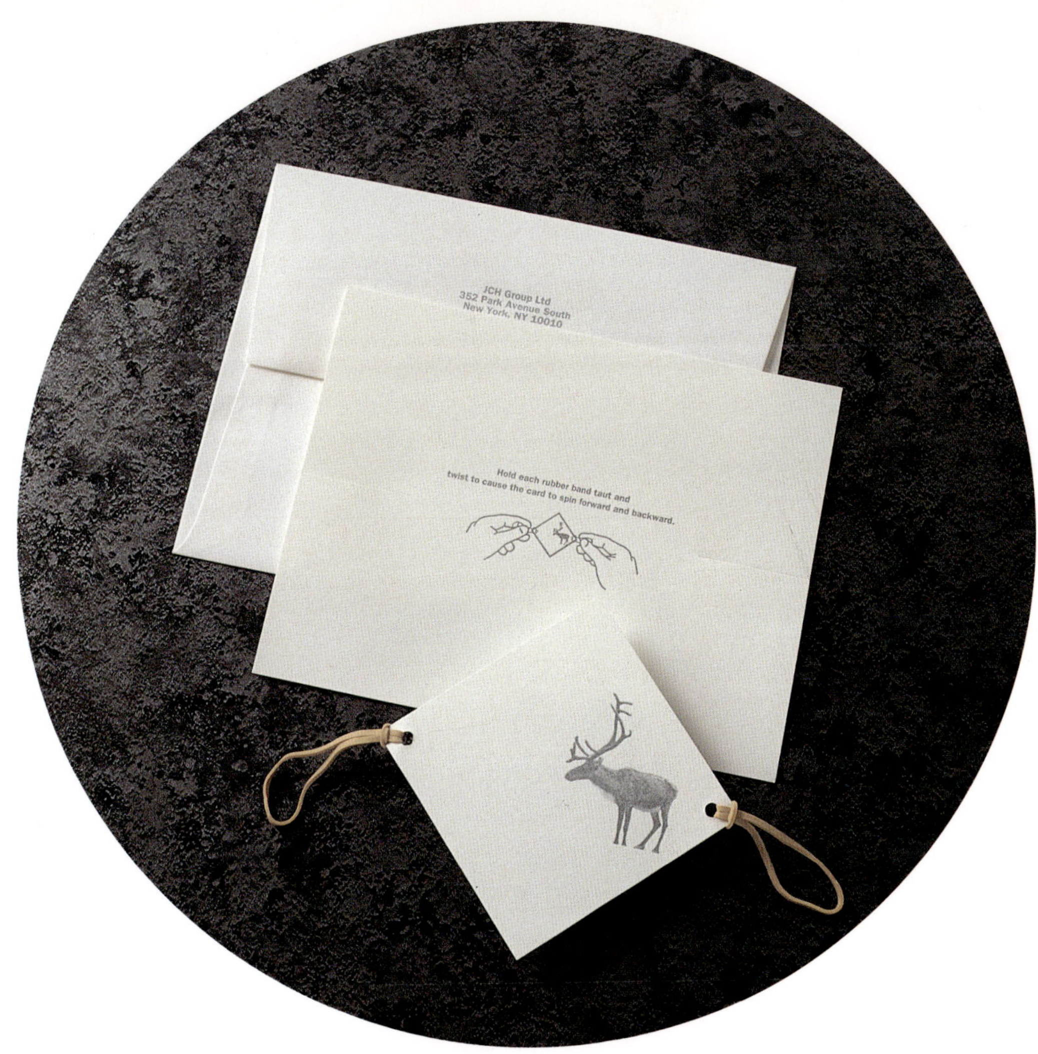

▲

Christmas card

クリスマス・カード

USA 1991

AD:Michael McGinn

Takaaki Matsumoto

D:Michael McGinn

DF:M Plus M

CL:JCH Group

TC:Typography and Prepress Service

印刷サービス

•

Due to the elasticity of the rubber, the card may be rotated. This causes the photo on the front and the letters on the back to overlap.

ゴムの力でカードが回転して、表の写真と、裏の文字が重なって見える。

▼

New year's card

ニューイヤーズ・カード

GERMANY 1991

D:Peter Biler

CL:Peter Biler

•

The vinyl card is linked to form a Mobius Strip.

ビニール製のカードをメビウスの輪のようにつなげて完成させる。

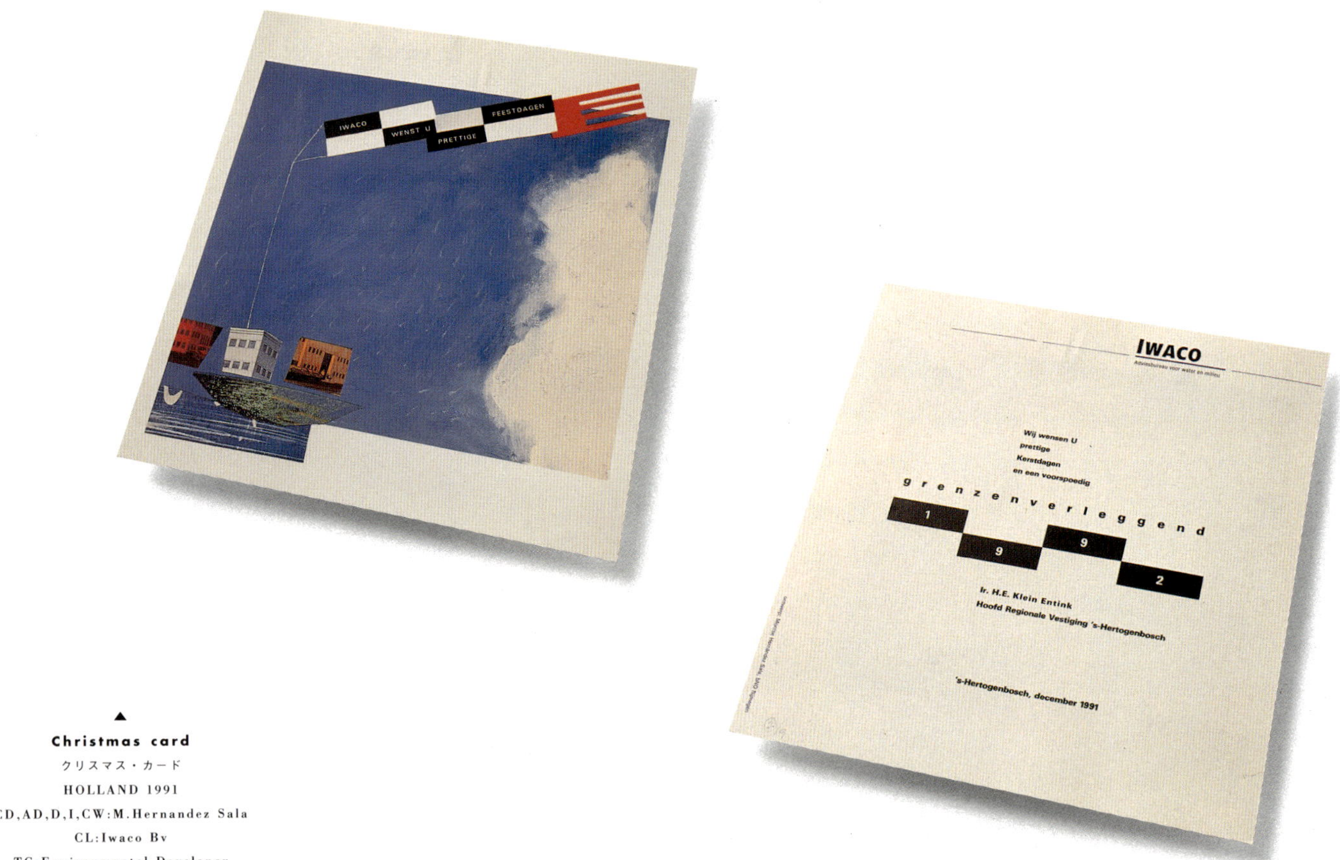

▲

Christmas card

クリスマス・カード

HOLLAND 1991

CD,AD,D,I,CW:M.Hernandez Sala

CL:Iwaco Bv

TC:Environmental Developer

環境開発

▼

Christmas card

クリスマス・カード

USA 1989

D:Rebeca Mendez

DF:Art Center College of Design.

Design Office

CL:Art Center College of Design

TC:Art College

美術大学

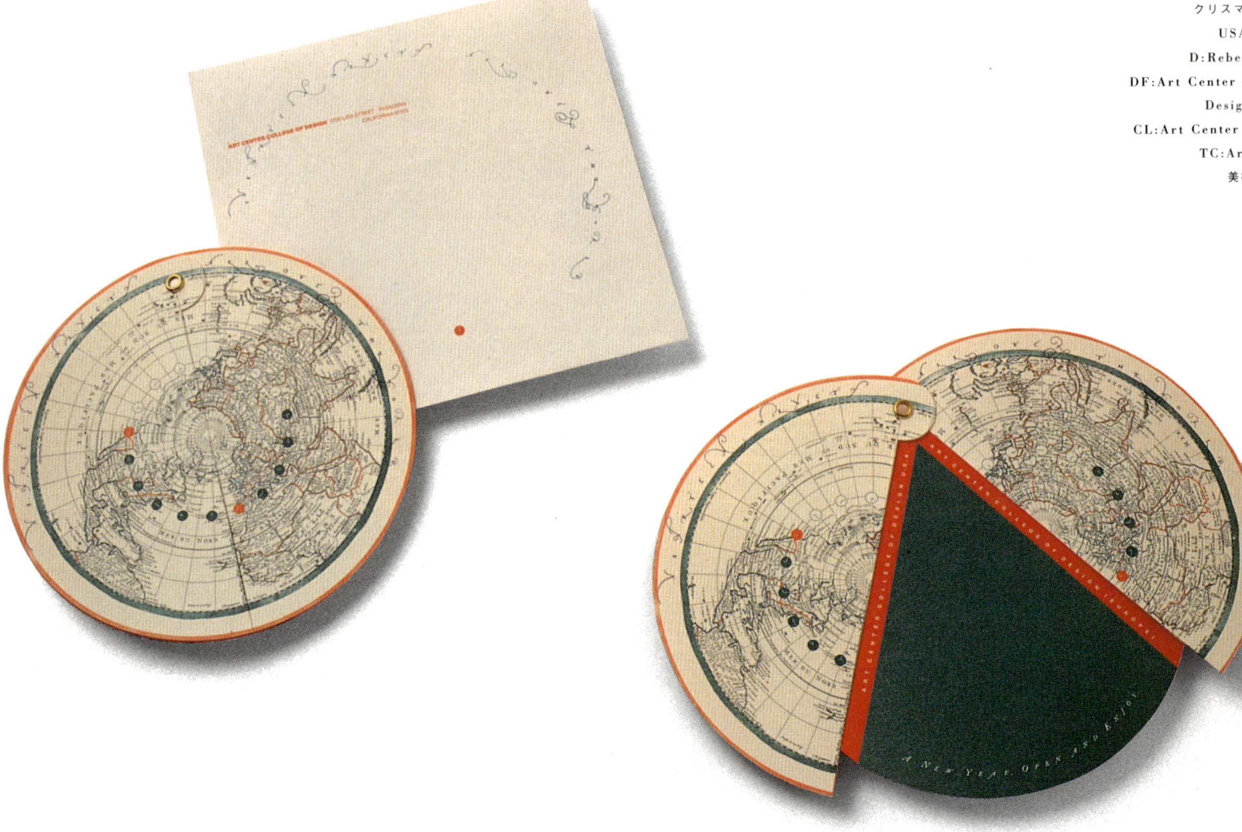

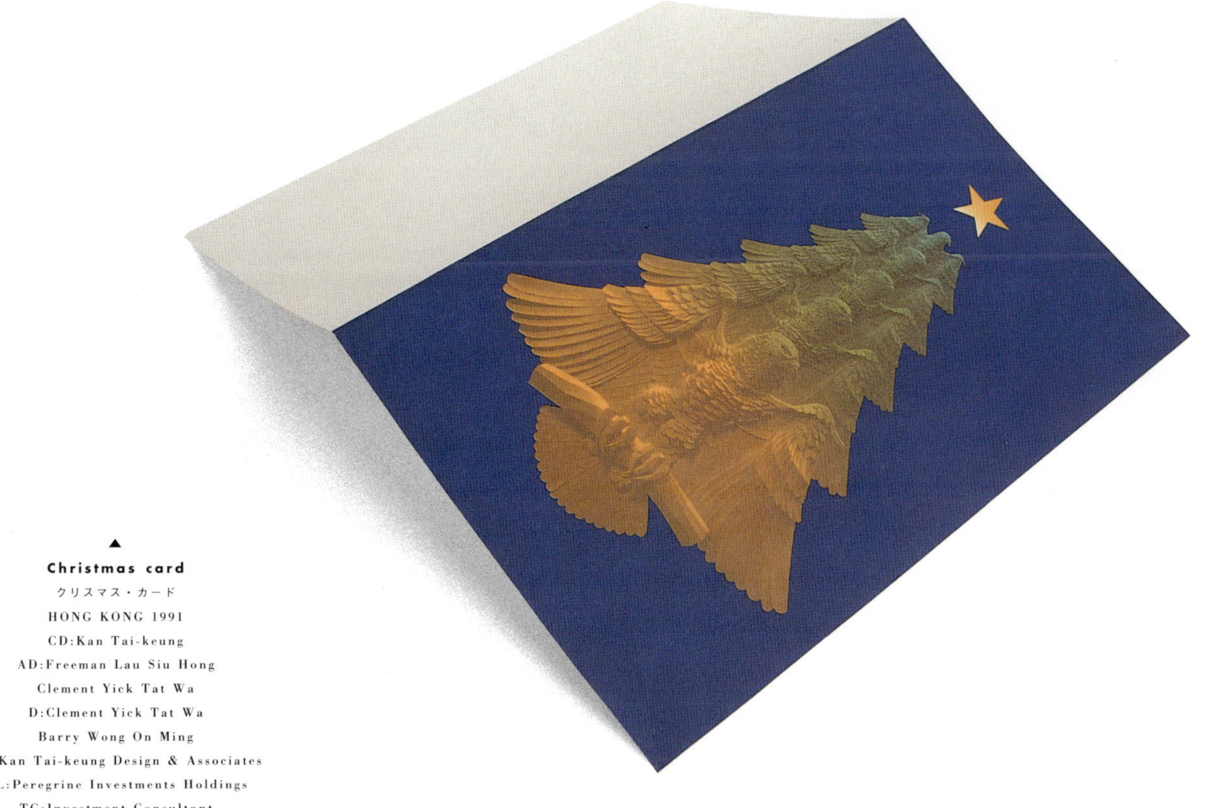

▲

Christmas card

クリスマス・カード

HONG KONG 1991

CD:Kan Tai-keung

AD:Freeman Lau Siu Hong

Clement Yick Tat Wa

D:Clement Yick Tat Wa

Barry Wong On Ming

DF:Kan Tai-keung Design & Associates

CL:Peregrine Investments Holdings

TC:Investment Consultant

投資コンサルタント

▼

Christmas card

クリスマス・カード

ENGLAND 1991

CD,AD,D,I,CW:Amelia Davies

P:Robert Shackleton

Amelia Davies

DF:Amelia Davies

CL:Cameo Reprographics

TC:Reprographics Service

複写

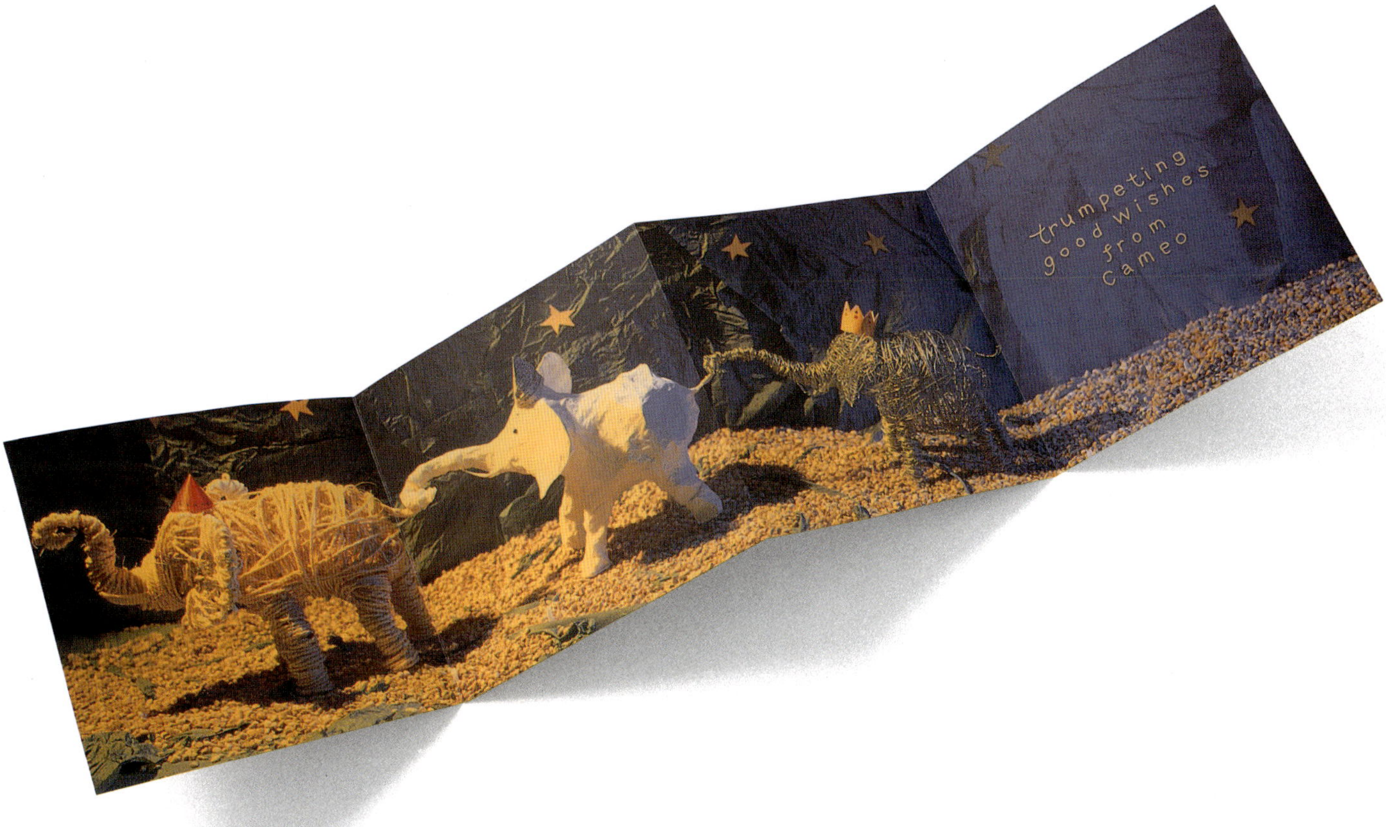

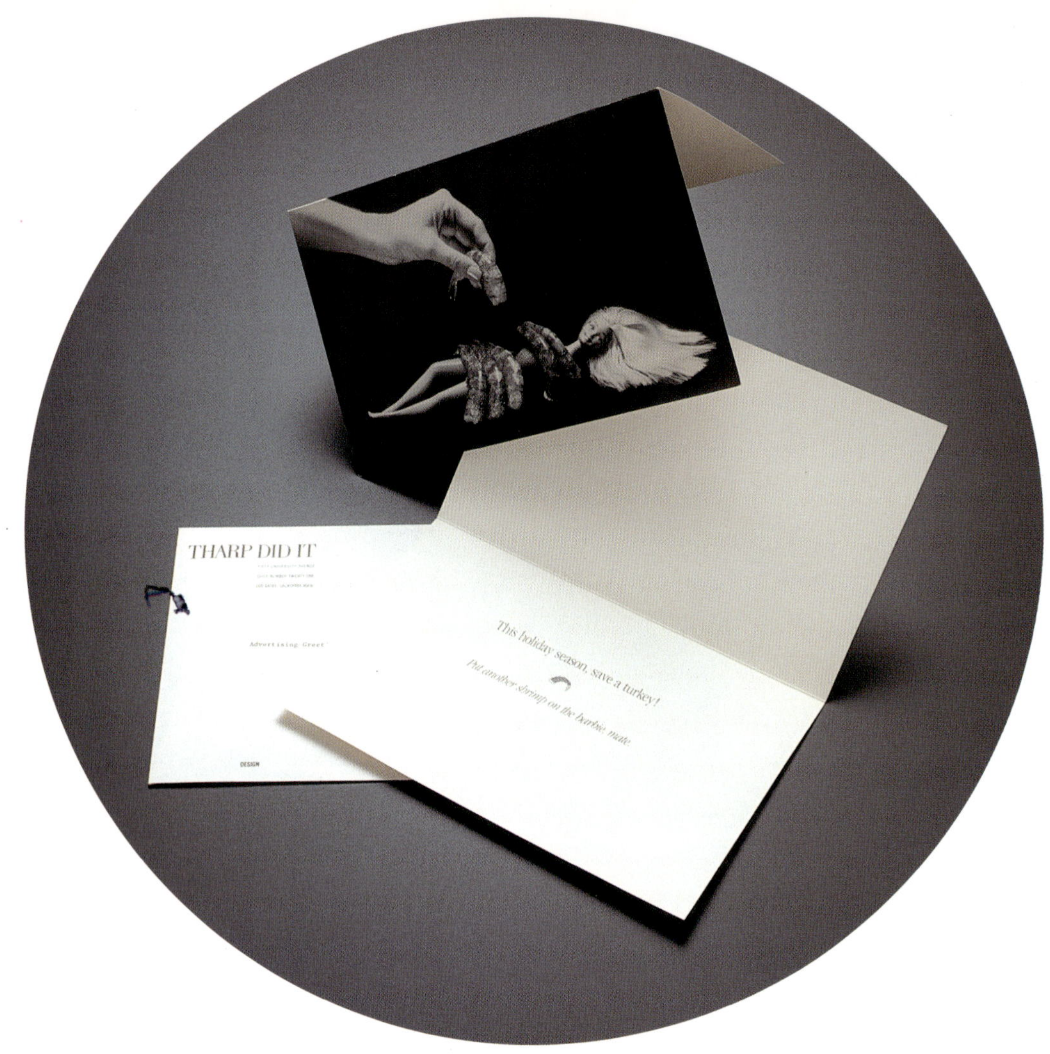

▲
Holiday card
ホリデー・カード
USA 1986
AD,D,CW:Rick Tharp
P:Kelly O'Connor
DF:THARP DID IT Los Gatos
San Francisco
CL:Steamer's Seafood Restaurant
TC:Restaurant
レストラン

▼
Halloween card
ハロウィーン・カード
CANADA 1989
CD:Marcello Grossutti
AD,D:Rosanna D'Agostino
P:Sidney Tabak
DF:Rushton Green and Grossutti
CL:Sidney Tabak
TC:Photographer
フォトグラファー

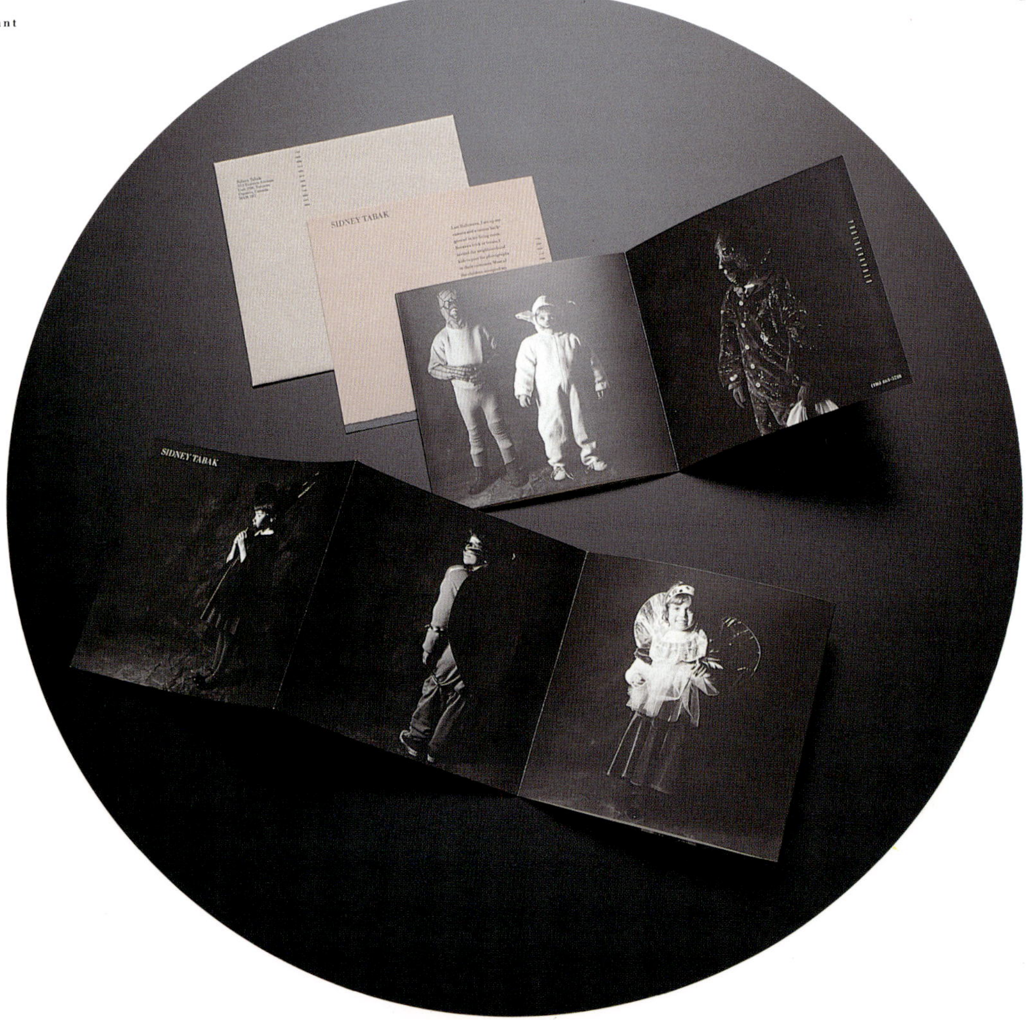

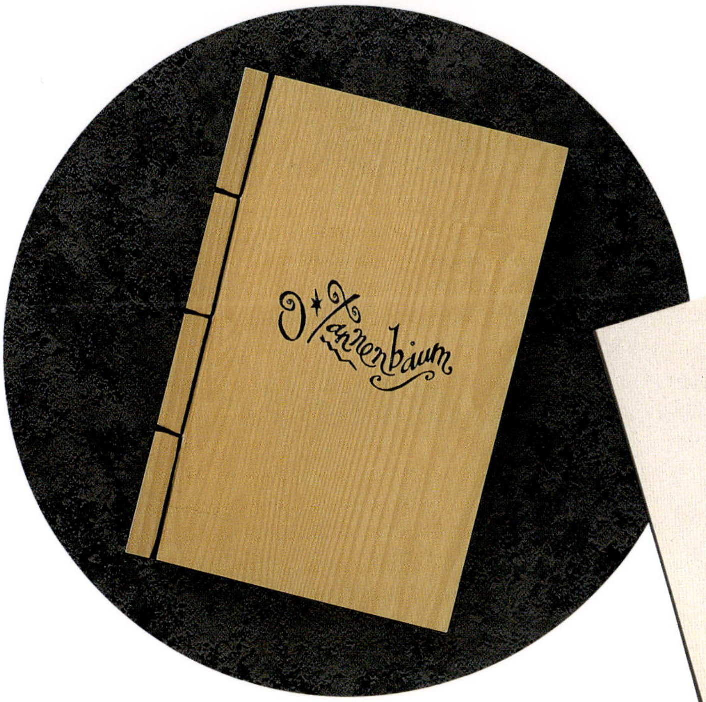

O Tannenbaum

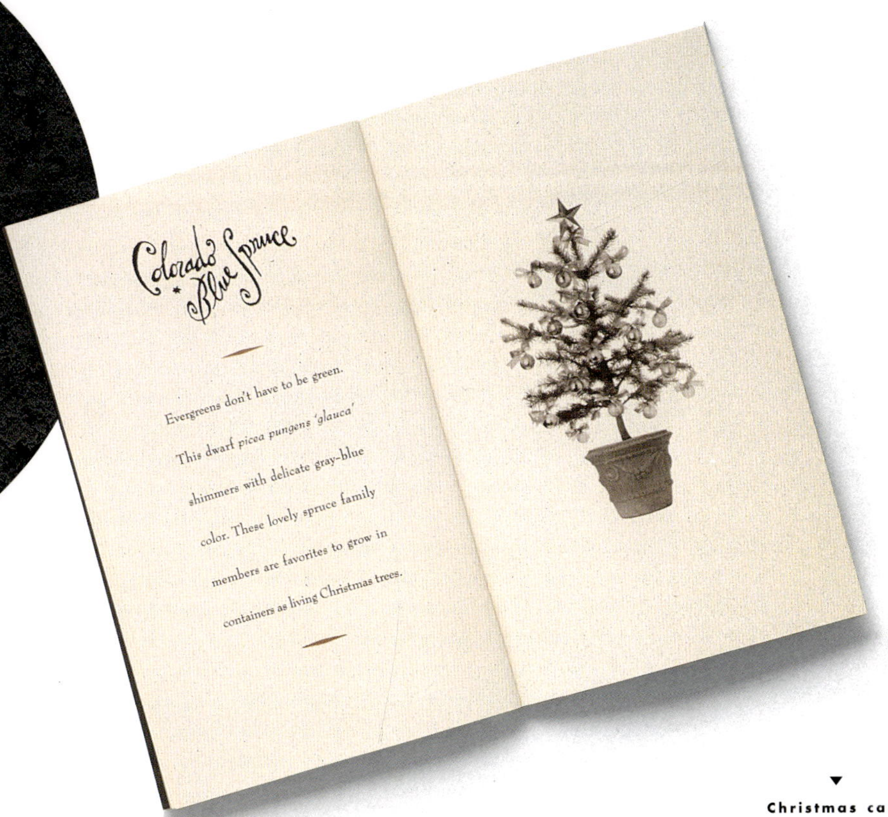

Colorado Blue Spruce

Evergreens don't have to be green.
This dwarf picea pungens 'glauca'
shimmers with delicate gray-blue
color. These lovely spruce family
members are favorites to grow in
containers as living Christmas trees.

▲
Holiday card
ホリデー・カード
USA 1989
AD:Jennifer Morla
D:Jennifer Morla
Jeanette Aramburu
P:Kathryn Kleinman
I:Jeanette Aramburu
CW:Peterson, Skolnick & Dodge
DF:Morla Design
CL:Morla Design
TC:Design Studio
デザイン

▼
Christmas card
クリスマス・カード
ITALY 1991
CD:Antonella Sala
CW:Grazia Lotti
CL:Tag Heuer
TC:Watch Maker
時計製造

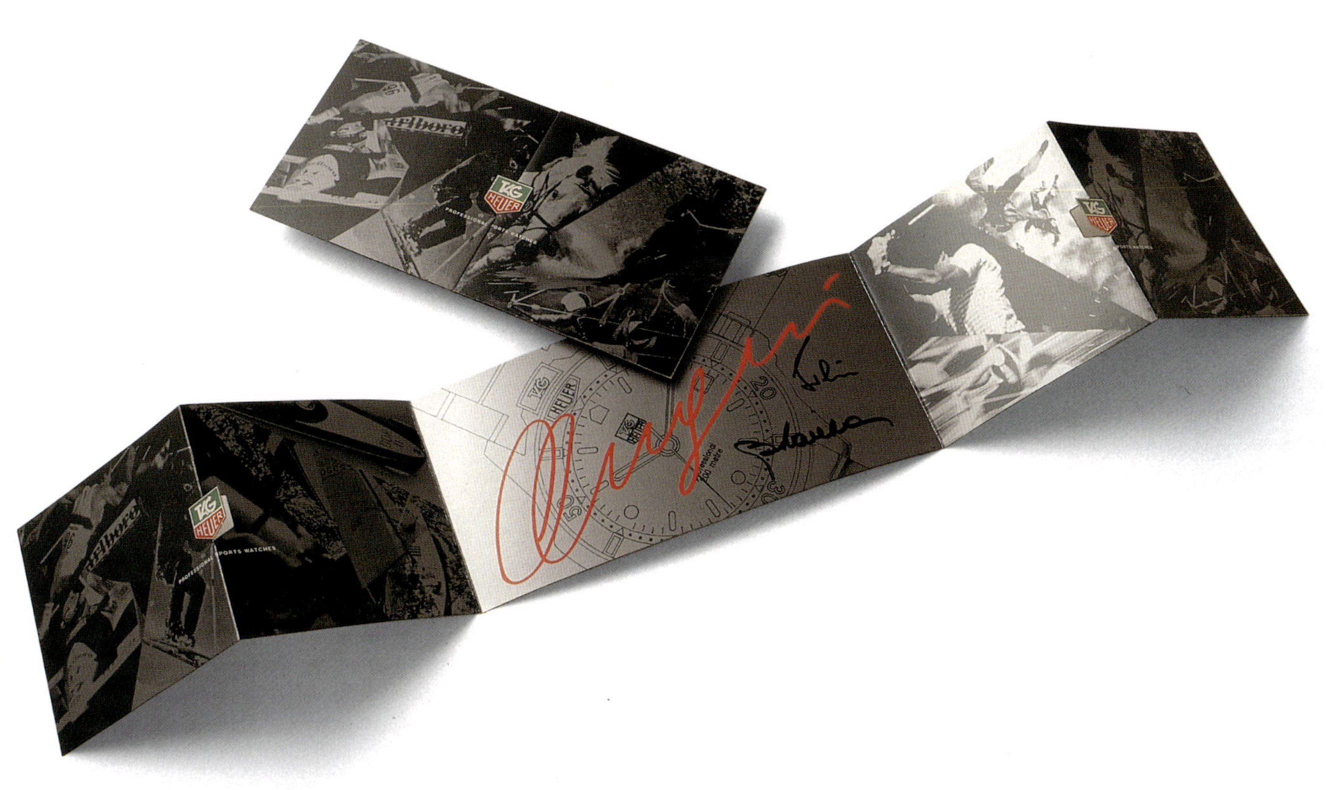

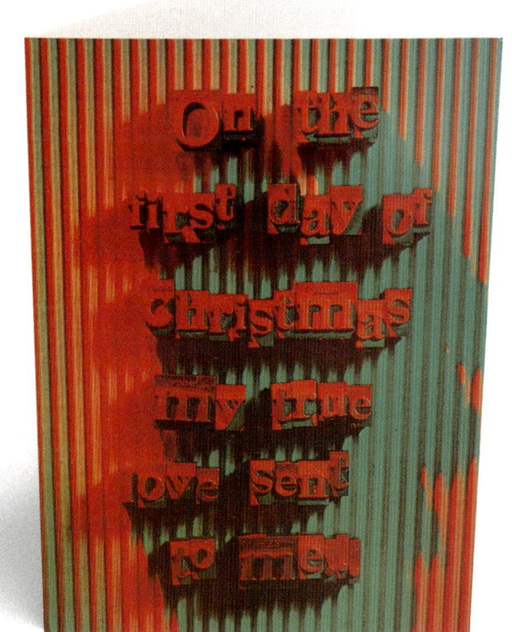

◀

Christmas card

クリスマス・カード

AUSTRALIA 1992

CD,AD,D:Andrew Hoyne

P:Rob Blackburn

DF:Andrew Hoyne Design

CL:Enzo Presley Ink Design

TC:Card Publisher

カード制作

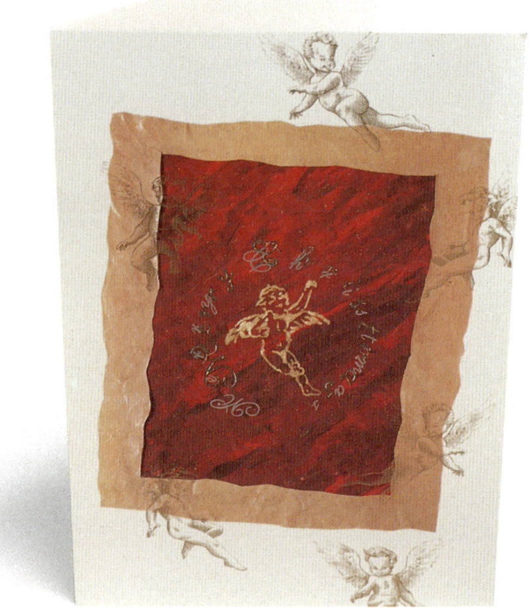

▶

Christmas card

クリスマス・カード

AUSTRALIA 1992

CD,AD,D:Andrew Hoyne

I:Andrew Hoyne

Zelko Zalak

DF:Andrew Hoyne Design

CL:Enzo Presley Ink Design

TC:Card Publisher

カード制作

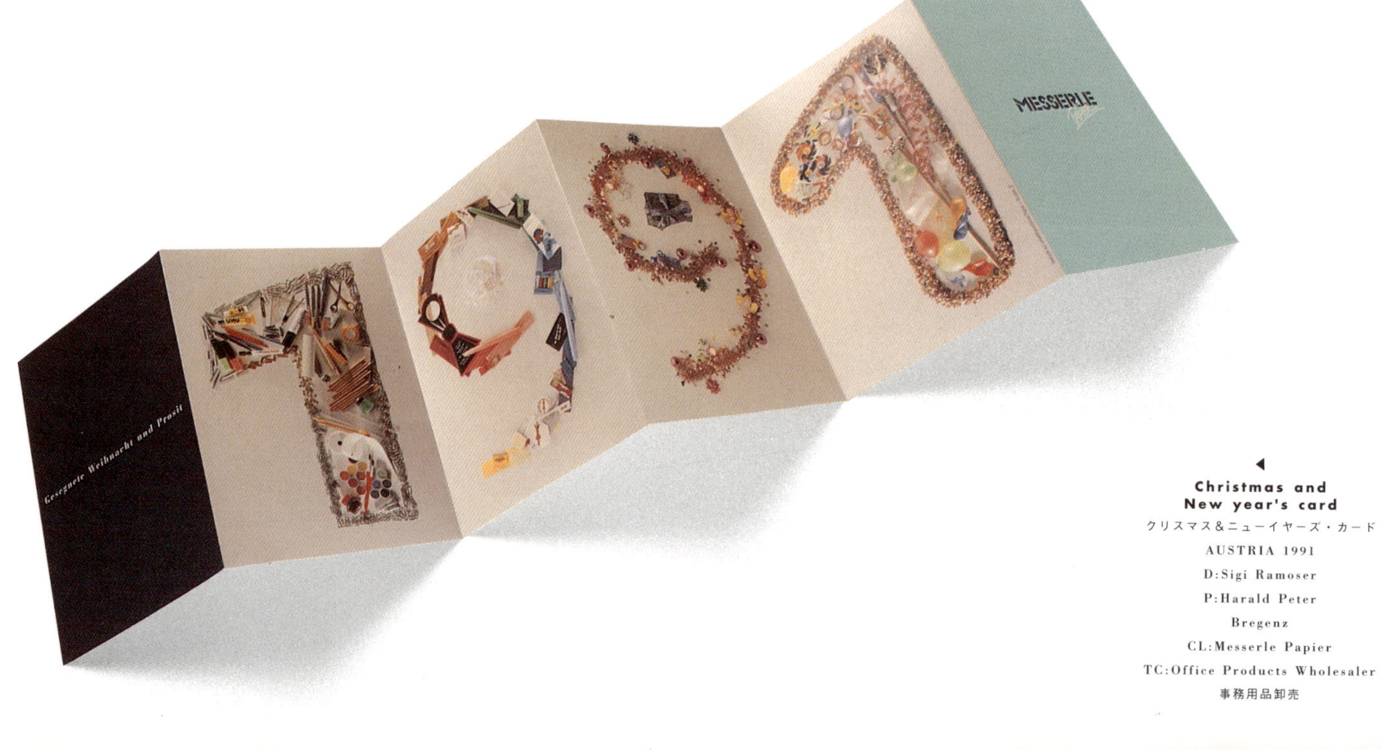

◀

Christmas and New year's card

クリスマス&ニューイヤーズ・カード

AUSTRIA 1991

D:Sigi Ramoser

P:Harald Peter

Bregenz

CL:Messerle Papier

TC:Office Products Wholesaler

事務用品卸売

◀
Christmas card
クリスマス・カード
ENGLAND 1990
CD,AD:Mary Lewis
D:Susanna Cucco
P:Laurie Evans
DF:Lewis Moberly
CL:Lewis Moberly
TC:Design Consultant
デザイン・コンサルタント

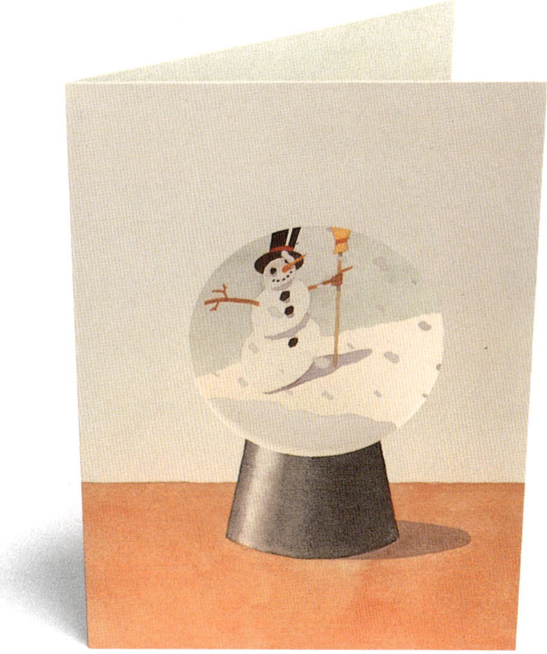

▶
Christmas card
クリスマス・カード
USA 1989
AD:The Museum of Modern Art, New York
I:Steven Guarnaccia
CL:The Museum of Modern Art, New York
TC:Museum of Art
美術館

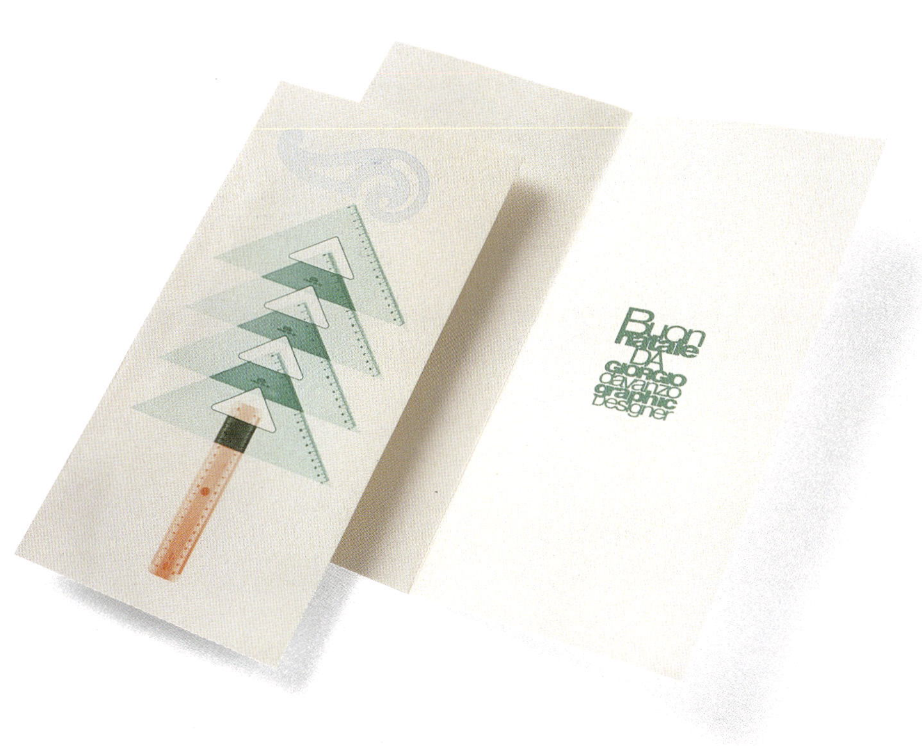

◀
Christmas and New year's card
クリスマス&ニューイヤーズ・カード
ITALY 1990
D:Giorgio Davanzo
DF:Giorgio Davanzo Design
CL:Giorgio Davanzo Design
TC:Advertising Agency
広告

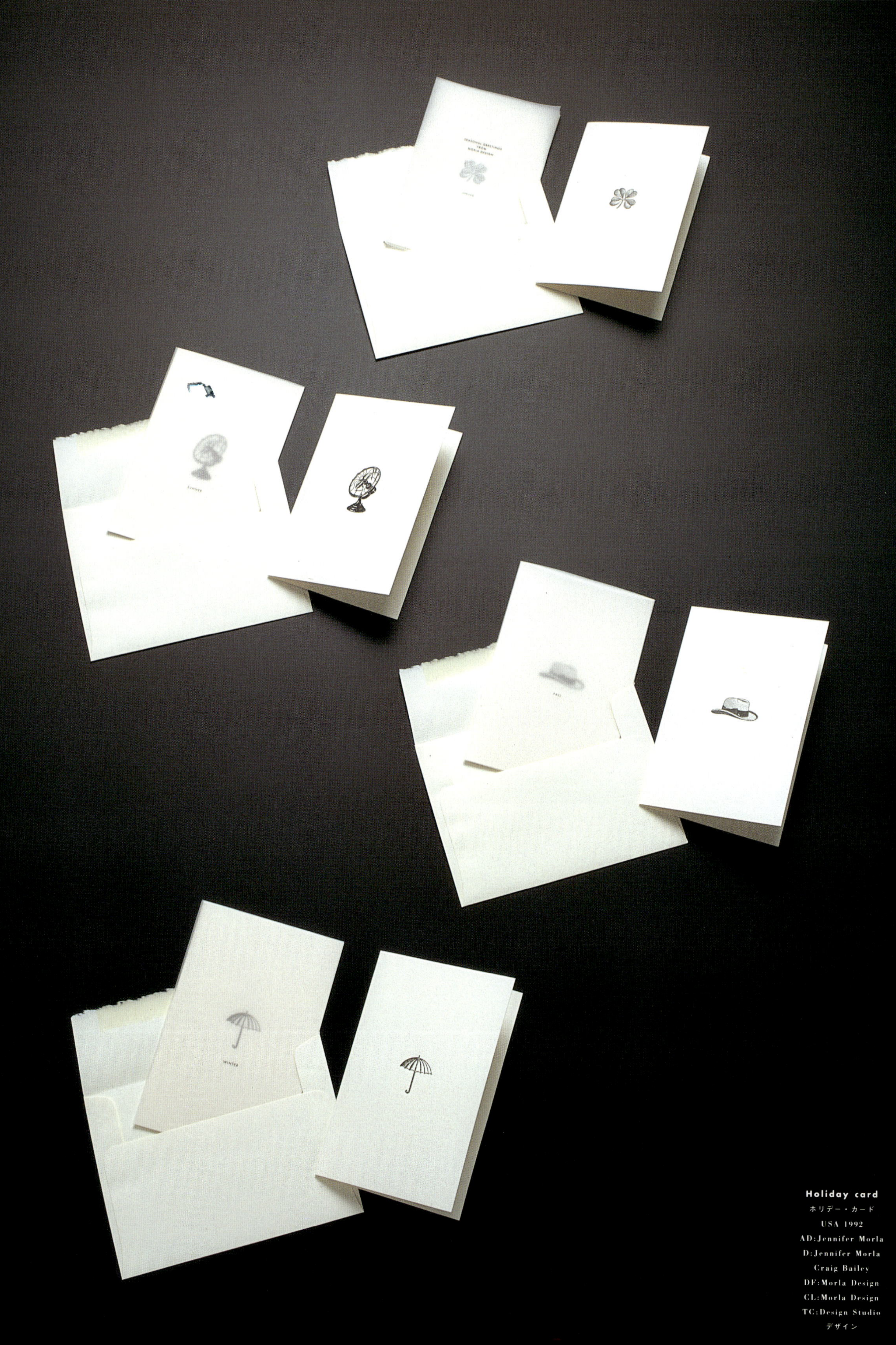

Holiday card
ホリデー・カード
USA 1992
AD:Jennifer Morla
D:Jennifer Morla
Craig Bailey
DF:Morla Design
CL:Morla Design
TC:Design Studio
デザイン

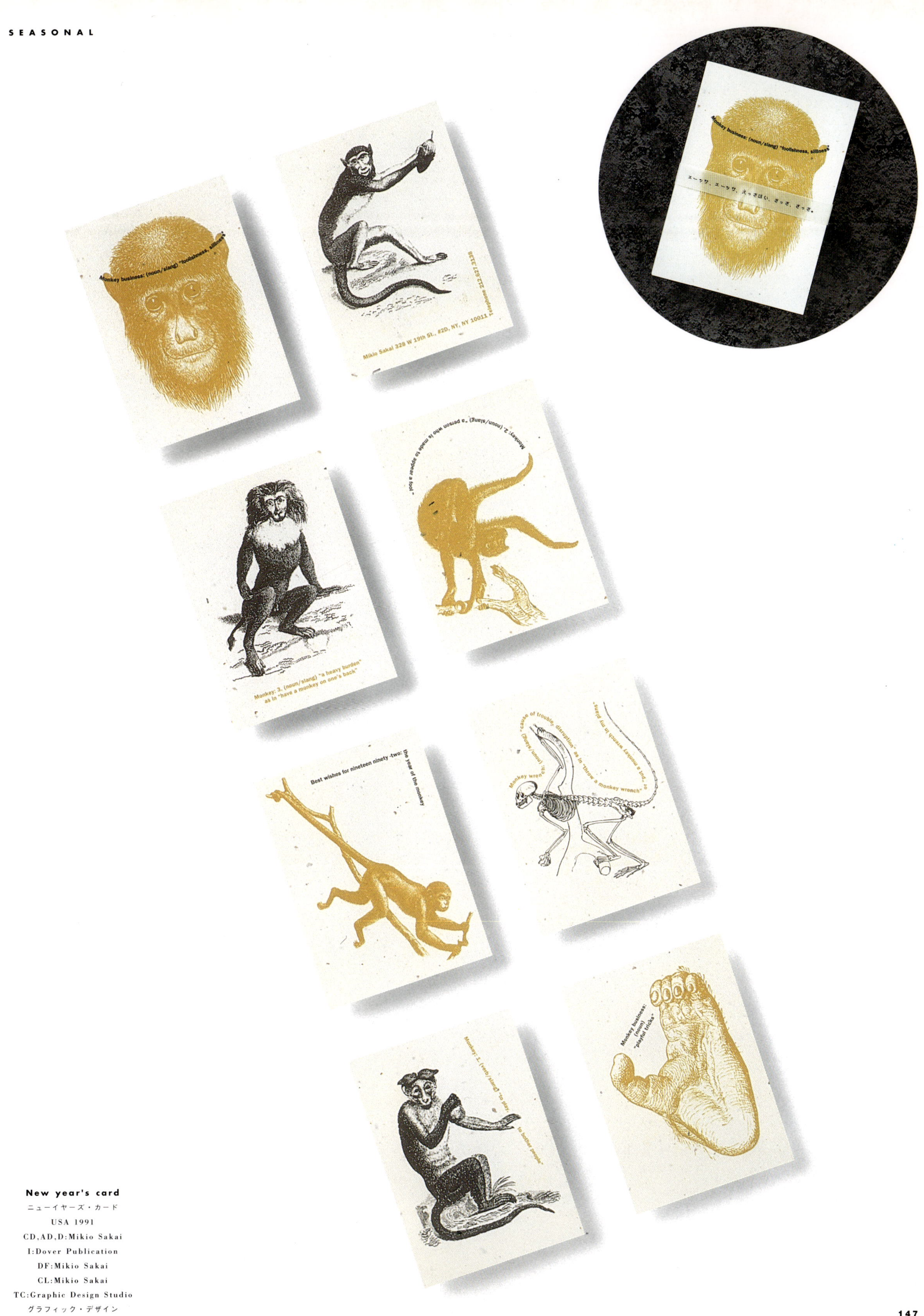

New year's card
ニューイヤーズ・カード
USA 1991
CD,AD,D:Mikio Sakai
I:Dover Publication
DF:Mikio Sakai
CL:Mikio Sakai
TC:Graphic Design Studio
グラフィック・デザイン

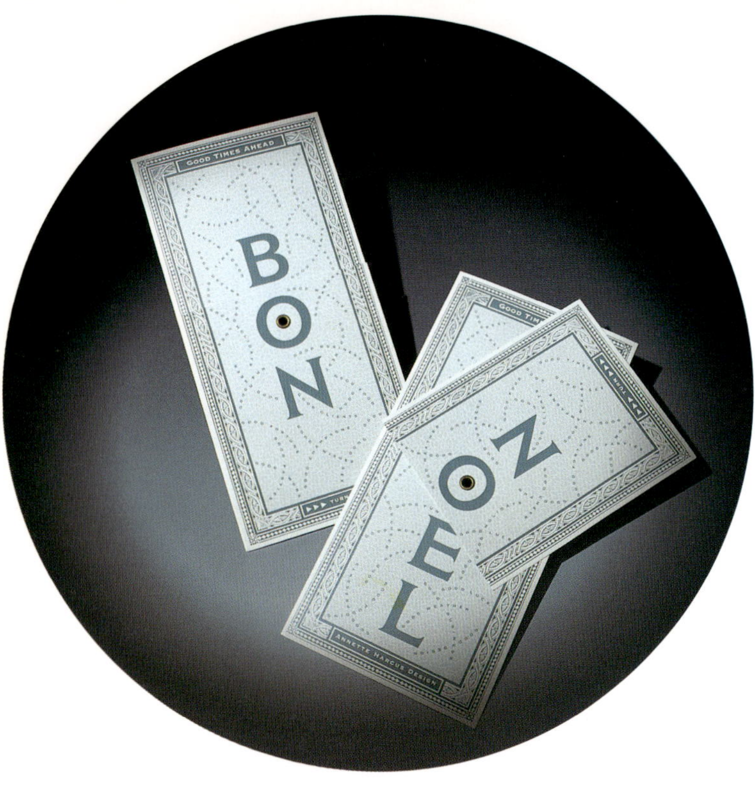

◀
Christmas card
クリスマス・カード
AUSTRALIA 1990
AD,D:Annette Harcus
I:Melinda Dudley
CW,DF:Annette Harcus Design
CL:Annette Harcus Design
TC:Graphic Design Studio
グラフィック・デザイン

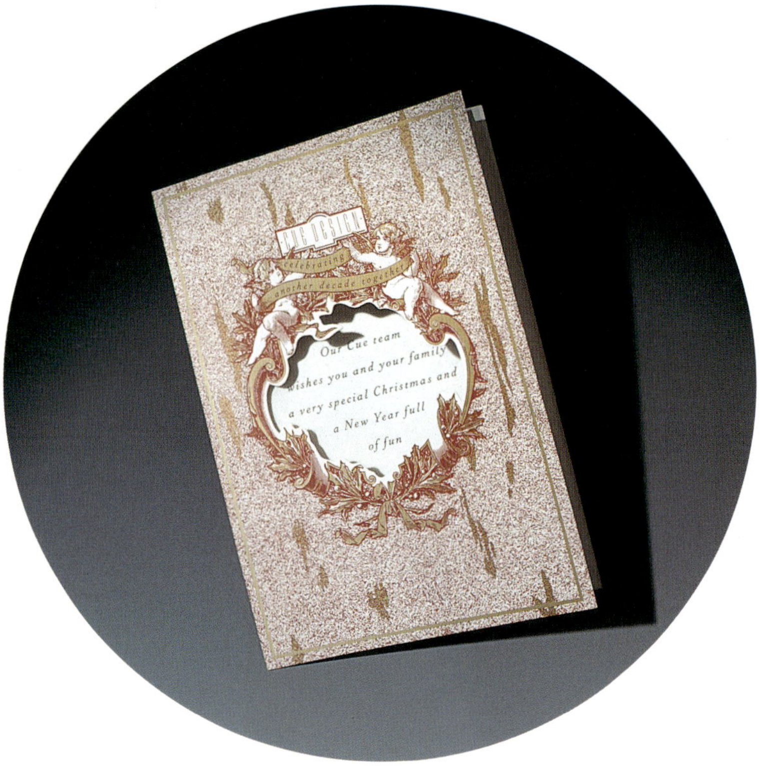

▶
Christmas card
クリスマス・カード
AUSTRALIA 1989
AD,CW:Annette Harcus
D:Marcella Paolacci
Annette Harcus
I:Melinda Dudley
DF:Annette Harcus Design
CL:CUE Design
TC:Fashion Boutique Chain
ファッション・ブティック・チェーン

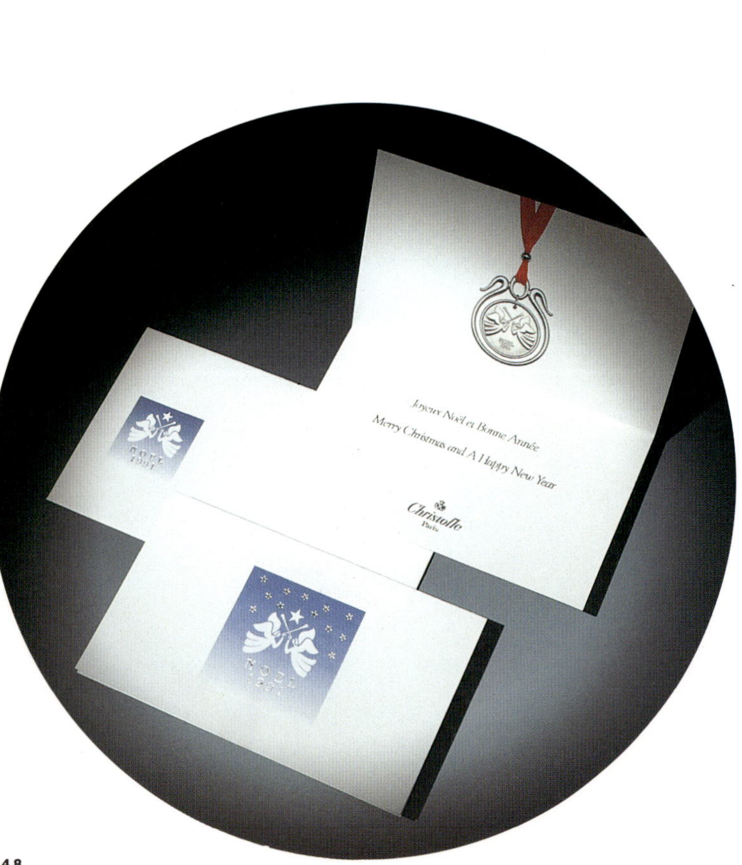

◀
Christmas card
クリスマス・カード
JAPAN 1991
CD:Daisuke Yamanaka
D:Mika Ikeda
CL:Blue Bell Japan
TC:Import Agent
輸入代理店

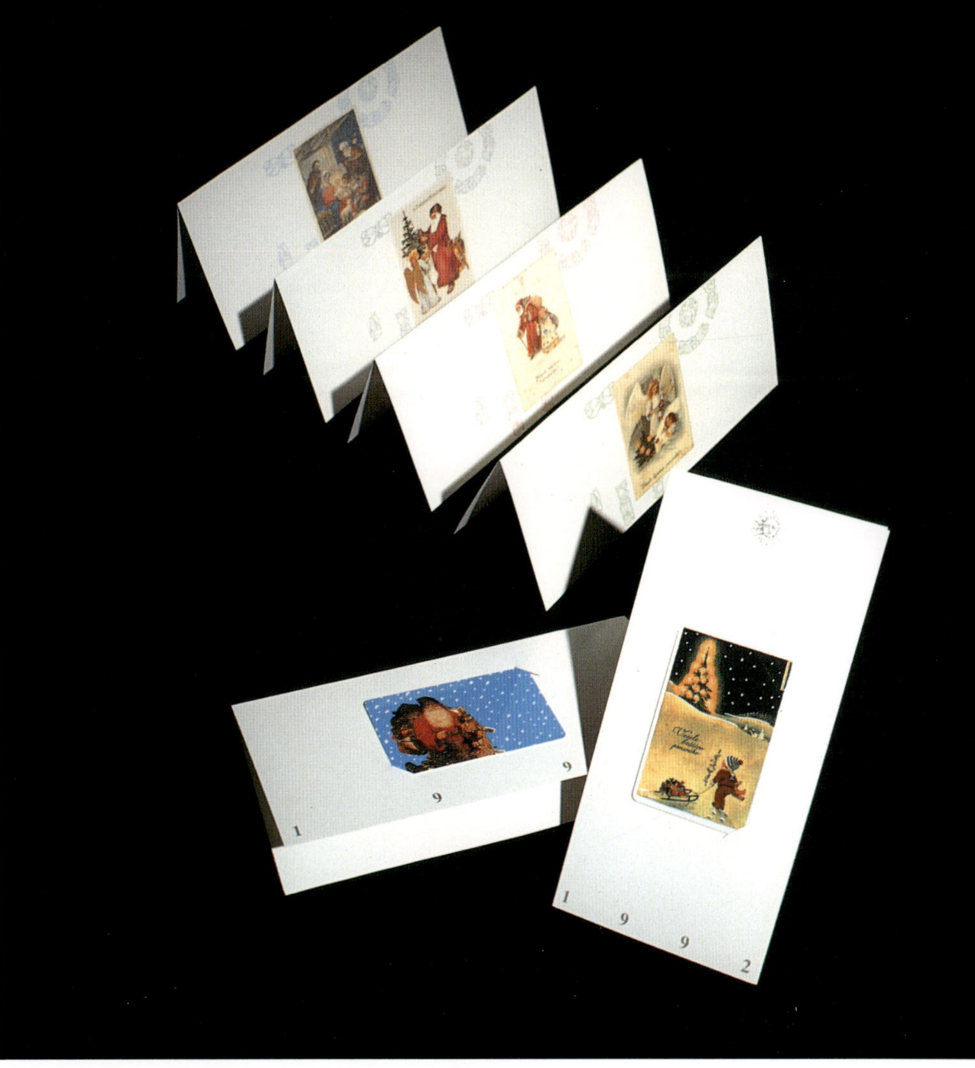

▶
Christmas card
クリスマス・カード
SLOVENIJA 1991
AD,D:Simon Sernec
DF:Design "SS" Creation
CL:Simon Sernec
TC:Design Studio
デザイン

▶
Christmas card
クリスマス・カード
SLOVENIJA 1991
AD,D:Simon Sernec
I:Archive and Simon Sernec
CL:Radece Papir
TC:Paper Mill
製紙

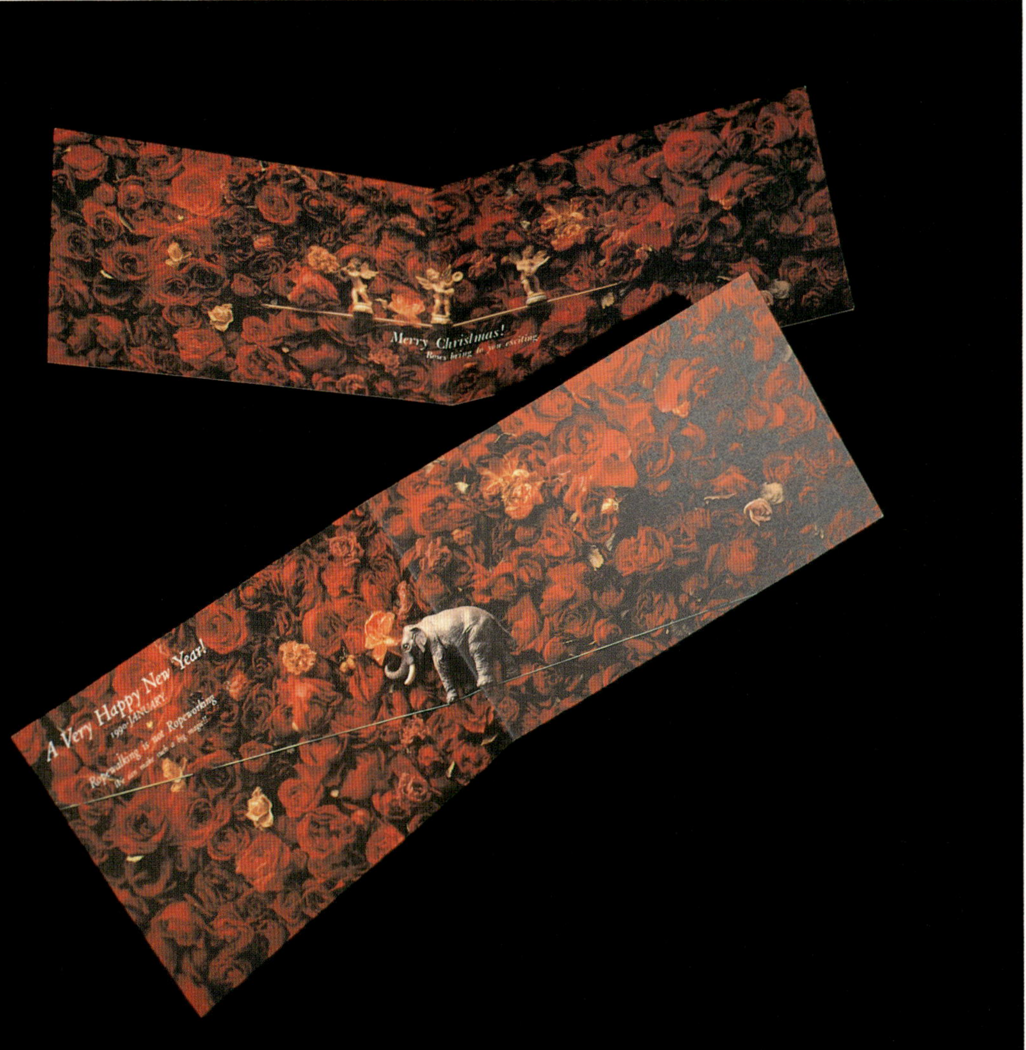

◀
Christmas card
クリスマス・カード
JAPAN 1989
CD,AD,D:Koji Kusatsugu
P:Tsuyoshi Fuseya
DF:Studio Vis
CL:Studio Vis
TC:Graphic Design Studio
グラフィック・デザイン

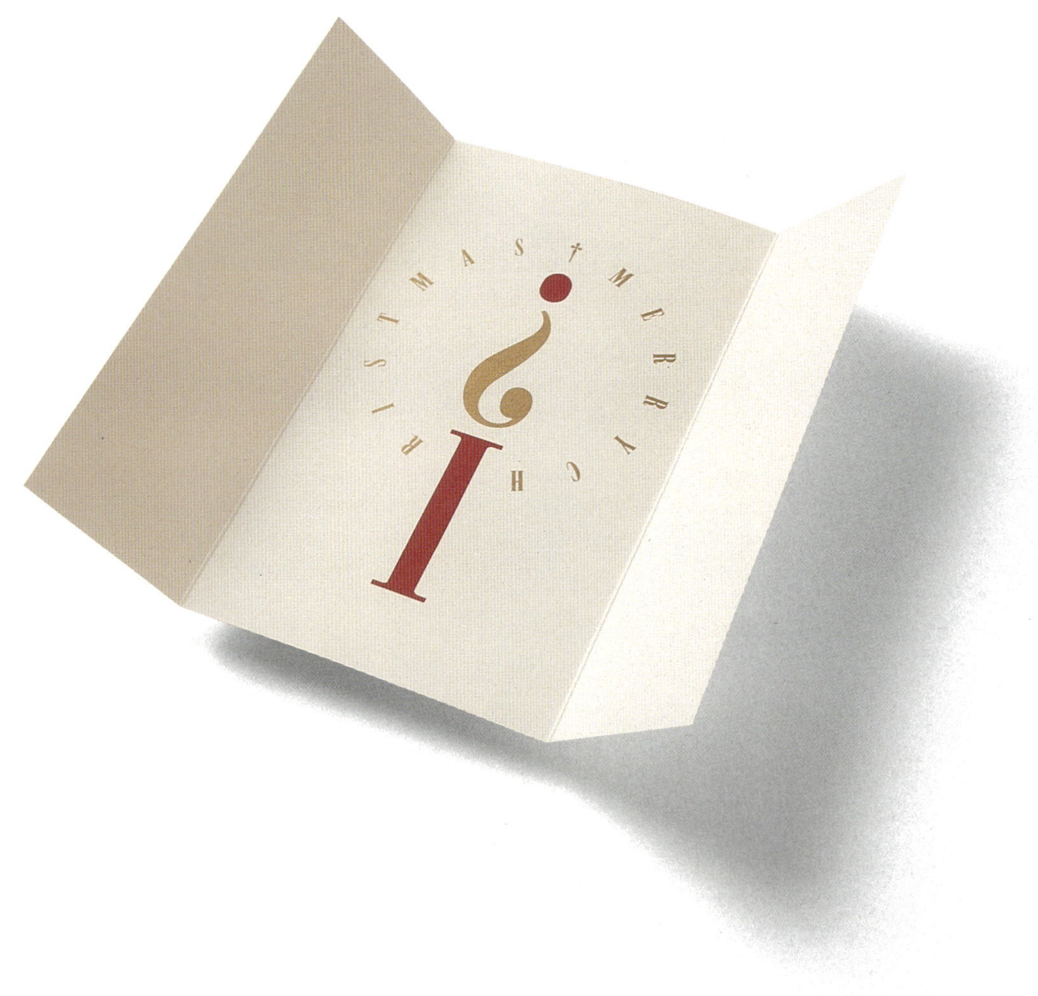

▲
Christmas card
クリスマス・カード
JAPAN 1990
CD,AD,D:Keisuke Unosawa
DF:Keisuke Unosawa Design
CL:Keisuke Unosawa
TC:Graphic Design Studio
グラフィック・デザイン

▼
New year's card
ニューイヤーズ・カード
JAPAN 1990
AD,D,CW:Keisuke Unosawa
DF:Keisuke Unosawa Design
CL:Keisuke Unosawa
TC:Graphic Design Studio
グラフィック・デザイン

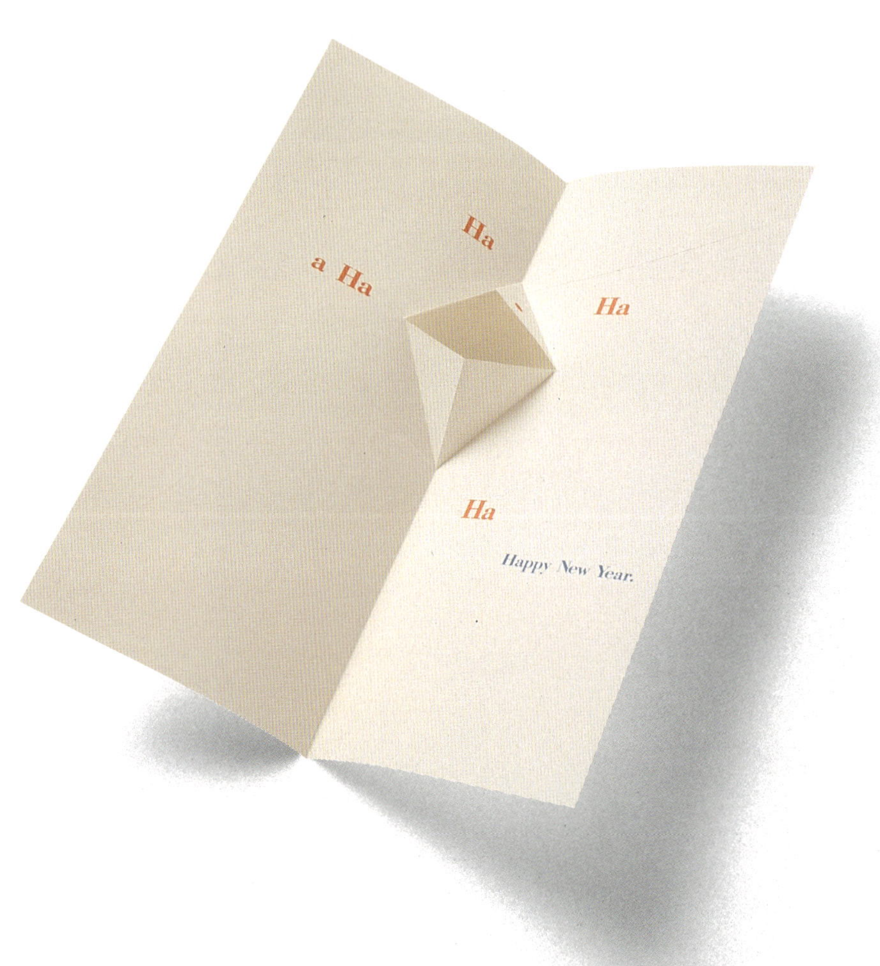

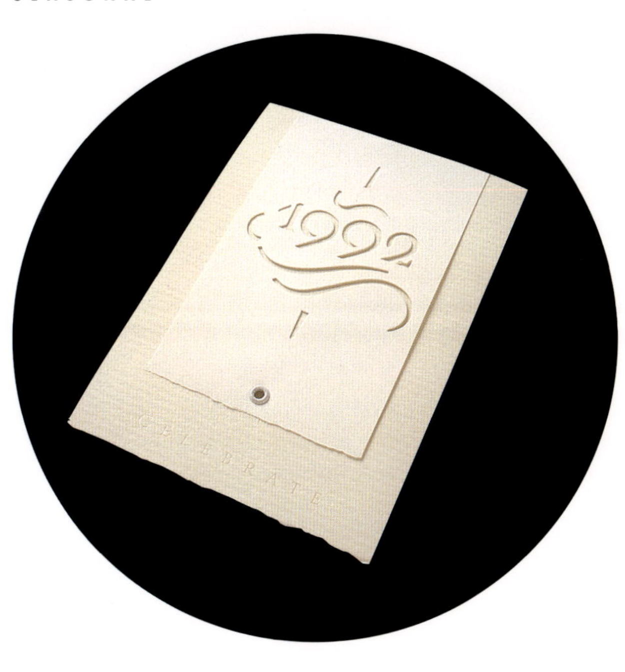

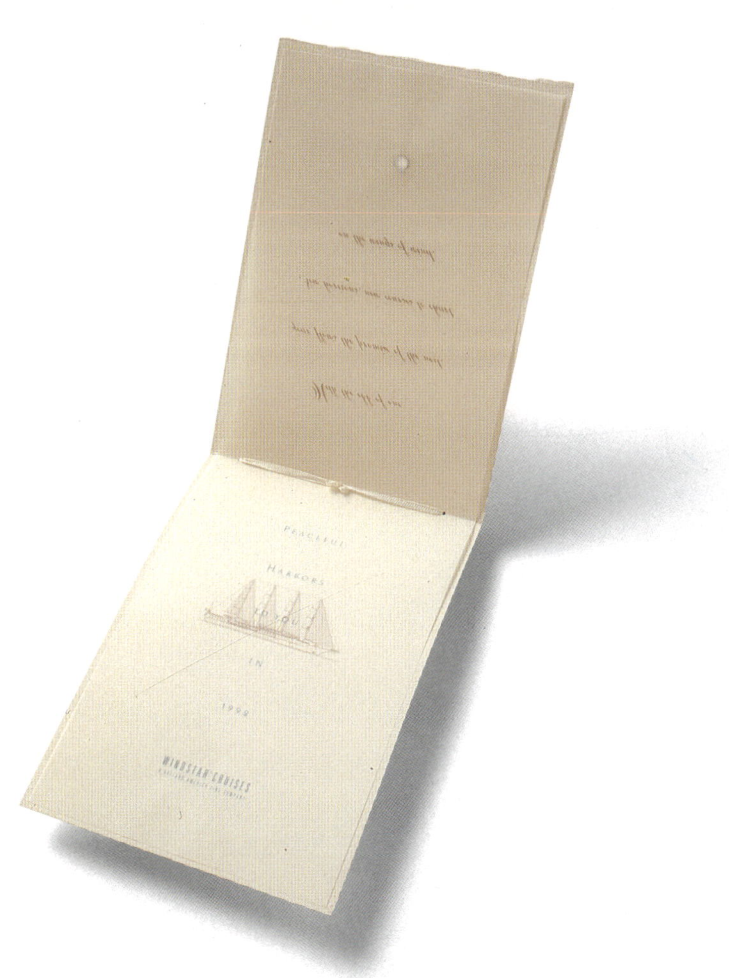

▲

New year's card
ニューイヤーズ・カード
USA 1991
AD:Jack Anderson
D:Jack Anderson
Denise Weir
Lian Ng
CW:Joan Brown
DF:Hornall Anderson Design Works
CL:Windstar Cruises
TC:Cruise Operator
客船サービス

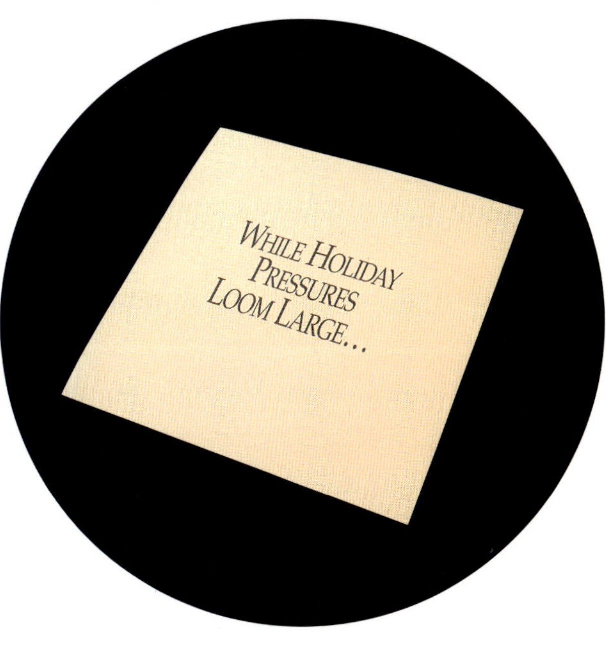

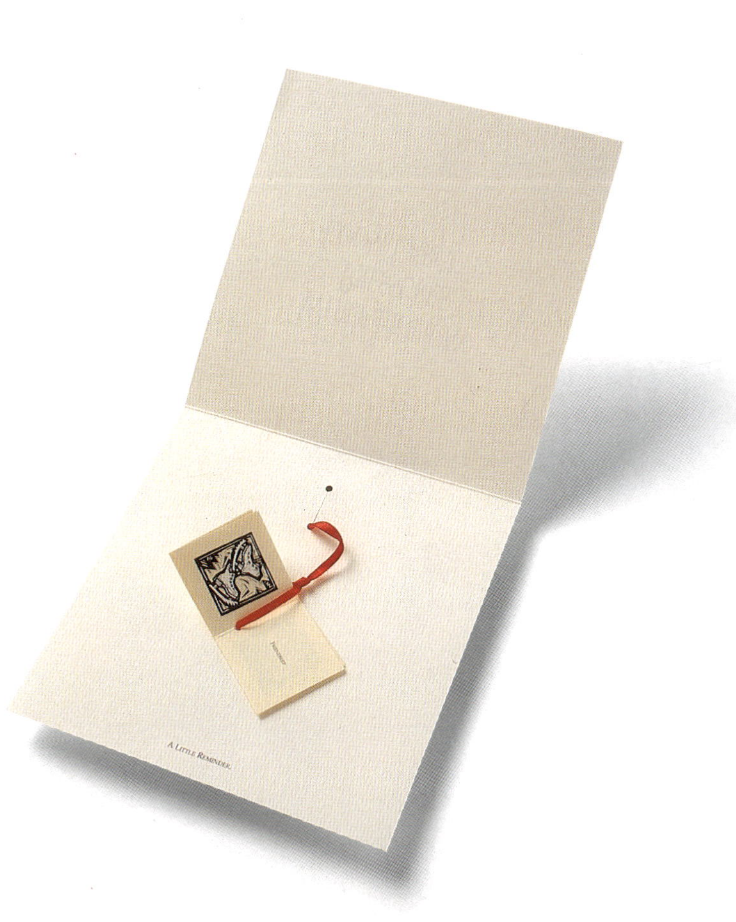

▲

Christmas card
クリスマス・カード
USA 1991
CD,AD,D:Ken Hanson
I:Jon Hargreaves
CW:Ken Hanson
Cheri Choudoir
DF:Hanson Graphic
CL:Hanson Graphic
TC:Graphic Design Studio
グラフィック・デザイン

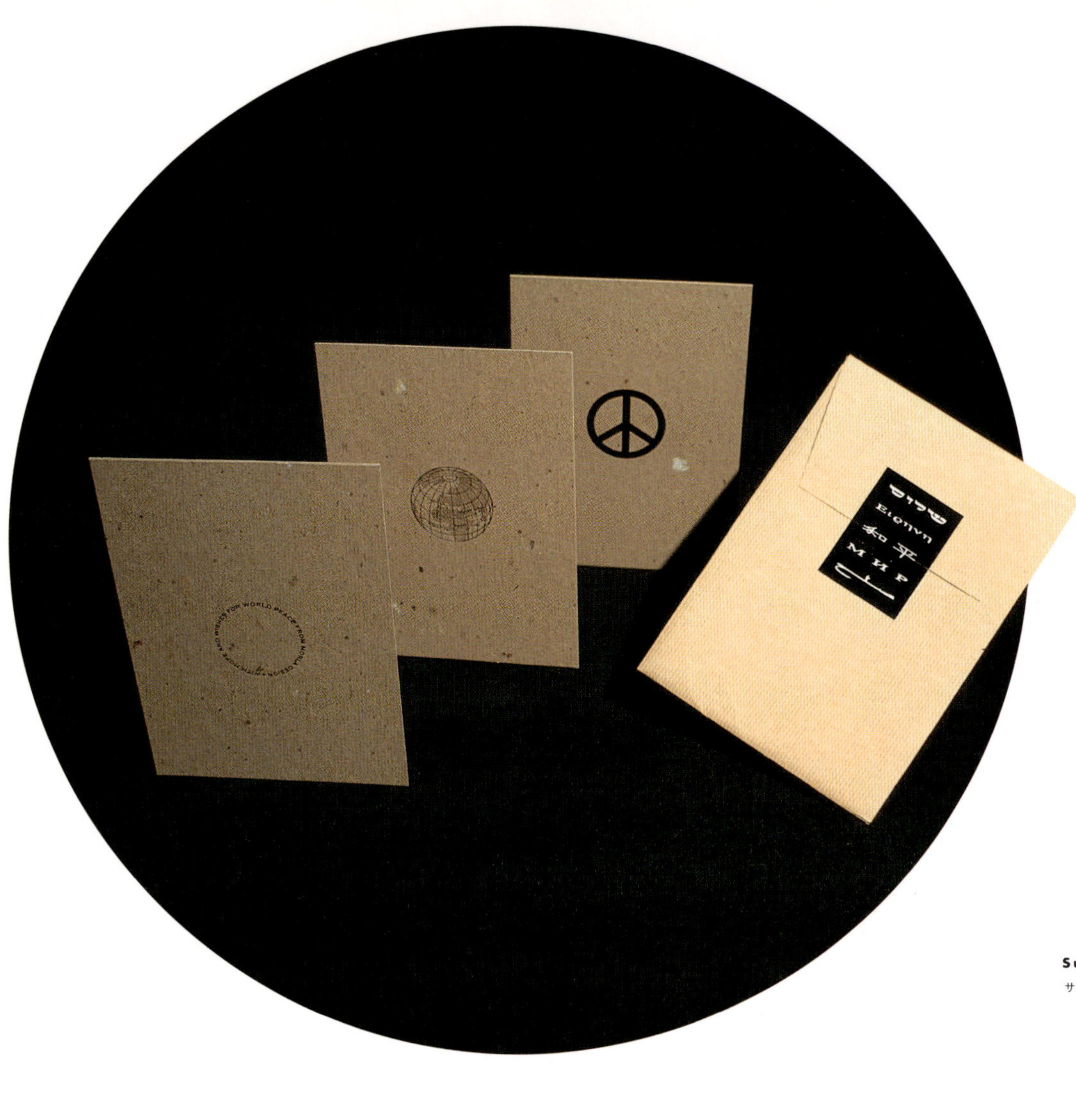

▲
Holiday card
ホリデー・カード
USA 1990
AD:Jennifer Morla
D:Jennifer Morla
Scott Drummond
Sharrie Brooks
Jeanette Aramburu
DF:Morla Design
CL:Morla Design
TC:Design Studio
デザイン

▼
Summer greeting card
サマー・グリーティング・カード
USA 1990
AD:Takaaki Matsumoto
Michael McGinn
D:Takaaki Matsumoto
DF:M Plus M
CL:M Plus M
TC:Design Studio
デザイン

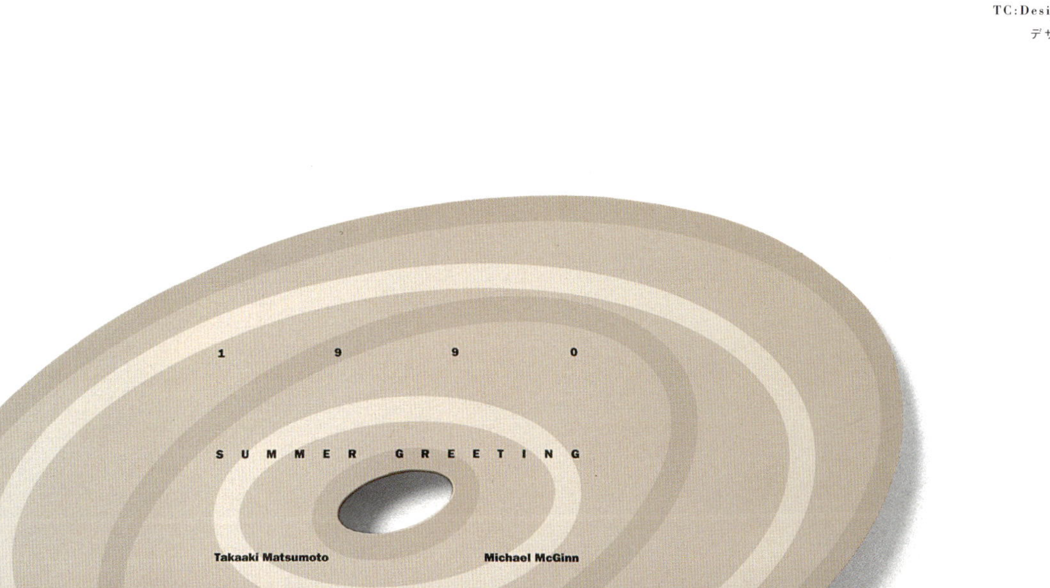

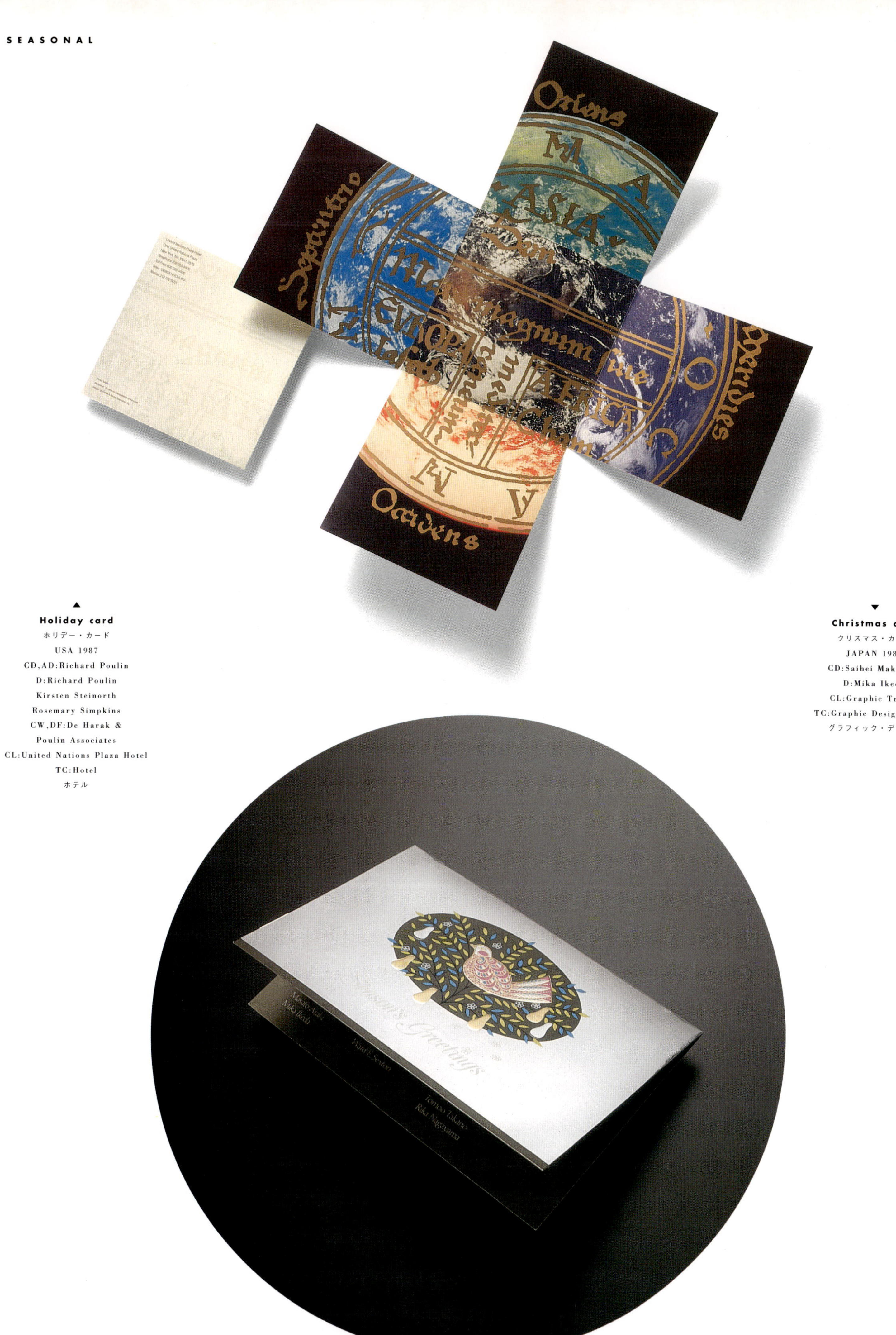

▲
Holiday card
ホリデー・カード
USA 1987
CD,AD:Richard Poulin
D:Richard Poulin
Kirsten Steinorth
Rosemary Simpkins
CW,DF:De Harak &
Poulin Associates
CL:United Nations Plaza Hotel
TC:Hotel
ホテル

▼
Christmas card
クリスマス・カード
JAPAN 1987
CD:Saihei Makinami
D:Mika Ikeda
CL:Graphic Traffic
TC:Graphic Design Studio
グラフィック・デザイン

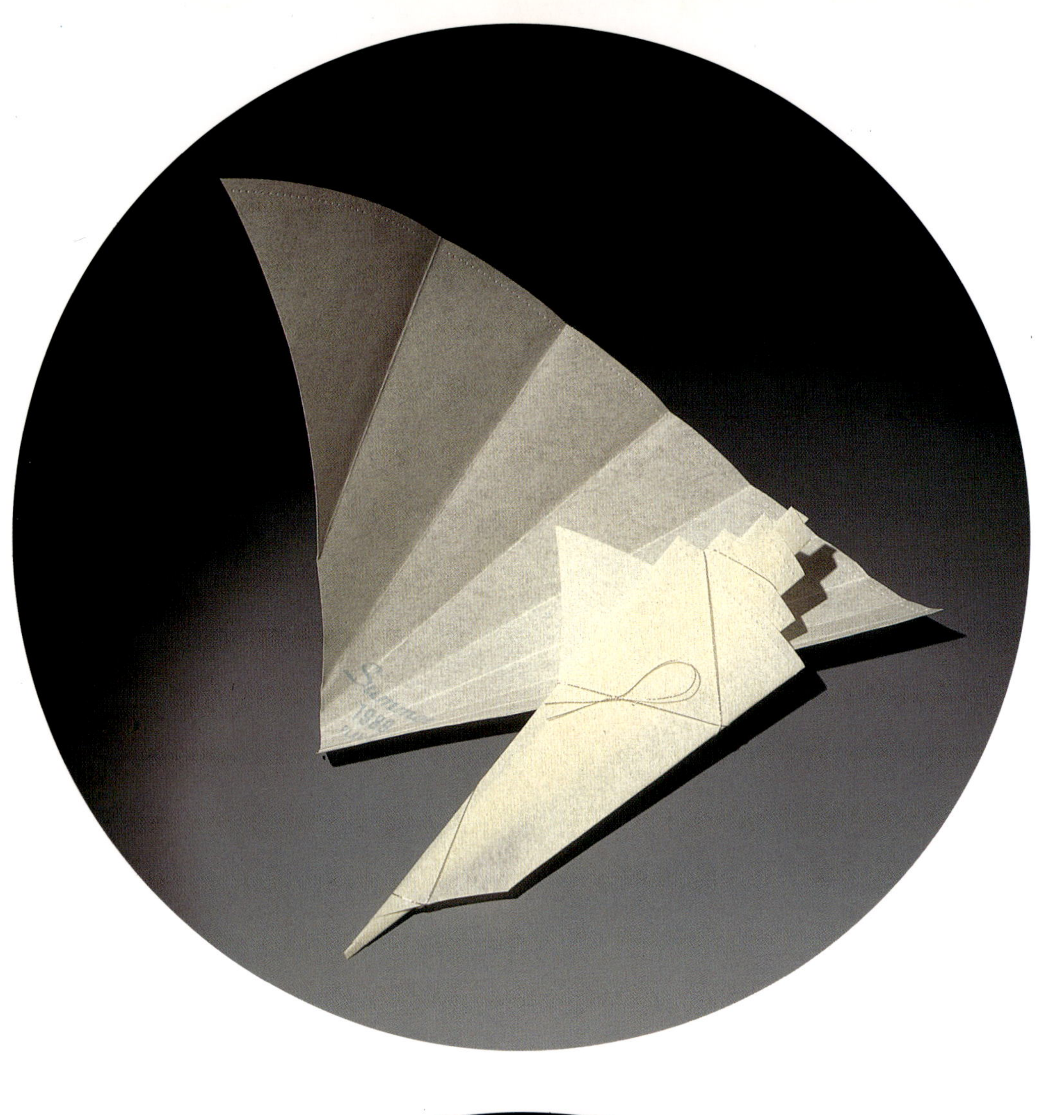

▲
Summer greeting card
サマー・グリーティング・カード
JAPAN 1989
CD,AD,D:Miyuki Yoshida
CL:Plan•Y
TC:Architectural Design, Package Design
建築設計、パッケージ・デザイン

▼
New year's card
ニューイヤーズ・カード
JAPAN 1990
CD,AD,D:Miyuki Yoshida
CL:Plan•Y
TC:Architectural Design, Package Design
建築設計、パッケージ・デザイン

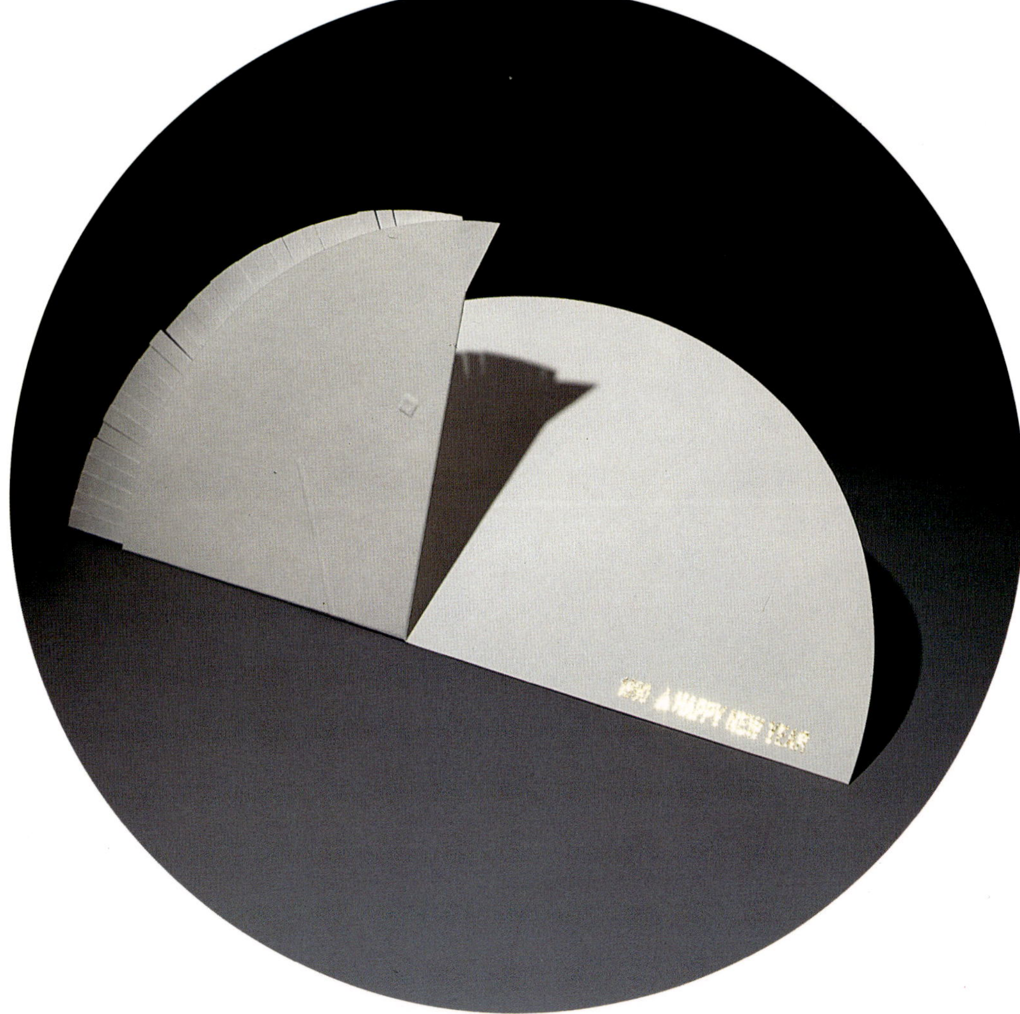

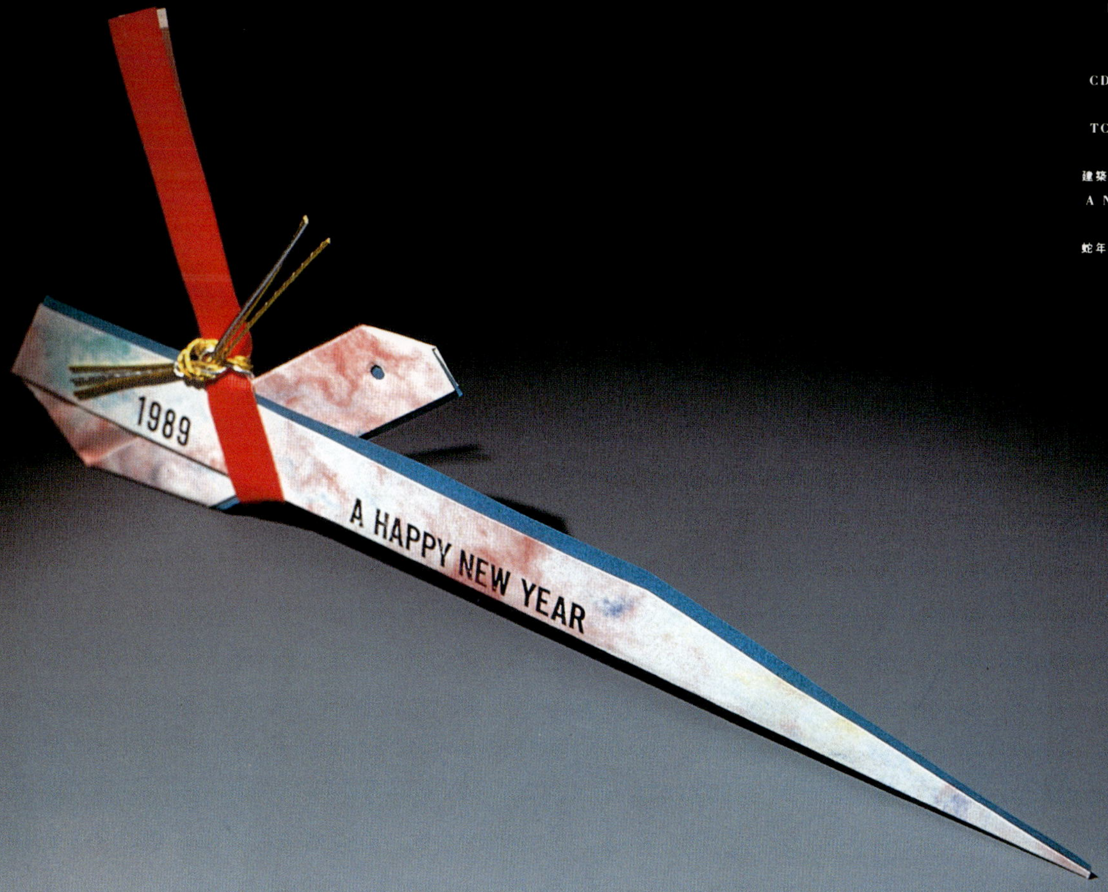

▲

New year's card

ニューイヤーズ・カード

JAPAN 1989

CD,AD,D:Miyuki Yoshida

CL:Plan•Y

TC:Architectural Design, Package Design

建築設計、パッケージ・デザイン

A New Year's card for the year of the snake.

蛇年のニューイヤーズ・カード。

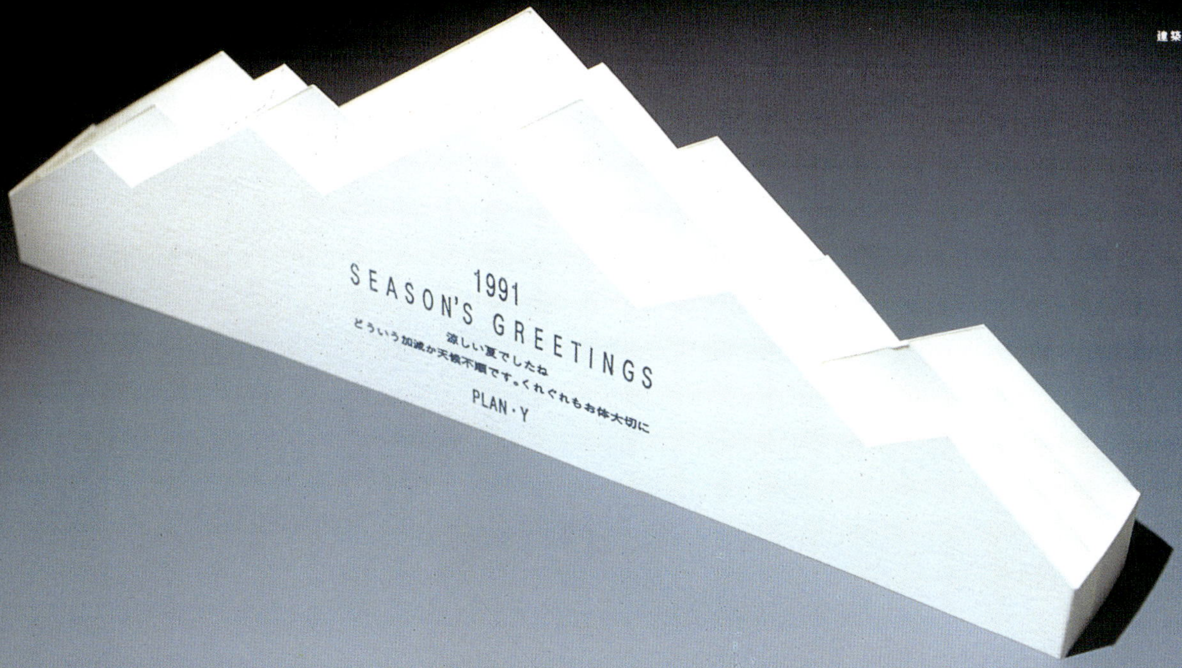

▼

Summer greeting card

サマー・グリーティング・カード

JAPAN 1991

CD,AD,D:Miyuki Yoshida

CL:Plan•Y

TC:Architectural Design, Package Design

建築設計、パッケージ・デザイン

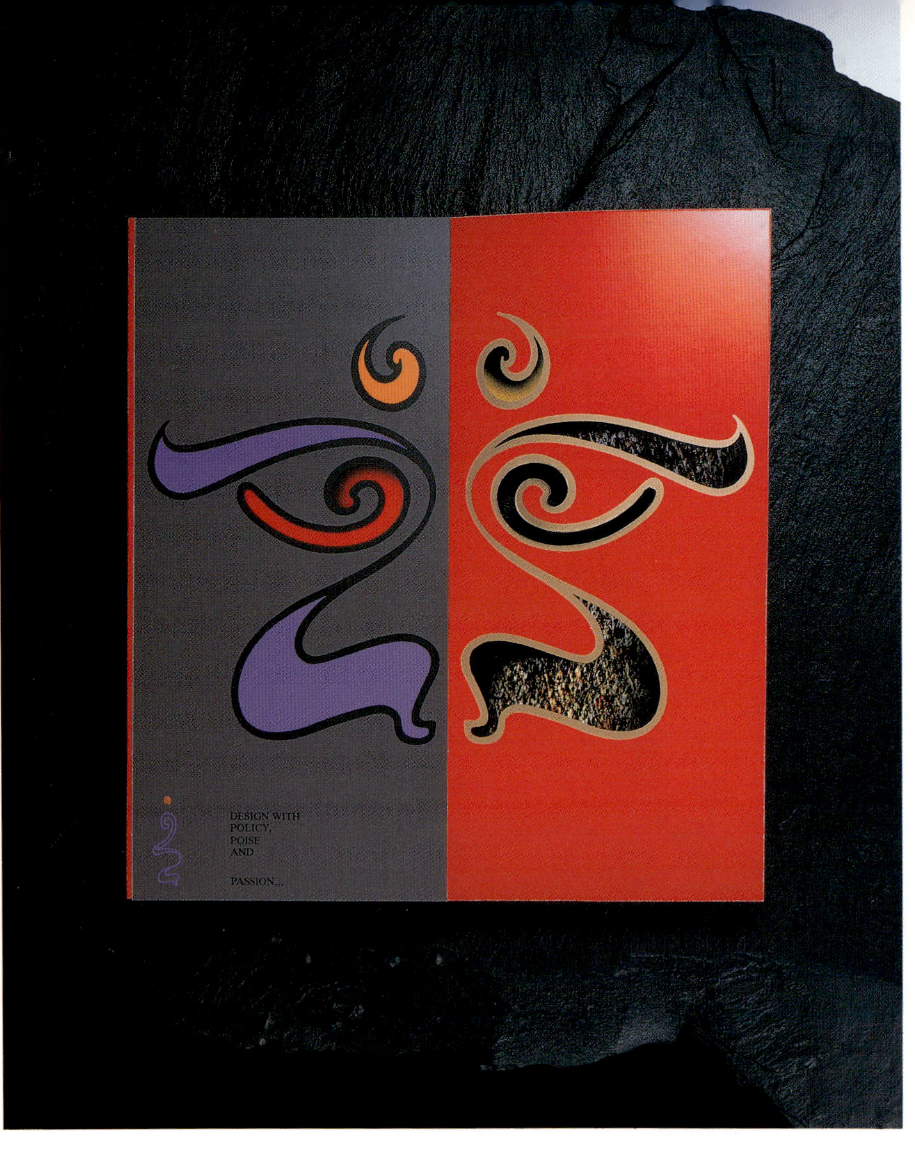

◀
New year's card
ニューイヤーズ・カード
JAPAN 1992
AD:Douglas Doolittle
CL:Douglas Design
TC:Graphic Design Studio
グラフィック・デザイン

▶
Christmas card
クリスマス・カード
TAIWAN 1991
AD,D:Chan Wing Kei,Leslie
DF:Leslie Chan Design
CL:Shiatzy International
TC:Apparel Retailer
アパレル

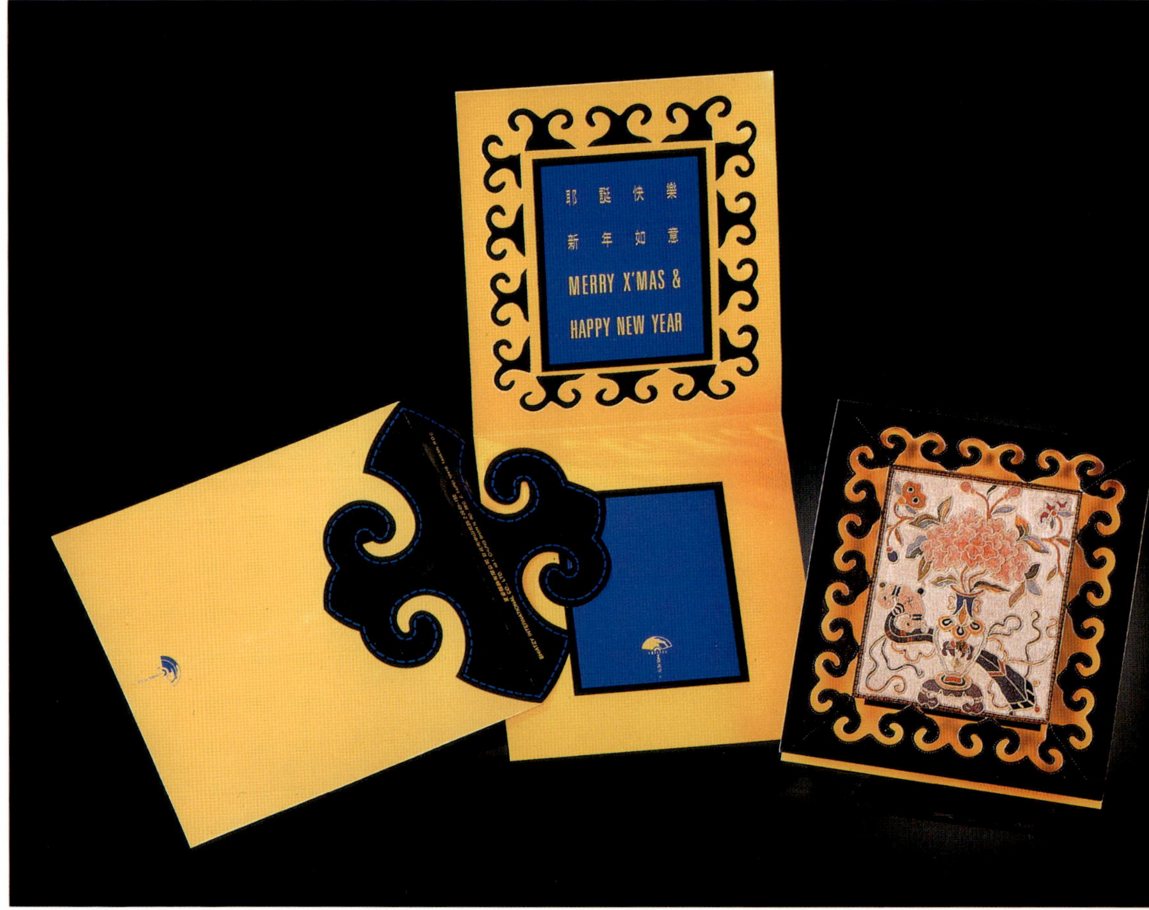

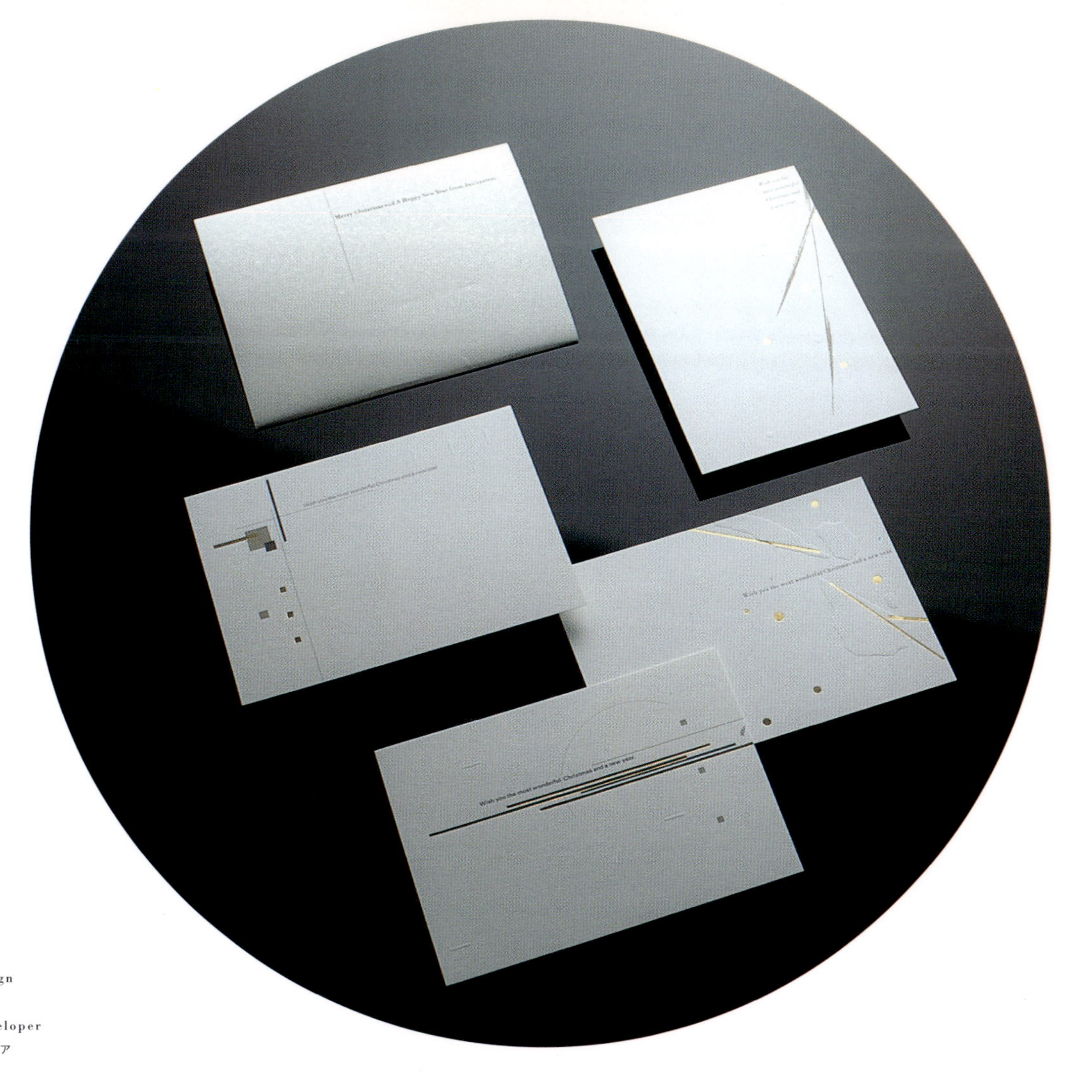

▲

Christmas card

クリスマス・カード

JAPAN 1991

AD:Takaaki Bando

D:Fujiko Uchimura

CW:Yoshimi Ishikawa

DF:Takaaki Bando Design

CL:Justsystem

TC:Computer Software Developer

コンピューター・ソフトウェア

研究開発、販売

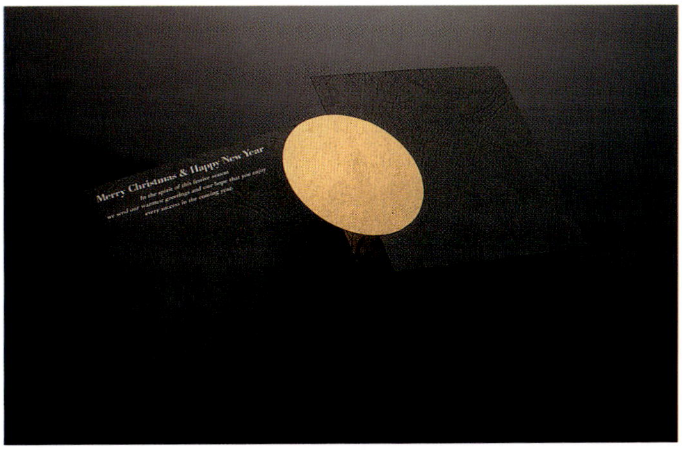

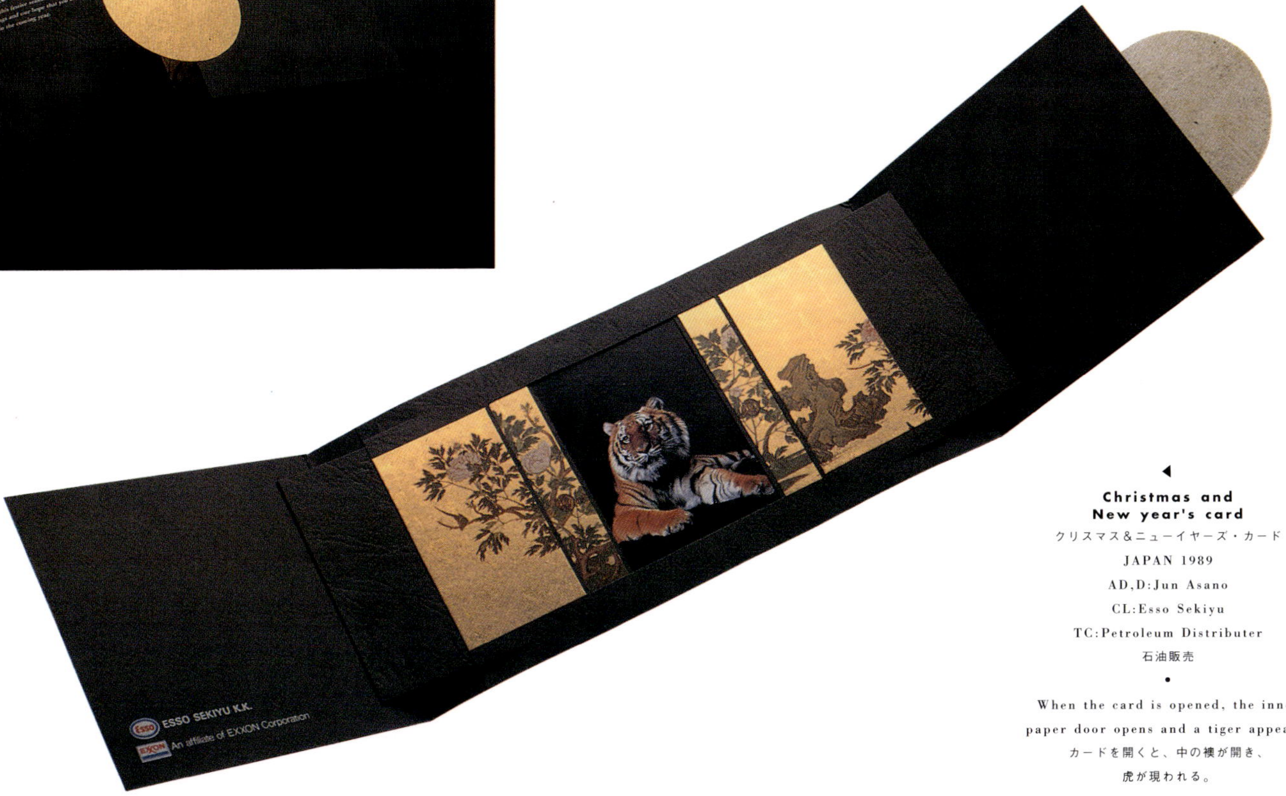

◀

Christmas and New year's card

クリスマス&ニューイヤーズ・カード

JAPAN 1989

AD,D:Jun Asano

CL:Esso Sekiyu

TC:Petroleum Distributer

石油販売

•

When the card is opened, the inner paper door opens and a tiger appears.

カードを開くと、中の襖が開き、

虎が現われる。

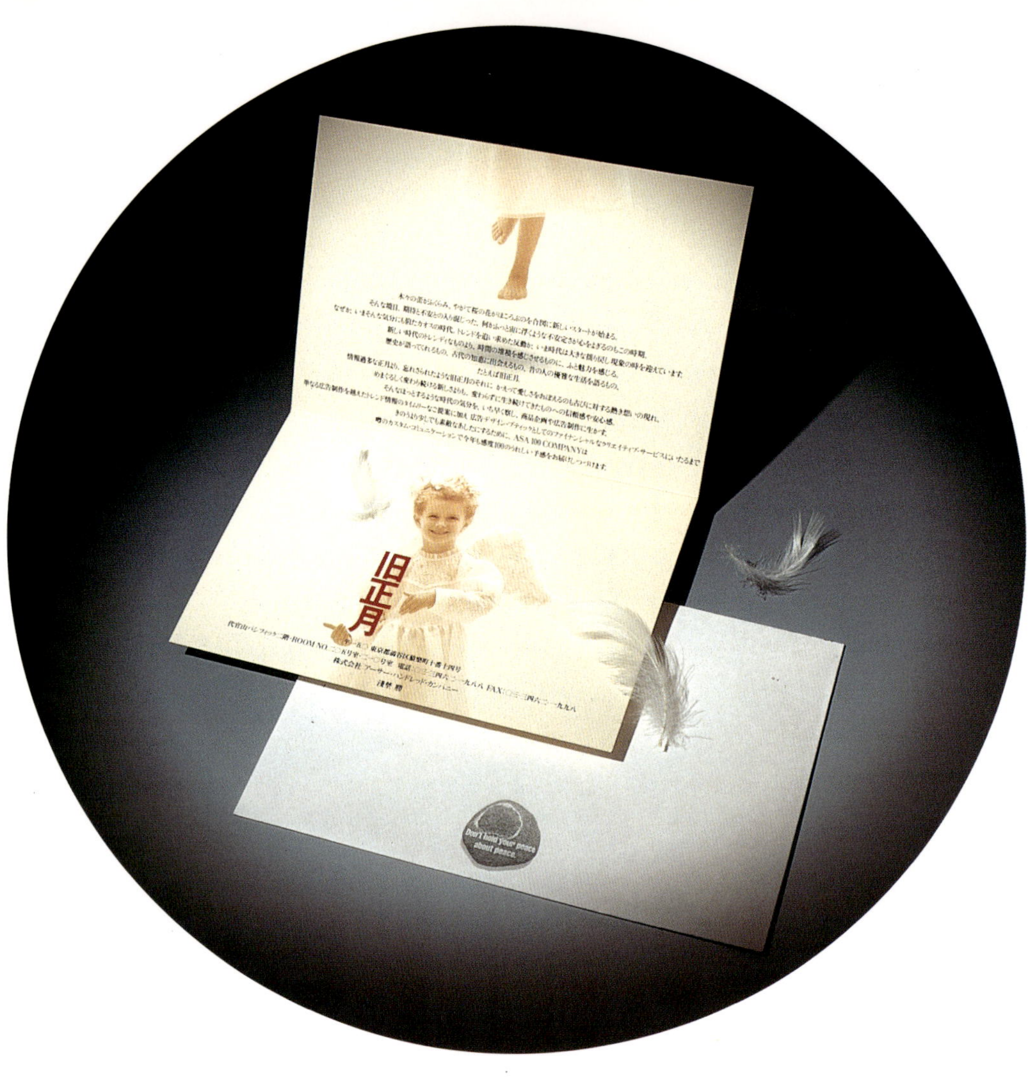

▲
New year's card
ニューイヤーズ・カード
JAPAN 1991
CD,AD,CW:Katsu Asano
D:Kinue Yonezawa
P:Hideo Fujii
DF:ASA 100 Company
CL:ASA 100 Company
TC:Design Studio
デザイン

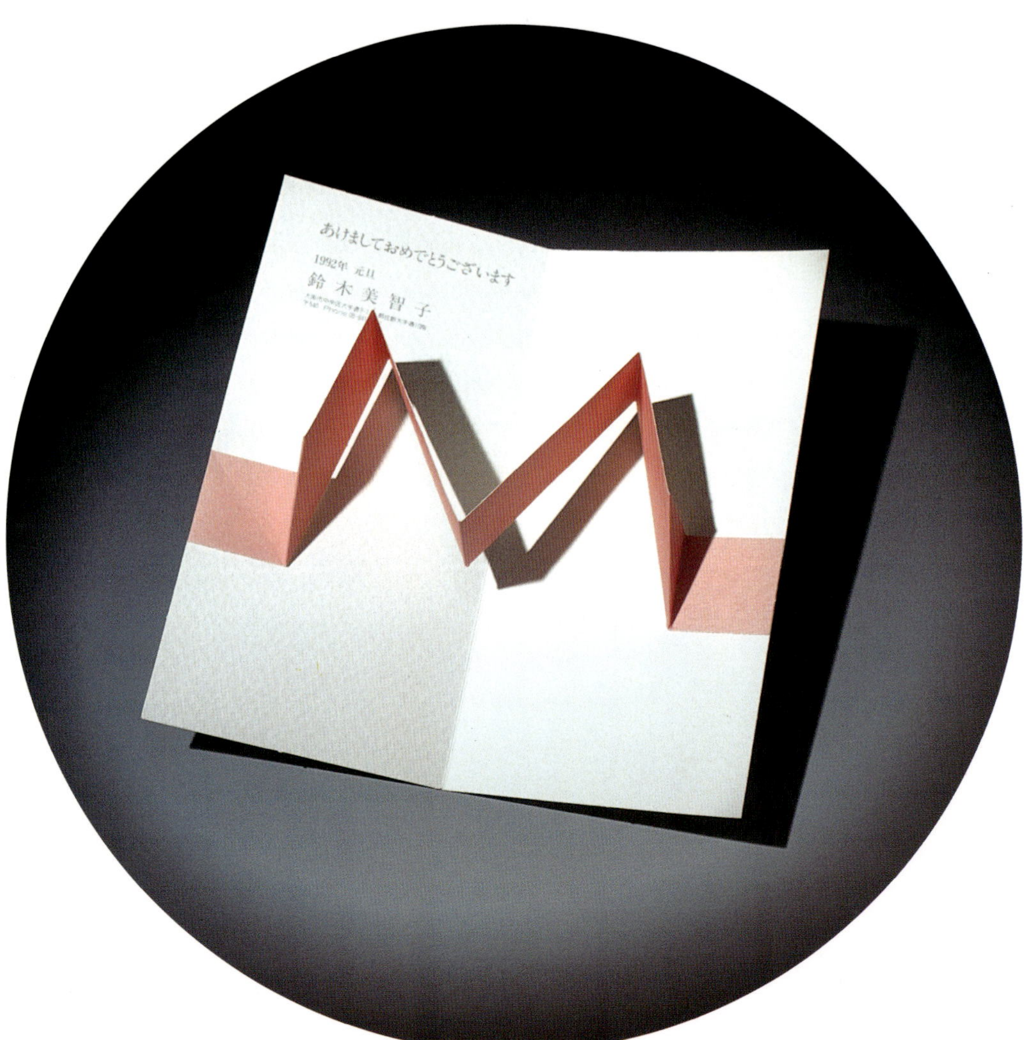

▼
New year's card
ニューイヤーズ・カード
JAPAN 1992
AD,D:Akio Okumura
CL:Michiko Suzuki

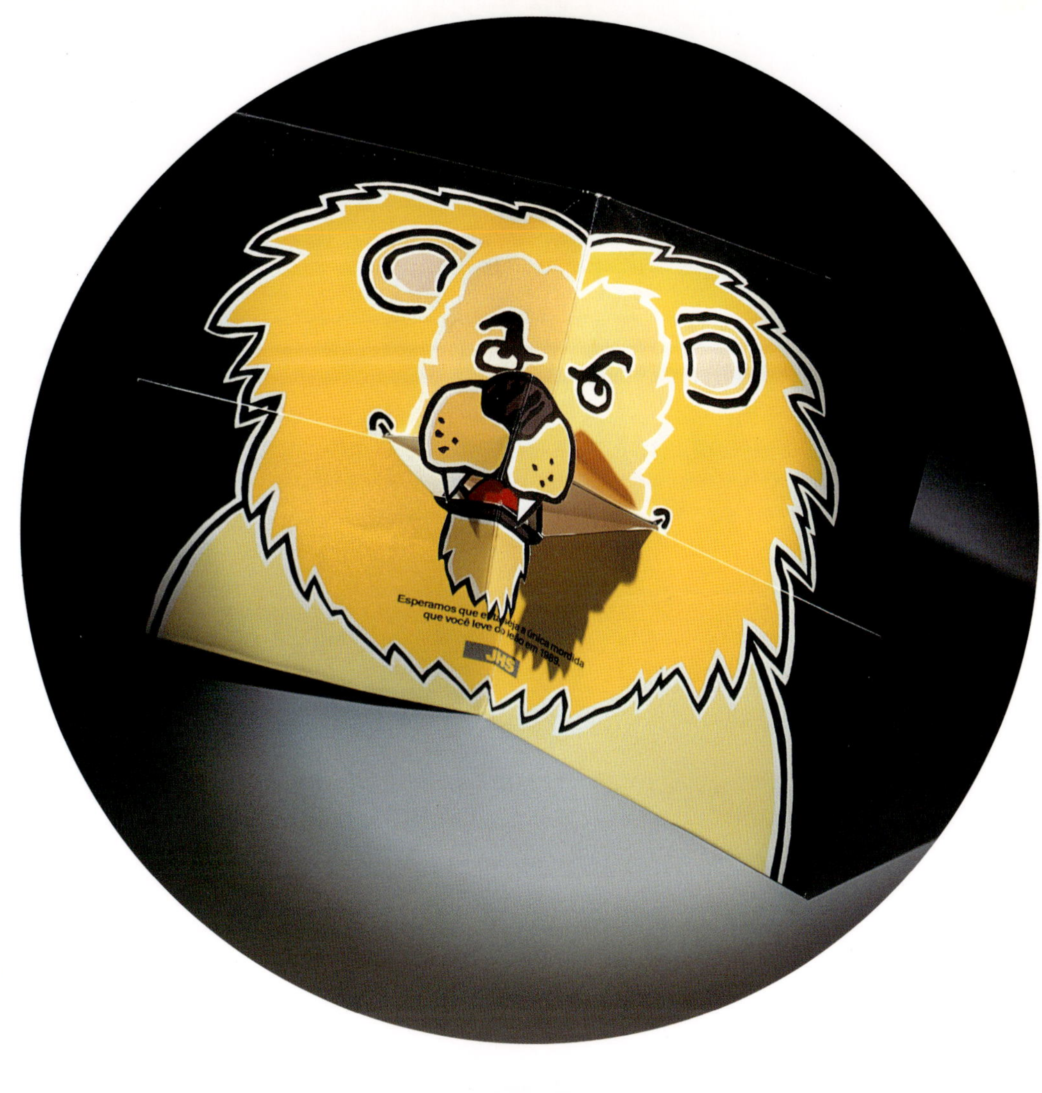

▲
New year's card
ニューイヤーズ・カード
BRASIL 1988
CD:Hugo Kovadloff
Milton Cipis
Claudio Novaes
D,I:Milton Cipis
DF:D Designers Associados
CL:JHS Construcão e Plane jamento
TC:Builder
建設

▼
Christmas and New year's card
クリスマス＆ニューイヤーズ・カード
JAPAN 1991
AD,D:Shinichiro Wada
I:Yasuhiko Kida
CL:Coca Cola (Japan)
TC:Beverage Vendor
清涼飲料水

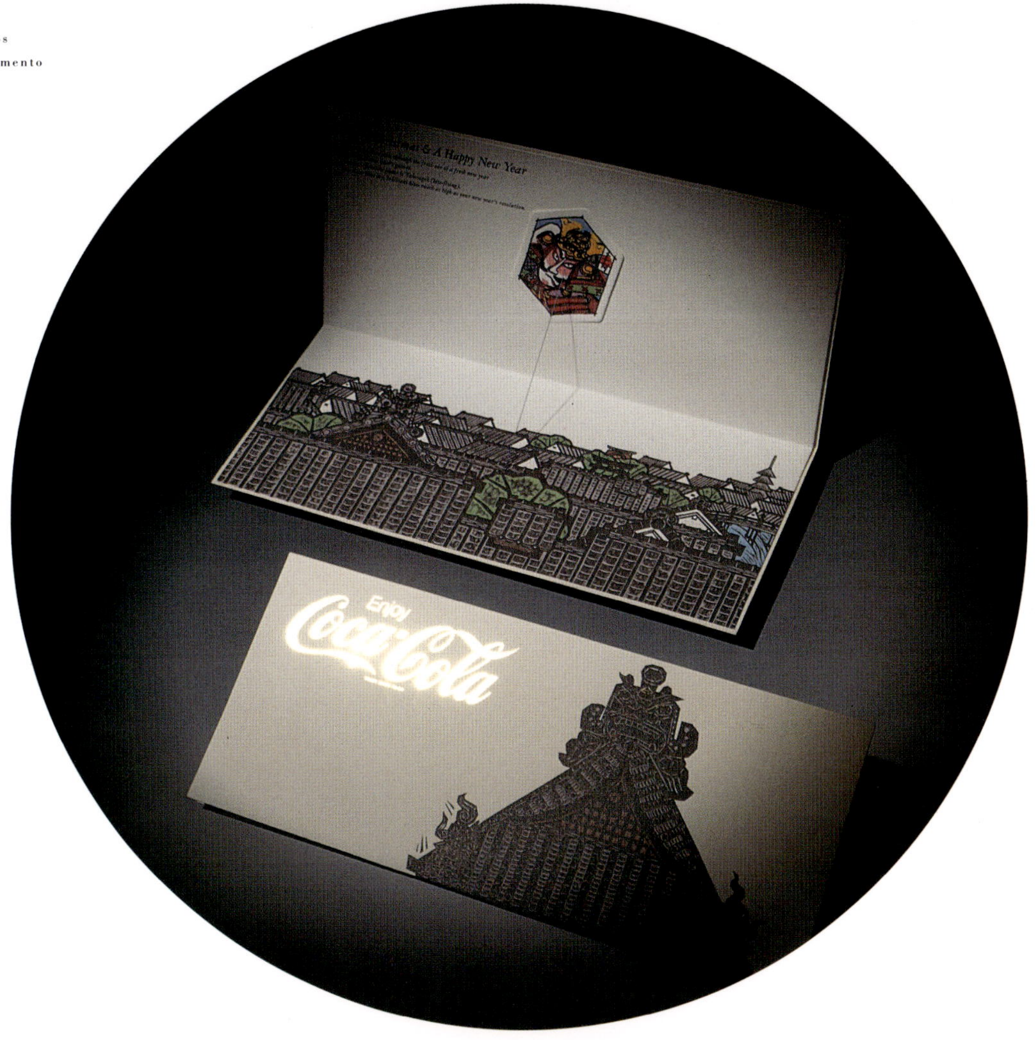

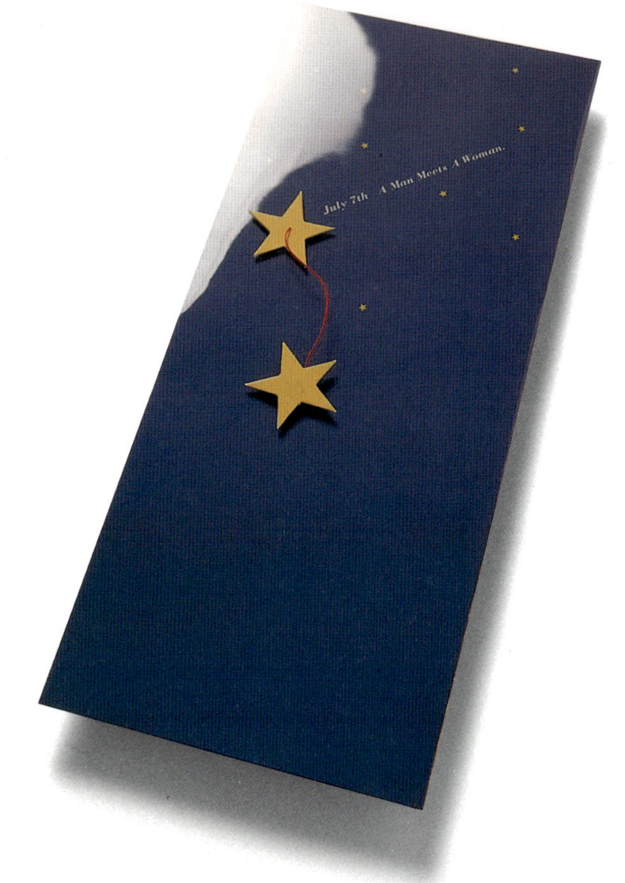

▲
Summer greeting card
セタカード
JAPAN 1989
CD,AD,D,CW:Keisuke Unosawa
DF:Keisuke Unosawa Design
CL:Keisuke Unosawa
TC:Graphic Designer
グラフィック・デザイン

▼
Christmas card
クリスマス・カード
JAPAN 1989
CD,AD,D,I:Keisuke Unosawa
DF:Keisuke Unosawa Design
CL:Keisuke Unosawa
TC:Graphic Design Studio
グラフィック・デザイン

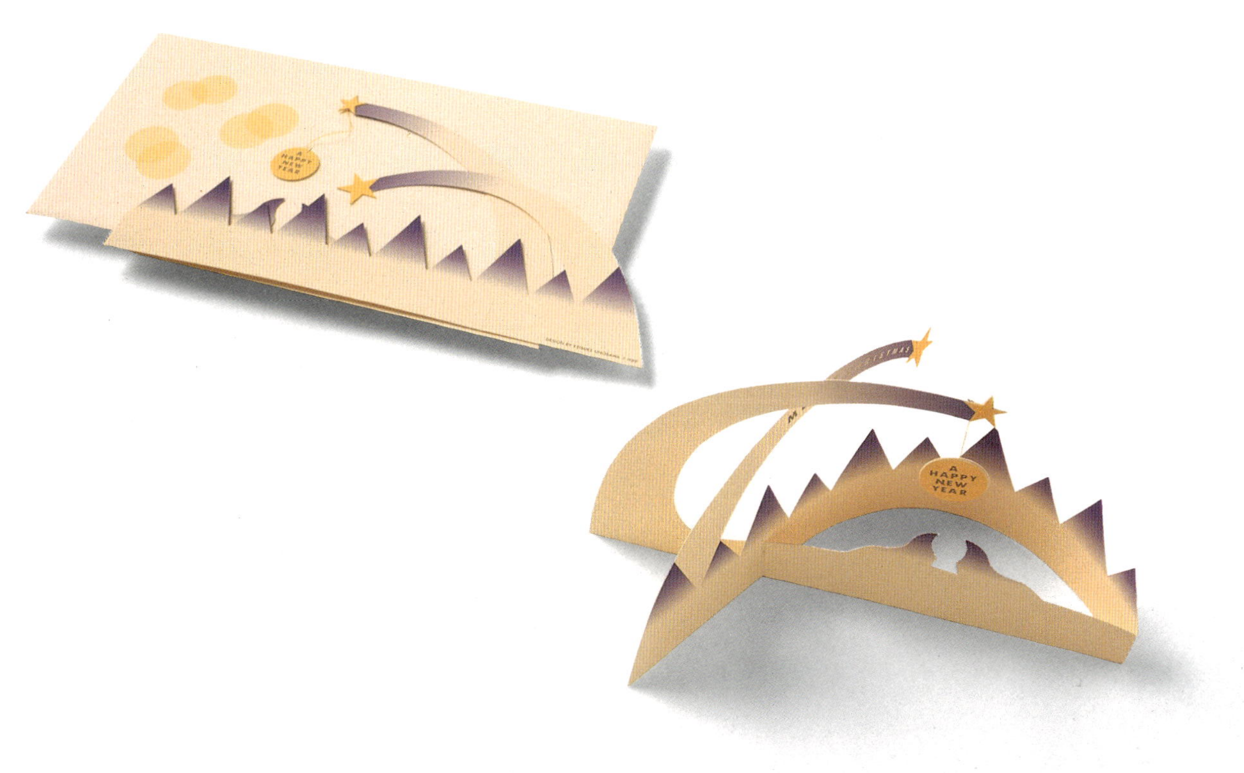

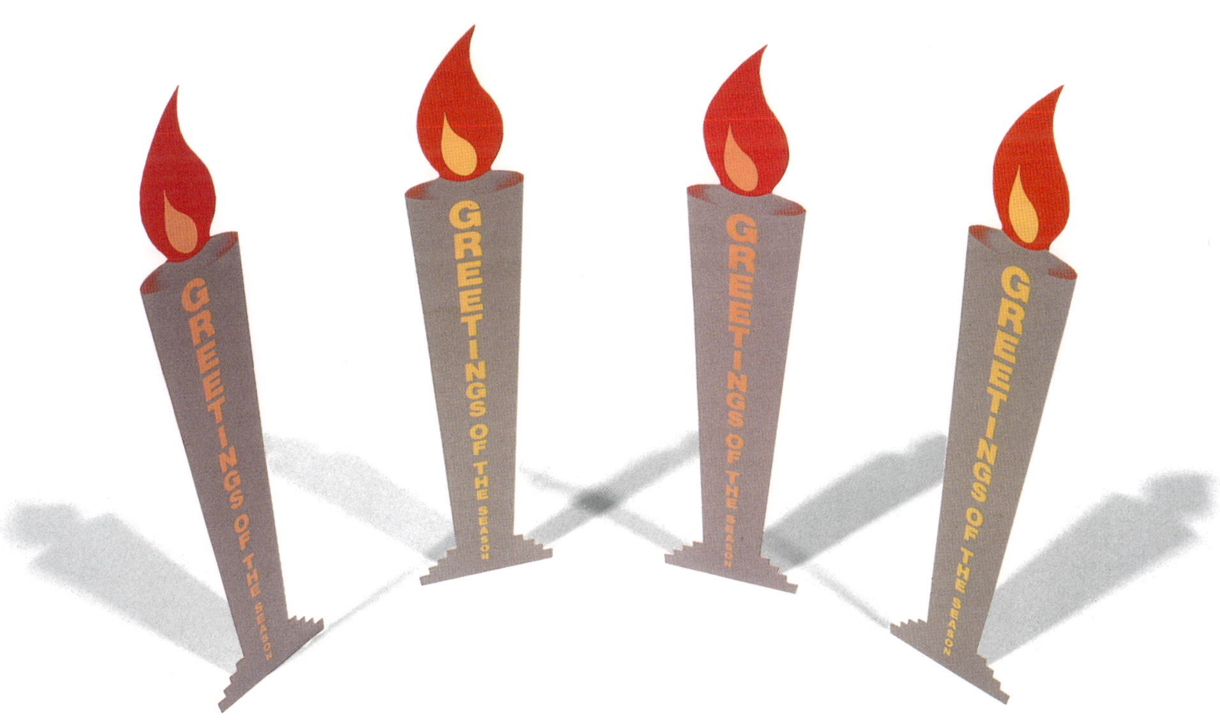

▲
Christmas card
クリスマス・カード
JAPAN 1990
CD,AD,D:Keisuke Unosawa
DF:Keisuke Unosawa Design
CL:Videoarts Japan
TC:Video Production,Sales
ビデオ企画制作、販売

▼
Summer greeting card
サマー・グリーティング・カード
JAPAN 1989
CD,AD,D,I:Keisuke Unosawa
DF:Keisuke Unosawa Design
CL:Keisuke Unosawa
TC:Graphic Designer
グラフィック・デザイン

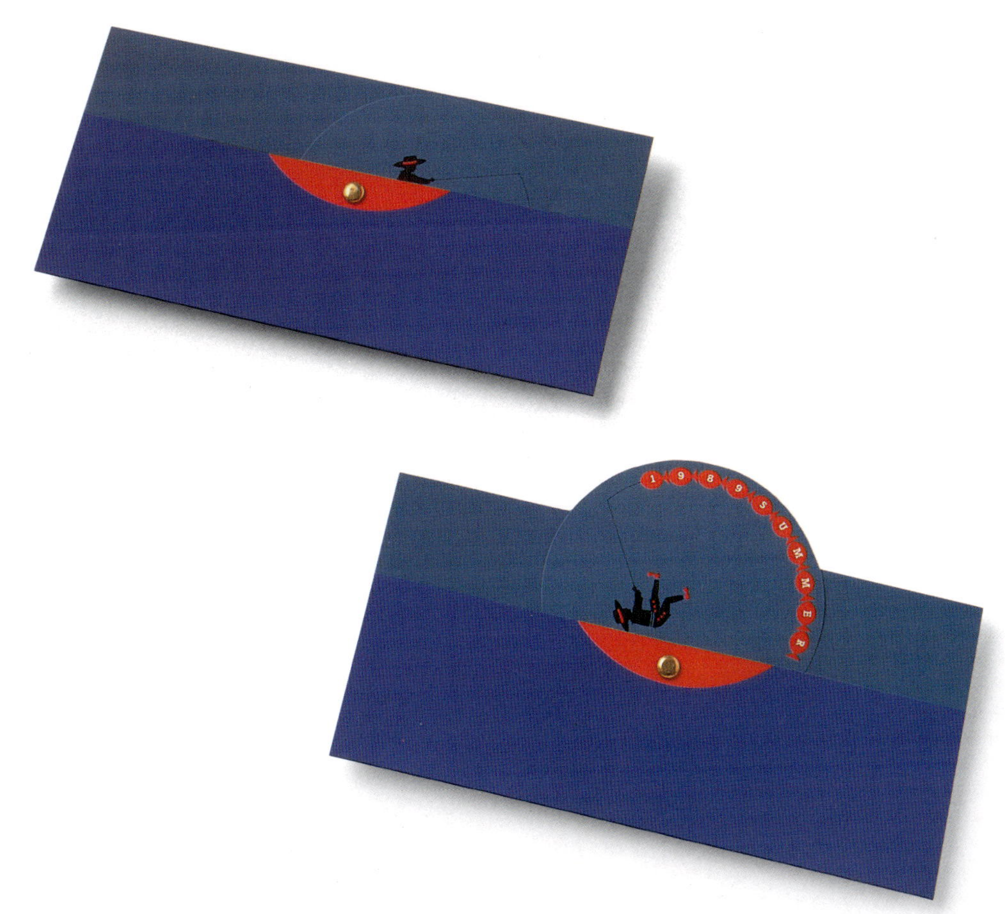

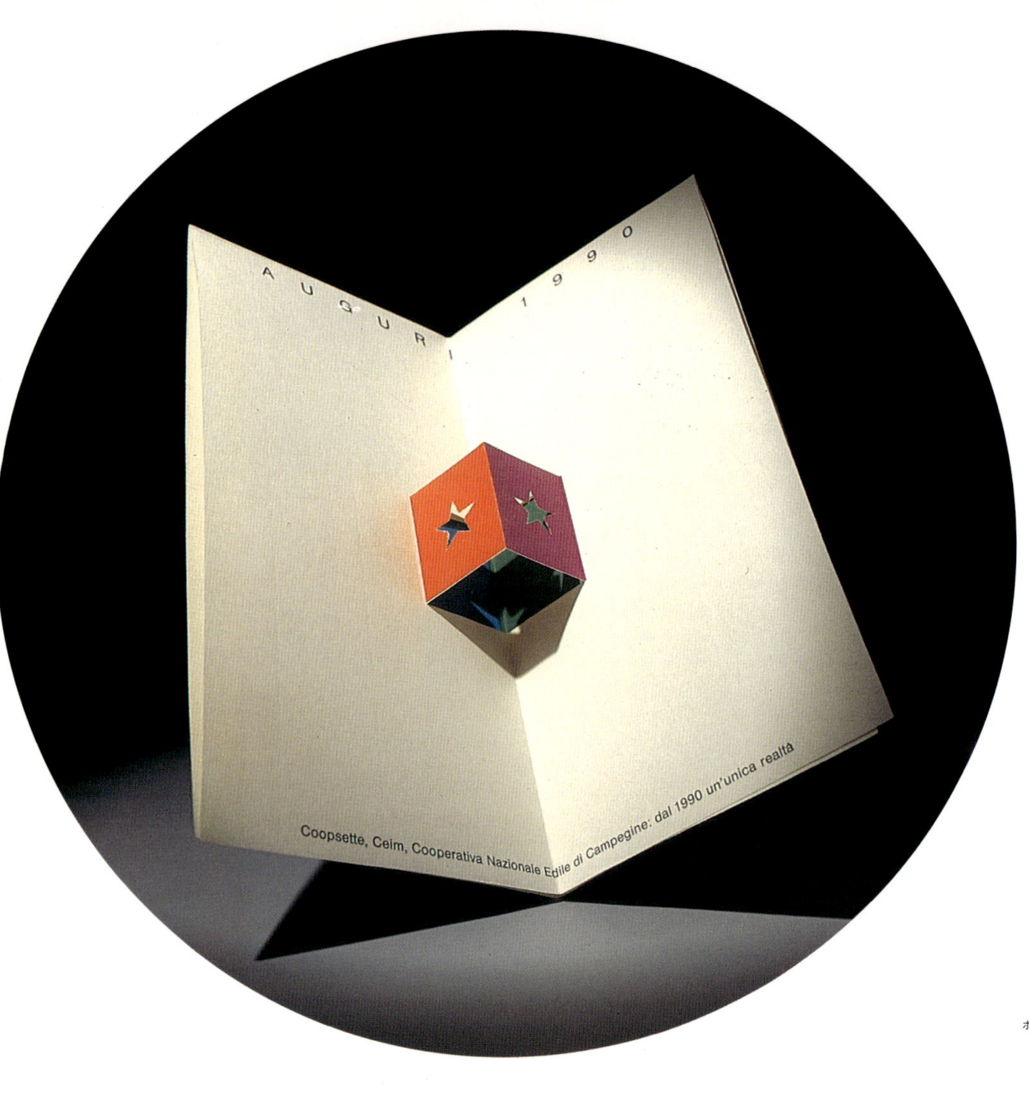

▲
New year's card
ニューイヤーズ・カード
ITALY 1989
CD,AD:Graziano Villani
D:Fabio Adranno
I:Nicoletia Marchi
CL:Coopsette
TC:Graphic Design Studio
グラフィック・デザイン

▼
Holiday card and invitation to a party
ホリデー・カード兼パーティー招待状
USA 1988
AD:Noel Davies
D:Meredith Kamm
Cathy Tetef-Davies
DF:Davies Associates
CL:CYP
TC:Architects
建築

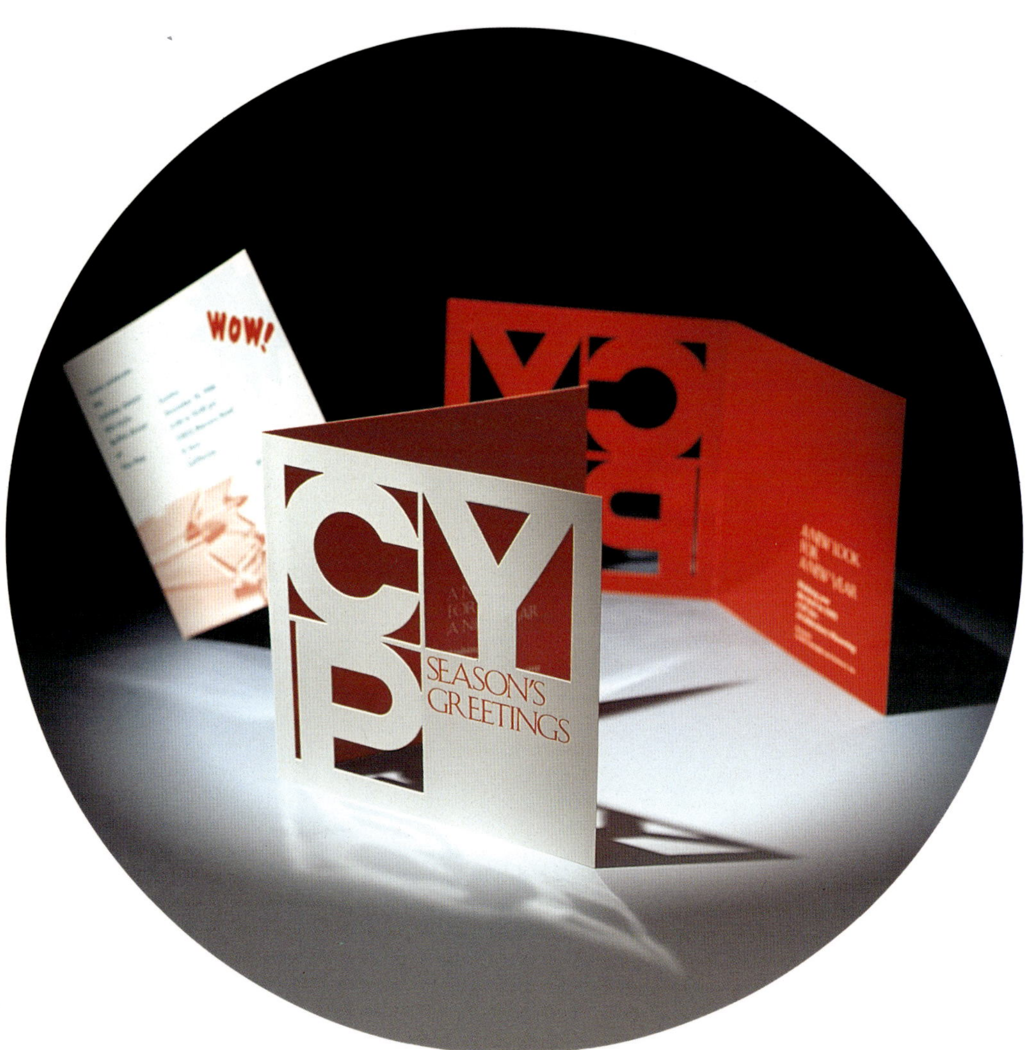

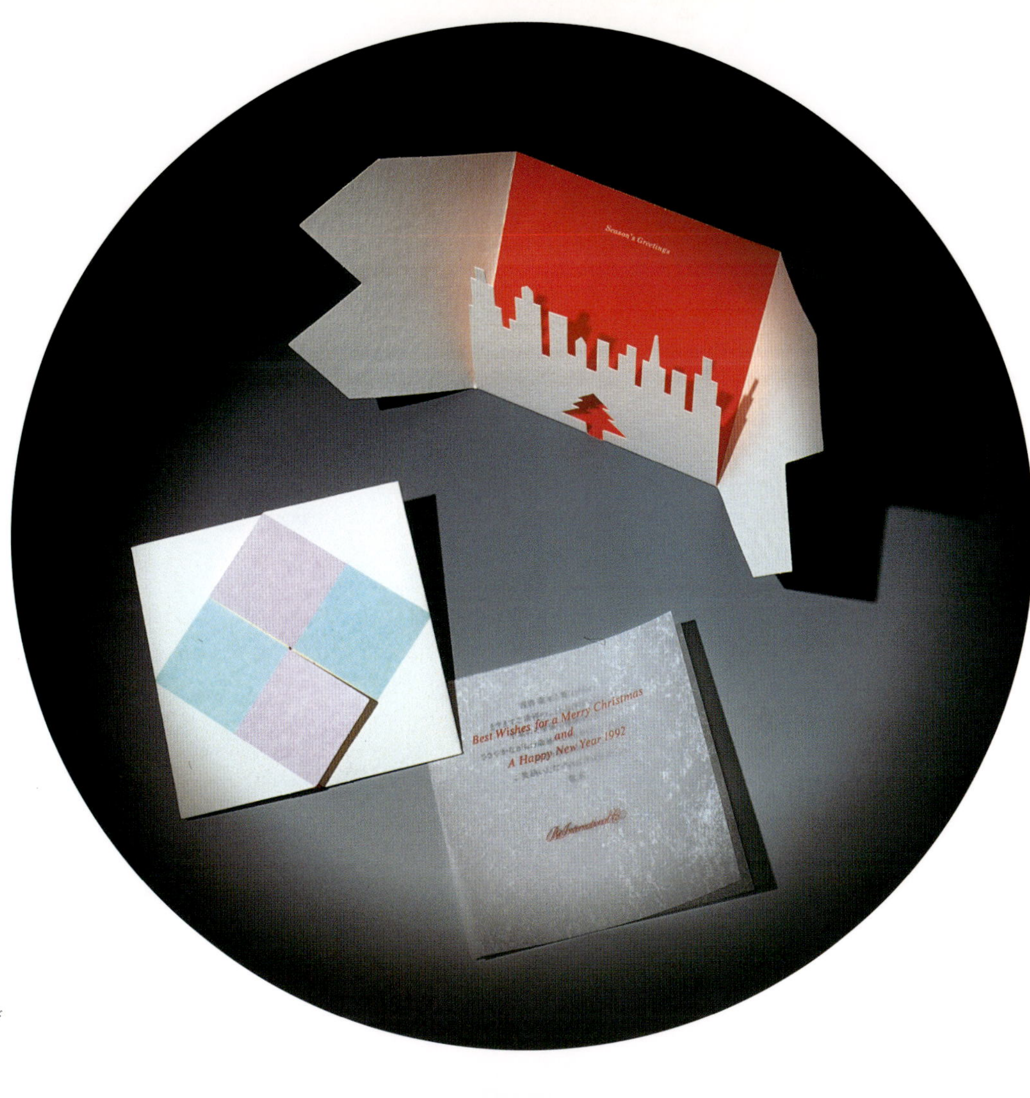

▲
Christmas and New year's card
クリスマス&ニューイヤーズ・カード
JAPAN 1991
D:Akihiko Tsukamoto
CL:Be International
TC:Interior Design
インテリア・デザイン

▼
Holiday card
ホリデー・カード
USA 1991
AD:Noel Davies
D:Cathy Tetef-Davies
Meredith Kamm
DF:Davies Associates
CL:R+T Development
TC:Real Estate Developer
不動産開発

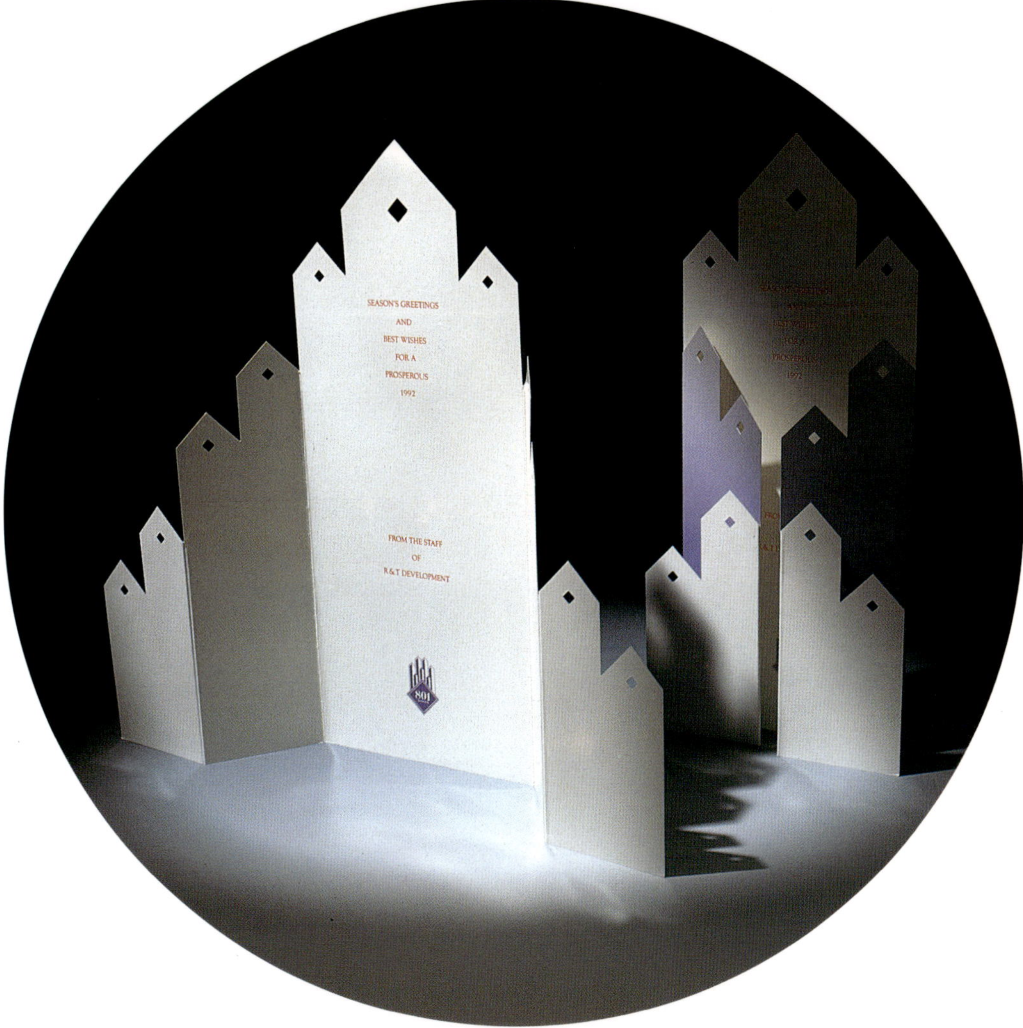

▶

New year's card

ニューイヤーズ・カード

HOLLAND 1991

CD,AD,D,I:Frans Koenigs

CL:Frans Koenigs

TC:Graphic Design Studio

グラフィック・デザイン

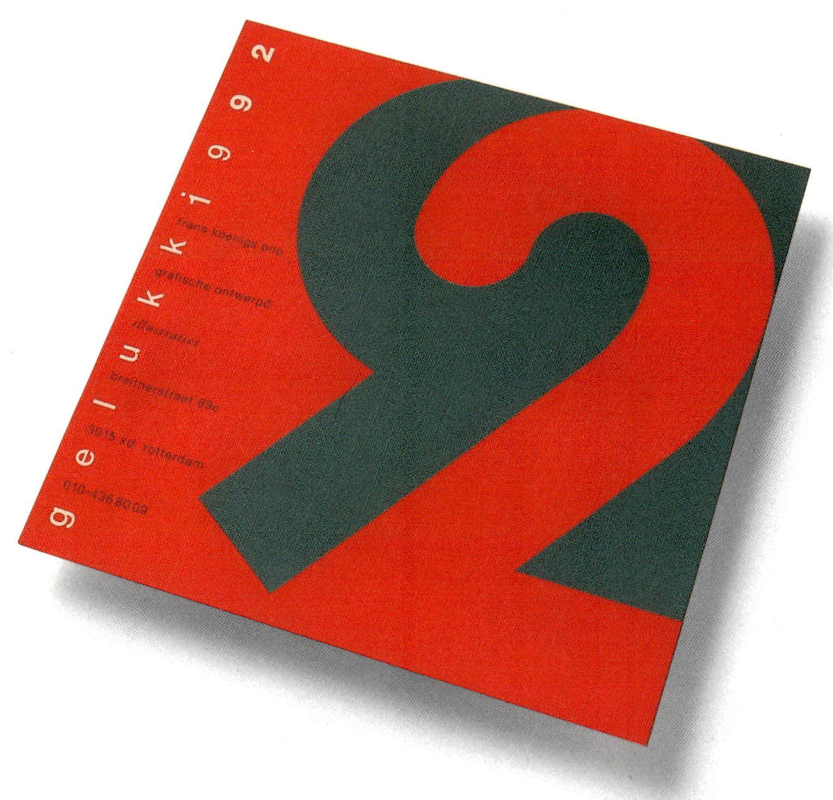

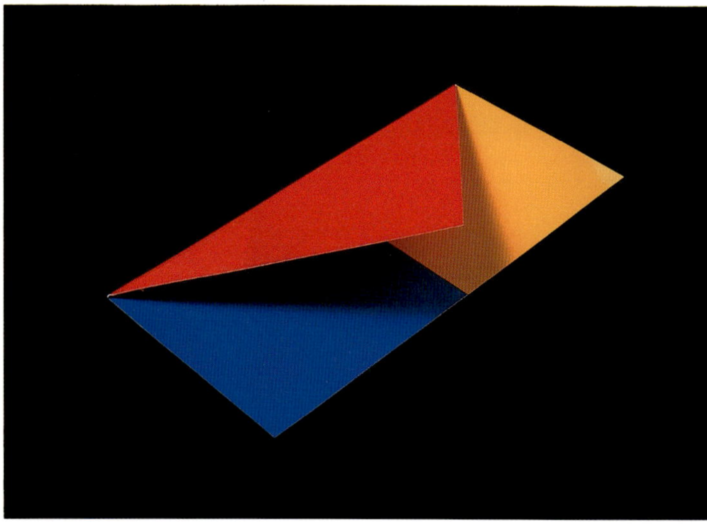

▲

New year's card

ニューイヤーズ・カード

ITALY 1988

CD,AD,D:Graziano Villani

CL:CS Coopstudio

TC:Graphic Design Studio

グラフィック・デザイン

▼

New year's card

ニューイヤーズ・カード

ITALY 1988

AD,D:Graziano Villani

CL:Tipografia Gamberini

TC:Graphic Design Studio

グラフィック・デザイン

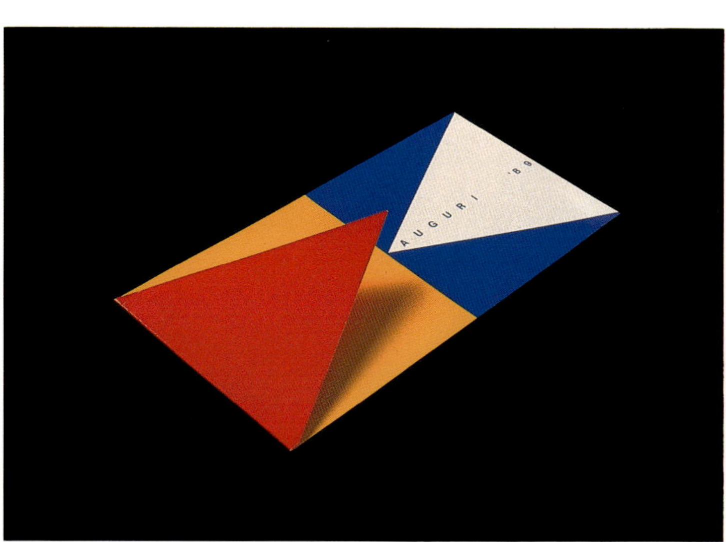

Christmas and New year's card
クリスマス&ニューイヤーズ・カード
ITALY 1989
D:Giorgio Davanzo
DF:Giorgio Davanzo Design
CL:Giorgio Davanzo Design
TC:Advertising Agency
広告

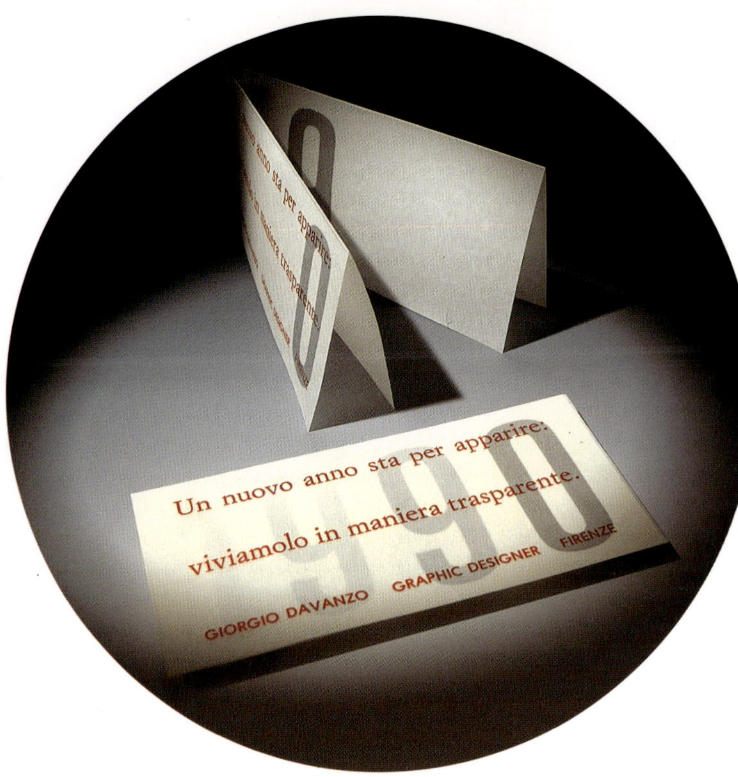

New year's card
ニューイヤーズ・カード
SWITZERLAND 1988
CD,AD,D,I,CW:Michael Baviera
DF:BBV Michael Baviera
CL:BBV
TC:Graphic Design Studio
グラフィック・デザイン

New year's card
ニューイヤーズ・カード
SWITZERLAND 1990
CD,AD,D,I,CW:Michael Baviera
DF:BBV Michael Baviera
CL:BBV
TC:Graphic Design Studio
グラフィック・デザイン

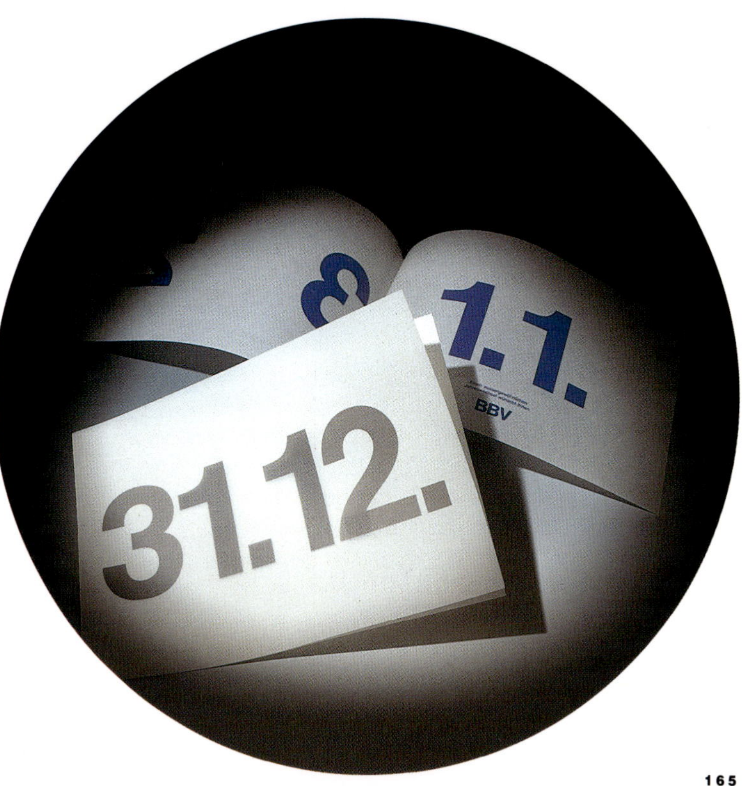

Christmas card
クリスマス・カード
ITALY 1990
AD,D:Giorgio Davanzo
DF:Giorgio Davanzo Design
CL:Luca Baggiani
TC:Advertising Agency
広告

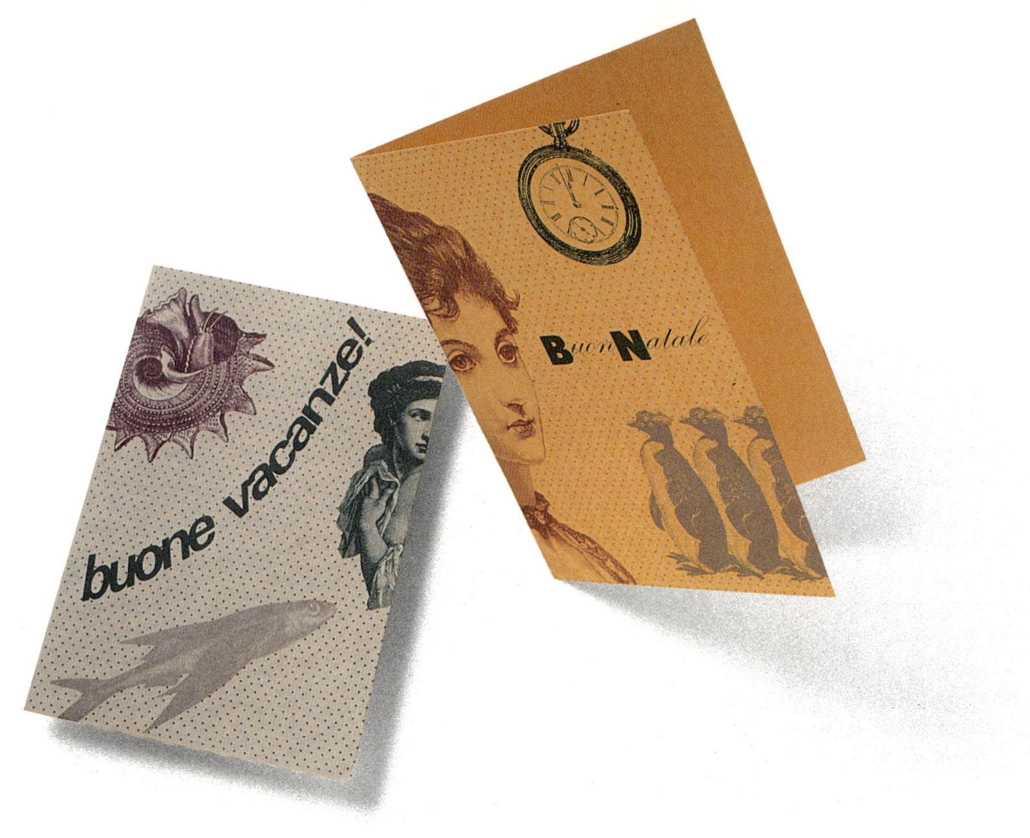

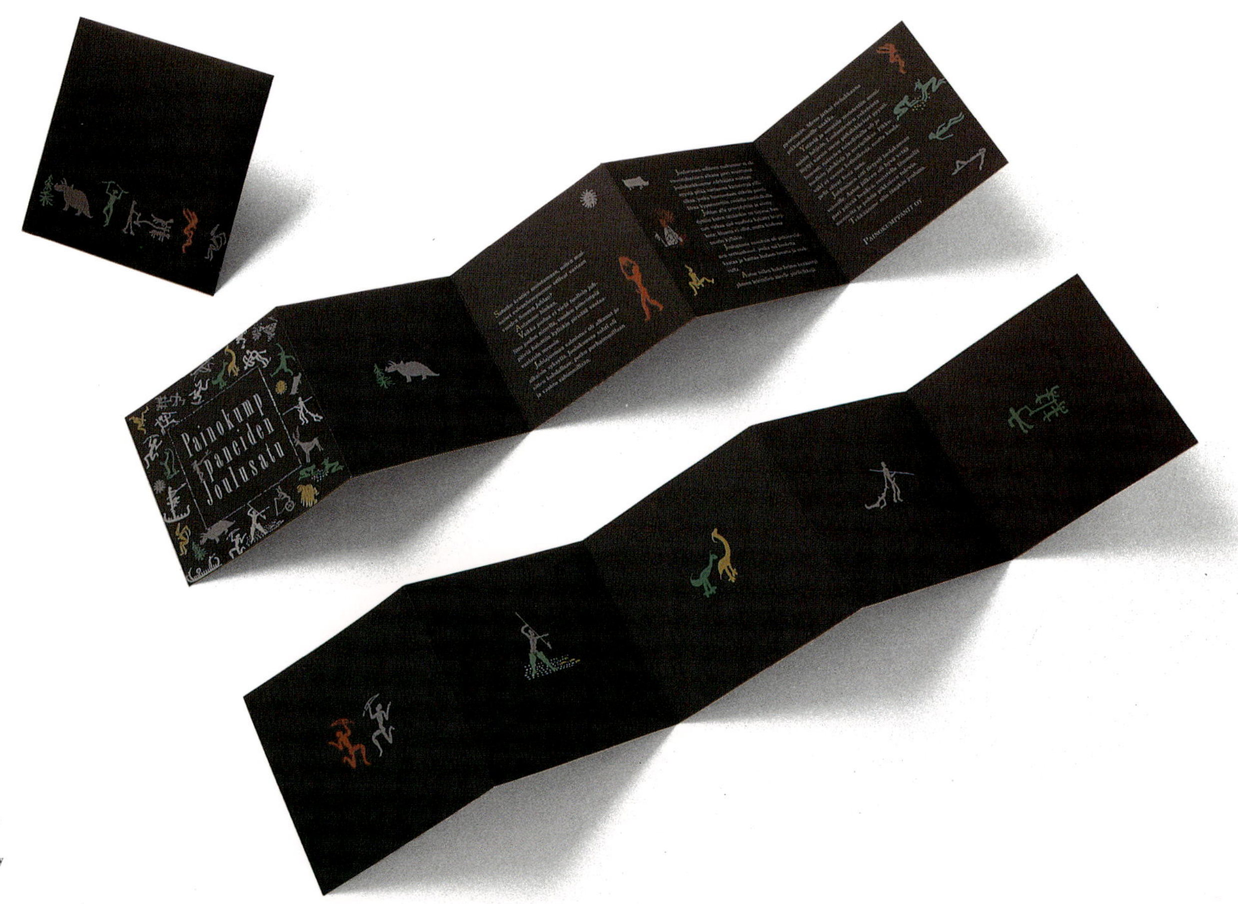

Christmas card
クリスマス・カード
FINLAND 1990
D,I:Viktor Kaltala
CW:Reijo Taajaranta
CL:Painokumppanit Oy
TC:Printer
印刷

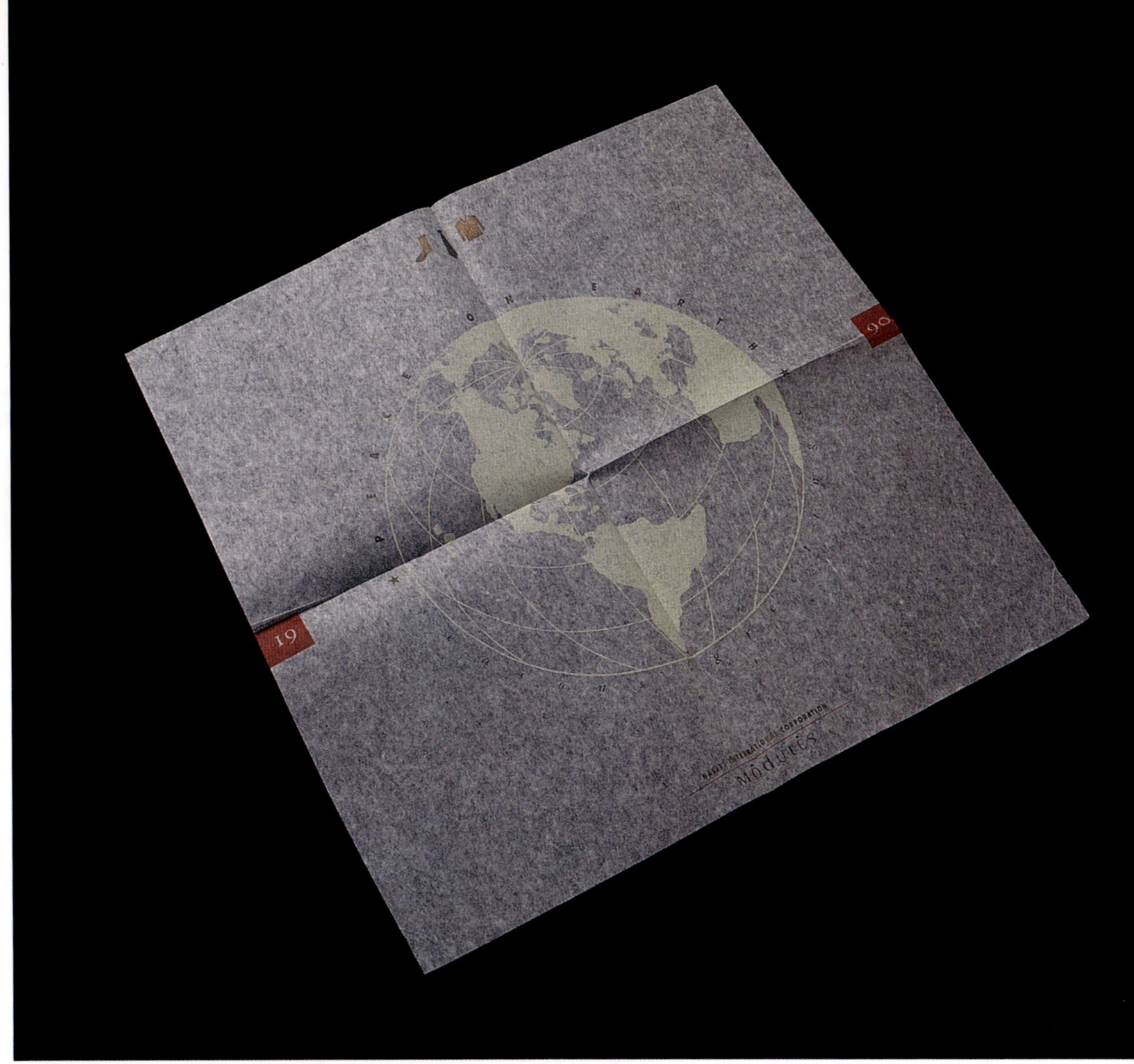

▶
New year's card
ニューイヤーズ・カード
USA 1990
CD:Toshiya Takahashi
D:Gail Rigelhaupt
I:Mike Samuel
DF:Rigelhaupt Design
CL:Nasett International
TC:Apparel Maker
アパレル

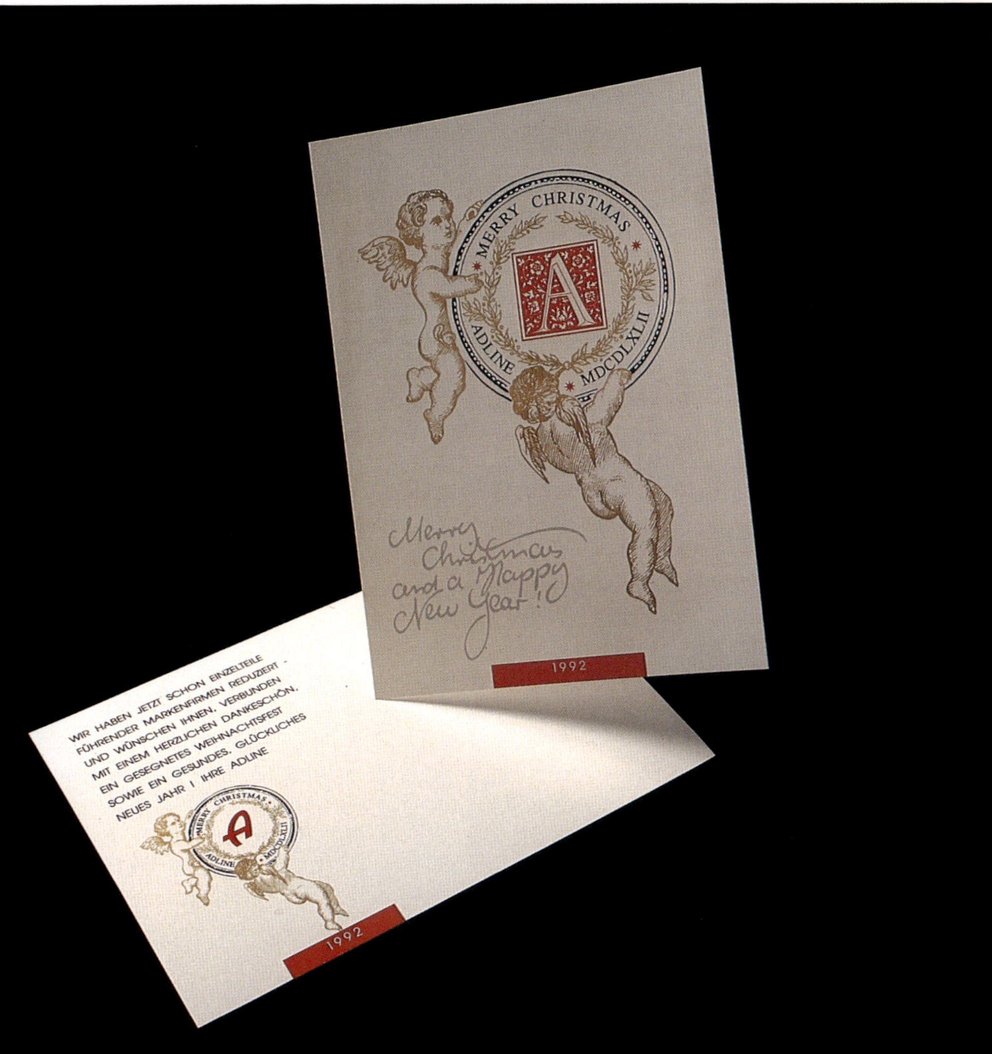

◀
Christmas card
クリスマス・カード
GERMANY 1991
D,I:Hans Georg lang
DF:Lane Art + Graphic Design
CL:Adline Exclusive Lady Fashion
TC:Fashion Boutique
ファッション・ブティック

▲

New year's card

ニューイヤーズ・カード

USA 1989

D:Gail Rigelhaupt

DF:Rigelhaupt Design

CL:Rigelhaupt Design

TC:Graphic Design Studio

グラフィック・デザイン

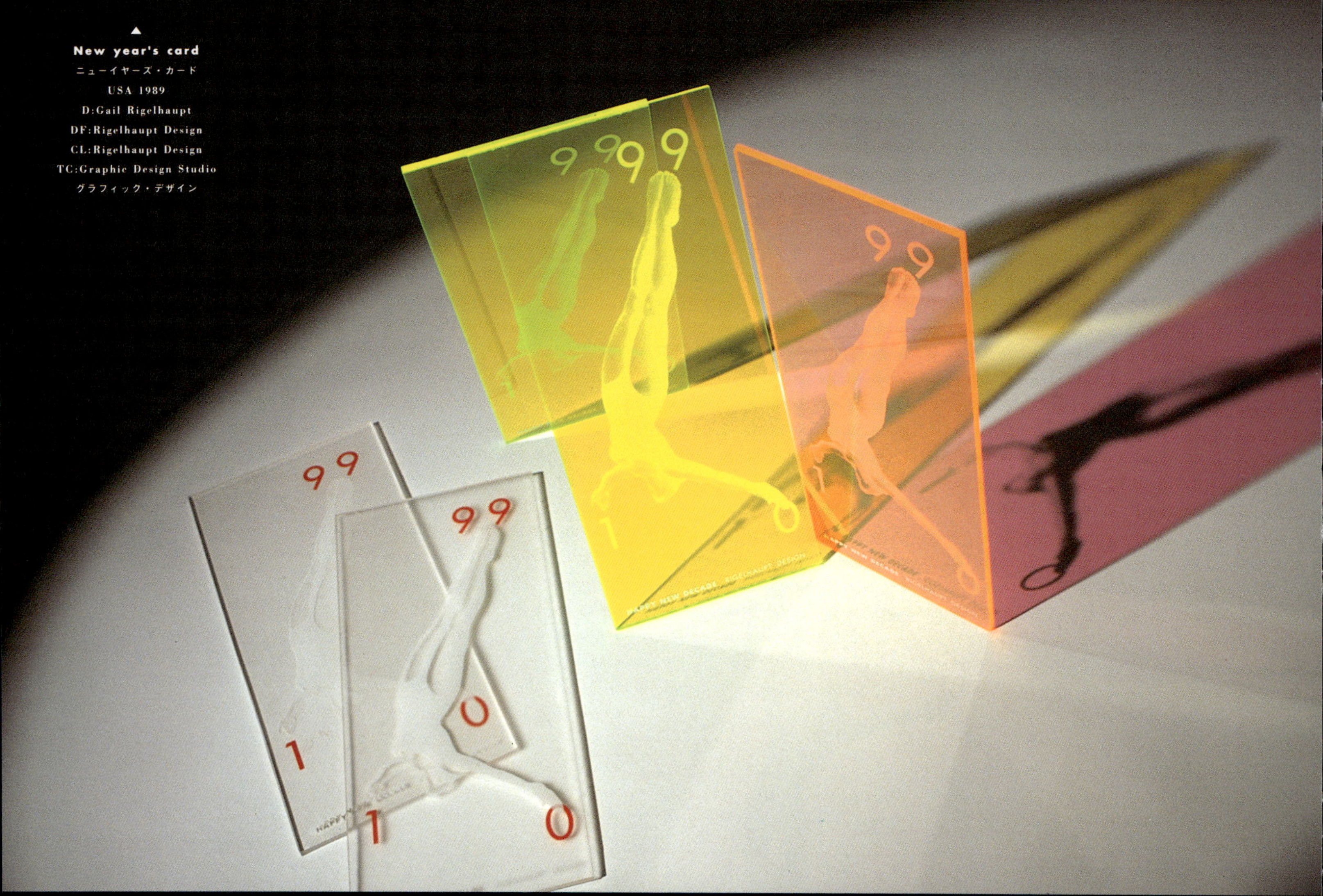

▼

Summer greeting card

サマー・グリーティング・カード

JAPAN 1992

CD,AD,D:Mikiko Shimizu

CL:Tokyo Can

TC:Apparel Maker

アパレル

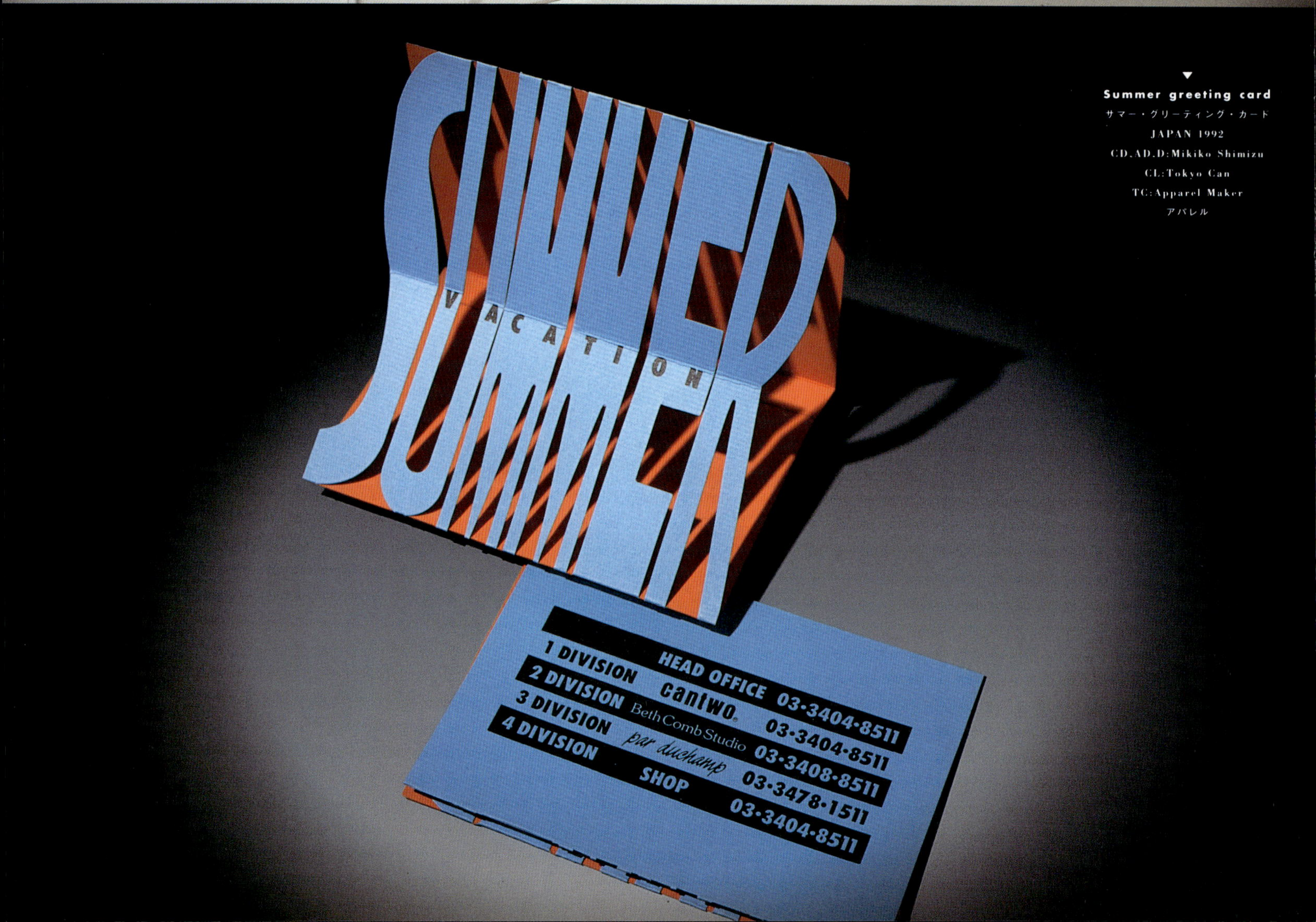

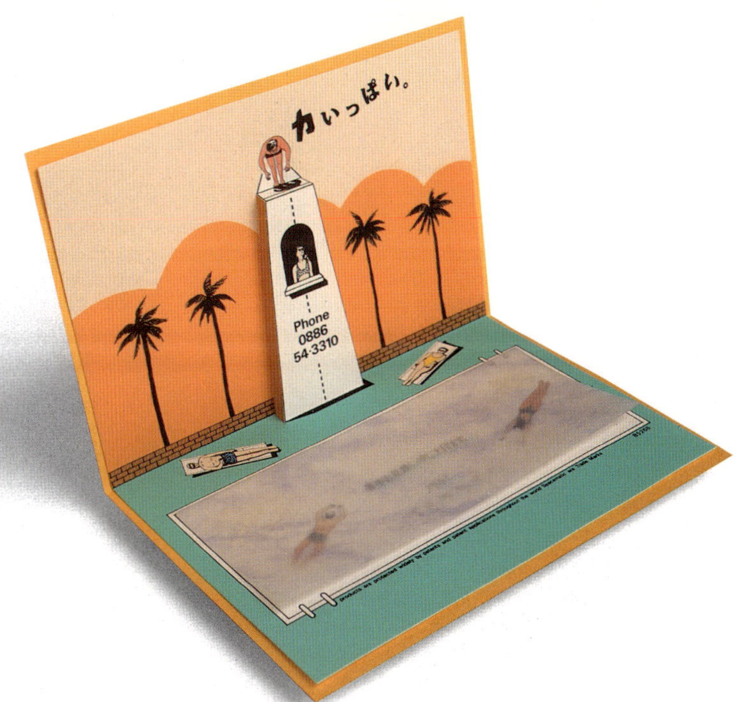

◀
Summer greeting card
サマー・グリーティング・カード
JAPAN 1991
AD,I:Kei Tamaki
D:Kei Tamaki
Shoichi Miyano
CW:Tokko Morino
DF:Granz Kohkokuseisakusho
CL:Granz Kohkokuseisakusho
TC:Graphic Design Studio
グラフィック・デザイン

▶
Summer greeting card
サマー・グリーティング・カード
JAPAN 1990
CD,AD,D:Keisuke Unosawa
DF:Keisuke Unosawa Design
CL:Keisuke Unosawa
TC:Graphic Design Studio
グラフィック・デザイン

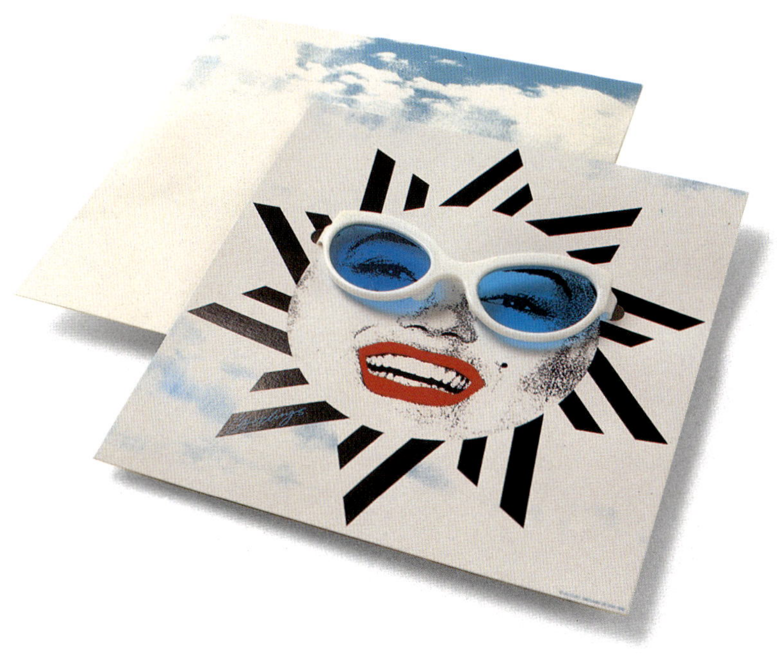

◀
New year's card
ニューイヤーズ・カード
BRASIL 1989
CD:Hugo Kovadloff
Milton Cipis
Claudio Novaes
D:Hugo Kovadloff
DF:D Designers Associados
CL:Neumeister Design Munchen
Axis Design Rio D Designers
TC:Industrial and
Graphic Design Studio
工業及びグラフィック・デザイン

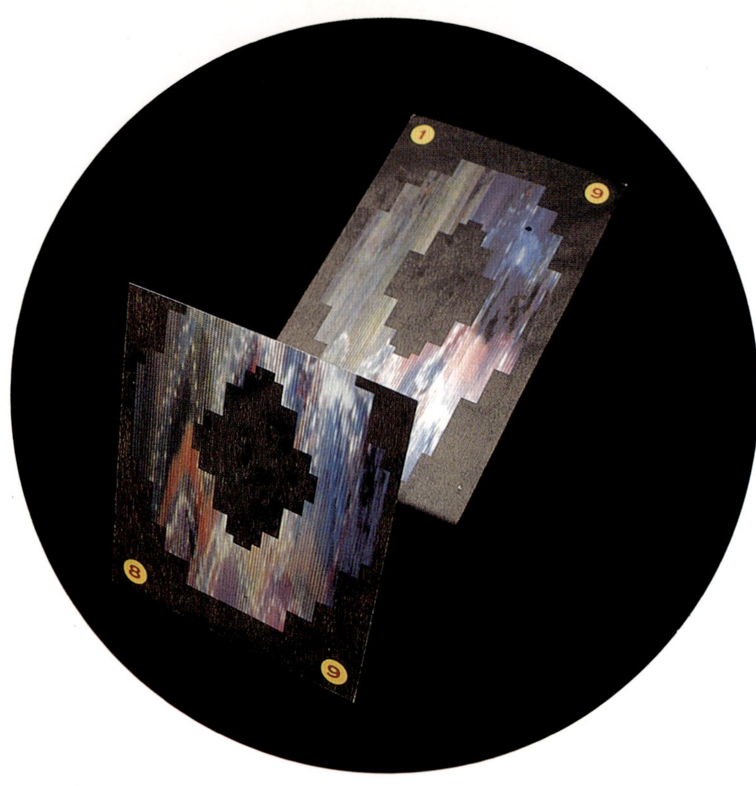

◀
New year's card
ニューイヤーズ・カード
USA 1988
AD:Takaaki Matsumoto
Michael McGinn
D:Takaaki Matsumoto
DF:M Plus M
CL:M Plus M
TC:Design Studio
デザイン

▶
New year's card
ニューイヤーズ・カード
USA 1991
CD,AD,D:Mikio Sakai
CL:Mikio Sakai
TC:Graphic Design Studio
グラフィック・デザイン

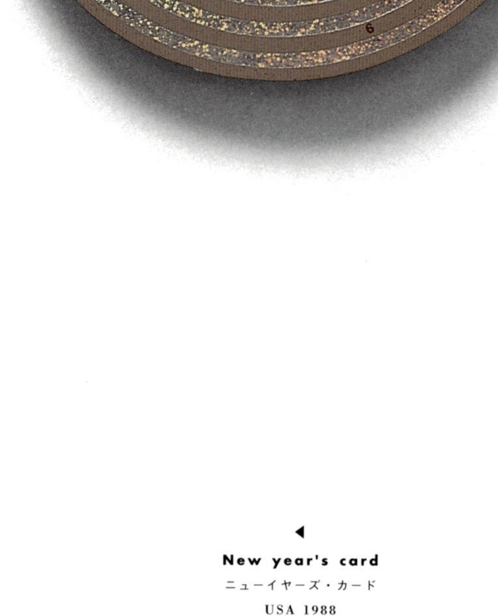

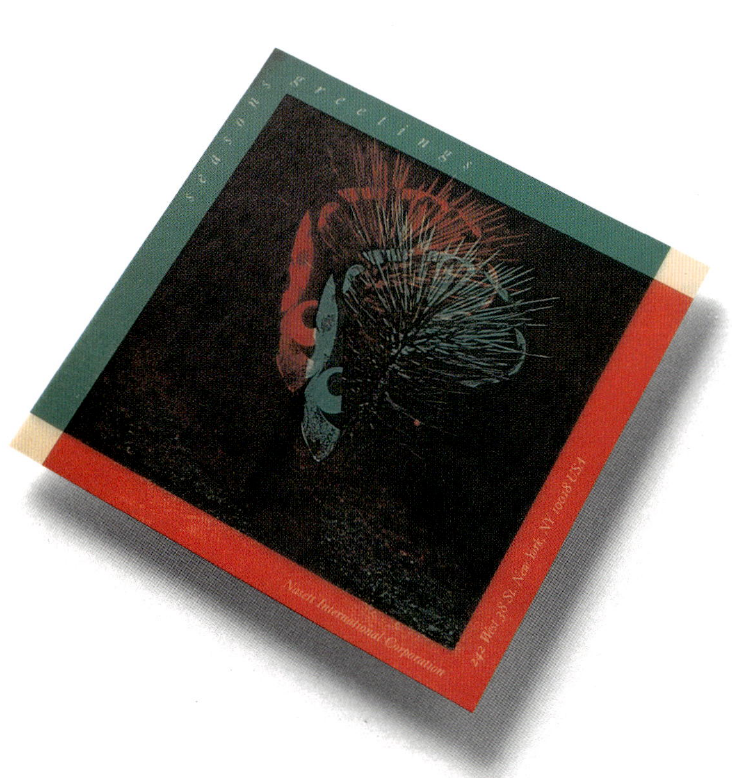

◀
New year's card
ニューイヤーズ・カード
USA 1988
CD:Toshiya Takahashi
D:Gail Rigelhaupt
P:Toshi Kazama
DF:Rigelhaupt Design
CL:Nasett International
TC:Apparel Maker
アパレル

▶

Summer greeting card

サマー・グリーティング・カード

USA 1989

AD:Takaaki Matsumoto

Michael McGinn

D:Michael McGinn

CW:Gary Kleinau

DF:M Plus M

CL:M Plus M

TC:Design Studio

デザイン

●

When the card is folded,

it becomes a sun-dial.

カードを折り曲げると日時計になる。

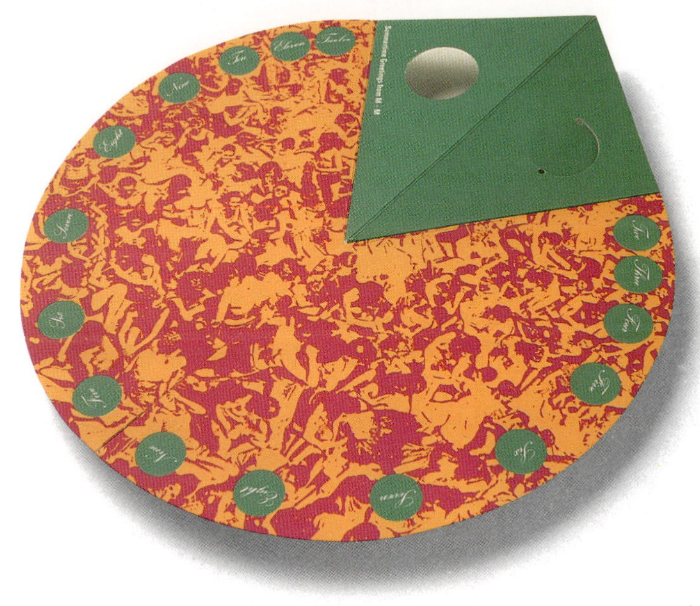

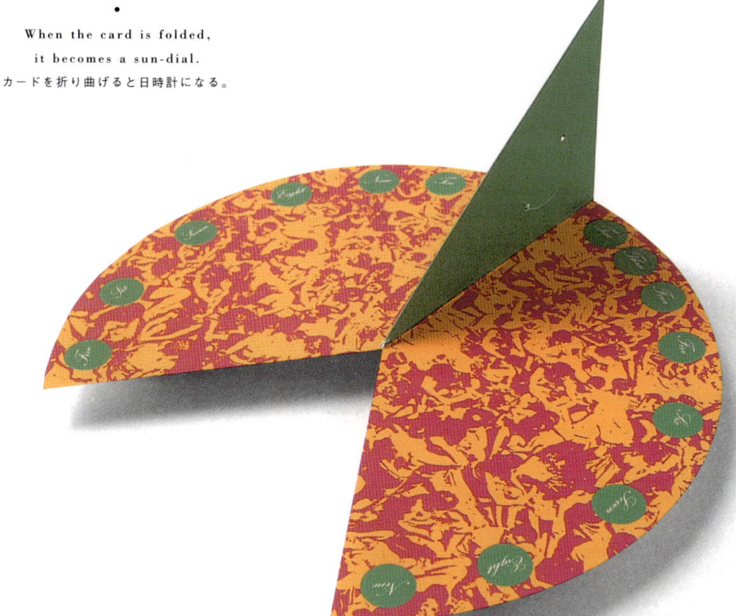

▼

Christmas card

クリスマス・カード

USA 1990

CD,AD,D,I:Ramina Y Khachi

DF:Ramina Yadgar Khachi Design

CL:Focal Point

TC:Communications Service

通信

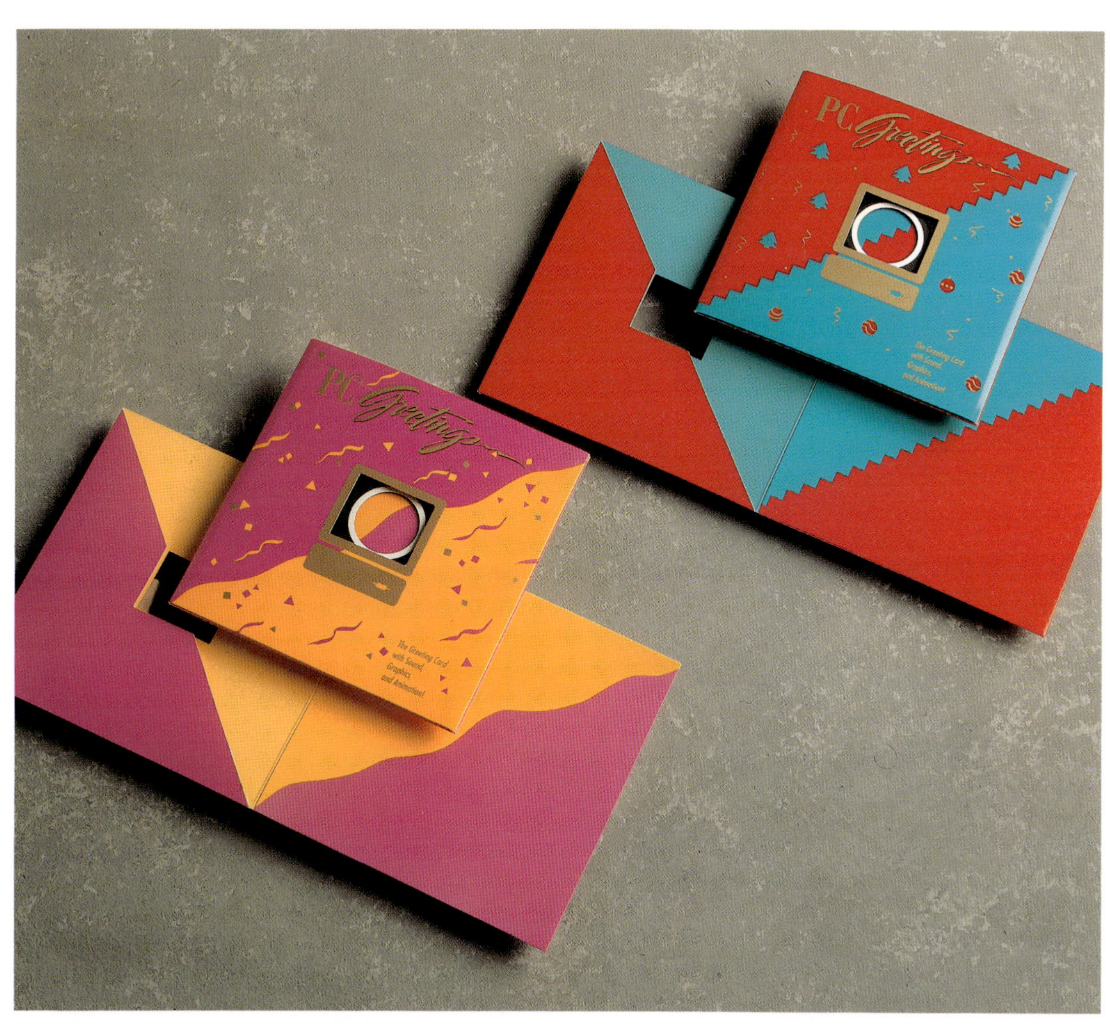

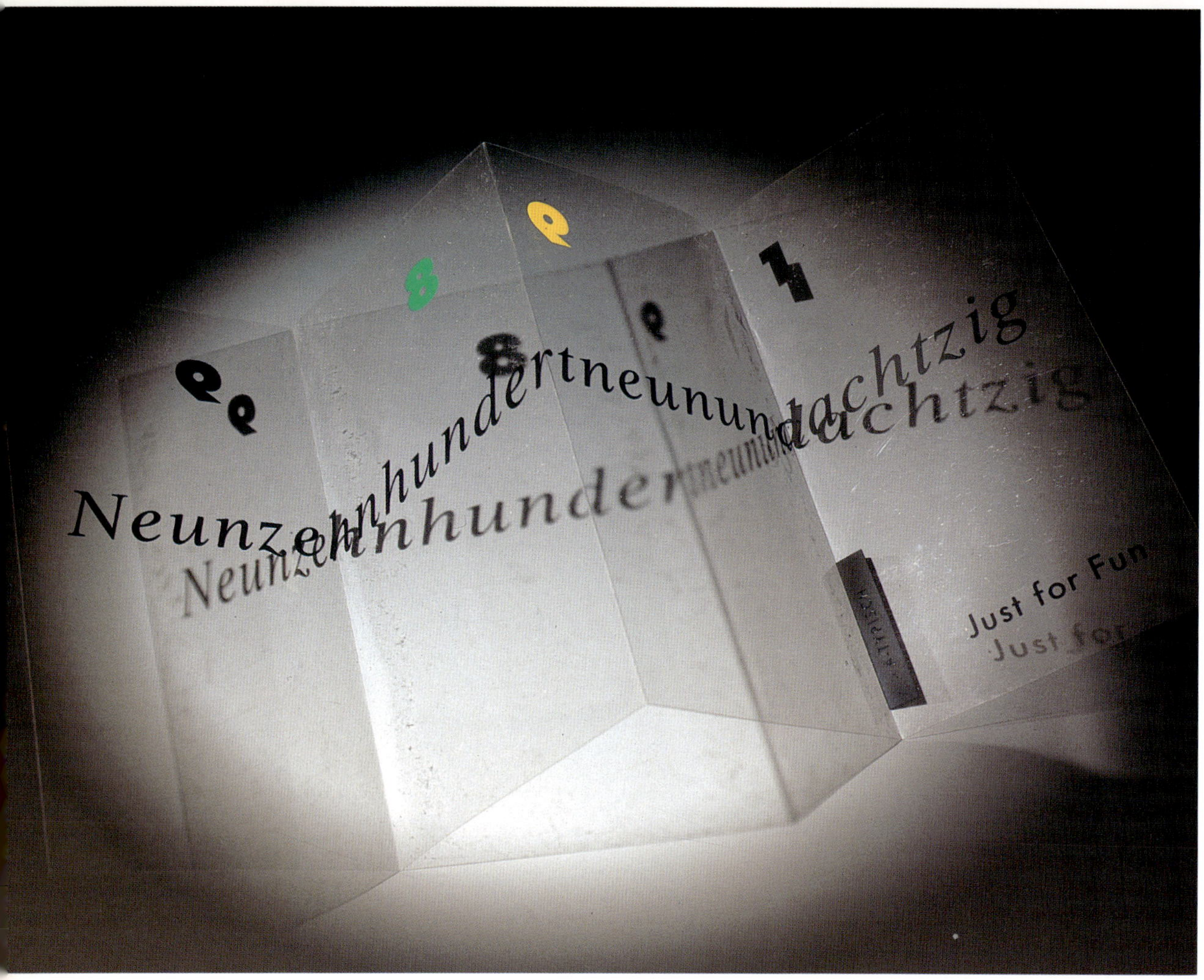

New year's card
ニューイヤーズ・カード
AUSTRIA 1988
AD,D:Kurt Dornig
CW:Hermann Brändle
DF:Dornig Grafik Design
CL:A-Typisch Projektmanagement
TC:Advertising Agency
広告

Christmas card
クリスマス・カード
AUSTRALIA 1989
AD,D,I,CW:Annette Harcus
DF:Annette Harcus Design
CL:ICM Australia
TC:Agriculture
農業

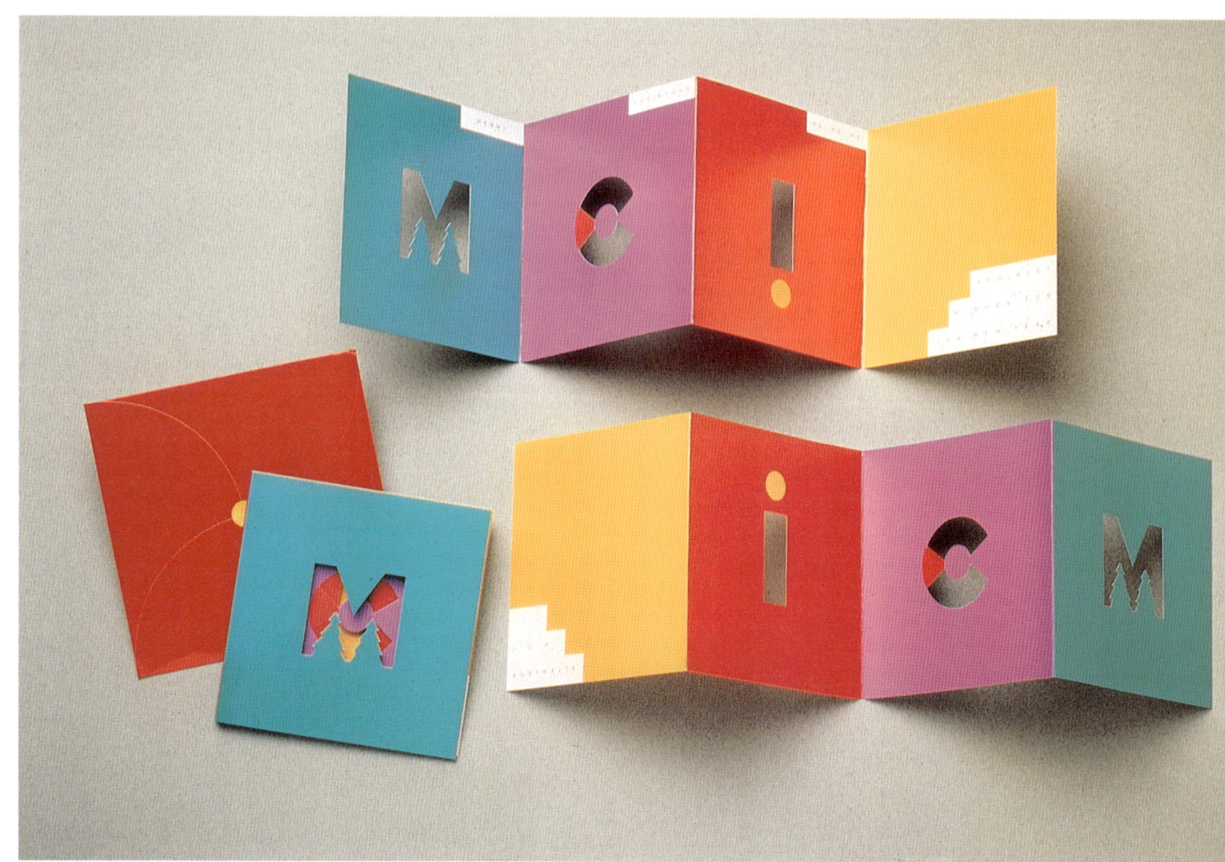

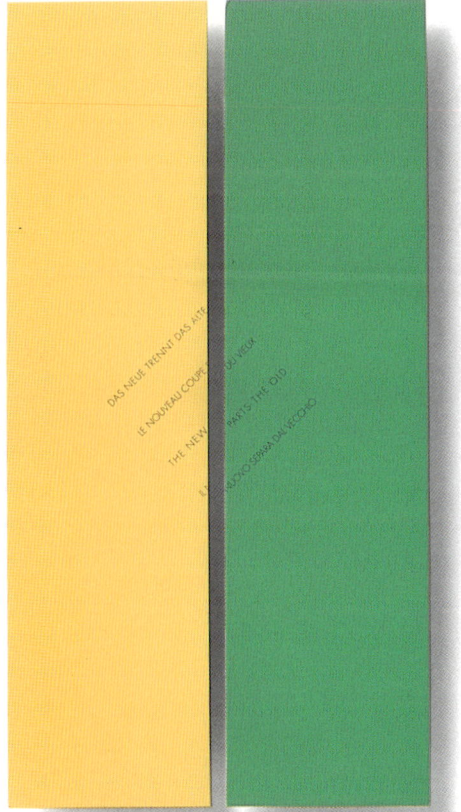

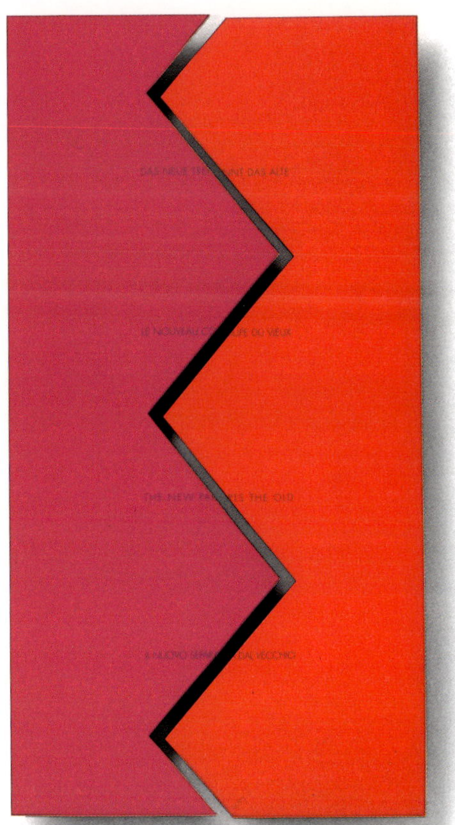

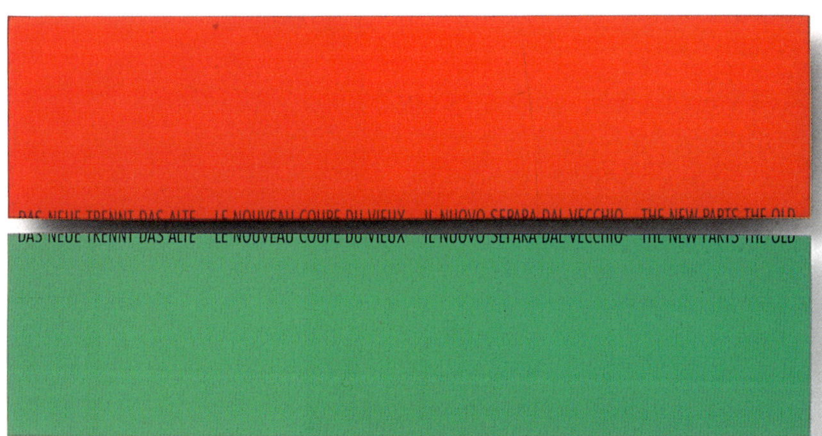

New year's card
ニューイヤーズ・カード
SWITZERLAND 1991
CD,AD,D,I,CW:Michael Baviera
DF:BBV Michael Baviera
CL:BBV
TC:Graphic Design Studio
グラフィック・デザイン

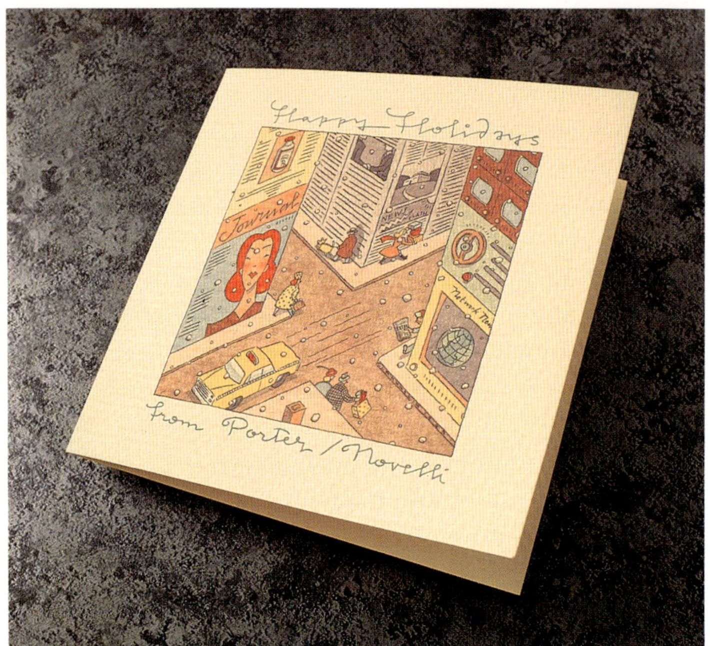

◀
Christmas card
クリスマス・カード
USA 1989
AD:Donald Burg
D,I:Steven Guarnaccia
CL:Porter
Novelli
TC:Public Relations Service
広報

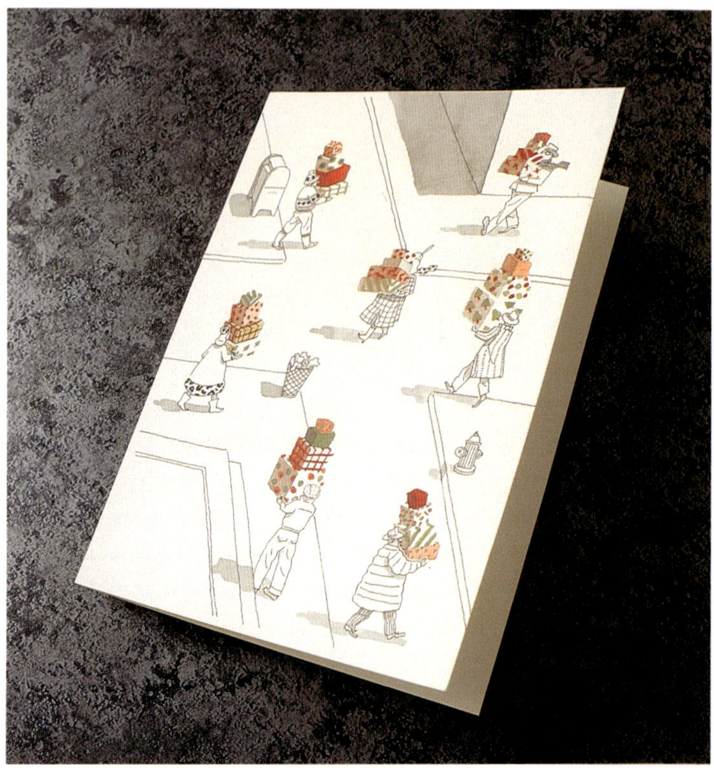

▶
Christmas card
クリスマス・カード
USA 1988
AD:The Museum of Modern Art,
New York
I:Steven Guarnaccia
CL:The Museum of Modern Art,
New York
TC:Museum of Art
美術館

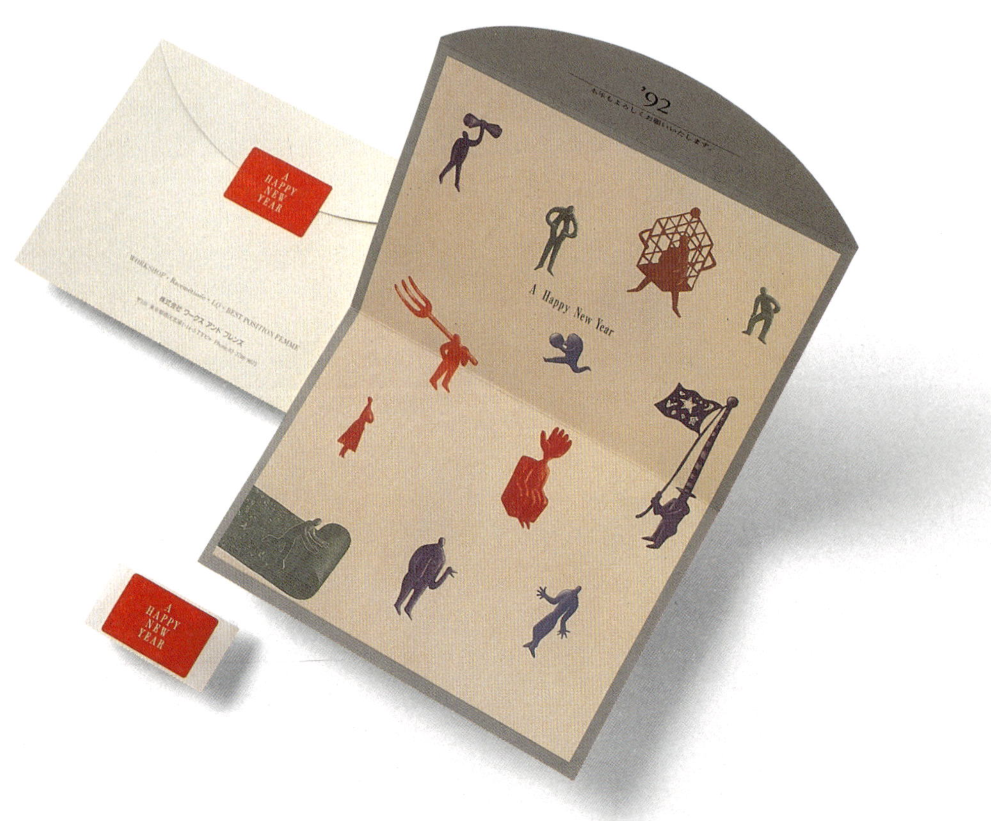

◀
New year's card
ニューイヤーズ・カード
JAPAN 1992
AD,D:Koichi Kurenuma
I:Akihiro Watabiki
DF:Genet Associates
CL:Work's & Friends
TC:Apparel Maker
アパレル

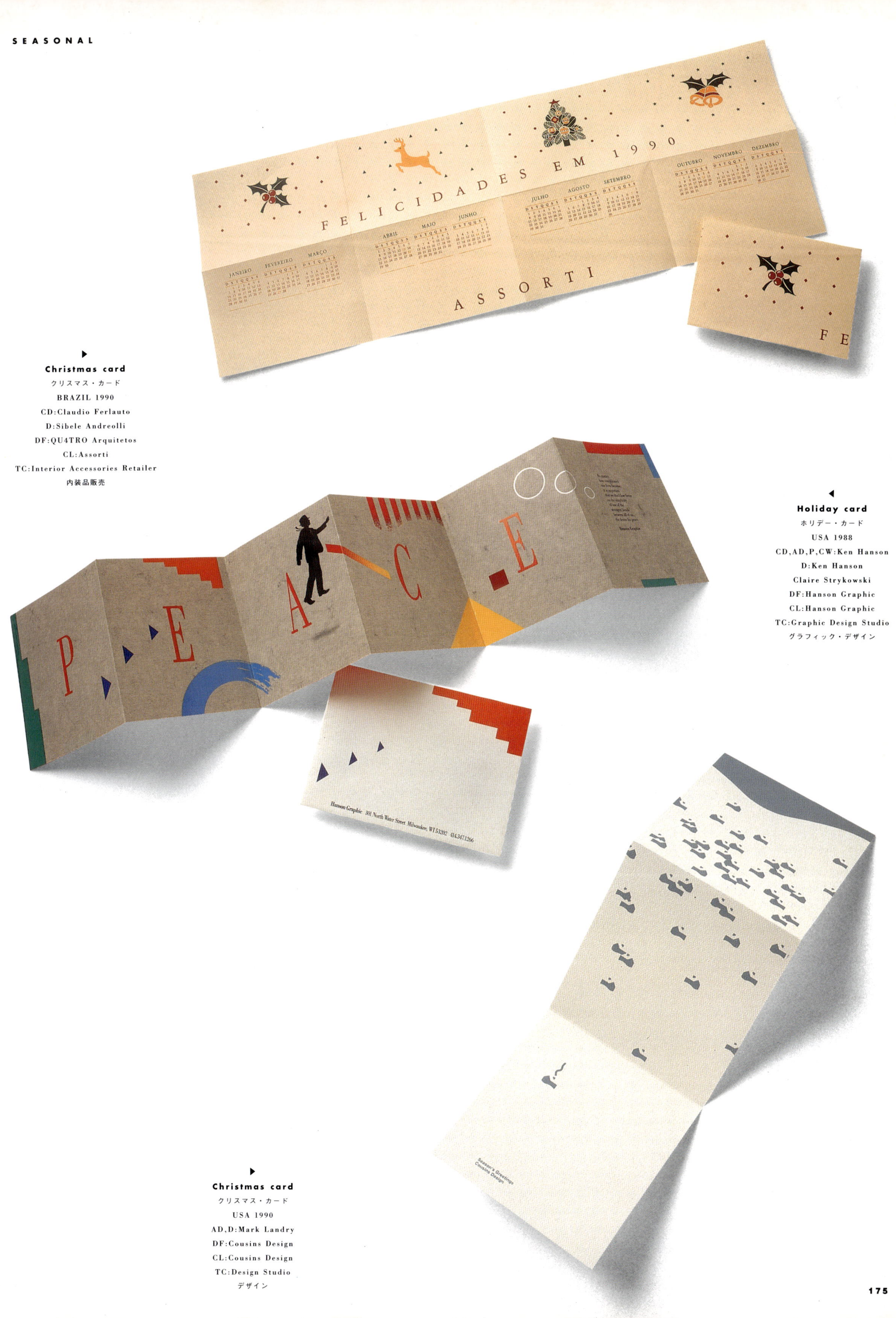

Christmas card
クリスマス・カード
BRAZIL 1990
CD:Claudio Ferlauto
D:Sibele Andreolli
DF:QU4TRO Arquitetos
CL:Assorti
TC:Interior Accessories Retailer
内装品販売

Holiday card
ホリデー・カード
USA 1988
CD,AD,P,CW:Ken Hanson
D:Ken Hanson
Claire Strykowski
DF:Hanson Graphic
CL:Hanson Graphic
TC:Graphic Design Studio
グラフィック・デザイン

Christmas card
クリスマス・カード
USA 1990
AD,D:Mark Landry
DF:Cousins Design
CL:Cousins Design
TC:Design Studio
デザイン

▲

Holiday card

ホリデー・カード

USA 1988

CD:Kris Kagelmann Holtz

AD,D:Tracy Gibbons

I:Clara Richardson

CW:Sandy Siegrist

DF:Janis Boehm Design

CL:Manpower

TC:Personnel Agency

人材派遣

•

When taken out of the envelope, the contents spring into a box shape.

封筒から出すとゴムの力で箱型になる。

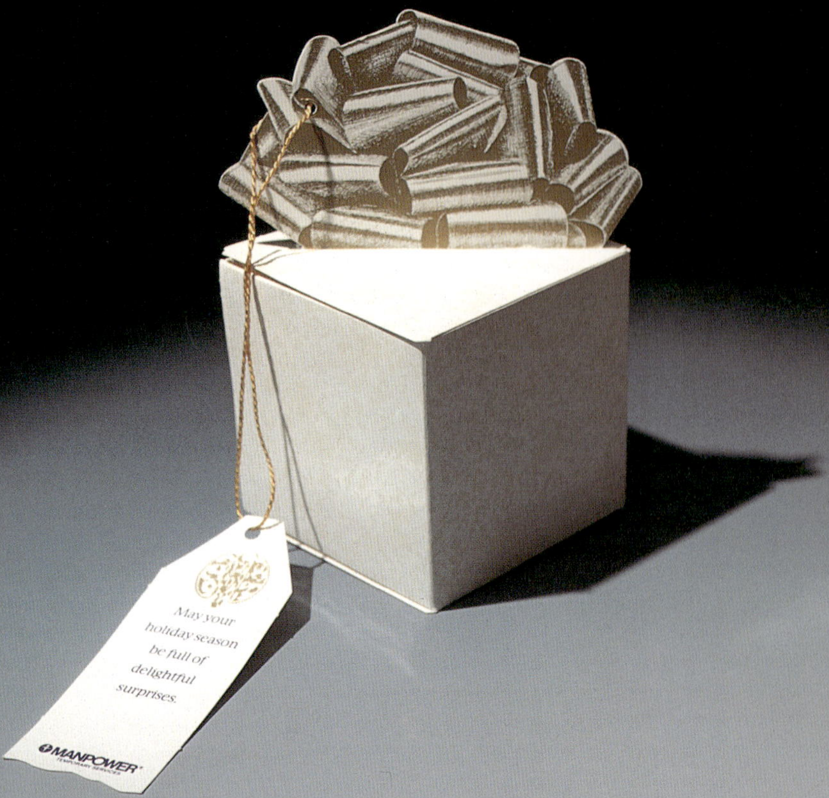

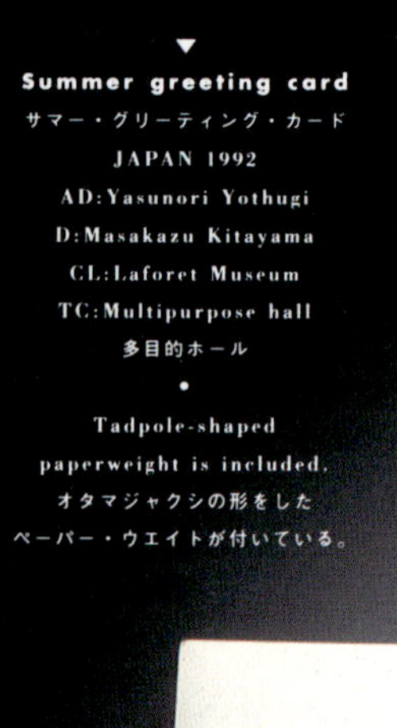

▼

Summer greeting card

サマー・グリーティング・カード

JAPAN 1992

AD:Yasunori Yothugi

D:Masakazu Kitayama

CL:Laforet Museum

TC:Multipurpose hall

多目的ホール

•

Tadpole-shaped paperweight is included.

オタマジャクシの形をしたペーパー・ウエイトが付いている。

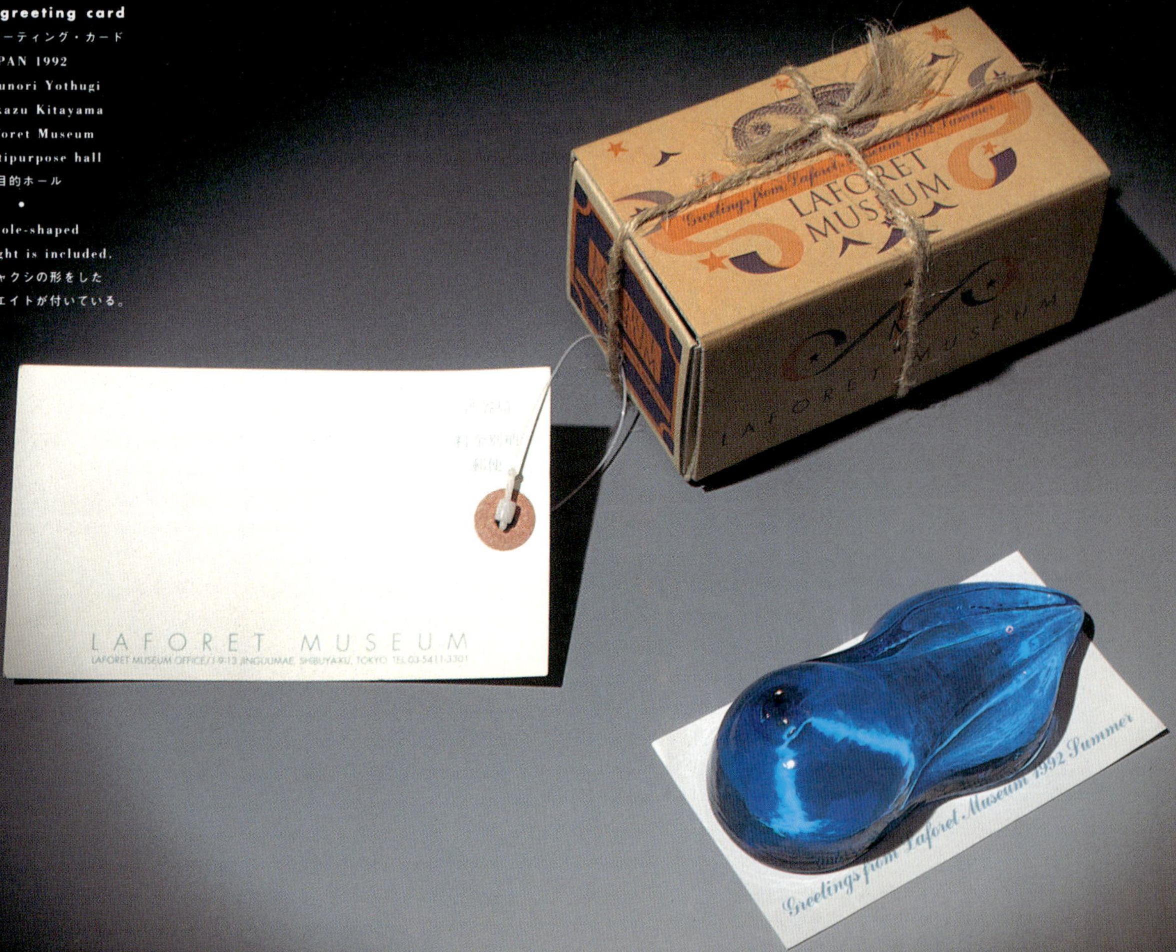

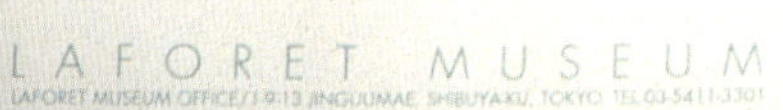

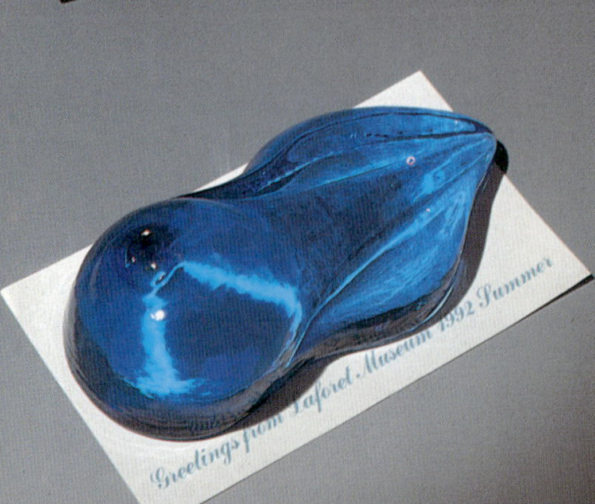

▼

New year's card
ニューイヤーズ・カード
USA 1991
AD:Michael McGinn
Takaaki Matsumoto
D:Takaaki Matsumoto
DF:M Plus M
CL:M Plus M
TC:Design Studio
デザイン

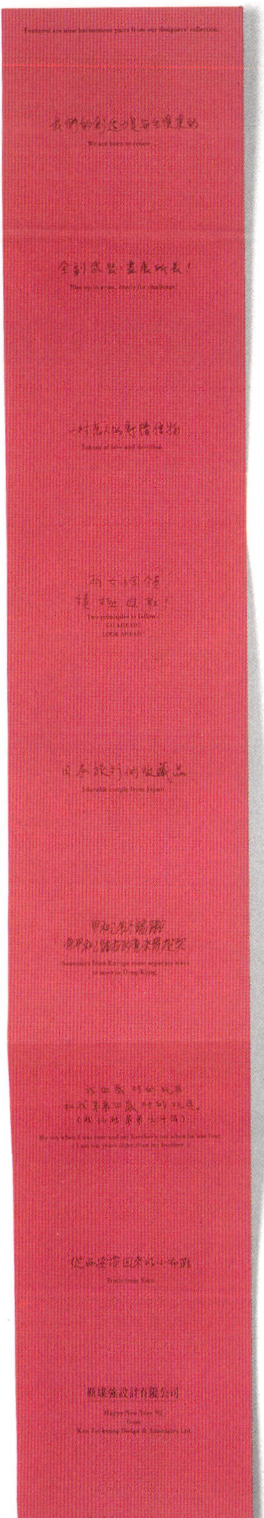

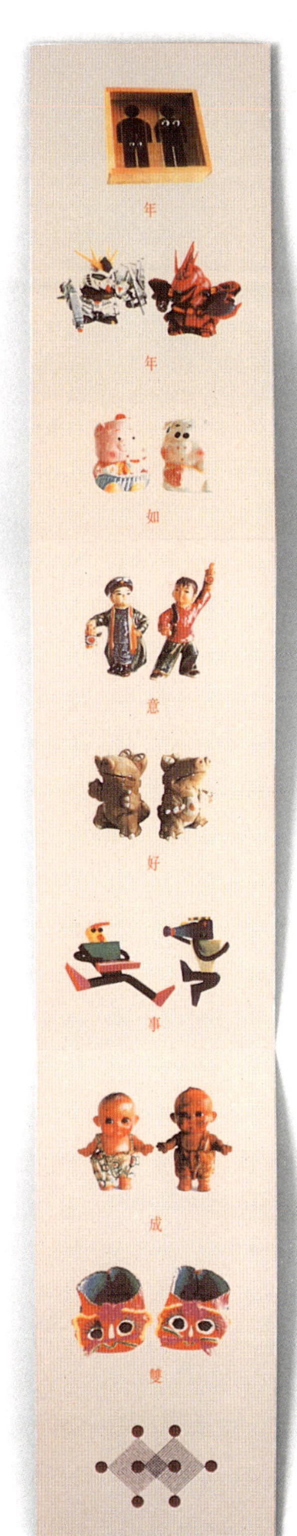

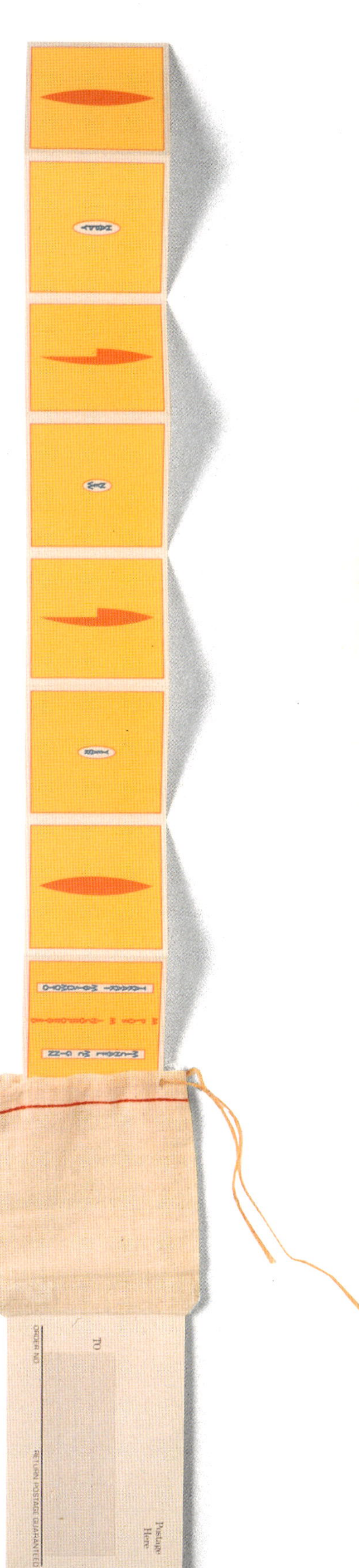

▲

New year's card
ニューイヤーズ・カード
HONG KONG 1991
CD,D:Kan Tai-keung
AD:Kan Tai-keung
Freeman Lau Siu Hong
Eddy Yu Chi Kong
DF:Kan Tai-keung
Design & Associates
CL:Kan Tai-keung
Design & Associates
TC:Graphic Design Studio
グラフィック・デザイン

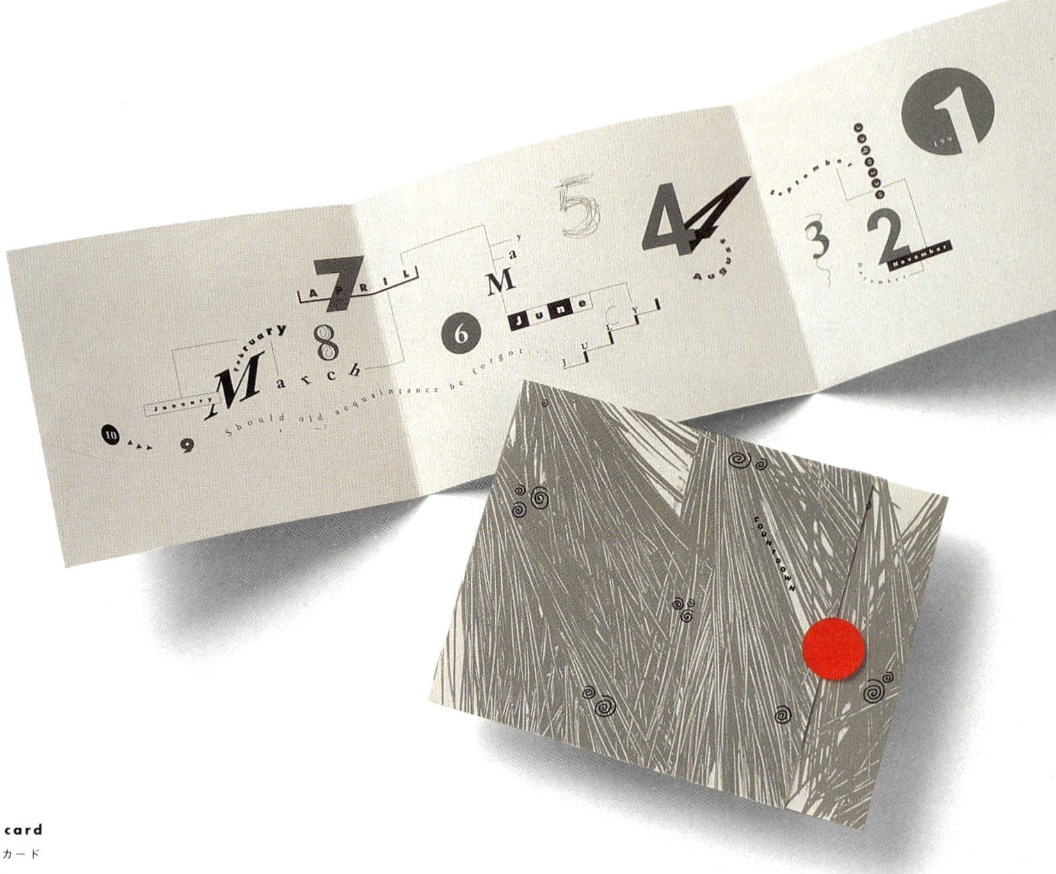

▲

New year's card

ニューイヤーズ・カード

USA 1991

CD,AD:Kathy Forsythe

D:Jane Cuthbertson

DF:Forsythe Design

CL:Forsythe Design

TC:Design Studio

デザイン

▼

Christmas card

クリスマス・カード

USA 1992

CD,AD,D,CW:Carlos Segura

DF:Segura

CL:Mrsa Architects

TC:Architects

建築

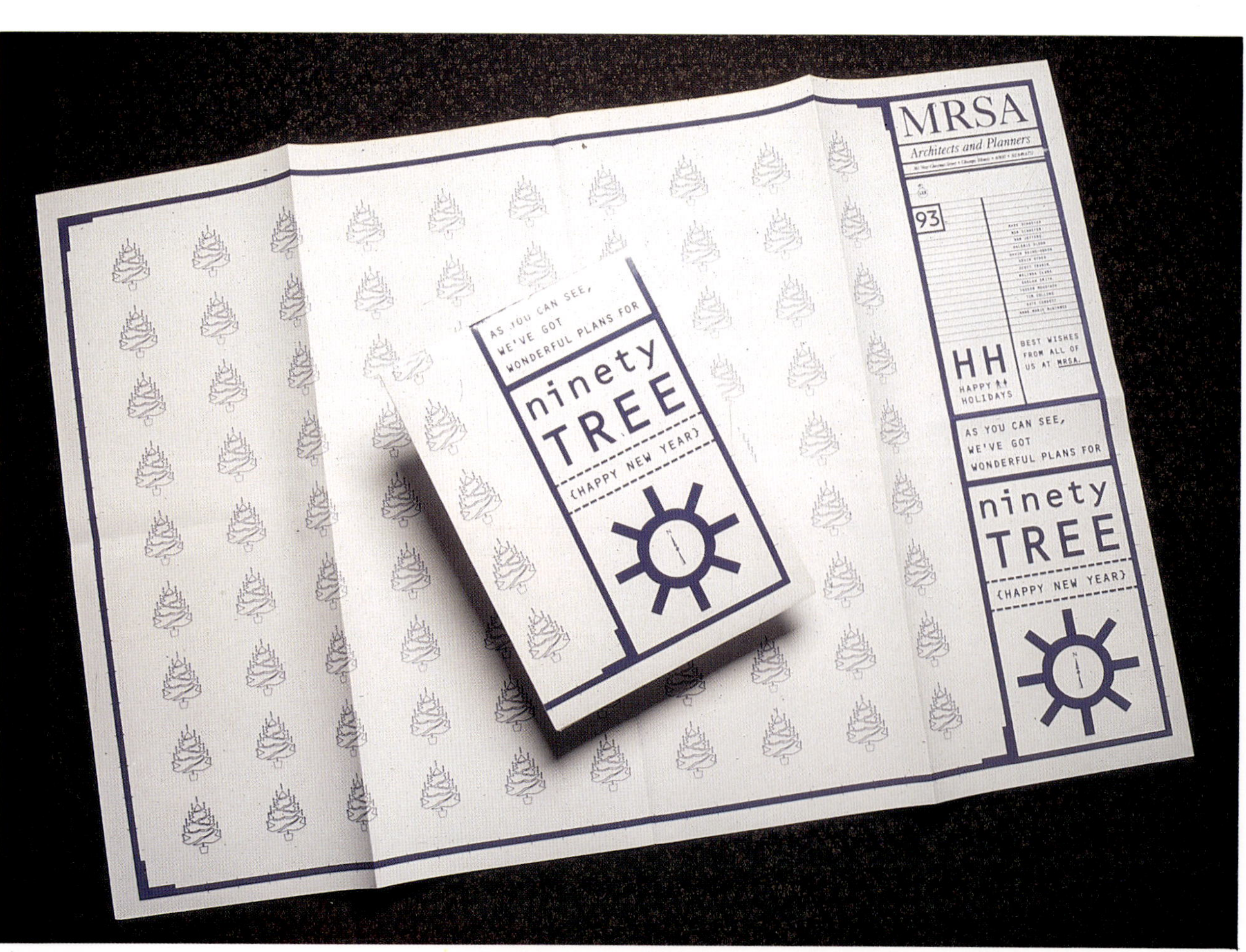

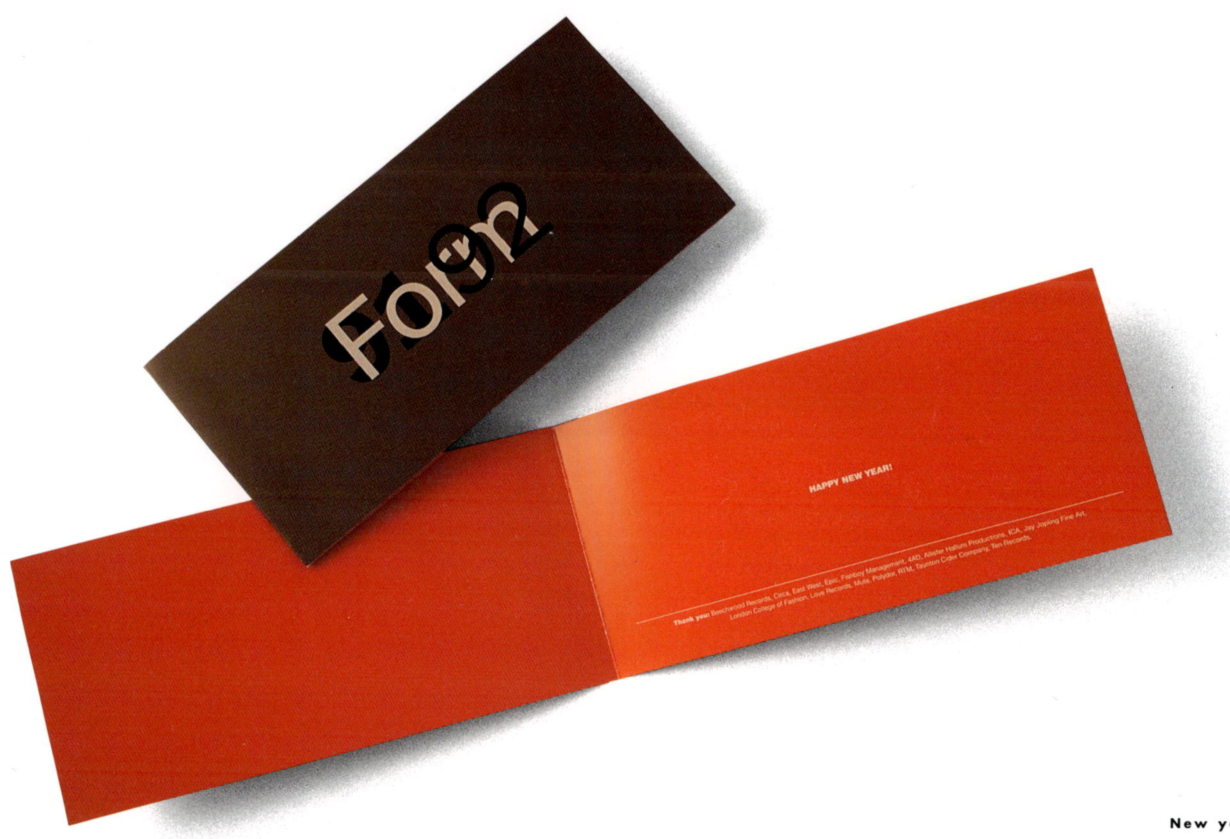

▲
New year's card
ニューイヤーズ・カード
ENGLAND 1991
D,CW:Paul West
Paula Benson
DF:Form
CL:Form
TC:Graphic Design Studio
グラフィック・デザイン

▼
New year's card
ニューイヤーズ・カード
USA 1990
CD,AD,P:Patricia McShane
D:Patricia McShane
Erik Adigard
I:Erik Adigard
DF:M.A.D.
CL:M.A.D.
TC:Graphic Design Studio
グラフィック・デザイン

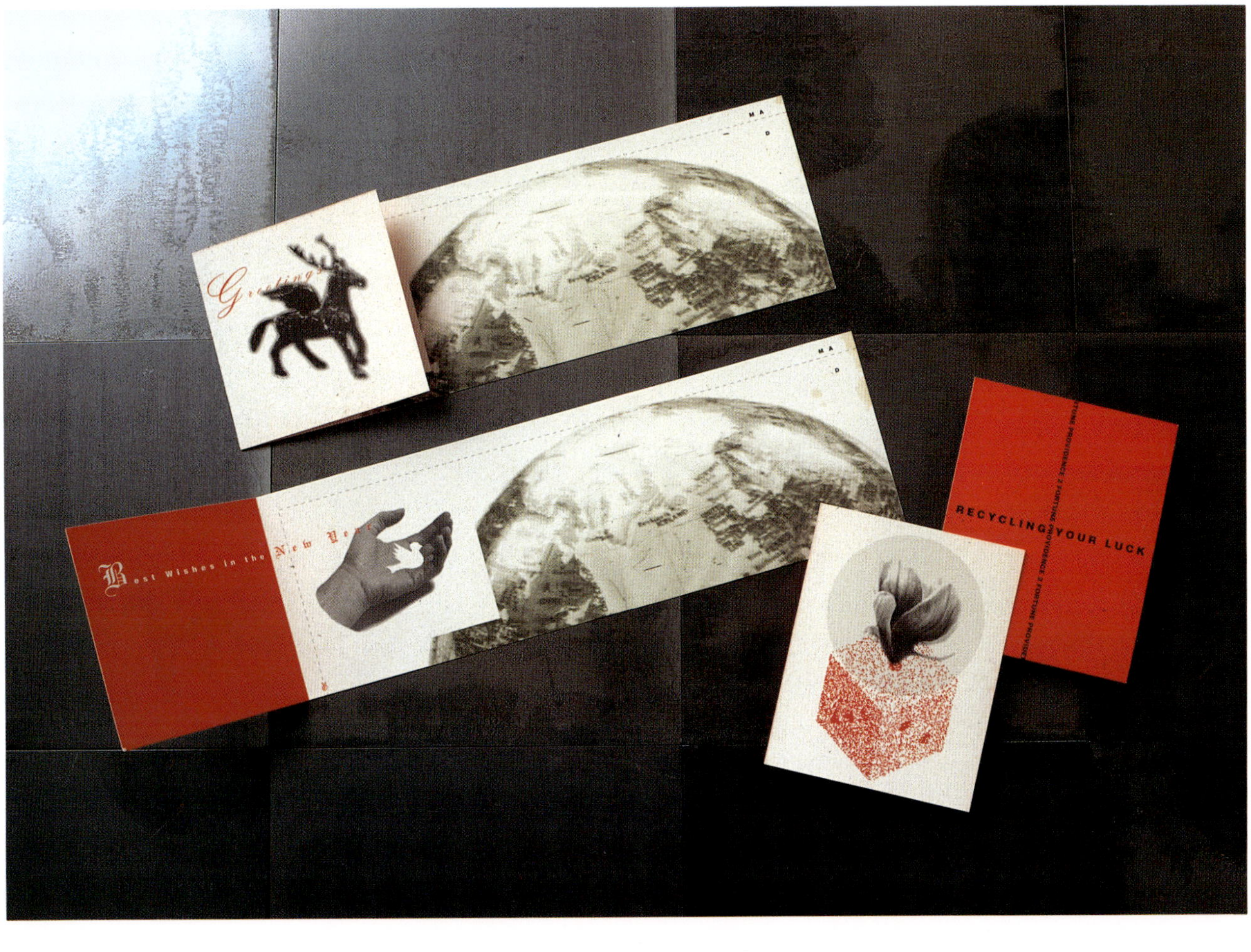

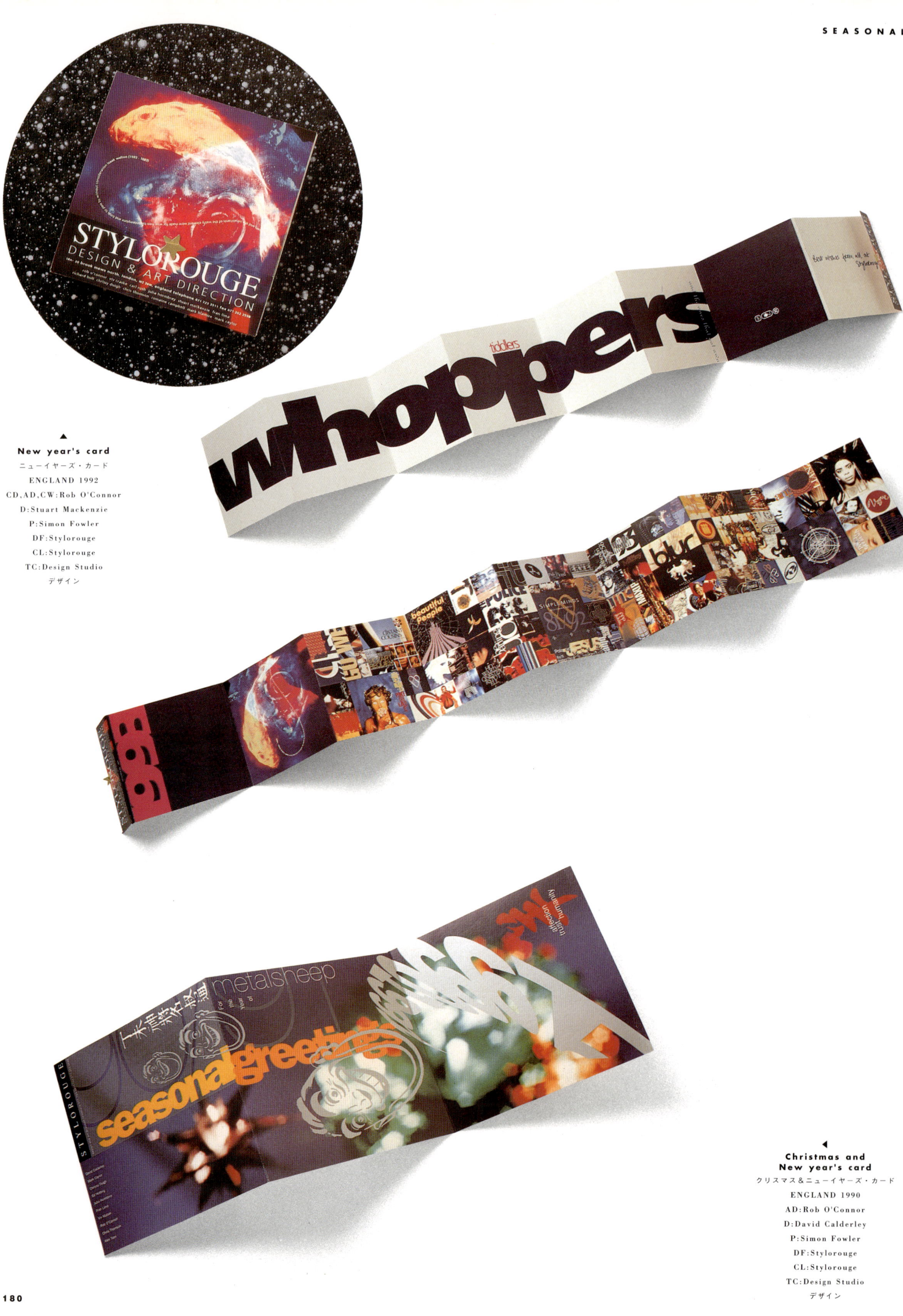

▲
New year's card
ニューイヤーズ・カード
ENGLAND 1992
CD,AD,CW:Rob O'Connor
D:Stuart Mackenzie
P:Simon Fowler
DF:Stylorouge
CL:Stylorouge
TC:Design Studio
デザイン

◀
Christmas and New year's card
クリスマス＆ニューイヤーズ・カード
ENGLAND 1990
AD:Rob O'Connor
D:David Calderley
P:Simon Fowler
DF:Stylorouge
CL:Stylorouge
TC:Design Studio
デザイン

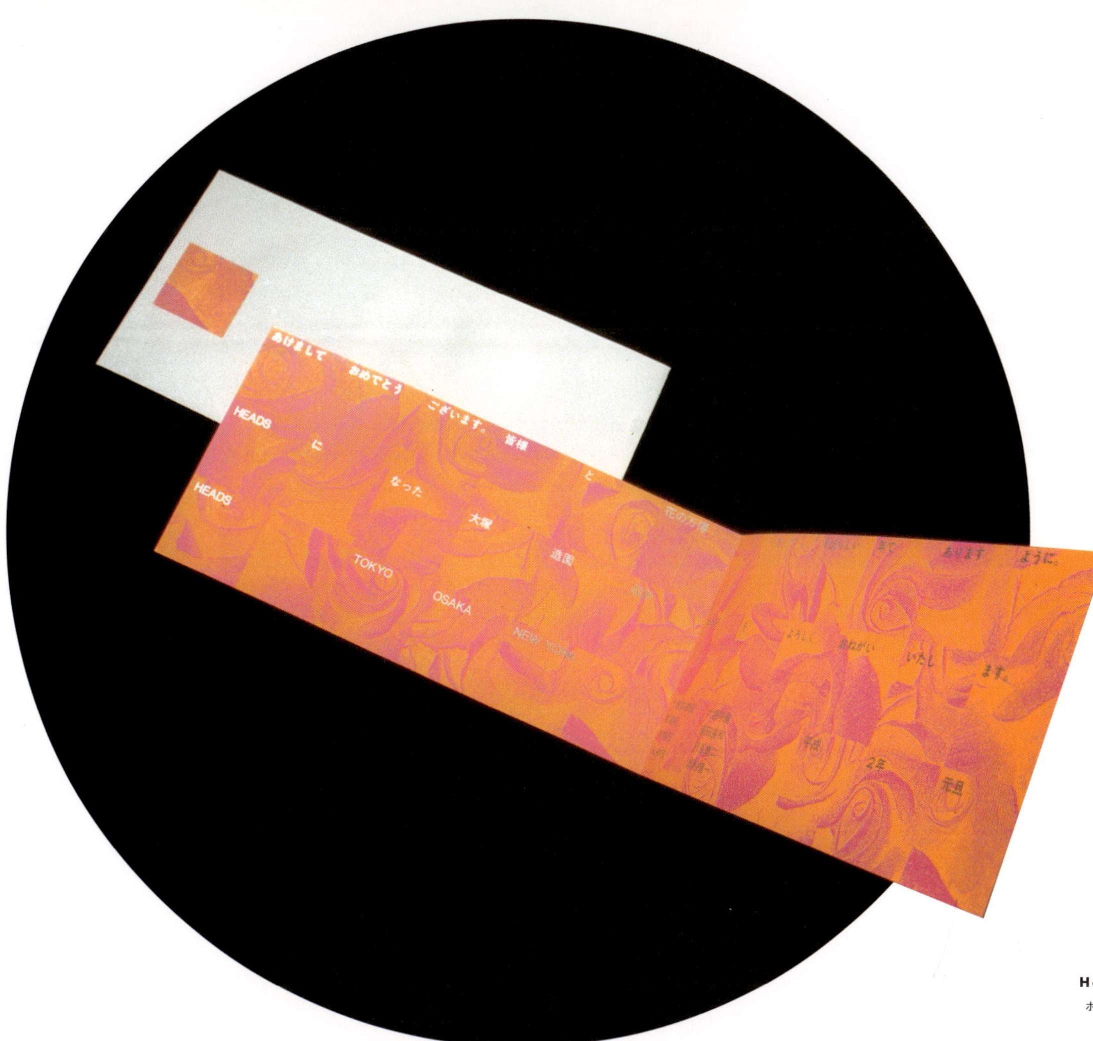

▲
New year's card
ニューイヤーズ・カード
USA 1989
CD,AD,D:Mikio Sakai
CW:Moriyasu Ohtsuka
CL:Heads
TC:Landscaping Service
造園

▼
Holiday card
ホリデー・カード
USA 1990
CD,AD:Richard Poulin
D:Rosemary Simpkins
CW:Richard Poulin
Rosemary Simpkins
DF:Richard Poulin Design Group
CL:United Nations Plaza Hotel
TC:Hotel
ホテル

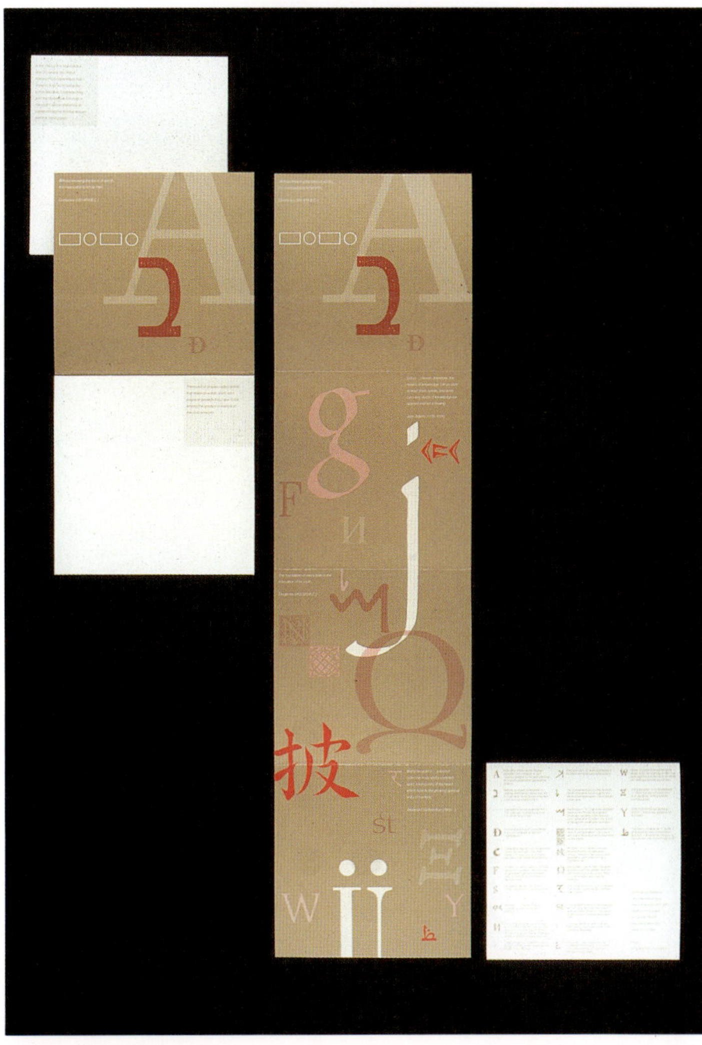

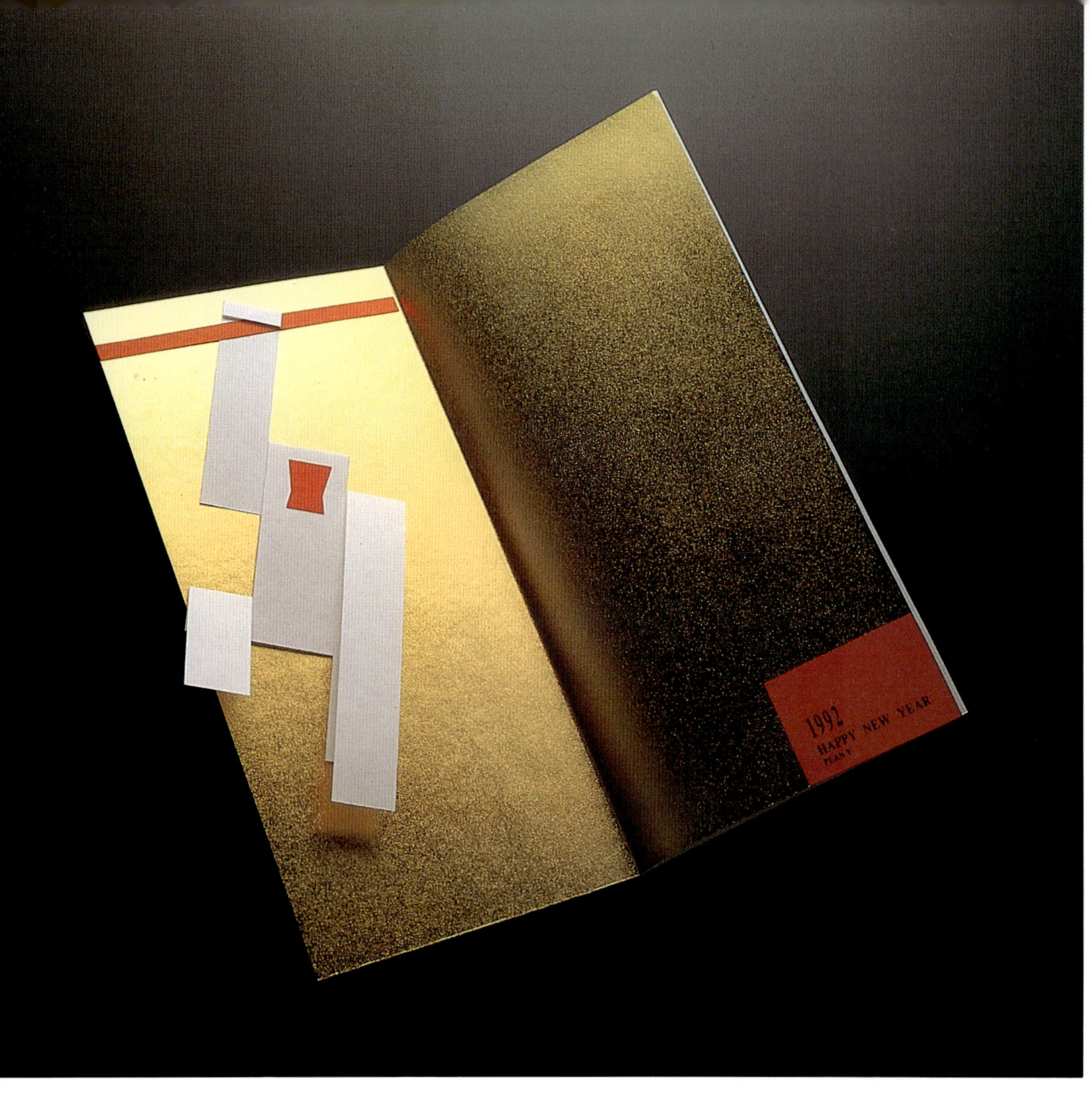

◀
New year's card
ニューイヤーズ・カード
JAPAN 1992
CD,AD,D:Miyuki Yoshida
CL:Plan•Y
TC:Architectural Design,
Package Design
建築設計、パッケージ・デザイン

▶
Summer greeting card
サマー・グリーティング・カード
JAPAN 1992
CD,AD,D:Miyuki Yoshida
CL:Plan•Y
TC:Architectural Design,
Package Design
建築設計、パッケージ・デザイン

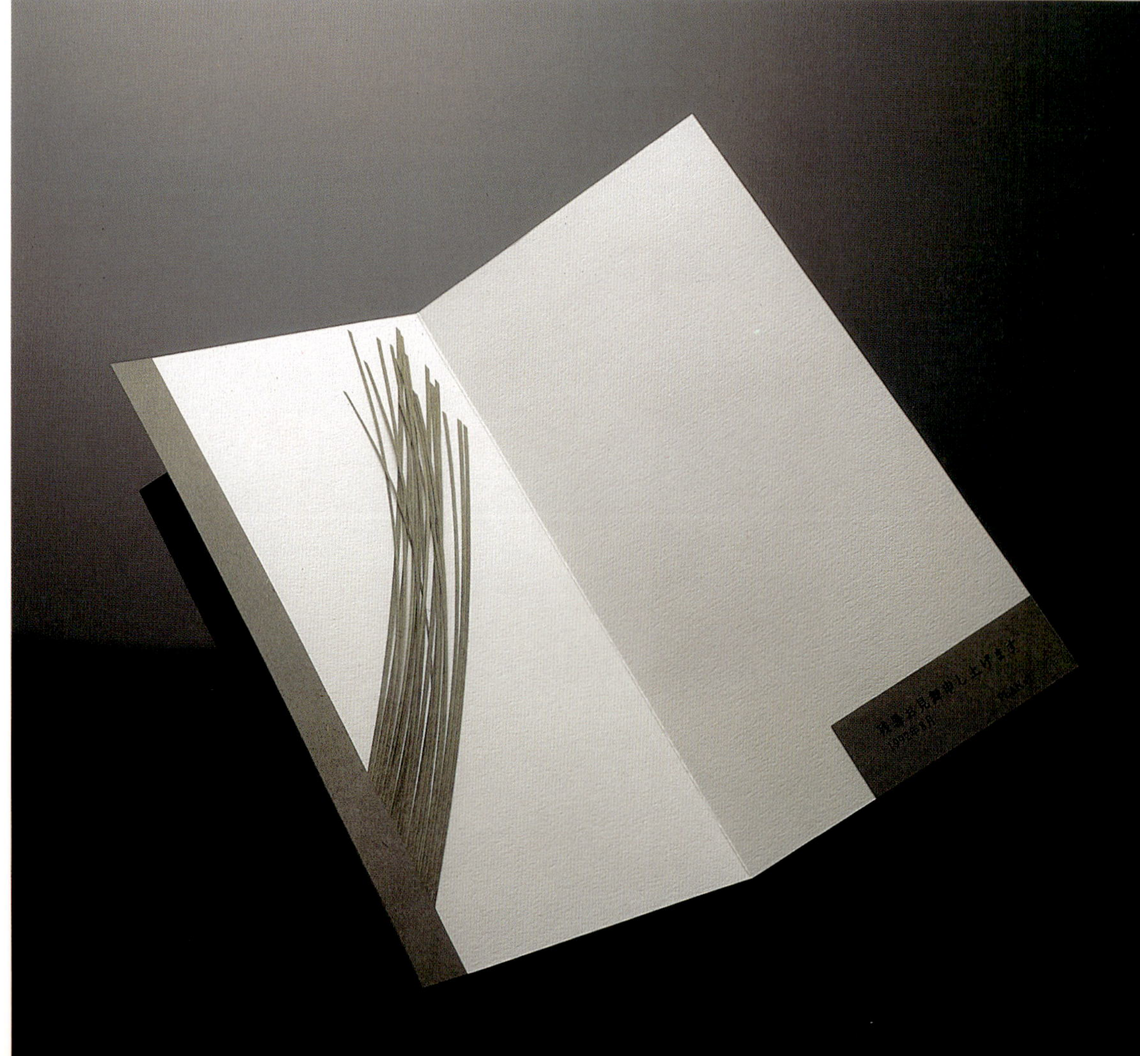

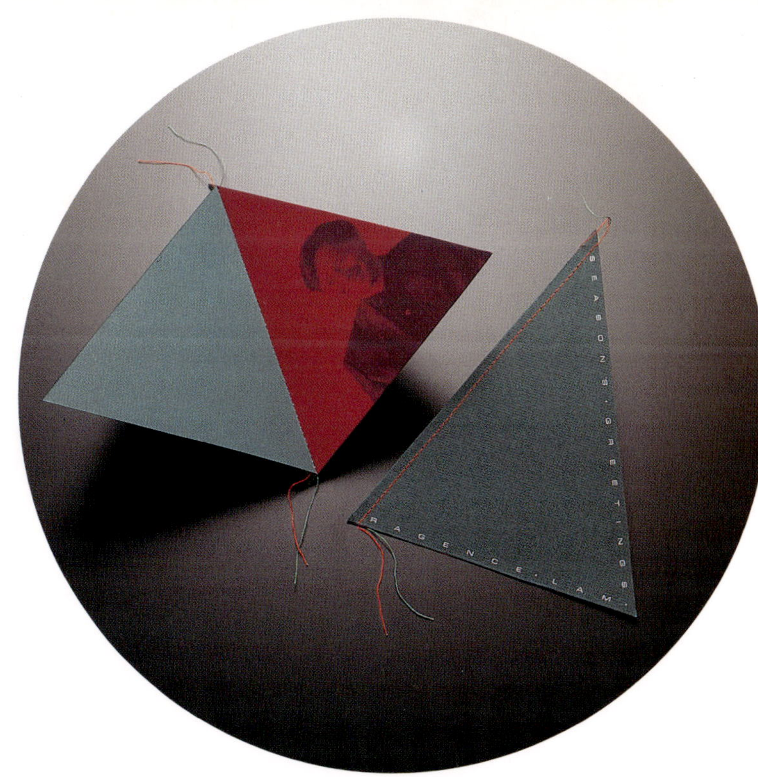

▶
Christmas card
クリスマス・カード
HONG KONG 1988
CD,AD,D:Kan Tai-keung
DF:Kan Tai-keung
Design & Associates
CL:Ragence Lam
TC:Fashion Designer
ファッション・デザイン

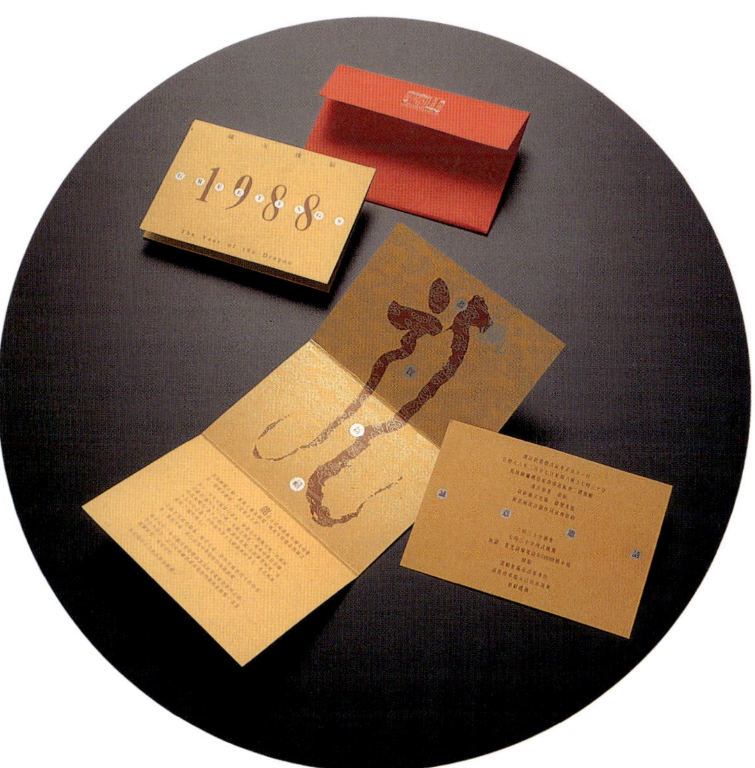

◀
New year's card
ニューイヤーズ・カード
HONG KONG 1988
CD:Kan Tai-keung
AD:Kan Tai-keung
Lau Siu-hong,Freeman
D:Lau Siu-hong,Freeman
DF:Kan Tai-keung
Design & Associates
CL:SS Design & Production
TC:Graphic Design Studio
グラフィック・デザイン

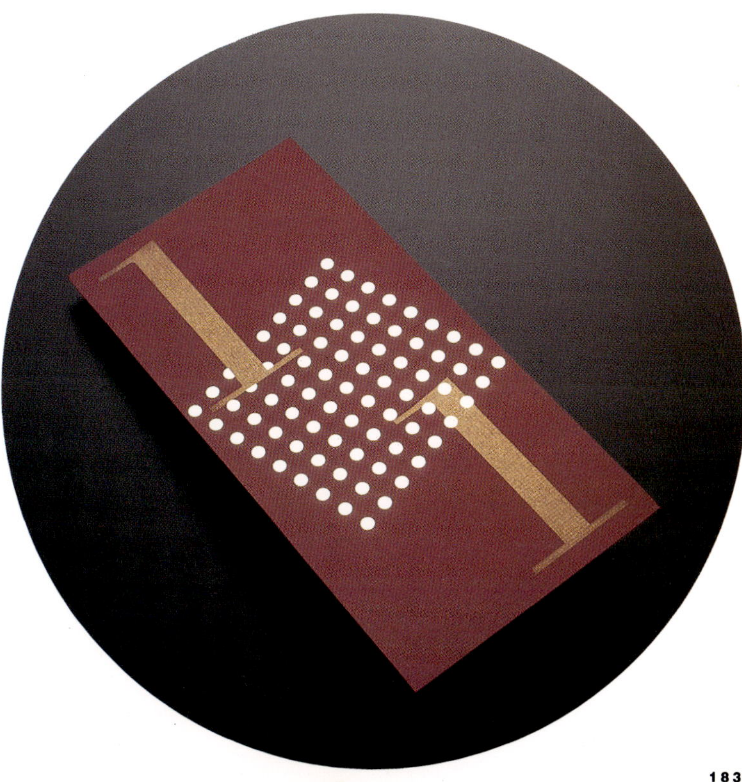

▶
New year's card
ニューイヤーズ・カード
HONG KONG 1990
CD:Kan Tai-keung
AD,D:Freeman Lau Siu Hong
DF:Kan Tai-keung
Design & Associates
CL:Kan Tai-keung
Design & Associates
TC:Graphic Design Studio
グラフィック・デザイン

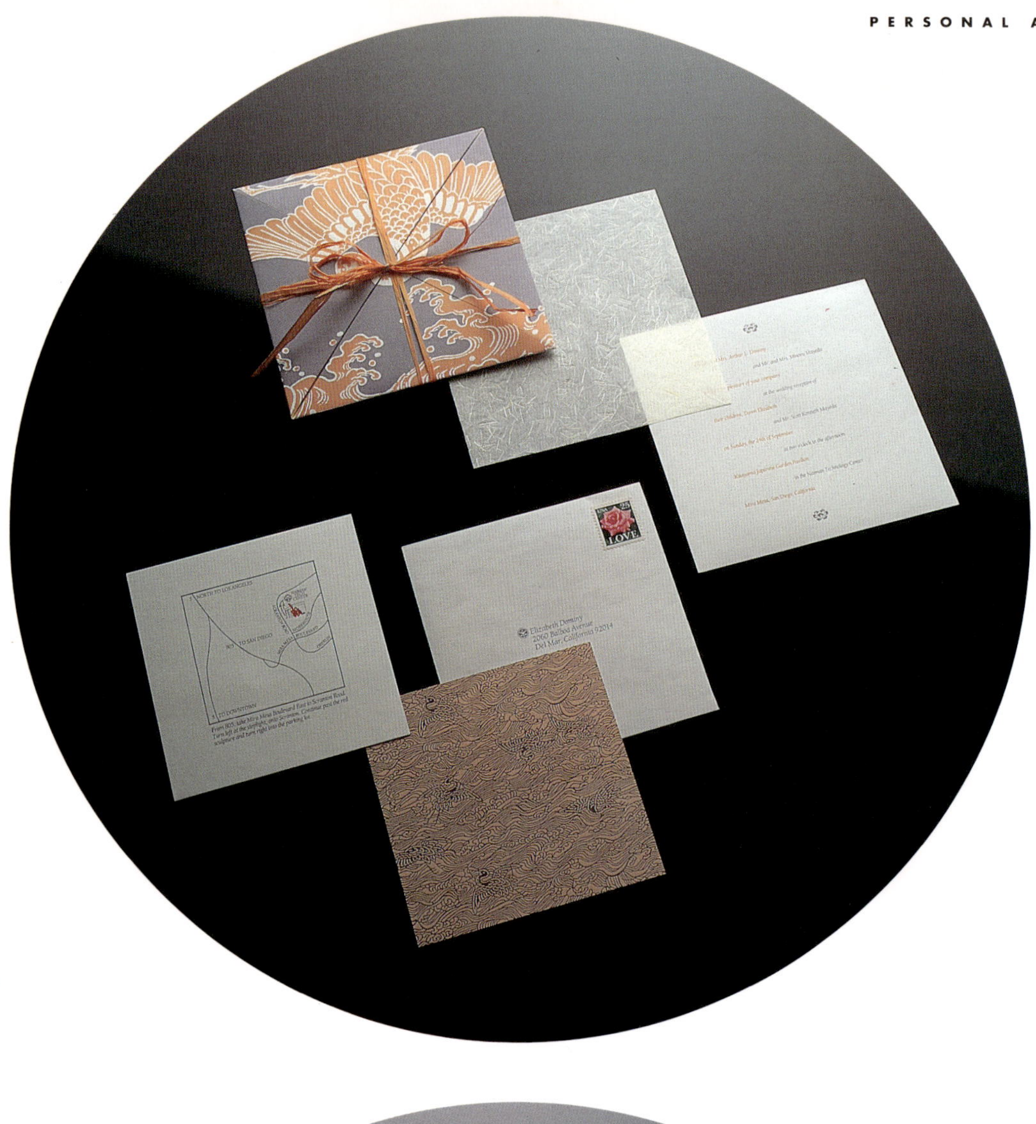

▲
Invitation to a wedding
結婚式招待状
USA 1989
AD,D:Scott Mayeda
I:Tokugawa Shogunate
CW:Dawn Dominy Mayeda
DF:Scott Mayeda, Art Direction and Design
CL:Art and Beth Dominy, Min and Sue Mayeda

▼
Invitation to a wedding
結婚式招待状
JAPAN 1992
D:Mie Takeda
CL:Mie Takeda

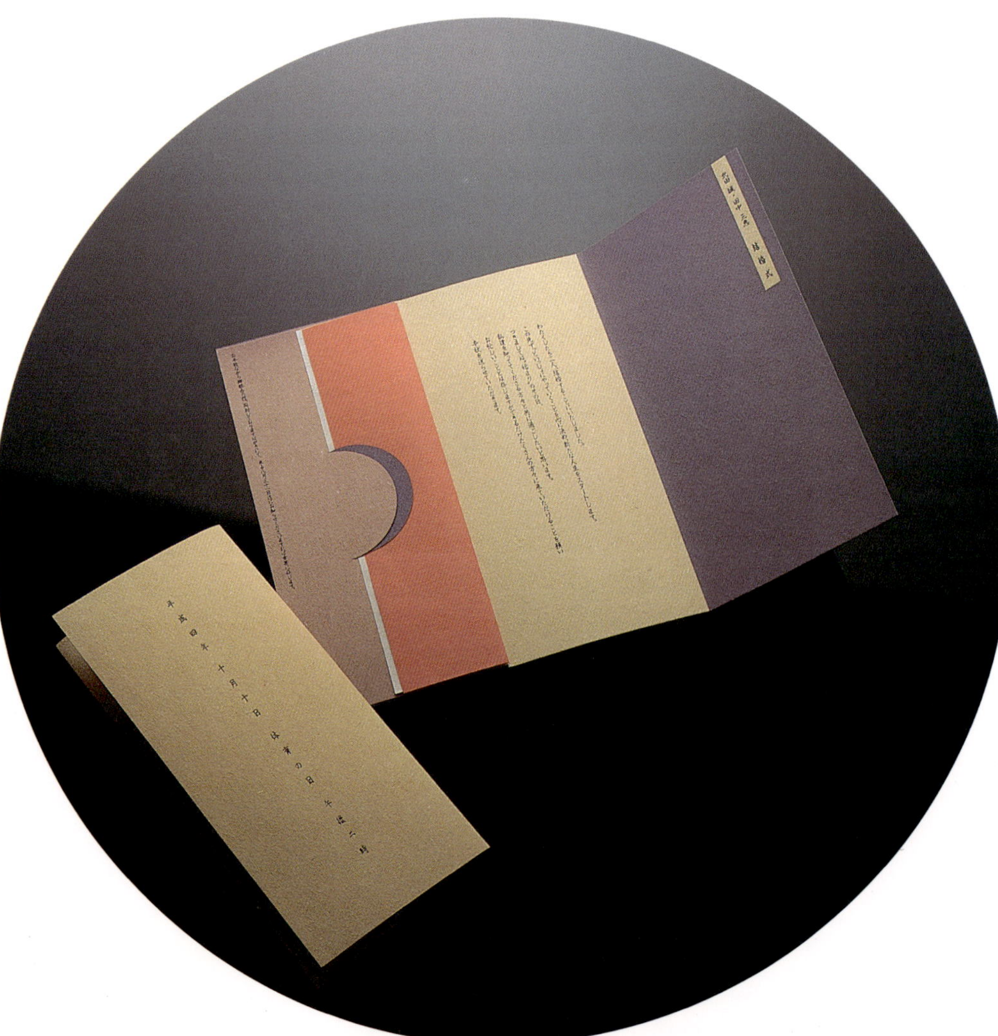

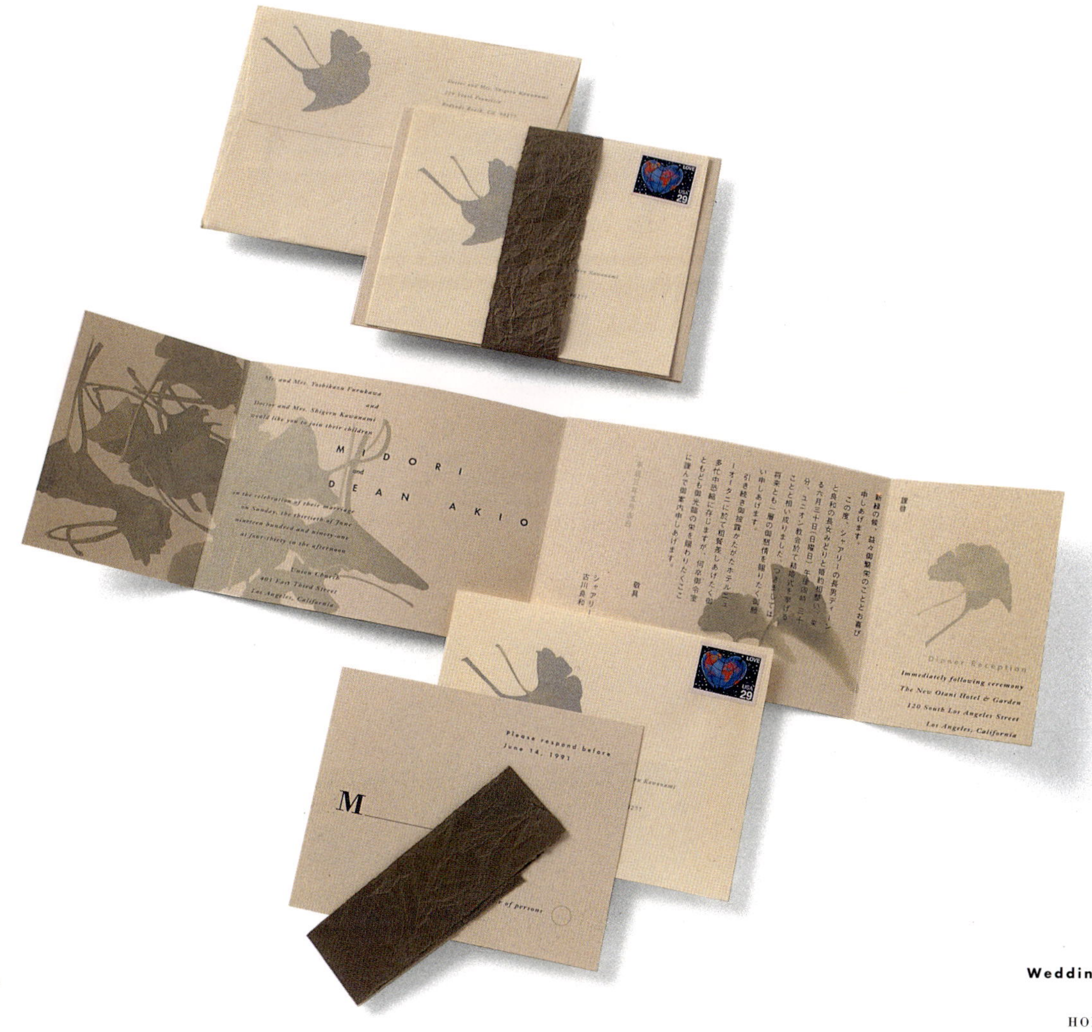

▲
Invitation to a wedding
結婚式招待状
USA 1991
AD,D,P:Craig Yamashita
DF:See Why Design
CL:Dean & Midori Yamashita

▼
Wedding announcement
結婚通知
HONG KONG 1991
CD,AD,D:Catherine Lam Siu Hung
DF:Cat Lam Design

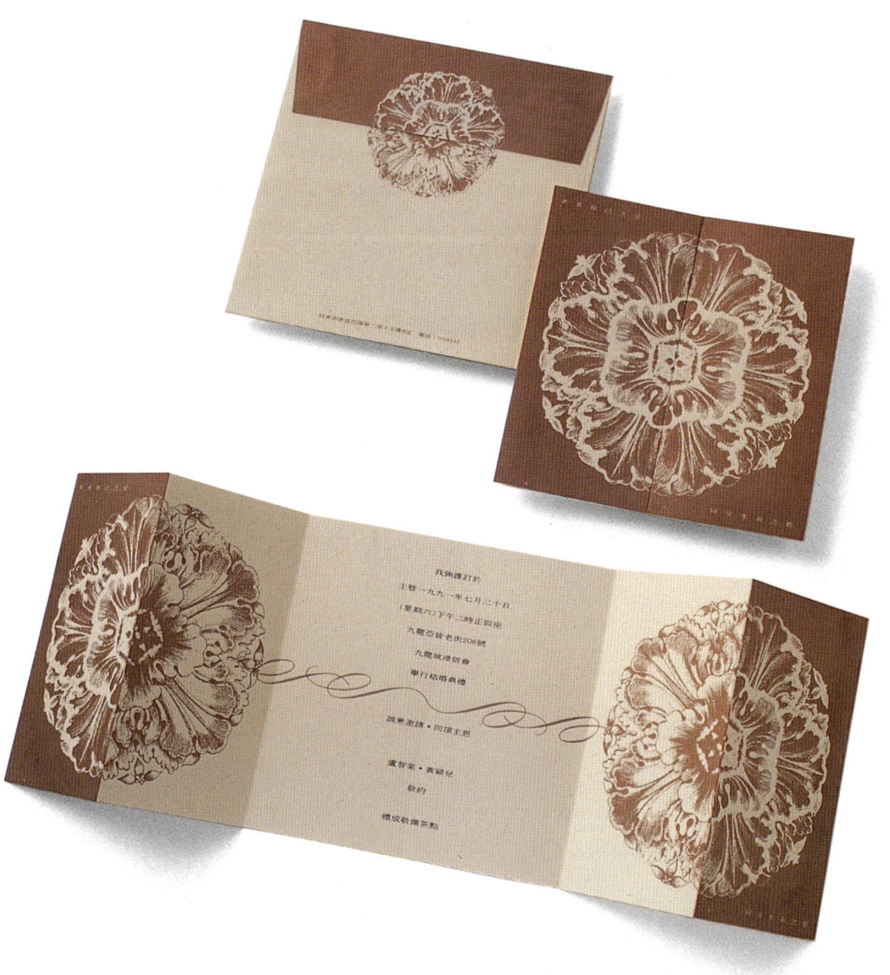

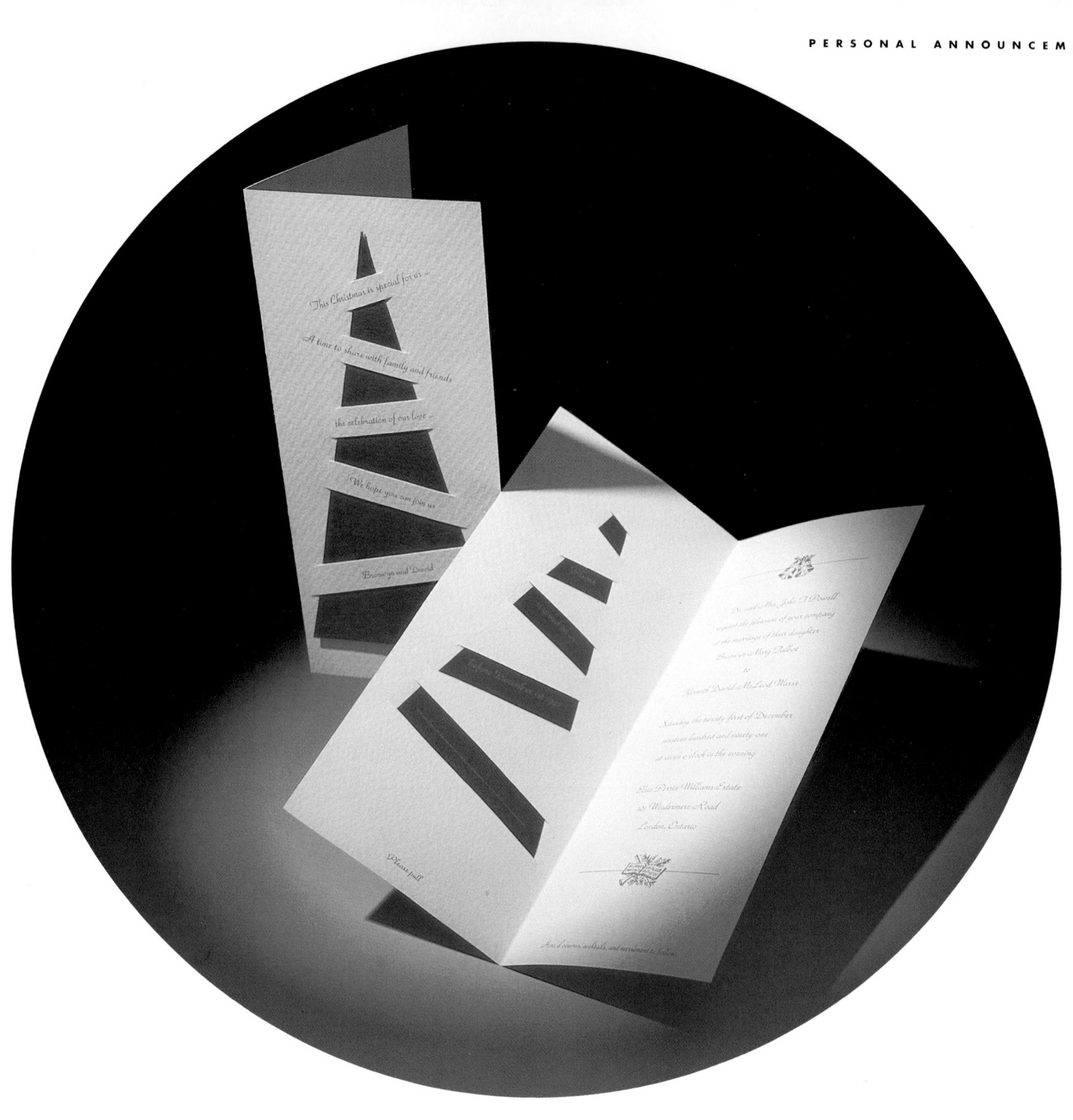

Invitation to a wedding
結婚式招待状
CANADA 1991
CD,AD,D:Andy Ip
CL:Bronwyn & David

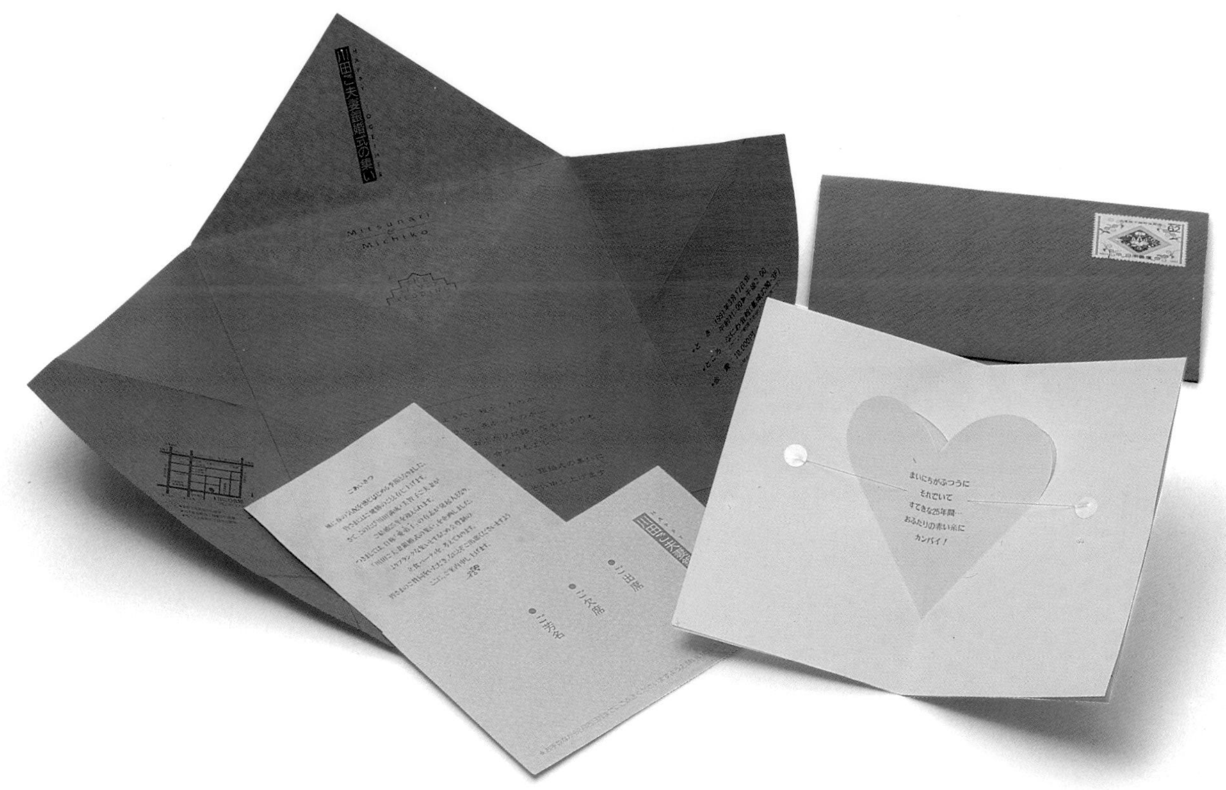

▲
Invitation to a silver wedding anniversary celebration
銀婚式招待状
JAPAN 1991
AD:Taiki Toriyama
D:Yasue Kodama
CW:Hiroco Toriyama
DF:Bird Design House
CL:The Silver Wedding Secretariat

▼
Wedding announcement
結婚通知
TAIWAN 1992
AD,D:Toto Tseng
CL:Gordon & Jessica

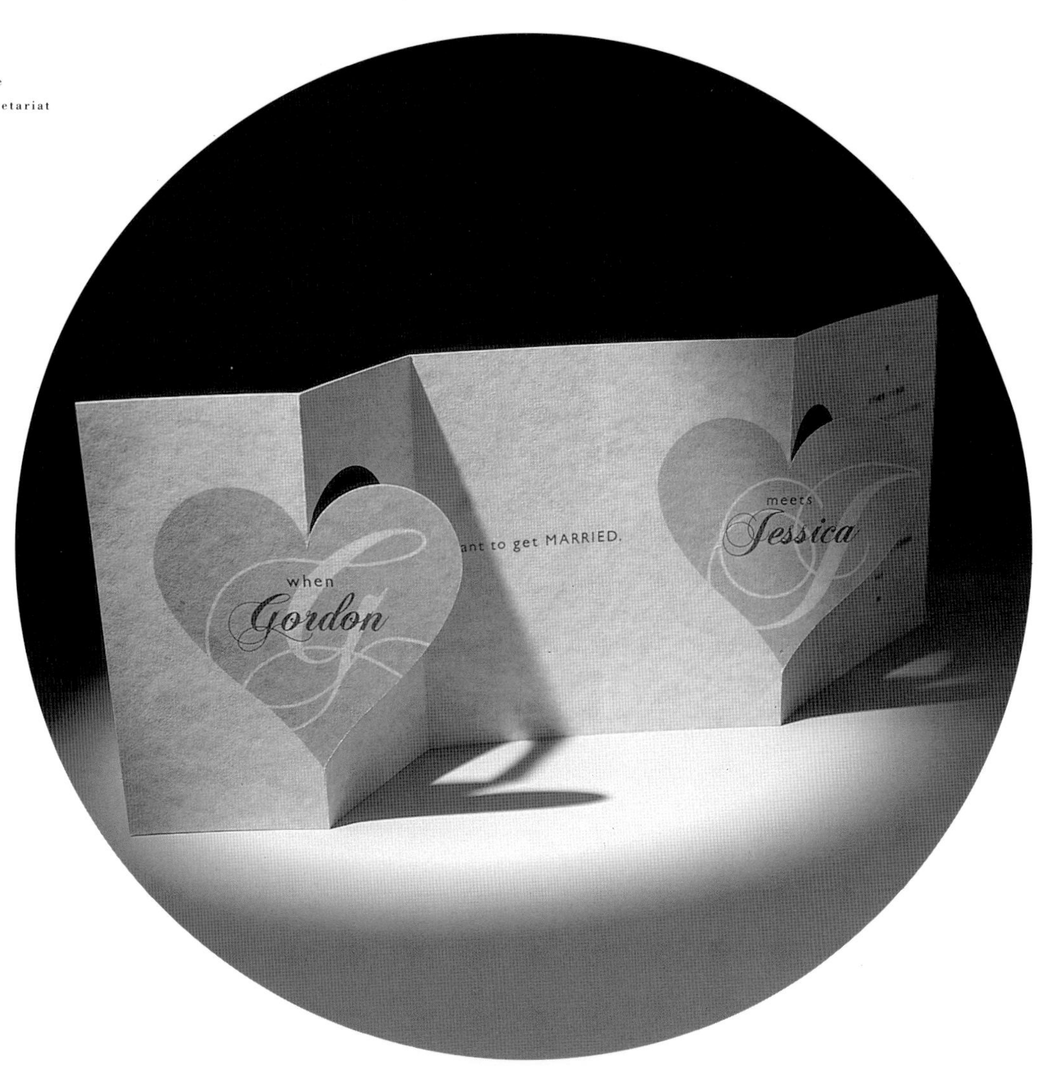

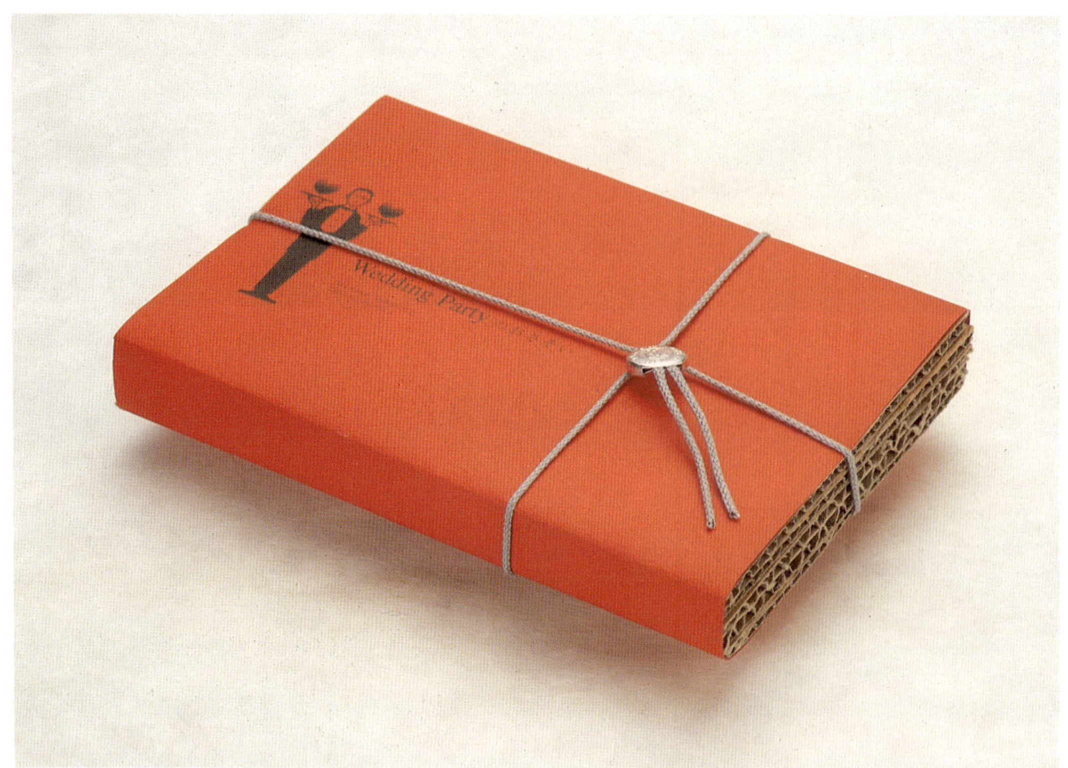

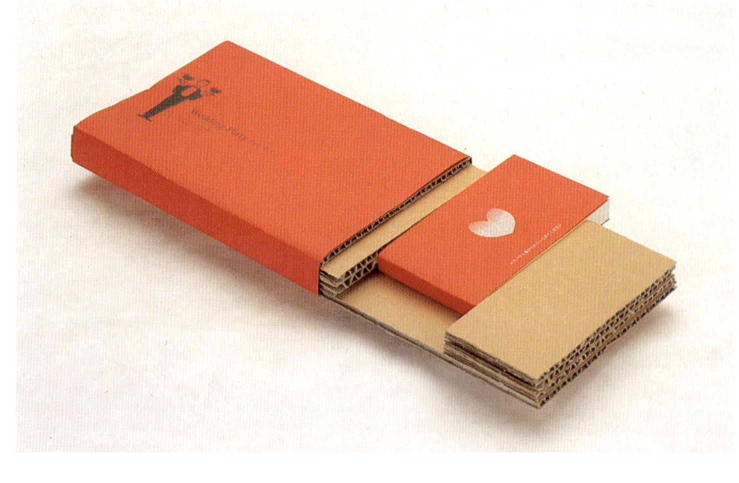

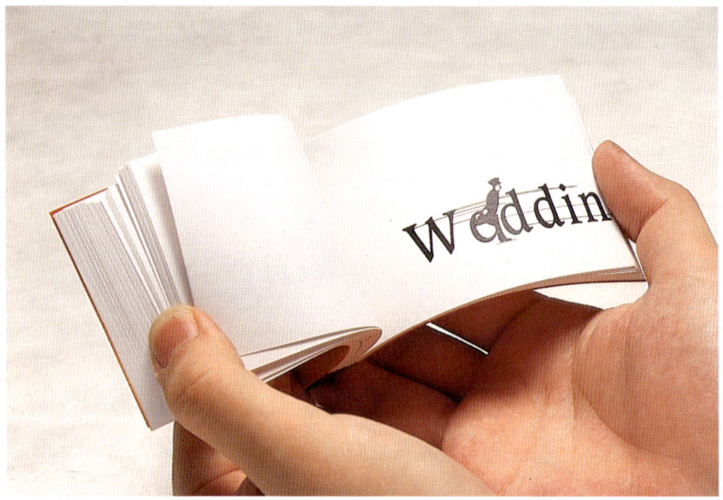

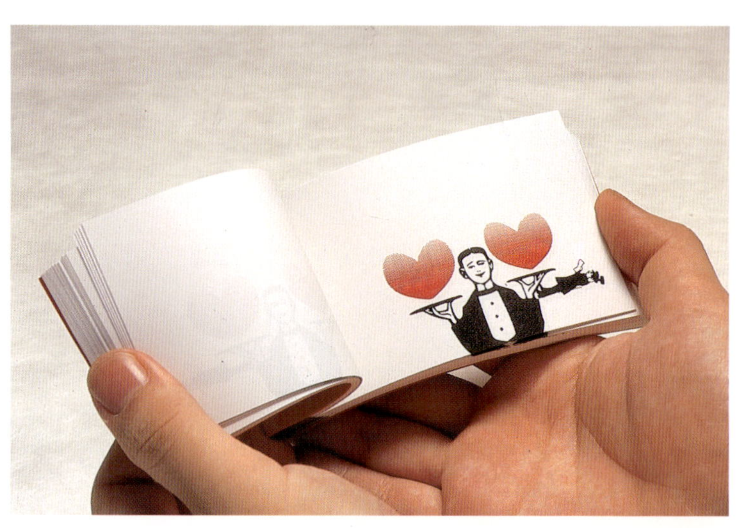

Invitation to a wedding

結婚式招待状

JAPAN 1992

AD,D:Masayuki Shimizu

DF:Heter-O-Doxy Protprast

CL:Daisuke Nakamoto

•

When you thumb throgh the pages of
the inner leaflet quickly,
the illustration is animated.

中の小冊子をめくっていくと
イラストが動いて見える。

Invitation to a wedding
結婚式招待状
SWITZERLAND 1992
AD,I,CW:Thomas Von Ah
D,P:Patricia Von Ah
DF:Vacd
CL:Andrea+Gill Ben-Zur

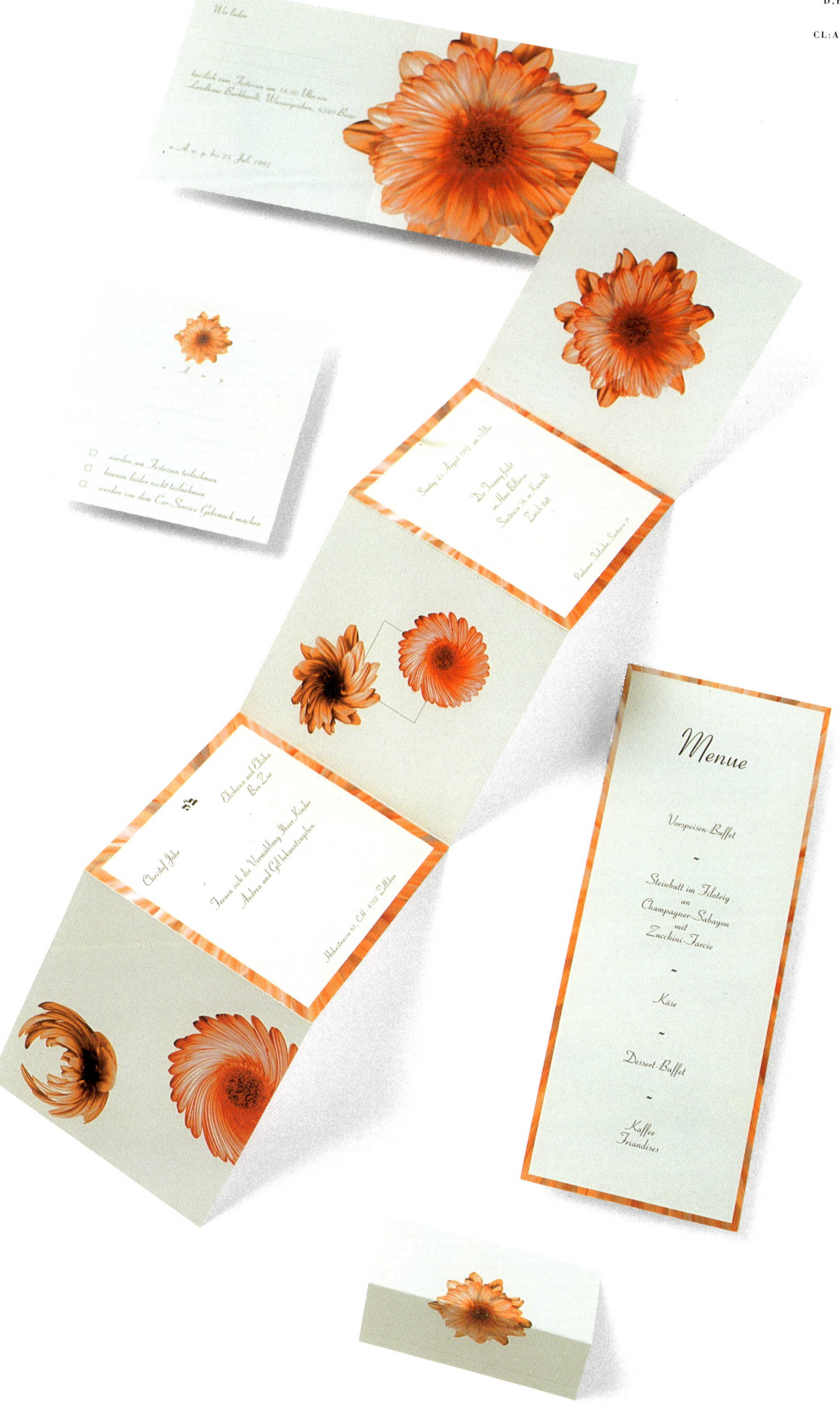

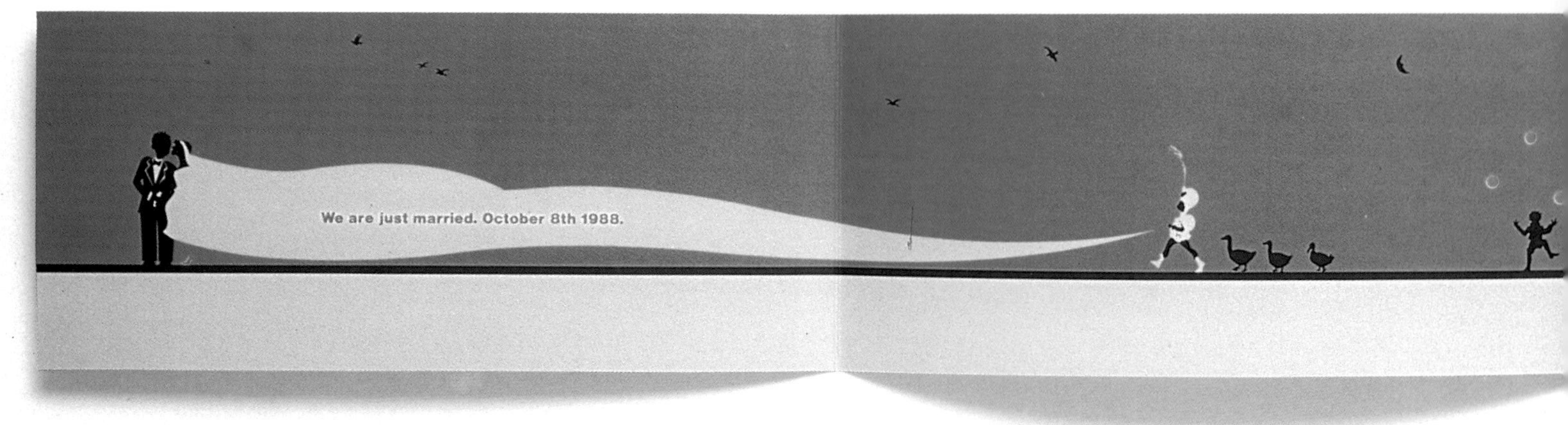

▲
Invitation to a wedding
結婚式招待状
JAPAN 1988
CD,AD,D:Keisuke Unosawa
DF:Keisuke Unosawa Design
CL:Keisuke Unosawa

◀
Invitation to a wedding
結婚式招待状
GERMANY 1990
CD,AD:Detlef Behr
DF:Detlef Behr,Graphik-Design AGD
CL:Frauke Thomas Kanigowski

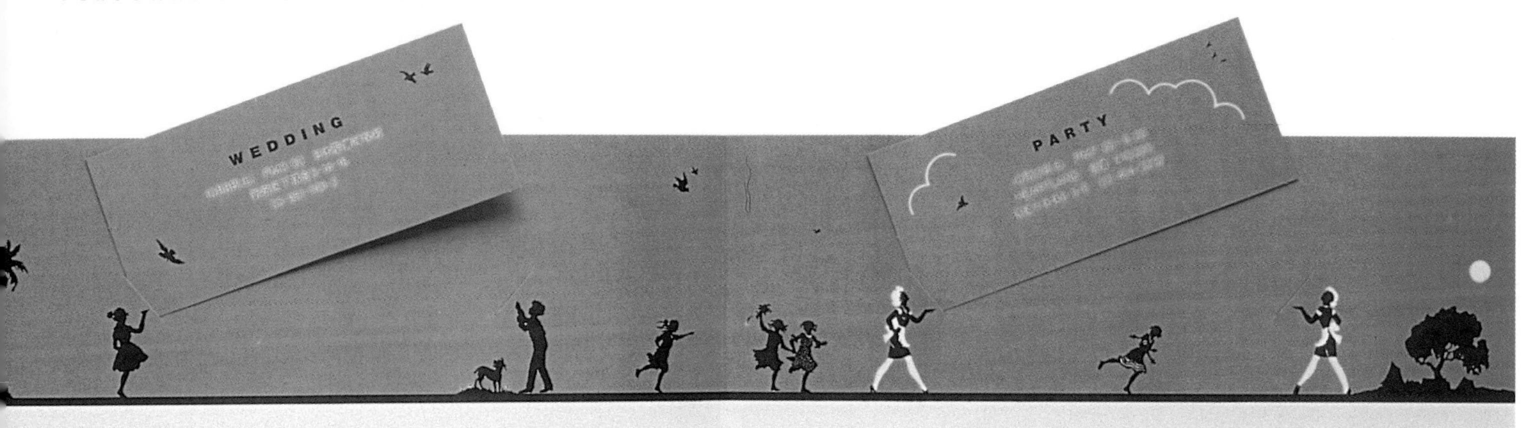

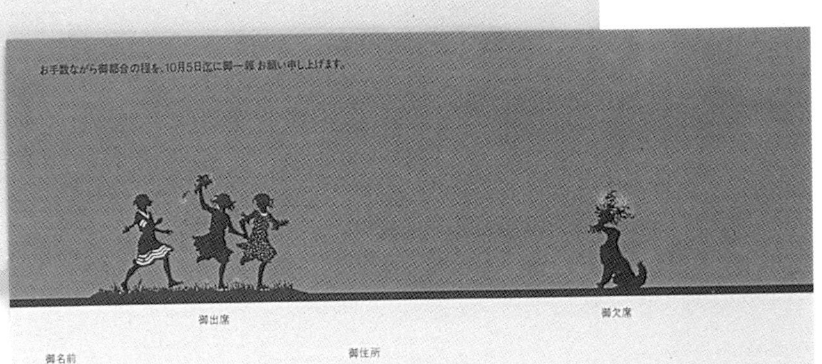

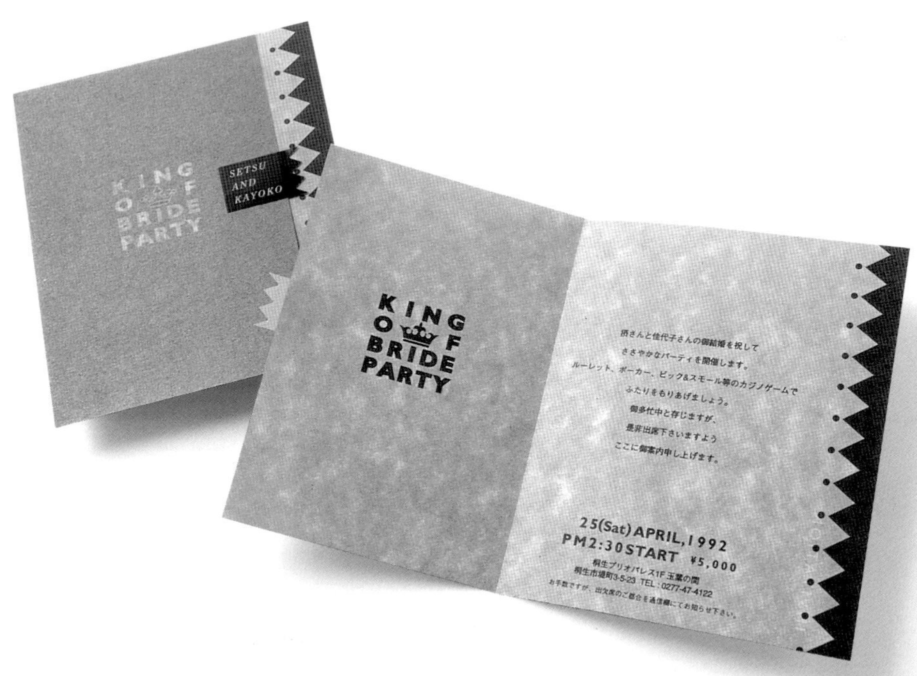

▶
Invitation to a wedding reception
結婚披露パーティー案内状
JAPAN 1992
AD,D:Joji Yano
DF:Yano Design Room
CL:Kayoko Hirasawa

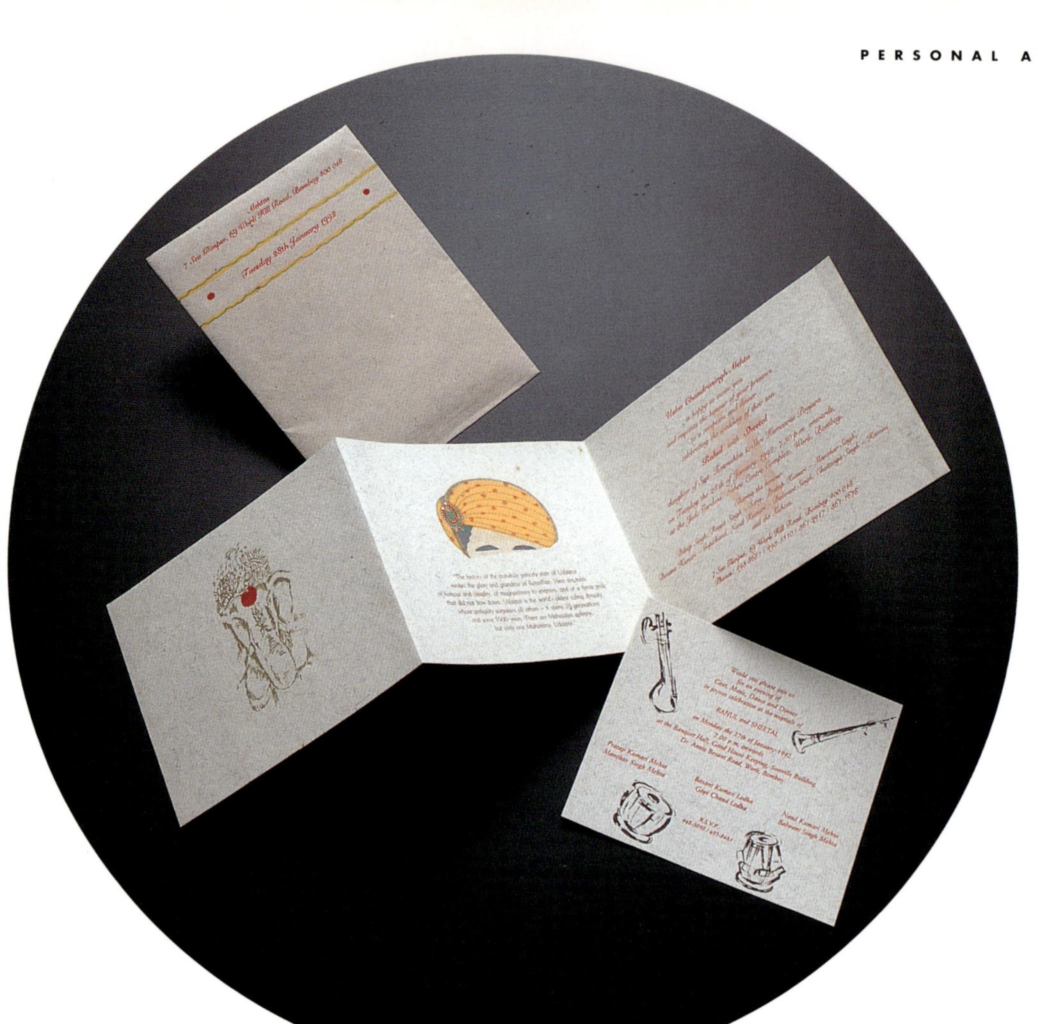

▲
Invitation to a wedding
結婚式招待状
INDIA 1992
CD,CW:Shailendra M.Kothari
AD:Naina Kothari
D,I:Quintessence Design Team
DF:Quintessence
CL:Usha Mehta

▼
Invitation to a wedding
結婚式招待状
USA 1990
AD,D:Michael Stanard
DF:Michael Stanard
CL:Beth Stanard & Scott Goldberg

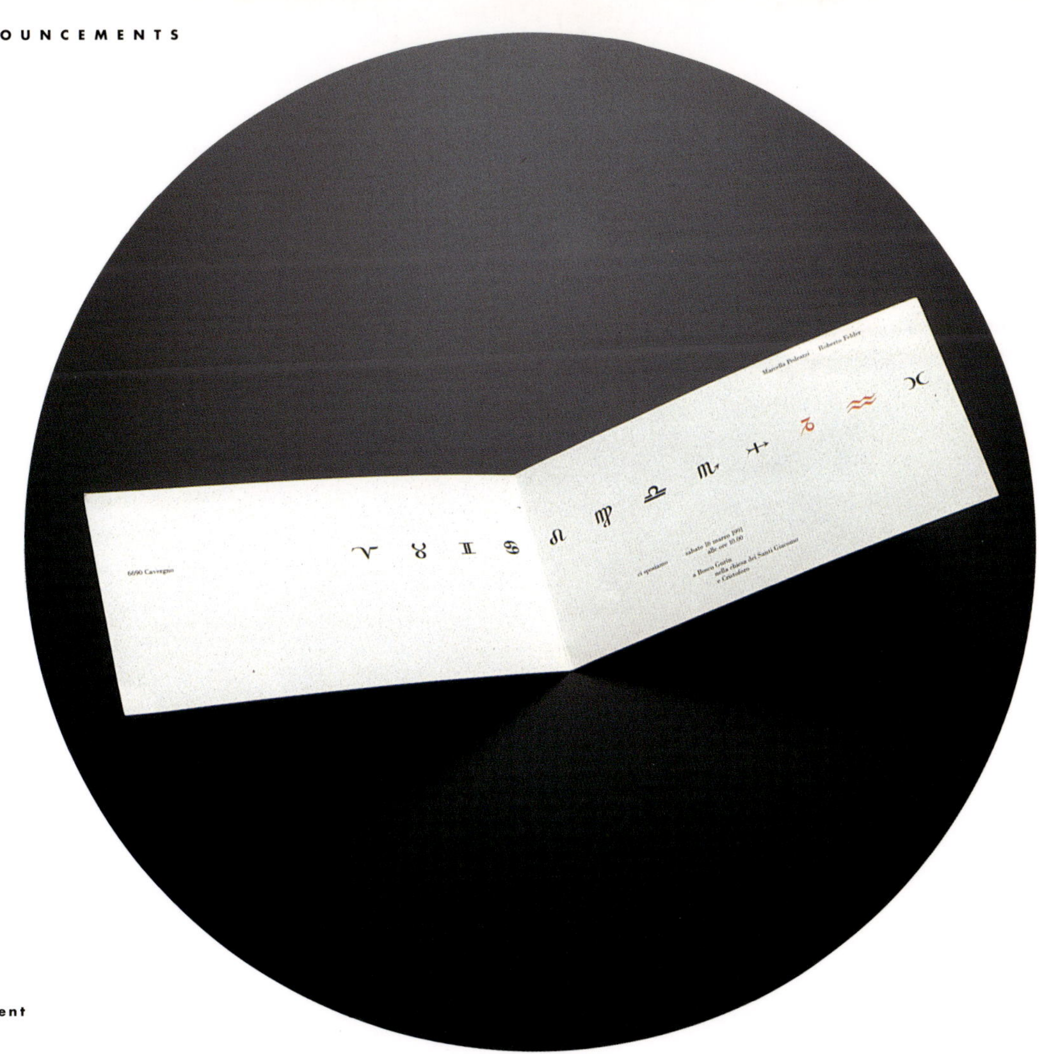

▲
Wedding announcement
結婚通知
SWITZERLAND 1991
CD,AD,D:Oberhulzer Tagli Knobec
DF:Oberhulzer Tagli Knobec
CL:Roberto Felder

▼
Invitation to a wedding
結婚式招待状
USA 1992
AD,D,I:Margo Sepanski
CW:David Hoedemaker
DF:NBBJ - Graphic Design
CL:David Hoedemaker

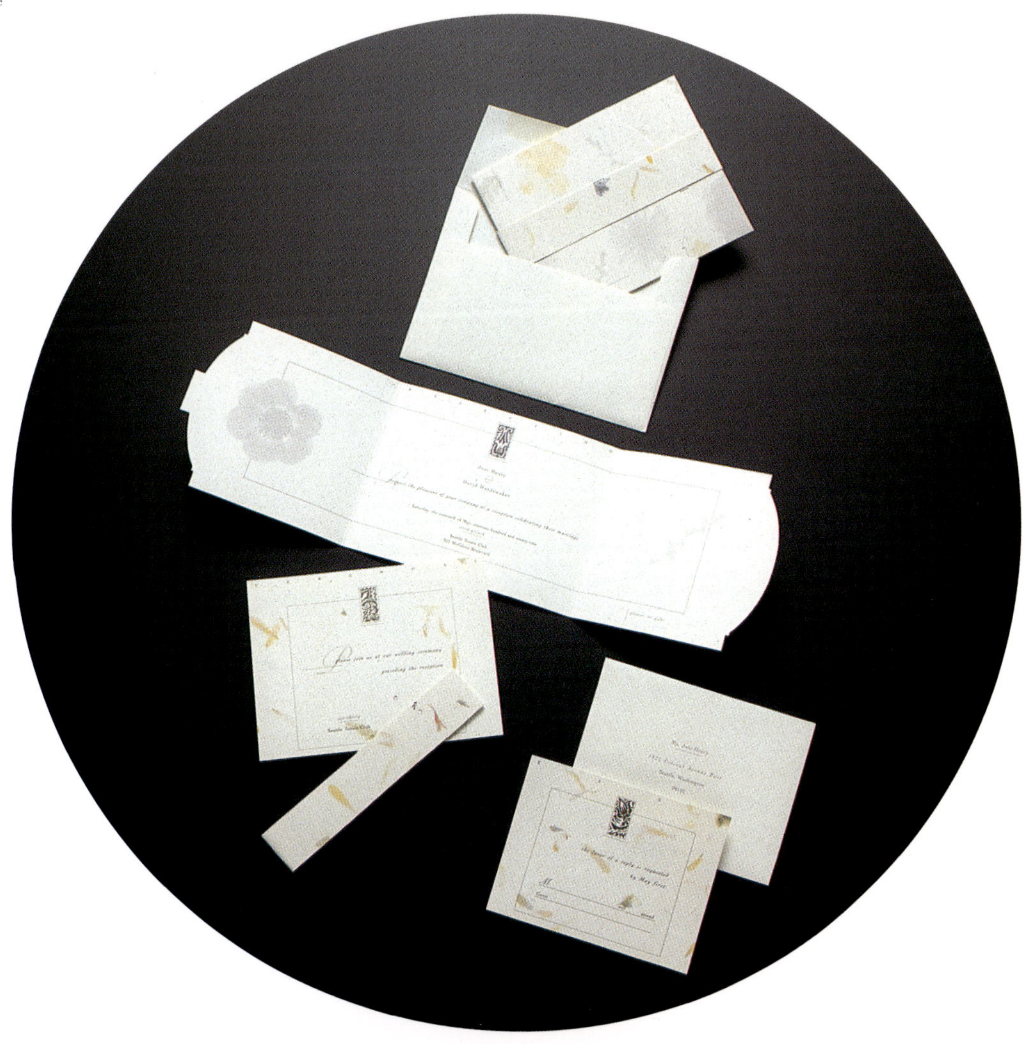

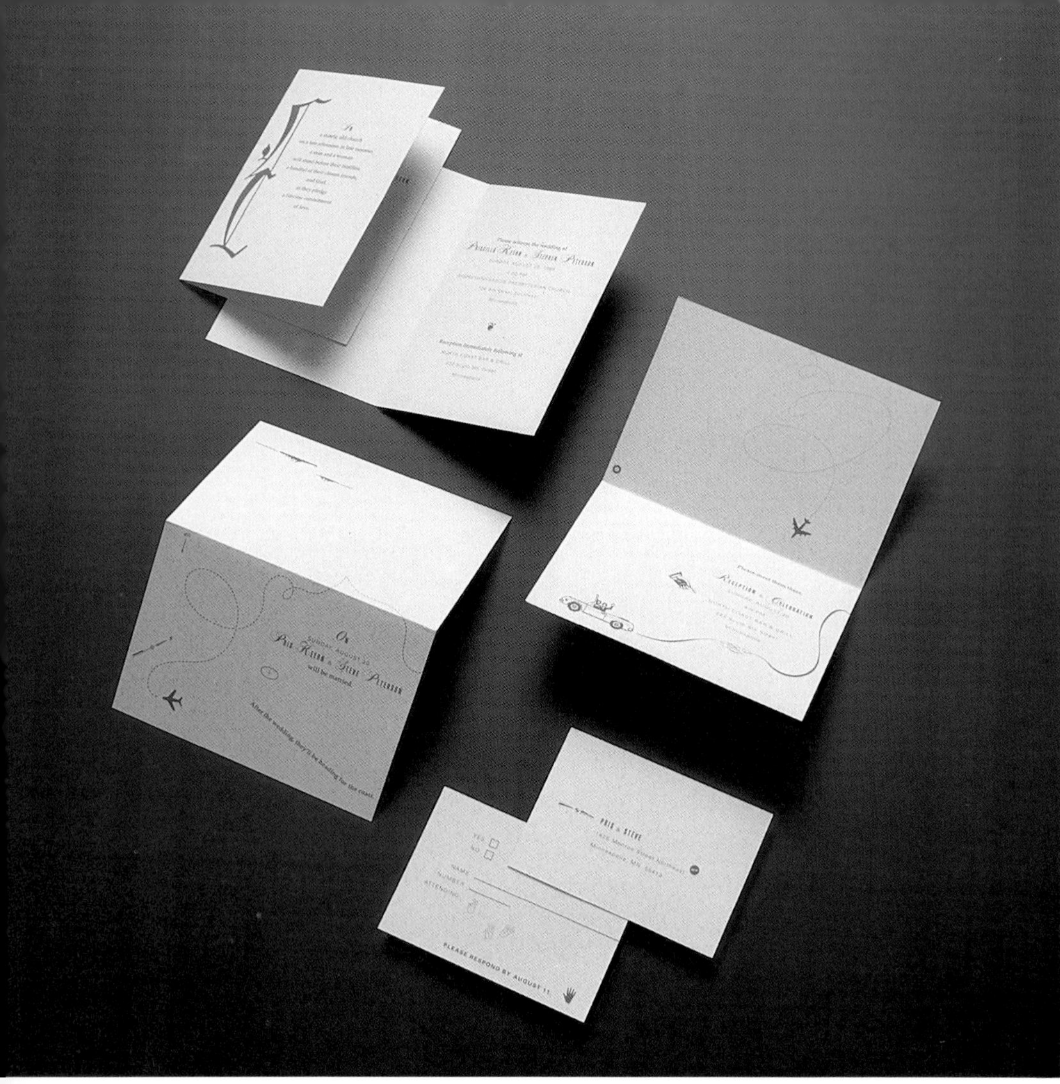

Invitation to a wedding
結婚式招待状
USA 1989
D:Donna Daubendiek
DF:Blind Design
CL:Kyia Downing

Wedding announcement
結婚通知
USA 1991
D:Timorse Daubendiek
Donna Daubendiek
CW:Z Heads Communications
DF:Coloured Blind
CL:Kris & Ellen Iegler

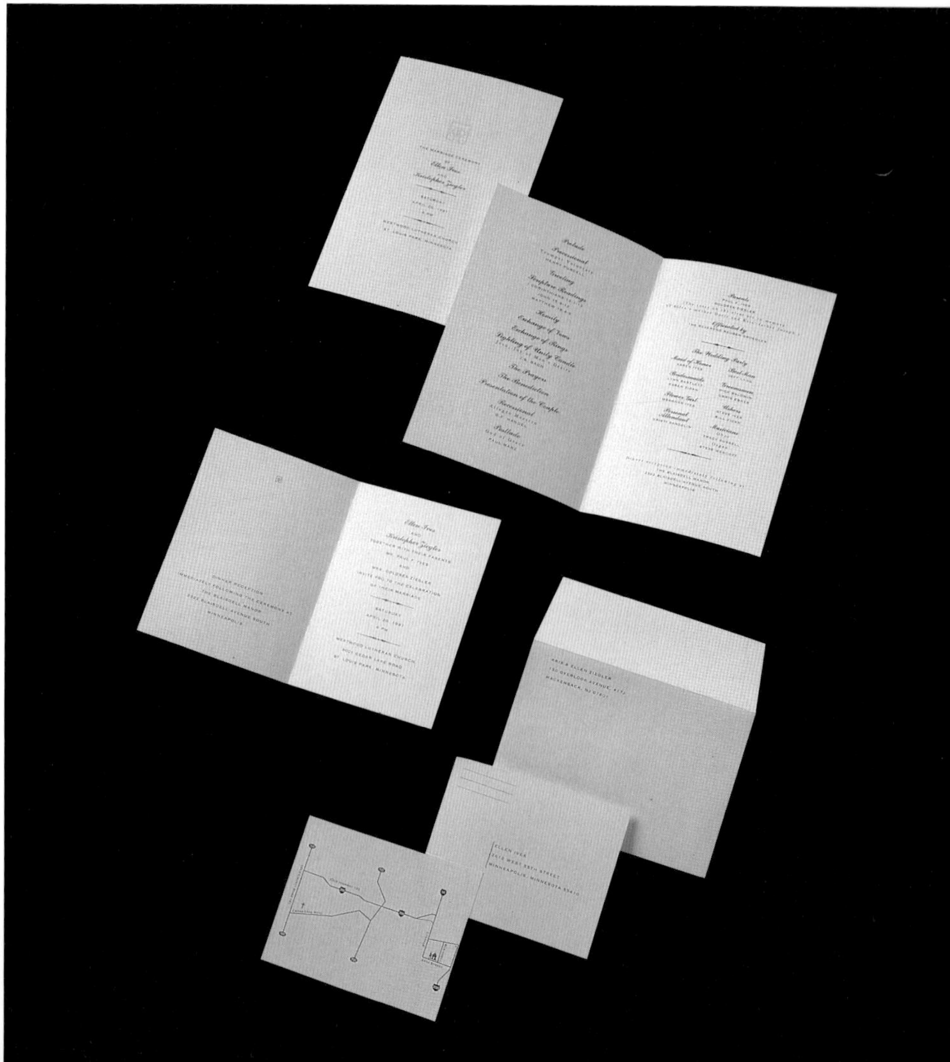

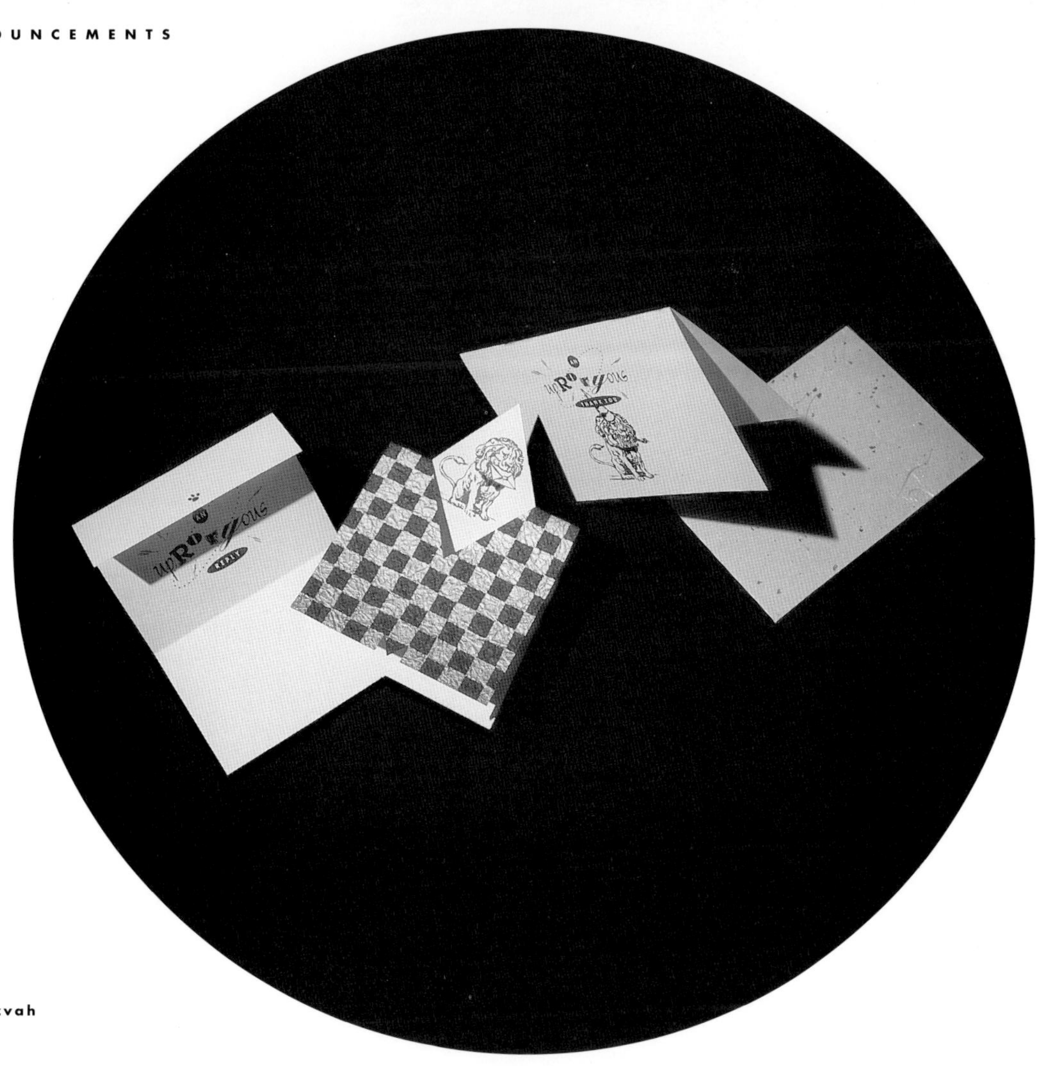

▲
Invitation to a Bar Mitzvah
バー・ミズヴァー招待状
CANADA 1992
CD,D,I:Dan Wheaton
AD:Ric Riordon
DF:The Riordon Design Group
CL:Rave-up Productions

▼
Invitation to a wedding
結婚式招待状
JAPAN 1991
AD,D:Yoko Kobayashi
CW:Seizo Kobayashi
CL:Yoko Kobayashi

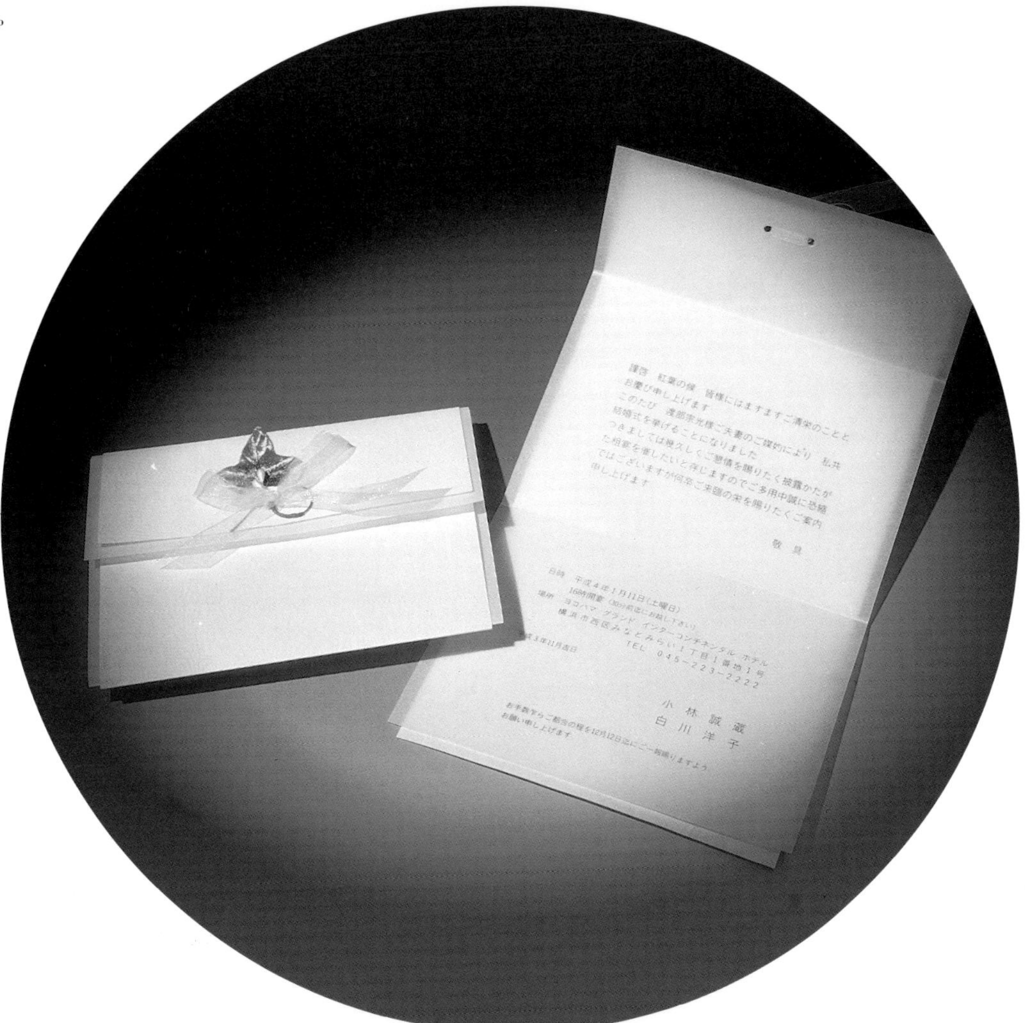

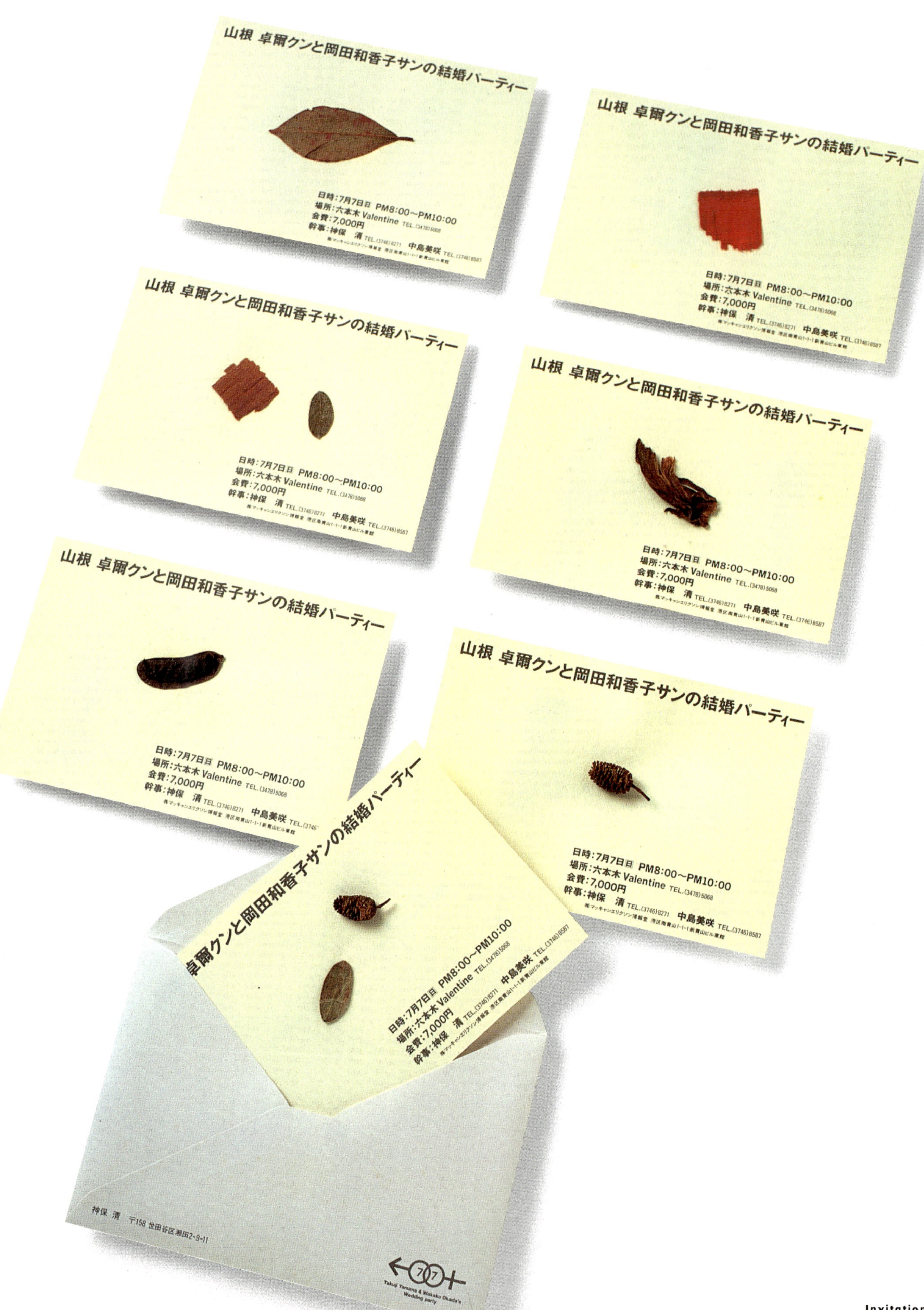

Invitation to a wedding reception
結婚披露パーティー招待状
JAPAN 1991
AD,D:Jun Asano
CL:Takuji Yamane

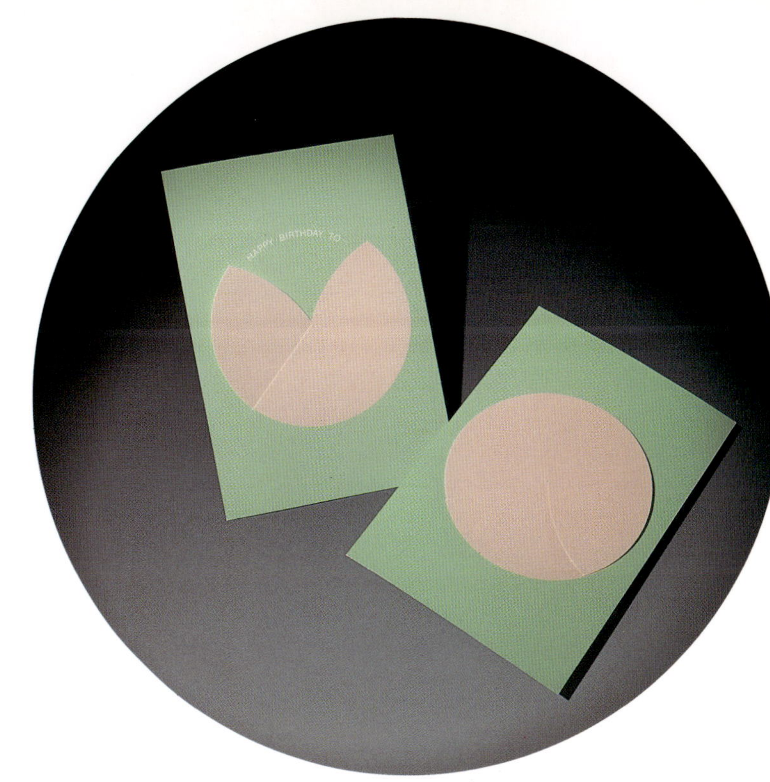

▶
Birthday card
バースデー・カード
JAPAN 1990
AD,D:Keisuke Unosawa
DF:Keisuke Unosawa Design
CL:Baby's

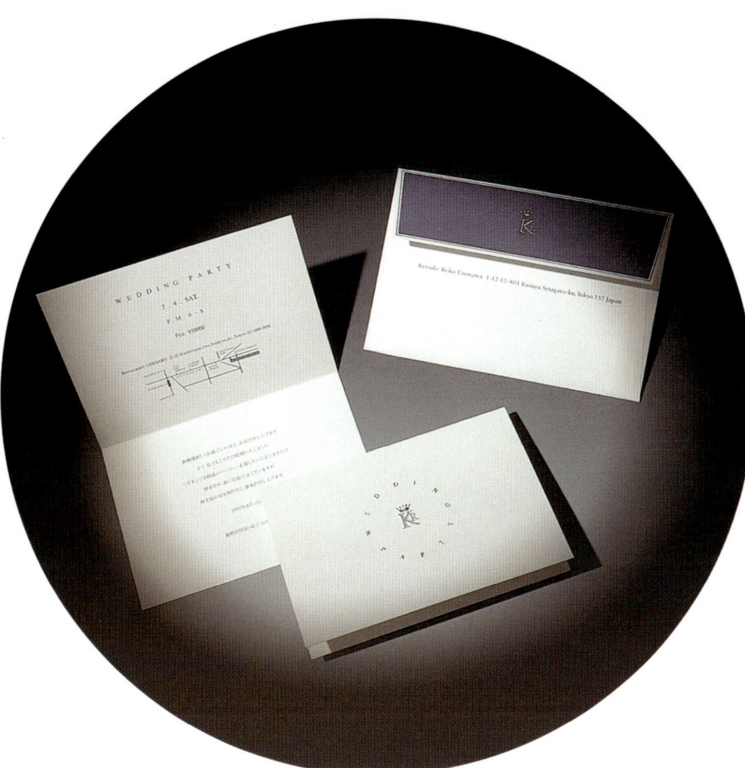

◀
Invitation to a wedding
結婚式招待状
JAPAN 1992
CD,AD,D:Keisuke Unosawa
CW:Keisuke Unosawa
Reiko Unosawa
DF:Keisuke Unosawa Design
CL:Keisuke Unosawa
Reiko Unosawa

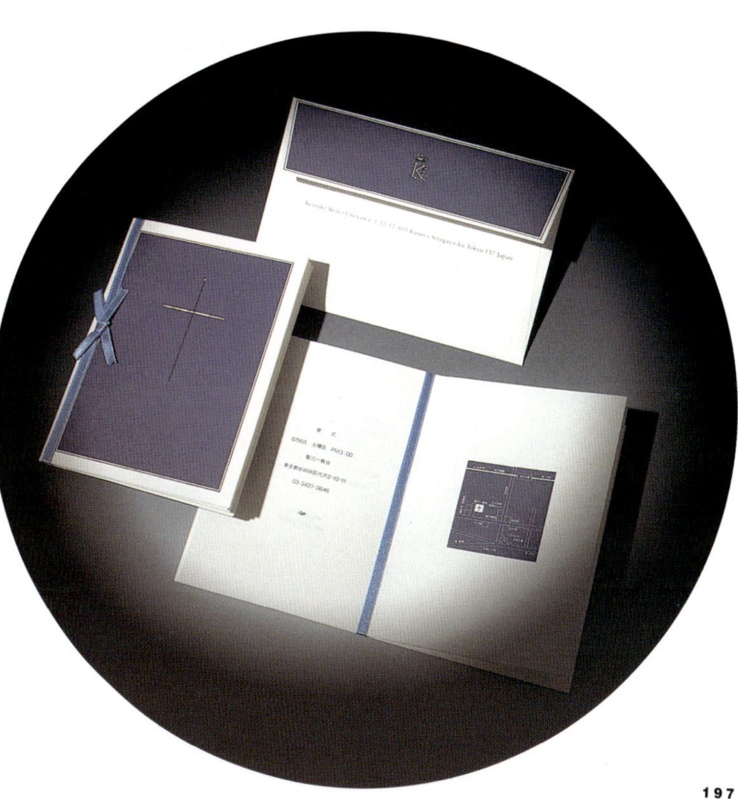

▶
Invitation to a wedding
結婚式招待状
JAPAN 1992
CD,CW:Keisuke Unosawa
Reiko Unosawa
AD,D:Keisuke Unosawa
DF:Keisuke Unosawa Design
CL:Keisuke Unosawa
Reiko Unosawa

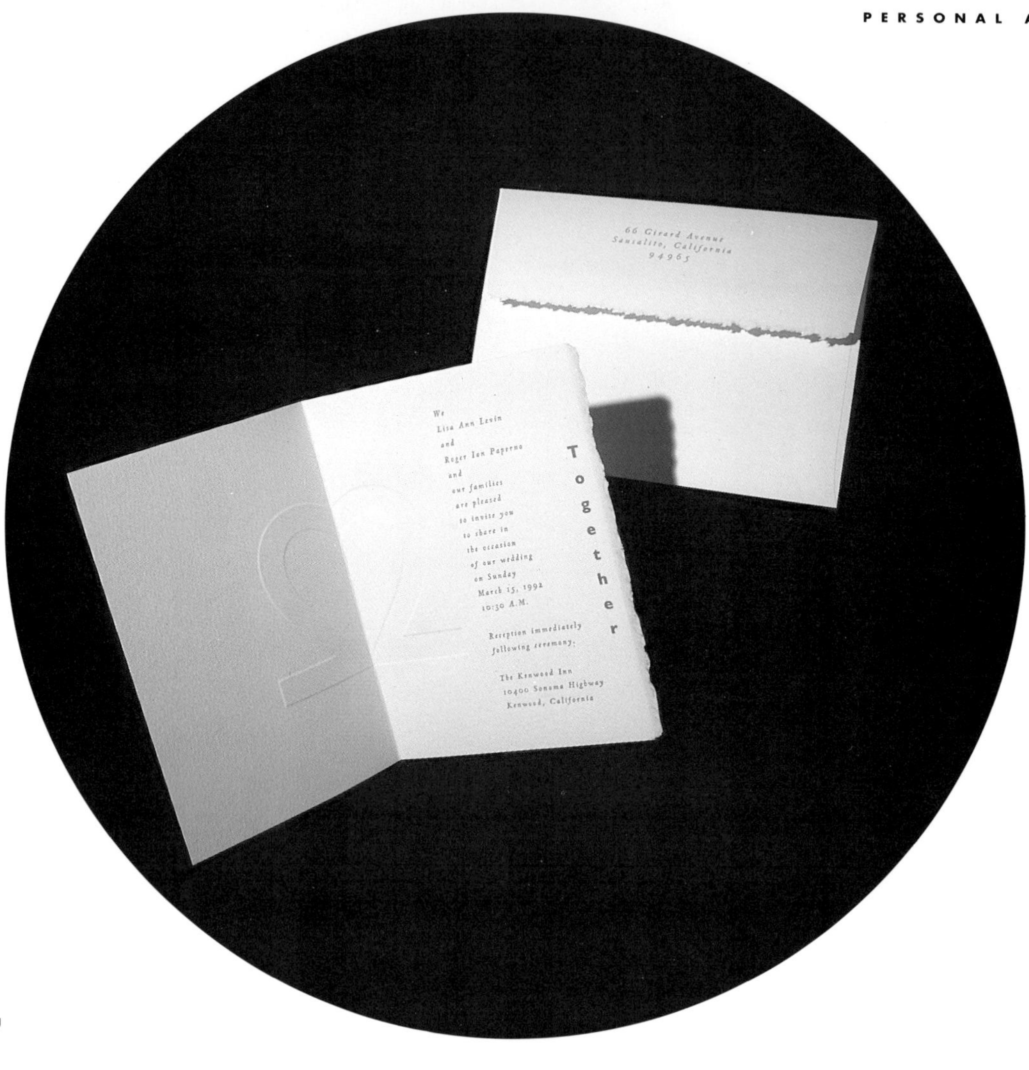

▲
Invitation to a wedding
結婚式招待状
USA 1992
CD,AD,D:Lisa Levin
DF:Lisa Levin Design
CL:Lisa Levin & Roger Paperno

▼
Invitation to a wedding
結婚式招待状
USA 1990
AD,D:Mark Landry
DF:Mark Landry Design
CL:Vincenza Birritteri

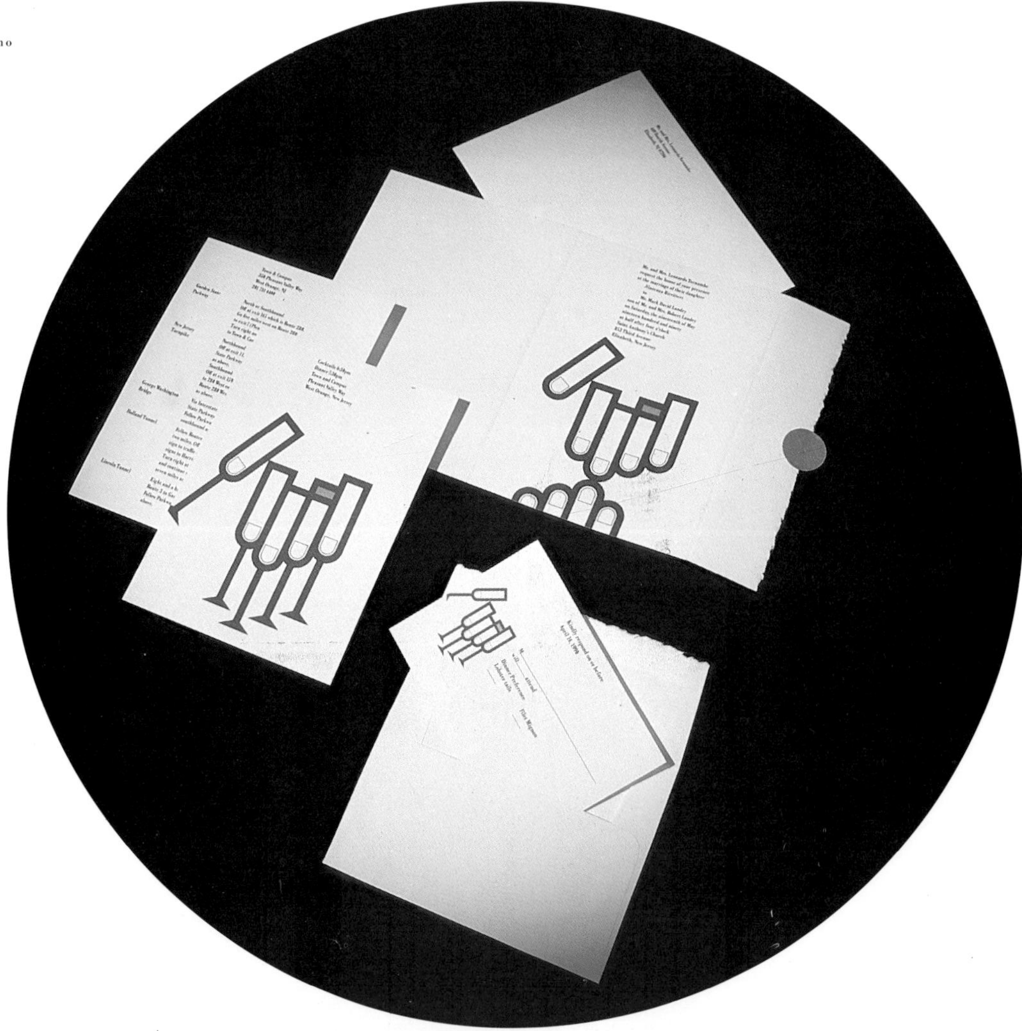

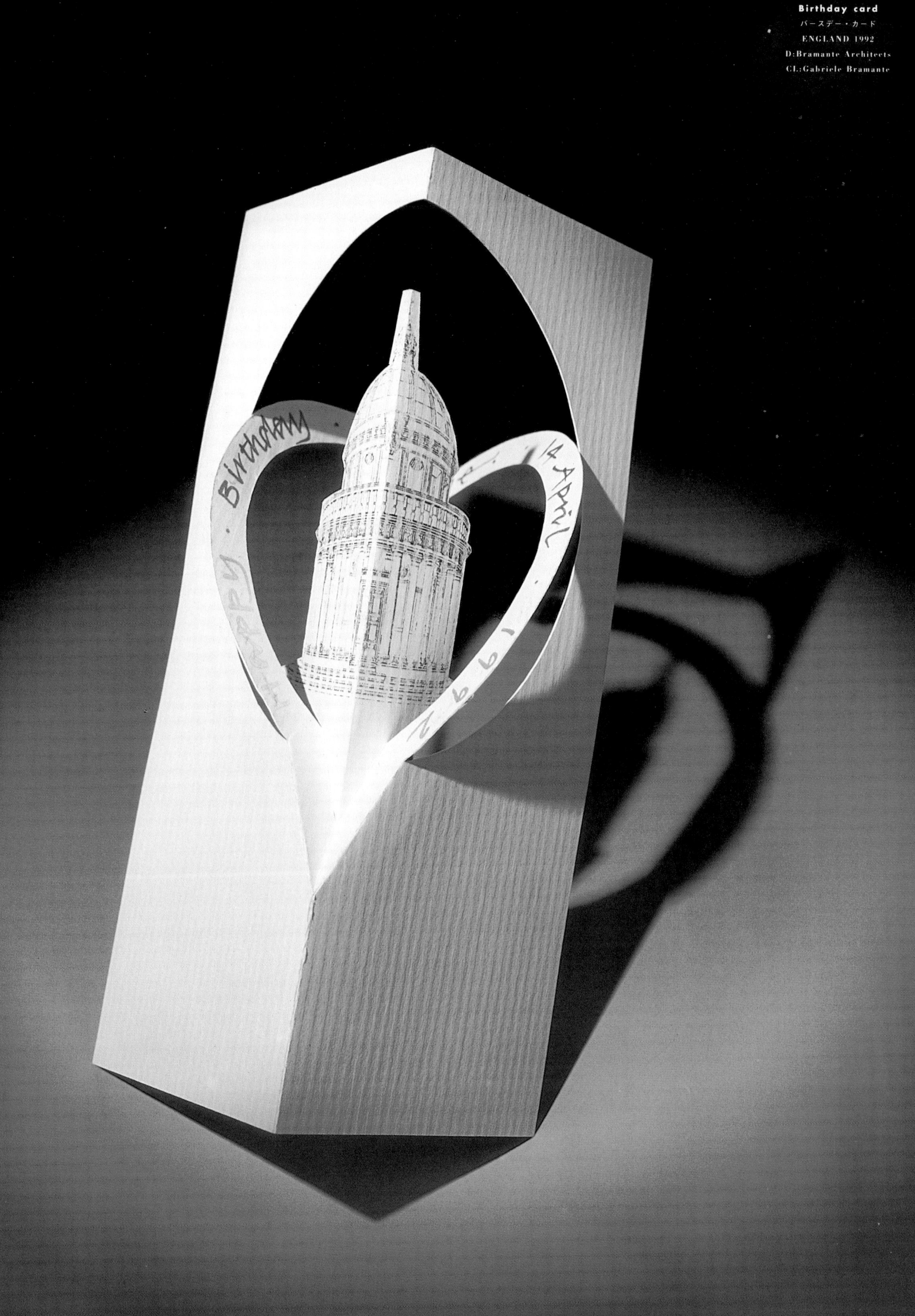

Birthday card
バースデー・カード
ENGLAND 1992
D:Bramante Architects
CL:Gabriele Bramante

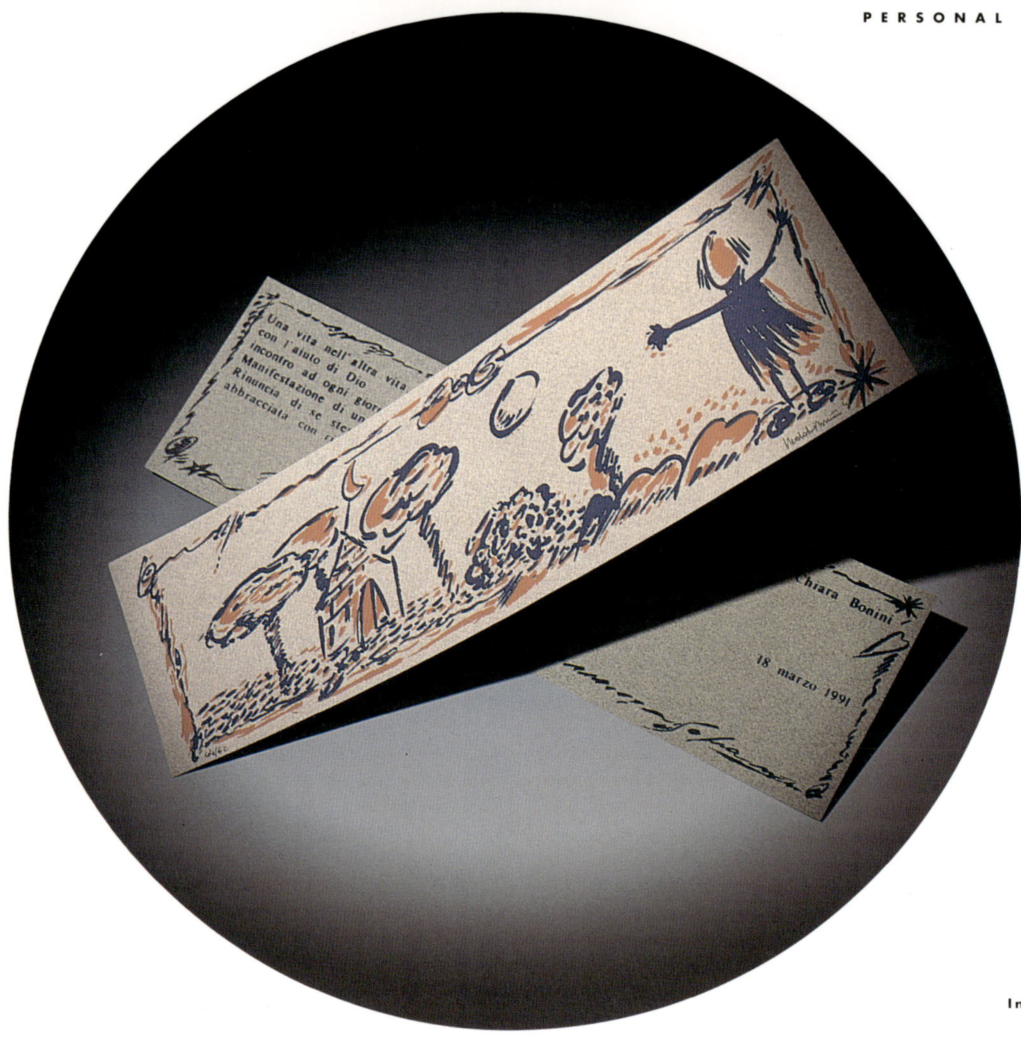

▲
Birth announcemant
出産通知
ITALY 1991
CD,AD,D,I,DF:Nedda Bonini
CW:Nevio Bonini
CL:Nevio Bonini e Luisa Scuderi

▼
Invitation to a Bar Mitzvah
バー・ミズヴァー招待状
ARGENTINE 1992
CD,AD,D,CW:Marcelo Sapoznik
DF:Marcelo Sapoznik Graphic Designer
CL:Martin Weis

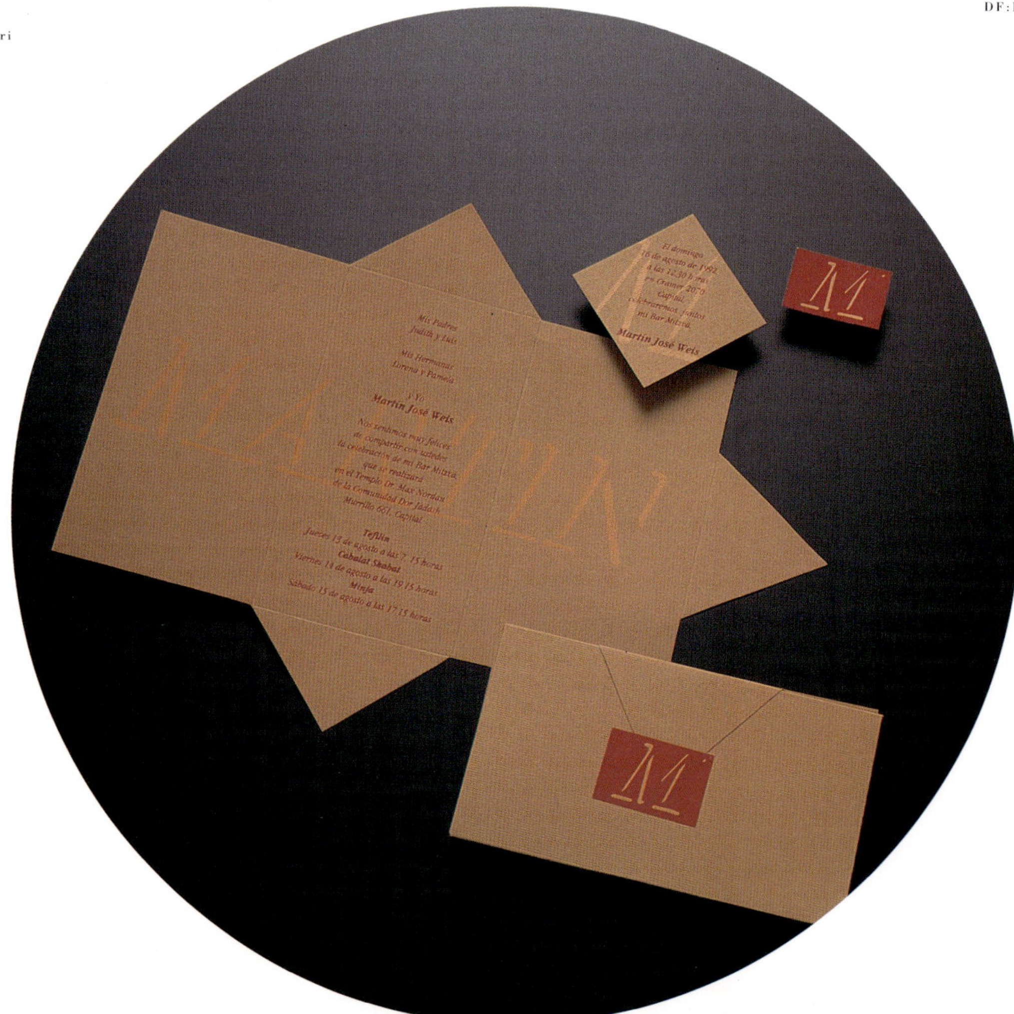

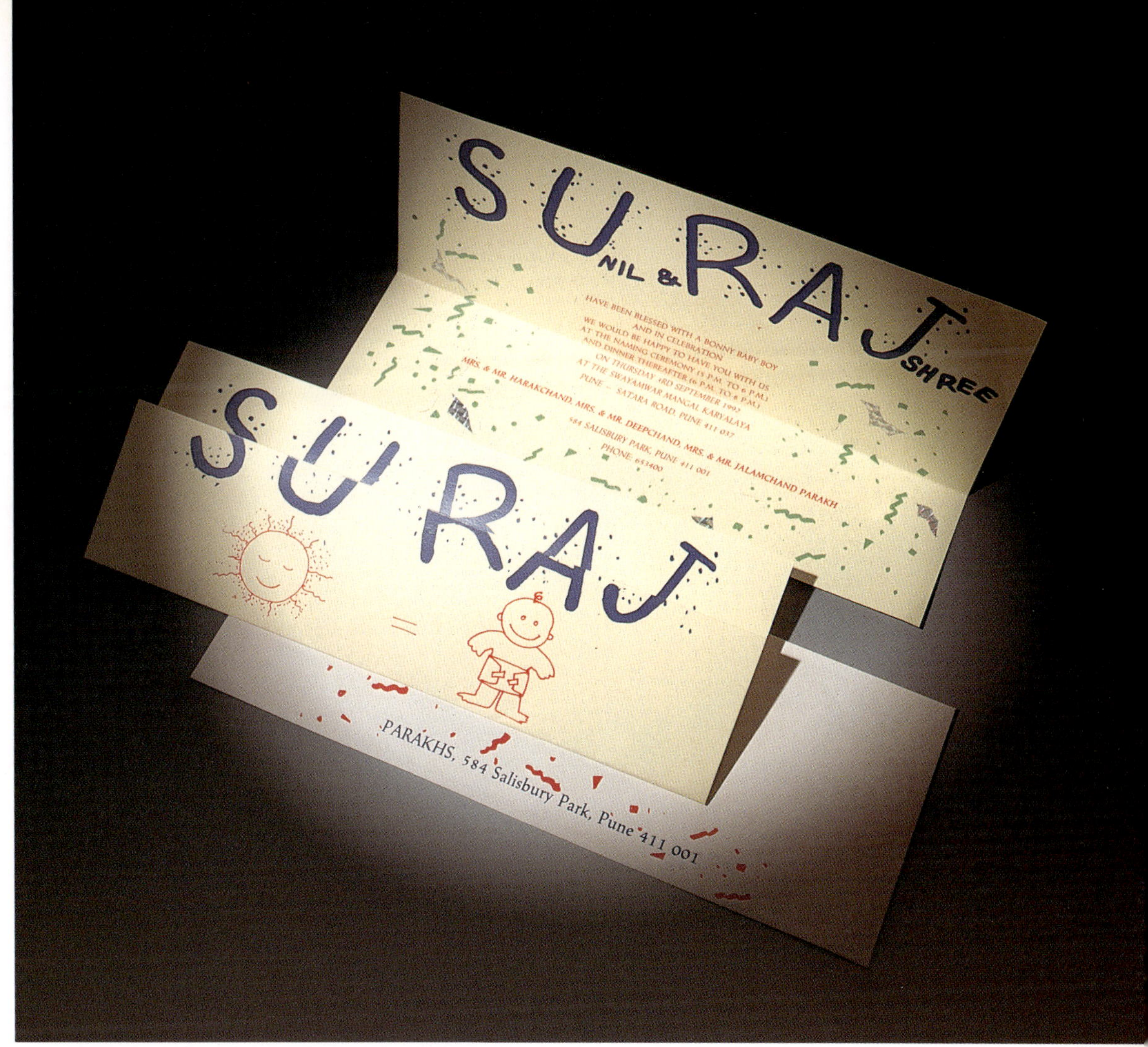

Invitation to a naming ceremony

命名式招待状

INDIA 1992

CD,CW:Shailendra M.Kothari

AD:Naina Kothari

D,I:Quintessence Design Team

DF:Quintessence

CL:Sunil & Rajshree Parakh

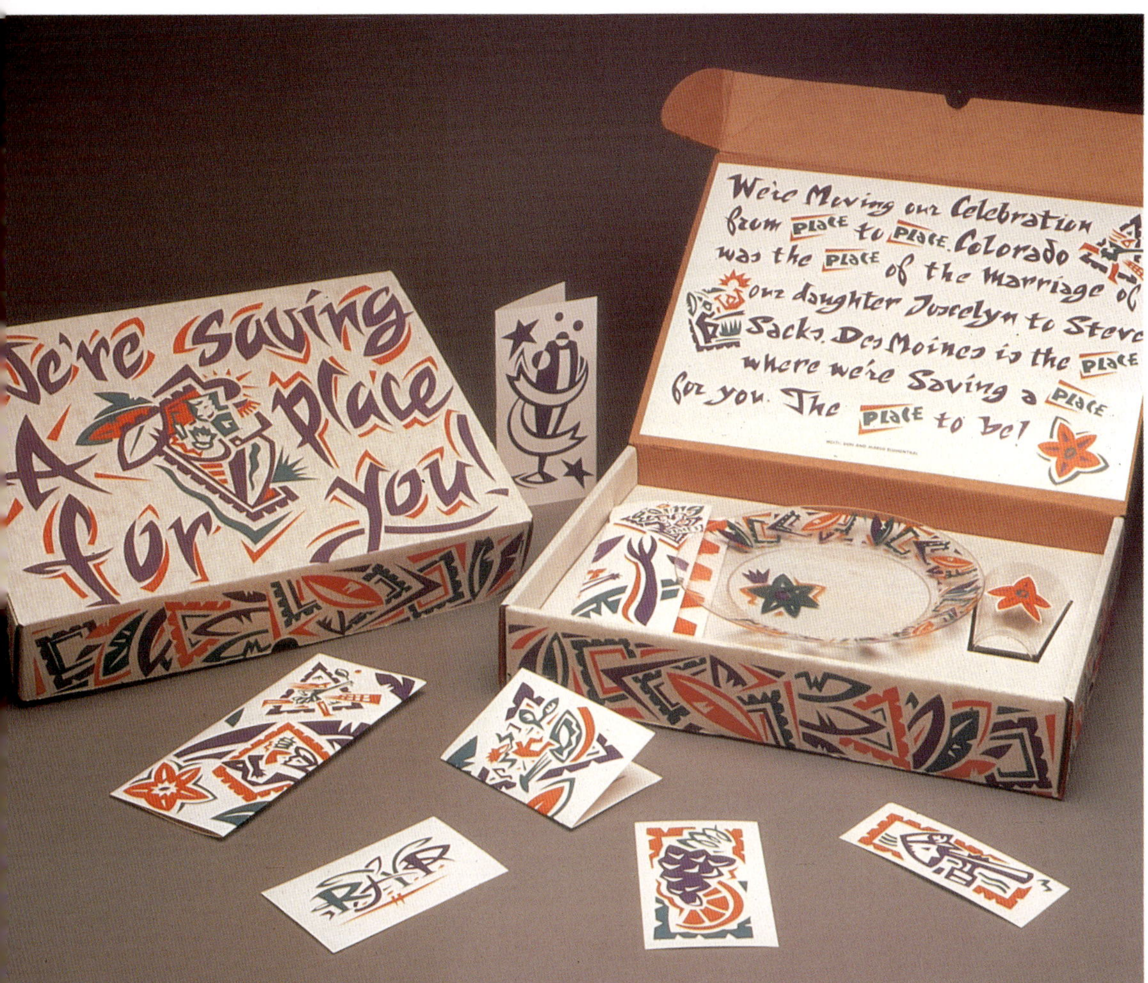

Invitation to a wedding reception

結婚披露宴招待状

USA 1992

AD,D,I:John Sayles

CW:Margo Blumenthal

DF:Sayles Graphic Design

CL:Blumenthal Family

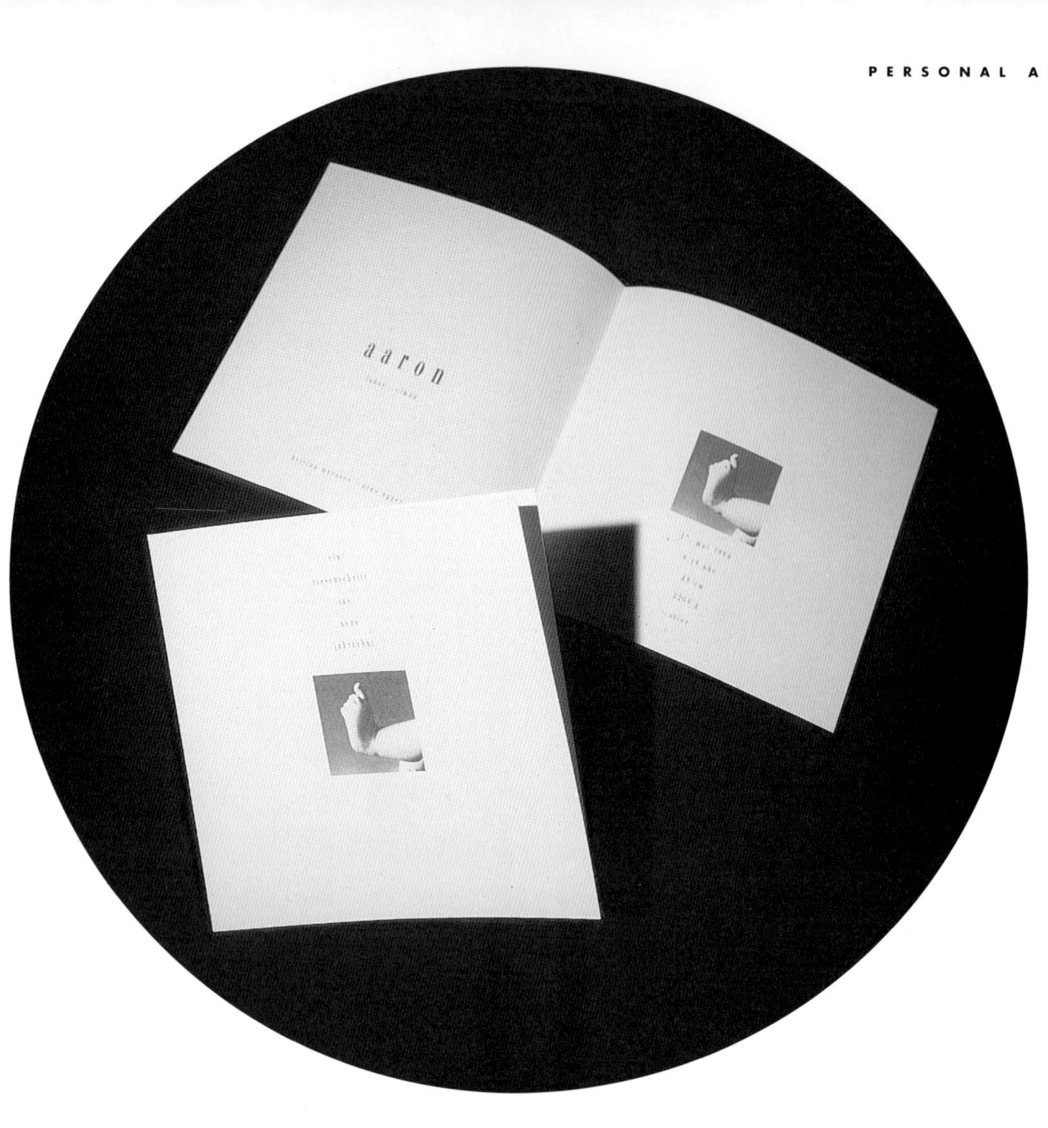

▲
Birth announcement
出産通知
AUSTRIA 1990
AD:Sigi Ramoser
CL:Bettina Morauec
Arno Egger

▼
Birth announcement
出産通知
CANADA 1991
CD,D,CW:Marcello Grossutti
DF:Rushton Green and Grossutti
CL:Maryann Grossutti

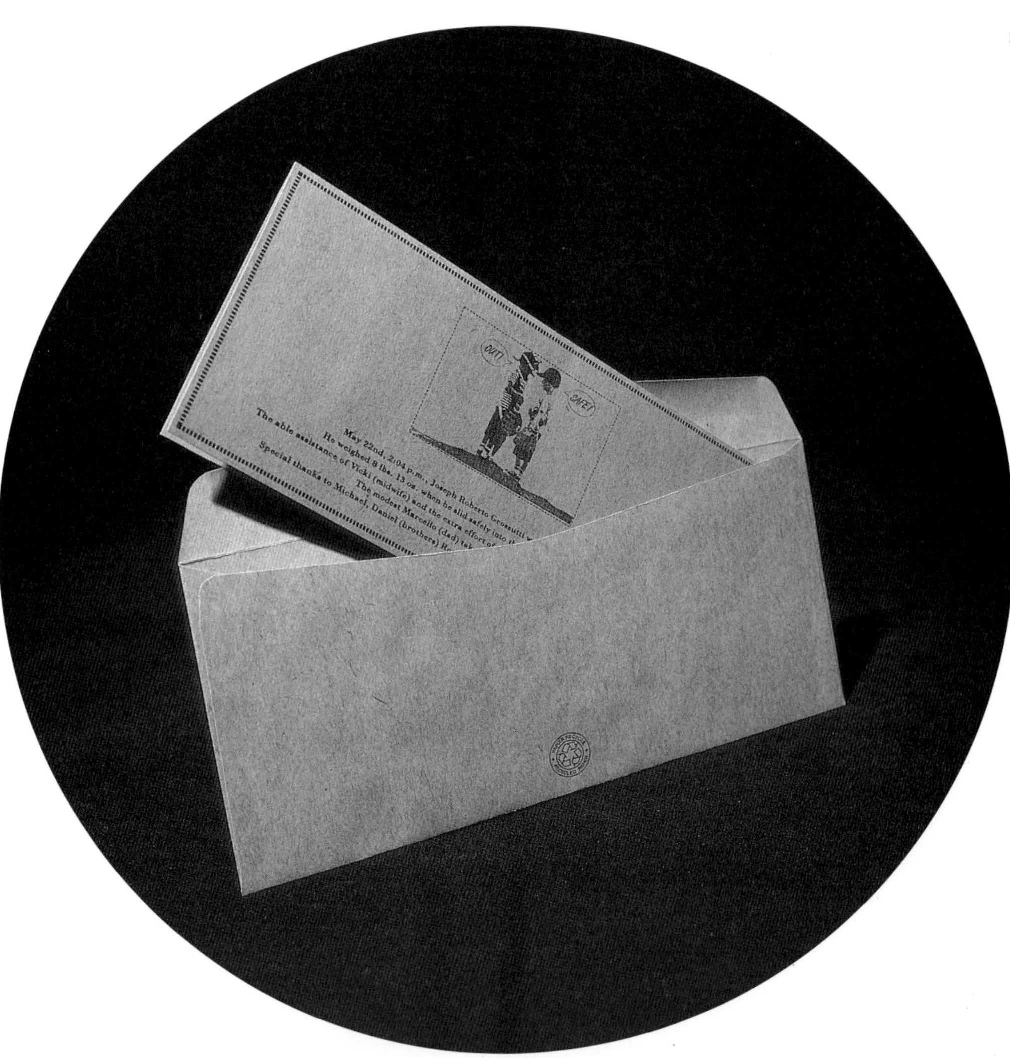

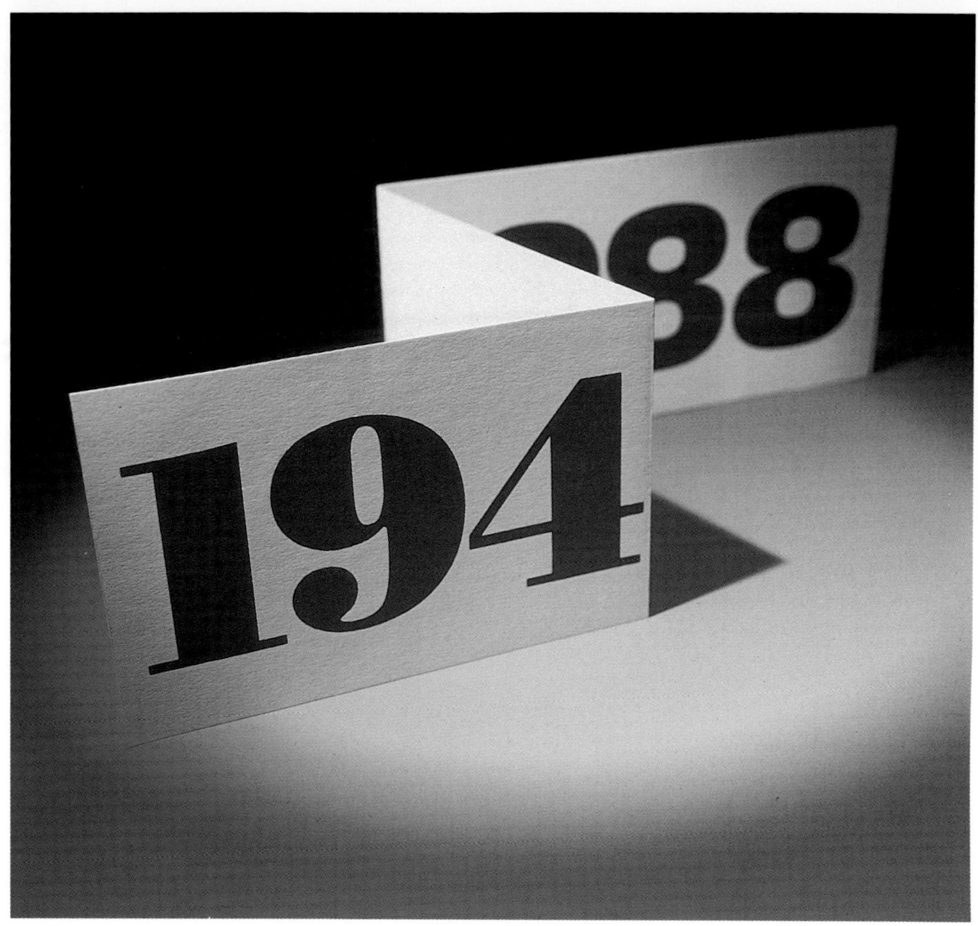

▼
Invitation to a wedding
結婚式招待状
CANADA 1989
AD,D,CW:Michéle Miodonski
DF:Applications in Design
CL:Ginny Townson
Paul Sedik

▲
Invitation to a wedding anniversary
結婚記念日招待状
CANADA 1988
AD,D:Michéle Miodonski
DF:Applications in Design
CL:Robb Collis

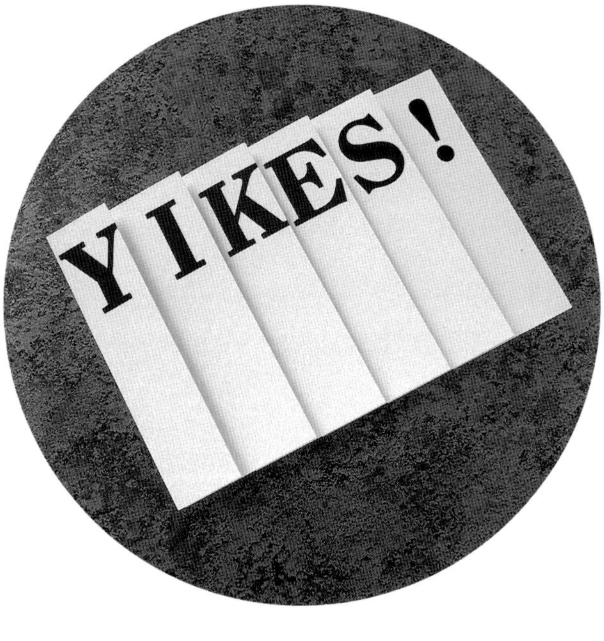

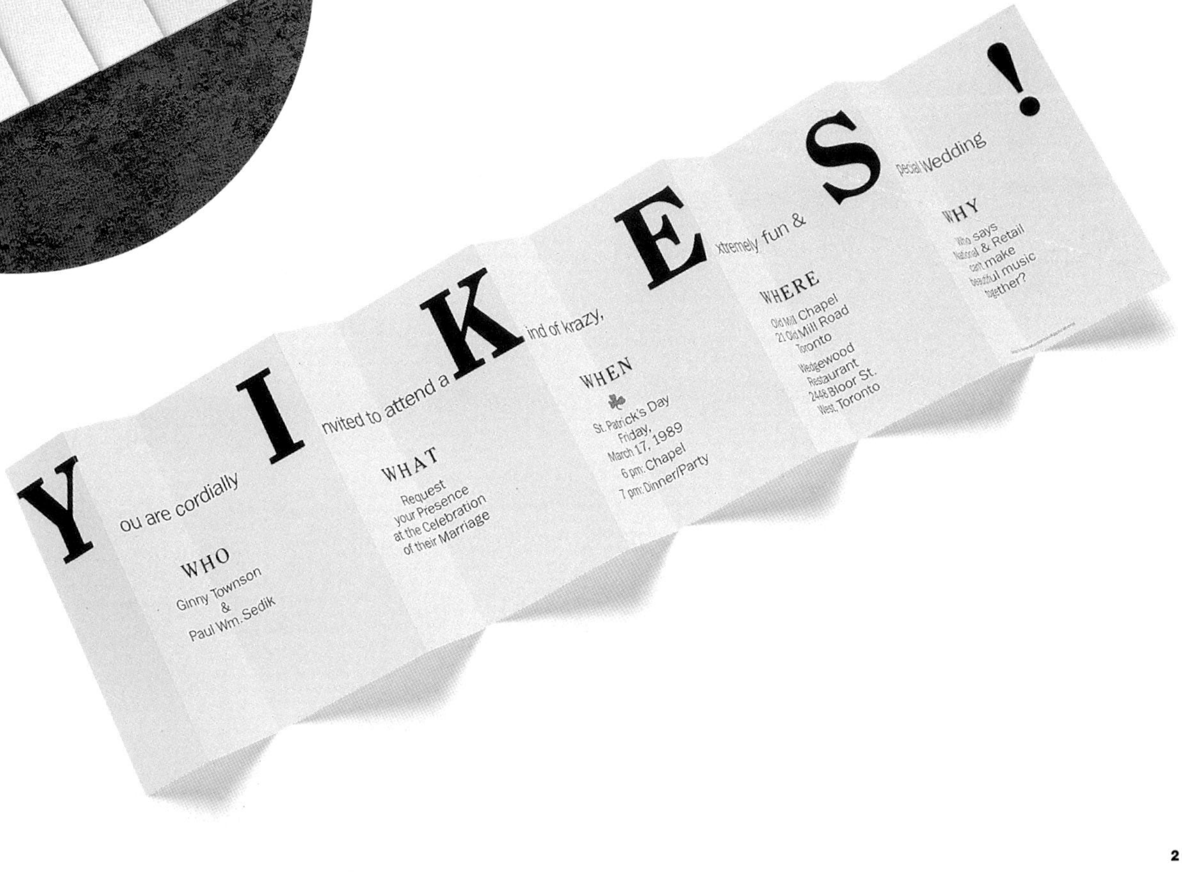

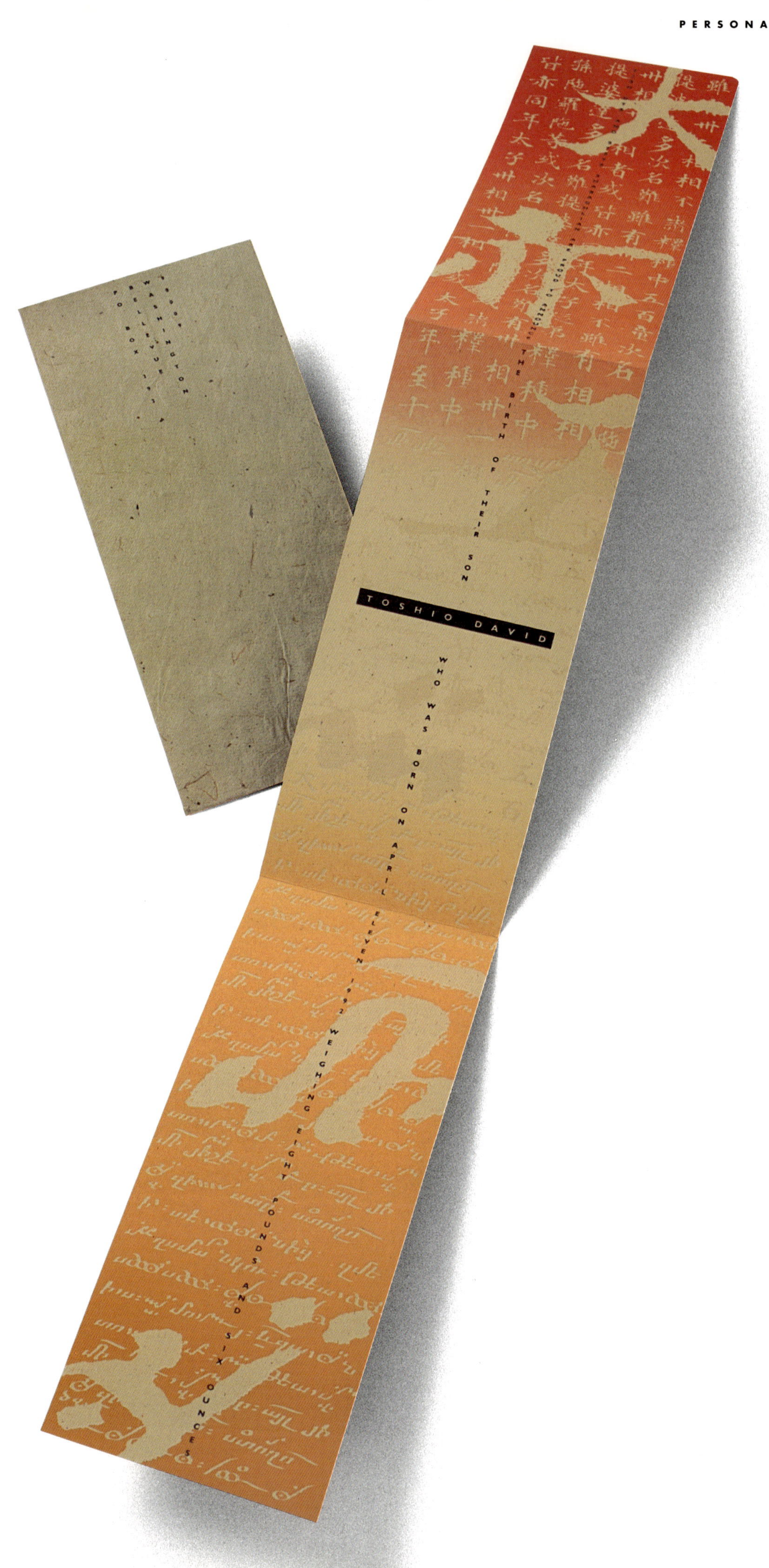

Birth announcement
出産通知
USA 1992
AD:Jack Anderson
D:Jack Anderson
Leo Raymundo
CW:Steve Shabaghlian
DF:Hornall Anderson Design Works
CL:Tish Oye and Steve Shabaghlian

Birth announcement
出産通知
USA 1991
AD,D:Lisa Fingerhut
DF:Michael Stanard
CL:Ruth Tamkin

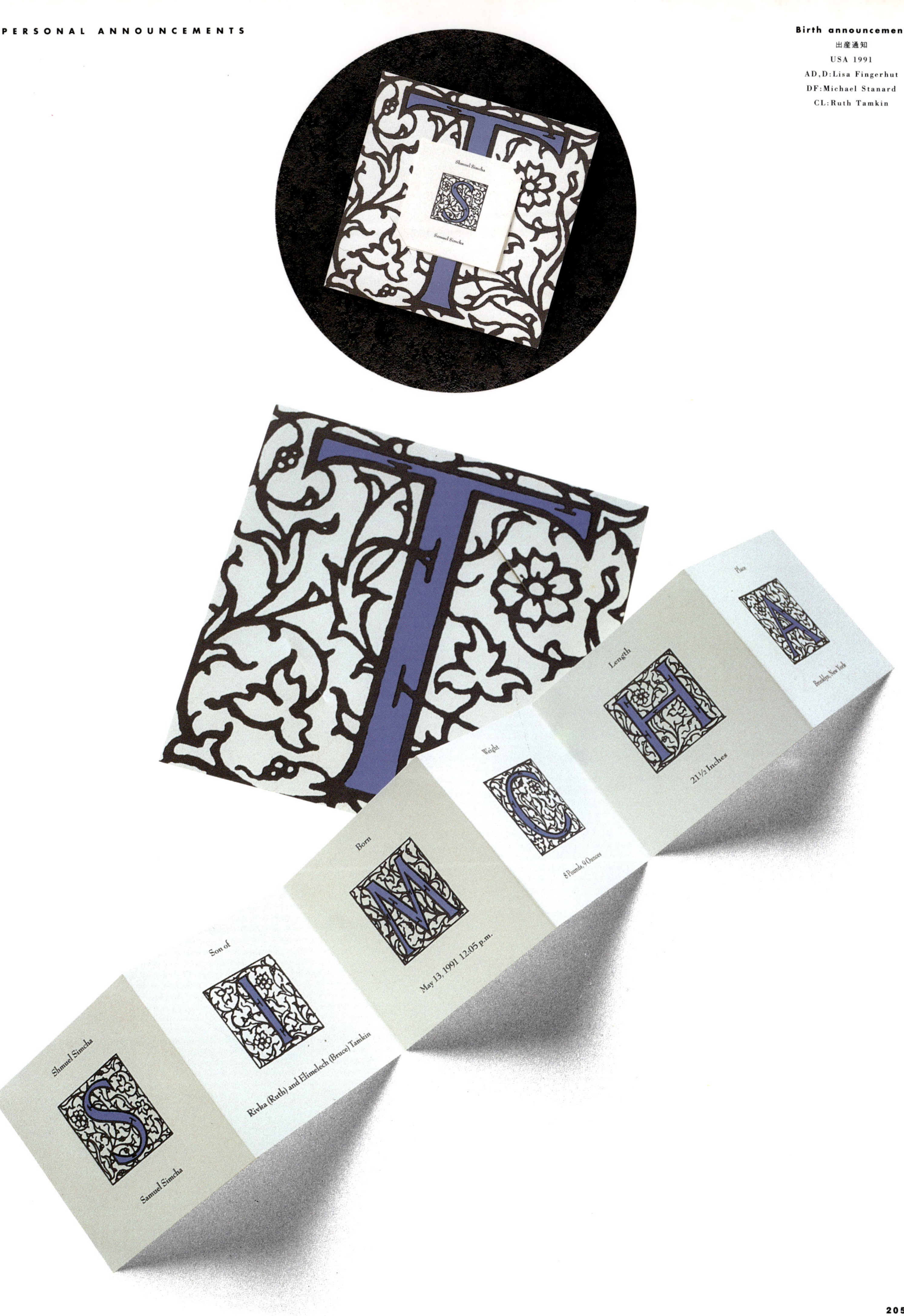

Birth announcement
出産通知
CANADA 1991
AD,D:Michéle Miodonski
CW:Franca Leeson
DF:Applications in Design
CL:Franca Leeson
Tim Hurson

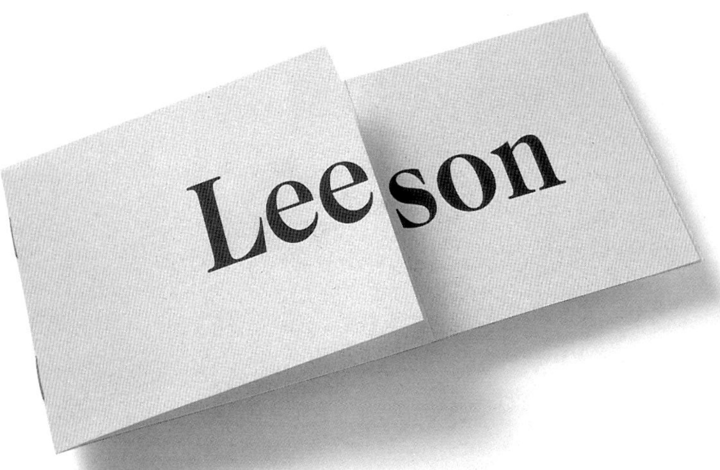

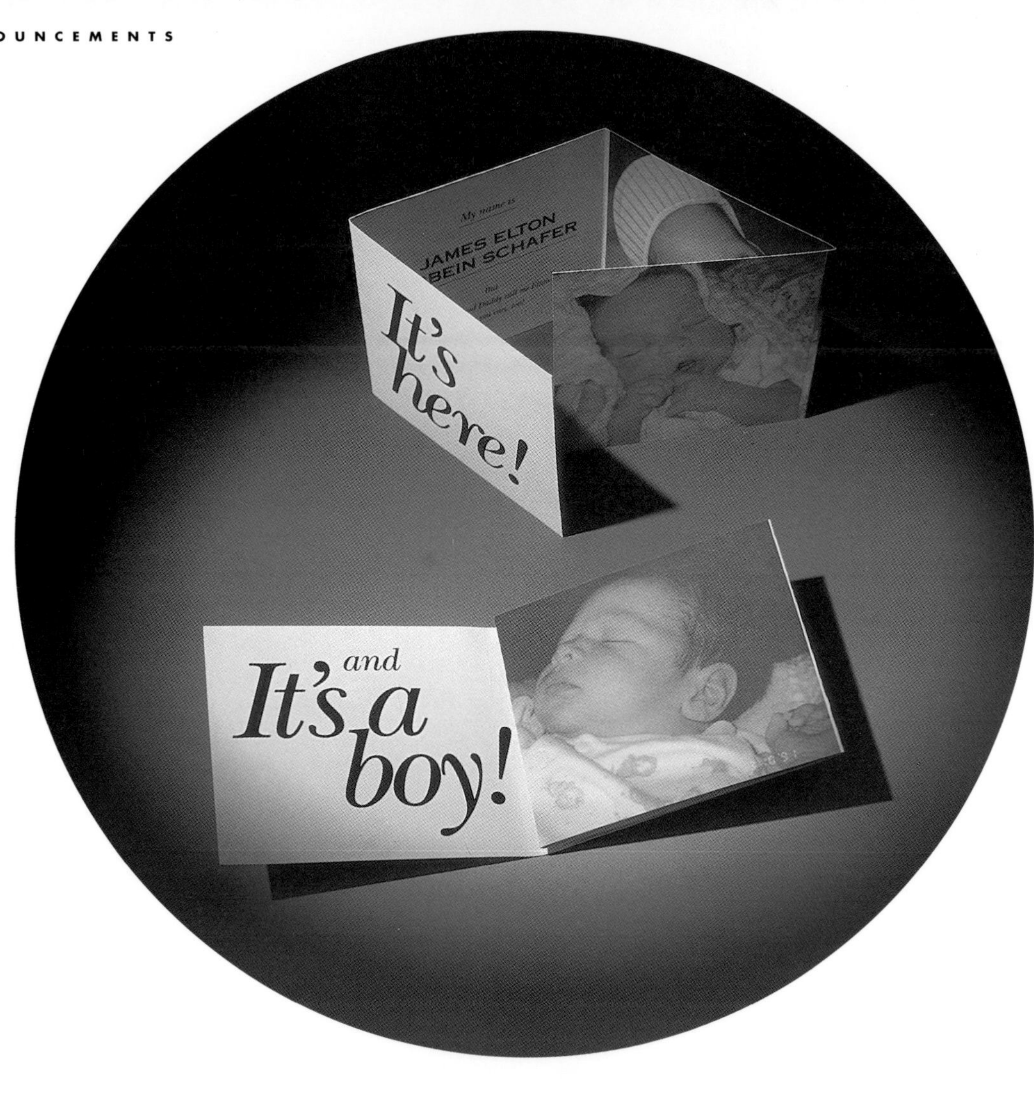

▲
Birth announcement
出産通知
USA 1991
CD,AD,D,P,CW:Pepe Orbein
DF:Pepe Orbein & Associates
CL:Pepe Orbein & Anita Schafer

▼
Birth announcement
出産通知
CANADA 1990
AD,D:Michéle Miodonski
DF:Applications in Design
CL:The Corners

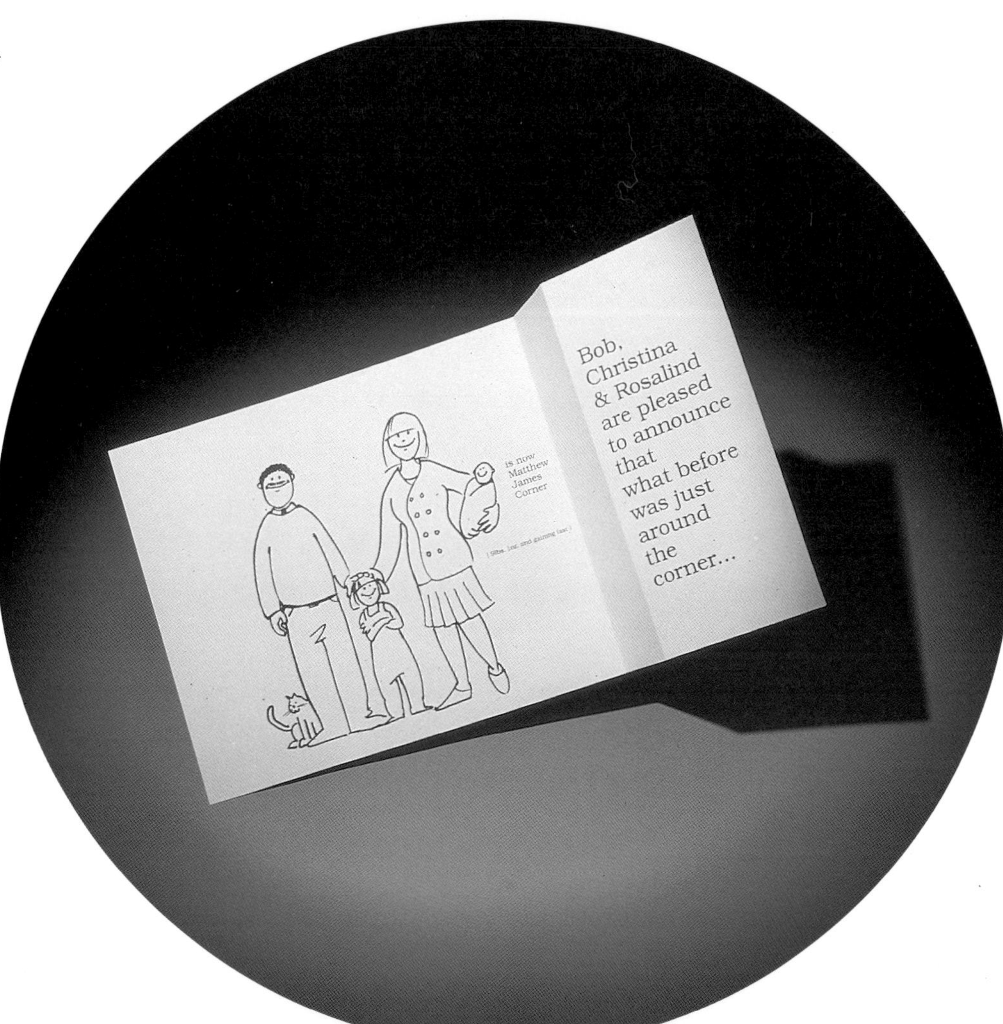

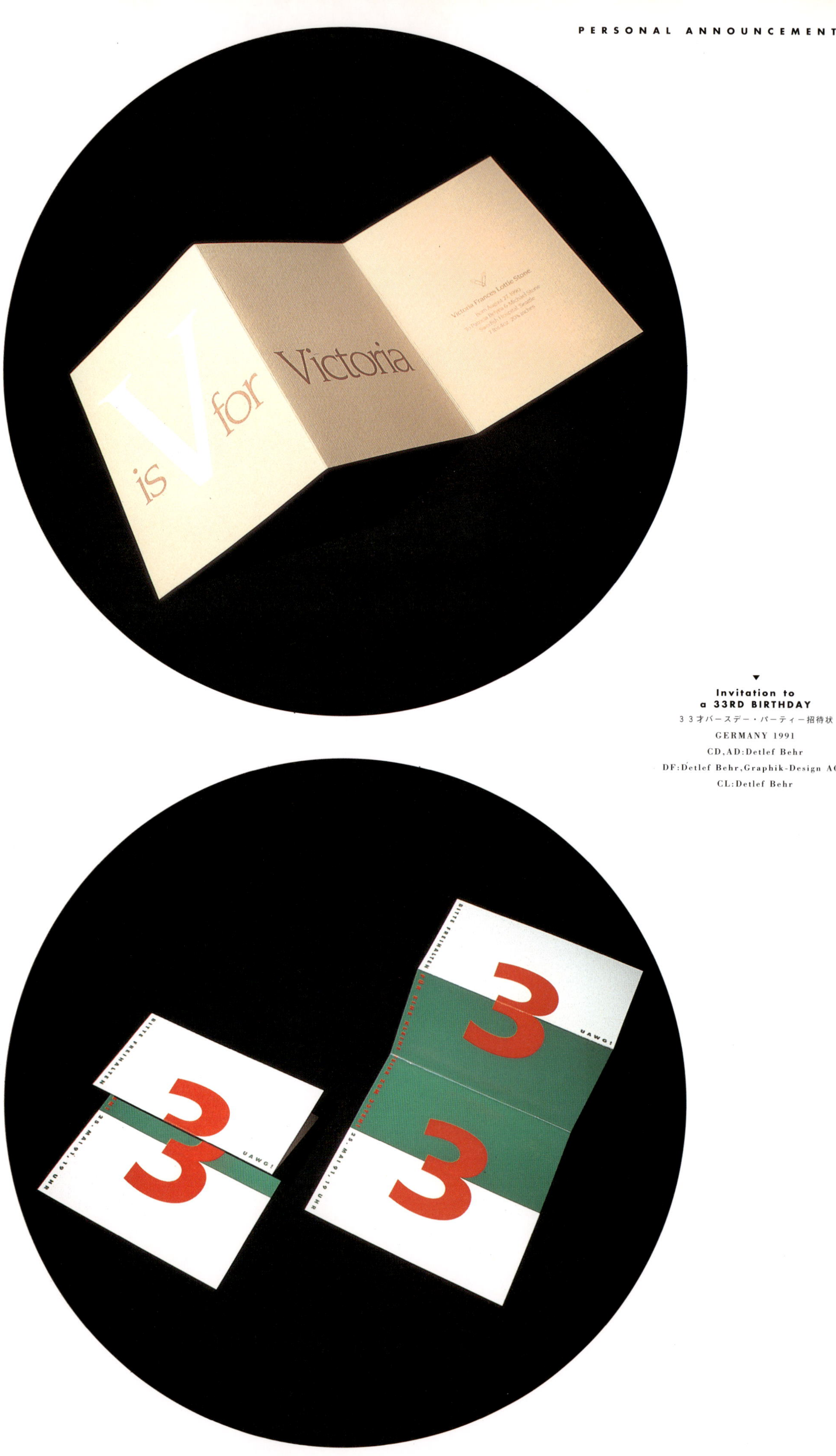

▲
Birth announcement
出産通知
USA 1990
D,CW:Patricia Belyea
DF:Belyea Design
CL:Patricia Belyea and Michael Stone

▼
Invitation to a 33RD BIRTHDAY
33才バースデー・パーティー招待状
GERMANY 1991
CD,AD:Detlef Behr
DF:Detlef Behr,Graphik-Design AGD
CL:Detlef Behr

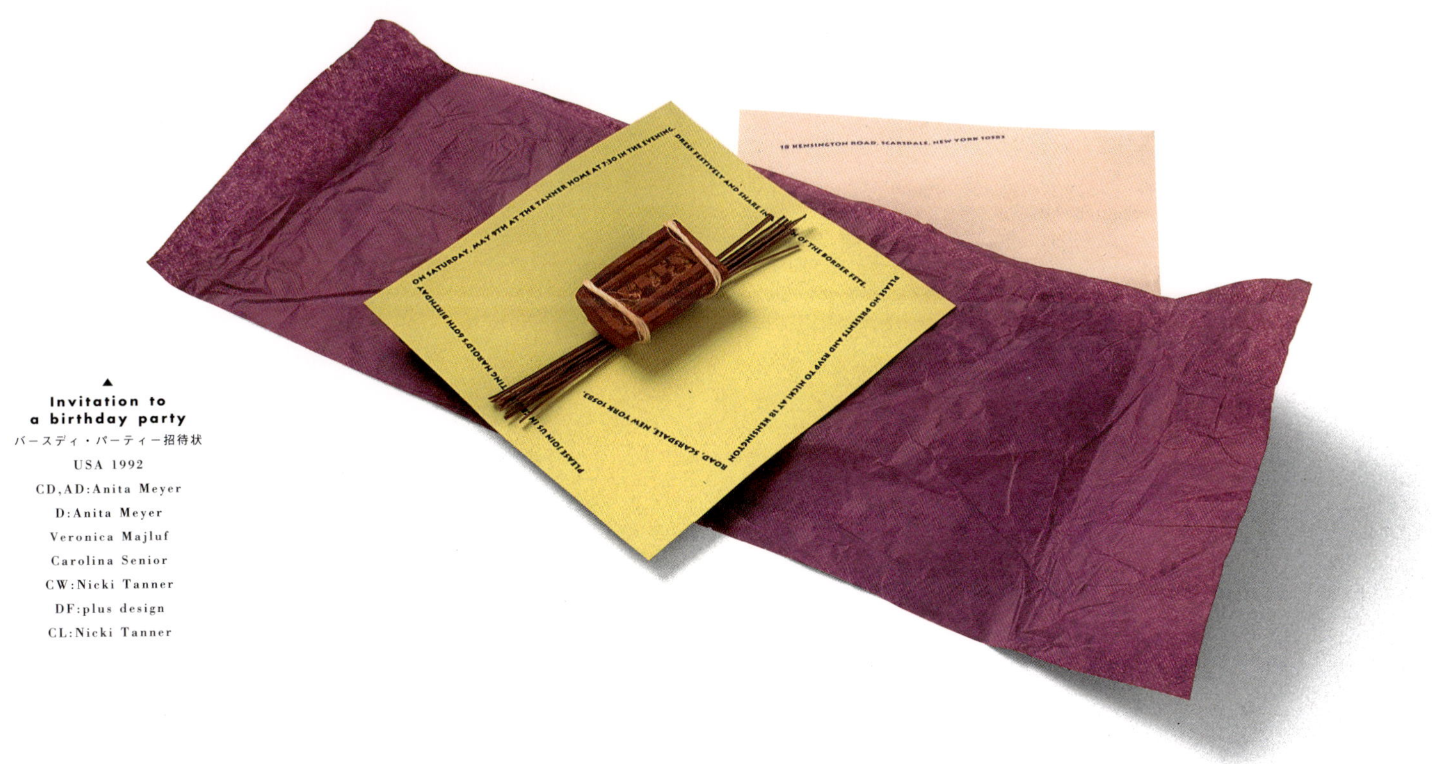

▲
Invitation to a birthday party
バースディ・パーティー招待状
USA 1992
CD,AD:Anita Meyer
D:Anita Meyer
Veronica Majluf
Carolina Senior
CW:Nicki Tanner
DF:plus design
CL:Nicki Tanner

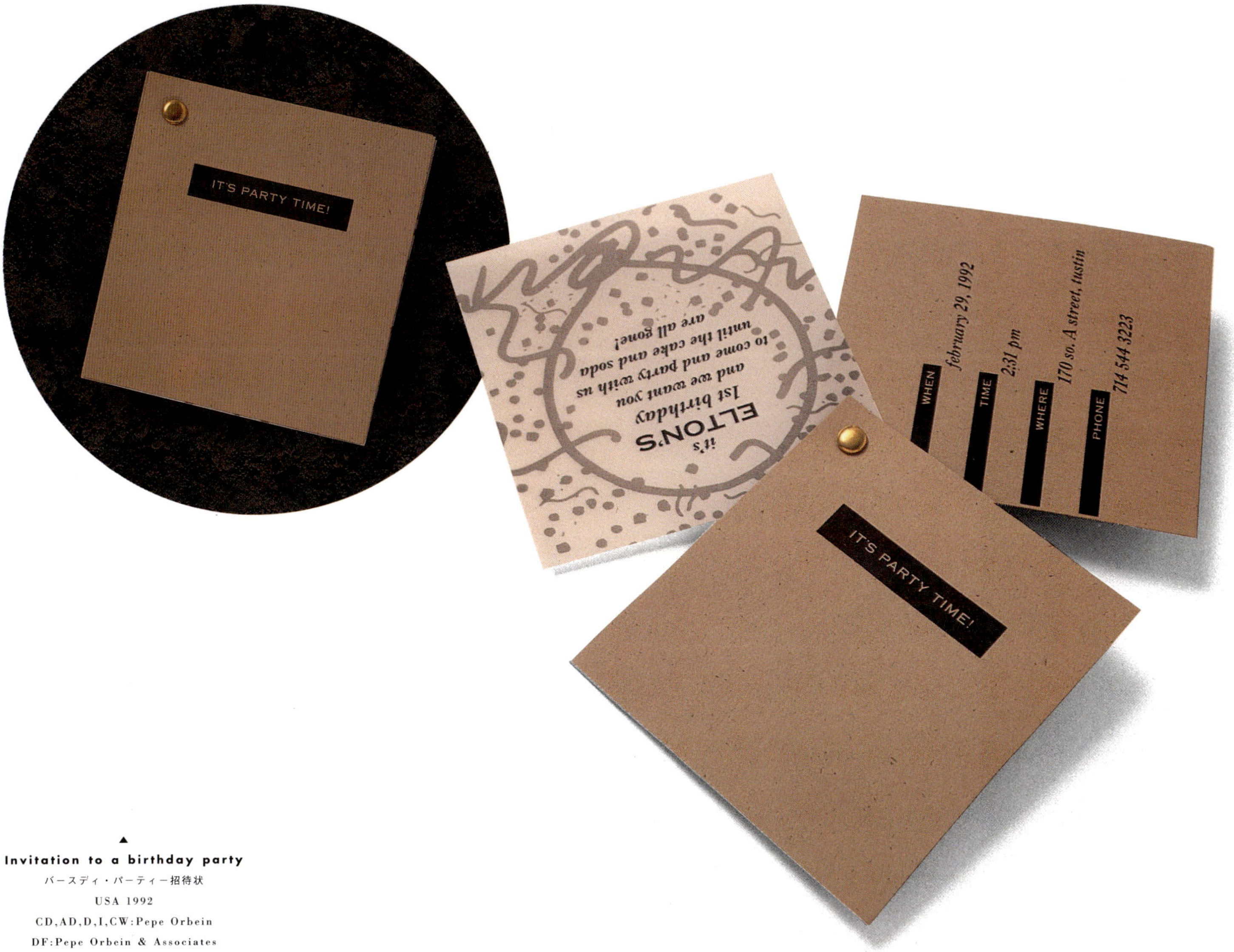

▲
Invitation to a birthday party
バースディ・パーティー招待状
USA 1992
CD,AD,D,I,CW:Pepe Orbein
DF:Pepe Orbein & Associates
CL:Pepe Orbein & Anita Schafer

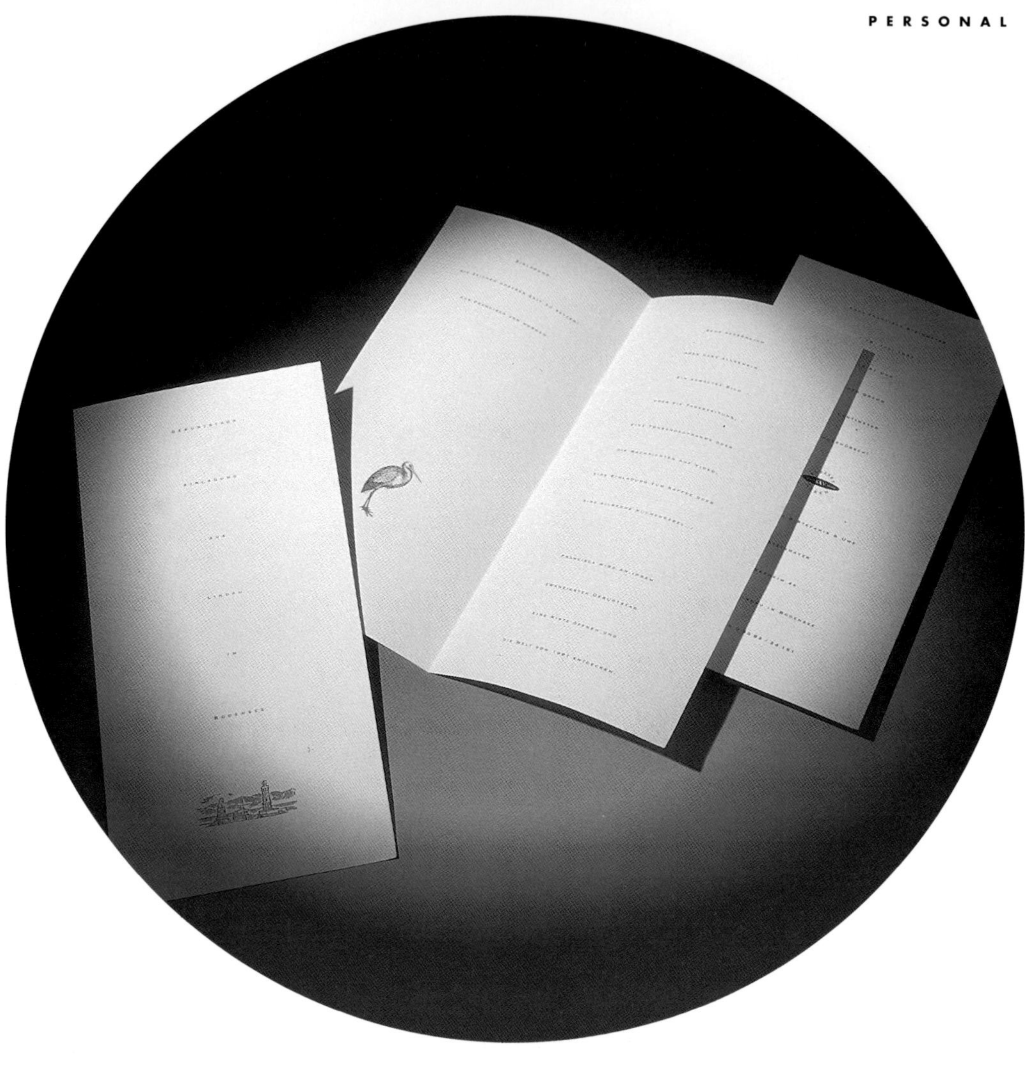

▲

Birth announcement

出産通知

GERMANY 1991

CD,AD,D:Uwe Steinmayer

CW:Stefanie & Uwe Steinmayer

CL:Family Steinmayer

▼

Birth announcement

出産通知

USA 1987

CD,AD,D:Rick Eiber

CW:Sam Angeloff

DF:Rick Eiber Design

CL:Sam Angeloff & Suky Hutton

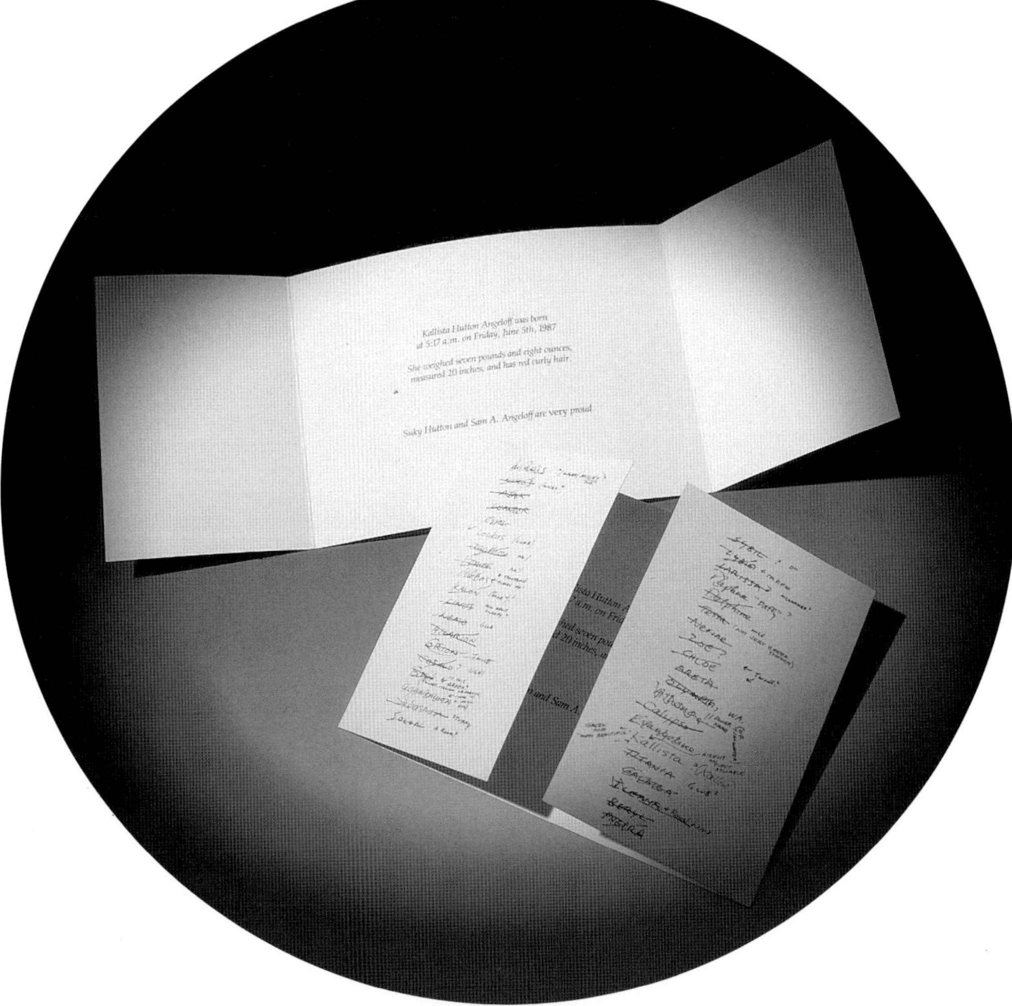

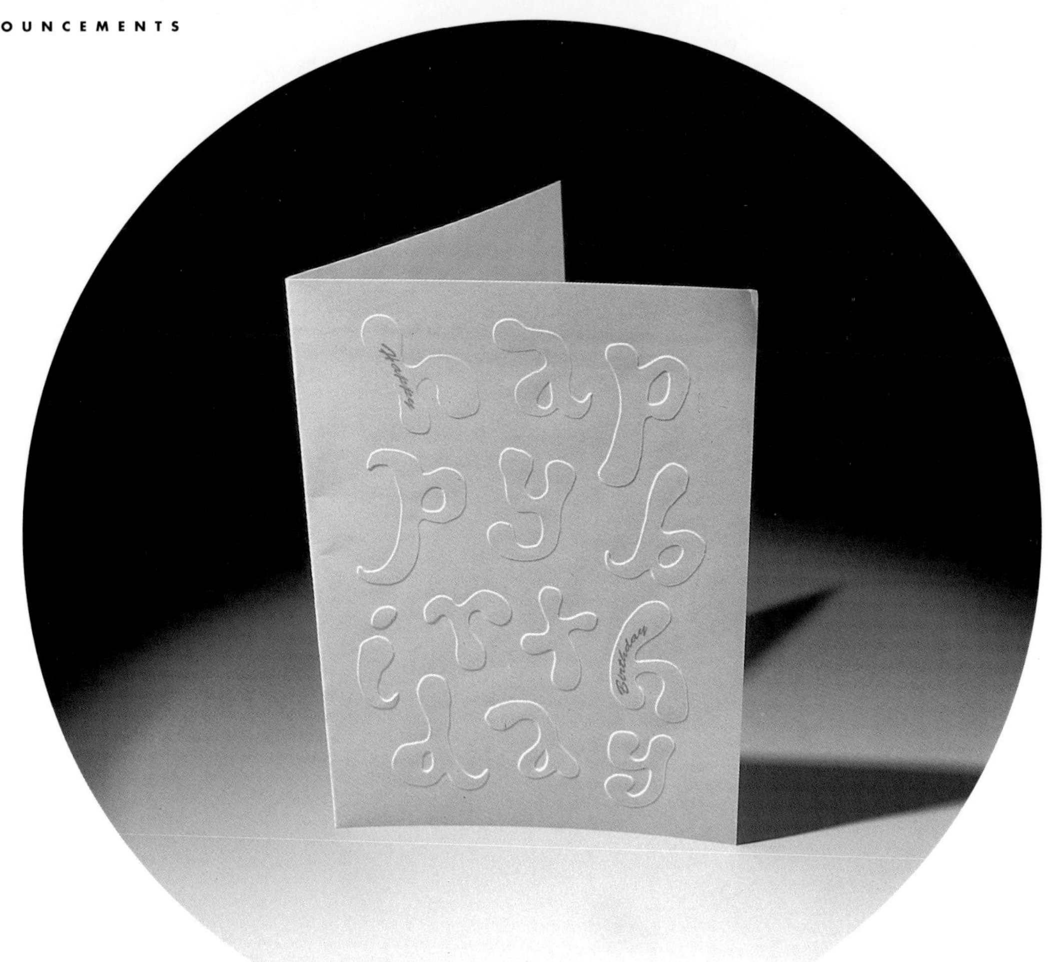

▲
Birthday card
バースデー・カード
AUSTRALIA 1992
CD,AD,D,I:Andrew Hoyne
DF:Andrew Hoyne Design
CL:Enzo Presley Ink Design

▼
Executive placement announcement
役員就任通知
USA 1989
AD:Michael Stanard
D:Marcos Chavez
DF:Michael Stanard
CL:Douglas S. Stanard

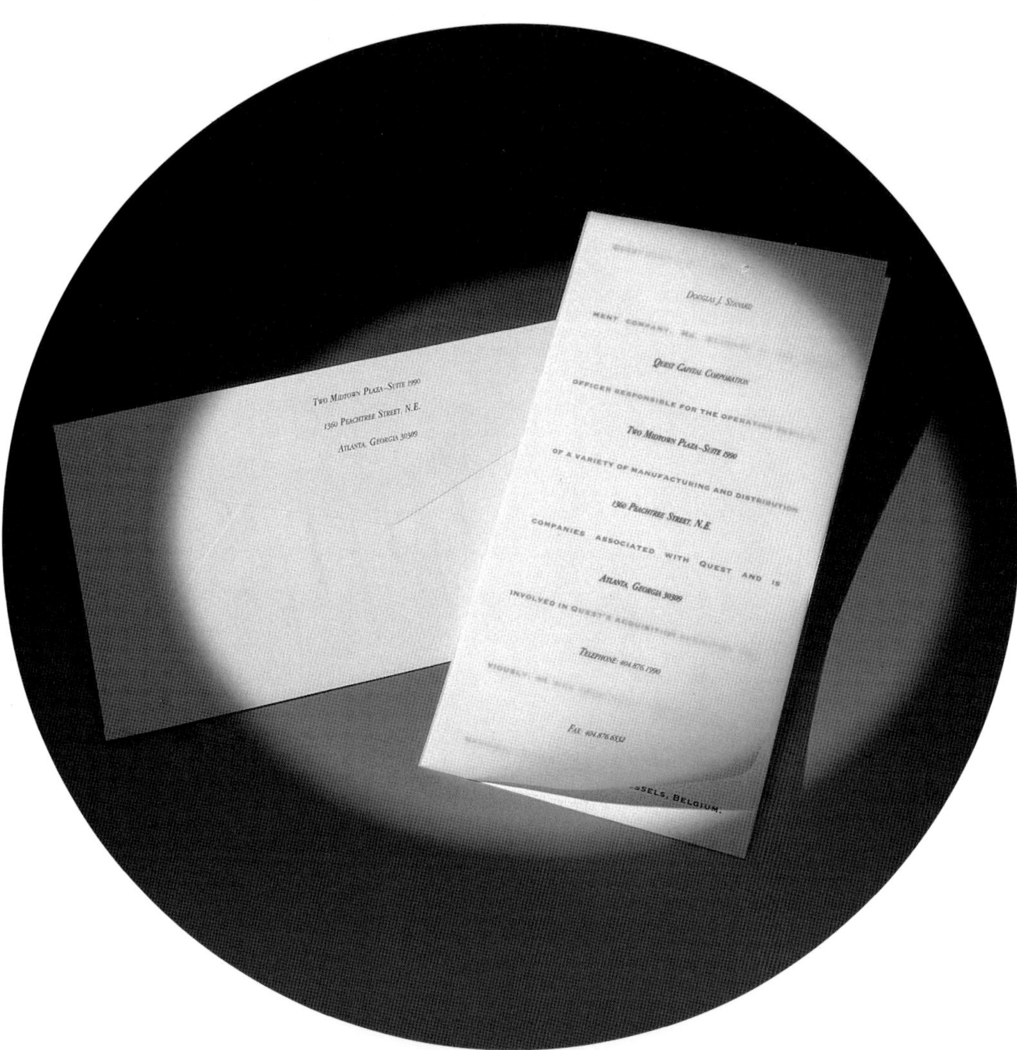

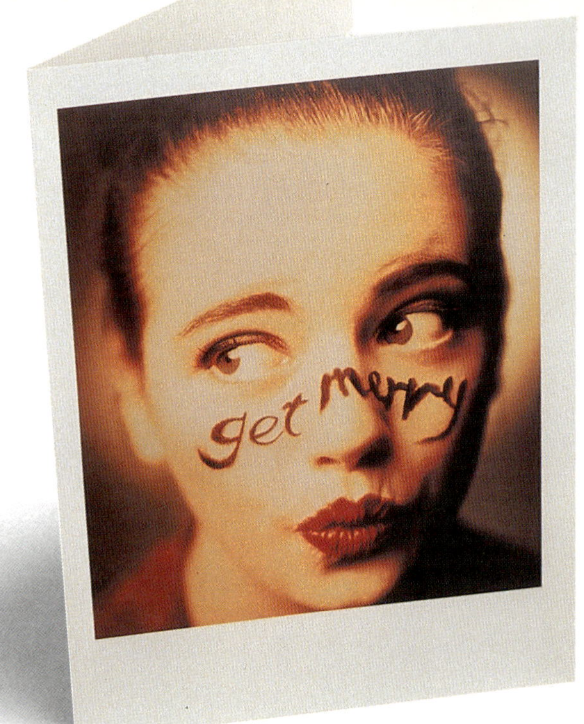

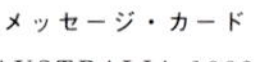

Message card
メッセージ・カード
AUSTRALIA 1992
CD,AD,D,I:Andrew Hoyne
P:Brad Taylor
DF:Andrew Hoyne Design
CL:Enzo Presley Ink Design

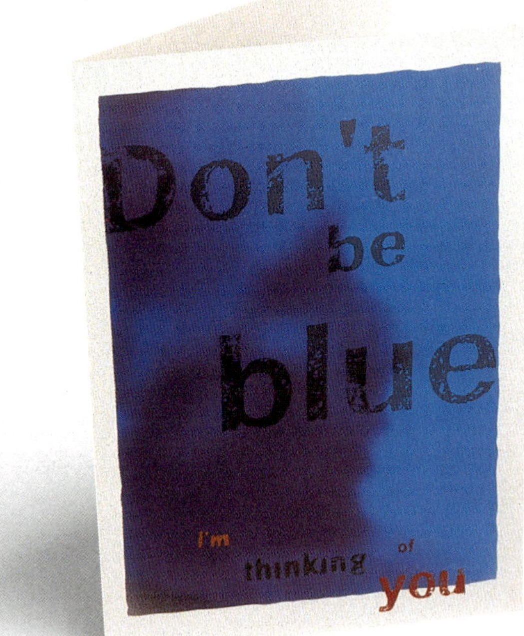

Message card
メッセージ・カード
AUSTRALIA 1992
CD,AD,D,I,CW:Andrew Hoyne
P:Rob Blackburn
DF:Andrew Hoyne Design
CL:Enzo Presley Ink Design
TC:Card Publisher

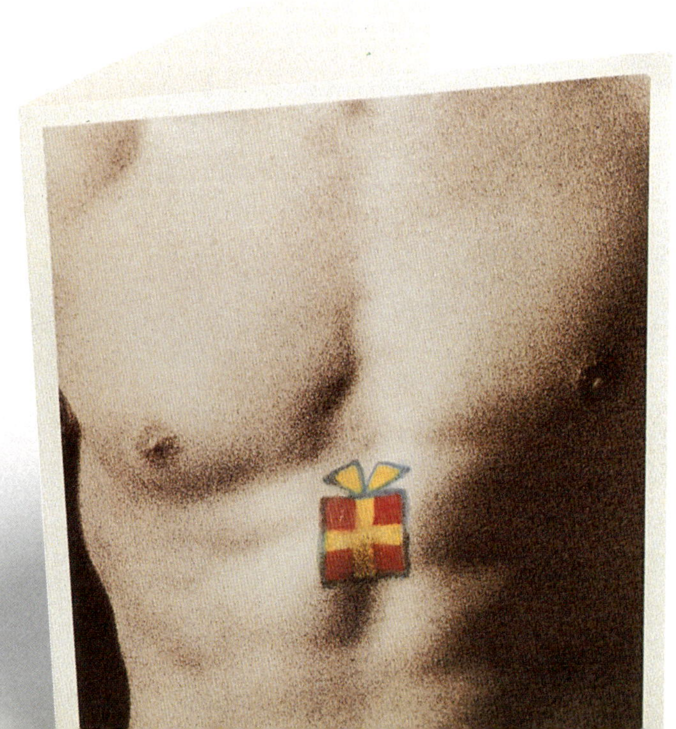

Message card
メッセージ・カード
AUSTRALIA 1992
CD,AD,D,I:Andrew Hoyne
P:Rob Blackburn
DF:Andrew Hoyne Design
CL:Enzo Presley Ink Design

◀
Message card
メッセージ・カード
AUSTRALIA 1992
CD,AD,D,I:Andrew Hoyne
DF:Andrew Hoyne Design
CL:Enzo Presley Ink Design

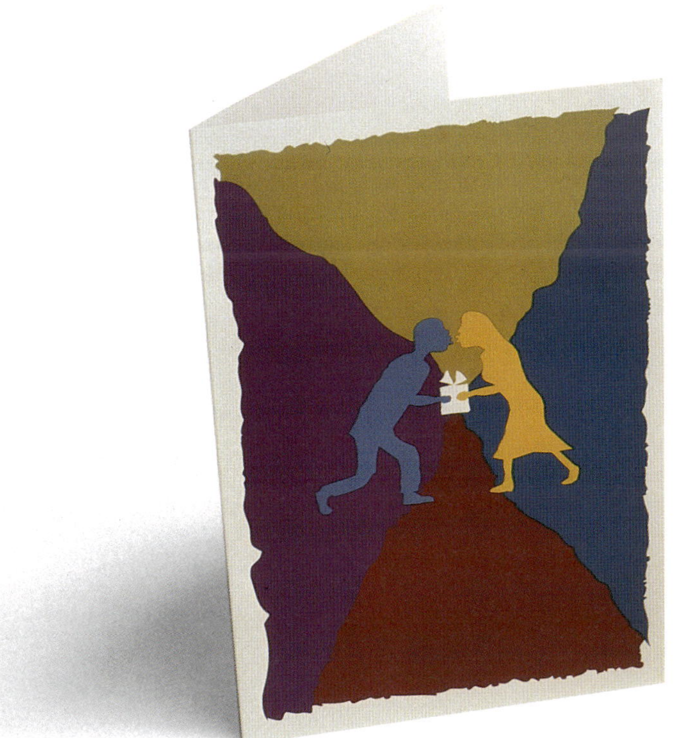

▼
Message card
メッセージ・カード
AUSTRALIA 1992
CD,AD,D:Andrew Hoyne
P:Rob Blackburn
DF:Andrew Hoyne Design
CL:Enzo Presley Ink Design
TC:Card Publisher
カード制作

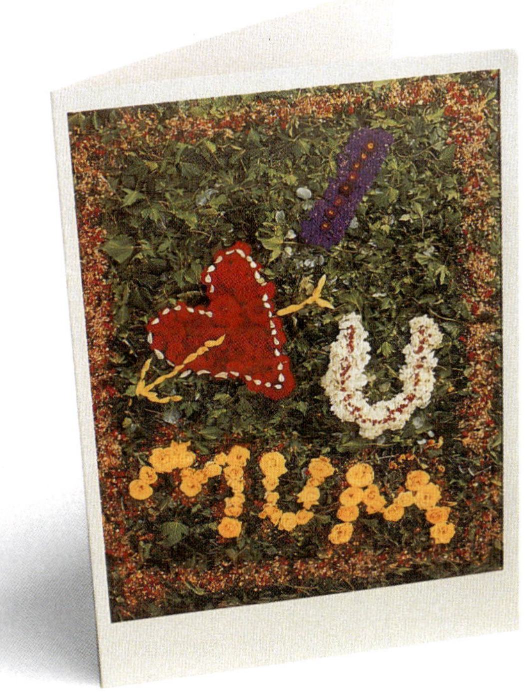

▶
Message card
メッセージ・カード
AUSTRALIA 1992
CD,AD,D,I:Andrew Hoyne
DF:Andrew Hoyne Design
CL:Enzo Presley Ink Design

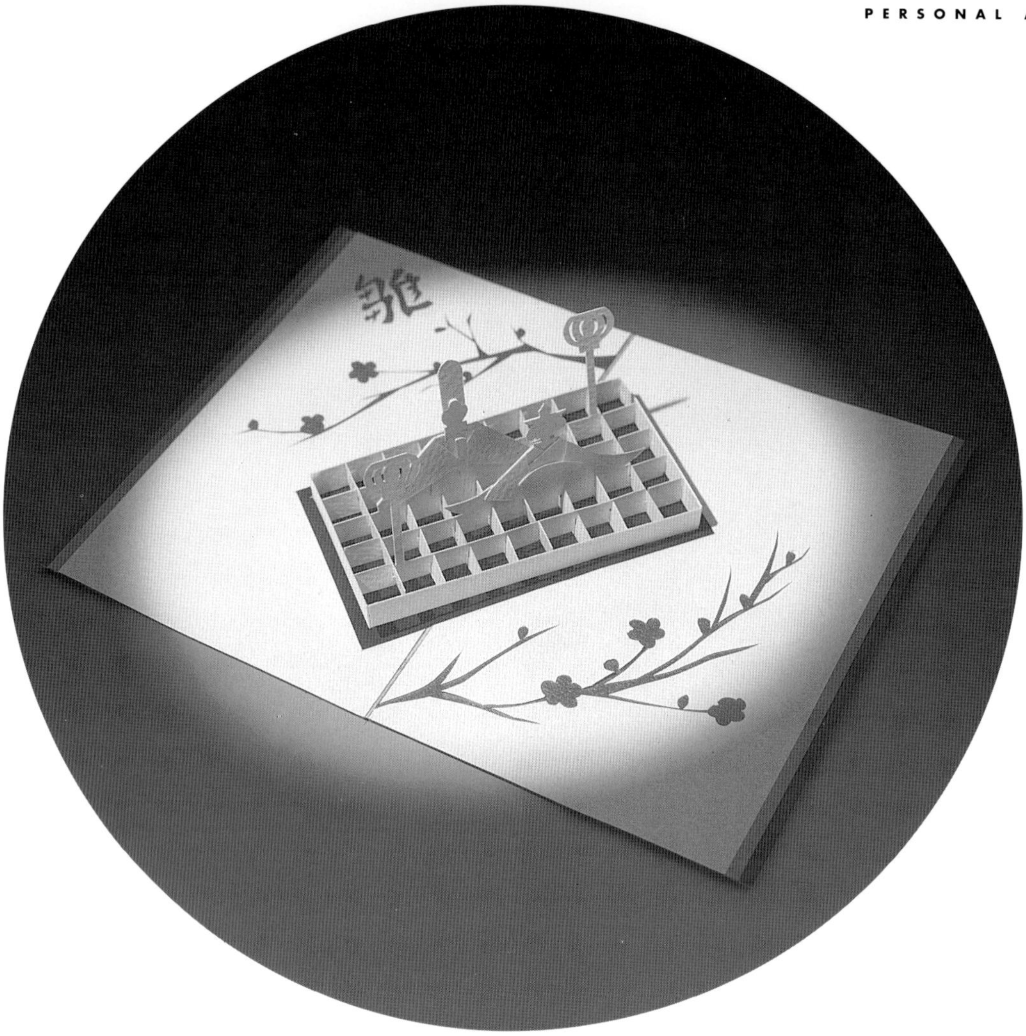

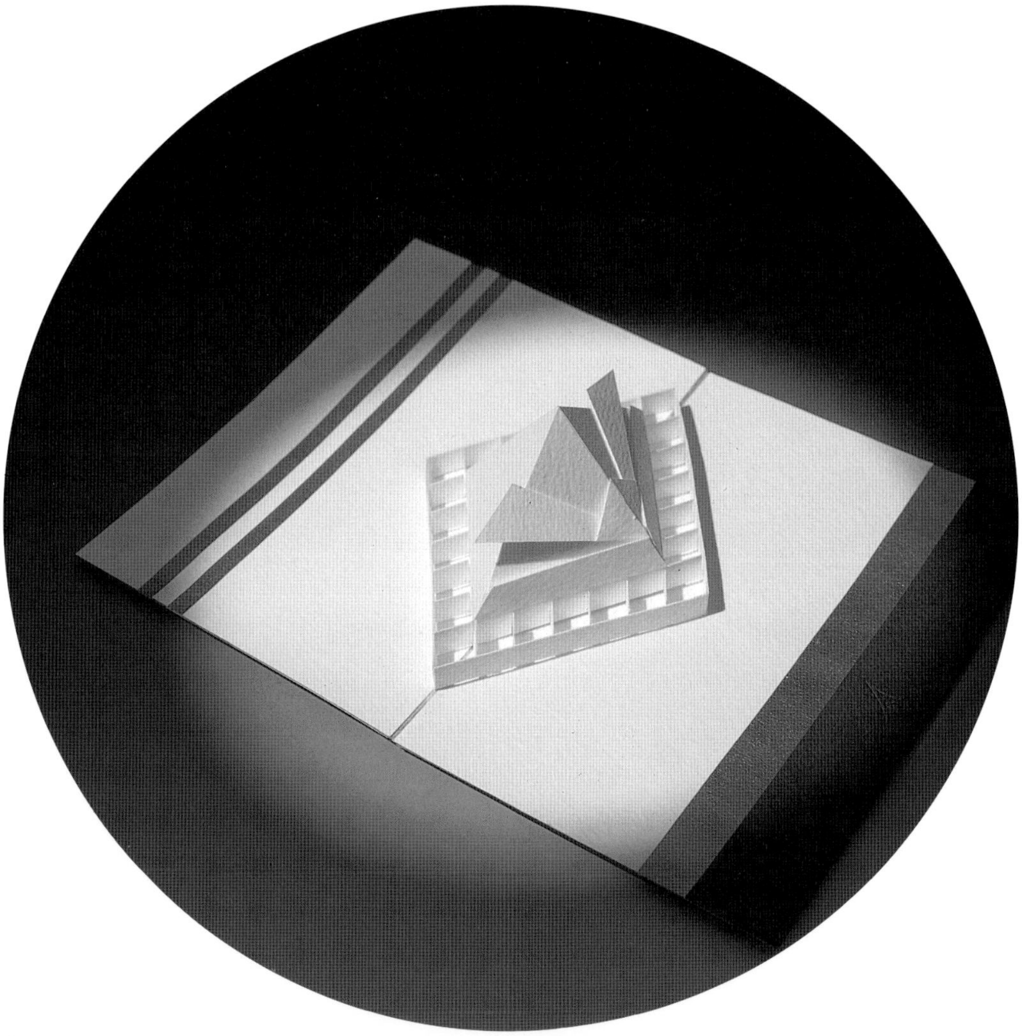

Multipurpose card
多目的カード
JAPAN 1992
D:Keiko Nakazawa
CL:Atelier Bouquet

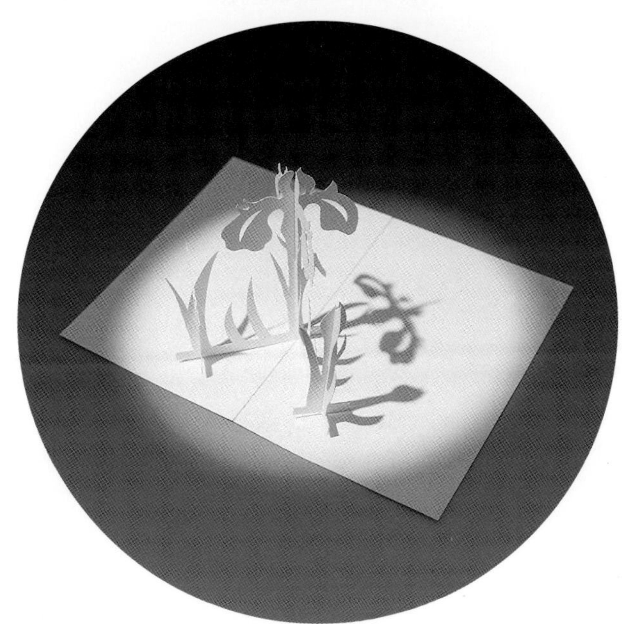

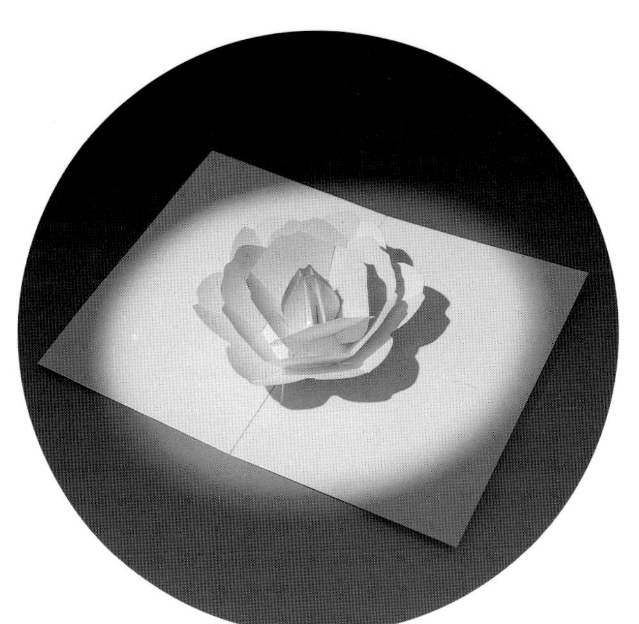

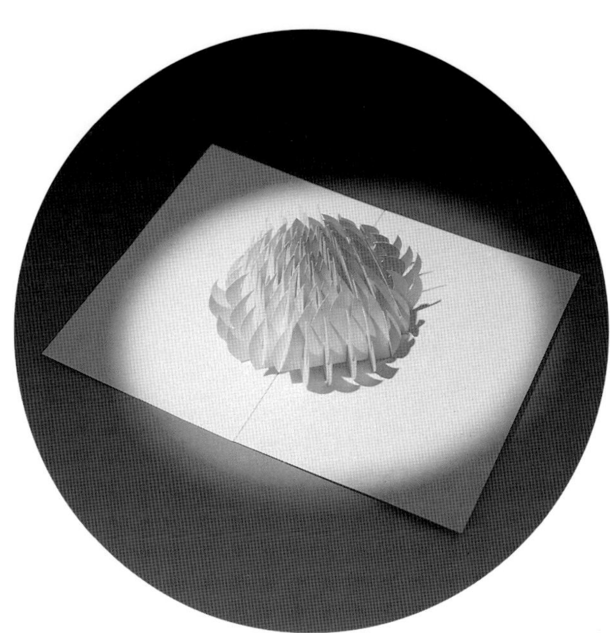

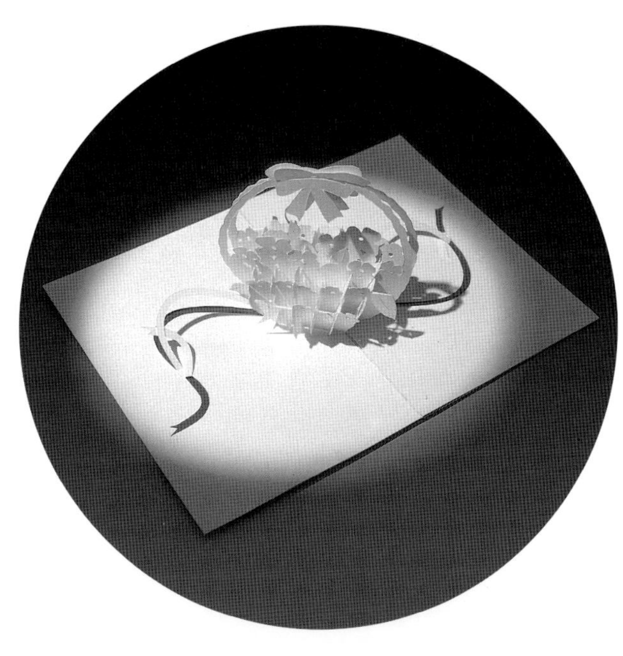

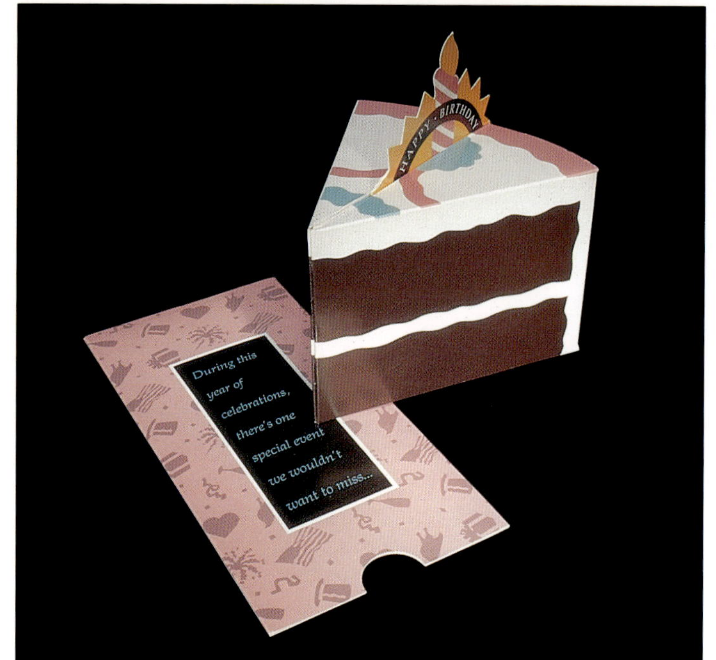

Birthday card
バースデー・カード
USA 1991
CD:Allison Hill
AD:Anthony Marterson
D,I:Tracy Sabin
DF:Sabin Design
CL:Turner Entertainment

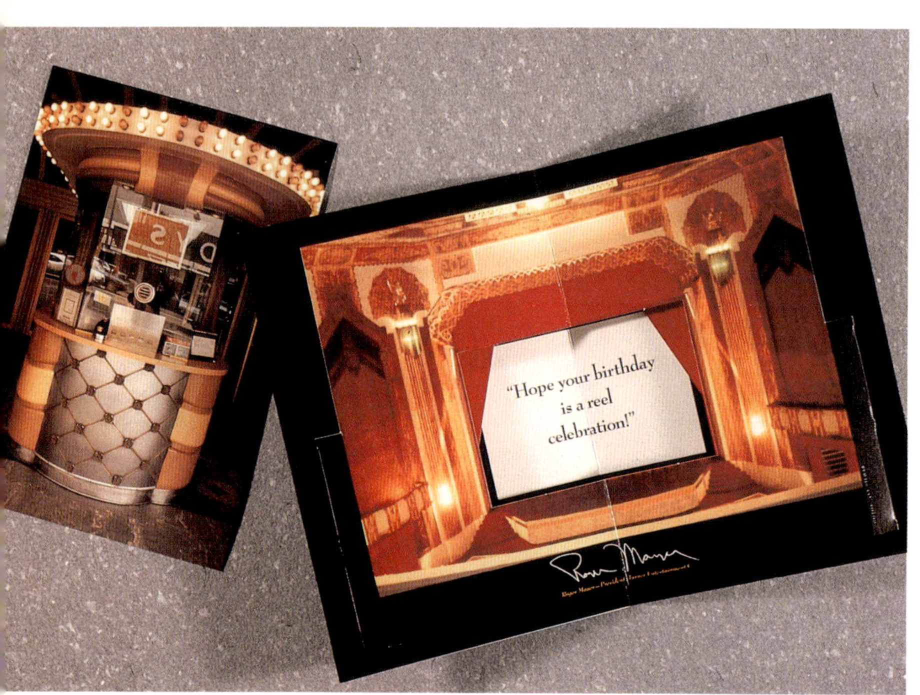

Birthday card
バースデー・カード
USA 1990
CD:Allison Hill
AD:Anthony Marterson
D:Tracy Sabin
P:Ave Pildas
DF:Sabin Design
CL:Turner Entertainment

Birthday card
バースデー・カード
USA 1992
CD:Allison Hill
AD:Anthony Marterson
D,I:Tracy Sabin
DF:Sabin Design
CL:Turner Entertainment

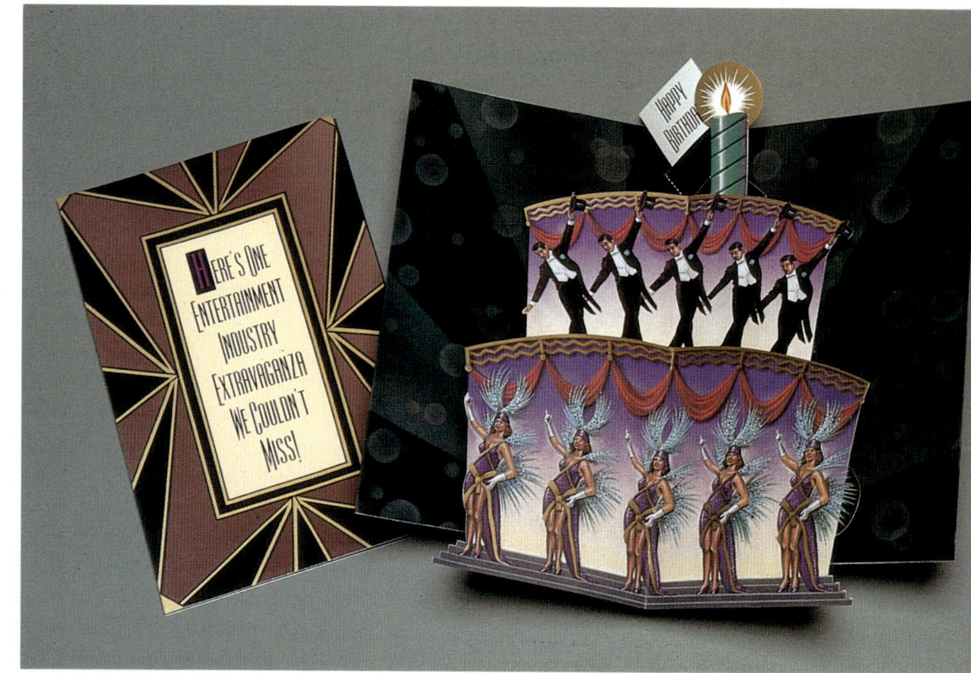

Submittor's Index

Submittor's Index

Submittor's Index

VOL. 3 ADVERTISING GREETING CARDS

Art Director
Kazuo Abe

Designers
Kazuo Abe
Shinji Ikenoue
Miyuki Kawanabe
Yoko Tanimoto

Editors
Tsutomu Hirata
Kazuhisa Yoshihara
Yuko Yoshio
Ayako Aoyama

Editorial Manager
Masato Ieshiro

Photographer
Kuniharu Fujimoto

English Translator and Consultant
write Away Co., Ltd.

English Consultant
Clive Avins

Thanks to
Megumi Hara
Naomi Sakuma

Publisher
Shingo Miyoshi

1993年 5月28日初版第1 版発行

定価 16,000 円（本体 15,534円）

発行所 ピエ・ブックス
〒170 東京都豊島区駒込4-14-6-407
Tel:03-3949-5010 Fax:03-3949-5650

製版、印刷、製版 弘陽印刷
〒116 東京都荒川区西日暮里4-8-12
Tel:03-3802-1221

Printed in Japan

ISBN4-938586-41-X C3070 P16000E

REQUEST FOR SUBMISSIONS

作品提供のお願い

P·I·E Books, as always, has several new and ambitious graphic book projects in the works which will introduce a variety of superior designs from Japan and abroad. Currently we are planning the collection series detailed below. If you have any graphics which you consider worthy for submission to these publications, please fill in the necessary information on the inserted questionnaire postcard and forward it to us. You will receive a notice when the relevant project goes into production.

ピエ・ブックスでは、今後も新しいタイプのグラフィック書籍の出版を目指すとともに、国内外の優れたデザインを幅広く紹介していきたいと考えております。今後の刊行予定として下記のコレクション・シリーズを企画しておりますので、作品提供していただける企画がございましたら、挟み込みのアンケートハガキに必要事項を記入の上お送り下さい。企画が近づきましたらそのつど案内書をお送りいたします。

A. POSTCARD GRAPHICS

A collection of various types of postcards including product advertising, direct mailers, invitations to events such as parties and fashion shows as well as birthday cards and seasonal greetings. In short all sorts of cards except the letter type which are mailed in envelopes.

A．ポストカード・グラフィックス

各シーズンのグリーティングカードをはじめとして、商品広告ＤＭ、パーティーやコレクション等のイベントのお知らせ、バースデイカードなど封書タイプを除く様々なポストカードをコレクションします。

B. ADVERTISING GREETING CARDS

A collection of letter-style direct mailers including sales promotional sheets, invitations to events such as exhibitions, parties and weddings. Some of these are quite simple, some have unusual shapes or dimensions (limited to cards inserted in envelopes).

B．アドバタイジング・グリーティングカード

販促用のＤＭ、展示会・イベントの案内状やパーティや結婚式などの招待状など、プレーンなものから形状の変わったもの・立体になったものまで封書タイプのＤＭをコレクションします。（封書タイプのものに限ります）

C. BROCHURE & PAMPHLET COLLECTION

A collection of brochures and pamphlets categorized according to the business of the client company. Includes sales promotional pamphlets, product catalogues, corporate image brochures gallery exhibitions, special events, annual reports and company profiles from all sorts of businesses.

C．ブローシュア＆パンフレット・コレクション

販促用パンフレット、商品カタログ、イメージ・カタログ、ギャラリーや展示会・イベントのパンフレット、アニュアル・リポート、会社案内など様々な業種のブローシュアやパンフレットを業種別にコレクションします。

D. POSTER GRAPHICS

A collection of posters, classified according to the business of the client. Fashion, department stores, automotive, food, home appliances and almost any sort of poster you might see on streets. Invitational posters for art exhibitions, concerts and plays as well as regional posters which will be seen for the first time outside of the local area where they were published.

D．ポスター・グラフィックス

ファッション、デパート、車、食品、家電など街角を飾る広告ポスター、美術展、コンサート、演劇などのイベント案内ポスター、見る機会の少ない地方のポスターなどを業種別にコレクションします。

E. BOOK COVER AND EDITORIAL DESIGNS

Editorial and cover designs for various types of books and magazines. Includes all sorts of magazines, books, comics and other visual publications.

E．ブックカバー＆エディトリアル・デザイン

雑誌、単行本、ヴィジュアル書、コミックなど様々なタイプの書籍・雑誌のエディトリアル・デザイン、カバー・デザインを紹介します。

F. CORPORATE IMAGE LOGO DESIGNS

A collection of C.I. materials mainly symbols and logos for corporations of all sorts, classified according to the type of business. In some cases, development samples and trial comps as well as the final designs are included. Includes logos for magazines and various products.

F．コーポレイト・イメージ・ロゴマーク・デザイン

企業やショップのシンボルマーク・ロゴマークを中心に幅広い業種にわたり分類しコレクションします。マークのみではなく展開例としてのアプリケーションも数多く紹介し、その他、雑誌や商品などの様々なロゴマークもコレクションします。

G. BUSINESS CARD AND LETTERHEAD GRAPHICS

A collection of cards such as the business cards of corporations and individuals as well as shopping cards for restaurants and boutiques, membership cards and various prepaid cards. This collection centers on business cards, letterheads and shopping cards of superior design.

G．ビジネスカード＆レターヘッド・グラフィックス

様々な企業や個人の名刺、レストランやブティックのショップカード、会員カード、プリペイドカードなど、デザイン的に優れたカードを名刺・ショップカードを中心にコレクション。またカードのみでなくレターヘッドも紹介します。

H. CALENDAR GRAPHICS

A collection of visually interesting calendars. We do not take into account the form of the calendar, i.e. wall hanging-type or note-type or desktop-type etc. So that the calendars represent the widest range of possibilities.

H．カレンダー・グラフィックス

ヴィジュアル的に優れたカレンダーをコレクションします。壁掛けタイプ、ノートタイプ、ダイアリー、日めくりタイプ、卓上タイプなど形状にはこだわらず幅広い分野の様々なタイプのカレンダーを紹介します。

I. PACKAGE AND WRAPPING GRAPHICS

A collection of packaging and wrapping materials of superior design from Japan and abroad. Includes related accessories such as labels and ribbons and almost anything else that comes under the heading of containing, protecting and decorating things.

I．パッケージ＆ラッピング・グラフィックス

商品そのもののパッケージデザインはもちろん、いろいろな物を包む、保護する、飾るというコンセプトで国内外の優れたパッケージ、ケース、ラッピング・デザイン及びラベル、リボンなどの付属アクセサリー類を幅広く紹介します。

DEMANDE DE SOUMISSIONS

AUFFORDERUNG ZU MITARBEIT

Comme toujours, P・I・E Books a dans ses ateliers plusieurs projets de livres graphiques neufs et ambitieux qui introduiront une gamme de modèles supérieurs en provenance du Japon et de l'étranger. Nous prévoyons en ce moment la série de collections détaillée cidessous. Si vous êtes en possession d'un graphique que vous jugez digne de soumettre à ces publications, nous vous prions de remplir les informations nécessaires sur l'étiquette à renvoyer située à la carte postale questionnaire insérée et de nous la faire parvenir. Vous recevrez un avis lorsque le projet correspondant passera à la production.

Wie immer hat P・I・E Books einige neue anspruchsvolle Grafikbücher in Arbeit, die eine Vielzahl von hervorragenden Designs aus Japan und anderen Ländern vorstellen werden. Momentan planen wir eine Serie mit den nachfolgend aufgeführten Themen.
Wenn Sie grafische Darstellungen besitzen, von denen Sie meinen, daß sie in diese Veröffentlichung aufgenommen werden könnten, geben Sie uns bitte die nötigen Informationen auf der entsprechenden Antwortseite am füllen Sie die beigelegte Antwortkarte aus und schicken Sie sie an uns. Wir werden Sie benachrichtigen, wenn das entsprechende Projekt in Arbeit geht.

A. Graphiques pour cartes postales
Une collection de divers types de cartes postales, y compris la publicité de produits, l'adressage direct, des invitations à des événements tels que soirées et défilés de mode, ainsi que des cartes d'anniversaire et des voeux de saison. En bref, toutes sortes de cartes, à part le type lettre qui sera envoyé dans des enveloppes.

B. Cartes de voeux publicitaires
Une collection d'adressages directs style lettre y compris des feuilles de promotion de ventes, des invitations à des événements tels qu'expositions, soirées et mariages. Certaines d'entre elles sont très simples, d'autres ont des formes ou dimensions inhabituelles (limitées aux cartes insérées dans des enveloppes).

C. Collection de brochures et de pamphlets
Une collection de brochures et de pamphlets triées en fonction des affaires de la société client. Comprend des pamphlets de promotion des ventes, des catalogues de produits, des brochures sur l'image de la société, des expositions de galerie, des événements spéciaux, des compte-rendus annuels et des profils de sociétés de toutes sortes d'affaires.

D. Graphiques sur affiche
Une collection d'affiches, classées en fonction du secteur d'affaires du client. La mode, les grands magasins, l'automobile, l'alimentation, les appareils électro-ménagers et presque tous les types d'affiche que vous pouvez voir dans les rues. Des affiches invitant à des expositions d'art, des concerts et des pièces ainsi que des affiches régionales qui seront vues pour la première fois en dehors de la région où elles ont été éditées.

E. Designs de couverture de livre et d'éditorial
Des designs de livre et d'éditorial de divers types de livres et magazines. Comprend toutes sortes de magazines, livres, bandes dessinées et autres publications visuelles.

F. Designs de logo d'image de société
Une collection de matériaux d'image de société, principalement des symboles et des logos pour sociétés de toutes sortes ; classés en fonction du type d'affaires. Dans certains cas, sont inclus des échantillons de développement et également des compositions d'essai ainsi que les designs finaux. Comprend des logos pour magazines et divers produits.

G. Graphiques pour en-têtes et cartes de visite
Une collection de cartes telles que les cartes de visite de sociétés et d'individus ainsi que les cartes de fidélité de restaurants et de boutiques, les cartes de membre et diverses cartes payées à l'avance. Cette collection se concentre sur les cartes de visite, les en-têtes et les cartes de fidélité d'une qualité supérieure.

H. Graphiques pour calendrier
Une collection de calendriers visuellement intéressants. Nous ne tenons pas compte de la forme du calendrier, c.-à-d., type à accrocher au mur, type carnet ou type bureau, etc. de telle sorte que les calendriers représentent la gamme de possibilités la plus large.

I. Graphiques pour emballage et paquetage
Une collection de matériaux d'emballage et de paquetage de qualité supérieure en provenance du Japon et de l'étranger. Comprend des accessoires en relation tels qu'étiquettes et rubans, et presque tout ce qui est destiné à contenir, protéger et décorer des choses.

A. Postkarten-Grafik
Zusammenstellung verschiedener Postkartenarten, und zwar für Produktwerbung, Direkt Mailing, Einladungen zu Parties und Modenschauen sowie Geburtstagskarten und Karten zu verschiedenen Jahreszeiten. Also alle Arten von Karten, ausgenommen Briefkarten.

B. Werbe-Grußkarten
Zusammenstellung briefähnlicher Direkt-Mailings, wie z.B. verkaufsfördernde Texte, Einladungen zu Anlässen wie Ausstellungen, Parties oder Hochzeiten. Einige von ihnen sind recht einfach gemacht, andere fallen durch ungewöhnliches Aussehen oder Größe auf (Karten dürfen Umschlaggröße nicht überschreiten).

C. Zusammenstellung von Broschüren und Druckschriften
Diese Zusammenstellung von Broschüren und Druckschriften ist nach den Tätigkeiten der Kundenfirmen geordnet. Sie beinhaltet verkaufsfördernde Broschüren, Produktkataloge, Corporate-Image-Broschüren, Galerieausstellungen, besondere Veranstaltungen und Firmenprofile für alle Arten von Unternehmen.

D. Postergrafik
Eine Zusammenstellung von Postern, die nach dem Geschäftsgebiet des Kunden geordnet sind. Mode Kaufhäuser, Kraftfahrzeuge, Nahrungsmittel, Haushaltsgeräte und fast jede Art von Postern, die auf der Straße zu sehen sind. Einladungsposter für Kunstausstellungen, Konzerte und Theaterstücke ebenso wie Poster mit regionalen Themen, die zum ersten Mal außerhalb des Gebietes, in dem sie aufgehängt wurden, zu sehen sein werden.

E. Bucheinbände und redaktionelles Design
Bucheinbände und redaktionelles Design für verschiedenste Buch- und Zeitschriftentypen. Dies schließt alle Arten von Zeitschriften, Büchern, Comics und anderen visuellen Publikationen ein.

F. Corporate-Image-Logo-Design
Dies ist eine Zusammenstellung von C.I.-Material, und zwar hauptsächlich von Symbolen und Logos für Firmen aller Art, nach Geschäftsgebieten geordnet. In manchen Fällen sind die Arbeiten der Entwicklungsphase und Probeexemplare ebenso miteinbezogen wie das endgültige Design. Logos für Zeitschriften und andere Produkte sind miteingeschlossen.

G.Visitenkarten und Briefkopt-Grafik
Dies ist eine Zusammenstellung verschiedener Visitenkarten, z.B. für Firmen und Einzelpersonen, Kreditkarten für Restaurants und Boutiquen, Mitgliedskarten und Vorverkaufskarten. Diese Sammlung konzentriert sich vor allem auf geschäftliche Karten, Briefköpfe und Geschäftseigene Kreditkarten mit herausragendem Design.

H. Kalendergrafik
Eine Zusammenstellung von optisch interessanten Kalendern. Es ist für uns dabei unwichtig, ob es sich um die Form des Wandkalenders, Tischkalenders oder Notizbuchkalenders handelt, sodaß die größtmögliche Vielfalt an Kalendern gezeigt werden kann.

I. Grafik auf Verpackungen und Verpackungsmaterial
Eine Zusammenstellung von Grafik auf Verpackungen und Verpackungsmaterial mit herausragendem Design aus Japan und anderen Ländern. Dazugehörige Accessoires wie Etiketten und Bänder sind eingeschlossen, ebenso wie fast alles, was als Behälter für Produkte dienen kann, sie ziert oder schützt.

THE P·I·E COLLECTION

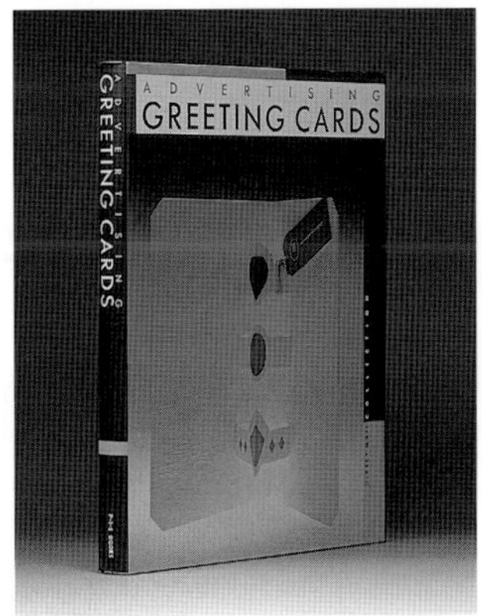

ADVERTISING GREETING CARDS 1
Pages: 224(144 in color) ¥15,000
業種別ダイレクトメールの集大成
A collection of more than 500 direct mail pieces selected from thousands used throughout Japan. Cards were selected for their distinctive design and include 3-D pop-ups, special die-cuts, folds and embossings.

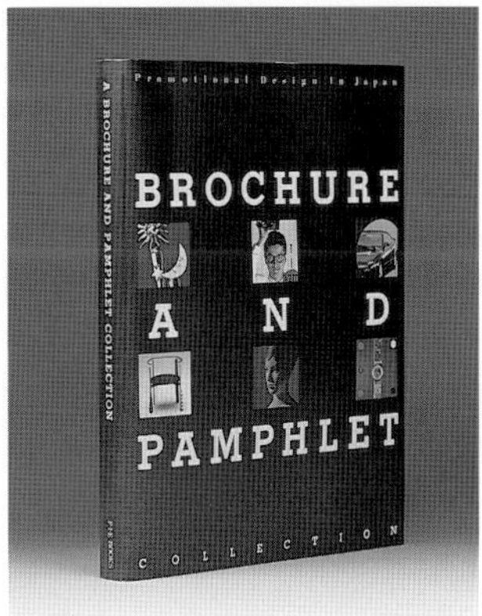

BROCHURE & PAMPHLET COLLECTION 1
Pages: 224(144 in color) ¥15,000
業種別カタログ・コレクション
Here are hundreds of the best brochures and pamphlets from Japan.
This collection will make a valuable sourcebook for anyone involved in corporate identity advertising and graphic design.

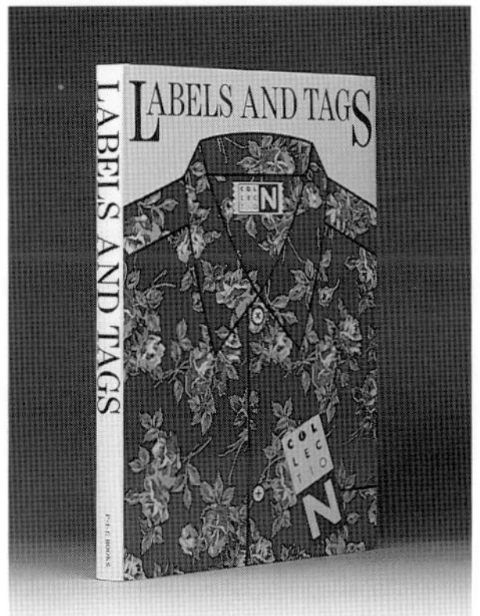

LABELS AND TAGS
Pages: 224(192 in color) ¥15,000
ファッションのラベル&タグ・コレクション
Over 1,600 garment labels representing 450 brands produced in Japan are included in this full-color collection.

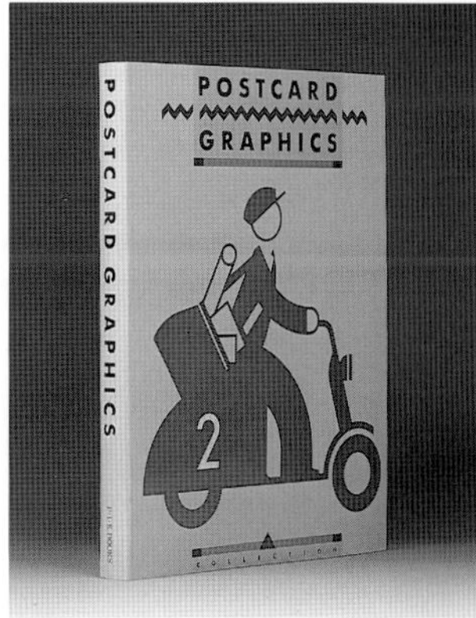

POSTCARD GRAPHICS 2
Pages: 240(208 in color) ¥16,000
好評！ 業種別ポストカードの第２弾
Here are 1,500 promotional postcards created by Japan's top design talent.
A wide range of clients are represented including 120 fashion houses and 90 major retailers. Presented in striking full color.

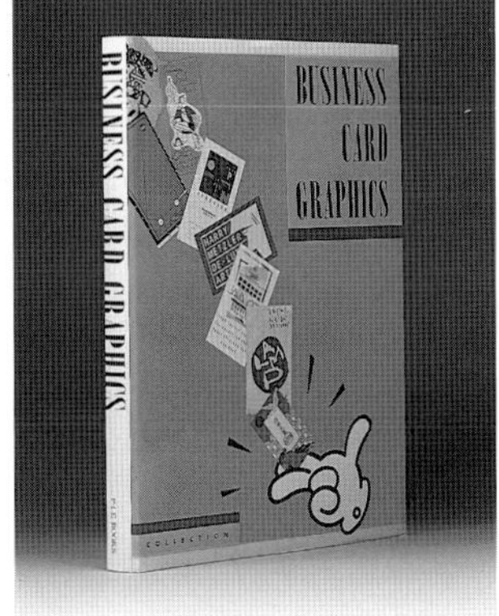

BUSINESS CARD GRAPHICS 1
Pages: 256(160 in color) ¥16,000
世界の名刺&ショップカード集大成
Over 1,200 business cards are presented in this international collection.
Created by 500 of the world's top design firms, designers will discover a wealth of new ideas in this remarkable collection.

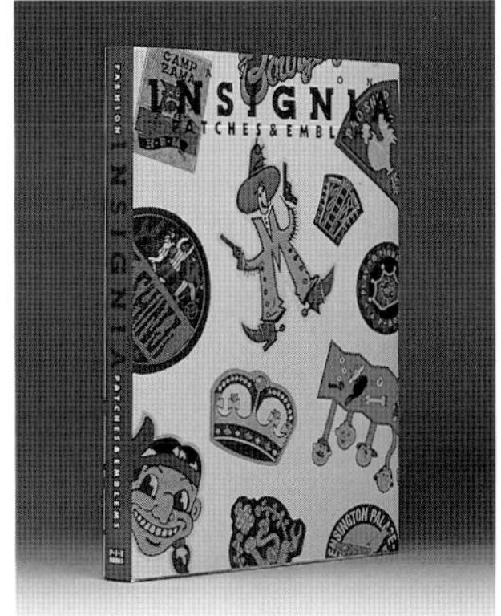

FASHION INSIGNIA
Pages: 224(208 in color) ¥16,000
ファッションのワッペン・コレクション
One thousand full-color emblems have been gathered in this beautiful and sometimes playful collection.
The great variety of color and shape demonstrates the versatility of embroidery art.

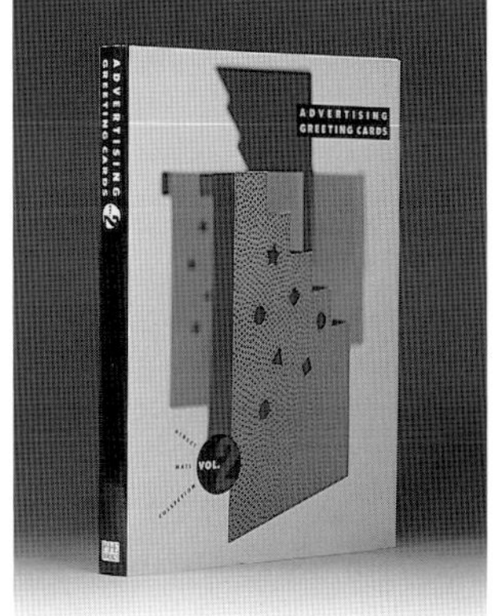

ADVERTISING GREETING CARDS 2
Pages: 224(176 in color) ¥16,000
世界のダイレクトメール・コレクション
500 visually remarkable works representing a variety of businesses. Pieces include new product announcements, invitation cards and direct mail envelopes. An excellent image bank for graphic designers.

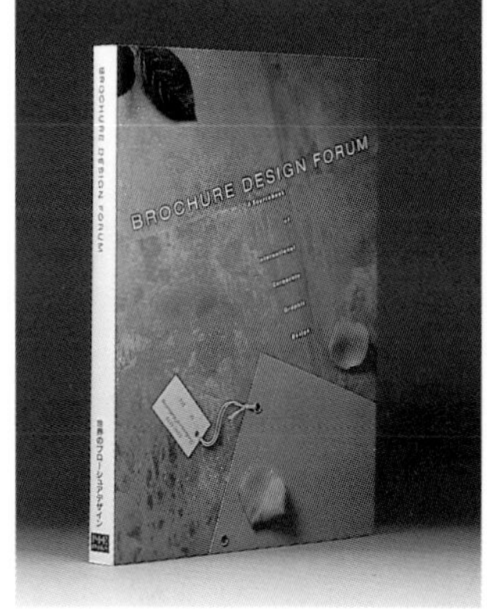

BROCHURE DESIGN FORUM 1
Pages: 224(192 in color) ¥15,000
世界のカタログ・コレクション
A large collection of international brochures from a variety of business categories. Showcases more than 250 eye-catching works.

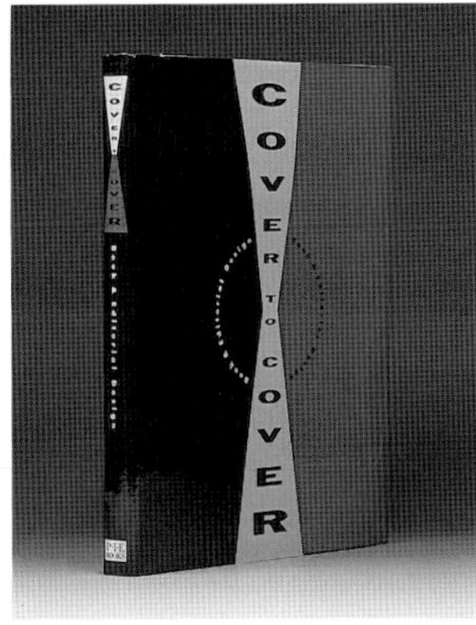

COVER TO COVER
Pages: 240(176 in color) ¥17,000
世界のブック&エディトリアル・デザイン
The latest trends in book and magazine design are illustrated with over 1,000 creative works by international firms.

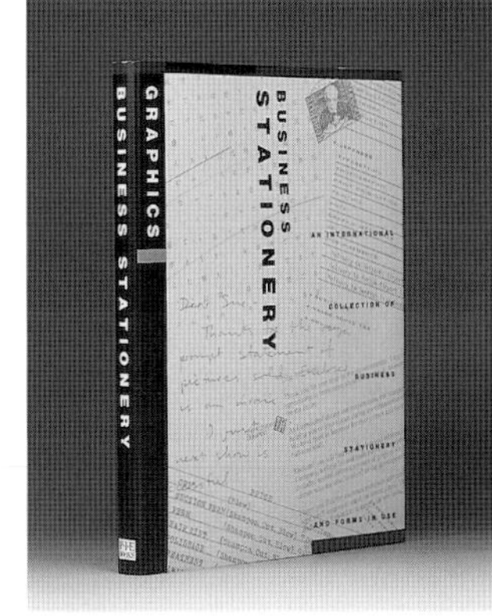

BUSINESS STATIONERY GRAPHICS 1
Pages: 224(192 in color) ¥15,000
世界のレターヘッド・コレクション
Creatively designed letterheads, business cards, memo pads, and other business forms and documents are included this international collection.

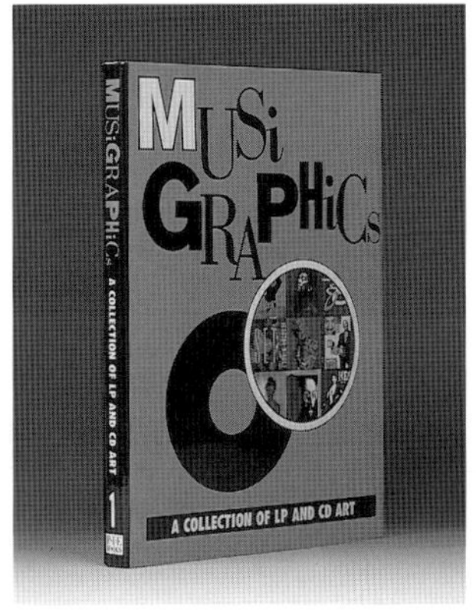

MUSIGRAPHICS 1
Pages: 224(192 in color) ¥16,000
世界のＬＰ&ＣＤグラフィックス
A collection of more than 600 of the world's most outstanding CD and LP covers, featuring design for all musical genres.

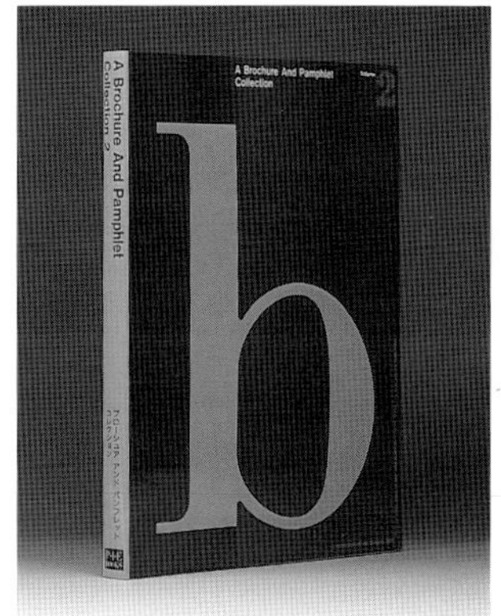

BROCHURE & PAMPHLET COLLECTION 2
Pages: 224(192 in color) ¥15,000
業種別カタログ・コレクション、第２弾
Features a selection of 1,000 brochures and pamphlets covering a wide range of products from Japan. The value of brochures in visual communication is demonstrated in this dazzling collection.

THE P·I·E COLLECTION

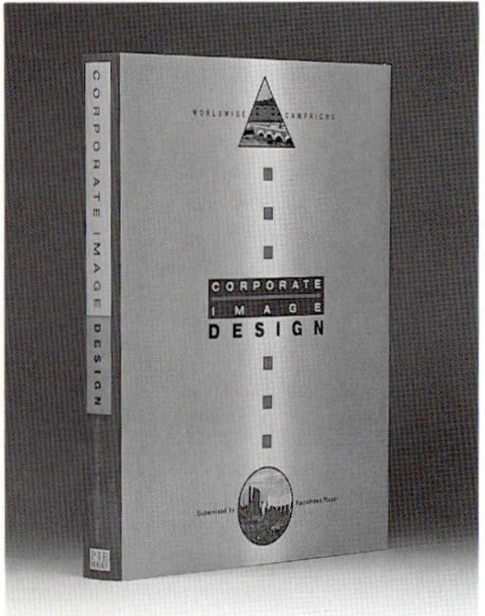

CORPORATE IMAGE DESIGN
Pages: 336(272 in color) ¥16,000
世界の業種別ＣＩ・ロゴマーク
This collection presents the best corporate identity projects from around the world. Creative and effective designs from top international firms are featured in this valuable source book.

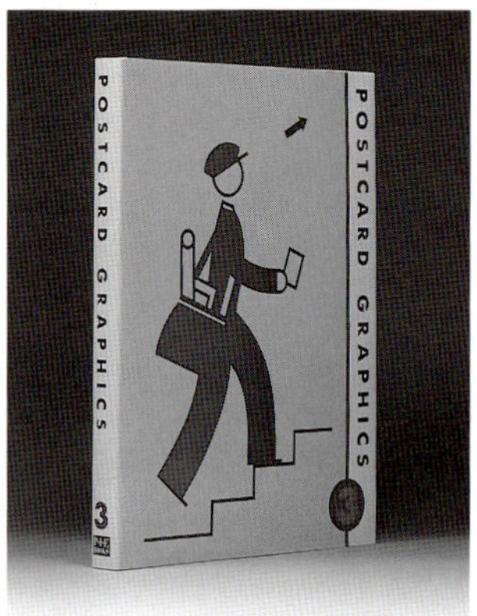

POSTCARD GRAPHICS 3
Pages: 232(208 in color) ¥16,000
世界の業種別ポストカード・コレクション
Volume 3 in the series presents more than 1,200 promotional postcards in dazzling full color. Top designers from the world over have contributed to this useful image bank of ideas.

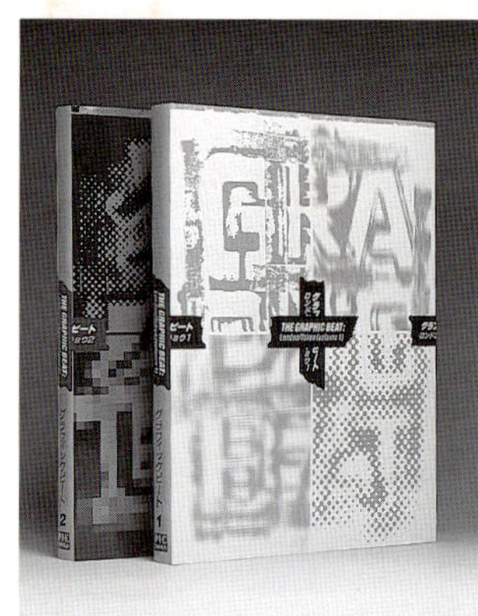

GRAPHIC BEAT LONDON/TOKYO 1 & 2
Pages: 224(208 in color) ¥16,000
音楽とグラフィックのコラボレーション
1,500 music-related graphic works from 29 of the hottest designers in Tokyo and London. Features Malcolm Garrett, Russell Miles, Tadanori Yokoo, Neville Brody, Vaughn Oliver and others.

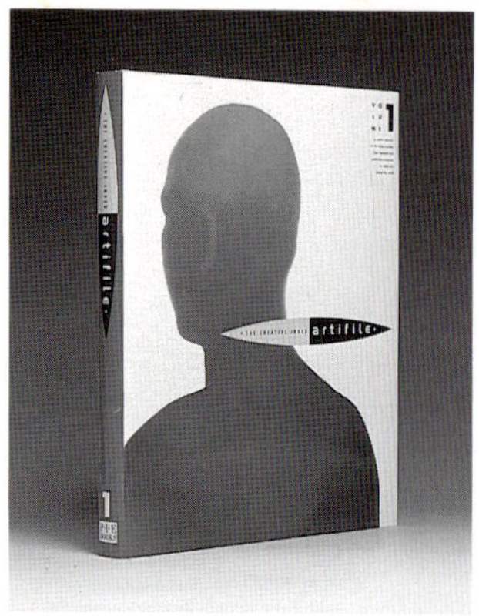

The Creative Index ARTIFILE
Pages: 224(Full color) ¥12,500
実力派プロダクション104社の作品集
Showcases the best works from 104 graphic studios in Japan and abroad. A variety of fields included such as advertising design, corporate identity, photography and illustration.

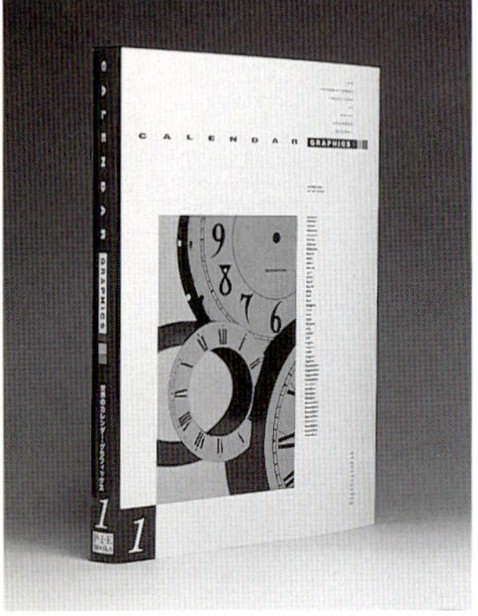

CALENDAR GRAPHICS
Pages: 224(192 in color) ¥16,000
世界のカレンダー・グラフィックス
An exciting collection of creatively designed calendars from around the world. A wide variety of styles included such as poster, book and 3-D calendars. Clients range from large corporations to retail shops.

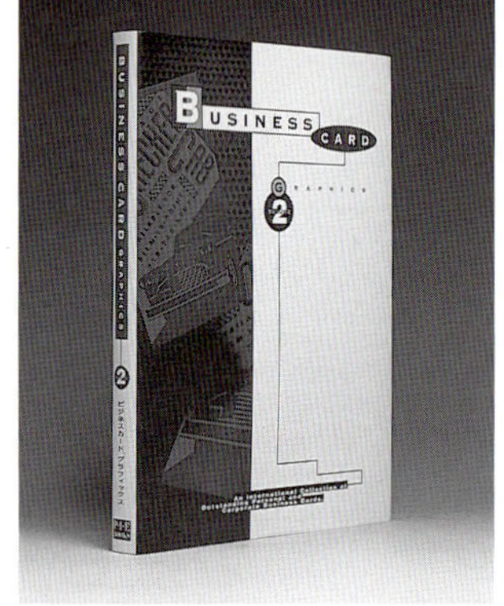

BUSINESS CARD GRAPHICS 2
Pages: 224(192 in color) ¥16,000
世界の名刺&ショップカード、第２弾
This latest collection presents 1,000 creative cards from international designers. Features hundreds of cards used in creative fields such as graphic design and architecture.

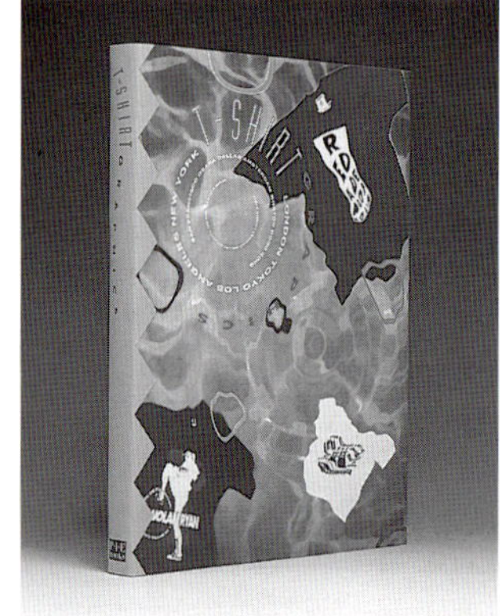

T-SHIRT GRAPHICS
Pages: 224(192 in color) ¥16,000
世界のＴシャツ・グラフィックス
This unique collection showcases 700 wonderfully creative T-Shirt designs from the world's premier design centers. Grouped according to theme, categories include sports, casual, designer and promotional shirts among others.

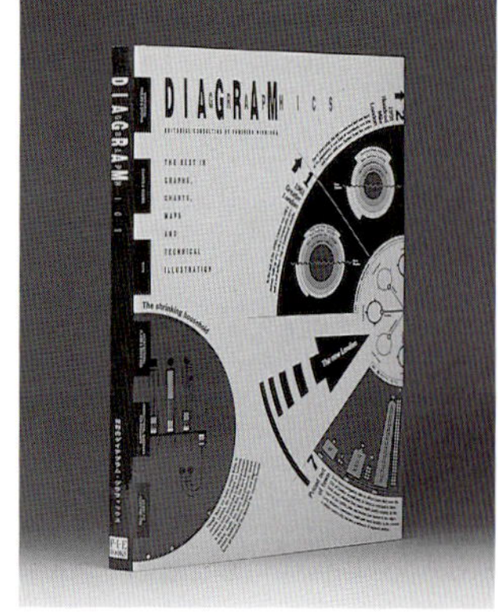

DIAGRAM GRAPHICS
Pages: 224(192 in color) ¥16,000
世界のダイアグラム・デザインの集大成
Hundreds of unique and lucid diagrams, charts, graphs, maps and technical illustrations from leading international design firms. Variety of media represented including computer graphics.

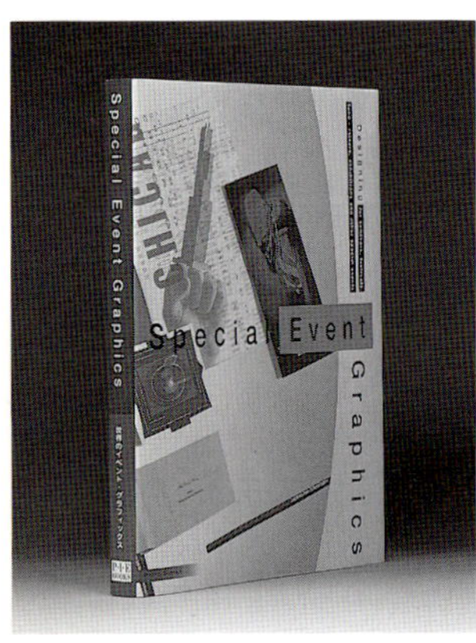

SPECIAL EVENT GRAPHICS
Pages: 224(192 in color) ¥16,000
世界のイベント・グラフィックス特集
This innovative collection features design elements from concerts, festivals, fashion shows, symposiums and more. International works include posters, tickets, flyers, invitations and various premiers.

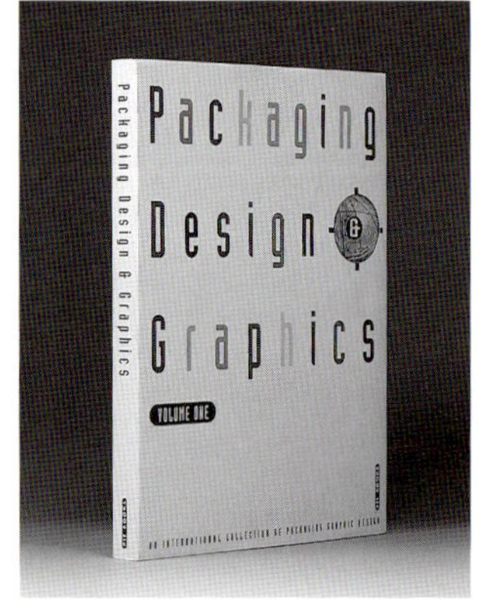

PACKAGING DESIGN & GRAPHICS 1
Pages: 224(192 in color) ¥16,000
世界の業種別パッケージ・デザイン
An international collection featuring 400 creative and exciting package designs from renowned designers.

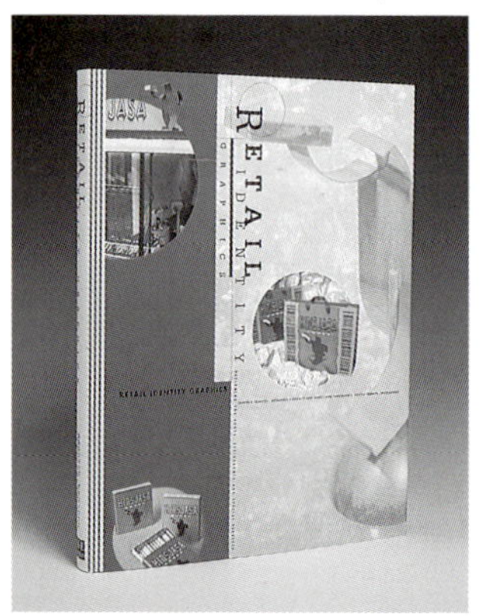

RETAIL IDENTITY GRAPHICS
Pages: 208(176 in color) ¥14,800
世界のショップ・グラフィックス
This visually exciting collection showcases the identity design campaigns of restaurants, bars, shops and various other retailers. Wide variety of pieces are featured including business cards, signs, menus, bags and hundreds more.

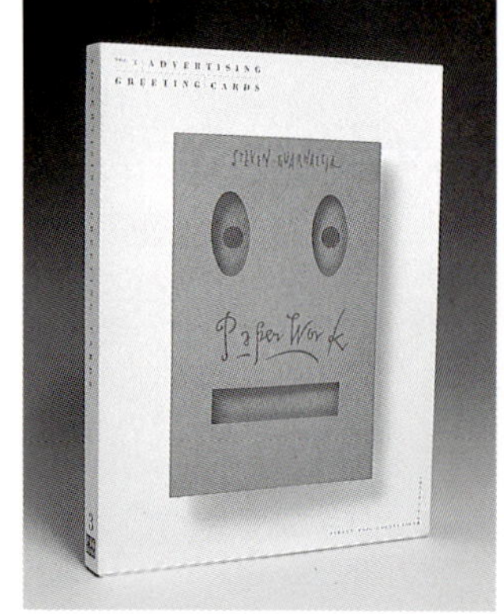

ADVERTISING GREETING CARDS 3
Pages: 224(176 in color) ¥16,000
世界のダイレクトメール集大成、第3弾
The best-selling series continues with this collection of elegantly designed advertising pieces from a wide variety of categories. This exciting image bank of ideas will interest all graphic designers and direct mail specialists.